ANTIQUES
Handbook
& Price Guide
2020~2021

Miller's Antiques Handbook & Price Guide 2020–2021
By Judith Miller

First published in Great Britain in 2019 by Miller's, a division of Mitchell Beazley,
imprints of Octopus Publishing Group Ltd., Carmelite House,
50 Victoria Embankment, London, EC4Y 0DZ
www.octopusbooks.co.uk

An Hachette UK Company
www.hachette.co.uk

Distributed in the USA by Hachette Book Group
1290 Avenue of the Americas, 4th and 5th Floors, New York, NY 10104

Distributed in Canada by Canadian Manda Group
664 Annette St., Toronto, Ontario, Canada, M6S 2C8

Miller's is a registered trademark of Octopus Publishing Group Ltd.
www.millersguides.com

ISBN: 978 1 78472 610 2

A CIP record for this book is available from the British Library

Set in Frutiger

Printed and bound in China

1 3 5 7 9 10 8 6 4 2

Publisher Alison Starling
Assistant Editor Katie Lumsden
Proofreader John Wainwright
Advertising Sales Julie Brooke
Indexer Hilary Bird
Art Director Juliette Norsworthy
Designer Ali Scrivens, T J Graphics
Senior Production Manager Peter Hunt

Photographs of Judith Miller page 7, by Chris Terry

Page 1: A George II and later red lacquered and gilt chinoiserie bureau bookcase. 91in (231cm) high $15,000-19,000 SWO
Page 3: A 1930s Lenci figure, 'Nella' by Helen Konig Scavini, date mark 11-XI-33. 9in (23cm) high $6,500-7,500 FLD
Page 4 from left to right: A Chinese Ming-style vase, with star motifs between formal bands. 8¾in (22.5cm) high $29,000-34,000 WW;
A Regency mahogany double-sided stool, in the manner of William Trotter. c1815 51½in (131cm) wide $32,000-38,000 DN;
A Wedgwood Fairyland lustre Malfrey vase and cover, "Ghostly Wood" pattern. c1926 13in (33cm) high $33,000-38,000 SWO;
A George II Channel Islands silver hot milk pitcher, by Guillaume Henry, Guernsey. c1727 4½in (11.5cm) high $29,000-35,000 MART;
A Tiffany Studios Favrile ruffled compote, etched "1529-1259M L.C. Tiffany-Favrile." c1918 6in (15cm) wide $1,900-2,500 DRA;
A Clarice Cliff "Conical" teapot, "Blue Autumn" pattern. c1930 5½in (14cm) high $1,800-2,300 FLD;
A George III Blue John campana urn, on a black marble plinth. 8¾in (22.5cm) high $6,500-7,000 WW;
A late 17thC bracket clock, by Thomas Tompion, London, with double-fusee bell-striking movement. c1690 14¼in (36cm) high $320,000-380,000 HAN
Page 7 from left to right: A Meissen teapot and cover, with Böttger luster glaze, "M.P.M." mark. c1722 6½in (16.5cm) wide $23,000-28,000 REEM;
A Chinese Republic period fan. 20¾in (52.5cm) wide $15,000-19,000 L&T
A late 19thC Black Forest bench, the bears with glass eyes. 31½in (80cm) wide $4,400-5,000 L&T

ANTIQUES
Handbook
& Price Guide

2020~2021

Judith Miller

MILLER'S

Contents

LIST OF CONSULTANTS

At Miller's we are extremely lucky to be able to call on a large number of specialists for advice. My colleagues and friends on the UK's BBC Antiques Roadshow have a wealth of knowledge and their advice on the state of the market is invaluable. It is also important to keep in touch with dealers, because they are really in the trenches dealing directly with collectors. Certain parts of the market have been extremely volatile over the past year, so up-to-date information is critical.

ASIAN

**John Axford &
Jeremy Morgan**
Woolley & Wallis
51-61 Castle Street
Salisbury SP1 3SU

Dan Bray
Gorringes
15 North Street
Lewes
East Sussex BN7 2PE

Adrian Rathbone
Hansons
Heage Lane
Derbyshire DE65 6LS

Lee Young
Duke's
Brewery Square
Dorchester DT1 1GA

Ling Zhu
Lyon & Turnbull
33 Broughton Place
Edinburgh EH1 3RR

CERAMICS

John Axford
Woolley & Wallis
51-61 Castle Street
Salisbury SP1 3SU

Ed Crichton
Lacy Scott & Knight
10 Risbygate St
Suffolk IP33 3AA

Fergus Gambon
Bonhams
101 New Bond Street
London W1S 1SR

Nic Saintey
Bearnes Hampton &
Littlewood
St Edmund's Court
Okehampton Street
Exeter EX4 1DU

CLOCKS

Paul Archard
Derek Roberts
25 Shipbourne Road
Tonbridge TN10 3DN.

DECORATIVE ARTS

Wayne Chapman
Lynways
www.lynways.com

Will Farmer
Fieldings
Mill Race Lane
Stourbridge DY8 1JN

Michael Jeffrey
Woolley & Wallis
51-61 Castle Street
Salisbury, SP1 3SU

John Mackie
Lyon & Turnbull
33 Broughton Place
Edinburgh EH1 3RR

Mike Moir
www.manddmoir.co.uk

Steven Moore
Burleigh Pottery
Middleport Pottery, Port Street,
Burslem ST6 3PE

David Rago
Rago Arts
333 North Main Street,
Lambertville, NJ 08530 USA

FURNITURE

Lennox Cato
1 The Square, Edenbridge
Kent TN8 5BD

Guy Schooling
Sworders
Cambridge Road
Stansted Mountfitchet
Essex CM24 8GE

JEWELLERY

Trevor Kyle
Lyon & Turnbull
33 Broughton Place
Edinburgh EH1 3RR

Gemma Redmond
5 Roby Mill, Wigan,
Skelmersdale WN8 0QF

MODERN DESIGN

John Mackie
Lyon & Turnbull
33 Broughton Place
Edinburgh EH1 3RR

SILVER

Duncan Campbell
Beau Nash
31 Brock Street
Bath BA1 2LN

Alastair Dickenson
90 Jermyn Street
London SW1 6JD

SPORTING

Graham Budd
Graham Budd
PO Box 47519
N14 6XD

TRIBAL

Alex Tweedy
Lyon & Turnbull
33 Broughton Place
Edinburgh EH1 3RR

Waddington's
275 King Street East,
Toronto, Ontario
Canada M5A 1K2

HOW TO USE THIS BOOK

Running head Indicates the subcategory of the main heading.

Page tab This appears on every page and identifies the main category heading as identified in the Table of Contents on pages 4-5.

Essential reference Gives key facts about the factory, maker, or style, along with stylistic identification points, value tips, and advice on fakes.

Closer look Does exactly that. We show identifying aspects of a factory or maker, point out rare colors or shapes, and explain why a particular piece is so desirable.

The object The antiques are shown in full color. This is a vital aid to identification and valuation. With many objects, a slight color variation can signify a large price differential.

Caption The description of the item illustrated, including when relevant, the period, the maker or factory, medium, the year it was made, dimensions, and condition. Many captions have **footnotes** that explain terminology or give identification or valuation information.

The price guide These price ranges give a ballpark figure of what you should pay for a similar item. The great joy of antiques is that there is not a recommended retail price. The price ranges in this book are based on actual prices, either what a dealer will take or the full auction price.

Source code Every item has been especially photographed at an auction house, a dealer, an antiques market, or a private collection. These are credited by code at the end of the caption, and they can be checked against the Key to Illustrations on pages 588-589.

Judith Picks Items chosen especially by Judith, either because they are important or interesting, or because they're good investments.

INTRODUCTION

Welcome to the 2020–2021 edition of *Miller's Antiques Handbook and Price Guide*—it is an unbelievable 40 years since we published the first black-and-white edition in 1979. The UK's BBC television station commissioned "Antiques Roadshow" in the same year, when antiques were still considered elitist, but the antiques world has changed since those heady days. In the early 1970s, there were many more antiques stores in every town, and more general auction sales where potential "sleepers" (unidentified treasures) could be found. There was no Internet. Collectors scoured the country and abroad to find a hidden gem. The recession and changing tastes have hit the antiques market hard. Many stores have closed, and many traditional areas of the market are struggling to survive. However, there are indications of an upturn. Many dealers have joined together in antiques centers, many display their antiques at fairs, and many now deal primarily online.

Across the board there is a certain cautious optimism about the future of the antiques trade. Some areas are strong, such as the Asian, Russian, and Indian markets. Any good-quality, top-end antique in original condition that is fresh to the market will excite collectors' interest.

This guide is, as always, packed with 8,000-plus images of antiques and fine decorative objects that are completely new to this edition. I am often asked if we update the prices in each edition; we don't—when we publish a new edition, we start from scratch to properly reflect changes and developments in the market.

I am also often asked, "Do antiques have a future?"

A Chinese Republic period fan. 20¾in (52.5cm) wide $15,000-19,000 L&T

It's an interesting question. Some people say young people seem less interested in collecting, favoring a more minimal look within their homes. Largely true, the consequence of this is, in fact, a transition from more traditional collecting fields to Mid-century and Modern. Indeed, there is a shortage of good antiques—the dealers' lament today is that having made a sale, the hardest part is finding good-quality antiques to replace it.

There is also the eco argument. Buying solid mahogany furniture is more ethical than buying disposable MDF pieces, and in many cases, buying secondhand is cheaper than brand new alternatives: no one is going to convince me MDF will prove a good investment. That solid, plain mahogany early- to mid-19th-century chest of drawers will still be a practical storage piece in 200 years' time, and if your taste is for Gastavian, then paint it.

The Internet has meant that antiques are now more accessible than ever—we can easily browse large numbers of pieces of different styles and periods. Due to the power of the Internet, auction houses outside the big cities are getting record prices for rare pieces.

I am constantly asked, "What is your advice on buying antiques? What is the next 'big' thing?" My answer is always the same. Buy what you like. Buy something that will bring you pleasure—if it increases in value, that's a bonus. I have included images of a few personal likes—a Meissen teapot, a 19th-century Chinese fan, and a Black Forest bench on this page—and note that, Meissen, when early, rare, and of exquisite quality, will always fetch record prices.

We live in uncertain times. With all the political upheaval in the United States and Brexit in Europe, who knows what the future will hold? However, in times of economic uncertainty, top-quality antiques are often seen as a good investment, and you have the added benefit of enjoying them.

Indeed, now is a great time to be buying antiques. So please use this guide to increase your knowledge, your commercial acumen, and your enjoyment. Those hidden treasures are still out there just waiting to be discovered!

Judith Miller.

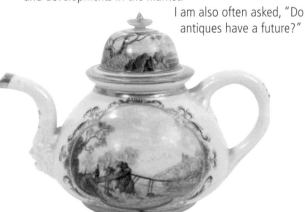

A Meissen teapot and cover, with Böttger luster glaze, underglazed blue "M.P.M." mark. c1722 6½in (16.5cm) wide $23,000-28,000 REEM

A late 19thC Black Forest bench, the bears with glass eyes. 31½in (80cm) wide $4,400-5,000 L&T

THE PORCELAIN MARKET

Although there is a feeling that the market is improving, there has been continued nervousness fueled by porcelain collectors' very real concern that the ceramic market is "soft." Private collectors are, however, prepared to buy when items are rare and of excellent quality. As mentioned by Steven Moore, ceramics specialist on the UK's BBC television "Antiques Roadshow," "2019 was the year that saw some ceramic pieces come out of the china cabinet and into the trophy cabinet. I'm thinking of pieces like the previously unrecorded teapot attributed to the John Bartlam factory in Cain Hoy, South Carolina [above], sold by Woolley and Wallis, and the Rothschild ceramics at Sotheby's."

There has been little change to the market over the last few years. The market leaders Sèvres and Meissen have continued to remain in demand, particularly for early 18th-century examples. The "golden age" of Meissen, from the early years of the factory to the end of the Seven Years War (1710–59) is still strong, and in this area collectors are even prepared to accept some damage. However, really high-quality figures from the late 19th century, if of superb quality, are still in demand. Dresden, Vienna, and Limoges pieces have to be particularly impressive to sell well. The Paris factories have also struggled, and buyers are still suspicious of many so-called "Samson" pieces that do not have the quality of the true Samson copies.

Another area that is still struggling is British blue and white from both the 18th and 19th centuries. Buyers will pay for pieces in exceptional condition and with a rare early pattern. Large platters are also in demand, but not if they have a common transfer-printed pattern. Some Worcester has also been in demand, but only really early pieces with rare hand-painted patterns. Later transfer-printed pieces have struggled to find prerecession prices, with many auctioneers combining pieces in job lots. If someone is considering starting a collection of 18th-century English porcelain, this could be a good time to start. Many pieces fail to find the price levels that I was paying 30 years ago.

Pieces that have continued to excite collectors are the "Girl-in-a-Swing" groups from a London factory possibly run by Charles Gouyn (also known as the St James' factory). These have that magical combination of superb quality and rarity. There has also been a great deal of research done on these groups, much by the English Ceramic Circle, which has stimulated the market.

Lowestoft continues to have a loyal group of collectors and prices remain strong—again, this is particularly true when rare shapes and patterns are offered. Nantgarw and Swansea are also still in demand due in part to rarity and superb quality. Unrecorded early Derby figures always excite the market. Royal Worcester ewers and vases painted by certain artists, such as Charles Baldwin, Harry Davis, and the Stintons, still have their collectors and prices have remained steady, but the pieces have to be of a good size and preferably fresh to the market.

Top Left: An important American porcelain teapot, attributed to John Bartlam, Cain Hoy, South Carolina, damaged.

c1765-69   *7in (17.5cm) wide*

$760,000+   **WW**

Above: A late 19thC Meissen figure of Count Bruhl's Tailor, after the model by J.J. Kändler.

16½in (42cm) high

$13,000-15,000   **BRI**

PORCELAIN

ESSENTIAL REFERENCE—BERLIN

The first Berlin porcelain factory was founded in 1752 by Wilhelm Kaspar Wegely. It produced Meissen-style decorative wares, typically floral vases, and copies of Meissen figures. The factory closed in 1757.

● In 1761, Johann Ernst Gotzkowsky purchased Wegely's old stock and, with support from Prussian king Frederick II, founded the Königliche Porzellan-Manufaktur Berlin (Royal Porcelain Manufactory Berlin), or KPM Berlin.

● Under Gotzkowsky, the factory developed its own late Rococo style. Gotzkowsky worked with Friedrich and William Meyer to create Classical figures, often painted in black, puce, and salmon pink. The factory also used porcelain as a vehicle for miniature painting. KPM Berlin is still active today.

● Wegely porcelain was marked with an underglaze blue "W." Gotzkowsky's pieces were marked with a scepter. From 1832, "KPM" was added. In the years 1849-70, pieces were marked with a Prussian eagle holding an orb and scepter.

A 19thC Berlin group, the infant Bacchus drinking wine, with a female attendant, underglaze blue mark, impressed "634," minor gilt rubbing.

7¾in (19.5cm) high

$280-350   FELL

A KPM Berlin group, of a putto with a chariot drawn by a ram.

$200-250   HALL

A late 19thC Berlin plaque, painted with a praying lady, impressed "KPM. SZ," incised "407-269," framed.

16in (40.5cm) high

$6,500-7,000   HT

A late 19thC KPM Berlin plaque, painted by R. Dittrich, impressed factory marks, titled "Heimathlos Nach Kray," framed.

9¾in (24.5cm) high

$1,800-2,300   TOV

A KPM Berlin plaque, with a classically draped maiden, impressed marks, scratches to enamel.

9in (23cm) high

$1,800-2,300   CHOR

A late 19thC KPM Berlin plaque, painted with "The Immaculate Conception," after Bartolomé Esteban Murillo, impressed "KPM," scepter mark, within a gilt frame.

plaque 10¾in (27.5cm) high

$1,900-2,500   TOV

BERLIN MARKS

KPM Berlin
Mark used from 1832

A late 19thC Berlin plaque, after Ludwig Sturm (1844-1926), inscribed "Kinder Lust v. Lasch 4, Sturm, Wien," incised "K.P.M.," in later gilt frame.

plaque 19¼in (49cm) high

$16,000-20,000   CA

A late 19thC Berlin plaque, with a portrait of a young lady, signed "Wagner," impressed factory marks, within a gilt frame.

3¼in (8.5cm) high

$230-280   TOV

ESSENTIAL REFERENCE—BOW

The Bow factory was founded in London c1744 by Thomas Frye and Edward Heylyn. Its porcelain wares were inexpensive and at first popular, but the factory declined in the 1760s and closed in 1776.

- Bow porcelain was white and chalky, with an irregular surface and granular texture. Its glassy glaze was of a gray-green hue. Its wares were usually painted in blues, yellows, and purples.
- Inspired by Asian designs, most early Bow wares were plain blanc-de-Chine or decorated in underglaze blue. Later enameled wares were based on the famille rose palette or Kakiemon designs.
- Bow figures were press molded instead of slip cast, which makes them heavy and less fine than those made by Chelsea or Derby.
- Early Bow is generally unmarked. From c1765, an anchor and dagger mark was painted in red enamel.

A Bow white-glazed figure of a pedlar, the stick broken off and repaired.
c1754   *6½in (16.5cm) high*
$2,300-2,500   **WW**

A Bow white-glazed figure of a female hunter and dog, beside a water fountain, minor damages.
c1752   *5in (13cm) high*
$700-800   **WW**

A Bow blue-and-white tea bowl, painted with a boat, islands with pagodas, "Q" mark to base.
c1752-54   *3¾in (9.5cm) diam*
$400-450   **WW**

A Bow white-glazed footed gravy boat, of silver shape, small chips to feet.
c1754   *7in (18cm) wide*
$700-800   **WW**

A small Bow blue-and-white fluted cream boat, painted with the "Desirable Residence" pattern.
c1755-60   *4¼in (11cm) long*
$300-400   **BELL**

A rare Bow blue-and-white dish, painted with islands, pagodas, trees, and a figure on a sampan.
c1755-58   *10¾in (27.5cm) long*
$650-750   **WW**

A rare Bow famille rose plate, with a chinoiserie figure, micro-fritting to rim.
c1756-58   *9¼in (23.5cm) diam*
$1,050-1,200   **HAN**

CLOSER LOOK—BLUE AND WHITE PINT MUG

The reverse is decorated with a Classical architectural ornament and a man holding a trowel.

This side depicts a man with a hunting flintlock rifle.

The mug is decorated in underglaze blue with the armorial of the Worshipful Company of Tylers and Bricklayers and the inscription "in God is all our trust."

It was probably made at the Bow factory. The base is marked "M W, E Jan, 1757," dating it to the factory's high point, when it employed around 3,000 people.

A rare Bow teapot stand, with a landscape by Jefferys Hammet O'Neal, wear to enamels, hairline crack.
c1758   *4¾in (12cm) wide*
$1,300-1,800   **HAN**

A rare English soft-paste porcelain pint mug, some chips on the rim, cracked handle.
1757   *5¾in (14.5cm) high*
$28,000-33,000   **STA**

A rare Bow duck tureen base, the plumage finely painted.

This form derives from George Edwards, "Natural History of Uncommon Birds" (1743-47), volume III, plate 157.

c1755-58   4¾in (12cm) wide
$2,300-2,800   **WW**

A rare Bow model of a pug, in polychrome enamels, some small chips.

c1755   4¼in (11cm) high
$3,800-4,500   **WW**

A Bow model of a canary, restoration to tail, wing, and flowers.

c1758   9½in (24cm) wide
$500-550   **HAN**

A rare Bow figure of Il Capitano, from the Commedia dell'Arte series, some restoration.

c1755   7¼in (18.5cm) high
$4,400-5,000   **WW**

A rare Bow figure of Pedrolino or Pierrot, from the Commedia dell'Arte series.

This figure was first modeled by Reinicke at Meissen, using an engraving by Francois Joullain in Louis Riccobini, "Histoire du Theatre Italien" (1731), and was faithfully copied by Bow.

c1755   6in (15cm) high
$2,500-3,200   **WW**

A Bow figure of Fame as a winged angel, on a cloud base, restoration to fingers.

c1756-58   7in (18cm) high
$2,000-2,500   **BE**

A Bow figure of a salt box player, some restoration.

c1758   4¾in (12cm) high
$1,500-1,900   **WW**

A set of Bow figures of the Adolescent Seasons, some restoration.

c1765   7in (17.5cm) high
$2,800-3,200   **WW**

ESSENTIAL REFERENCE—CAUGHLEY

Caughley was founded in the 1750s by Ambrose Gallimore in Caughley, Shropshire, England, as the Salopian China Manufactory. It continued production until it was purchased by John Rose of the Coalport factory in 1799.

- Gallimore worked closely with Thomas Turner and later Robert Hancock, both previously employees of the Worcester factory. Together, they produced and decorated soft-paste porcelain, made with soapstone and clay imported from Devon and Cornwall.
- Caughley wares included a range of tableware, homeware, and miniature "toy" items. These were decorated in blue and white, with occasional gilded or enameled details.
- Caughley designs emulated Chinese porcelain, with a French influence in later decades. The best-known Caughley patterns include "Fisherman" and "Willow," both later adopted by other factories, including Worcester.
- Wares were usually marked "S" for Salopian or "C" for Caughley.

A Caughley teapot, painted with the rare "Bird in the Ring" pattern, lacking cover, "S" mark.

This is a copy of the Worcester version of this pattern and is the only Caughley example known.

c1776-79   4¼in (10.5cm) high

$700-800   HALL

A Caughley coffee cup and saucer, transfer-printed with the "Bridge and Windmill" pattern, "S" mark, minor chip to saucer.

c1780

$650-700   PW

A Caughley mask-head pitcher, transfer-printed with the "Fisherman" or "Pleasure Boat" pattern, inscribed "God Speed the Plough."

c1780-90   9in (23cm) high

$1,300-1,800   HALL

GOD SPEED THE PLOUGH.

A rare Caughley mustard spoon, transfer-printed with the "Floret" pattern.

c1777-82   4in (10cm) long

$1,000-1,150   HALL

A Caughley butter pot and cover, transfer-printed with the "Gillyflower II" pattern, "S" mark.

c1776-79   4¼in (10.5cm) wide

$700-800   HALL

A Caughley toy cider pitcher, painted with the "Island" pattern, reversed "S" mark.

c1780-90   2in (5cm) high

$900-1,000   HALL

A rare Caughley rice spoon, painted with the "Maltese Cross" pattern, "C" mark.

5¼in (13.5cm) long

$1,500-1,800   HALL

A Caughley chestnut basket, cover, and stand, transfer-printed with the "Ripe Pomegranate" pattern.

The chestnuts in this basket would have been roasted and peeled, then eaten. The piercing to the basket is functional, allowing for the escape of steam from the hot chestnuts.

c1780-90   basket 8¼in (21cm) wide

$1,500-2,000   HALL

CAUGHLEY MARKS

Marks used 1775-99

A Caughley punch bowl, transfer-printed with the "Punch Bowl Sprays" pattern, with monogrammed initials "E.H REA," glaze craze to foot rim.

10¼in (26cm) diam

$700-8000   **HALL**

A deep Caughley bowl, painted with the rare "Rock and Willow" pattern, "C" mark, chip.

c1778-85   *4in (10cm) diam*

$750-900   **HALL**

A Caughley mug, transfer-printed with the "Thorny Rose" pattern, "S" mark.

c1776-80   *4¾in (12cm) high*

$1,150-1,400   **HALL**

A Caughley vase, transfer-printed with the "Sliced Apple" pattern, originally one of a pair.

c1778-86   *5in (12.5cm) high*

$900-1,000   **HALL**

A Caughley mask-head pitcher, painted with the "Salopian Rose Sprays" pattern, initialed, "S" mark, firing crack, dated.

The monogram reads "J," "I," or "T H" and "1790." This may possibly refer to a member of the Hill family of Hawkstone who turned 21 that year.

1790   *7½in (19cm) high*

$1,300-1,800   **HALL**

A Caughley pounce pot, transfer-printed with sprigs, "C" mark.

Pounce is a fine powder made predominantly from cuttlefish bone, which was used to dry ink and make rough surfaces suitable for writing on. After sprinkling the paper, ink would generally take around ten seconds to dry before the paper could safely be folded without the risk of blotting.

c1776-85   *3¼in (8cm) high*

$2,800-3,500   **HALL**

A rare Caughley eye bath, painted with the "Locre Sprigs" pattern, hairline crack, and filled chip.

These eye baths were used to wash out people's eyes with boric acid when they became infected. Initially, in the 16thC, the wealthy had eye baths made of silver. It was not until the 18thC that they were made of earthenware or porcelain and came into more general use.

c1785-93   *2¼in (5.5cm) high*

$1,000-1,050   **HALL**

A Caughley chocolate cup and saucer, painted with the "Salopian Sprig" pattern, "S" mark.

c1785-92   saucer 6in (15.5cm) diam

$450-500   **HALL**

A Caughley dry mustard pot, transfer-printed with the "Travellers" pattern, "S" mark, chip to rim.

After 1720, the processing of mustard seeds in a mill resulted in a fine flour, which came to be commercially known as "Durham mustard." Mustard pots would contain either dry or prepared mustard and were common in 18thC kitchens.

c1778-85   *3½in (9cm) high*

$1,500-1,900   **HALL**

A Caughley dessert plate, with a blue-painted scene with a gilt spangled border, from the "Star and Spangles" service, impressed "Salopian" mark, gilding rubbed.

c1785-93   *8¼in (21cm) diam*

$650-750   **HALL**

ESSENTIAL REFERENCE—CHELSEA

The Chelsea factory was founded in London c1744 by Flemish silversmith Nicholas Sprimont. Sprimont focused on luxury porcelain goods, aiming his products at "the Quality and Gentry." Chelsea's phases can be defined by its changing marks.

- Early pieces, chiefly small-scale tableware, such as pitchers, beakers (a type of drinking cup), teapots, and salts, were marked with an incised triangle. These were influenced by French Rococo style and by Sprimont's past as a silversmith.
- Pieces from the Raised Anchor period (c1749-52) were in part inspired by Asian Kakiemon shapes and by Meissen designs.
- In the Red Anchor period (c1752-56), Chelsea changed its porcelain formula. The new wares were finished with a clear bluish glaze. Chelsea began to produce its famous Rococo tureens in the shapes of fruit, vegetables, and animals.
- In the Gold Anchor period (c1756-69), inspired by Sèvres, Chelsea wares became more elaborate in form and design. A new, thick, blush glaze was introduced. Wares were painted in a brighter palette and often gilded.
- In c1769, the Chelsea factory was purchased by William Duesbury, owner of the Derby porcelain factory

A Chelsea "Scolopendrium" molded large tea bowl, raised anchor mark, short firing crack to lower body.

Scolopendrium is a variety of fern, sometimes known as "hart's-tongue" fern.

c1750-52   3¾in (9.5cm) diam
$1,900-2,300   BE

A Chelsea beaker, in the Kakiemon style, raised anchor mark.

c1750-52   2¼in (5.5cm) high
$2,500-3,200   BE

A Chelsea "Scolopendrium" beaker and saucer, painted with insects and floral sprays, raised anchor marks, firing cracks to beaker, restored chip to saucer.

c1750-52   saucer 5in (13cm) diam
$5,000-6,300   BE

A Chelsea plate, after Meissen, in the Kakiemon style, red anchor mark.

c1752-54   9½in (24cm) wide
$750-800   WW

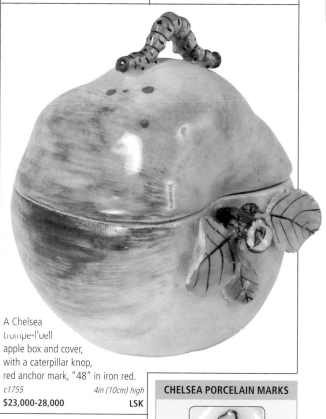

A Chelsea trompe-l'oeil apple box and cover, with a caterpillar knop, red anchor mark, "48" in iron red.

c1755   4in (10cm) high
$23,000-28,000   LSK

A Chelsea coffee cup and saucer, with crabstock handle, painted with Meissen-style flowers, red anchor marks, red "21" to saucer, minor glaze cracks.

c1755
$750-900   PW

A Chelsea mug, painted with a Meissen-style bouquet, red anchor mark, minor wear to rim.

c1756-58   3½in (9cm) high
$700-800   BE

A pair of Chelsea dishes, with fruit and butterflies, some glaze crackling, gold anchor marks.

10in (25.5cm) wide
$450-550   CHEF

CHELSEA PORCELAIN MARKS

Mark used 1752-56

Mark used c1756-69

A Chelsea botanical Hans Sloane-type plate, gold anchor mark, two pieces reattached.

c1758   9¼in (23.5cm) diam

$1,300-1,800   **HAN**

A Chelsea silver-form dish, painted with two birds in a landscape, gold anchor mark.

c1765   9¾in (24.5cm) wide

$1,600-2,100   **BE**

A gilt-metal-mounted Chelsea vase and cover, painted with Classical figures, some repairs and losses.

The scene is from an engraving of "Aeneas Bearing Anchises from Troy." The original painting, by Carle van Loo in 1729, is now in the Louvre.

c1765   10¾in (27cm) high

$13,000-18,000   **TEN**

A Chelsea gilt-metal-mounted étui or bodkin case, the top as the head of Columbine.

c1760   4¾in (12cm) high

$3,200-3,800   **BE**

A Chelsea rose box and cover, small chips.

c1753-55   3in (7.5cm) high

$5,500-6,500   **WW**

A Chelsea bonbonnière, the gold mount inscribed "Votre Amitie Fait/ Mon Bonheur" (your friendship makes my happiness).

c1755-60   1¾in (4.5cm) long

$7,000-8,000   **BE**

A Chelsea bonbonnière, with gilt-metal mounts and enamel cover, minor stress cracks, crazing to enamel.

c1760   2½in (6.5cm) long

$2,800-3,200   **BE**

A Chelsea bonbonnière, a maiden blindfolding Cupid, titled "Aimant Aveuglement," gilt-metal mounts, hardstone base.

c1760   2in (5cm) high

$2,500-3,200   **WW**

A Chelsea gold-mounted bonbonnière, with three children and a dog, the boy wearing a sash inscribed "La Curiousité Des Belles."

c1760   5½in (14cm) high

$7,500-9,000   **WW**

A Chelsea figure of Autumn, from the Rustic Seasons, red anchor mark, some restoration. **The figures in this series were copied from Meissen, and also copied by Longton Hall.**
c1755   *5¼in (13.5cm) high*
$1,900-2,500   **WW**

A Chelsea figure of a Levantine lady, modeled by Joseph Willems after Meissen, red anchor mark, some restoration.
c1755   *6in (15cm) high*
$2,100-2,500   **WW**

A Chelsea figure, "The Night-Watchman's Companion," gold anchor mark, some restoration. **This figure derives from Meissen's Cris de Paris series.**
c1760   *6in (15cm) high*
$1,900-2,500   **WW**

A Chelsea figure of one of the Nine Muses, probably Thalia, on an associated stand for Erato, with gold anchor and impressed "R" marks, the figure numbered "1," some restoration.
c1760-65   *15¾in (40cm) high*
$5,500-6,500   **WW**

A Chelsea figure of a gardener, gold anchor mark, some restoration.
c1760-65   *9in (23cm) high*
$2,300-2,800   **WW**

A Chelsea figure of a musician, gold anchor mark, minor restoration.
c1762   *6in (15cm) high*
$1,900-2,500   **WW**

A Chelsea flower-holder "Chinaman" figure, gold anchor mark, some restoration.
c1762   *7¾in (20cm) high*
$1,000-1,250   **WW**

A pair of Chelsea figures of Imperial Shepherds, gold anchor marks, small damages.
c1765   *12½in (32cm) high*
$9,000-10,000   **WW**

A Chelsea candlestick group, modeled in the Fable manner, gold anchor mark, one ear restored, some chips.
c1760   *8¾in (22cm) high*
$3,500-4,300   **WW**

A Chelsea 18ct gold-mounted scent bottle, modeled as Harlequin, with chained head stopper, some firing cracks, some restoration.

Harlequin was one of the principle stock characters of the Italia Commedia dell'Arte, a comic Italian theatrical form that flourished throughout Europe from the 16thC to 18thC. Harlequin was a comic figure of a valet or servant, characterized by his checkered costume.

c1950   3¼in (8.5cm) high
$13,000-15,000   SWO

A Chelsea 18ct gold-mounted scent bottle, of a lady playing a hurdy-gurdy, stopper mount in poor condition, some chips and staining, chain missing.

c1950   3¼in (8.5cm) high
$13,000-15,000   SWO

A Chelsea 9ct gold-mounted scent bottle, of a shepherdess tending lambs, inscribed "Votre Douceur Fait Mon Bonheur," chain broken, some chips and restoration, in a shagreen case.

3¼in (8.5cm) high
$9,000-10,000   SWO

A Chelsea scent bottle, modeled as a boy and his dog, now with dragonfly stopper.

c1950   3in (7.5cm) high
$1,500-2,000   SWO

A Chelsea gold-mounted scent bottle, with flower stopper, some losses and chips, stopper repaired.

c1950   3¼in (8cm) high
$5,500-6,500   SWO

A Chelsea scent bottle, modeled as a lady cradling her baby, some restoration.

c1950   3¼in (8.5cm) high
$6,500-7,000   SWO

A Chelsea 15ct gold-mounted scent bottle, modeled as a flower seller with dog, cracked in half and restored, some damages.

c1950   3¼in (8.5cm) high
$5,000-5,700   SWO

A Chelsea gold-mounted scent bottle, of a flower-encrusted vase, some losses and restoration, stopper stuck in.

3in (7.5cm) high
$9,000-10,000   SWO

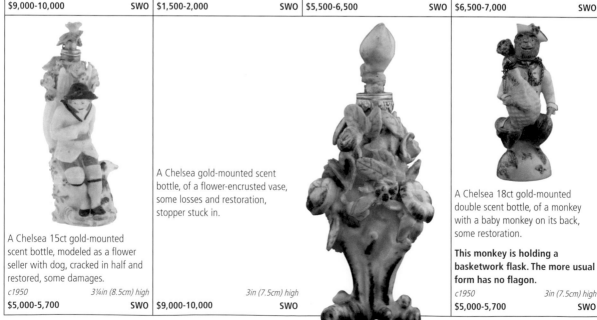

A Chelsea 18ct gold-mounted double scent bottle, of a monkey with a baby monkey on its back, some restoration.

This monkey is holding a basketwork flask. The more usual form has no flagon.

c1950   3in (7.5cm) high
$5,000-5,700   SWO

ESSENTIAL REFERENCE—COALPORT

The Coalport factory was founded by John Rose in the 1790s in Shropshire, UK. After John Rose's death in 1841, the company continued under the name John Rose & Co.

● Rose had previously trained at Caughley, and purchased the Caughley factory in 1799. He bought the Nantgarw factory in 1819 and took on former Nantgarw employees William Billingsley and Samuel Walker as his chief painter and chemist, respectively.

● Coalport concentrated on table and decorative wares. In the second half of the 19thC, it also began to produce flower-encrusted Rococo pieces and Sèvres-style vases.

● Its varied decorative patterns included Neoclassical designs, Imari decoration, landscape scenes, and bouquets of summer flowers. These were often set against a solid dark blue ground. Green and beige grounds were also common.

A rare Coalport commemorative beaker, painted with military motifs, inscribed "Wenlock Loyal Volunteers."

The Wenlock Loyal Volunteers were formed in 1799 in response to the threat of invasion from France. Thomas Turner, proprietor of the Caughley factory, was a captain. Only a handful of commemorative pieces are recorded. Most are in museum collections.

c1800   3¼in (8.5cm) high

$2,300-2,800   **WW**

A Coalport tea kettle and cover, applied with flowers and leaves, with swan knop, painted "CD" mark.

c1825   6in (15.5cm) high

$450-500   **SWO**

A pair of Coalport vases and covers, pattern no.A1412, printed mark.

c1875-81   7in (17.5cm) high

$1,000-1,050   **HALL**

A Coalport câchepot and stand, painted with birds, with lion masks, on paw feet, the base broken and reglued.

c1815-20   7½in (19cm) high

$180-230   **WW**

A late 19thC Coalport jeweled cabinet cup and saucer, pattern no.T309, retailers' mark for Ovington Brothers, printed green factory mark.

saucer 4in (10cm) diam

$300-400   **HALL**

A Coalport cabinet plate, with a hand-painted woman, by J. Keeling.

8¾in (22.5cm) diam

$450-500   **PSA**

A Coalport cabinet plate, by Frederick Chiver (1881-1965), signed, printed green factory mark and gilt pattern number.

8¾in (22.5cm) diam

$250-320   **HALL**

A Coalport vase, with a hand-painted woman, by E.N. Sutton, heavily gilded.

10¾in (27.5cm) high

$2,500-3,200   **PSA**

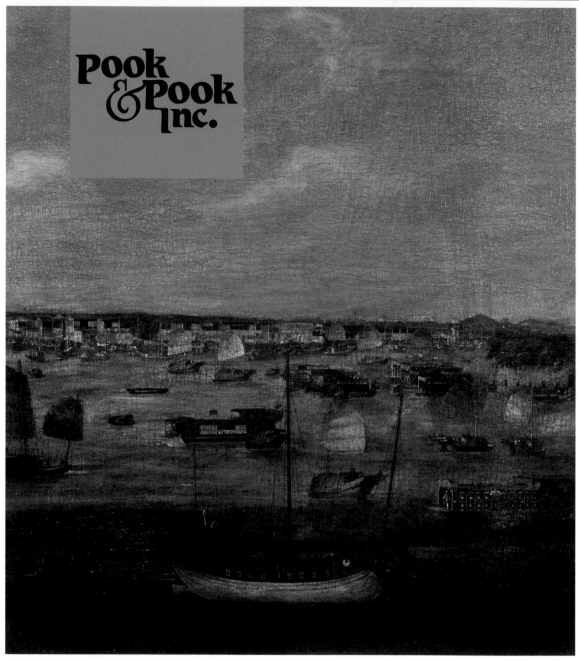

ESSENTIAL REFERENCE—DERBY

A porcelain factory was founded in Derby, UK, in c1748 by Frenchman André Planché. In 1756, it was bought by John Heath and William Duesbury, previously decorators for Chelsea. In 1770, they bought out the Chelsea factory, and operated together as Chelsea-Derby until 1784. In 1811, the company was acquired by Robert Bloor, who managed the factory until its closure in 1848.

- Early Derby soft-paste porcelain is fine grained, glazed in grayish white or grayish green. Its early wares were mostly figures. These were pastoral and allegorical subjects, often left in white. In the 1750s and 60s, Derby figures were typically Rococo in style, standing on scrolled bases.
- After 1756, Derby's range expanded to include tureens, baskets, and other tableware. Tea wares often cracked during use, so examples are rare.
- After the acquisition of Chelsea, the paste became a pure white and the glaze a clear blush. New designs included landscapes, detailed flowers, and exotic birds. Many patterns were loose copies of Chelsea or Sèvres designs.

A pair of Derby sweetmeat figures of a gallant and companion, attributed to Andrew Planché, some restoration.
c1753-55   6¼in (16cm) high
$3,200-3,800   WW

A Derby "pale family" figure of a lady, one finger lacking, minor chips.

The design was adapted from a Meissen figure by J.J. Kandler. The "pale family" refers to the figures of c1755-56, which were lightly decorated beneath a white glaze.
c1755-58   5½in (14cm) high
$3,800 4,400   BE

A Derby figure, "The Farmer's Wife," some chips.
c1757   6in (15cm) high
$650-700   WW

A pair of Derby figures of vintners, some chips, the man's hat restored.
c1758   5in (13cm) high
$1,300-1,800   WW

A rare set of Derby figures from the Four Quarters of the Globe series, emblematic of Asia, Africa, the Americas, and Europe, some damages and restoration.

This series was first created by Kändler at Meissen around 1745, and adapted a few years later by Meyer using children instead. Meyer's series was copied at Chelsea, and it is probable that this Derby series derives from Chelsea instead of the German originals.
c1760   9¾in (25cm) high
$4,400-5,700   WW

A Derby figure of Jupiter, paper label for the R. Parker collection.
c1760-65   9¾in (24.5cm) high
$1,800-2,300   WW

A Derby sweetmeat figure of a kneeling man.
c1765   8½in (21.5cm) high
$1,900-2,500   WW

DERBY PORCELAIN MARKS

Mark used c1782-1800

Mark used c1782-1825
In red c1806-25

BLOOR DERBY

Mark used c1820-40

A Derby mythological figure of Leda and the Swan, some restoration.

c1765   *10¼in (26cm) high*

$1,600-2,000   **WW**

A Derby mythological figure of Europa and the Bull, chip to horn.

c1765   *11¼in (28.5cm) high*

$2,300-2,800   **WW**

A Derby figure of a map seller, restoration to hat, minor chips.

c1765   *6¼in (16cm) high*

$1,050-1,200   **TEN**

A Derby group of children playing Hazard, incised "95," some damage.

This group is copied from a 1736 painting by François Boucher, entitled "Country Fair." A similar version was produced at Sèvres, modeled by Falconet.

c1780   *6in (15cm) high*

$500-650   **WW**

A pair of Derby figures of dancers, each incised "No. 317," some restoration.

c1790   *8in (20.5cm) high*

$750-900   **WW**

A Derby bisque figure of a shepherd, sheep, and dog, modeled by William Coffee, incised "396."

William Coffee (1773-c1846) was a modeler at the Derby China Manufactory in the 1790s. He worked for other local factories, both as a modeler and a traveling salesman, before establishing his own business as a sculptor in 1803. In c1816-17, he moved to the United States, where he continued to work as a sculptor, later with the patronage of Thomas Jefferson.

14¼in (36cm) high

$6,500-7,000   **HAN**

A Derby bisque figure of a shepherdess at gate, possibly modeled by William Coffee, incised "395."

$3,200-3,800   **HAN**

An early 19thC Derby group, of two maidens awakening Cupid, incised "195."

13in (33cm) high

$450-500   **FLD**

A Bloor Derby figure of John Liston in the role of Paul Pry, hands restored.

c1820   *6¼in (16cm) high*

$130-190   **CHOR**

A Derby coffee cup, painted with birds, possibly bitterns, hairline to handle.
c1758-60   2¼in (5.5cm) high
$550-650   BE

A pair of Derby baskets, painted with fruiting branches and moths, one replacement handle, hairline cracks.
c1760
$2,300-2,800   TEN

A Derby inkstand.
c1760   8¾in (22cm) wide
$1,500-1,900   WW

A Derby partridge tureen and cover, minor chips to flowers.
c1760   5in (13cm) long
$1,300-1,800   BE

A Derby basket and cover, with applied flowers and bird finial, small chips.
c1765   6in (15.5cm) high
$1,900-2,500   WW

A pair of Chelsea-Derby custard cups and covers, minor damages.
c1770   3¾in (9.5cm) high
$2,800-3,300   WW

A Derby wine taster.
Derby wine tasters in polychrome enamels are uncommon.
c1765-70   3¼in (8cm) wide
$450-500   WW

A Derby trout head stirrup cup, crack and chip restored.
c1800   ¾in (2cm) long
$700-880   HAN

A Derby vase, painted with a child, spaniel, and lady, marks in red, chip to base.
c1805   12¾in (32.5cm) high
$800-900   CHEF

An English porcelain plaque, probably Derby, by James Rouse Sr. (1802-88), signed, framed, and glazed.

James Rouse Sr. was apprenticed to Robert Bloor at the Nottingham Road Works, Derby, UK. He left Derby in c1826 and worked for John Rose at Coalport. In 1871, he left Coalport and worked for Ridgway before heading back to Derby in 1875 to work for Sampson Hancock in King Street. In 1882, he moved again to work at the factory on Osmaston Road.

plaque 7½in (19cm) wide
$700-750   DN

A Richard Chaffers Liverpool mug, printed with the arms of the Ancient and Honourable Society of Bucks, signed "Sadler Liverpool," chip to inside rim.

The print is after an engraving by H. Copeland, dated 1748, and is attributed to Jeremiah Evans. It can be found on Worcester and Longton Hall porcelain.

c1760   *4¾in (12cm) high*

$550-500   **WW**

A Chaffers Liverpool famille verte coffeepot and cover, minor nibbles to cover.

8in (20.5cm) high

$1,900-2,500   **HAN**

A Christian's Liverpool famille rose gravy boat, painted with Chinese figures, small chips.

c1765   *6in (15.5cm) wide*

$550-650   **BELL**

A William Reid Liverpool Rococo cream pitcher, stress crack to front.

c1755-58   *4¼in (11cm) high*

$1,900-2,500   **HAN**

A Philip Christian Liverpool tea canister and cover, painted with the arms of Brougham impaling Lamplugh.

A tea and coffee service was made for Peter Brougham, possibly on the occasion of a proposed marriage to his cousin, Elizabeth Falconer, prior to her death in May 1769.

c1768   *4¼in (11cm) high*

$1,300-1,800   **WW**

A William Reid Liverpool tankard, painted with an Asian figure and a dog.

c1756-58   *3½in (9cm) high*

$2,800-3,500   **HAN**

A William Reid Liverpool shell salt.

c1756-61   *4½in (11.5cm) wide*

$3,200-3,800   **WW**

A William Reid Liverpool famille verte teapot stand.

c1758   *4¼in (11cm) wide*

$1,900-2,500   **HAN**

A William Reid Liverpool teapot, marked "6," cover lacking, the spout chipped.

c1756-60   *7in (17.5cm) wide*

$500-650   **WW**

ESSENTIAL REFERENCE—LOWESTOFT

The Lowestoft factory was founded in 1757 by Robert Browne and three partners in Suffolk.

- It made phosphate porcelain, similar to Bow, with a tendency to discoloration. The glaze is of a greenish or grayish tone.
- In the factory's first ten years, it made wares decorated in underglaze blue, influenced by Worcester and by Chinese blue-and-white ceramics.
- From the mid-1760s, overglaze colors and underglaze blue printing were introduced. The factory also began to produce figures, often of dogs, cats, and sheep.
- The factory closed in 1800.

A Lowestoft miniature teapot and cover, decorator's mark "17," two chips to lid.
c1765   *3¼in (8cm) high*
$1,900-2,500   **LOW**

A Lowestoft miniature sucrier and cover, decorator's mark, chip inside lid.
c1765   *2in (5cm) high*
$2,300-2,800   **LOW**

A Lowestoft tea caddy, decorator's mark "2."
c1765-68   *3¾in (9.5cm) high*
$2,300-2,800   **LOW**

A Lowestoft vase, painted with a pagoda and landscape.
c1765   *4¼in (11cm) high*
$2,300-2,800   **LOW**

A Lowestoft feeding cup, decorator's mark "5."

This is a rare shape for 18thC English porcelain. Lowestoft was the only factory to produce feeding cups in any quantity.
c1768   *3½in (9cm) high*
$1,900-2,500   **KEY**

A Lowestoft teapot and cover, painted with Chinese figures, minor firing cracks, one glaze flaw.
c1770-75   *5in (12.5cm) high*
$1,000-1,500   **BE**

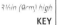

A 1780s Lowestoft milk pitcher and cover, with flower knop, crescent mark.
$950-1,050   **LOW**

A Lowestoft coffee cup and saucer, painted with Chinese figures, minor glaze flaws.
c1770-80   *saucer 4¾in (12cm) diam*
$1,300-1,900   **BE**

LOWESTOFT MARKS

Mark used c1775-90

A Lowestoft vase and cover, painted with Asian figures.
c1770-80   *5½in (14cm) high*
$1,900-2,500   **BE**

A Lowestoft tea canister and silver cover, painted in the "Curtis" pattern, the cover hallmarked "R.P.," London 1773, decorated by "T. Rose."
c1770-80   *4in (10cm) high*
$800-950   **BE**

A Lowestoft tea bowl and saucer, with unusual Asian-style decoration of chickens and figures, some hairline cracks.
c1775
$3,200-3,800   **LOW**

A Lowestoft enameled mug, painted with a bridge scene.
c1775-80   *3½in (9cm) high*
$3,800-5,000   **LOW**

A Lowestoft coffee cup and saucer, "Tobacco Leaf" pattern, decorator's mark "2," minor staining.
c1780
$1,150-1,400   **LOW**

A Lowestoft mug, painted with Asian figures.
c1775-80   *3½in (9cm) high*
$1,500-2,000   **BE**

A Lowestoft polychrome coffee cup.
c1780
$450-500   **LOW**

A Lowestoft sparrowbeak pitcher, with an Asian woman and child.
c1780-85
$650-750   **LOW**

A Lowestoft teapot and lid, small crack, chip to lid.
c1780-85
$750-800   **LOW**

A Lowestoft garniture vase, chips to rim, small stress cracks from base.
c1785   *6in (15cm) high*
$3,200-3,800   **LOW**

A Lowestoft vase, painted with the "Curtis" pattern, small chip to rim.
c1785   *4¼in (11cm) high*
$2,300-2,500   **LOW**

A Lowestoft "Royal Commemorative" mug, with scroll handle, inscribed "Long Live The King," with paper label.

In 1788-89, George III had his first episode of serious ill health. However, from March 1789, he was in remission for 12 years and reigned as a much loved monarch and a symbol of security in the era of France's revolutionary chaos. This rare decoration and inscription is thought to celebrate the King's return to health in the 1790s and is apparently unrecorded.
c1790-95   *3¼in (8.5cm) high*
$8,000-9,000   **BE**

A Lowestoft inkpot, inscribed "HL."

Hewling Luson was the owner of the Gunton Estate, near Lowestoft, where clay deposits were found by one of his tenants, Lowestoft founder Philip Walker. This inkpot was probably a presentation piece to Hewling Luson's son and the distinctive script of the initials are the work of Robert Allen.
c1790-95   *2¾in (7cm) diam*
$5,500-6,500   **BE**

A 1790s Lowestoft tea bowl and saucer, with cornflower sprays.
$700-800   **LOW**

A rare Lowestoft swan, in the white.
c1770-80   *2¾in (7cm) long*
$6,500-7,500   **BE**

CLOSER LOOK—LOWESTOFT FIGURES

These Lowestoft figures are modeled as musicians in contemporary dress and dancing poses, the male holding a triangle, the female with a mandolin or lute.

Despite restoration to both figures, their rarity ensures their value. This pair was the first to come onto the market in the last thirty years.

A Lowestoft cat, some chips, lacking part of its tail.

Although badly damaged, this cat commands a high price due to its rarity.
c1780   *2½in (6.5cm) high*
$5,500-7,000   **JN**

A Lowestoft ram, on a pad base with glazed vent hole, small chips to extremities.

During its final two decades of production, the factory made some unsophisticated animal models: a pair of pugs, a cat, three bird groups, a ram, and an ewe. All are considered rarities.
c1785-90   *2in (5cm) high*
$3,800-4,400   **PBE**

Each is mounted on a four-scroll base decorated with flowers.

Lowestoft's white-glazed figures are thought to be the forerunners of enameled figures produced a decade or so later.

A pair of Lowestoft musicians.
c1770   *larger 7½in (19cm) high*
$6,500-7,500   **KEY**

ESSENTIAL REFERENCE—MEISSEN

True hard-paste porcelain was first developed in Europe in 1708 by Johann Friedrich Böttger and Walther von Tschirnhausen. Böttger, an alchemist famed for his claims that he could create gold, had been ordered by Augustus the Strong, Elector Prince of Saxony and King of Poland, to assist the scientist von Tschirnhausen in his porcelain experiments. In 1710, Augustus the Strong set up the Meissen factory near Dresden. It was Europe's first hard-paste porcelain factory.

- The factory prospered under J.G. Höroldt, who was appointed as chief painter in 1720. Johann Joachim Kändler joined as chief modeler from 1733, and helped produce some of Meissen's most striking figures.
- Early decoration was highly influenced by Asian design. Copies of Japanese Kakiemon wares were produced, and many pieces were inspired by Chinese famille verte.
- From the 1730s, European themes became more popular, and pieces were decorated with harbor scenes, landscapes, or naturalistic flowers, known as "Deutsche Blumen" (German flowers).
- From the 1750s, wares were made in the newly popular Rococo style, embellished with scrolled bases and painted in pastel colors.
- Meissen's shapes, decoration, and crossed swords mark were widely copied by other European porcelain makers.
- In the 19thC, Meissen produced pieces in the popular Neo-classical, Biedermeier, Empire, and Gothic Revival styles. Meissen continued into the 20thC, where new designs were produced by Paul Scheurich and Max Esser. The factory is still active today.

A rare Meissen teapot and cover, with Böttger luster glaze, painted with landscape vignettes, underglazed blue "M.P.M." mark, some gilding wear and chips.

The underglaze blue "M.P.M." (Meissener Porzellan Manufaktur) mark is believed to have been used for only one year before the factory introduced the blue crossed swords mark in 1723. This teapot may have been decorated by young Johann Gregorius Höroldt (1696-1775), who worked as a porcelain painter for Meissen for fifty-plus years.

c1722   *6½in (16.5cm) wide*
$23,000-28,000   **REEM**

A Meissen Hausmaler teapot and cover, blue crossed swords mark, some wear.

c1720-25   *6¼in (16cm) high*
$2,300-2,800   **WW**

A Meissen plate, attributed to Christian Friedrich Herold, with maritime scenes and Chinese figures, blue crossed swords mark, some restoration.

c1725   *9½in (24cm) diam*
$5,000-6,300   **SOU**

A Meissen chinoiserie tea bowl and saucer, numbered "50," minor wear to gilding.

c1723-25   *saucer 5in (12.5cm) diam*
$2,500-3,200   **HAN**

A Meissen Kakiemon beaker and trembleuse saucer, blue crossed swords marks, small filled rim chip.

c1730   *5in (12.5cm) high*
$1,150-1,500   **WW**

A Meissen cabinet plate, with courting couples, blue crossed swords mark.

c1735-40   *9¼in (23.5cm) diam*
$3,200-3,800   **WW**

A Meissen pitcher, with a harbor scene, a Rococo shield, and amorini, blue crossed swords mark and gilt dot, lacking lid, some scratches and rubbing.

c1735   *6¾in (17cm) high*
$4,400-5,000   **MOR**

MEISSEN MARKS

Mark used 1723-40

Mark used 1763-74

Mark used c1774-1814

Mark used 19thC-c1925

CLOSER LOOK—"SWAN" SERVICE PLATE

This plate is from the "Schwanenservice" or "Swan service," created by J.J. Kändler and Johann Friedrich Eberlein for Count von Brühl, in c1737-42. The service consisted of 2,200 individual parts, one of the largest ever made.

The plate is molded in the form of a shallow seashell, decorated with swans in relief, and painted with flowers on the rim.

It is further decorated with the crest of Count von Brühl and his wife, Countess Franziska Kolowrat-Krakowsky. Count von Brühl was First Minister of the Electorate of Saxony from 1746 and director of the Meissen factory 1733-63.

More than half the "Swan" service is thought to have been destroyed in World War II, so pieces are rare. The high quality of the porcelain and the ties to Count von Brühl further increase the value.

A Meissen plate, underglaze blue sword mark.

1738   16½in (42cm) diam

$25,000-32,000   MTZ

A Meissen cup and saucer, blue crossed swords mark, gilt number "1," impressed "23" to saucer, small chip to saucer.

c1740   saucer 5in (13cm) diam

$2,300-2,800   HAN

A Meissen gold-mounted snuff box, painted with courting couples, discharge mark.

c1740   3in (7.5cm) long

$2,300-2,800   WW

A rare Meissen gold-mounted snuff box, with courting couples and Commedia dell'Arte figures.

c1760   3¼in (8cm) long

$15,000-19,000   WW

A Meissen figure of Harlequin, later decorated in bright enamels, some damages.

c1745   5¾in (14.5cm) high

$500-650   MOR

A Meissen snuff box, with osier-type molding, painted with "Deutsche Blumen," the interior lid with a spaniel, gilt-metal mounts, paper Hasse Collection label

c1760   3¼in (8cm) long

$4,400-5,000   WW

A Meissen figure of a woman playing a hurdy-gurdy, blue crossed swords mark.

c1750   figure 6in (15cm) high

$1,150-1,400   JN

A miniature Meissen bottle, blue crossed swords mark, painted "k.H.C."

This is from the "Red Dragon" service, made for the Saxon Royal Court Pantry, Dresden.

c1740-50   3in (7.5cm) high

$2,800-3,200   HAN

A mid-18thC Meissen monkey band figure, modeled by Peter Reinicke, blue crossed swords mark, some restoration.

6in (15cm) high

$1,500-1,800   WW

A mid-18thC Meissen Harlequin scent bottle, faint blue crossed swords mark, some damages.

3¼in (8cm) high

$1,800-2,300 WW

A pair of Meissen figures of a blacksmith and woodcutter, the blacksmith incised "50," small blue crossed swords mark, minor chips and hairlines.

The puce scrolls on the bases and the very small blue marks are more commonly found on English copies of Meissen pieces than on Meissen originals, but there are some comparable examples. This pair is extremely rare.

c1750 8¾in (22cm) high

$8,000-9,500 FELL

A Meissen figure of a fox, blue crossed swords mark, some restoration.

c1760 4in (10cm) wide

$500-650 WW

A Meissen group, "The Good Mother," blue crossed swords mark, incised "E69," some damages.

c1860 8¾in (22cm) high

$650-750 CHOR

A pair of 19thC Meissen groups, blue crossed swords marks, incised "H81" and "82."

5¾in (14.5cm) high

$1,900-2,500 JN

A 19thC Meissen figure of a gardener, numbered "59" and "692," minor losses to extremities.

7½in (19cm) high

$400-450 APAR

A Meissen group, after the original by Michel Victor Acier and Johann Carl Schönheit, blue crossed swords mark, marked "G32," "57," and "10," some losses and chips.

c1875-80 10¾in (27cm) high

$1,050-1,200 SWO

A pair of Meissen figures, after the originals by Johann Carl Schönheit, impressed "B65," canceled and ground out crossed swords mark, some damages.

c1875-80 19¼in (49cm) high

$4,400-5,700 SWO

CLOSER LOOK—MEISSEN EWER

This Meissen ewer is decorated to symbolize "The Element Water."

The spout is shell molded above painted insects, with a ribbon-tied reed handle surmounted by a winged putto.

The body is molded with a fleet of warships at sea between an applied figure of a Nereid (sea nymph) and Neptune in a shell chariot.

The foot is molded with bulrushes and applied with stylized dolphins.

A Meissen ewer.

c1880 26in (66.5cm) high

$10,000-11,000 MEA

A late 19thC Meissen centerpiece bowl on stand, blue crossed swords marks, some damages and losses.

22¾in (58cm) wide

$15,000-19,000 **BELL**

A Meissen group, by Gustav Deloy, blue crossed swords mark, incised "Nu. P114."

c1890

$1,300-1,800 **JN**

A late 19thC Meissen parrot, blue crossed swords mark, incised model "No 53X" and "89."

13in (33cm) high

$1,000-1,050 **BELL**

A Meissen model of Zemira, after the original by J.J. Kändler, blue crossed swords mark, rubbed inscription, "Chien favorit de feu SM l'Imperatrice Catherine de Russie," losses to tassels.

Catherine II of Russia, better known as Catherine the Great, loved greyhounds. Her most treasured companion was Zemira, named after the heroine from a Beauty and the Beast opera, Zemira and Azor. Zemira joined Catherine for daily walks and slept on a silk cushion in her chambers. After Zemira's death, Catherine is said to have been so upset that she shut herself in her room for several days. Catherine had Zemira's tombstone engraved with an epitaph written by the French ambassador Count Ségur: "Here lies Zemira and the mourning graces ought to throw flowers on her grave... The gods, witnesses of her faithfulness, should have rewarded her for her loyalty with immortality."

c1850-70 *17in (43cm) long*

$10,000-11,000 **BE**

A late 19thC Meissen parrot, blue crossed swords mark, incised, some restoration.

10¾in (27.5cm) high

$550-700 **BELL**

A Meissen parrot, blue crossed swords mark.

12in (30.5cm) high

$1,500-1,900 **JN**

A late 19thC Meissen Bolognese hound, after the original by J.J. Kändler, underscored blue crossed swords mark, tail detached.

9in (23cm) high

$750-900 **BELL**

An early 20thC Meissen "Onion" part dinner service, with 48 plates, a tureen and cover, 2 gravy boats, a fish dish, 5 serving dishes, blue crossed swords marks, one dish with cancellation marks.

$13,000-18,000 **DN**

A Meissen goat, modeled by Eric Hoesel, blue crossed swords mark, incised "No. V107."
c1925   *12½in (32cm) high*
$1,300-1,800   **JN**

A rare Meissen Japanese chin, modeled by Eric Hoesel, blue crossed swords mark, incised "N148."
c1915   *4½in (11.5cm) high*
$1,500-2,000   **JN**

A pair of Meissen figures of the Senses, blue crossed swords mark, impressed "No.122," incised "E2," firing crack to base of one.
5in (12.5cm) high
$1,800-2,300   **CHOR**

A Meissen figure of a girl, doll, and baby carriage, by Konrad Hentschel, incised "W124," blue crossed swords.

Konrad Hentschel (1872-1907) designed a series of figures for Meissen in the Art Nouveau style c1905. They were seen as a refreshing change from the earlier "old" figures produced by Meissen and became an instant success.
c1905   *5in (12.5cm) high*
$1,800-2,300   **TW**

An early 20thC Meissen Schneeballen vase, encrusted with blossom, branches, and birds, minor restoration, the parrot previously broken off.
19¼in (49cm) high
$15,000-19,000   **CHOR**

A Meissen group of lovers, modeled by Alfred König, blue crossed swords mark, incised '4257'.
c1912   *9in (23cm) high*
$2,500-3,200   **JN**

A Meissen figure of two girls, modeled after the original by Alfred König, blue crossed swords mark, impressed "Y.181" and "34."
7¾in (20cm) high
$2,500-3,200   **BE**

An Art Nouveau Meissen figure of a girl, attributed to Alfred König, model H.157, impressed marks, crossed swords mark.
8in (20.5cm) high
$2,300-2,800   **WW**

A Meissen porcelain figure group, modeled by Paul Scheurich (1883-1945), No.A1226, blue crossed swords mark, incised and impressed "1186," incised "Scheurich."
14¼in (36cm) high
$3,200-3,800   **CAN**

ESSENTIAL REFERENCE—NANTGARW

In 1813, William Weston Young and William Billingsley, previously a decorator at Derby, set up a factory at Nantgarw, Wales.

- In 1814, the company moved to Swansea, Wales, and merged with Lewis Weston Dillwyn's Cambrian Pottery. In 1817, Dillwyn left the business and Billingsley and Young returned to Nantgarw and reopened the factory. It was purchased by Coalport in 1819 and remained open until 1823.
- The porcelain was so fine that it was exceptionally difficult to fire and a large proportion was lost in the kiln. Nantgarw chiefly made tea wares and flatwares. Large hollow wares are particularly rare.
- Nantgarw porcelain is usually translucent and almost pure white when held to the light. The glaze tends to be thick and smooth.
- Billingsley was especially known for his flower painting. Decorating was done either at Nantgarw or in London.
- Nantgarw wares tend to be impressed "NANTGARW CW" (CW for China Works).

A Nantgarw dessert dish, decorated in London, impressed "NANT GARW CW" to base.
c1818-20   *9½in (24cm) diam*
$1,900-2,500   JON

A Nantgarw dish, painted in the manner of William Pollard, impressed "Nantgarw CW," incised "B."

Impressed letters and incised numerals are occasionally found in conjunction with the usual Nantgarw mark; their significance is discussed by David M. Phillips in "Swansea Nantgarw Review No 2."
c1818-20   *11¾in (30cm) wide*
$950-1,050   WW

A Nantgarw plate, decorated by Mortlock's, London, impressed "NANT GARW CW," inscribed "Mortlock's" in gold.

It is unusual for pieces made at Nantgarw and painted in London to be marked with their London decorator.
9in (23cm) diam
$650-750   JON

A Nantgarw plate, impressed "NANT GARW CW."
9½in (24cm) diam
$750-900   JON

A Nantgarw fan-handled dish, impressed "NANT GARW CW."
9in (23cm) wide
$750-900   JON

A Nantgarw tureen, cover, and stand, from the Brace service, with pineapple knop.
c1818-20   *5in (13cm) high*
$5,000-6,300   JON

A Nantgarw cup and saucer.
$500-650   JON

CLOSER LOOK—MASONIC TUMBLER

This tumbler is gilt-decorated with Masonic symbols, with a set square and compass on the obverse.

The reverse is intricately decorated with the sun as a deity.

The tapered body has gilt bands on the top and bottom.

It is probably one of only six ever made, originally sold in 1821 by Nantgarw founder William Billingsley to a Mr. Hopkin-Jones, at 4 shillings 6 pence (about $16) each.

A rare Nantgarw Masonic tumbler.
1819   *3¼in (8cm) high*
$6,500-7,500   JON

A mid-to-late 18thC Sèvres biscuit figure of a girl, "La Petite Fille a la Cage," incised "F" to base, some chips and firing cracks.

8½in (21.5cm) high

$400-450   **BELL**

A Sèvres biscuit figure, possibly modeled by Josse-François-Joseph Leriche, titled "M'elle LAFOREST (l'ainé) role de Jeanette," incised marks.

This figure depicts Mademoiselle La Forrest in her role as Jeanette in A.L. De Beaunoir's play "Jeanette ou Les Battus ne payent pas toujours l'amende," a one-act comedy.

c1780   *11in (29cm) high*

$650-700   **WW**

A pair of Sèvres stands, painted by Pierre Antoine Merault (fl.1754-91) and François Binet (fl.1750-75), painted marks, glazed-over rim chip, minor wear.

1756/59   *10¾in (27.5cm) wide*

$550-650   **TEN**

Two Sèvres cups and saucers, painted by François Aloncle, date codes to one.

c1760   *saucer 5¼in (13.5cm) diam*

$2,500-3,200   **WW**

A pair of Sèvres serving dishes, interlaced "LL" mark to one, some wear.

c1760   *13¾in (35cm) wide*

$2,300-2,800   **WW**

A Sèvres pitcher and basin, crowned interlaced "LL" marks, some wear to enamel.

c1760-70   *10¼in (26cm) high*

$2,800-3,300   **WW**

A Sèvres coffee cup and saucer, probably decorated in London, with an oeil-de-perdrix ground, blue interlaced "LL" marks.

c1760-70   *saucer 5¼in (13.5cm) diam*

$550-700   **WW**

A Sèvres pot and cover, blue interlaced "LL" marks, date code "L."

c1764   *2¾in (7cm) high*

$450-500   **WW**

SÈVRES MARKS

Mark used 1769-93

A pair of Sèvres orange-tubs, blue interlaced "LL" marks, date code "M" above "S," hairline cracks, one finial reattached.

c1765   *5¾in (14.5cm) high*

$550-650   **BELL**

A pair of Sèvres pots and covers, painted by Claude Antoine Tardy, blue interlaced "LL" marks, painter's mark, date code.

1766   *4in (10cm) diam*

$2,300-2,800   **WW**

A Sèvres cup and saucer, the saucer incised "pate no. 43," blue interlaced "LL" mark, painter's initials "SC," date code.

1768   *saucer 4¼in (11cm) diam*

$650-750   **WW**

A Sèvres saucer dish, gray interlaced "LL" mark, gilder's mark, date code "Z."

1777   *8½in (21.5cm) diam*

$1,900-2,500   **LC**

A pair of Sèvres dessert plates, in the "Jardin" design, stacking wear, some rubbing, dated.

These plates are almost certainly from a service of 48 delivered to MM Boyd Kerr et Compagnie, Paris-based British bankers, acting as intermediaries for Jacques Gordon, possibly James Gordon MP.

1789   *9½in (24cm) diam*

$1,500-2,000   **CHOR**

A Sèvres bowl, molded with feuilles-de-choux, blue interlaced "LL" mark, painter's mark "a," script "G," date code "Q."

1796   *10¼in (26cm) diam*

$450-550   **MOR**

A pair of French Empire porcelain and ormolu-mounted faux tortoiseshell urns, possibly Sèvres or Dihl & Guerhard, the mounts attributed to Pierre-Philippe Thomire (1751-1843).

19in (48.5cm) high

$38,000-44,000   **WW**

A 19thC Sèvres porcelain tea for two set.

tray 13in (34cm) wide

$25,000-32,000   **HANN**

A Sèvres cabinet plate, depicting "Le Mort de Gaston de Foix en 1512," from "Bataille de Ravenies," the border with portrait medallions including Louis XIV and Marie Antoinette.

12½in (34cm) long

$2,500-3,200   **HAN**

A Sèvres Imperial teapot, with monkey decoration, dated.

Having been made for Royalty, this teapot is highly desirable, despite restoration to the handle, which has previously been broken and repaired.

1833   *6¼in (16cm) high*

$19,000-25,000   **K&O**

A Sèvres plate, painted with Raoul de Beaumont, incised marks, printed date, painted inscription, minor glaze scratches, and gilt rubbing.

The Beaumont and later Beaumont-Brienne family were the Viscounts of Maine, France, from the 10thC to the 14thC.

1835   *9½in (24cm) diam*

$5,000-5,700   **PW**

A Sèvres chocolate cup and saucer, incised fabrication marks, the saucer with stenciled mark for Louis XVIII, minor wear.

c1814-24   *saucer 6¼in (16cm) diam*

$2,800-3,200   **BE**

A late 19thC Sèvres cup and saucer, painted marks.

saucer 5in (12.5cm) diam

$1,900-2,500   **DUK**

A Sèvres reticulated teacup and saucer, with bamboo-style handle.

c1884

$1,500-2,000   **HAN**

A pair of late 19thC to early 20thC Sèvres "Summer" and "Winter" plates, overglaze blue painted factory mark.

9¾in (25cm) diam

$400-500   **HALL**

A late 19thC to early 20thC Sèvres-style parcel-gilt biscuit jardinière, with ram's mask handles, molded with putti, blue interlaced "LL" mark, some loss and wear.

18in (46cm) diam

$2,300-2,800   **BELL**

A Sèvres Art Nouveau-style floor vase, designed by A. Gumery, inscribed "A. GUMERY," printed factory marks to interior, dated.

1913   *23¼in (59cm) high*

$9,500-10,500   **DN**

A Vauxhall teapot, with a Chinese cover, restoration to spout, star crack to base, chips to rim.
c1755
$700-800 PW

A Vauxhall milk pitcher, metal replacement handle, some faults.
c1758-60 *3¼in (8cm) high*
$300-400 WW

A Vauxhall cream boat, with interior cailloute panel, restoration to rim.
c1760-65 *5½in (14cm) long*
$650-750 WW

A Vauxhall tea bowl and saucer, painted in the Imari palette, minor faults to foot rims.
c1755
$950-1,050 PW

A Vauxhall porcelain group of two putti and a dolphin.
c1755 *6¾in (17cm) high*
$1,400-1,900 BELL

A pair of Vauxhall porcelain figures of a gardener and his companion.
c1755 *6in (15cm) high*
$1,300-1,800 DN

A pair of Vauxhall porcelain figures.
c1755 *5in (13cm) high*
$800-950 DN

A rare Vauxhall figure of a man, reclining on a scrolled base, restoration to right arm.
c1760 *6in (15.5cm) high*
$2,500-3,200 WW

PORCELAIN

A pair of late 19thC Vienna tea caddies and covers, blue beehive marks, some rubbing and scratches.

8¾in (22.5cm) high

$400-450   MOR

A 19thC Vienna tureen, cover, and stand, with drinking and gambling scenes, underglaze blue marks, broken and reglued.

10¼in (26cm) high

$500-650   SWO

A gilt-metal-mounted Vienna tankard and cover, titled "Darius," blue shield mark, minor surface scratches.

c1900   6¼in (16cm) high

$1,500-2,000   TEN

A 19thC Vienna dish, depicting Aeneas saving Anchises, blue beehive mark.

13½in (34.5cm) wide

$1,150-1,500   BELL

A late 19thC Vienna charger, depicting Neptune, signed "Rob Pilz," painted mark and title to base, minor surface wear.

14in (35.5cm) diam

$1,300-1,800   DRA

A pair of Vienna plaques, one titled "Reflection," the other "Erbluht," both signed "Wagner."

The Wagners were a family of artists working for KPM and other German porcelain makers in the 19thC. The signature "Wagner" also appears on Vienna wares. Pieces signed "Wagner," especially portraits, tend to be of high quality.

7¼in (18.5cm) high

$650-750   GWA

A 19thC Vienna cabinet plate, depicting Ruth, marked and titled to base, minor wear.

9½in (24cm) diam

$700-750   APAR

A 19thC Vienna-style tray, painted with "The Spirit of the Alps," after Konrad Dielitz, signed "P Hoffmann," titled on reverse, blue shield mark.

20in (50.5cm) diam

$2,300-2,800   WW

VIENNA MARK

Mark used 1784 onward

ESSENTIAL REFERENCE—WORCESTER

The first Worcester factory was established in 1751 by a team of fifteen men, headed by Dr. John Wall. It produced tableware, tea and coffee services, inkwells, and more, made from soft-paste porcelain with a greenish or bluish glaze, often with Chinese-style decoration.

● After Dr. Wall's retirement in 1783, the Worcester factory was purchased by Thomas Flight. It was managed by the family for nearly sixty years, known variously as Flight (1783-92), Flight & Barr (1792-1804), Barr, Flight & Barr (1804-13), and Flight, Barr & Barr (1813-40). Thomas Flight introduced hard-paste porcelain. In the early 19thC, the factory continued to produce tableware and mantel-shelf pieces, increasingly in Neoclassical and Rococo designs.

● At the same time, two further Worcester factories were operating: that of Humphrey Chamberlain, founded c1786; and that of Thomas Grainger, founded c1806. Chamberlain's and Flight's merged in 1840 to form Chamberlain & Co. Henry Kerr and Richard William Binns took over the management of the Chamberlain & Co. works 1852-62.

● In 1862, Kerr left the company and Binns continued to manage the factory alone. It became known as Royal Worcester, and focused on the production of figures and vases. It is especially known for its Japonaise wares and its individually decorated vases and pot pourris in Classical shapes.

A Worcester pickle dish, painted with a "Long Eliza" figure, small rim chips.

"Long Eliza" is the term for elongated female figures often found on Chinese porcelain and later imitated by English factories. This design derives from Limehouse and is seen on Lund's Bristol and early Worcester porcelain. Lund's examples tend to be slightly narrower than Worcester ones (see page 47).

c1751-52   *4in (10cm) high*
$1,500-1,900   **WW**

A Worcester tea bowl and saucer, painted with the "Romantic Rocks" pattern, workman's marks, some rim chips.

c1755   *5in (12.5cm) high*
$950-1,050   **WW**

A Worcester cream pitcher, painted with the "Indian Fisherman" pattern, workman's mark, minor damages.

c1755-56   *4in (10cm) high*
$1,150-1,400   **WW**

A Worcester mug, painted with the "The Walk In The Garden" pattern.

1755-65   *5¾in (14.5cm) high*
$500-650   **JN**

A Worcester tea bowl and saucer, printed with the "Two Swan Precipice" pattern.

c1757-60   *saucer 4½in (11.5cm) wide*
$1,300-1,800   **WW**

A Worcester coffee cup, painted in the "Solid Fence Pavilion" pattern, workman's mark.

c1760   *3in (7.5cm) high*
$550-650   **TEN**

A Worcester guglet, or water bottle, and basin, painted with the "Willow Bridge Fisherman" pattern, open crescent mark, script "W," the bowl broken and repaired.

The term "guglet" is believed to derive from the sound made by liquid pouring out of the wide neck of such shaped bottles. The flared neck of this bottle is less common at Worcester than the narrow truncated opening on similar bottles.

c1760-65   *11in (28cm) high*
$1,300-1,800   **WW**

WORCESTER MARKS

Mark used c1755-75

Mark used c1755-90

A Worcester dish, by Robert Hancock, printed in black with the King of Prussia, after a portrait by Antoine Pesne, signed "RH Worcester," dated.

Robert Hancock was an engraver and painter who joined the Worcester Porcelain Company in 1756. He later became a partner of the firm. At Worcester, he engraved copper plates for transfer-printing on porcelain, adapting many designs from contemporary engravings and paintings.

1757   *7in (17.5cm) diam*
$2,000-2,500   **WW**

A Worcester slop bowl, printed in black with Britannia and figures, one with a banner reading "Marine Society," the interior with a portrait of George II, chip to rim.

The source for this print is an engraving by Thomas Major after a drawing by Samuel Wale from Motives for the Establishment of the Marine Society, London 1757. The society, the world's first maritime charity, had been set up the previous year to support the navy at the start of the Seven Year's War.

c1760   *6½in (16.5cm) wide*
$750-900   **WW**

A Worcester "Pitt the Elder" mug.

c1760   *3¼in (8.5cm) high*
$2,800-3,300   **H&C**

A Worcester mug, printed with the "Tree Grafters" and "Whitton Anglers" patterns, slight glaze flaw.

c1765   *3¼in (8.5cm) high*
$650-750   **HAN**

A Worcester coffeepot and cover, printed with the "Milkmaids" pattern, later colored with polychrome enamels, overglaze blue crossed swords mark.

c1770   *8in (20cm) high*
$550-700   **WW**

A Worcester cream boat, painted in famille verte enamels, restoration to handle, glaze frit to lip.

c1752-53   *4¼in (11cm) wide*
$1,150-1,500   **BE**

A Worcester coffee can, painted with flowers and insects, some factory faults, chip to rim.

c1753   *2¼in (5.5cm) high*
$1,400-1,800   **PW**

A Worcester coffee cup, painted with the "Snake in a Basket" pattern, glaze flaw to rim.

c1753-54   *2¼in (6cm) high*
$1,400-1,800   **BE**

A Worcester coffee cup, with grooved loop handle, printed with the "The Fortune Teller, no. 2" pattern, after Robert Hancock.

c1754-55   *2¼in (6cm) high*
$1,400-1,800   **BE**

A Worcester cauliflower tureen, cover, and stand.

c1757-60   *stand 8½in (21.5cm) long*
$2,000-2,500   **WW**

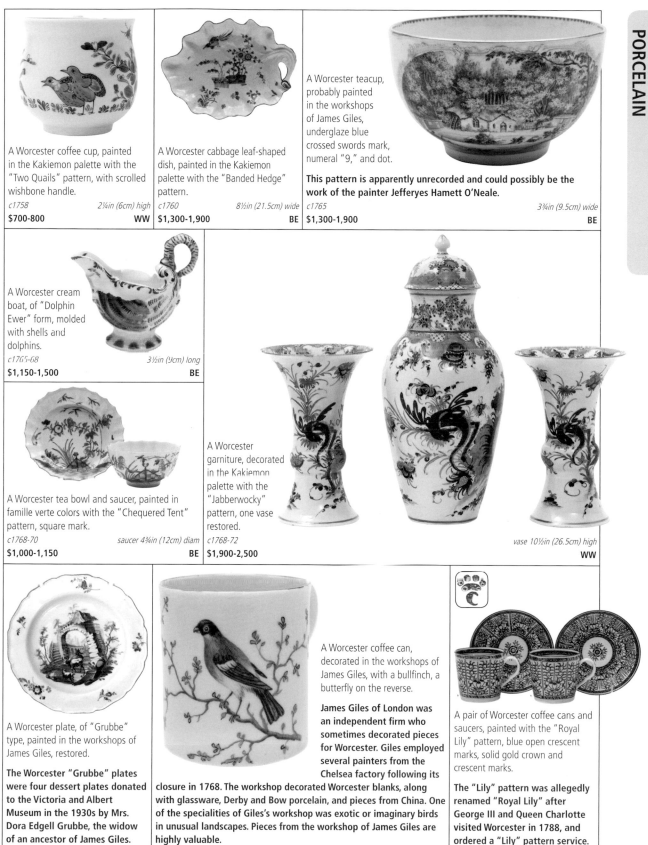

A Worcester coffee cup, painted in the Kakiemon palette with the "Two Quails" pattern, with scrolled wishbone handle.

c1758 2¼in (6cm) high

$700-800 WW

A Worcester cabbage leaf-shaped dish, painted in the Kakiemon palette with the "Banded Hedge" pattern.

c1760 8½in (21.5cm) wide

$1,300-1,900 BE

A Worcester teacup, probably painted in the workshops of James Giles, underglaze blue crossed swords mark, numeral "9," and dot.

This pattern is apparently unrecorded and could possibly be the work of the painter Jefferyes Hamett O'Neale.

c1765 3¾in (9.5cm) wide

$1,300-1,900 BE

A Worcester cream boat, of "Dolphin Ewer" form, molded with shells and dolphins.

c1765-68 3½in (9cm) long

$1,150-1,500 BE

A Worcester tea bowl and saucer, painted in famille verte colors with the "Chequered Tent" pattern, square mark.

c1768-70 saucer 4¾in (12cm) diam

$1,000-1,150 BE

A Worcester garniture, decorated in the Kakiemon palette with the "Jabberwocky" pattern, one vase restored.

c1768-72

$1,900-2,500 BE

vase 10½in (26.5cm) high

WW

A Worcester plate, of "Grubbe" type, painted in the workshops of James Giles, restored.

The Worcester "Grubbe" plates were four dessert plates donated to the Victoria and Albert Museum in the 1930s by Mrs. Dora Edgell Grubbe, the widow of an ancestor of James Giles.

c1770 8¾in (22.5cm) wide

$2,300-2,800 WW

A Worcester coffee can, decorated in the workshops of James Giles, with a bullfinch, a butterfly on the reverse.

James Giles of London was an independent firm who sometimes decorated pieces for Worcester. Giles employed several painters from the Chelsea factory following its closure in 1768. The workshop decorated Worcester blanks, along with glassware, Derby and Bow porcelain, and pieces from China. One of the specialities of Giles's workshop was exotic or imaginary birds in unusual landscapes. Pieces from the workshop of James Giles are highly valuable.

c1770-72 2¼in (6cm) high

$9,500-10,500 BE

A pair of Worcester coffee cans and saucers, painted with the "Royal Lily" pattern, blue open crescent marks, solid gold crown and crescent marks.

The "Lily" pattern was allegedly renamed "Royal Lily" after George III and Queen Charlotte visited Worcester in 1788, and ordered a "Lily" pattern service.

c1788-90 saucers 5¼in (13.5cm) diam

$1,300-1,900 BE

A rare pair of early 19thC Chamberlain's vases, one with Stafford's of New Bond Street label, one with restoration.

6¼in (16cm) high

$7,500-8,000   **LSK**

A pair of Flight soup bowls, from "The Celebrated Hope" service ordered by the Duke of Clarence, decorated by John Pennington, blue Flight mark.

c1790   *9¾in (24.5cm) diam*

$1,300-1,900   **DUK**

A pair of Flight & Barr beakers, incised "F&B" and crowned script marks "Flight & Barr Worcester/ Manuf. to their Maj."

c1800   *4in (10cm) high*

$2,300-2,800   **BE**

A Flight & Barr pitcher, painted with a portrait of George III, probably by John Pennington (1773-1841), script crown mark to base.

The use of the painted Flight & Barr mark is recorded c1792-1807, although the company was chiefly known as Barr, Flight & Barr from 1804.

c1807   *6¾in (17cm) high*

$3,800-4,400   **H&C**

A Flight & Barr triple-spill vase, painted by Thomas Baxter, incised "B" mark, minor wear to gilding.

The rare orange ground, combined with the quality of Thomas Baxter's shell painting, makes this vase especially desirable.

c1800-05   *5¾in (14.5cm) high*

$28,000-33,000   **BE**

A Barr, Flight & Barr vase, with dolphin handles, painted with Tintern Abbey, Monmouthshire, crown mark, script title and marks.

c1805-10   *13in (33cm) high*

$11,000-13,000   **BE**

A pair of Flight, Barr & Barr urns, of Neoclassical design, impressed and script marks.

c1815-20   *7¾in (20cm) high*

$7,00-7,500   **BE**

A Barr, Flight & Barr dessert service, by William Billingsley, with 2 tureens and covers, 2 dishes, and 24 plates, impressed and printed marks, one plate chipped, restoration to finials, some gilt rubbing.

William Billingsley (1758-1828) was born in Derby and apprenticed at the William Duesbury Derby China Works. He left Derby in 1795 and later worked for Barr, Flight & Barr, Nantgarw, Swansea, Coalport, and the Torksey Porcelain Manufactory, Lincolnshire. He was a highly talented painter, particularly known for his depictions of flowers.

c1810   *plates 8¼in (21cm) diam*

$19,000-25,000 for the set   **H&C**

A Flight, Barr & Barr "King Fisher" vase and cover, possibly painted by William Doe, titled to reverse, script marks, chip to flambé finial.

c1815-20   *7¼in (18.5cm) high*

$8,000-9,000   **BE**

WORCESTER MARKS

BFB

Mark used c1807-13

FLIGHT, BARR & BARR
Proprietors of the
Royal Porcelain Works
WORCESTER
Established 1751

Mark used c1813-40

A Flight, Barr & Barr pastille burner and stand, impressed and script marks, cracked.

c1825-30   *6¾in (17cm) high*

$800-950   **BE**

A Royal Worcester fruit-painted vase and cover, by Harry Ayrton, signed.

Harry Ayrton (1905-76) started at the Royal Worcester factory in 1920 and worked there until his retirement in 1970.

$4,400-5,000   **HAN**

A pair of framed Royal Worcester plaques, by Harry Davis, with puce factory marks, signed, date code.

1920   *4in (10cm) diam*

$5,500-6,500   **LC**

A pair of Royal Worcester ewers, by Harry Davis, signed, with printed factory marks.

Harry Davis (1885-1970), the son of a Royal Worcester china figure maker, was apprenticed at Royal Worcester at the age of 14. He is known for his landscapes and depictions of nature.

11½in (29cm) high

$11,000-14,000   **HALL**

A Royal Worcester plate, by John Freeman, signed, black printed mark.

9½in (24cm) diam

$700-750   **FELL**

CLOSER LOOK—"HUNTING" VASE

This vase is of campana form, with a pineapple finial and rope-twist fox-head handles.

Each side is painted with a hunting scene, "Swishing at a rasper" and "Going in and out clever" on a claret ground.

It would have been the center vase of a "HuntingH garniture.

The vase is marked in script. "Flight, Barr & Barr/Royal Porcelain Works, Worcester/ London House 1, Coventry Street."

A Flight, Barr & Barr "Hunting" vase and cover.

c1830   *20in (51cm) high*

$15,000-19,000   **BE**

An Aesthetic movement Royal Worcester vase, in the style of Christopher Dresser, with puce and molded marks.

Besides the typically Aesthetic Japonaise bird and foliage design, the grotesque handles are reminiscent of one of Dresser's most famous designs for Ault Pottery, known as the "Tongue Vase."

1877   *13½in (34cm) high*

$550-650   **HAN**

A Royal Worcester vase, decorated by William Jarman, signed, green printed mark with date code.

1910   *14¼in (36cm) high*

$550-650   **FLD**

WORCESTER PORCELAIN MARKS

Mark used 1852-62

Mark used 1891-

A Royal Worcester vase, by Arthur Lewis, signed, with puce marks, marked "1410."

1909   *11in (28cm) high*
$2,500-3,200   **HAN**

A Royal Worcester reticulated goblet, attributed to George Owen, printed green mark, date code.

George Owen (1845-1917) began working for Royal Worcester in 1859. He is especially known for his pierced or reticulated porcelain, where an inner wall of porcelain is left intact inside an outer wall with piercings, emulating the style of many Chinese ivory carvings. This technique required a particularly high level of skill.

1878   *7¾in (19.5cm) high*
$5,000-7,500   **LSK**

A Royal Worcester reticulated cup and saucer, attributed to George Owen, green backstamp, indistinct date code, and gilder's mark.

c1882
$7,500-8,000   **BE**

A Royal Worcester reticulated vase and cover, by George Owen, with incised signature, gilt marks, and "169."

1912   *6½in (16.5cm) high*
$15,000-19,000   **HAN**

An early 20thC Royal Worcester reticulated ewer vase, by George Owen, signed, gilt mark, and "1581."

6¼in (16cm) high
$13,000-18,000   **HAN**

A pair of Royal Worcester plaques, "Off Hastings" and "The Port of Havre," painted by Raymond Rushton, signed and titled, puce marks, and date code, framed.

1919   *6in (15cm) wide*
$1,600-2,000   **BE**

A Royal Worcester vase, painted by D. Shinnie, signed.

D. Shinnie was a painter and decorator at Royal Worcester, active in the second half of the 20thC.

$1,300-1,800   **HAN**

An early 20thC Royal Worcester Art Nouveau vase, shape 1686, monogrammed "RJD," puce mark, indistinct date code, some damages.

18¾in (47.5cm) high
$700-800   **FLD**

A framed Royal Worcester plaque, by John Stinton, signed, puce mark to reverse.

plaque 4¼in (10.5cm) diam
$1,900-2,500   **GWA**

A pair of Royal Worcester vases and covers, by John Stinton, puce marks.

John Stinton was born in 1854. His father worked for Royal Worcester, but he himself did not discover porcelain painting until the age of 35. He was a talented painter, best known for his depictions of British cattle and castles. He lived to be 102 years old.

11½in (29.5cm) high
$2,300-2,800   **HAN**

A Baddeley-Littler pitcher, glaze blemish to rim.

c1780-85   *3¼in (8.5cm) high*

$650-750   **PW**

A Calcut Jackfield blue-and-white cabbage leaf pitcher, transfer-printed with the "Elephant" pattern.

The Calcut China Manufactory operated in the Jackfield area of Shropshire, UK. Very little documentation survives regarding the factory, but it is probable that it was operational by late 1794 and had been subsumed into John Rose's Coalport factory by the end of 1796. See Roger S. Edmundson, "Northern Ceramic Society Journal" (2011), 27, 75.

c1794-96   *7¾in (20cm) high*

$1,500-2,000   **HALL**

Judith Picks

This teapot was purchased at a Lincolnshire sale for £15 ($19) and, two years on, sold at auction for £460,000 ($580,000) plus premium. It is now in the Metropolitan Museum, New York. It is probably America's oldest porcelain teapot, only identified very recently. It is the seventh recorded piece of John Bartlam's porcelain and bears significant similarities to his other designs, and to fragments excavated from the site of his factory in Cain Hoy, South Carolina.

John Bartlam was born in England and apprenticed to a potter in Staffordshire. He left England c1763 and traveled to South Carolina, where he established

himself as a potter in Cain Hoy. South Carolina was then one of the wealthiest areas of North America, and residents were eager for the latest and finest ceramics from England. The area also had easy access to kaolin clay.

Bartlam therefore endeavored to make porcelain to rival that being imported from England, probably with the help of someone with experience in the British porcelain industry. By 1768, Bartlam was having financial difficulties. His factory relocated to Charleston in 1770. By 1772, his financial situation was again precarious, and he moved farther north to Camden, New Jersey, where he produced pottery until 1776. He died c1781.

An important American porcelain teapot, attributed to John Bartlam, Cain Hoy, South Carolina, printed in underglaze blue with two cranes, the reverse with a version of the "Man on the Bridge" pattern, the cover lacking, the handle broken off and reattached.

c1765-69   *7in (17.5cm) wide*

$760,000+   **WW**

A Chantilly saucer, painted in the Kakiemon pallette with the "Two Quails" pattern, red hunting horn mark.

Chantilly was a French factory that produced soft-paste porcelain wares from c1725, including figures, jardinières, teapots, beakers, plates, pitchers, and coffeepots. Pieces were often decorated in the typical Japanese Kakiemon colors of iron red, turquoise, blue, yellow, gold, and black. The factory closed c1789.

c1730-35   *5in (12.5cm) wide*

$1,600-2,000   **WW**

A Chantilly beaker, painted in the Kakiemon pallette with the "Two Quails" pattern, red hunting horn mark.

c1730-40   *2¼in (6cm) high*

$2,300-2,800   **WW**

A Davenport tray, decorated with a "Japan" pattern, highlighted in gilding.

18½in (47cm) long

$500-550   **TRI**

A pair of 20thC Dresden jardinières, with gilt ram-head handles, blue printed marks.

8¾in (22cm) high

$650-750   **BELL**

PORCELAIN

A Frankenthal figure of Venus, probably modeled by Adam Bauer, blue crowned "CT" monogram, some restoration, dated.

1775   9¾in (24.5cm) wide

$1,300-1,800   WW

A Frankenthal figure of a fruit vendor, blue crowned "CT" monogram, workmans' marks "AB" and "GHM."

c1760   5½in (14cm) high

$1,050-1,200   WW

A late 18thC Furstenberg group of Europe and America, by Anton Carl Luplau, incised "f" mark, some restoration.

7in (18cm) high

$500-650   WW

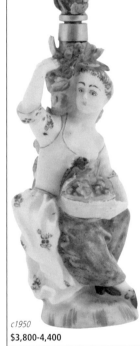

A "Girl-in-a-Swing"-type gold-mounted scent bottle, modeled as a lady holding a basket, some chips and losses.

The "Girl-in-a-Swing" group of small porcelain figures, scent bottles, and other wares were originally attributed to Chelsea. A specific figure, of a girl in a swing, shed doubt on this, and many wares are now thought to have been made elsewhere, at the so-called "Girl-in-a-Swing" factory, possibly run by Charles Gouyn (d.1785).

c1950   3¾in (9.5cm) high

$3,800-4,400   SWO

A "Girl-in-a-Swing"-type gold-mounted scent bottle, some restoration, some incomplete leaves.

c1950   3¾in (9.5cm) high

$5,500-7,000   SWO

A Continental étui, possibly Kelsterbach, modeled as a crying swaddled baby.

c1765   4¼in (11cm) high

$1,000-1,150   WW

A rare Limehouse gravy boat, crack to rim.

Although relatively little known today, Limehouse was probably the first English factory to make blue-and-white porcelain.

c1746-48   6½in (16.5cm) wide

$3,800-4,400   WW

A pair of Longton Hall figures of a nun and her novice, the nun's book titled "Of Absolution," the novice's "Of Purgatory," some restoration.

Longton Hall was one of the earliest of the famous Staffordshire factories. It was founded at Longton Hall by salt-glaze manufacturer William Littler in 1749 and continued production until 1760.

c1755   5in (12.5cm) high

$1,500-2,000   WW

A pair of Longton Hall figures of a sportsman and companion, the man's head and wrist broken and reglued.

c1755   7in (18cm) high

$1,600-2,000   DN

A Longton Hall figure of Summer, minor losses to flowers.

c1758   5in (13cm) high
$1,300-1,800   **WW**

A Lund's Bristol pickle dish, painted with a "Long Eliza" figure, some repairs.

See page 39 for a similar pickle dish made by Worcester.

c1750   4in (10cm) long
$1,900-2,500   **WW**

A Lund's Bristol pickle dish, painted with a "Long Eliza" figure, one clean crack.

Analysis of similar dishes has shown the inclusion of soaprock in the body, indicating an attribution to Lund's Bristol, rather than Worcester.

c1750   3in (7.5cm) long
$1,300-1,800   **WW**

A Mennecy silver-mounted snuff box and cover, with Kakiemon flowers, Paris discharge mark.

c1740   3¼in (8cm) long
$2,500-3,200   **WW**

A Mintons part dinner service, retailed by Thomas Goode & Co., London, with 24 plates, 4 coffee cups and saucers, 3 tureens and covers, 7 serving dishes, printed and impressed marks, date code, a saucer cracked.

1882
$5,000-6,300   **DN**

A German porcelain snuff box, perhaps Nymphenburg.

c1770   3in (7.5cm) wide
$800-900   **WW**

A pair of Paris Empire-style Locre Russinger Pouyat vases, underglaze blue crossed torches marks, minor wear to gilt.

c1820   13in (33cm) high
$2,900-3,300   **BE**

A Paris part coffee service, with a milk pitcher, a sucrier and cover, six cups and saucers, two surplus lids, wear to gilding, chip to sucrier.

c1830
$500-650   **DN**

PORCELAIN

A garniture of Pinxton bough pots, painted en camaïeu, one titled "Butterley Hall," two signed "Sarah or S Jessop," cracks and chips to larger pot, minor wear to all gilding.

As well as being a talented decorator, Sarah Jessop was the wife of William Jessop, the noted civil engineer, best known for his work on canals, harbors, and as the cofounder of the Butterley Iron Works, Derbyshire.

c1800 *largest 9¾in (24.5cm) wide*
$10,500-12,000 **CHOR**

A Plymouth figure of Autumn, as a putto squeezing grapes into a goblet.

c1768 *6in (15cm) high*
$800-950 **WW**

A Plymouth shell salt, some restoration.

c1768-70 *5in (13cm) long*
$950-1,050 **WW**

A pair of Potschappel urns and covers, by Carl Thieme, after Antoine Watteau, blue 'T' marks, some chips.

1900 *22¾in (58cm) high*
$1,000-1,050 **DN**

A Ridgway "Rococo revival" part tea and coffee service, with teapot, cover, and stand, a milk pitcher, a slop bowl, a dish, 13 teacups, 11 coffee cups, and 12 saucers, iron red fractional mark, "2/1008," some damages.

c1835
$500-650 **DN**

A Saint Cloud white-glazed tea bowl and saucer, applied with prunus blossom.

Saint Cloud was the first major porcelain factory in France. The business enjoyed the patronage of Philippe, duc d'Orléans, King Louis XIV's brother. It was initially established as a faience earthenware factory in 1666, but by the 1690s was producing soft-paste porcelain. Saint Cloud closed in 1766.

c1730-40 *saucer 4¾in (12cm) wide*
$650-750 **WW**

A Saint Cloud cup and trembleuse saucer, painted with tied gourds and auspicious objects in the Chinese manner.

Trembleuse cups and saucers were first developed in Paris in the 1690s. The saucer would be made with a well in the center in which the cup could snugly sit, ensuring that people with unsteady hands were able to safely drink hot chocolate and later tea and coffee.

c1730-40 *saucer 5in (13cm) diam*
$650-750 **WW**

A St James's Charles Gouyn étui, some restoration.

c1755-59 *4in (10cm) high*
$2,500-3,200 **BE**

A Staffordshire porcelain porter mug, painted with the "Independent Taliho" stagecoach, inscribed "Henry Truslove," some faults and wear.

Dunchurch, near Rugby, UK, was an important staging post for stagecoaches and the mail coach. The "Independent Tally-Ho" was one of the London-to-Birmingham coaches that passed through regularly. There were several coaching inns at Dunchurch, including The Bell, which was under the management of Henry Truslove in 1828.

c1825-30 *5in (12.5cm) high*
$650-750 **WW**

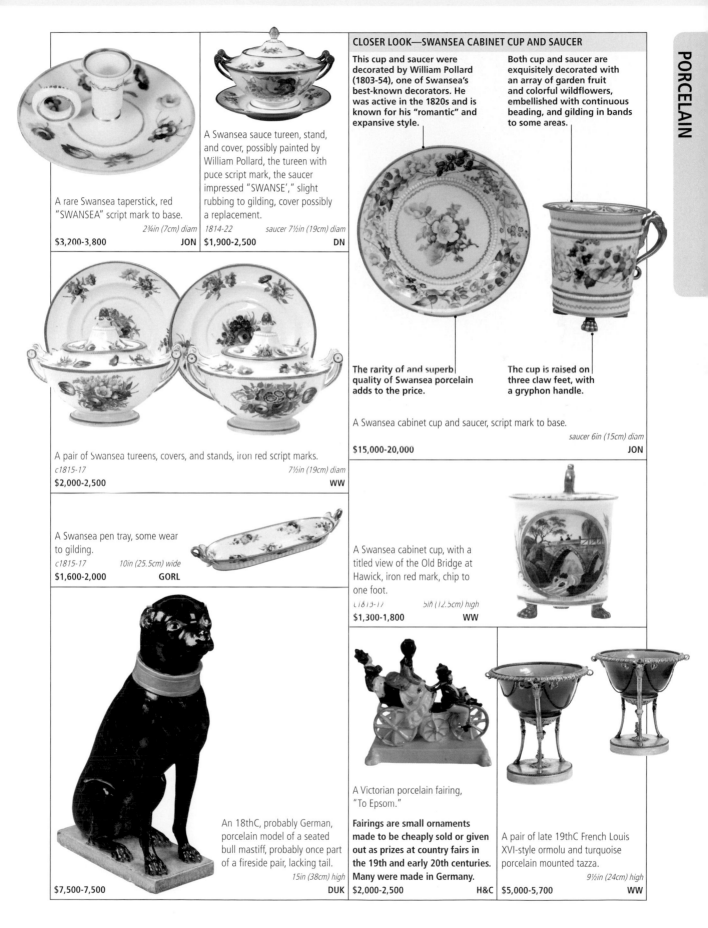

A rare Swansea taperstick, red "SWANSEA" script mark to base.

2¾in (7cm) diam

$3,200-3,800   **JON**

A Swansea sauce tureen, stand, and cover, possibly painted by William Pollard, the tureen with puce script mark, the saucer impressed "SWANSE'," slight rubbing to gilding, cover possibly a replacement.

1814-22   saucer 7½in (19cm) diam

$1,900-2,500   **DN**

CLOSER LOOK—SWANSEA CABINET CUP AND SAUCER

This cup and saucer were decorated by William Pollard (1803-54), one of Swansea's best-known decorators. He was active in the 1820s and is known for his "romantic" and expansive style.

Both cup and saucer are exquisitely decorated with an array of garden fruit and colorful wildflowers, embellished with continuous beading, and gilding in bands to some areas.

The rarity of and superb quality of Swansea porcelain adds to the price.

The cup is raised on three claw feet, with a gryphon handle.

A Swansea cabinet cup and saucer, script mark to base.

saucer 6in (15cm) diam

$15,000-20,000   **JON**

A pair of Swansea tureens, covers, and stands, iron red script marks.

c1815-17   7½in (19cm) diam

$2,000-2,500   **WW**

A Swansea pen tray, some wear to gilding.

c1815-17   10in (25.5cm) wide

$1,600-2,000   **GORL**

A Swansea cabinet cup, with a titled view of the Old Bridge at Hawick, iron red mark, chip to one foot.

c1815-17   5in (12.5cm) high

$1,300-1,800   **WW**

An 18thC, probably German, porcelain model of a seated bull mastiff, probably once part of a fireside pair, lacking tail.

15in (38cm) high

$7,500-7,500   **DUK**

A Victorian porcelain fairing, "To Epsom."

Fairings are small ornaments made to be cheaply sold or given out as prizes at country fairs in the 19th and early 20th centuries. Many were made in Germany.

$2,000-2,500   **H&C**

A pair of late 19thC French Louis XVI-style ormolu and turquoise porcelain mounted tazza.

9½in (24cm) high

$5,000-5,700   **WW**

THE POTTERY MARKET

As with most areas, pottery collectors have been affected by the economic climate. As always, when good, rare, early, and, especially, dated pieces come fresh to the market, top prices are paid. Mid-priced and low-end pieces have struggled, particularly if they were produced in large quantities, such as some of the more common transfer-printed Staffordshire patterns. However, the best meat platters have weathered the dip in fortune of Staffordshire pearlware; the Durham Ox series remains a favorite with collectors. Delftware again has to be early and of a rare shape and decoration to achieve strong prices—the tile tableau (opposite) is a good example. For the more modest collector who is interested in delft and slipware, it is an excellent time to buy. At many sales, there is strong competition for the top-end pieces, but the market is generally sluggish for the more common pottery.

As in the previous edition of *The Miller's Antiques Handbook and Price Guide*, the American market for pottery is generally stronger than the UK market. Good quality pre-1830 pottery is still in demand. Business is mainly through the Internet, because we are still not seeing the number of American buyers traveling around the country as in the past, although there are indications that the collectors are returning.

Victorian pottery and Staffordshire figures have to be exceptionally rare to attract any interest. The Staffordshire dogs (above) are good quality, early, in excellent condition, and have the added embellishment of delicate cushions. There is still the problem of fake "Staffordshire" coming from the Far East—I have seen examples on both sides of the Atlantic. They are really easy to spot, because they don't have the same quality of period examples. If you are in any doubt, you should buy from a reputable dealer or auction house. Again, it is worth taking a look at good, original "right" pieces to "get your eye in."

It is around the time when we published the first *Miller's Antiques Handbook and Price Guide* that 19th-century pot lids were in great demand. As with many areas, rarity drives the prices. At Andrew Hilton's Historical & Collectable Auctions, rare lids showing the Bay of Naples, "How I love to laugh" and "Pet rabbits" all sold for in excess of $2,500. But as Andrew Hilton said, "At the other end of the market, lids selling at £20 [$25] were making £40 in the 1970s" (the equivalent of about $300 today). As in most markets, there is a limited number of top-end collectors and, when they have got all they want, the market sinks until newcomers arrive." This rings true for the pottery market in general.

There have been some dramatic prices paid for some early pottery, particularly the Italian *maiolica istoriato* ware plates, dishes, and apothecary jars created in the 16th century. Interest in good and early (16th century) Hispano Moresque pottery remains strong, but little comes to the market. Mason's ironstone has to be an interesting shape with good strong colors to make any money. Good-quality early Wedgwood, particularly if the piece has unusual color combinations, seems to be selling better in the US sale rooms. American stoneware also continues to have a strong collectors' market, particularly for rare shapes and makers, and the more unusual designs. Redware has seen a sluggish period where only the most unusual pieces fetch high prices.

Top Left: A pair of Staffordshire
pottery spaniels.
c1850   *9¾in (25cm) high*
$2,800-3,300   **BELL**

Above: An unusual 18thC manganese tiled tableau, probably Dutch,
several tiles cracked.

35¾in (91cm) wide

$6,500-7,500   **CHOR**

An English delft plate, probably Bristol, with a portrait of George I, initialled "GR," cracked.

c1714   *8¾in (22cm) diam*

$7,000-8,000   **H&C**

A Bristol delft plate, depicting a smoldering bottle kiln.

This is a rare and interesting subject.

c1720   *8¾in (22.5cm) diam*

$4,400-5,700   **WW**

A Bristol delft "Farmhouse" plate, painted with a cockerel, between sponged trees.

c1720-30   *9in (23cm) diam*

$3,200-3,800   **WW**

A Bristol delft bowl, with "piecrust" rim, painted with a lake landscape and Chinese figures, large star crack, some chips.

c1740-50   *13½in (34cm) diam*

$7,500-8,000   **BE**

A mid-18thC delft charger, possibly Bristol, filled glaze chips on the rim.

11½in (29cm) diam

$1,300-1,800   **PW**

A Bristol delft "King of Prussia" plate, with a portrait of Frederick the Great below the letters "K P," minor rim chips.

During the Seven Years War (1756-63), Frederick II of Prussia was an ally and a popular figure in Great Britain.

c1760   *8¾in (22cm) diam*

$1,900-2,500   **BE**

A documentary Liverpool delft plate, the reverse inscribed "Richard Bury of Royley in the Township of Wrighton, 1750."

Several other named and dated delft pieces have been recorded, including several plates featuring the names of landowners in the Oldham and Bury areas of Lancashire, possibly those associated with the coal-mining industry. Richard Bury (c1715-90) is mentioned in the Quarter Sessions at Rochdale on October 3, 1757, for nonrepair of a stretch of the Kings Highway, leading to the sluice carrying water to the coal pits.

1750   *8¾in (22cm) diam*

$1,000-1,150   **WW**

A delft plate, Liverpool or Dublin, painted with the "La Pêche" pattern, chip to rim.

This design, commonly seen on Caughley and Worcester porcelain, is copied from a design by Jean Pillement, engraved by P.C. Canot and published in 1759.

c1770   *9in (23cm) wide*

$550-700   **WW**

A London delft Royal portrait blue-dash charger, painted with William III, inscribed "WR," fine hairline crack, some glaze flaking.

There were several London factories producing delft pieces in the 17thC and 18thC, most notably at Aldgate, Bermondsey, Lambeth, Southwark, and Vauxhall.

c1690   *13½in (34cm) diam*

$13,000-18,000   **DN**

A delft dish, probably London, painted with portraits of William and Mary, initialled "WMR," minor glaze loss to rim, one small chip.

c1690   *8¼in (21cm) diam*

$5,500-7,000   **H&C**

A delft dish, possibly London, painted with a portrait medallion of Queen Anne, initialed "AR," glaze loss to rim.

c1702   *9in (23cm) diam*

$7,000-7,500   **H&C**

A London delft plate, attributed to Vauxhall, depicting a working pot kiln.

c1750   *8¾in (22.5cm) diam*

$4,400-5,700   **HALL**

An English delft dish, depicting William III, initialled "KW," restored.

c1690   *13½in (34cm) diam*

$3,200-3,800   **H&C**

CLOSER LOOK—DELFT PILL SLAB

This delft pottery slab would have been used for rolling out pills.

It is painted in blue with the arms of the Worshipful Company of Apothecaries, a London livery company founded in 1617.

The arms feature Apollo, two unicorns and a rhinoceros.

Beneath is painted the motto "OPIFER QUE PER ORBEM DICOR" ("Throughout the world they speak of me as a bringer of help") and the arms of the City of London.

A London delft pill slab, hairline crack, flat glaze chips, minor wear.

c1740   *10¾in (27cm) high*

$9,500-10,500   **TEN**

A rare Vauxhall delft teapot and cover, minor chip to cover rim, typical fritting.

c1720   *4in (10cm) high*

$8,000-9,500   **HAN**

An early 18thC dated delft marriage plate, painted with a "merryman"-style cartouche of winged griffons, a crown, and cherub's head, inscribed "TGD 1705," hairline crack, minor glaze losses.

1705   *10in (25.5cm) diam*

$700-800   **BE**

An early 18thC delft posset pot, painted with Chinese figures, the cover lacking, some faults.

12½in (31.5cm) wide

$2,800-3,200   **WW**

ESSENTIAL REFERENCE—DUTCH DELFT

Tin-glazed pottery was made in the Netherlands from the late 15thC. While potteries were established in Haarlem, Rotterdam, and Amsterdam, the town of Delft rose to prominence in the mid-17thC, hence the term Dutch Delft.

- From the mid-16thC, pottery was painted in high-fired colors, such as copper green, yellow, and ocher, and boldly outlined in cobalt blue. Early wares included household objects, such as dishes, plates, syrup jars, and pots. Early patterns tended to be inspired by Italian designs.
- From the late 16thC, tiles were made in large quantities for both floors and walls. These were often decorated in simple patterns and repeated motifs.
- In the 17thC, when blue-and-white Chinese porcelain was imported to the Netherlands, Dutch pottery began to emulate its patterns. Pottery was produced in blue and white. When imports from China ceased in the mid-17thC, due to China's invasion from Manchuria, the demand for blue-and-white pottery in the Netherlands became even greater. Repeated floral patterns, Dutch landscape, and biblical subjects were common.
- The increasing popularity of English creamware throughout Europe led to the decline of the tin-glazed industry in the Netherlands from the early 19thC.

A mid-to-late 17thC Dutch Delft pewter-mounted pitcher, by De Metaale Pot, marked "LVE" to base, some chips.

12½in (32cm) high

$11,000-14,000 RMA

A Dutch Delft dish, with a portrait of Queen Mary, initialed "KM," hairline crack.

c1690 *13½in (34cm) diam*

$1,900-2,500 H&C

An early 18thC Dutch Delft teapot and cover, red "LF" monogram mark for Lambertus van Eenhoorn, the handle broken off and reglued, some chipping.

Lambertus van Eenhoorn was the son of Wouter van Eenhoorn and brother of Samuel van Eenhoorn, both of whom ran De Grieksche A factory. Lambertus ran De Metaale Pot (The Metal Pot) factory from the death of its previous owner in 1691 until his own death in 1721.

6in (15cm) high

$1,050-1,200 WW

An 18thC Dutch Delft tobacco jar, painted "Duinkerker" and "5," painted marks, with associated brass cover.

15in (38cm) high

$3,200-3,800 DUK

A pair of 18thC Dutch Delft "kraak" chargers, by De Metaale Pot.

13½in (34.5cm) diam

$1,300-1,800 L&T

An early to mid-18thC Dutch Delft cuspidor, with tobacco harvesting scenes, some small rim chips.

5in (13cm) diam

$10,000-11,000 RMA

A rare 18thC Dutch Delft yellow ground "Sample" or "Hundred Antiquities" plate.

8¾in (22.5cm) diam

$20,000-23,000 RMA

A pair of early 19thC Dutch Delft six-tile panels of Roman soldiers.

The source material for these tile panels could be a series of Virtue and Vices (these emblematic of War) by Jacques de Gheyn II. Soldiers, especially Dutch soldiers, were a popular subject for Delft tiles in the 17thC.

15in (38cm) high

$900-1,000 DN

ESSENTIAL REFERENCE—FAIENCE

The term faience, otherwise spelt faïence or fayence, refers to tin-glazed pottery made in France, Germany, Spain, and Scandinavia. It is distinguished from tin-glazed pottery made in Italy, called maiolica, or made in the Netherlands, called Dutch Delft, or in England, called delft.

● The name faience came from the similarity in design between early 16thC French earthenware and the maiolica made in Faenza, Italy. French faience soon took on its own style, influenced by Baroque styles and Chinese blue-and-white ceramics.

● The majority of German faience dates from the late 17thC to early 19thC. Early German faience pieces often resemble Dutch Delft. Such patterns were later replaced by a more native style, featuring birds, foliage, buildings, landscapes, double-headed eagles, and coats of arms.

● In Spain, production of faience wear was led by a factory in Alcora, north of Valencia, where high-quality "loza fina" faience ware was made. Painted designs often included landscapes, figures, and animals.

● Many faience factories across Continental Europe struggled and ultimately closed in the late 18thC due to competition with porcelain and with English creamware.

A pair of 18thC French faience "Chinaman" figures, attributed to the Charles Hannong workshop, Strasbourg.

12¼in (31cm) high

$5,000-7,500 RMA

A rare 18thC French faience playing cards dish, possibly by Ferrat, Moustiers, or Nevers, minor surface chips and glaze loss.

This piece has a tag on the back for the collection of G. Papillon, former conservator of the Sèvres ceramics museum.

9½in (24cm) diam

$3,800-5,000 RMA

A late 18thC French faience albarello, Paris or Rouen, inscribed "Ung. de Styrace," some restoration.

Unguent de Styrace is recorded as being used as a form of poultice to help clean infected wounds.

7in (18cm) high

A French faience tureen and cover, with associated stand.

c1770-80   13½in (34cm) wide

$400-500 WW | **$300-400** WW

An early 18thC Frankfurt faience vase, blue circle mark to base, cover lacking.

10¾in (27.5cm) high

$750-900 WW

A Höchst faience figure, possibly from the Commedia dell'Arte series.

c1760   6in (15cm) high

$700-800 WW

A set of four Antonibon faience plates, blue star marks.

Tin-glazed earthenware made at Antonibon, Nove, in Northern Italy, is typically closer to the French style, so it is generally referred to as faience instead of maiolica.

c1775   9¼in (23.5cm) diam

$1,000-1,150 WW

A large mid-18thC Spanish faience syrup jar, initialed "SP," a banner reading "A:Di:Boragne," some glaze chipping.

13½in (34cm) high

$700-800 WW

A Spanish faience albarello and cover, probably Talavera, inscribed with "IHS," and "C. Ammon," the base inscribed "JHC," some glaze chipping, dated.

1773   12in (30.5cm) high

$650-900 WW

A 15thC Montelupo maiolica pitcher, painted in enamels with an owl, some glaze wear and chipping.

6½in (16.5cm) high

$5,000-5,700 **WW**

A Montelupo maiolica dish, broken and cleanly repaired.

c1500 *14¼in (36.5cm) diam*

$2,500-3,200 **WW**

An early 16thC Montelupo maiolica armorial albarello, inscribed "Pill Cotie" beneath the arms of Luigi di Antonio Aldobrandini of Florence, handles inscribed "Bo," cracked.

5in (13cm) high

$1,900-2,500 **WW**

A mid-16thC Italian maiolica albarello, attributed to Pesaro, inscribed "Confet o cingul orum," inscribed "RB," some restoration.

Previously attributed to Faenza or Castel Durante, similar jars inscribed "RB" (probably for a pharmacy) are now believed to have been made at Pesaro.

10½in (26.5cm) high

$8,000-9,000 **WW**

A Montelupo maiolica albarello, decorated with Persian palmettes, some restoration.

c1520 *8¾in (22cm) high*

$2,800-3,300 **WW**

A Venetian maiolica albarello.

c1560-80 *6in (15cm) high*

$1,900-2,500 **WW**

A pair of 16thC Antwerp maiolica "A foglie" albarelli, one inscribed "MITRIDATUM," the other "CERASA-COND," some chips and hairlines, minor glaze loss.

As Antwerp became an important European hub, Italian maiolica artists moved from Venice and other areas in Italy to Antwerp, Guido di Savino being the most famous. Antwerp maiolica was only made during a short time span, as artisans moved north to Dutch cities, such as Delft and Haarlem, during the Inquisition and Spanish rule in the late 1570s and early 1580s.

9¾in (24.5cm) high

$18,000-20,000 **RMA**

A pair of mid-16thC Faenza maiolica albarelli, with portraits inscribed "Vargel" and "Fabio," "Sy. De onphafu" and "Dia. Fribuf," some restoration.

12½in (32cm) high

$9,500-10,500 **WW**

A rare "Faenza" maiolica vessel, with a siren handle, a grimacing grotesque mask forming the aperture.

One comparable boot is in the Ashmolean Museum, Oxford, and another at Waddesdon Manor, the latter with the mark of the Faenza potter Don Pino Bettisi. It is unclear whether these vessels had a celebratory purpose, comparable to the tradition of drinking from a bride's shoe at a wedding, or were merely novelty objects.

c1580 *9¼in (23.5cm) high*

$7,500-9,000 **DUK**

An Italian maiolica albarello, probably Siena, inscribed "F Di Cappi," surface chip, dated.

Caper flowers were used as a culinary spice and an anti-inflammatory.

1613   *6in (15cm) high*
$2,300-2,800   **WW**

A Castelli maiolica charger, from the workshop of Francesco Grue, with Alexander the Great accepting the keys to Nysa, hairline cracks and chips, some repairs.

c1650   18½in (47cm) diam
$4,400-5,000   **TEN**

An Italian maiolica syrup or wet drug jar, possibly Deruta, inscribed "Sy. di Lupoli," restored, dated.

The label refers to Syrup of Hops, which has a sedative effect used to treat bouts of delirium and sleeplessness.

1676   11½in (29cm) high
$2,500-3,800   **WW**

A pair of early 18thC Laterza maiolica albarelli, marked "GE."

10¾in (27cm) high
$1,500-1,900   **WW**

An 18thC Sicilian maiolica jar.

8¾in (22cm) high
$500-650   **WW**

An 18thC Castelli maiolica basin and cover, the base broken and reglued.

18½in (47cm) diam
$2,500-3,200   **TEN**

An 18thC Italian maiolica syrup jar, inscribed "PLANTAGINIS," small chip to foot.

Plantain has a variety of medicinal uses, including as an expectorant and diuretic when taken internally, or for fistulae and ulcers as an external lotion.

8½in (21.5cm) high
$650-750   **WW**

A mid-18thC Castelli maiolica plaque.

12½in (32.5cm) long
$750-900   **WW**

A Castelli maiolica plaque, painted with a lady and attendants.

c1730   7¼in (18.5cm) high
$2,300-2,800   **WW**

ESSENTIAL REFERENCE—ENGLISH REDWARE

English Redware was inspired by Chinese Yixing stoneware.

● It was first made in the Netherlands, and probably introduced to the Staffordshire area by migrant potters in the late 17thC or early 18thC. English Redware is sometimes described as "Elers ware," after Dutch brothers John and David Elers, who settled in Staffordshire in 1686.

● It fell out of fashion in England in the mid-to-late 18thC, as white stoneware and creamware grew in popularity.

A Staffordshire glazed redware pitcher and cover, decorated in cream slip, some chipping.
c1745   *5½in (14cm) high*
$450-500   **WW**

A Staffordshire redware punch pot and cover, some chipping.
c1760   *7¾in (19.5cm) high*
$300-350   **TEN**

A Staffordshire redware milk pitcher.
c1760   *3¼in (8cm) high*
$500-550   **WW**

An early 19thC Spode redware teapot and cover, impressed mark, some chips, glued break to handle.
8in (20.5cm) long
$1,300-1,800   **SK**

ESSENTIAL REFERENCE—AMERICAN REDWARE

Redware was brought to North America by German and Dutch settlers in the 17thC. After it fell out of fashion in England, it remained popular in the American colonies, where clay was abundant, making redware pieces affordable.

● Redware was often decorated with simple patterns in liquid clay slip, or with the more complex sgraffito technique.

● Pieces were finished with a lead-based glaze to ensure they were waterproofed for cooking and food storage.

● Whiteware and stoneware began to take over in the 19thC, but redware production continued in areas of Pennsylvania, North Carolina, and Virginia into the 20thC.

A German redware charger, with sgraffito decoration and an inscribed verse.
c1800   *21in (53.5cm) diam*
$2,300-2,800   **POOK**

A 19thC Connecticut redware charger, large reglued break.
12½in (32cm) diam
$300-400   **POOK**

A 19thC Long Island redware charger, old rim chip.
12in (30.5cm) diam
$700-750   **POOK**

An early 19thC New England redware jar, attributed to Hartford, Connecticut.
8in (20.5cm) high
$750-800   **POOK**

A 19thC New England redware crock, some chips.

10¾in (27.5cm) high

$450-500 **POOK**

A 19thC New England slip-decorated redware charger, with coggled rim.

12in (30.5cm) high

$650-750 **SK**

A Pennsylvania Bucks County sgraffito redware charger, attributed to Conrad Mumbauer, dated.

1810 *11¾in (30cm) diam*

$3,800-4,400 **POOK**

A 19thC Pennsylvania redware loaf dish.

15¾in (40cm) wide

$1,200-1,400 **POOK**

A 19thC Pennsylvania redware charger, old rim chip.

14½in (37cm) diam

$1,300-1,800 **POOK**

A 19thC Pennsylvania redware plate, glaze loss to center.

11¼in (28.5cm) diam

$500-550 **POOK**

A 19thC Pennsylvania slip-decorated redware toddy plate, some cracks and chip.

5¾in (14.5cm) diam

$450-550 **SK**

A 19thC Pennsylvania redware bird rattle, chip to base.

3in (7.5cm) high

$1,000-1,050 **POOK**

A large 19thC American redware jar, some cracks and repairs.

13½in (34.5cm) high

$1,500-2,000 **SK**

Three 18thC creamware pedestal dishes, crack to one.

max 11in (28cm) wide

$750-900   MOR

A pair of 18thC Continental creamware groups, probably Italian.

15½in (39.5cm) high

$1,300-1,800   DUK

A creamware teapot, transfer-printed with a portrait of John Wesley, the reverse with verse.

John Wesley (1703-91) was one of the founders of Methodism, along with his brother Charles Wesley, Robert Kirkham, and William Morgan. He was ordained as a deacon of the Church of England in 1725, and in 1726 became a fellow of Lincoln College, Oxford, where he helped establish the Holy Club, known as "Methodist" due to its prescribed method of studying the Bible. Concerned that the poor felt excluded from the Church, Wesley began to address the public in open areas, something which became a key feature of Methodism.

c1750

$2,000-2,500   HAN

A transfer-printed creamware teapot, depicting John Wesley within a ring of 15 preachers, some hairline and crazing.

c1760

$1,900-2,500   HAN

A Staffordshire Whieldon-type creamware puzzle jug or pitcher, the neck incised "IL" within the date, some restoration.

1752   *7in (18cm) high*

$80-950   WW

A Whieldon-type creamware plate.

c1760   *9¼in (23.5cm) diam*

$650-750   WW

A Whieldon creamware pug, some restoration.

Thomas Whieldon (fl.1740-80) was a leading Staffordshire potter, briefly the partner of Josiah Wedgwood and later High Sheriff of Staffordshire.

c1760   *3¼in (8cm) high*

$1,000-1,150   TEN

A miniature creamware Whieldon-type teapot and cover, cracked.

c1770   *5½in (14cm) wide*

$450-500   WW

A William Greatbatch creamware teapot and cover, printed and overpainted with "The Prodigal Son Receives His Patrimony," the reverse with "The Prodigal Son Taking Leave," some chips and staining, minor cracks.

William Greatbatch (1735-1813) was an important Staffordshire potter, active from the mid-18thC to the early 19thC. He ran his own pottery and was also employed by Josiah Wedgwood to supply block molds for the Wedgwood factory.

c1770-82   *5in (12.5cm) high*

$900-1,000   TEN

A creamware coffeepot and cover, hairline crack.
c1770   *11½in (29cm) high*
$400-500   **TEN**

A creamware mug, painted with a piper, some restoration.
c1770   *6½in (16.5cm) high*
$700-800   **TEN**

A Wedgwood creamware jelly mold cone, impressed mark to base, small chip to top.
c1780   *8¼in (21cm) high*
$1,000-1,150   **WW**

A Neale & Co. creamware figure of Apollo, some chipping.
c1795-1800   *6in (15cm) high*
$450-500   **WW**

A late 18thC Wilson creamware jelly mold cone, the base pierced with eight holes, impressed mark.

Robert Wilson was part of Neale & Co., a partnership which dissolved in 1792. The factory continued under Robert and David Wilson into the 19thC, and continued to use earlier molds and styles.

8in (20.5cm) high
$1,400-1,800   **WW**

A Bovey Tracey documentary creamware tea canister, inscribed "Mary Coombs, Exeter," one cherub restored, dated.
1796   *5in (13cm) high*
$1,500-1,900   **BE**

An Italian creamware cardinal on a horse, probably Naples, some restoration, horse's leg detached, some glaze flakes.
c1800   *18in (46cm) high*
$2,500-3,200   **TEN**

A pair of early 19thC Herculaneum creamware plates, with printed portraits of Nelson, impressed marks.
9¾in (25cm) diam
$800-950   **WW**

A Staffordshire creamware cat, some chipping.
c1800   *3¼in (8.5cm) high*
$700-800   **WW**

A creamware slip-decorated creamer, some chips.
c1800   *4in (10cm) high*
$3,200-3,800   **SK**

A pair of early 19thC Leeds Pottery creamware plates, painted with a Chinese man, impressed marks.
9½in (24cm) diam
$300-400   **WW**

A Wedgwood creamware part service, printed with the "Waterlily" pattern, with two chargers, a tureen and cover, two plates, a mug, an oval stand, and a sauce ladle.

This design derives from prints in the Botanist's Repository and the Botanical Magazine, from 1803-06. The design was probably inspired by the interests of Josiah Wedgwood's eldest son John, who was a founding member of the Royal Horticultural Society.
c1810
$2,300-2,800   **WW**

A creamware cow creamer and cover, with mottled manganese and green glaze.
c1800   *6¾in (17cm) long*
$550-700   **TEN**

A creamware model of a horse, minor restoration.
c1800-20   *6in (15cm) high*
$1,300-1,800   **BE**

An early 19thC creamware pitcher, printed with Masonic designs, glaze chips to spout, prints retouched.
10½in (26.5cm) high
$250-380   **PW**

A 19thC Liverpool creamware mug, transfer-printed with the "Success to the Duke of York & His Brave Army," restored.
6in (15cm) high
$400-500   **POOK**

A Wedgwood creamware charger, painted with Meissen-style songbirds, impressed mark.
c1820   *14¼in (36cm) diam*
$450-500   **WW**

ESSENTIAL REFERENCE—PEARLWARE

Pearlware was introduced by Wedgwood c1779 in an attempt to improve creamware.

- **Pearlware included more white clay and flint in the body than creamware and thus was of a whiter color. Cobalt oxide was added to the glaze, giving it a bluish-white tint.**
- **Pearlware included dishes, plates, teapots, coffeepots, pitchers, and figural groups.**
- **Pearlware was often decorated in underglaze blue by painting or transfer-printing. Designs included the chinoiserie "Willow" pattern, and many varieties of Classical designs and English landscapes.**

A rare pearlware bonbonnière, modeled as the head of a lady.
c1780   *3¼in (8cm) long*
$2,500-3,200   **WW**

A slip-marbled pearlware pitcher, repaired spout, some scratches and chips.
c1800   *9in (23cm) high*
$9,000-9,500   **SK**

An early 19thC pearlware plate, transfer-printed with a woman playing a harp, inscribed "Erin Ma Vournin!" (My Beloved Ireland, or Ireland Vien of My Heart), and "To the battle men of Erin,/To the front of battle go,/Every breast a shamrock wearing,/Burns to meet his country's foe," hairline to rim.

This piece is undated, but is thought to be associated with the Irish Republican movement. It was possibly produced to commemorate an uprising.
7in (18cm) diam
$700-800   **BE**

A pearlware transfer-printed pitcher, with Masonic decoration, chipping to rim, star hairline to base.
12½in (32cm) high
$450-500   **HAN**

A rare pearlware pug dog bonbonnière or snuff box, decorated in Portobello-type colors, the interior inscribed "Rose," with a pewter hinged lid and mount.
c1800   *2¾in (7cm) long*
$1,900-2,500   **WW**

A pearlware quart mug and cover, crack to base and rim, repair to lid.
c1790   *7in (18cm) high*
$3,200-3,800   **SK**

A pearlware pitcher, painted with a barge inscribed "J Yates Colton 18 tons" and "Victoria," inscribed "Joseph Tomlinson Little Haywood," the handle restored, dated.

The 1841 census lists Joseph Tomlinson as a publican in the village of Little Haywood while William White, "History, Gazetteer and Directory of Staffordshire of 1834" mentions John Yates of Colton, "an extensive maltster and corn merchant." Possibly the latter commissioned this pitcher as a gift for the former.
1839   *10¼in (26cm) high*
$450-500   **WW**

A copper luster banded pearlware mug, printed with an unusual named portrait of George IV, restored.
1821   *3¼in (8cm) high*
$750-900   **H&C**

CLOSER LOOK—BOXING TANKARD

This tankard depicts a boxing match between rivals Richard Humphreys and Daniel Mendoza, fought at Odiham, Hampshire, on January 9, 1788, with a key naming the eight attendants.

The rivalry between Humphreys and Mendoza was arguably one of the reasons for boxing's surge in popularity in the late 18thC.

The tankard is signed "Jno Aynsley, Lane End" for John Aynsley, a Staffordshire pottery company founded in 1775. Today, Aynsley continues as part of Belleek Pottery in Ireland.

Despite repairs and surface scratches, the tankard keeps its value due to the interest of the subject matter.

A John Aynsley pearlware tankard, minor damages.
c1788   *5in (12.5cm) high*
$6,500-7,000   **BELL**

A large late 18thC Staffordshire Enoch Wood pearlware statue, possibly depicting Salmacis.

Salmacis is a naiad, or nymph, in Greek mythology.

28¾in (73cm) high

$3,800-4,400   **FLD**

A Staffordshire Pratt-type pearlware group of St. George and the Dragon, some restoration.

c1800   *11¾in (30cm) high*

$950-1,050   **DN**

An Obadiah Sherratt pearlware bust, of Reverend John Wesley.

c1820   *12¼in (31cm) high*

$3,200-3,800   **WW**

A Staffordshire pearlware figure group, "Savoyard with Dancing Bear."

8½in (21.5cm) high

$700-800   **SWO**

An early 19thC Staffordshire pearlware group, "The Dandies" or "Dandy and Dandizette," some restoration.

7¼in (18.5cm) high

$2,300-2,800   **BELL**

A pair of Walton pearlware groups, "Flight into Egypt" and "Return from Egypt," depicting Mary, Joseph, baby Jesus, and a donkey, some restoration.

John Walton was a Staffordshire figure potter active c1805-30s.

c1820   *7½in (19cm) high*

$2,500-3,200   **BELL**

A Staffordshire pearlware group, "Gretna Green," (a Scottish town) in the manner of Obadiah Sherratt, some restoration.

c1830   *8¼in (21cm) wide*

$1,300-1,800   **BELL**

A pair of Staffordshire pearlware figures of Geoffrey Chaucer and Isaac Newton, on square marbled bases, some restoration and minor damages.

12in (31cm) high

$1,900-2,500   **CHIL**

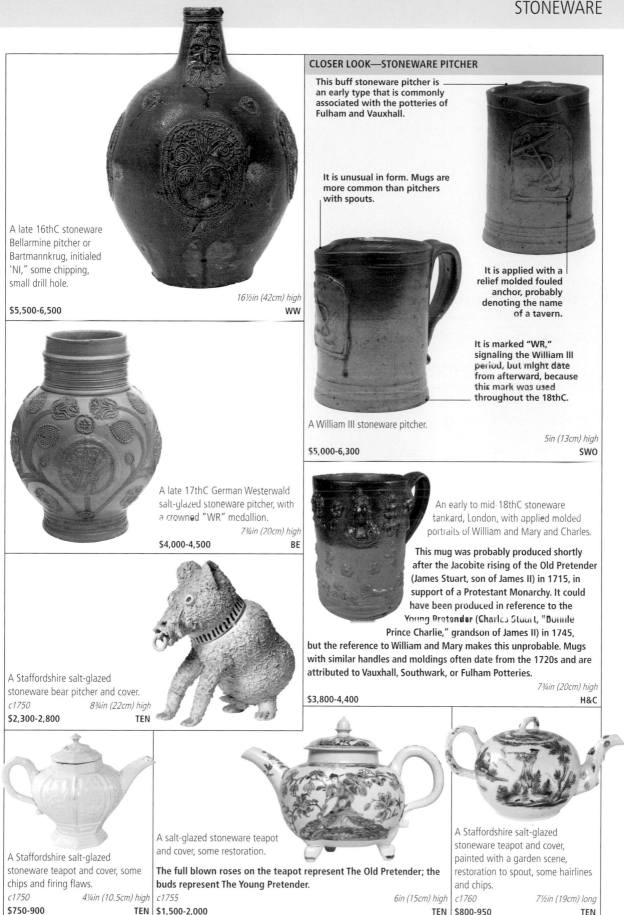

A late 16thC stoneware Bellarmine pitcher or Bartmannkrug, initialed 'NI," some chipping, small drill hole.

16½in (42cm) high

$5,500-6,500
WW

A late 17thC German Westerwald salt-glazed stoneware pitcher, with a crowned "WR" medallion.

7¾in (20cm) high

$4,000-4,500
BE

A Staffordshire salt-glazed stoneware bear pitcher and cover.
c1750   8¾in (22cm) high
$2,300-2,800
TEN

CLOSER LOOK—STONEWARE PITCHER

This buff stoneware pitcher is an early type that is commonly associated with the potteries of Fulham and Vauxhall.

It is unusual in form. Mugs are more common than pitchers with spouts.

It is applied with a relief molded fouled anchor, probably denoting the name of a tavern.

It is marked "WR," signaling the William III period, but might date from afterward, because this mark was used throughout the 18thC.

A William III stoneware pitcher.

5in (13cm) high

$5,000-6,300
SWO

An early to mid-18thC stoneware tankard, London, with applied molded portraits of William and Mary and Charles.

This mug was probably produced shortly after the Jacobite rising of the Old Pretender (James Stuart, son of James II) in 1715, in support of a Protestant Monarchy. It could have been produced in reference to the Young Pretender (Charles Stuart, "Bonnie Prince Charlie," grandson of James II) in 1745, but the reference to William and Mary makes this unprobable. Mugs with similar handles and moldings often date from the 1720s and are attributed to Vauxhall, Southwark, or Fulham Potteries.

7¾in (20cm) high

$3,800-4,400
H&C

A Staffordshire salt-glazed stoneware teapot and cover, some chips and firing flaws.
c1750   4¼in (10.5cm) high
$750-900
TEN

A salt-glazed stoneware teapot and cover, some restoration.

The full blown roses on the teapot represent The Old Pretender; the buds represent The Young Pretender.

c1755   6in (15cm) high
$1,500-2,000
TEN

A Staffordshire salt-glazed stoneware teapot and cover, painted with a garden scene, restoration to spout, some hairlines and chips.
c1760   7½in (19cm) long
$800-950
TEN

A Staffordshire salt-glazed stoneware coffeepot and cover, one hairline crack, minor wear.

c1760 9½in (24cm) high

$1,800-2,300 TEN

A 19thC salt-glazed stoneware pub dispensing pitcher, with relief-molded hunting scenes, profile portraits, and a Royal coat of arms, tap hole to bottom.

23in (58.5cm) high

$2,800-3,300 MART

A 19thC stoneware bottle, "Irish Reform Cordial, Daniel O'Connell Esq.," by Denby and Codnor Park, Bournes Potteries Derbyshire.

Daniel O'Connell (1775-1847) was a lawyer and one of the first Irish nationalist leaders. He campaigned for Catholic emancipation in Ireland and was the first Catholic MP.

8in (20.5cm) high

$400-450 AST

An early 19thC salt-glazed stoneware bottle, inscribed "Warrens Liquid Blacking Wholesale & for Exportation 14 St Martins Lane."

Warren's Blacking was a leading manufacturer of shoe black, or shoe polish, in the 19thC. The polish was sold as a liquid in bottles or as a paste in pots. Charles Dickens famously worked at Warren's Blacking Factory as a child while his father was in debtor's prison.

7in (18cm) high

$750-900 MART

A Doulton & Watts Lambeth Pottery stoneware Nelson flagon, impressed "TRAFALGAR 1805 ENGLAND EXPECTS EVERY MAN TO DO HIS DUTY," some faults.

This half-length model is particularly rare in bottle form, although it is sometimes seen as a pitcher.

c1840-50 16¼in (41.5cm) high

$2,300-2,800 WW

A salt-glazed stoneware Sir Robert Peel spirit flask, holding corn and a scroll reading "Bread for the Millions," the base embossed "Sir R. Peel," chips to base.

c1846 9¾in (24.5cm) high

$400-500 BE

A 19thC Western Pennsylvania three-gallon stoneware crock, inscribed "Hamilton & Jones 3."

13½in (34.5cm) high

$5,000-5,700 POOK

A large 19thC Pennsylvania stoneware lidded crock, some flakes and chips, sprayed hairlines.

11½in (29cm) diam

$450-500 POOK

A two-gallon stoneware pitcher, probably Maryland or Virginia, old chips, small hairline, dated.

1843 13¾in (35cm) high

$950-1,050 POOK

ESSENTIAL REFERENCE—TRANSFER-PRINTING

Transfer-printing was developed in the mid-18thC as a quicker and cheaper alternative to painting ceramics by hand.

- The design would be engraved onto a copper plate. The plate was then covered in ink and the design transferred to the ceramic surface using paper, then sealed under a clear glaze.
- Transfer-printed pieces were usually blue and white, because underglaze cobalt blue was most suited to withstanding the heat of a kiln.
- The technique was used by Worcester, Spode, Davenport, and many other factories.
- Transfer-printed ware featuring American landscapes and buildings was made in Staffordshire and exported to North America.

A mid-19thC Davenport earthenware punch bowl, printed and impressed marks, surface scratches and glaze loss.

17¾in (45cm) diam

$800-950   **BELL**

A Jones & Son tazza, from the "British History" series, the well transfer-printed with "The Death of Nelson," the sides with "Charles I Ordering the Speaker to Give up the Five Members," crack to foot.

c1826-28   *11¼in (28.5cm) wide*

$1,500-1,900   **WW**

A Spode "Indian Sporting Series" platter, transfer-printed with "Battle Between a Buffalo and a Tiger," printed marks.

9in (23cm) long

$800-950   **HAN**

A 19thC Staffordshire meat platter, transfer-printed with the "Bee Keeping" pattern.

21¾in (55.5cm) long

$1,900-2,500   **HAN**

Judith Picks

The Durham Ox was a shorthorn bull bred in 1796 by Charles Colling (1751-1836) of Ketton Hall, near Darlington, England. It was famous for its shape, size, and massive weight, with contemporary estimates ranging from 2,400 to 3,780 lb. In 1801, it was bought by John Day for £250 ($13,900 in today's money). Day and his wife traveled the country for several years, transporting the Durham Ox in a specially built four-horse cart, and displaying it to paying customers. The Durham Ox proved such a success that it could bring its owners up to £100 a day. Dozens of inn and pubs at which it had stopped changed their original names to "The Durham Ox."

An early 19thC Staffordshire meat platter, transfer-printed with the "Durham Ox" pattern, some restoration.

19¾in (50cm) long

$750-900   **HAN**

A 19thC Staffordshire plate, transfer-printed with a portrait medallion of King George III.

9in (23cm) diam

$700-750   **POOK**

A 19thC Staffordshire plate, transfer-printed with "Sacred to the Memory of George III," two rim repairs.

10in (25.5cm) diam

$650-750   **POOK**

A Victorian foot bath, transfer-printed with children and animals, an Asian landscape on the interior, some crazing, staining, and cracks.

21¼in (54cm) wide

$900-1,000   **BELL**

POTTERY

CLOSER LOOK—ARMS OF PENNSYLVANIA PLATTER

This platter is widely considered one of the most desirable pieces of Historical Staffordshire to collectors.

It is transfer-printed with the "Arms of Pennsylvania" design, with a border of flowers and foliage.

It is impressed "T. Mayer," for Thomas Mayer, a skilled potter based in Staffordshire, born c1800.

The quality of the transfer-printing is incredibly clear.

A 19thC Historical Staffordshire "Arms of Pennsylvania" platter, some small knife marks.

21in (53.5cm) wide

$38,000-44,000   **POOK**

An early 19thC Historical Staffordshire antislavery/constitution plate, transfer-decorated with "CONGRESS SHALL MAKE NO LAW..." inscription.

9½in (24cm) diam

$450-500   **SK**

A 19thC Staffordshire coffeepot, transfer-printed with a spread eagle, some chips.

11in (28cm) high

$1,150-1,500   **SK**

An early 19thC Historical Staffordshire pitcher, transfer-printed with the "Views of the Erie Canal" pattern, small chip to handle.

7¾in (20cm) high

$950-1,050   **SK**

A 19thC Historical Staffordshire fruit bowl, the interior transfer-printed with "Commodore MacDonnough's Victory," the exterior with "Dixcove on the Gold Coast of Africa."

10½in (26.5cm) diam

$9,000-10,000   **POOK**

A Historical Staffordshire coffeepot, transfer-printed with the "Lafayette at Franklin's Tomb" pattern, flake to spout, chip to lid.

12¼in (31cm) high

$1,200-1,400   **POOK**

A Historical Staffordshire fruit bowl and undertray, transfer-printed with the "Landing of Lafayette" pattern, by James and Ralph Clewes, Cobridge, England.

c1824-36   *12in (30.5cm) wide*

$1,500-2,000   **SK**

A 19thC Historical Staffordshire soup tureen and cover, transfer-printed with the "Louisville, Kentucky" pattern, two small repaired chips.

15in (38cm) wide

$12,000-14,000   **POOK**

A Staffordshire agateware pitcher and cover, with recumbent lion dog finial, small damages.

Agateware is made from the combination of different colored clays, creating an overall marbled effect.

c1755   *5¾in (14.5cm) high*

$3,800-4,400   WW

A Staffordshire pottery "Porter" mug, transfer-printed with "Porter/Super Fine/Peace and Roast Beef to the Friends of Liberty," hairline to base.

c1805-10   *3¼in (8cm) high*

$500-550   BE

A Staffordshire Prattware Wesleyan Chapel moneybox.

$1,300-1,800   HAN

A Staffordshire treacle-glaze bear pitcher and cover, holding a dog, with monkey handle.

c1830   *11in (27.5cm) high*

$650-750   TEN

CLOSER LOOK—PIPE-SMOKING SPANIELS

While common Staffordshire dogs are not particularly desirable, rare models, such as these pipe-smoking spaniels, can fetch higher prices.

Staffordshire pottery pipe-smoking dogs were inspired by the painting "A Quiet Pipe," by Edwin Henry Landseer (1802-73).

Both spaniels have characterful faces and detailed fur, with enamel details.

Their front legs are separately molded on an unusual foliate scroll base.

A pair of 19thC Staffordshire pottery pipe-smoking spaniels, flaking to black enamel.

8¼in (21cm) high

$2,300-2,800   BELL

A 19thC Staffordshire pottery leopard, cracks and chips, flaking to enamel.

7½in (19cm) high

$750-900   CHOR

A mid-19thC Staffordshire pottery rabbit.

9in (23cm) wide

$1,150-1,500   PW

A pair of 19thC Staffordshire pottery "Disraeli" greyhounds, one with a hare in its mouth, minor chips, losses to enamel.

These "Disraeli" Staffordshire dogs are painted with a similar haircut to Benjamin Disraeli (1804-81), Prime Minister 1868 and 1874-80.

27½in (70cm) high

$500-650   BELL

A 19thC Staffordshire figure of Daniel O'Connell, flaking to enamels.

16in (40.5cm) high

$750-900 BELL

A 19thC Staffordshire figure, modeled as Mr. Barton and Miss Rosa Henry as Selim (or Giaffier) and Zuleika from "The Bride of Abydos."

13in (33cm) high

$400-500 FLD

A Staffordshire pottery elephant, "Jumbo," scratches to enamel.

Jumbo was an African elephant obtained by London Zoo in 1865. In 1881, he became dangerous and the American showman P.T. Barnum purchased him. His stay in the Americas was short-lived. He was killed by a locomotive in Ontario, Canada, in 1885, at 24 years old.

c1885 *10¾in (27.5cm) high*

$2,300-2,800 BELL

A Staffordshire group, "The Alphington Ponies," titled "A Present from Torquay."

The Misses Durnford moved from Alphington to Torquay with their mother and became locally notorious for promenading around the town identically dressed in outlandish costume and heavily made up. They became known as "The Alphington Ponies," because they often rode out in a carriage with ponies. Their brother was so irritated by their habits and clothing that he offered to increase their allowance if they stopped. They refused.

c1845 *4¾in (12cm) high*

$300-400 WW

A pair of Staffordshire pottery figures of Emily Stanford and James Blomfield Rush, some chips.

The Rush and Stanford figures were produced immediately after the 1849 trial of the notorious murders at Stanfield Hall. Norfolk tenant farmer and fraudster Rush shot and killed his landlord and the landlord's son. Stanford, who refused to give him an alibi, was found not guilty.

c1849 *10in (25cm) high*

$1,900-2,500 CHIL

A 19thC Staffordshire figure of Louis Napoleon, some minor wear.

This is a rare large figure, decorated in excellent polychrome enamels and in good condition.

23½in (60cm) high

$4,400-5,000 BELL

A 19thC Staffordshire figure of Field Marshal Lord Raglan, on a gilt titled base.

Lord Raglan (1788-1855) served in the British army in the Napoleonic wars and later in the Crimean war. He lost part of his right arm in the Battle of Waterloo, hence the figure's missing right hand. He is best known today, alongside the Earl of Lucan and the Earl of Cardigan, for his part in instigating the disastrous charge of the Light Cavalry Brigade in 1854.

13in (33cm) high

$450-500 BELL

An early 20thC Staffordshire bust of General William Booth (1829-1912), founder of the Salvation Army, with "Blood and Fire" shield to his chest.

13½in (34.5cm) high

$1,150-1,250 FLD

An early Whitaker & Co. "Bear in a Ravine" pot lid, attributed to Ridgway, minor glaze defect.

3in (7.5cm) diam

$3,200-3,800   H&C

An early "Bears with Valentines" pot lid, attributed to Ridgway.

This design comes from an engraving featured in Alfred Elwes's children's book, "The Adventures of a Bear."

2¾in (7cm) diam

$2,500-3,200   H&C

A "Performing Bear" pot lid, attributed to Ridgway, small rim chip.

2¾in (7cm) diam

$1,600-2,300   H&C

A "Bears Reading Newspapers" pot lid, attributed to Ridgway.

2¾in (7cm) diam

$2,300-2,800   H&C

A "Spanish Lady" pot lid, attributed to the Pratt factory, from a painting by G. Herbert.

3¼in (8cm) diam

$2,500-3,200   H&C

An early "Belle Vue Tavern with Cart" pot lid, attributed to the Pratt factory.

5in (12.5cm) diam

$750-1,000   H&C

An early "Pegwell Bay" pot lid, attributed to T.J. & J. Mayer.

3½in (9cm) high

$1,500-2,000   H&C

A "Garden Terrace" pot lid, attributed to J. Ridgway & Bates, with base.

c1850   *2¼in (6cm) diam*

$2,300-2,800   H&C

A Bates, Brown-Westhead & Moore "Pet Rabbits" pot lid, after the Le Blond print.

c1850   *4in (10cm) diam*

$4,400-5,000   H&C

POTTERY

A T.J. & J. Mayer "Great Exhibition Closing Ceremony" pot lid.

This design comes from W. Simpson's painting "The Transept looking towards the Grand Entrance."

4¾in (12cm) diam

$950-1,050   H&C

A "Jenny Lind" pot lid, attributed to Ridgway.

Born in Stockholm in 1820, Jenny Lind traveled to England in 1847, where she became a famous singer.

3in (7.5cm) diam

$2,300-2,800   H&C

A "Royal Arms and Allied Flags of Crimea" pot lid, with flags of Turkey, Great Britain, and France.

3¼in (8.5cm) diam

$3,500-4,000   H&C

ESSENTIAL REFERENCE—JOHN WILKES

John Wilkes (1725-98) was an English radical, journalist, and politician. He was elected Member of Parliament in 1757, but he was repeatedly expelled for his radical views.

- **He founded his political radical newspaper, "The North Briton," in 1862. The inscription on this mug refers to its 45th issue, in which Wilkes attacked George III's 1763 speech endorsing the Paris Peace Treaty. A warrant was put out for his arrest for libel, but Wilkes was cleared.**
- **Wilkes was a hero to American Founding Fathers Samuel Adams and John Hancock, because he criticized the British government's taxation policy in the colonies and supported the rebels in 1776.**
  - **The few surviving objects with Wilkes' name carry a premium among political memorabilia collectors.**

A rare mid-to-late 18thC creamware mug, painted with John Wilkes, titled "Wilkes & Liberty No.45."

c1763   5in (12.5cm) high

$16,000-20,000   WW

A George III Prattware tea caddy, inscribed "God Save the King" and "Super Fine Tea," the silver cover inset with a coin, chip to one corner.

4¼in (11cm) high

$1,900-2,500   CHEF

A creamware mug, commemorating the betrothal of Princess Charlotte, with a caricature of the Princess and three figures from Punch, one holding a placard inscribed "A Prize of 30,000£ Huzza."

This is seemingly the only commemorative ever produced to take against the otherwise adored Princess. This scene derides her Civil List allocation.

1816   4½in (11.5cm) high

$4,400-5,000   H&C

An early 19thC Staffordshire "Long Live Queen Caroline" commemorative pitcher, printed with a portrait and hunting scenes, restored chips.

Caroline of Brunswick (1768-1821) married George, Prince of Wales, in 1795. Their marriage was an unhappy one. Following the birth of their daughter Princess Charlotte, the couple separated, and Caroline later left the country. When Prince George became King in 1820, Charlotte traveled back to England to claim her title. The new King attempted to pass a bill to divorce her, but the bill was so unpopular it was dropped. Queen Charlotte was refused entry to the coronation service and died in London three weeks after her husband had been crowned.

8¾in (22cm) high

$500-550   PW

A pearlware mourning cup and saucer, printed with Princess Charlotte and "HRH Princess Charlotte Died Nov 6 1817 at 21."

c1818   saucer 5½in (14cm) diam

$160-230   WW

A Meyer Prattware commemorative Crimea War paste pot, "Landing of the British Army."

Prattware has recently had a considerable boost from new collectors from Australia and New Zealand.

c1842-55

$5,000-5,700   H&C

ESSENTIAL REFERENCE—NELSON

Admiral Lord Horatio Nelson (1758-1805) was a British naval commander, famous for his victories against the French during the Napoleonic Wars.

- Nelson was the sixth son of a clergyman. He grew up in Norfolk, joined the Navy at the age of 12 and was a captain by 20.
- When Great Britain entered the French Revolutionary Wars in 1793, Nelson was given command of the Agamemnon. He won victories against the Spanish off Cape Vincent in 1797 and against Napoleon's fleet at the Battle of the Nile in 1798. He was promoted to vice admiral in 1801.
- Before the battle at Cape Trafalgar in October 1805, which ultimately saved Great Britain from threat of French invasion, Nelson famously sent off the signal to his fleet: "England expects that every man will do his duty." He was killed by a French sniper a few hours later.
- Nelson's status as a national hero ensured that many commemorative pieces were made to celebrate his victories and to mourn his death. He remains one of Great Britain's most important national figures, and Nelson commemoratives are popular with collectors today.

A creamware Nelson Battle of the Nile pitcher, marked "Silk," some restoration and crazing, dated.
1805 *9¾in (25cm) high*
$900-950 **PW**

A Prattware pitcher, with Nelson driving Neptune's chariot, inscribed "JW," some restoration, dated.
1809 *6in (15.5cm) high*
$750-900 **WW**

An early 19thC creamware mug, printed with Nelson, the interior modeled with a frog, star crack to base.
5½in (14cm) high
$650-750 **WW**

An early to mid-19thC Liverpool creamware pitcher, printed with Nelson, the reverse with a ship, painted with "William Baker born September 12th 1806," chipping to foot, crack to spout.
8¾in (22.5cm) high
$800-950 **WW**

A mug, transfer-printed with Britannia holding a portrait of Nelson before a monument, star crack to base.
c1805 *8in (20.5cm) high*
$500-550 **WW**

A 19thC Nelson teapot and cover, possibly Leeds, some restoration.
8½in (21.5cm) high
$300-400 **WW**

An early to mid-19thC pearlware pitcher, printed with Nelson, inscribed "England Expects that Every Man Will do His Duty," the reverse with Britannia weeping at a tomb.
6in (15cm) high
$300-400 **WW**

A Copeland subscriber's issue tyg, printed with a naval battle, Nelson, and Britannia, the inside rim inscribed "England Expects That Every Man Will Do His Duty," printed mark.

1905 was the 100th anniversary of Nelson's death.
c1905 *5¾in (14.5cm) high*
$750-900 **WW**

A Staffordshire pearlware Toby jug, an upright barrel between his feet.

Pitchers known as Toby jugs emerged in the early 18thC. There are several theories on where the name "Toby" came from; it may be a reference to Sir Toby Belch in Shakespeare's "Twelfth Night" or Toby Fillpot, an infamous drinker from the 18thC song "The Brown Jug."

c1780   *9¾in (25cm) high*

$1,050-1,200   **WW**

A creamware Wood-type "Long Face" Toby jug, restoration to hat.

While the market for Toby jugs is deflated in comparison to the market 20 years ago, a niche market for them still exists and shows some signs of picking up. Condition and age play an enormous part in the value of a Toby jug, and rare or early examples in very good condition can reach four figures.

c1780-90   *10¾in (27cm) high*

$1,900-2,500   **WW**

A late 18thC Ralph Wood-type "Ordinary" Toby jug.

9in (23cm) high

$1,900-2,500   **FLD**

A late 18thC Ralph Wood-type "Ordinary" Toby jug, restored.

10¼in (26cm) high

$300-400   **FLD**

A late 18thC Ralph Wood-type "Ordinary" Toby jug, some damages.

9¾in (25cm) high

$1,150-1,400   **FLD**

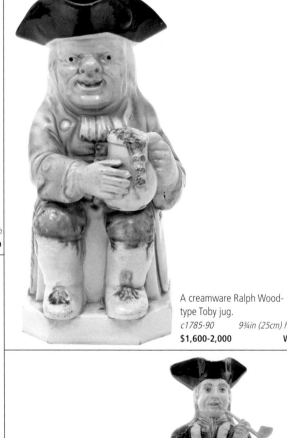

A creamware Ralph Wood-type Toby jug.

c1785-90   *9¾in (25cm) high*

$1,600-2,000   **WW**

A creamware Toby jug, in Whieldon-type running glazes, hat restored.

c1790   *9½in (24cm) high*

$1,300-1,800   **WW**

A 19thC Staffordshire Wood-type "The Sailor Toby" jug, some damages.

12in (30.5cm) high

$1,400-1,900   **FLD**

A 19thC Squire Toby jug, brown painted mark to base, some damages.

12½in (32cm) high

$450-500   **FLD**

A rare early 19thC Mexborough (Yorkshire) Toby jug, holding a miniature Toby jug, a dog between his feet, impressed crown mark, some good restoration.

10¼in (26cm) high

$3,200-3,800 **WW**

An early 19thC pearlware pottery Toby jug, probably Scottish.

9¾in (24.5cm) high

$750-900 **BE**

A pearlware Toby jug, with some marbled decoration.

c1810 10in (25.5cm) high

$650-750 **H&C**

A "Hearty Good Fellow" Toby jug, holding a pipe and jug of ale, restoration to hat.

c1810 11½in (29.5cm) high

$400-450 **WW**

A "Squire" Toby jug, some chipping, replacement pipe.

c1810-20 11½in (29.5cm) high

$900-1,000 **WW**

A pearlware "Hearty Good Fellow" Toby jug, restored.

c1820 9¼in (23.5cm) high

$650-750 **H&C**

A 19thC Staffordshire "Thin Man" Toby jug, seated, holding a jug and a pipe.

9¾in (25cm) high

$1,800-2,300 **FLD**

A Prattware "Martha Gunn" Toby jug, holding a gin bottle and glass, restoration to hat.

Martha Gunn (1726-1815) was a famous dipper. A dipper was the operator of a bathing machine used by women bathers. She worked as an attendant at Brighton from her youth until her late 80s, and was a favorite with George, Prince of Wales, later Prince Regent and King George IV.

c1800 10¼in (26cm) high

$1,300-1,800 **WW**

A "Martha Gunn" Toby jug.

c1820-40 10¼in (26cm) high

$700-800 **WW**

A Wedgwood & Bentley caneware hare's head stirrup cup, impressed mark, firing crack.

The Wedgwood pottery was founded in Staffordshire in 1759 by Josiah Wedgwood. Thomas Bentley was his Wedgwood's business partner from 1768 to Bentley's death in 1780. Wedgwood is still active today.

c1770 *7in (18cm) high*

$4,400-5,000 **BRI**

A Wedgwood & Bentley agateware vase, labeled medallion mark, adapted to be a lamp.

c1770 *10¾in (27.5cm) high*

$750-900 **CHEF**

A Prestige Wedgwood & Bentley black basalt candlestick, "Minerva Goddess of Wisdom," from a limited edition of 200, boxed with certificate.

1775 *13¾in (35cm) high*

$650-750 **PSA**

A 19thC Wedgwood Jasperware "Portland" vase.

9¾in (25cm) high

$1,150-1,500 **PSA**

A mid-to-late 19thC near pair of Wedgwood Jasperware ormolu-mounted Zodiac vases and covers, top covers lacking.

13in (33cm) high

$1,300-1,800 **WW**

A Wedgwood Jasperware "Trafalgar" vase, with sphinx handles, impressed "Wedgwood" to base, small chips.

This vase commemorates the centenary of the Battle of Trafalgar in 1805.

c1905 *9¾in (25cm) high*

$800-950 **BELL**

A pair of Wedgwood black basalt portrait plaques, impressed "WEDGWOOD."

c1865 *4in (10cm) high*

$550-700 **JN**

A pair of late 19thC Wedgwood basalt "wine" and "water" ewers, impressed marks, some damages.

15in (38cm) high

$1,300-1,800 **BELL**

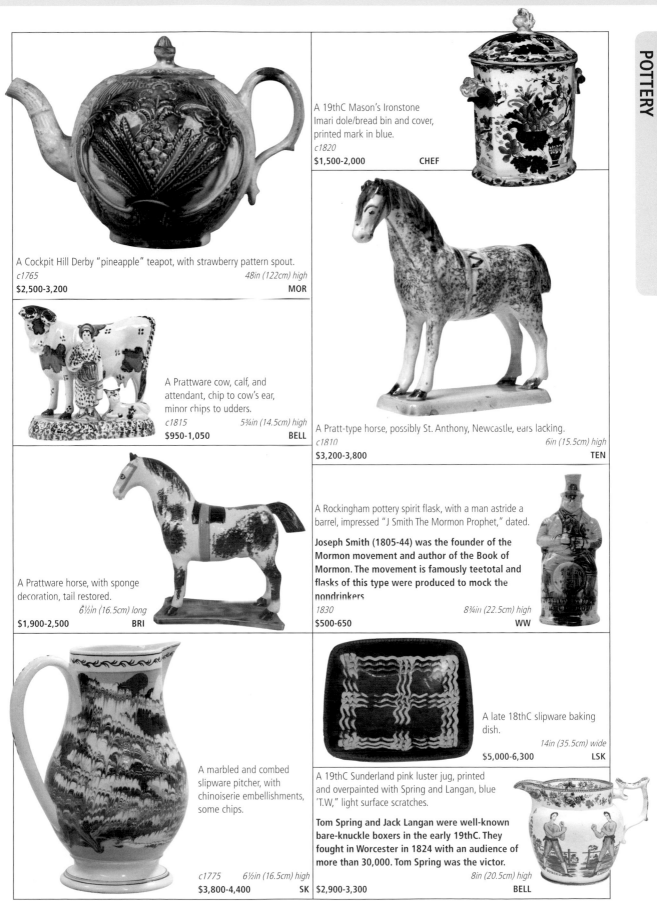

A Cockpit Hill Derby "pineapple" teapot, with strawberry pattern spout.
c1765   *48in (122cm) high*
$2,500-3,200   MOR

A 19thC Mason's Ironstone Imari dole/bread bin and cover, printed mark in blue.
c1820
$1,500-2,000   CHEF

A Prattware cow, calf, and attendant, chip to cow's ear, minor chips to udders.
c1815   *5¾in (14.5cm) high*
$950-1,050   BELL

A Pratt-type horse, possibly St. Anthony, Newcastle, ears lacking.
c1810   *6in (15.5cm) high*
$3,200-3,800   TEN

A Prattware horse, with sponge decoration, tail restored.
6½in (16.5cm) long
$1,900-2,500   BRI

A Rockingham pottery spirit flask, with a man astride a barrel, impressed "J Smith The Mormon Prophet," dated.

Joseph Smith (1805-44) was the founder of the Mormon movement and author of the Book of Mormon. The movement is famously teetotal and flasks of this type were produced to mock the nondrinkers.
1830   *8¾in (22.5cm) high*
$500-650   WW

A marbled and combed slipware pitcher, with chinoiserie embellishments, some chips.
c1775   *6½in (16.5cm) high*
$3,800-4,400   SK

A late 18thC slipware baking dish.
14in (35.5cm) wide
$5,000-6,300   LSK

A 19thC Sunderland pink luster jug, printed and overpainted with Spring and Langan, blue 'T.W," light surface scratches.

Tom Spring and Jack Langan were well-known bare-knuckle boxers in the early 19thC. They fought in Worcester in 1824 with an audience of more than 30,000. Tom Spring was the victor.
8in (20.5cm) high
$2,900-3,300   BELL

THE ASIAN MARKET

Over the past few years, Asian works of art, whether jade or ceramic, have bucked the trend in a depressed economic climate, and it seems that not a week passes by without some record price being achieved. However, the market is getting a lot more discerning, with top prices being reserved for rare pieces with Imperial provenance. Also, prices have been fluctuating; a lot may fetch a record price in Hong Kong, but a similar piece may fail to meet its much lower reserve in London, or the reverse.

The Chinese collectors are particularly discerning and are looking for excellent-quality, rare Imperial pieces. As in many areas it helps if they are "fresh to market."

There was considerable excitement at the Drouot sale in Paris in December 2018, when a bronze dragon head estimated at €20,000, sold for €3million ($2.75million). This was fueled by speculation that this was one of the five missing heads from the zodiac fountain in the Haiyantang area of the Yuanmingyuan (the Old Summer Palace in Beijing), designed by Jesuit Giuseppe Castiglione for the Qianlong emperor. The heads were removed by the French and British forces that looted the palace in the Second Opium War in 1860, and they have since become symbolic of China's humiliation by the Imperial West.

On the market for Japanese antiques, Lee Young, Managing Director and Head of Asian Art at Duke's Auctions in Dorchester, England, said, "We have, over the last few years, seen a noticeable increase in the number of buyers for Japanese items, resulting in higher prices in key areas, such as cloisonné and mixed metal wares. However, the regained vigor of the Japanese market is still considerably overshadowed by the incredible strength of the Chinese market. With European and American collectors now often unable to compete with new and extremely affluent Chinese purchasers intent on buying back their heritage."

The strength in the Japanese market is increasing. There is a strong demand for rare and unusual Chinese snuff bottles, but they must be top quality. Good-quality jade continues to excite buyers. But the problem with ivory continues. In the United States, it may not be illegal to own or inherit ivory, but it's not legal to buy or sell it, and the rules vary, depending on the state you live in. In the UK, the government passed a bill in December 2018 banning the sale of all ivory, with exceptions as follows:

- Items that contain only a small amount of ivory. Such items must be comprised of less than 10 percent ivory by volume and made prior to 1947.
- Musical instruments. These must have an ivory content of less than 20 percent and made prior to 1975.
- Portrait miniatures. A specific exemption for pre-1918 portrait miniatures, which were often painted on thin slivers of ivory.
- Sales to and between accredited museums. This applies to museums accredited by Arts Council England, the Welsh Government, The Scottish Government, or the Northern Ireland Museums Council in the UK, or, for museums outside the UK, The International Council of Museums.
- The rarest and most important items of their type. Items of outstanding artistic, cultural, or historic significance, and made prior to 1918. Such items will be subject to the advice of specialists at institutions.

Because of the ongoing uncertainty, we have decided to exclude ivory items from this chapter, because they are extremely difficult to value.

CHINESE REIGN PERIODS AND MARKS

Imperial reign marks were adopted during the Ming dynasty, and some of the most common are illustrated here. Certain emperors forbade the use of their own reign mark to avoid experiencing the disrespect of a broken vessel bearing their name being thrown away. This is where the convention of using earlier reign marks comes from—a custom that was enthusiastically adopted by potters as a way of showing their respect for their predecessors.

It is worth remembering that a great deal of Imperial porcelain is marked misleadingly, and pieces bearing the reign mark for the period in which they were made are, therefore, especially sought after.

EARLY PERIODS AND DATES

Xia dynasty	c2000-1500 BC	Three Kingdoms	221-280	The Five Dynasties	907-960
Shang dynasty	1500-1028 BC	Jin dynasty	265-420	Song dynasty	960-1279
Zhou dynasty	1028-221 BC	Northern and Southern dynasties	420-581	Jin dynasty	1115-1234
Qin dynasty	221-206 BC	Sui dynasty	581-618	Yuan dynasty	1260-1368
Han dynasty	206 BC-220 AD	Tang dynasty	618-906		

EARLY MING DYNASTY REIGNS

Hongwu	1368-98	Zhengtong	1436-49
Jianwen	1399-1402	Jingtai	1450-57
Yongle	1403-24	Tianshun	1457-64
Hongxi	1425	Chenghua	1465-87
Xuande	1426-35		

MING DYNASTY MARKS

Hongzhi
1488-1505

Zhengde
1506-21

Jiajing
1522-66

Wanli
1573-1619

Chongzhen
1628-44

QING DYNASTY MARKS

Kangxi
1662-1722

Yongzheng
1723-35

Qianlong
1736-95

Jiaqing
1796-1820

Daoguang
1821-50

Xianfeng
1851-61

Tongzhi
1862-74

Guangxu
1875-1908

Xuantong
1909-11

Hongxian
1915-16

A Chinese Han pottery horse and rider.
206 BC-AD 220   11in (28cm) high
$650-750   CHEF

CLOSER LOOK—TANG POTTERY HORSE

This Tang pottery horse stands with one foreleg raised. It has a molded face and mane and a detailed plaited tail.

It retains the remains of cold-painted decoration and would have once been fully painted.

It is fitted with a saddle with fan-type guards, with rosettes and conch shells molded on its chest, and rosettes and tassels molded on each side of its rump.

The horse is in restored excavated condition, with authentication certificate, sample no.C112b25, dated February 20, 2012.

A Chinese Tang painted pottery horse.
618-906   20½in (52cm) high
$6,500-7,000   TEN

A Chinese Tang chestnut-glazed pottery horse, traces of pigment to saddle.
618-906   18in (45.5cm) high
$5,500-6,500   JN

A Chinese Tang phosphatic-splashed meiping.
618-906   10¾in (27cm) high
$2,500-3,200   ROS

A Chinese Song Cizhou brown-splashed black-glazed jar.

This pottery was produced in Handan (formerly Cizhou), Hebei province, primarily during the Song dynasty. Most vessels were simply decorated, often in brown, gray, cream, and sometimes turquoise. Pale backgrounds were often achieved by applying a coat of slip to the vessel before firing.
960-1279   7¼in (18.5cm) high
$16,000-20,000   WW

A Chinese Tang or later phosphatic-splashed ewer.
618-c906   7¾in (19.5cm) high
$5,000-5,700   WW

A Chinese Song Jun ware bowl, with tonal lavender to celadon glaze.

Jun ware is a type of pottery from one of the five kilns of the Song dynasty: Ru, Guan, Ge, Ding, and Jun. Jun ware is mostly of opalescent blue, sometimes splashed or mottled in purple or crimson. The Jun kiln produced its wares for the Imperial household.
960-1279   6in (15.5cm) wide
$2,500-3,200   FLD

A reproduction Chinese Jun ware ceramic tripod censer, the base with spur marks.

This censer is a reproduction of a Song dynasty Jun ware piece, made within the last few years. Despite not being original, its high quality means that it is still a desirable item.
5½in (14cm) diam
$3,800-4,400   JN

A Chinese Song ding bowl, the interior incised with stylized flowerheads, the exterior with concentric bands.
960-1279   3¾in (9.5cm) wide
$9,500-10,000   WW

A Chinese Southern Song celadon-glazed Longquan-type tripod censer, with wood cover and stand, some crazing and chips, finial reattached.

c1127-1279   *4¼in (11cm) wide*

$14,000-18,000   **DN**

A Chinese Guan-type vase, with a grayish crackled celadon glaze, raised on a short foot.

Guan was one of the five kilns of the Song dynasty, characterized by a wash of brown slip and pale green, blue, or purple glazes. Guan ware was later replicated in the Ming and Qing dynasties.

6in (15cm) high

$100,000-110,000   **WW**

A Chinese Yuan celadon dish, with a dragon chasing a pearl.

In Chinese mythology, the dragon is a symbol of strength and good fortune, often portrayed in art, textiles, and ceramics as chasing a luminous or flaming pearl, against a sky of clouds and flames. The five-clawed dragon, in particular, was used as a symbol of the Chinese emperors. The pearl is a symbol of wisdom, related to yang energy in early Taoism.

1260-1368   12in (30.5cm) diam

$4,400-5,000   **CHEF**

A Chinese Yuan/Ming Longquan celadon stoneware dish.

This dish was recovered from a shipwreck near Mergui in Burma. Longquan celadon stoneware was produced in the town of Longquan from the Song to the mid-Qing dynasties. Decoration was typically incised or molded, with a transparent green glaze.

13¾in (35cm) diam

$900-1,000   **JN**

A Chinese Yuan/Ming Longquan celadon bottle vase, on wood stand.

8¾in (22cm) high

$1,300-1,800   **JN**

A Chinese Ming Longquan celadon bowl.

11½in (29.5cm) diam

$8,000-9,500   **WW**

A Chinese Ming Longquan celadon dish, carved with a spray of camelia.

14in (35.5cm) diam

$7,000-7,500   **WW**

A 17thC to 18thC Chinese celadon-glazed porcelain kendi, with ribbed sides and spout.

A kendi is a type of pouring vessel with no handle and a spout on the side.

6in (15cm) high

$650-750   **JN**

A rare Chinese Yongzheng Imperial pale blue-ground celadon ru-type vase, decorated with vertical flanges, six-character mark.

The shape of this vase is directly derived from a Shang dynasty bronze lei.

1723-35   13in (33cm) high

$200,000-250,000   **WW**

A 19thC Chinese celadon-ground porcelain bottle vase, slip-decorated with dragons chasing pearls.

23in (58.5cm) high

$5,500-6,500   **JN**

A 16thC to 17thC Chinese Dehua blanc-de-chine censer, minor glaze imperfections and scratches.

Blanc-de-Chine ('White from China") is the European term for a type of monochrome white Chinese porcelain made at Dehua, Fujian province, produced from the Ming dynasty onward. Large quantities were exported to Europe in the early 18thC and it was copied at Meissen and elsewhere.

6in (15cm) diam

$750-900   **GORL**

A Chinese early Qing blanc-de-Chine "rhinoceros horn" libation cup, molded with a deer, two dragons to reverse.

6in (15.5cm) high

$950-1,050   **WW**

A Chinese early Qing blanc-de-Chine model of Guanyin, on a wave and lotus stand, her head broken off, marked "He Chaozong."

Guanyin is the bodhisattva (Buddha-to-be) of compassion and mercy.

Provenance: From the Annette Worsley-Taylor family collection, acquired no later than the early 20thC. That this item has been off the market for 100 years increases its desirability. It is badly damaged, with the head broken off and reattached with a wooden stump, and the neck badly ground down. However, interest has recently increased in the artist He Chaozong, and undamaged pieces by him can fetch more than $1,250,000.

14¾in (37.5cm) high

$60,000-65,000   **WW**

A Chinese late Qing Dehua blanc-de-Chine qilin, on a plinth, decorated with Taoist emblems, impressed Boji Yuren seal mark.

The Boji Yuren seal mark approximates to "virtue extends to all, including fishermen." A qilin, or kylin, is a mythical beast with the hooves of a horse, the body of a deer, the tail of an ox, and the horn of a unicorn.

12in (30.5cm) high

$300-350   **BRI**

A 17thC Chinese blanc-de-chine water dropper, formed as a crab.

5¼in (13.5cm) long

$4,400-5,000   **WW**

An 17thC to 18thC Chinese blanc-de-chine bombé censer, with lion mask handles, impressed seal mark, with wood cover, nick to foot rim.

4¼in (11cm) wide

$2,800-3,300   **BELL**

A 19thC Chinese blanc-de-chine Guanyin riding a Buddhistic lion, possibly by Su Xuejin (1869-1919), impressed Boji Yuren seal mark.

11in (28cm) high

$7,000-7,500   **JN**

A 20thC Chinese blanc-de-chine standing figure of Guanyin, holding a lotus spray.

22½in (57cm) high

$1,400-1,800   **L&T**

A bronze-mounted 18thC Chinese blanc-de-chine gu vase, incised with leaves, dragon mask, and tongue handles.

15¼in (39cm) high

$2,800-3,500   **CHEF**

ASIAN CERAMICS

A Chinese Yuan or early Ming guan-type mallet vase, minor surface scratches, some glaze cracks.

9½in (24cm) high

$60,000-65,000   TEN

A Chinese Ming Guan-type hexafoil dish, allover crackle to glaze.

6¼in (16cm) diam

$80,000-90,000   TEN

An 18thC Chinese Claire-de-Lune glazed scribe's box and cover.

8¾in (22cm) long

$50,000-57,000   GORL

A Chinese porcelain bottle vase, carved with stylized foliage, six-character Xuande reign mark, some spotting.

15¼in (39cm) high

$5,500-7,000   TEN

A Chinese white-glazed soft-paste porcelain vase, carved with archaic designs and borders, elephant-head handles, incised Qianlong mark.

1736-95   *9½in (24cm) high*

$38,000-44,000   JN

An early 19thC Chinese white crackled glaze molded porcelain vase, with dragon panels.

This piece was bought in Rangoon in 1928 from the collection of a Tuchan warlord.

17¾in (45cm) high

$7,500-9,000   JN

One of a pair of 18thC to 19thC Chinese bowls, six-character Kangxi mark, on hardwood stands.

These bowls are engraved with the bajixiang, which are the Eight Buddhist Emblems.

bowls 5½in (14cm) wide

$50,000-57,000 the pair   JN

A Chinese porcelain bowl and cover, of archaic bronze form, the cover with four flanges, Qianlong seal mark.

10¾in (27.5cm) wide

$6,500-7,500   JN

A Chinese bowl, incised with dragons chasing pearls, six-character Qianlong seal mark.

1736-95   *5½in (14cm) diam*

$5,500-6,500   WW

A Chinese vase, with dragon roundels and Buddhist emblems, on a 19thC spinach jade and ivory-mounted stand, Qianlong mark to vase, chips to extremities.

4¼in (11cm) high

$4,400-5,000   BELL

A Chinese Daoguang archaistic ritual food "fu" vessel, with elephant-head handles, six-character mark.

1821-50   *9in (23cm) high*

$4,400-5,000   WW

A pair of Chinese Kangxi hounds.
1662-1772   *6in (15.5cm) high*
$3,200-4,400   **L&T**

A Chinese Qianlong bottle vase,
painted with a Buddhist lion.
1736-95   *12¼in (31cm) high*
$1,300-1,900   **L&T**

A 18thC to 19thC Chinese "lu tou
zun" vase, decorated in gilt with
deer in a mountainous landscape,
with stag-head handles, six-
character Qianlong mark.
18½in (47cm) high
$7,500-9,000   **L&T**

A 19thC Chinese "yuhuchun" vase, with white
rim and foot rim, apocryphal six-character
Yongzheng mark.

**Chinese makers in the Qing dynasty and
later often added apocryphal marks
(reign marks of former Emperors) to
their pieces. This was sometimes
done in order to pass a piece off
as older than it was to buyers.
However, it was also done as a
sign of respect and reverence
for earlier periods in history.
For example, Qing pieces in
Ming style often carry a Ming
emperor's reign mark. Some pieces
with apocryphal marks may also be
direct copies of earlier pieces.**
14¾in (38cm) high
$3,800-4,400   **L&T**

A mid-20thC
Chinese bottle
vase, with
pâte-sur-
pâte-style
decoration of
a fisherman
before a
mountain, blue
four-character
seal mark.

**The very fine translucent
body and the high-quality
workmanship of the decoration
makes this a valuable piece.**
8¼in (21cm) high
$6,500-7,500   **LC**

A Chinese Southern Song Longquan
stoneware jar and cover, the
shoulders molded with a cat and
a kitten, with bird finial.
1127-1279   *8¾in (22cm) high*
$5,000-6,300   **JN**

An 18thC Chinese Qing green crackled glaze vase.
4½in (11.5cm) high
$950-1,050   **L&T**

An 18thC Chinese porcelain rouleau vase, with
turquoise-green glaze.
17¾in (45cm) high
$4,400-5,000   **JN**

A 19thC Chinese
imitation bronze
porcelain bottle
vase, with panels of
dragons amid cloud
scrolls, reserved on a
linked wan swastika
ground, molded
Qianlong mark.

**This vase was bought
in Rangoon in 1927
from the collection of a Tuchan warlord.**
15¼in (38.5cm) high
$3,800-5,000   **JN**

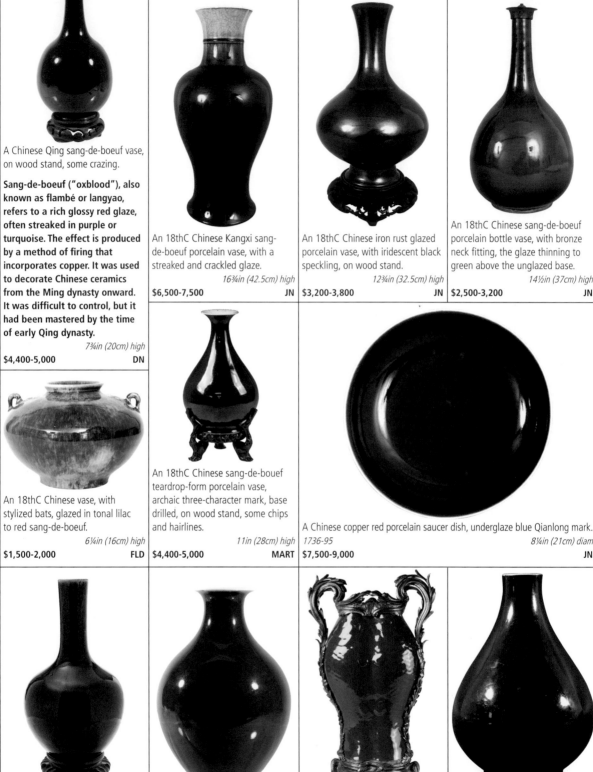

A Chinese Qing sang-de-boeuf vase, on wood stand, some crazing.

Sang-de-boeuf ("oxblood"), also known as flambé or langyao, refers to a rich glossy red glaze, often streaked in purple or turquoise. The effect is produced by a method of firing that incorporates copper. It was used to decorate Chinese ceramics from the Ming dynasty onward. It was difficult to control, but it had been mastered by the time of early Qing dynasty.

7¾in (20cm) high

$4,400-5,000   **DN**

An 18thC Chinese Kangxi sang-de-boeuf porcelain vase, with a streaked and crackled glaze.

16¾in (42.5cm) high

$6,500-7,500   **JN**

An 18thC Chinese iron rust glazed porcelain vase, with iridescent black speckling, on wood stand.

12¾in (32.5cm) high

$3,200-3,800   **JN**

An 18thC Chinese sang-de-boeuf porcelain bottle vase, with bronze neck fitting, the glaze thinning to green above the unglazed base.

14½in (37cm) high

$2,500-3,200   **JN**

An 18thC Chinese vase, with stylized bats, glazed in tonal lilac to red sang-de-boeuf.

6¼in (16cm) high

$1,500-2,000   **FLD**

An 18thC Chinese sang-de-bouef teardrop-form porcelain vase, archaic three-character mark, base drilled, on wood stand, some chips and hairlines.

11in (28cm) high

$4,400-5,000   **MART**

A Chinese copper red porcelain saucer dish, underglaze blue Qianlong mark.

1736-95   *8¼in (21cm) diam*

$7,500-9,000   **JN**

An 18thC to 19thC Chinese sang-de-boeuf vase, glaze thinning at neck, on wood stand.

16¼in (41cm) high

$4,000-4,800   **BE**

A 19thC Chinese copper red vase, apocryphal Qianlong mark, glaze fault.

8¼in (21cm) high

$5,500-7,000   **DN**

A 19thC Chinese porcelain sang-de-boeuf glazed double-fish vase, with 19thC French ormolu mounts.

18½in (47cm) high

$2,500-3,800   **ROS**

A 19thC Chinese sang-de-boeuf vase, underglaze blue apocryphal Qianlong six-character mark.

7in (18cm) high

$3,800-4,400   **LC**

ESSENTIAL REFERENCE—YIXING TEAPOTS

From the early 16thC, clay teapots and other red stonewares were produced in Yixing, in the Eastern province of Jiangsu.

- They were very popular with the upper classes, especially among scholars.
- Because Yixing teapots were washed out only with water, the clay would absorb the aroma and flavor of tea over time. After many years of use, a scholar could brew tea simply by pouring boiling water into the empty pot.
- Yixing wares were exported to Europe from the mid-17thC to the late 18thC and influenced Dutch and Staffordshire redware (see pages 58-59).

A Chinese early Qing Yixing teapot and cover, by Chen Bo Fang, the handle as a geranium stem, the spout as a leaf, the cover as an upturned flower, signed to lid.

7¼in (18.5cm) high

$25,000-32,000 **WW**

A Chinese enameled Yixing teapot and cover, with sprays of chrysanthemum and bamboo, six-character Qianlong mark.

1736-95 *7in (17.5cm) wide*

$6,500-7,500 **WW**

A 17thC to 18thC Chinese Yixing teapot and associated cover, with metal mounts to handle, oval seal, and five-character mark to base, "jing xi hui meng chen."

The mark refers to Hui Mengchen, a Yixing potter active in the late Ming and early Qing dynasties.

7in (17.5cm) high

$13,000-15,000 **WW**

A Chinese Qing Yixing teapot and cover, molded with chrysanthemums and clouds, surmounted with a buffalo.

5½in (14cm) high

$4,400-5,000 **WW**

An 18thC Chinese Yixing teapot and cover, with a dragon's head spout and dragon's tail handle, with a Buddhist lion dog finial.

6¼in (16cm) high

$9,000-10,000 **WW**

An 18thC Chinese Yixing teapot and cover, with molded vine leaves and squirrels, the handle, spout, and cover formed as vine branches.

8¾in (22cm) high

$7,000-7,500 **WW**

A Chinese Qing pewter-encased Yixing teapot and cover, by Yang Peng Nian, with a jade handle and glass replacement knop, incised by Wang Qia with poems about tea, four-character seal mark.

6¼in (16cm) high

$8,000-9,000 **WW**

A Chinese Qing turquoise-glazed Yixing teapot, seal marks to cover reading "zhi yuan," four-character seal to base.

7½in (19cm) high

$1,900-2,500 **WW**

A Chinese Qing Yixing duan ni vase, with a figure among bamboo, inscribed with a poem, impressed mark to base "li yong gogn so chui pin."

Duan ni is a rare clay, typically of a yellowish white color.

9¼in (23.5cm) high

$5,500-6,500 **WW**

A Chinese Qing Yixing jar and cover, with enameled colored bands, marked "shou" to lid.

"Shou" is the Chinese character for longevity.

8¾in (22cm) high

$3,800-4,400 **WW**

ASIAN CERAMICS

ESSENTIAL REFERENCE—BLUE-AND-WHITE CERAMICS

- The use of underglaze blue decoration in China dates from the Tang dynasty and rose to prominence under the Mongol Yuan dynasty in the late 13thC and 14thC.
- Jingdezhen, Jiangxi province, became the center of the Chinese porcelain industry, producing blue-and-white ceramics, from Imperial wares to export pieces.
- Blue-and-white ceramics made in the Ming dynasty, especially those from the Chenghau period or before, are generally considered to be of the highest quality.
- The shade of blue varied considerably over time. Cobalt imported from Persia produced a dark blue-black color, while blues derived from local ores were often lighter.
- Chinese blue-and-white porcelain was very popular with the export market in the late 16thC and 17thC. Pieces were imported in vast quantities to Europe and imitated in many European factories.

A Chinese Jiajing porcelain box and cover, painted with birds in flight, six-character mark, some cracks.

1521-67   *11¾in (30cm) wide*

$15,000-20,000   JN

A Chinese Wanli porcelain vase, with two five-clawed dragons, six-character mark.

1573-1620   *20½in (52cm) high*

$32,000-38,000   JN

A Chinese Wanli or later elephant kendi, some glaze fritting.

1573-c1620   *9in (23cm) high*

$11,000-12,000   DN

A Chinese Jiajing "peony" yuhuchunping vase, six-character mark, neck restored.

Provenance: Purchased from Sotheby's London, March 8, 1954. That it has been off the market for 60 years very much increased the desirability of this piece. Jeremy Morgan, Senior Specialist of Asian Art at Woolley & Wallis, has said that finely painted 16thC Ming pieces are currently on the rise and have increased in value in the last 12 to 18 months.

1522-66   *12¼in (31cm) high*

$110,000-120,000   WW

A Chinese Transitional porcelain double-gourd vase, minor surface wear.

The Transitional period in Chinese ceramics refers to the years when the Ming dynasty had lost control of the Imperial porcelain factories in Jingdezhen, Jiangxi province, and the Qing dynasty was yet to gain control of them. It is usually dated from the death of the Wanli emperor in 1620 to the arrival of Zang Yingxuan as Director of the Imperial factories in 1683.

11¼in (28.5cm) high

$5,500-6,500   TEN

A Chinese late Ming or Kangxi "scholar's table" bowl, painted with mythical sea creatures, minor firing blemishes.

5¼in (13.5cm) diam

$13,000-18,000   DN

A 17thC Chinese ewer, zoomorphic handle and three further mask handles, painted with mythical animals and some of the "Eight Treasures," some firing faults.

The "Eight Treasures," or "Eight Precious Things," are Chinese symbols of good fortune, often featuring in ceramic decoration from the Yuan dynasty onward. The symbols are a jewel (symbolizing the granting of wishes), a coin (symbolizing wealth), a lozenge (victory), a pair of books (learning), a mirror (counteracting evil), a jade gong (celebration), a pair of rhinoceros horns (happiness), and an artemisia leaf (good luck and health).

7½in (19cm) high

$3,800-4,400   DN

A Chinese Transitional "sleeve" vase, with a scene from the "Water Margin," long crack to body.

c1640   *19in (48cm) high*

$32,000-38,000   WW

A Chinese Transitional bombé-shaped incense burner, painted with six figures of Immortals.

c1640   *7¾in (20cm) diam*

$8,000-9,500   **WW**

A pair of mid-17thC Chinese "Eight Horses of Mu Wang" bowls, apocryphal Jiajing marks, some hairlines and chips.

In Chinese legend, the chariot of Emperor Mu, the fifth emperor of the Zhou dynasty, was pulled by eight horses. Each horse had a different power, such as galloping without touching the ground or possessing wings.

7in (17.5cm) diam

$1,500-2,300   **HAN**

A mid-17thC Chinese Transitional gu vase or brush pot, painted with insects and birds, firing crack to unglazed base.

Dan Bray, Valuer at Gorringes Auctioneers, has said that "larger pieces of blue-and-white porcelain from the Transitional and Kangxi period are particularly popular with mainland Chinese buyers at the moment."

9¾in (24.5cm) high

$6,500-7,500   **GORL**

A Chinese Kangxi jar, painted with courtiers on a terrace, with a reticulated wood cover carved with the bajixiang (Eight Buddhist Emblems).

1662-1722   *8¼in (21cm) high*

$9,500-10,500   **WW**

A Chinese, probably Kangxi, vase, painted with mountainous landscapes and flowers, with replacement hardwood and metal cover and ebonized stand.

19¼in (49cm) high

$5,500-6,500   **LC**

A Chinese Kangxi rouleau vase, painted with two sages and a xianren, some hairlines and glaze fritting.

1662-1722   *18¼in (46.5cm) diam*

$6,500-7,500   **GORL**

A Chinese Kangxi flask, painted with figurative scenes, the neck with Buddhist emblems, four-character Xuande mark, cover missing, some fritting.

1662-1722   *11¼in (28.5cm) high*

$2,800-3,500   **BELL**

A pair of Chinese Kangxi jars, painted with phoenix among flowers, with pierced wood covers, one section reglued.

1662-1722   *9¼in (23.5cm) high*

$3,800-4,400   **CHEF**

A pair of Chinese Kangxi "yen yen" vases, painted with deer and cranes.

1662-1722   *18in (45.5cm) high*

$25,000-38,000   **WW**

A Chinese Kangxi porcelain vase, painted with a village landscape, mountains, and fisherman.
1662-1722   *31½in (80cm) high*
$11,000-14,000   **ROS**

A Chinese Kangxi porcelain vase, painted with foliage and vases, the base unglazed.
c1700   *19in (48.5cm) high*
$7,000-7,500   **JN**

A Chinese Kangxi vase, painted with ladies and boys in a garden, with wood cover and stand.
1662-1722   *8in (20.5cm) high*
$4,400-5,000   **WW**

A Chinese Kangxi vase, painted with peony scrolls, with a pierced hardwood cover.
1662-1722   *vase 18½in (47cm) high*
$4,300-4,800   **DUK**

A Chinese Kangxi bowl, painted with foliage, Chenghua six-character mark, minor firing blemishes.
1662-1722   *6in (15.5cm) diam*
$2,500-3,200   **DN**

A Chinese Kangxi porcelain vase and cover, painted with lotus, peony, and other flowers, with a stepped lotus bud finial.
c1700   *24in (61cm) high*
$4,400-5,000   **JN**

A pair of Chinese Kangxi bottle vases, painted with birds, blossoms, and rocks.
1662-1722   *7¾in (20cm) high*
$5,000-6,300   **WW**

A Chinese Kangxi porcelain bowl, painted with figures in a landscape and a waterside shrine, minor stain, lacking cover.
1662-1722   *9½in (24cm) diam*
$5,000-6,300   **BE**

A pair of Chinese Kangxi gilt-metal-mounted porcelain jars and covers, painted with prunus blossom, with a crackled-ice ground.
1662-1722   *6½in (16.5cm) high*
$1,400-1,800   **JN**

A Chinese Yongzheng Ming-style porcelain dish, painted with scrolling lotus, the base unglazed.

1723-35   *14½in (37cm) diam*

$3,800-5,000   **JN**

A near pair of Chinese Yongzheng "mandarin duck and pond" saucer dishes, character mark, some firing flaws.

1723-35   *6in (15.5cm) diam*

$4,400-5,000   **GORL**

CLOSER LOOK—YONGZHENG DISH

The dish is decorated with three gardenia flowers on leafy branches in the center, within a border of four further flowers, each highlighted with white slip.

Its distinctive six-character mark within a double circle dates it to the Yongzheng period, 1723-35.

The rare, unusual, and striking reverse decoration with raised slip detailing is inspired by Ming and Yuan ceramics.

It is in very good condition, with only minor surface scratches and some rim fritting.

A Chinese Yongzheng dish.

Provenance: Formerly the property of Alexander Robertson Esquire, who purchased the dish in Chicago, Illinois, in 1911.

13in (33cm) diam

$350,000-400,000   **HAN**

A Chinese Ming-style porcelain vase, six-character Yongzheng mark.

8in (20.5cm) high

$1,300-1,800   **JN**

A Chinese porcelain bottle vase, painted with peony and the bajixiang, Qianlong mark, on carved hardwood stand.

The bajixiang, the "Eight Buddhist Emblems" or "Eight Auspicious Symbols," were introduced to China with Buddhism in the Yuan dynasty. The symbols are the dharma (symbolizing knowledge), conch shell (symbolizing the thoughts of Buddha), victory banner (victory of Buddha's teaching), parasol (protection and spiritual power), lotus flower (purity and enlightenment), treasure vase (treasure and wealth), fish pair (happiness and freedom from restraint), and the endless knot (harmony).

vase 13in (33cm) high

$2,500-3,200   **JN**

A Chinese Ming-style yuhuchunping porcelain vase, decorated with a garden scene, Qianlong mark.

A yuhuchunping is a distinctive kind of Chinese bottle or pear-form vase.

11½in (29cm) high

$2,500-3,200   **JN**

A Chinese Ming-style porcelain vase, decorated with archaic bands of dragons and key-fret, Qianlong mark.

7¾in (20cm) high

$2,500-3,800   **JN**

A Chinese Qianlong bottle vase, with Ming-style lotus flowers within foliate scroll ground, six-character mark.

1736-95   *14½in (37cm) high*

$9,000-10,000   **HAN**

A Chinese Qianlong "dragon" dish, with five-clawed dragons chasing pearls, six-character mark.

From the Ming dynasty onward, the five-clawed dragon was a symbol of Imperial power. It was used on wares only for the emperor.

1736-95 *10in (25.5cm) diam*

$13,000-19,000 **L&T**

A Chinese porcelain hu vase, decorated with scrolling lotus, Qianlong mark.

14in (35.5cm) high

$2,500-3,200 **JN**

A Chinese porcelain bottle vase, decorated with scrolling flowerheads, Qianlong mark.

19in (48.5cm) high

$5,500-7,000 **JN**

A Chinese Qianlong Imperial wine cup, decorated with the bajixiang (Eight Buddhist Emblems), six-character mark.

1736-95 *2¾in (7cm) high*

$9,500-10,500 **WW**

A Chinese porcelain stem bowl, with Ming-style "heaped and piled" scrolling lotus, extended Qianlong mark.

1736-95 *6¼in (16cm) diam*

$1,800-2,300 **JN**

A Chinese Ming-style porcelain vase, with molded horse-head handles, with bands of formal decoration, Qianlong mark.

16in (40.5cm) high

$1,300-1,800 **JN**

A Chinese Ming-style porcelain moon flask, with scrolling lotus and flowerheads, Qianlong mark.

The moon flask, also "bianhu" or "baoyueping," is characterized by a circular body, representing the moon, a flat base, narrow cylindrical neck, and two arched side handles. "Baoyue" literally means "embracing the moon."

16in (40.5cm) high

$1,900-2,500 **JN**

An 18thC Chinese kendi, with panels of plants, hairline to rim, some losses to glaze.

7½in (19cm) high

$1,050-1,200 **CHOR**

A Chinese Ming-style vase, with star motifs between formal bands.

Vases of this shape typically date from the Qianlong period (1736-95). This was cataloged as Ming-style, not genuine Ming, but several bidders on the day believed it to be a true Qianlong example.

8¾in (22.5cm) high

$29,000-34,000 **WW**

An 18thC Chinese vase, with lotus blossoms and foliage, with elephant-head handles.

13½in (34cm) high

$15,000-19,000   WW

An 18thC Chinese saucer dish, ten-character horizontal mark, some kiln dust to glaze, initialed "N.Y." to foot rim.

14½in (37cm) diam

$5,500-6,500   MART

A 18thC Chinese Ming-style dish, with a lotus bouquet centered within a floral border, broken and repaired.

20½in (52cm) diam

$15,000-19,000   BELL

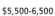

A pair of Chinese late Qing triple-gourd vases, adapted as lamps, one with star crack to base, some firming blemishes.

17¾in (45cm) high

$5,500-6,500   DN

A mid-19thC Chinese porcelain bottle vase, painted with children presenting gifts to an official.

12¼in (31cm) high

$1,900-2,500   ROS

A Chinese probably Tongzhi "Phoenix" plate, apocryphal six-character Kangxi mark, one hairline crack.

6½in (16.5cm) diam

$6,500-7,500   DN

One of a pair of 19thC Chinese footed bowls, painted with lotus, four-character mark for "well-shaded hall," the second bowl broken through bottom of the stem.

Despite extensive damage to the lower half of the second bowl, this pair is still desirable.

5¼in (13.5cm) high

$18,000-23,000 the pair   BELL

A 19thC Chinese tripod censer jar and cover, decorated with lotus and Buddhist emblem, with fu lion finial, handles reattached, some chips.

14¼in (36cm) high

$4,000-4,800   PSA

A 19thC Chinese saucer dish, painted with pomegranates, blue eight-character mark.

13in (33cm) diam

$1,050-1,200   LC

A Chinese Guangxu truncated bowl, decorated with chrysanthemums, marked, some scratches, firing crack to foot.
1875-1908   *9in (23cm) diam*
$2,800-3,200   **DRA**

A Chinese Ming-style Guangxu porcelain bottle vase, with "heaped and piled" bands of flowerheads, six-character mark.
1875-1908   *15¼in (38.5cm) high*
$38,000-44,000   **JN**

A Chinese Guangxu "hundred deer" snuff bottle, "shou" characters on the neck, single deer and five-character "su yun dao ren zhi" mark to base.

Suyun Daoren (1839-95), also known by his monk's name Liu Cheng Yin, or Liu Duo Shen, was one of the most powerful eunuchs in the court of the Empress Dowager Ci Xi and one of her most trusted political advisors.
1875-1908   *4¼in (11cm) high*
$3,200-3,800   **WW**

A 20thC Chinese porcelain bottle vase, painted with dragons, with lion mask handles, apocryphal Qianlong mark.
19¼in (49cm) high
$4,400-5,000   **ROS**

An early 20thC Chinese crackled glaze rouleau vase, with mounted warriors and foot soldiers, signed within battle standard, impressed character mark.
24in (61cm) high
$1,400-1,800   **MART**

A Chinese Yuan-style meiping porcelain vase, decorated with a dragon and phoenix, the base unglazed.
13¾in (35cm) high
$3,200-3,800   **JN**

A Chinese moon flask, painted with flowers, vines, and plantain leaves.
9¾in (25cm) high
$8,000-9,500   **L&T**

A Chinese Ming-style porcelain moon flask, decorated with lotus.
12½in (32cm) high
$5,000-6,300   **JN**

A Chinese bottle vase, with animals and vases, apocryphal six-character Kangxi mark, firing flaw to base.
15½in (39.5cm) high
$1,900-2,500   **CHOR**

A pair of 17thC Chinese Transitional famille verte porcelain jars, painted with squirrels and vines, bases unglazed.

The famille verte ("green family") palette is characterized by the use of green, yellow, blue, red, and purple overglaze enamels. This palette was favored in the reign of Emperor Kangxi (1661-1722).

12½in (34cm) high

$3,800-5,000   **JN**

A Chinese famille verte "month" cup, painted with prunus blossom, the reverse with a poem and seal mark, six-character Kangxi mark.

This would have been one from a set of 12 cups, each depicting a different month of the year. The prunus blossom here represents the first month of the year.

2½in (6.5cm) diam

$950-1,050   **JN**

A Chinese Kangxi famille verte bowl, painted with warriors, officials, and figures, the rim with auspicious objects, some minor frits, with stand and case.

1662-1722   *15¼in (39cm) diam*

$19,000-25,000   **BE**

A Chinese, probably Kangxi, famille verte vase and cover with lion finial, with a tiger hunting scene.

23¼in (59cm) high

$11,000-12,000   **LC**

A Chinese Kangxi famille verte bottle vase, painted with magpies and the "three friends of winter."

The "three friends of winter" refer to the pine, bamboo, and plum trees. This vase has a paper label for the BADA Art Treasures Exhibition 1932 to base.

1662-1722   *7¾in (19.5cm) high*

$2,300-2,800   **WW**

A Chinese Kangxi famille verte tea bowl and saucer, with Buddhist emblems, a hare to base of tea bowl.

From the collection of John Snelgrove, a captain of the East India Company.

1622-1722   *saucer 4¼in (11cm) diam*

$1,900-2,500   **WW**

A Chinese Kangxi famille verte rouleau vase, with a battle scene, with chrysanthemums on the shoulder, a river landscape on the neck.

1662-1722   *17¾in (45cm) high*

$23,000-28,000   **WW**

A Chinese Kangxi famille verte porcelain dish, with floral panels, the interior rim with insect vignettes.

c1700   *12in (30.5cm) wide*

$1,500-2,300   **JN**

ASIAN CERAMICS

A garniture of three Chinese Kangxi famille verte vases, with panels of animals and flowers, some chips, the jar with hairline cracks.

1662-1722   *max 15¾in (40cm) high*

$11,000-13,000   **CHOR**

A Chinese Kangxi famille verte "yen yen" vase, painted with warriors and beasts in battle.

c1685-1710   *17¾in (45cm) high*

$2,800-3,300   **PW**

A Chinese Yongzheng porcelain famille verte vase, with scholars and butterflies, with "shou" characters, some restoration, minor scratching.

1723-35   *14½in (37cm) high*

$3,200-3,800   **TEN**

A mid-19thC Chinese famille verte porcelain hu vase, with warring soldiers, with Buddhist lion mask handles.

20in (51cm) high

$3,300-3,800   **ROS**

A pair of 19thC Chinese famille verte stoneware floor vases, enameled with exotic objects, one rim chip, one body crack.

35¾in (91cm) high

$2,300-2,800   **LSK**

A pair of 19thC Chinese famille verte porcelain saucer dishes, with scholars and attendants, some scratches and chips.

15¾in (40cm) diam

$2,800-3,500   **DN**

A 19thC Chinese famille verte porcelain bowl, with figural panels, iron red lingzhi mark to base.

11in (28cm) diam

$700-800   **JN**

A probably 19thC Chinese porcelain famille verte "yen yen" vase, depicting five lion dogs and a brocade ball, blue concentric rings.

17in (43cm) high

$1,500-1,900   **BE**

A 19thC to 20thC Chinese famille verte porcelain rouleau vase, with a terrace scene, four-character Kangxi mark.

17¾in (45cm) high

$1,300-1,800   JN

A Chinese late Qing or Republic hardwood table screen with famille verte plaque, with five scholars on a veranda within a landscape.

The quality of decoration suggests that this plaque may be an unsigned piece by the famous Republic porcelain painter He Xuren.

15¼in (39cm) high

$7,000 7,500   L&T

A pair of Chinese famille verte vases, with warriors, officials, and landscapes, gilded with auspicious objects, insects, and foliage.

13½in (34cm) high

$1,150-1,500   BE

A pair of Chinese famille verte garden seats, with vignettes of birds and flowers.

$3,800-4,400   GKID

A Chinese famille verte vase, with birds and flowers, on hardwood stand.

vase 13½in (34.5cm) high

$1,500-2,000   MOR

A Chinese famille verte porcelain brush pot, with figures and mythical beasts in landscape with inscription, minor wear.

5¾in (14.5cm) high

$9,500-10,500   TEN

A Chinese famille verte porcelain brush pot, the base unglazed.

5½in (14cm) high

$1,500-2,000   JN

A 19thC Chinese famille rose-verte porcelain jardinière, painted with ducks, the base unglazed.

15¾in (40cm) diam

$2,800-3,300   JN

A Chinese famille rose-verte porcelain model of a seated Buddha, his robes with "shou" characters, the base unglazed.

8¾in (22cm) high

$1,500-2,000   JN

ASIAN CERAMICS

ESSENTIAL REFERENCE—FAMILLE ROSE

The famille rose ("pink family") palette was created in the early 18thC.

● It includes shades of opaque pink and carmine, sometimes made using gold. Opaque yellow and whites were used to enable painters to blend and shape colors.

● These colors originated from Europe, so they were often known as "foreign" in China.

● Famille rose patterns typically feature foliage, flowers, symbols, and panels of people.

● The famille rose palette was widely copied on ceramics in European factories, such as Meissen, Chelsea, and Chantilly.

A rare pair of Chinese Yongzheng famille rose porcelain bowls, painted with trees and flowers, with "an hua" decoration of two dragons chasing a pearl, six-character Hongzhi mark within double circle.

The appearance of lily, peony, orchid, prunus blossom, and incised dragons on one bowl suggests these may have been a gift to a retiring official, wishing him a long, happy, and restful retirement from his career at the Imperial court. When "an hua," or "secret decoration," is used, a new design becomes visible in certain light.

1723-35   *3¾in (9.5cm) diam*

$23,000-28,000   **ROS**

A Chinese Qianlong famille rose ginger jar and cover, with five-clawed dragons, seal mark, on hardwood stand, star crack to lid.

1736-95   *7¾in (20cm) high*

$110,000-140,000   **HAN**

A rare Chinese Yongzheng famille rose porcelain bowl, painted with a chrysanthemum, orchid, and lingzhi, six-character mark.

Lingzhi represents immortality and longevity, while the orchid stands for love and beauty, and the chrysanthemum symbolizes a life of ease. The appearance of these three together suggest that this bowl was a gift, meant to bestow sentiments of a long and happy marriage upon the drinker.

1723-35   *3½in (9cm) diam*

$16,000-19,000   **ROS**

A pair of Chinese Qianlong famille rose "double-peacock" tureens and covers, with Rococo scroll handles and finials, repair to one handle.

1736-95   *14½in (37cm) wide*

$4,000-4,800   **BE**

A Chinese famille rose porcelain butterfly vase, with ruyi scepter-form handles, Qianlong mark.

9in (23cm) high

$5,000-5,700   **JN**

One of a pair of Chinese famille rose "Madame de Pompadour" plates, the rim with cartouches of fish and eagles.

It has been suggested by art historians that this design was commissioned by Madame de Pompadour, the famous mistress of King Louis XV. The eagles symbolize King Louis XV. The fish represent Madame de Pompadour, whose surname was Poisson.

c1745   *9in (23cm) diam*

$3,200-3,800 the pair   **WW**

A Chinese Qianlong famille rose porcelain vase, painted with figural riverside terrace scenes, converted to a lamp.

1736-95   *37in (94cm) high*

$3,200-3,800   **JN**

CLOSER LOOK—FAMILLE ROSE TEA CADDIES

These tea caddies are painted on the front and back with blossoming branches and flowering stems. The accompanying poems are eulogies to flowers and trees.

The enameled sides are densely decorated with lotus flowers and scrolling tendrils on a yellow or iron red outlined ground.

The two red seals suggest the caddies were produced under the supervision of the celebrated ceramicist Tan Ying (1682-1756).

Both have repairs to the neck and lacked covers, but the aesthetic appeal of the decoration makes them a highly desirable pair.

A pair of Chinese Qing famille rose porcelain tea caddies.

6½in (16.5cm) high

$230,000-280,000   **TOV**

A Chinese Qianlong famille rose Buddhist Emblem altar vessel, with twin carp within a ring, on a lotus pedestal, seal mark.

Sets of eight Buddhist Emblems were produced to ornament altars.

1736-95   *11½in (29cm) high*

$90,000-100,000   FLD

A rare Chinese export Qianlong famille rose "cornucopia" wall vase, the base with a Chinese landscape.

Ling Zhu, Asian Art Specialist at Lyon & Turnbull, said that "the quality of the painting matches that of Imperial famille rose pieces," and that therefore "some of the bidders believe this was done by an artist working in the Imperial court.'

1736-95   *9½in (24cm) high*

$30,000-35,000   L&T

A Chinese Qianlong famille rose "tobacco-leaf" trumpet vase.

1736 95   *16¼in (41cm) high*

$7,000-7,500   MAL

A Chinese Qianlong famille rose "tobacco-leaf" tankard.

1736-95   *6in (15cm) high*

$3,200-3,800   MAL

An 18thC Chinese Qing famille rose meiping vase, painted with a scholar on horseback, and a boy carrying books and supplies.

It is possible that the scholar depicted is on his way to Beijing to take the Imperial Civil Service Examination.

7½in (19cm) high

$4,400-5,000   L&T

ESSENTIAL REFERENCE—TOBACCO-LEAF

"Tobacco-leaf" pieces are among the most luxurious of all 18thC China trade porcelain. The complex floral pattern, picked out in famille rose overglaze enamels, often combined with underglaze blue and gold, was highly popular, and the design was often used on export porcelain created for the European and American market. The name is something of a misnomer. The pattern was once thought to depict the flowering nicotiana plant—hence the name—but it actually depicts the wide serrated leaves of hibiscus, peony, and passion flowers. It was probably based on an 18thC textile pattern.

A set of six Chinese Qianlong famille rose "tobacco-leaf" meat plates.

1736-95   *max 18in (46cm) long*

$40,000-45,000   MAL

A Chinese Qianlong famille rose "tobacco-leaf" tureen, with lotus bud handles, the cover with a fruit finial.

1736-95   *7½in (19cm) wide*

$18,000-23,000   MAL

CLOSER LOOK—"HONG" PUNCH BOWL

This punch bowl is intricately decorated with a panoramic view of the "hongs"—the offices, factories, warehouses, and living spaces for foreign merchants in Canton, China.

The buildings are embellished with their national flags, including those of the United States, Great Britain, France, and Spain. The American flag was added only in the late 1780s, dating this bowl to c1790.

The interior is decorated with foliate swags hung from a gilt lattice border.

"Hong" punch bowls were created specifically for the export market, made in the Southern Chinese town of Jingdezhen, then carried to Canton to be decorated.

A Chinese famille rose porcelain "Hong" punch bowl.

c1790   *14¼in (36.5cm) diam*

$110,000-120,000   TEN

A pair of Chinese Jiaqing famille rose yellow-ground porcelain gu vases, enameled with the bajixiang (Eight Buddhist Emblems), six-character mark.
1796-1820   *10¾in (27.5cm) high*
44,000-50,000   **FELL**

A Chinese Jiaqing famille rose cricket cage, pierced with trellis work, one end with a bayonet fitting and cover, with spike finial, slight wear, firing crack to edge.
1796-1820   *8¾in (22cm) long*
$5,000-5,700   **GORL**

A late 18thC to early 19thC Chinese famille rose porcelain Guanyin and child.
20in (51cm) high
$10,000-11,000   **ROS**

A Chinese Daoguang famille rose sgraffito yellow-ground medallion bowl, six-character mark, hairline cracks.
1821-50   *5½in (14cm) diam*
$11,000-14,000   **GORL**

A Chinese Daoguang famille rose "cats" snuff bottle, four-character mark.
1821-50   *2¼in (6cm) high*
$9,500-10,500   **WW**

A Chinese Daoguang famille rose porcelain pebble-form "butterflies" snuff bottle.
1821-50   *2½in (6.5cm) high*
$3,800-5,000   **WW**

A Chinese Daoguang famille rose porcelain snuff bottle, with a scholar, a poem on the reverse, four-character mark.
The scholar depicted is based on Qiu Sheng Fu, a Confucian scholar of the Qin and Western Han dynasties of ancient China.
1821-50   *2¼in (6cm) high*
$3,800-5,000   **WW**

A Chinese Daoguang famille rose "sixteen boys" snuff bottle, four-character mark.
1821-50   *2¼in (6cm) high*
$5,500-6,500   **WW**

A Chinese Daoguang famille rose "crickets" snuff bottle, four-character mark.
1821-50   *2¼in (5.5cm) high*
$5,500-6,500   **WW**

A Chinese Daoguang famille rose porcelain "three rams" snuff bottle, four-character mark.
1821-50   *2¾in (7cm) high*
$4,400-5,000   **WW**

A Chinese Daoguang famille rose "European subject" vase, with two medallions of Roman figures, four-character Qianlong mark, on ivory stand.

1821-50 without stand 3½in (9cm) high
$15,000-18,000   **L&T**

A Chinese Daoguang famille rose bowl, painted with the bajixiang (Eight Buddhist Emblems), seal mark, minor scratches.

This bowl is very finely painted, which makes it more desirable.

1821-50   *4¼in (10.5cm) diam*
$9,500-10,500   **GORL**

A Chinese famille rose porcelain bowl, decorated with chrysanthemum, peony, and prunus, red Daoguang mark.

6¼in (16cm) diam
$2,000-2,500   **BE**

A mid-19thC Chinese famille rose "bats and peaches" porcelain charger.

19in (48cm) diam
$5,000-6,300   **ROS**

A Chinese Xianfeng famille rose "monkeys" snuff bottle, the rim gilded, four-character mark.

1851-61   *2¼in (6cm) high*
$1,600-2,000   **WW**

A pair of Chinese famille rose porcelain vases, with elephant mask handles, enameled with four figures from the "Wu Shuang Pu," with poetic texts, Xianfeng mark.

15in (38cm) high
$3,800-4,400   **BE**

A Chinese Tongzhi famille rose "marriage" basin, painted with butterflies, fruit, and "shuangxi" characters, with a gilt "fu" character, six-character mark.

The Chinese character "fu" means fortune or good luck.

1862-74   *16½in (42cm) diam*
$19,000-25,000   **WW**

A 19thC Chinese famille rose vase, with folk heroes from the "Wu Shuang Pu."

The "Wu Shuang Pu" ("Table of Peerless Heroes"), published in the late 17thC by Jin Guilang, illustrates 40 imagined portraits of Chinese folk heroes, warriors, and poets.

24¾in (63cm) high
$7,500-9,000   **WW**

A Chinese Guangxu famille rose yellow-ground part service, comprising five dishes, seven bowls and six covers, five saucer dishes, seven cup stands, six bowls, and a replica spoon, each with characters for "longevity without limit," six-character marks, some chips and cracks, some dishes reglued, wear to gilding.

1875-1908   *dishes 7¼in (18.5cm) diam*
$19,000-25,000   **DN**

ASIAN CERAMICS

A late 19thC Chinese famille rose vase, painted with scholars, iron red Qianlong mark.

16¼in (41.5cm) high

$3,200-3,800   **BELL**

A 19thC to 20thC Chinese famille rose porcelain jardinière, with birds and foliage, the base unglazed.

16in (40.5cm) diam

$2,000-2,500   **JN**

A Chinese Republic famille rose "nine peaches" tianqiuping bottle vase, six-character Qianlong mark.

In Chinese mythology, peaches symbolize immortality. The number nine represents perfection and the eternal. Ling Zhu, Asian Art Specialist at Lyon & Turnbull, said that this item was a good example of the "surging prices paid for fine quality Republic period porcelain in recent years."

1912-49   *12½in (31.5cm) high*

$25,000-32,000   **L&T**

A Chinese Republic famille rose revolving vase, constructed in three sections, with panels of dragons, the internal section with flowers, clouds, and bats, six-character Qianlong mark.

From the collection of Hugh Malcolm (1886-1961), Managing Director of the Rising Sun Petroleum Company in Japan (today known as Shell) from 1924-36. He lived in Kobe and Yokohama between 1913-36.

1912-49   *9¼in (23.5cm) high*

$23,000-28,000   **WW**

A Chinese Republic famille rose vase, with a figure in a pavilion, six-character mark, on wood stand, some wear to gilt rim.

1912-49   *11in (28cm) high*

$38,000-44,000   **DN**

A pair of Chinese Republic or later famille rose vases, painted with Zhong Kui and a lady, four-character Qianlong mark.

Zhong Kui is a figure in Chinese mythology, often depicted performing an exorcist's dance or subduing demons. His image was thought to ward off evil, especially at the Chinese New Year or the time of Double Five, the fifth day of the fifth lunar month.

c1912-49   *7½in (19cm) high*

$23,000-28,000   **WW**

A Chinese Republic famille rose figure of Wang Xi Zhi, a goose to his left side, four-character marks, "ruan jin kai zao," and "fu jian hui guan," on a stand.

Wang Xi Zhi (303-361), a Chinese official from the Jin dynasty (265-420), was a celebrated calligrapher. He is said to have reared geese and supposedly learned the technique of twisting his wrist while writing from observing the birds turning their necks.

1912-49   *6½in (16.5cm) high*

$5,000-5,700   **WW**

A 20thC Chinese famille rose teapot and cover, with a bird among wisteria in the Dowager Empress style, six-character Tongzhi mark.

6in (15.5cm) high

$900-1,000   **WW**

A 20thC Chinese famille rose Cantonese-style fish bowl or jardinière.

22¼in (56.5cm) high

$1,800-2,300   **DN**

A pair of mid-20thC Chinese famille rose vases, with flowers and birds, six-character Qianlong mark, on wood stands.

8¼in (21cm) high

$5,000-5,700   **WW**

A mid-19thC Chinese Canton famille rose porcelain vase, with warriors, on a ground of peony and pomegranate, with dragon handles.

Until 1842, all European trade with China was confined to the port of Guangzhou (Canton). Most pieces were made elsewhere in China and transported across long distances to reach the port.

24in (61cm) high

$7,500-9,000 ROS

A pair of mid-19thC Chinese Canton famille rose vases, with gilt lion dog and puppy handles, painted with figures and mythical beasts, one with reattached rim section.

17¾in (45cm) high

$1,900-2,500 DE

A pair of mid-19thC Chinese Canton famille rose porcelain vases, with mythical beast handles, one repair, wear to gilding.

23in (58.5cm) high

$2,300-2,800 TEN

A pair of mid-19thC Chinese Canton famille rose porcelain garden seats, with panels of figural scenes, one cracked.

19in (48cm) high

$3,800-5,000 TOV

A 19thC Chinese Canton famille rose punch bowl, enameled with figural panels, on a gilt floral scroll ground.

15¾in (40cm) high

$650-900 L&L

A 19thC Chinese Canton famille rose vase, with panels of scholars and beauties in a garden, with four lion-mask handles.

17¼in (44cm) high

$650-750 L&T

A pair of 19thC Chinese Canton porcelain vases and covers, with vases, butterflies, fruit, and foliage, with elephant-head handles.

15¾in (40cm) high

$2,500-3,200 JN

A pair of 19thC Chinese Canton famille rose porcelain vases, with figural and landscape panels.

24¼in (61.5cm) high

$2,500-3,200 JN

A 19thC Chinese Canton famille rose porcelain moon flask and cover, with figures, butterflies, and foliage, with bat-form handles.

17¼in (44cm) high

$900-1,000 JN

A 19thC Chinese Canton famille rose punch bowl, the interior painted with Bijin in a landscape, the exterior with horsemen, warriors, boatmen, and dignitaries, on hardwood stand, hairline crack.

Bijin, or Bijin-ga, is a term for beautiful women, used in several Asian languages, including Japanese, Chinese, and Korean.

15¾in (40cm) diam

$2,800-3,500 MOR

A Chinese Qianlong armorial porcelain famille rose punch bowl, with the arms of Cooke quartering Warren and Twysden in pretence, long crack, minor wear.
1736-95   *11¼in (28.5cm) diam*
$2,000-2,500   **TEN**

A Chinese Qianlong armorial porcelain famille rose punch bowl, with the arms of Lewin with Pollard in pretence, chip to rim, minor wear.
1736-95   *11¾in (30cm) diam*
$1,400-1,800   **TEN**

A Chinese Qianlong armorial porcelain famille rose tea bowl and saucer, with the arms of Marshall, small flake to saucer.
1736-95
$500-650   **TEN**

A Chinese Qianlong armorial porcelain famille rose tea bowl and saucer, with the arms of Browne, minor surface wear.
1736-95
$500-650   **TEN**

A Chinese Qianlong armorial famille rose porcelain platter, with the arms of Hutchinson impaling Calthrop, surface wear, restored rim chip and crack.
1736-95   *15in (38cm) wide*
$650-750   **TEN**

A mid-18thC Chinese armorial plate, with the arms of Taswell.
9in (23cm) diam
$450-500   **WW**

An 18thC Chinese porcelain armorial charger for the Dutch market.
17½in (44.5cm) diam
$1,300-1,800   **CAN**

A pair of 18thC Chinese export rose mandarin armorial shrimp dishes, with the arms of Seton of Tough (Scotland) with the motto "Forward ours."
9½in (24cm) long
$1,300-1,800   **FRE**

A Chinese famille rose armorial plate, painted with shields and gilt foliage.
10¾in (27cm) diam
$300-350   **HANN**

A Chinese probably Kangxi doucai "Phoenix and Bamboo" conical cup, painted with a phoenix and bamboo shoots, six-character Chenghua mark, minor scratches.

Doucai can be translated as "colors that fit together" or "contrasting colors." Invented during the Xuande period (1426-35), and mostly associated with Chenghua's reign (1465-87), Doucai pieces are decorated in underglaze cobalt blue outlines, with colored enamels added over the fired glaze. The technique was revived in the 18thC.

3¾in (9.5cm) diam

$9,500-10,500   DN

A Chinese Qing doucai bowl, with scholars in a landscape, the interior centered with a four-character Yongle mark, two rim chips.

4¼in (11cm) diam

$3,200-3,800   DN

A Chinese doucai porcelain saucer dish, decorated with formal scrolling lotus, Qianlong mark.

8¼in (21cm) diam

$1,150-1,400   JN

A Chinese doucai porcelain dish, with a horse above waves, six-character Yongzheng mark.

7¾in (20cm) diam

$750-900   JN

A Chinese doucai porcelain jue stand, with a peach among wave scrolls, surrounded by peonies and "shou" characters, four-character Qianlong mark.

A jue is a type of Chinese ritual bronze vessel or goblet.

6¾in (17cm) diam

$3,200-3,800   BE

A 20thC Chinese doucai sectional calendar vase, Qianlong mark.

9in (23cm) high

$3,200-3,800   JN

An early 19thC Chinese doucai dish, painted with precious objects, heightened in gilt.

8in (20.5cm) wide

$400-450   PW

A Chinese doucai "Bamboo" wine cup, enameled with bamboo, apocryphal six-character Yongzheng mark, hairline to rim.

2¼in (6cm) diam

$1,800-2,000   DN

A Chinese Wanli Imperial wucai "dragon" dish, painted with a five-clawed red dragon chasing a pearl, the rim with four phoenix, six-character mark.

Wucai means "five enamels." Decoration is chiefly in red, green, and yellow, with outlines in dark cobalt blue. With the white porcelain body, this makes five colors. Wucai decoration originated in the Ming period, especially during the reign of Jiajing (1522-66), Longqing (1567-72), and Wanli (1573-1620). It was revived in the Qing dynasty.

1573-1620   *6¼in (16cm) diam*
$6,500-7,500   **WW**

A Chinese Transitional wucai vase, painted with elderly scholars examining a scroll, accompanied by attendants.

19½in (49.5cm) high
$7,000-7,500   **L&T**

A Chinese Transitional wucai vase, with an official and two attendants, inscribed with "jia guan jin jue" characters.

c1640   *7¾in (19.5cm) high*
$2,500-3,200   **WW**

A Chinese Shunzhi wucai vase, with floral roundels, the neck with scroll and cracked-ice motifs, some firing faults and wear.

1644-61   *10¼in (26cm) high*
$3,800-4,400   **DN**

A Chinese Transitional wucai porcelain vase, painted with squirrels amid vines, the base unglazed.

c1650   *15½in (39.5cm) high*
$4,400-5,000   **JN**

A mid-17thC Chinese wucai vase and cover, painted with ladies and boys in a garden, a cracked-ice band on the shoulder.

12½in (31.5cm) high
$5,000-6,300   **WW**

A 19thC Chinese wucai meiping, with a dragon and phoenix with a flaming pearl, on wood stand, six-character Kangxi mark.

17½in (44.5cm) high
$3,800-5,000   **CHEF**

A 19thC Chinese wucai porcelain jar and cover, with boys and court figures on a terrace.

13¾in (35cm) high
$3,800-4,400   **L&T**

A 19thC Chinese Kangxi-style wucai jar and cover, with figures in a landscape, including an emperor, some damages and wear.

19¾in (50cm) high
$4,400-5,000   **GORL**

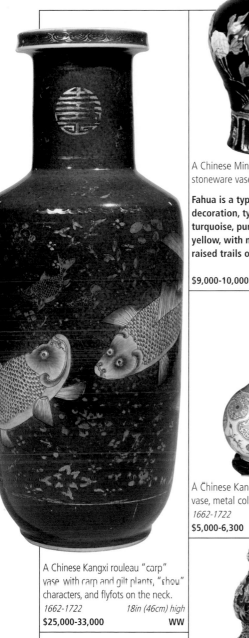

A Chinese Kangxi rouleau "carp" vase, with carp and gilt plants, "shou" characters, and flyfots on the neck.
1662-1722   *18in (46cm) high*
$25,000-33,000   **WW**

A Chinese Ming fahua meiping stoneware vase, base unglazed.

Fahua is a type of Chinese decoration, typically in bold blue, turquoise, purple, green, and yellow, with motifs outlined by raised trails of white slip.
8¼in (21cm) high
$9,000-10,000   **JN**

A Chinese Kangxi iron red and gilt vase, metal collar to rim.
1662-1722   *17¼in (44cm) high*
$5,000-6,300   **CHEF**

A Chinese Qing molded porcelain double-gourd "wu fu" snuff bottle and stopper, with bats amid vines, restoration to rim.

Bats are symbols of happiness and fortune in China. "Fu" in Chinese means both "fortune" and "bat," so that "wu fu" can be translated as "five blessings" or "five bats."
4½in (11.5cm) high
$13,000-18,000   **DN**

CLOSER LOOK—KANGXI IMPERIAL WATERPOT

Apple-shaped water pots such as this belong to a class of wares produced during the Kangxi period for scholars' tables, known as badama or "The Eight Great Numbers."

The in-curved rim is encircled with scrolling leaves and lotus flowerheads between concentric blue bands.

It is decorated in underglaze copper red, with four stylized flower sprays of lotus, chrysanthemum, peony, and hibiscus.

The base holds a six-character Kangxi Imperial mark.

A Chinese Kangxi Imperial waterpot.
1662-1722   *3¾in (9.5cm) diam*
$65,000-80,000   **WW**

A Chinese Kangxi enameled biscuit susancai "nine horses" dish, painted with horses amid auspicious objects, hairline cracks and rim chips.

Susancai can be translated as "plain three-colored," and it is the name given to a style of decoration originating in the Kangxi period, featuring green, brown, and yellow hues on a black, yellow, or white ground.
1662-1722   *12¾in (32.5cm) diam*
$2,800-3,200   **GORL**

A Chinese Qing susancai dish, painted pomegranates, the reverse with camellia blossoms, with incised dragons chasing pearls, six-character Kangxi mark.
14¼in (36cm) diam
$7,000-7,500   **WW**

A Chinese Ming-style porcelain vase, with scrolling lotus and ribboned emblems, Qianlong mark.
14¾in (37.5cm) high
$2,300-2,800   **JN**

A Chinese Qianlong bowl, with incised and green painted birds among peach branches, six-character zhuanshu script marks and mark.
4¾in (12cm) diam
$9,000-10,000   **LC**

A pair of Chinese Qianlong Imperial yellow and blue-ground "dragon" dishes, with five-clawed dragons chasing pearls, six-character marks.

Dishes of this color and pattern were produced for the use of a fifth-rank Imperial concubine.

1736-95 *10in (25.5cm) diam*

$50,000-57,000 WW

A pair of Chinese Qianlong dogs, with iron red patched coats.

.1736-95 *9in (23cm) long*

$19,000-25,000 DUK

A Chinese porcelain vase, with dragons among scrolling lotus, six-character Qianlong mark, minor surface wear.

10¼in (26cm) high

$1,400-1,800 TEN

An 18thC Chinese Ming-style moon flask, with geometric patterns enclosing a centered hexagonal star with a stylized lotus head.

This moon flask would originally have had two handles, but these have been broken off. However, its fine painting and aesthetic appeal means it is still a desirable piece. Copper red porcelain is popular in the present market.

7in (18cm) high

$68,000-80,000 WW

An 18thC Chinese export "Hongs of Canton" punch bowl, with the Canton waterfront, the Western "hongs" identified by their flags, the interior with a ship, restored.

14¼in (36.5cm) diam

$44,000-50,000 HALL

A probably 18thC Chinese porcelain vase, with a five-clawed dragon and phoenix among flowers, part of neck missing.

The depiction of the Imperial five-clawed dragon makes this a desirable vase, despite severe damage to the neck.

16¼in (41cm) high

$15,000-19,000 TEN

An 18thC to 19thC Chinese porcelain vase, with birds among flowering prunus, some hairline cracks.

18in (46cm) high

$13,000-15,000 BELL

A pair of Chinese mid-Qing fish bowls, with fish, shrimp, and crabs, with a border of ruyiheads.

15¼in (39cm) wide

$7,500-9,000 L&T

An 18thC or 19thC Chinese "Eight Immortals" saucer dish, the exterior with the Eight Taoist Immortals, the interior with Shoulao beside a deer, four-character Caihua Tangshi mark, crack and chips to rim.

Shoulao, or Shouxing, is the god of longevity in Chinese mythology. He is usually depicted as a bearded old man with a high brow and crooked staff.

5¾in (14.5cm) diam

$15,000-19,000 DN

A Chinese Daoguang Imperial porcelain dish, with flowerheads and foliage, six-character mark, losses to rim.

1821-50   *5¾in (14.5cm) wide*

$30,000-35,000   **T&F**

A Chinese yellow-ground bowl, with goats, the interior with three goats within a border of lucky charms, Daoguang mark.

This was purchased in the 1950s for no more than a dollar.

6in (15cm) diam

$38,000-44,000   **HAN**

A Chinese Daoguang "dragon" cup, with two dragons chasing pearls, six-character mark.

1821-50   *1¾in (4.5cm) high*

$7,000-7,500   **WW**

A 19thC Chinese famille jaune finger bowl, decorated with cranes, six-character mark.

4¼in (10.5cm) diam

$550-650   **WHP**

A 19thC Chinese Qing sancai glaze joss stick holder, modeled as a figure on a qilin, with a "Chinese Porcelain Company" paper label.

6¾in (17cm) high

$1,600-2,000   **DUK**

A Chinese Ming-style porcelain tripod censer, six-character Tongzhi mark, on wood stand.

12½in (32cm) wide

$7,500-9,000   **JN**

A Chinese porcelain plaque, by Lin Yin Chang, in the Qianjiang palette, with the Yangtze River, inscribed "Wide river reaches to the sky" "Painted for the Mayor of Jingdezhen, Mr Lin Sun," framed, wear and chips.

c1880 10¾in (27.5cm) diam

$5,000-6,300   **CHOR**

A late 19thC Chinese porcelain vase, decorated with figures.

23¾in (60.5cm) high

$6,300-7,500   **POOK**

A Chinese Republic-style porcelain vase, with a carp leaping from water weeds, seal mark to base.

6in (15cm) high

$750-800   **JN**

A pair of Chinese Republic porcelain vases, with cockerels in a yard to one side, artist colophon on the other side, Liu Yucen seal mark to base.

Liu Yucen (1904-69) was the youngest of the "Eight Friends of Zhushan," a group of porcelain painters active in late 19thC to mid-20thC China. The group, led by Wang Yi, played a key role in revitalizing the Chinese porcelain industry after the fall of the Qing dynasty.

13¼in (33.5cm) high

$450-500   **APAR**

A pair of Chinese Republic porcelain Meiping vases, decorated with prunus blossom in the Yongzheng Imperial style, with a poem referring to immortality, "One Thousand Autumns," Yongzheng mark.

c1920   *7½in (19cm) high*

$9,500-10,000   **CHOR**

A pair of 20thC Chinese Daya Zhai-style grisaille-decorated vases and covers, after Guangxu originals, Yong Qng Chang Chun four-character marks, some scratches.

These vases are based on 1870s originals, which had been intended to furnish a restored Yuanming Yuan (Old Summer Palace) after its destruction in 1860. The restoration never happened, and the original porcelain was stockpiled in the Forbidden City. The mark Daya Zhai refers to "Studio of the Greater Odes," which has never been identified.

24½in (62cm) high

$5,000-6,300   **DN**

A Chinese porcelain vase, with elephant mask handles, mounted as a lamp, six-character mark, broken and re-glued.

vase 9½in (24cm) high

$5,000-6,300   **CHT**

A 20thC Chinese vase, with storks below a setting sun.

72in (183cm) high

$2,500-3,200   **SWO**

A pair of Chinese porcelain famille noire vases, with figures in landscapes, apocryphal six-character Kangxi marks, some wear.

19¾in (50cm) high

$1,900-2,500   **BE**

A Chinese porcelain "dragon" bowl, with dragons chasing pearls, red six-character mark.

6in (15.5cm) diam

$700-800   **BE**

A Chinese Wang Bingrong-style porcelain moon flask, with molded dragon panels, molded seal mark.

Wang Bingrong was a notable potter and porcelain carver, active in the Tongzhi to Guangxu periods (1862-1908).

14in (35.5cm) high

$300-400   **JN**

A Chinese, painted in gilt with bats and the long life character, apocryphal Daoguang mark, repair to handle, wear to gilding.

10½in (26.5cm) high

$950-1,050   **DN**

ESSENTIAL REFERENCE—SATSUMA

Satsuma porcelain was produced in the towns of Satsuma and Kyoto from the mid-19thC.

- Satsuma designs are distinctive: a cream ground, with a finely crackled glaze, and enameled and gilded decoration.
- They often feature panels depicting miniature scenes and landscapes, surrounded by ornate borders.
- The demand for Satsuma porcelain in the West grew rapidly after it was shown at international exhibitions.
- Later Satsuma pieces can therefore vary in quality, from items of very high craftsmanship to those made more cheaply for foreign department stores.

A 19thC Japanese porcelain Satsuma vase, with overlapping framed panels.

15in (38cm) high

$6,500-7,500   WHYT

A 19thC Japanese Satsuma three-footed porcelain box, the lid with a figural scene, marked, some crazing and wear.

7½in (19cm) diam

$4,400-5,000   DRA

A Japanese Meiji Imperial Satsuma earthenware vase, painted with a collection of porcelain vases and koros, the base with description of the decoration, with Keihou artist's mark and Shimazu mark.

14½in (37cm) high

$9,000-10,000   JN

A Japanese Meiji Satsuma jar and cover, with figural panels and smaller floral panels, Shozan mark, signed in gilt.

5in (13cm) high

$1,900-2,500   L&T

A Japanese Meiji Satsuma earthenware vase, with figural and floral panels, maker's marks to base.

11¾in (30cm) high

$2,800-3,500   JN

A Japanese Satsuma Meiji earthenware jar and cover, painted with immortals, signed, minor surface wear.

14½in (37cm) high

$1,900-2,500   TEN

A pair of miniature Japanese Meiji Satsuma vases, painted with a celestial scene, signed.

2¼in (6cm) high

$1,900-2,500   ROS

A Japanese Meiji Satsuma vase, painted with four panels, of an Imperial procession, birds and flowers, a hunting party and a rooster, chicken and chick, Kinkozan Tsukuru seal mark.

The Kinkozan family were potters active c1645-1927, when their factory closed.

12½in (32cm) high

$16,000-20,000   LC

A Japanese Meiji Satsuma pottery pot pourri, with gilt-metal strapwork cover, Kinkozan mark.

4¾in (12cm) high

$1,900-2,500   HW

A late 19thC Japanese Satsuma coffeepot and cover, decorated with robed figures, the handle and spout formed as a dragon, gilt ten-character mark.

11½in (29cm) high

$750-900   FLD

A Japanese Imari porcelain jar, with panels of flowering branches, lacking cover, minor wear.

Imari porcelain was traditionally made in the town of Arita. It was extensively exported to Europe in the 17thC and 18thC, shipped from the port of Imari. Designs were influenced by Japanese textiles, with imagery featuring landscapes, birds, and women in detailed kimonos, often in a palette of cobalt blue, reddish-orange, and gold.

c1700　　　　　　　　　　*20½in (52cm) high*

$3,800-5,000　　　　　　　　　　　　　TEN

An early 18thC Japanese Imari vase and cover, with phoenix flying over paulownia, with shishi finial.

36¼in (92cm) high

$4,200-4,800　　　　　　　　WW

A 18thC Japanese Imari bowl and cover, with panels of hawks, flowers, and butterflies, restored.

19in (48.5cm) high

$900-1,000　　　　　　　WW

An early 18thC Japanese Imari vase and cover.

23in (58.5cm) high

$3,200-3,800　　　　　　DUK

A pair of 18thC Japanese Edo Imari jars and covers, the covers with silver finials.

12½in (32cm) high

$700-800　　　　　　L&T

A 19thC Japanese Imari charger, with a deer and boys playing mahjong, the sides with peacocks, the base marked "fuki choshun" (wealth and everlasting spring), on wood stand.

22½in (57cm) high

$450-500　　　　　　WW

A pair of Japanese Meiji Imari vases and covers.

16in (40.5cm) high

$500-650　　　　　　TRI

A pair of Japanese late Meiji Imari porcelain jars and covers, with shi shi knops, one cover broken and reglued, one chipped.

21¾in (55cm) high

$450-500　　　　　　BE

A Japanese late Meiji Imari porcelain bottle vase, embossed with dragons.

19¾in (50cm) high

$300-400　　　　　　BE

A rare Japanese Edo Nabeshima-style celadon shaku-zara dish, incised with three books and two paint brushes, the ground with kikko (hexagonal cells).

Nabeshima ware refers to the porcelain plates, bowls, and dishes made at the kilns directly operated by the Nabeshima clan, a Japanese samurai kin group who ruled the Saga Domain between the 1640s and 1871.

12in (30.5cm) diam

$5,000-6,300   **WW**

An 18thC Japanese Arita Nabeshima plate, some rim chips, one section reglued.

8in (20cm) diam

$6,500-7,000   **CHEF**

A 17thC Japanese Arita kraak dish, chip to rim.

12½in (32cm) diam

$400-450   **CHEF**

A late 17thC Japanese Arita vase, painted with flowers, trees, and geese, some cracking to foot, brass support.

16in (40.5cm) high

$1,500-2,000   **CHEF**

An early 18thC Japanese Kakiemon beaker.

Kakiemon is a delicate porcelain with a distinctive palette of iron red, blue, turquoise, yellow, gold, and black. The name comes from a family of potters working in Arita, who are believed to have introduced overglaze enameling on porcelain in the 1640s. It was a style regularly copied in Europe.

3in (7.5cm) diam

$800-950   **BE**

A Japanese Meiji porcelain vase, by Makuzu Kozan, decorated with Omodaka leaves and flowers in relief, seal mark "makuzu gama kozan sei.

10¾in (27cm) high

$5,000-5,700   **DN**

A Japanese Meiji Kutani porcelain jar, with decorated reserves of fish, birds, and flowers, some surface dimples.

Kutani pottery originated in the 17thC in the village of Kutani and enjoyed great popularity in the 19thC. It was typically decorated with overglaze painting in vivid blues, greens, yellows, purples, and reds. In the Meiji era, much Kutani pottery was exported to Europe.

17¾in (45cm) high

$700-750   **CHOR**

A late 19thC Japanese Arita porcelain bottle, painted with birds perched on branches, minor rim chips.

10in (25.5cm) high

$2,500-3,200   **TOV**

A 19thC Japanese Hirado cockerel and hen.

max 19in (48cm) high

$2,500-3,200   **CHEF**

ASIAN WORKS OF ART

A Chinese Canton enamel bowl, painted with flowers and "shou" character roundels, the interior with roundel surrounded by the bajixiang (Eight Buddhist Emblems), Qianlong mark, some restoration, some stress cracks.

7¼in (18.5cm) diam

$7,000-8,000   DN

An 18thC Chinese Canton enamel box and cover.

4½in (11.5cm) long

$1,050-1,200   L&T

An 18thC to 19thC Chinese Canton enamel dish, with a scrolling lotus and ruyi design.

7¼in (18.5cm) diam

$1,900-2,500   JN

A Chinese late Qing enamel "carps" dish, the exterior with phoenix and flowerheads, raised on foot.

22¾in (57.5cm) diam

$8,000-9,500   WW

A 19thC Chinese Canton enamel vase, with bronze neck rim.

14¾in (37.5cm) high

$1,500-2,000   JN

One of a pair of 19thC Chinese Canton enamel ewers, of Middle Eastern form, with painted bat, bird, fish, and floral decoration, some losses.

12½in (32cm) high

$650-750 the pair   REEM

A late 19thC to early 20thC Chinese Canton enamel sweetmeat set.

12½in (32cm) diam

$650-750   L&T

An early 20thC Chinese Canton enamel hanging lantern.

9½in (24cm) high

$18,000-23,000   DUK

ESSENTIAL REFERENCE—CLOISONNÉ

Cloisonné is an ancient technique for decorating metal objects.

- The technique was known in the Byzantine Empire and had spread to China by the 14thC.
- It involves firing enamel powder in compartments, "cloisons" in French, formed by metal wires soldered to the main surface.
- Early cloisonné pieces used dark green, cobalt blue, red, yellow, and white, often on a turquoise background. Rose pink was added in the 18thC.

A 16thC Chinese Ming cloisonné bowl, decorated with Buddhistic lions, the copper interior undecorated.

8½in (21.5cm) diam

$4,400-5,700　　JN

A 17thC to 18thC Chinese cloisonné seal paste box and cover, some corrosion to inside, minor losses.

2¾in (7cm) wide 4oz

$6,500-7,500　　DN

A pair of Chinese Qianlong cloisonné cups, with stylized lotus flowerheads, four-character marks.

1736-95　　2¾in (7cm) high

$19,000-25,000　　WW

A Chinese Qianlong cloisonné enamel bottle vase, four-character Qianlong mark and further mark, minor surface wear and enamel loss.

1736-95　　5¾in (14.5cm) high

$15,000-19,000　　TEN

A Chinese Qianlong Imperial cloisonné tripod censer, with Ming-style lotus scrolls, four-character mark and further character.

The further character can be read as "cheng" (pure/clear water) or "deng" (letting articles in the water fall to the bottom). This character is also found below the Qianlong reign mark on some Imperial glass wares and is believed by some scholars to be a serial number from the Chinese classic poem, "Qianziwen" ("The One Thousand Word Essay"), with a strong connection to the Imperial workshops.

1736-95　　3½in (9cm) diam

$60,000-65,000　　CAN

A Chinese cloisonné bottle, with dragons flanking a red "shou" character, with gilt copper eagle mask handles, four character Qianlong mark.

4½in (11.5cm) high

$2,300-2,800　　CHEF

A Chinese Qing cloisonné "lotus" vase, gilt rim, foot rim, and inner neck, four-character Qianlong mark, small damages.

13in (33cm) high

$1,900-2,500　　DN

A pair of 19thC Chinese cloisonné magpies, some wear.

11in (28cm) high 18oz each

$9,500-10,500　　DN

A pair of 19thC Chinese Qing cloisonné magpies.

7in (17.5cm) long

$1,500-1,900　　L&T

A pair of early to mid-20thC Chinese cloisonné cranes.

30¼in (77cm) high

$3,200-3,800　　JN

FREEMAN'S

AUCTIONS | PRIVATE SALES | APPRAISALS | TRUSTS & ESTATES

FREEMANSAUCTION.COM

A Japanese Meiji cloisonné vase and cover, with phoenix and dragons, with a kiku finial.

11¾in (30cm) high

$1,150-1,500   BELL

A pair of Japanese Meiji cloisonné vases, with koi fish.

12½in (31.5cm) high

$14,000-17,000   L&T

A Japanese Meiji silver and cloisonné millefleur censer and cover, the legs issuing from lion masks, with two elephant-head handles.

7in (18cm) high 17.9oz

$10,500-11,000   L&T

A pair of Japanese Meiji cloisonné enamel chargers, with magpies on maple trees, raised on a short circular foot.

23¾in (60.5cm) wide

$4,400-5,000   L&T

A pair of Japanese Meiji or Taisho cloisonné ground vases, from the studio of Hayashi Kodenji, impressed lozenge marks to bases, star crack to one, some pitting to enamels, tarnishing to silver wire. **These are a particularly unusual shape for the maker and in excellent condition, considering that they are top heavy and liable to fall over.**

12½in (31.5cm) high

$19,000-25,000   GORL

A Japanese Meiji cloisonné vase in the style of Hayashi Kodenji (1831-1915), the mouth and foot with silver mount.

7½in (19cm) high

$3,800-4,400   L&T

A Japanese Meiji cloisonné vase, the rims with silver mount.

8¾in (22.5cm) high

$800-950   L&T

A late 19thC Japanese cloisonné box, by Hayashi Kodenji (1831-1915), marked, some wear.

5¼in (13.5cm) wide

$1,300-1,800   DRA

A pair of Japanese cloisonné vases, with birds of prey on a pine tree.

12¼in (31cm) high

$3,200-3,800   GWA

A Japanese cloisonné censor and cover, possibly by Sato, marked.

6in (15cm) high

$750-900   HT

A Chinese Ming gilt-bronze incense burner, modeled as a luduan, the base with a later applied Japanese nine-character mark.

Luduan are mythical beasts with rounded bodies and clawed feet. They are believed to have the ability to detect the truth, travel over great distances in a very short time, and speak all the languages of the world.

17¾in (45cm) high 494oz

$25,000-32,000   **WW**

A Chinese late Ming bronze bodhisattva of Ksitigarbha, standing on a double lotus platform with a dog.

Ksitigarbha, the Essence of the Earth, is one of the eight principal Mahayana students, or "heart sons," of the Buddha, Shakyamuni. Ksitigarbha is known for his vow to take responsibility for the instruction of all beings in the six worlds between the death of Gautama Buddha and the rise of Maitreya, as well as his vow not to achieve Buddhahood until all hells are emptied. He is therefore often regarded as the bodhisattva who brings help and comfort to those in the underworld realm of hell beings.

31¾in (80.5cm) high

$19,000-23,000   **SWO**

CLOSER LOOK—BRONZE DING

This bronze ding, in the form of a cauldron, is incised in gold and silver with dragons and scrolling designs.

The carved wooden cover is topped with a jade mandarin duck finial.

It is raised on three tapered legs and placed on a carved wood stand.

The stand and cover are probably 18thC or 19thC, but the vessel itself is attributed to the early Ming period, which substantially increases the value.

A Chinese Ming bronze ding, on a later wood stand, some cracks, chips, and hairlines, losses to metalwork.

11¾in (30cm) high

$32,000-38,000   **CHOR**

A Chinese late Ming bronze incense burner, decorated with dragons chasing jewels, the handles shaped as chilong dragons, four-character seal mark to base reading "hu wen ming zh."

5¼in (13.5cm) wide 27oz

$15,000-19,000   **WW**

A Chinese late Ming or early Qing gilt-bronze figure of Guanyin, seated in dhyanasana with hands in dhyanamudra, traces of red lacquer, wear to gilding.

14¼in (36cm) high

$60,000-65,000   **DN**

A Chinese early Qing bronze incense burner, with mythical creatures, with lion mask handles, six-character Xuande mark.

5¼in (13.5cm) high 41¾oz

$8,000-9,500   **WW**

A rare 17thC to 18thC Chinese bronze Islamic market vase, cast with two panels of Arabic script, "Glory be to God."

This vase would have formed an incense set, including a censer, box, and cover.

5¾in (14.5cm) high 28.6oz

$15,000-19,000   **ROS**

A 17thC to 18thC Chinese bronze vase, cast with flowers and fruit, with elephant-head handles.

9in (23cm) high 48¼oz

$7,000-8,000   **WW**

A 17thC to 18thC Chinese bronze "qian qing gong" tripod censer and stand, Zhengde mark.

8¾in (22cm) wide 137.4oz

$5,000-6,300   **ROS**

A 18thC Chinese bronze fang ding form censer, archaistic four-character seal mark, on hongmu wood stand with silver wire inlay, polished.

Just 15 years ago, there was little market for bronze censers that had been polished and had their patina removed. Yet the current fashion in China is for plain polished bronze censers dating from the 16thC to 18thC, almost always with apocryphal Xuande marks. The vast majority seen are circular on a tripod base (ding) or a circular foot (gui). It is rare to find a plain example of a rectangular-form (fang-ding) censer such as this.

6in (15cm) wide 67½oz

$25,000-32,000   **GORL**

An 18thC Chinese bronze gold-splash censer, with lion mask handles, six-character Xuande mark.

5½in (14cm) wide 18.6oz

$9,500-10,500   **ROS**

A late 18thC to 19thC Chinese Qing bronze gold-splash tripod censer, Xuande two-character seal mark, some surface wear, casting hole to interior.

Gold-splash decoration is generally very popular with collectors.

7½in (19cm) wide 49.6oz

$9,000-10,000   **DN**

A 19thC Chinese archaistic gold-splashed bronze fang ding censer, in Western Zhou-style, cast with mythical beasts on zoomorphic feet, pierced wood cover, lacking finial, some scratches.

7¾in (20cm) high

$7,500-8,000   **GORL**

A Chinese Tang-style bronze mirror, cast in relief with dragons and Chinese characters, on carved hardwood stand.

14in (35.5cm) high

$4,000-4,800   **WW**

A Chinese late Qing bronze tripod censor, six-character Xuande mark.

11in (28cm) wide

$2,800-3,300   **HAN**

A Chinese bronze p'ou form wine vessel, decorated with taotie, phoenix, and geometric bands, with four-character mark within a three-clawed dragon.

The taotie is a demonic beast in Chinese mythology.

8½in (21.5cm) high

$1,600-2,000   **MART**

A Chinese Qing tiehua iron picture, in a wooden frame.

49¼in (125cm) high

$2,300-2,800   **WW**

A Chinese cast iron water cistern, the sides cast with Taoist panels, with inscription reading, "Dated to the sixth year of Qianlong in the fifth month on an auspicious day the world enjoyed peace, the nine regions shared their joy, this is recorded in this inscription," some rusting.

Such cisterns were used to store water in case of fires. They would have been found in temples and larger buildings. Supersize gilded examples can be seen in the Imperial Palace, Beijing.

1741   *24in (61cm) diam*

$1,400-1,900   **CHEF**

A Chinese silver tea set and kettle on stand, by Hung Chong, Shanghai, decorated with snarling dragons, character marks, kettle, stand, and burner marked "HC."

c1860-1930   *68oz*

$3,800-5,000   **BRI**

A Chinese Qing gold and silver inlaid tripod incense burner, decorated with taotie masks and other mythical beasts.

19½in (49.5cm) high 578¾oz

$3,200-3,800   **WW**

A late 19thC to early 20thC Chinese silver tray, maker's mark "WO."

21½in (54.5cm) high 67.6oz

$3,800-4,400   **BE**

A Chinese silver teapot, with embossed and chased decoration, maker's mark "N.M."

c1900   *7¼in (18.5cm) high 15¼oz*

$1,400-1,900   **PSA**

A pair of late 19thC to early 20thC Chinese enameled silver beakers, decorated with characters, maker's marks to bases.

3½in (9cm) high 16¾oz

$500-650   **JN**

A Chinese silver bowl, by Luen Wo, Shanghai, applied with a dragon.

c1920   *7¾in (19.5cm) diam 26¾oz*

$1,900-2,500   **WW**

A 1920s to 1930s Chinese silver and enamel trinket box, a carved tiger's eye centered on the lid, base stamped "Silver made in China," some scratches.

4¼in (11cm) long 8.6oz

$550-650   **APAR**

A Chinese silver cocktail shaker, by Wing Nam and Co., Hong Kong, inscribed "Presented to Mrs E.R.C. MacVicker by the Crew of H.M.S Otus, as a token of esteem 1933-35."

c1935   *9in (23cm) high 11oz*

$750-900   **WW**

A Chinese three-piece tea set, comprising a teapot, sugar bowl, and milk pitcher, with dragon handles, with Chinese character marks, with unmarked claw-ended sugar tongs, decorated with dragons, some dents, teapot lid loose.

32¼oz

$4,400-5,700   **BELL**

A pair of 19thC Japanese Meiji bronze vases and stands, in the manner of Otake Norikuno, decorated with raised carp.

18½in (47cm) high

$25,000-32,000   **HANN**

A Japanese Meiji bronze elephant, with ivory inset tusks, signed "Seiya saku," cast three-character mark, tail broken and reglued.

24¾in (63cm) long

$1,900-2,500   **GORL**

A Japanese Meiji bronze group of an elephant being attacked by two tigers, signed "Morimitsu," lacking tusks.

34¼in (87cm) long

$6,500-7,500   **BE**

A Japanese Meiji bronze tiger, signed with seal mark verso.

20¾in (53cm) wide

$1,400-1,900   **LSK**

A Japanese Meiji patinated bronze stork standing on a turtle, base signed.

15½in (39.5cm) high

$300-350   **TRI**

A pair of Japanese Meiji bronze rats, signed to base.

larger 3¾in (9.5cm) long

$550-700   **APAR**

A Japanese Meiji bronze figure of a peasant smoking a pipe, on a rootwood base, bronze signed to base, the pipe replaced, surface wear.

15¼in (39cm) high

$1,300-1,800   **APAR**

A Japanese Meiji bronze fisherman, on wood stand, fishing rod loose, surface wear.

36¼in (92cm) high

$2,500-3,200   **TEN**

A Japanese, probably Meiji, bronze fuchi, with gold inlay, three-character signature, "?-kane-tomo?."

A fuchi is part of a katana, a Japanese sword. It is the metal bordering piece or collar between the sword's guard and handle.

1½in (4cm) long

$250-320   **FELL**

A late 19thC to early 20thC Japanese inlaid bronze vase and cover, surmounted by a warrior riding an eagle, the body with dragon handles and a warrior scene, signed to lid, some losses, re-glued quiver.

20in (51cm) high

$1,600-2,000   **CHEF**

A near pair of Japanese Meiji iron dishes, inlaid with nunome zogan panels, one signed "Made by Komai living Kyoto Japan," the other "Made by Komai."

Nunome zogan is a traditional Japanese decoration technique of silver or gold inlay, probably imported to Japan from Syria in the 12thC. The technique is closely associated with the Komai family, prominent metalsmiths operating in Kyoto in the 19thC, who widely used and developed the technique.

6in (15cm) diam

$3,200-3,800   **L&T**

A Japanese iron plate, with nunome zogan panels of dragons, landscapes, and flowers, the base signed "Kyoto no ju Komai sei" (made by Komai of Kyoto).

c1880   10¾in (27.5cm) diam

$4,400-5,000   **WW**

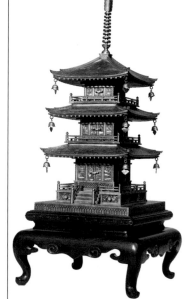

A Japanese Komai-style iron model of a pagoda, decorated in gold and silver nunome zogan, with opening doors and drawers, bells hung at the corners.

The panels include decoration of the Kiyomizu-dera temple and of Mount Fuji.

c1910-15   14½in (37cm) high

$25,000-32,000   **WW**

A Japanese Meiji or Taisho silver elephant, with a cartouche with gilt seal of Koreyoshi.

18½in (47cm) long 187.9oz

$25,000-32,000   **L&T**

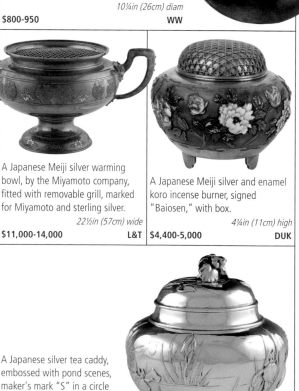

A pair of Japanese iron vases, decorated in nunome zogan with landscape panels, both signed "Kyoto no ju Komai sei" (made by Komai of Kyoto).

The landscapes depicted may be inspired by the Omi Hakkei, the traditional eight views of Omi province, where Japan's largest lake is located, a few miles east of Kyoto.

c1880   8½in (21.5cm) high

$32,000-38,000   **WW**

A 20thC Japanese iron plate, decorated in nunome zogan with a dressed rat and Daikoku carrying a sack, with Komai Seibei/Otojiro II seal mark and inscription for Kinzan.

In Japanese mythology, Daikoku is the god of wealth and the guardian of farmers. Kinzan was a gold mine in the Izu Peninsula, Japan; this mark possibly relates to the riches in the god's sack.

10¼in (26cm) diam

$800-950   **WW**

A Japanese Meiji silver warming bowl, by the Miyamoto company, fitted with removable grill, marked for Miyamoto and sterling silver.

22½in (57cm) wide

$11,000-14,000   **L&T**

A Japanese Meiji silver and enamel koro incense burner, signed "Baiosen," with box.

4¼in (11cm) high

$4,400-5,000   **DUK**

A Japanese silver tea caddy, embossed with pond scenes, maker's mark "S" in a circle within a fan-shaped punch.

4¼in (11cm) high 9¾oz

$1,000-1,150   **WW**

A Chinese Qing rhinoceros horn "loquat" libation cup.

3in (7.5cm) wide 6¼oz

$35,000-40,000 **WW**

A Chinese Qing rhino horn libation cup, carved in high relief with a pagoda, figures, flowers, and blossom.

Collectors should keep in mind that CITES Export licences are unlikely to be granted for items made of horn. CITES is the Convention on International Trade in Endangered Species of Wild Fauna and Flora, an international agreement between governments that came into force in 1975, requiring a permit for import and export of certain species or materials. Pieces such as this rhino horn libation cup will probably have to remain in the country of purchase.

4in (10cm) high 5.9oz

$25,000-30,000 **HAN**

A 17thC Chinese rhinoceros horn "nine dragon" libation cup, with nine chilong dragons.

Provenance: From the collection of William Cleverley Alexander. William Cleverley Alexander (1840-1916) was one of the most noted connoisseurs of his day, renowned for his taste in Western paintings and Asian works of art. The collection was started in 1867 and included items from the Tang, Song, Ming, and Qing dynasties.

6in (15.5cm) wide 9oz

$65,000-70,000 **WW**

A Chinese early Qing bamboo "prunus" libation cup.

5½in (14cm) wide

$10,000-11,000 **WW**

A 19thC Chinese Qing bamboo brush pot, carved with figures.

5½in (14cm) high

$1,400-1,900 **L&T**

A Chinese bamboo wrist rest, carved with a landscape, inscribed "Blessings from the Three Fortune Gods," stain to reverse, dated.

1875 *11½in (29cm) high*

$2,300-2,800 **DN**

A 19thC or early 20thC Chinese "Seven Sages" bamboo brush pot.

The Seven Sages of the Bamboo Grove were a group of Chinese scholars, writers, and musicians in the mid-3rdC AD who gathered together in a bamboo grove to enjoy their respective talents and reject the outside world.

8¼in (21cm) high

$450-500 **DN**

A Chinese bamboo brush pot, signed "Lao Tong," carved with the essay "Valediction to Dong Shaonan" by Han Yu, dated Spring, wuchen year.

6¾in (17cm) high

$3,200-3,800 **L&T**

A Chinese bamboo group of Shoulao and five attendants, some worm damage and losses.

12¾in (32.5cm) high

$3,800-4,400 **GORL**

An 18thC Chinese Qing bamboo figure of Zhongli Quan.

Zhongli Quan, also known as Han Zhongli, is one of the Baxian, Eight Immortals of Taoism. His fan supposedly had the power to revive the dead.

3¼in (8.5cm) high

$3,800-5,000 **L&T**

ASIAN WORKS OF ART

A Chinese Kangxi hardwood bitong, probably zitan, carved with nine scholars and an acolyte preparing tea, the rim inlaid in mother-of-pearl and silver wire.

6¼in (16cm) high

$80,000-90,000   WW

A Chinese Qing aloeswood section, carved with Shoulao holding a ruyi scepter, with further Immortals and the characters "zhi ri."

14in (35.5cm) high

$9,500-10,500   WW

A Chinese Qing carved wood elephant pole stand, painted with polychrome and gilt lacquer.

20¾in (52.5cm) high

$9,500-10,500   WW

A 17thC to 18thC Chinese wood figure of a Wenchang, old cracks to wood.

Wenchang, or Wendi, is the Chinese god of literature.

5in (13cm) high

$1,900-2,500   DN

An 18thC to 19thC Chinese giltwood carving of Amitayus, traces of gilt painted molded gesso, inscription to reverse.

16½in (42cm) high

$11,000-12,000   ROS

A 18thC to 19thC Chinese carved sandalwood casket and cover, by Sung Sing Gung.

This casket was exhibited at the International Exhibition or Great London Exposition in 1862.

15¼in (39cm) long

$2,500-3,200   HANN

A 19thC Chinese rosewood stand, carved with stylized chi-dragons and tight scrolls, joints reattached, some chips.

9in (23cm) wide

$1,900-2,500   GORL

A Chinese wood carving of Guanyin holding a child, probably Huangyang wood, minor nicks and knocks.

9¾in (24.5cm) high

$3,000-3,500   DN

A late 18thC to early 19thC Japanese Edo carved hardwood Hozuki fruit, by Toyomasa, signed.

1¾in (4.5cm) long

$3,200-3,800   PW

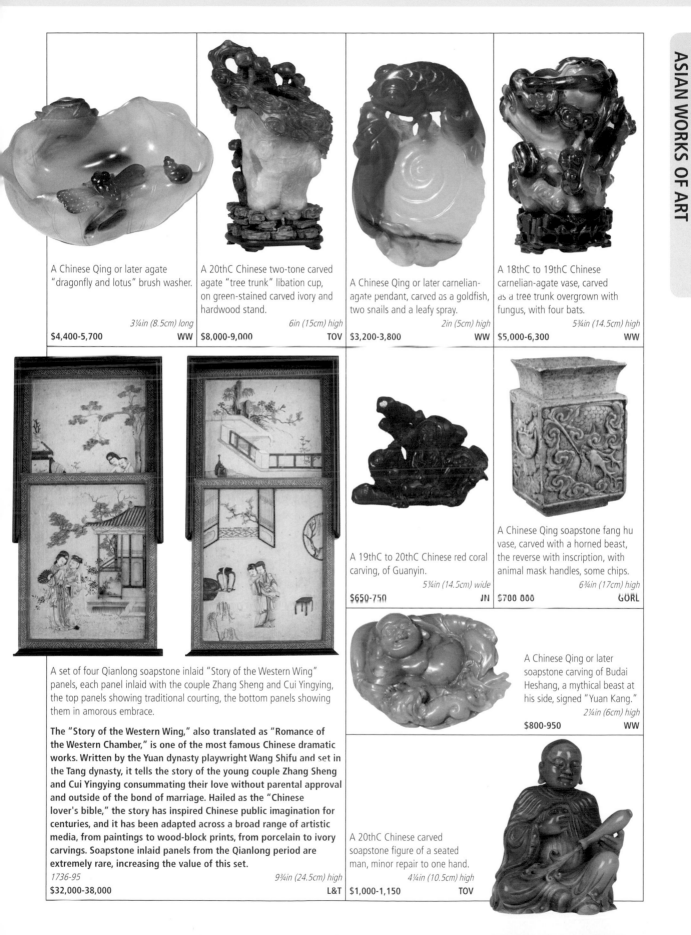

A Chinese Qing or later agate "dragonfly and lotus" brush washer.

3¼in (8.5cm) long

$4,400-5,700 WW

A 20thC Chinese two-tone carved agate "tree trunk" libation cup, on green-stained carved ivory and hardwood stand.

6in (15cm) high

$8,000-9,000 TOV

A Chinese Qing or later carnelian-agate pendant, carved as a goldfish, two snails and a leafy spray.

2in (5cm) high

$3,200-3,800 WW

A 18thC to 19thC Chinese carnelian-agate vase, carved as a tree trunk overgrown with fungus, with four bats.

5¾in (14.5cm) high

$5,000-6,300 WW

A set of four Qianlong soapstone inlaid "Story of the Western Wing" panels, each panel inlaid with the couple Zhang Sheng and Cui Yingying, the top panels showing traditional courting, the bottom panels showing them in amorous embrace.

The "Story of the Western Wing," also translated as "Romance of the Western Chamber," is one of the most famous Chinese dramatic works. Written by the Yuan dynasty playwright Wang Shifu and set in the Tang dynasty, it tells the story of the young couple Zhang Sheng and Cui Yingying consummating their love without parental approval and outside of the bond of marriage. Hailed as the "Chinese lover's bible," the story has inspired Chinese public imagination for centuries, and it has been adapted across a broad range of artistic media, from paintings to wood-block prints, from porcelain to ivory carvings. Soapstone inlaid panels from the Qianlong period are extremely rare, increasing the value of this set.

1736-95 *9¾in (24.5cm) high*

$32,000-38,000 L&T

A 19thC to 20thC Chinese red coral carving, of Guanyin.

5¾in (14.5cm) wide

$650-750 JN

A Chinese Qing soapstone fang hu vase, carved with a horned beast, the reverse with inscription, with animal mask handles, some chips.

6¾in (17cm) high

$700,000 GORL

A Chinese Qing or later soapstone carving of Budai Heshang, a mythical beast at his side, signed "Yuan Kang."

2¼in (6cm) high

$800-950 WW

A 20thC Chinese carved soapstone figure of a seated man, minor repair to one hand.

4¼in (10.5cm) high

$1,000-1,150 TOV

ESSENTIAL REFERENCE—JADE

Jade has a long history in China, and traditionally it has been prized almost as much as gold. It has long been carved into jewelry and ritual, ceremonial, or decorative items, with pieces of worked Chinese jade found dating from c4000 BC.

- Jade technically refers to two separate minerals, nephrite and jadeite, although items carved from other stones are sometimes also referred to as jades.
- Most Chinese jades are fashioned from nephrite, which was mined in eastern central Asia. Its color can vary from creams and whites to greens and blacks. Jadeite can contain green, white, and red within a single piece.
- Ming dynasty jades tend to be carved from different colored stones and have a soft polish, while Qing dynasty jades are often white, almost translucent.
- Heavier, more elaborate pieces will probably be more recent, but, in general, jade is difficult to date.
- Jade is a hard material, so it must be worked on with saws, disks, and drills. It is also brittle and easily scratched, so condition is important.
- The small size of Chinese jades, and the intricacy of their carvings, ensure their popularity today.
- The jade market is fairly unpredictable; it is not uncommon for Chinese jades to go to auction undated, with low estimates, and sell for much more than expected.

A Chinese Qing white jade "goose" pendant, four-character mark "qiu jiang su yan" to reverse.

2in (5cm) high

$25,000-32,000   **WW**

A Chinese celadon jade ceremonial tablet, carved Gui rising from waves, dragons chasing a pearl, with russet, brown, and white inclusions.

7in (17.5cm) high

$3,800-5,000   **DN**

A carved Chinese Qinglong white jade "landscape" pendant, surmounted by a pair of dragons, carved with a sage and attendant, signed "San Qiao," marked.

3¼in (8cm) high

$38,000-44,000   **L&T**

A Chinese white carved jade pendant, with gilt-metal clasp.

2in (5cm) wide

$2,300-2,800   **JN**

A white jade pendant, surmounted by ruyihead clouds, carved with a boy on a water buffalo, the reverse inscribed "yu fu" (jade amulet).

2¼in (6cm) high

$5,500-7,000   **L&T**

A Chinese white jade double belt buckle, carved with a chilong grasping a sprig of lingzhi, the hook a dragon's head, some old repairs.

4½in (11.5cm) long

$5,000-6,300   **DN**

A Chinese probably Ming celadon jade "chilong" disk, with light russet inclusions.

2¾in (7cm) long

$8,000-9,000   **L&T**

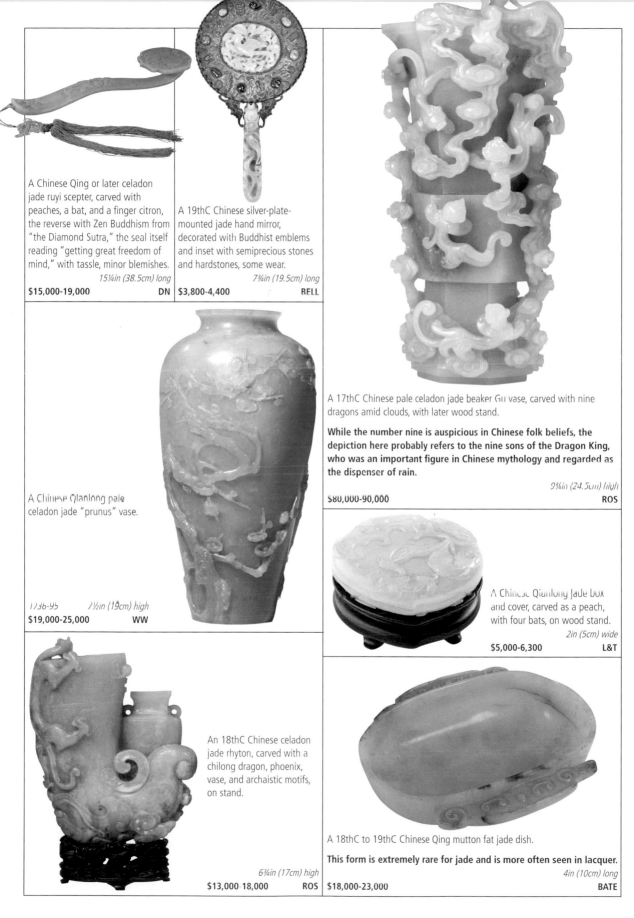

A Chinese Qing or later celadon jade ruyi scepter, carved with peaches, a bat, and a finger citron, the reverse with Zen Buddhism from "the Diamond Sutra," the seal itself reading "getting great freedom of mind," with tassle, minor blemishes.

15¼in (38.5cm) long

$15,000-19,000 DN

A 19thC Chinese silver-plate-mounted jade hand mirror, decorated with Buddhist emblems and inset with semiprecious stones and hardstones, some wear.

7¾in (19.5cm) long

$3,800-4,400 BELL

A 17thC Chinese pale celadon jade beaker Gu vase, carved with nine dragons amid clouds, with later wood stand.

While the number nine is auspicious in Chinese folk beliefs, the depiction here probably refers to the nine sons of the Dragon King, who was an important figure in Chinese mythology and regarded as the dispenser of rain.

9¾in (24.5cm) high

$80,000-90,000 ROS

A Chinese Qianlong pale celadon jade "prunus" vase.

1736-95   7½in (19cm) high

$19,000-25,000 WW

A Chinese Qianlong jade box and cover, carved as a peach, with four bats, on wood stand.

2in (5cm) wide

$5,000-6,300 L&T

An 18thC Chinese celadon jade rhyton, carved with a chilong dragon, phoenix, vase, and archaistic motifs, on stand.

6¾in (17cm) high

$13,000-18,000 ROS

A 18thC to 19thC Chinese Qing mutton fat jade dish.

This form is extremely rare for jade and is more often seen in lacquer.

4in (10cm) long

$18,000-23,000 BATE

ASIAN WORKS OF ART

A 19thC or 20thC Chinese white jade double "fruit" box and cover, on wood stand, the cover broken and reattached.

5in (13cm) long

$9,000-10,000   **DN**

A celadon jade vase and cover, with dragons in pursuit of a pearl.

4¾in (12cm) wide

$11,000-14,000   **L&T**

An archaistic jade tripod censer and cover, carved with archaistic scrolls forming taotie masks, with four-petal finial, of a grayish tone with dark patches.

9½in (24cm) high

$19,000-25,000   **L&T**

A Chinese Qing pale celadon jade carving of a luohan, with a small Buddhist lion.

"Luohan" is the Chinese word for "an arhat," a person within Buddhism who has achieved nirvana (enlightenment).

5in (12.5cm) wide

$9,500-10,500   **WW**

A Chinese jadeite carved celadon and russet vase, carved with cranes, a stag, a bat, lunzhi fungus, prunus, and a pine tree, some damages.

7in (18cm) wide

$4,400-5,000   **DN**

A Chinese Qing white jade carving of a boy.

3in (7.5cm) long

$6,500-7,000   **WW**

A Chinese celadon jade crouching scholar figure.

3¾in (9.5cm) high

$7,500-9,000   **BAM**

A celadon jade carving of fishermen on a boat, with russet veins.

7in (18cm) long

$11,000-12,000   **L&T**

A Chinese Qing pale celadon jade carving of a mountain, with five scholars and an attendant boy.

4½in (11.5cm) high

$11,000-12,000   **WW**

An 18thC Chinese Qing pale green nephrite jade boulder carving, with four children and an elephant in a mountain landscape, on later wood stand.

6in (15cm) high

$25,000-32,000   **CHEF**

A Chinese jade boulder, with two figures in landscape, the reverse with a deer, minor surface abrasions, some russet inclusions.

3½in (9cm) high

$4,400-5,000   **TEN**

A Chinese celadon and dark brown mottled jade mountain carving, carved with a gentleman and boy, on wood stand.

10¾in (27.5cm) high

$14,000-18,000   **MART**

A Chinese Qing white jade carving of a finger citron and a bat, with russet markings.

The finger citron, also known as Buddha's hand, is a fruit segmented into fingerlike sections.

4¾in (12cm) long

$27,000-35,000   **WW**

A Chinese Qing white jade carving of two mandarin ducks, on wood stand.

2in (5cm) long

$5,500-6,500   WW

A Chinese Qing yellow-green jade carving of a hound.

2¾in (7cm) long

$3,200-3,800   WW

A late Chinese Qing pale celadon jade carving of a boy on a water buffalo, on wood stand.

3½in (9cm) wide

$2,500-3,200   BE

A Chinese late Qing pale celadon jade model of a bear.

2½in (6.5cm) long

$18,000-23,000   L&T

A Chinese Qing white and gray jade carving of two hounds.

2¾in (7cm) long

$19,000-25,000   WW

An 18thC Chinese pale celadon jade carving of a qilin.

4¼in (10.5cm) long

$10,000-11,000   WW

A Chinese white-gray and russet jade carving of a cat.

2in (5cm) long

$6,500-7,500   SOU

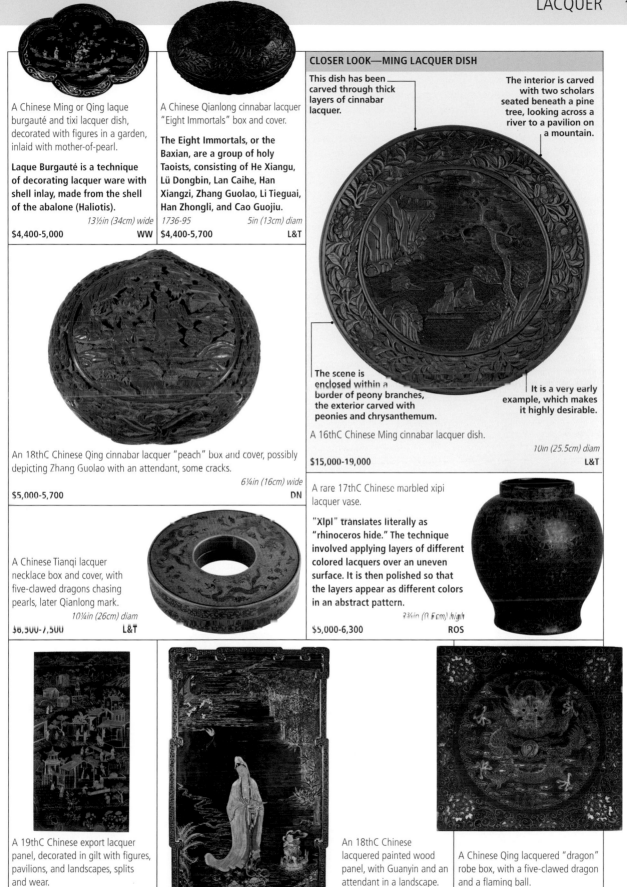

A Chinese Ming or Qing laque burgauté and tixi lacquer dish, decorated with figures in a garden, inlaid with mother-of-pearl.

Laque Burgauté is a technique of decorating lacquer ware with shell inlay, made from the shell of the abalone (Haliotis).

13½in (34cm) wide

$4,400-5,000　　　　WW

A Chinese Qianlong cinnabar lacquer "Eight Immortals" box and cover.

The Eight Immortals, or the Baxian, are a group of holy Taoists, consisting of He Xiangu, Lü Dongbin, Lan Caihe, Han Xiangzi, Zhang Guolao, Li Tieguai, Han Zhongli, and Cao Guojiu.

1736-95　　　　5in (13cm) diam

$4,400-5,700　　　　L&T

CLOSER LOOK—MING LACQUER DISH

This dish has been carved through thick layers of cinnabar lacquer.

The interior is carved with two scholars seated beneath a pine tree, looking across a river to a pavilion on a mountain.

The scene is enclosed within a border of peony branches, the exterior carved with peonies and chrysanthemum.

It is a very early example, which makes it highly desirable.

A 16thC Chinese Ming cinnabar lacquer dish.

10in (25.5cm) diam

$15,000-19,000　　　　L&T

An 18thC Chinese Qing cinnabar lacquer "peach" box and cover, possibly depicting Zhang Guolao with an attendant, some cracks.

6¼in (16cm) wide

$5,000-5,700　　　　DN

A Chinese Tianqi lacquer necklace box and cover, with five-clawed dragons chasing pearls, later Qianlong mark.

10¼in (26cm) diam

$6,500-7,500　　　　L&T

A rare 17thC Chinese marbled xipi lacquer vase.

"Xipi" translates literally as "rhinoceros hide." The technique involved applying layers of different colored lacquers over an uneven surface. It is then polished so that the layers appear as different colors in an abstract pattern.

7¾in (0.5cm) high

$5,000-6,300　　　　ROS

A 19thC Chinese export lacquer panel, decorated in gilt with figures, pavilions, and landscapes, splits and wear.

35¾in (91cm) high

$2,500-3,200　　　　DN

An 18thC Chinese lacquered painted wood panel, with Guanyin and an attendant in a landscape.

69in (175.5cm) high

$5,000-6,300　　　　BELL

A Chinese Qing lacquered "dragon" robe box, with a five-clawed dragon and a flaming ball.

25½in (65cm) wide

$1,900-2,500　　　　L&T

ASIAN WORKS OF ART

ESSENTIAL REFERENCE—NAMBAN CASKET

In the late 16thC, Europeans began to arrive in Japan to establish Christian missions and to trade. To furnish the new churches, and to contribute to export trade, Japanese lacquer workers began to make items in traditional European forms, such as chests, boxes, coffers, cabinets, or caskets, but using traditional Japanese decorative designs. These items were named "Namban" or "Nanban," translating literally as "southern barbarians," after the foreign settlers who had promoted their creation. Namban lacquer pieces are similar in design to the Kodaiji lacquer pieces made in Kyoto in the late Momoyama and early Edo period; both feature gold hiramakie on a roironuri, or black ground. However, Namban pieces are typically further decorated with mother-of-pearl panels and shell inlay, and often combine Japanese designs with Western geometric borders.

A rare Japanese Momoyama Namban lacquer casket, decorated in gold hiramakie and inlaid in mother-of-pearl on a black ground.

c1574-1600   *9in (23cm) wide*

$7,500-9,000   **BRI**

A pair of Japanese Meiji lacquer and Shibayama bottle vases, on three elephant-head feet, some losses, minor surface wear.

Shibayama is a type of Japanese inlay, popular during the Meiji period on both objets d'art and furniture. It was created from a variety of materials, including mother-of-pearl, ivory, glass, horn, tortoiseshell, and jade. The pieces would be individually carved, then set into a wood, lacquer, or ivory ground.

8¾in (22cm) high

$9,000-10,000   **TEN**

A Japanese Meiji Shibayama lacquered "kankodori" box and cover, signed "Masahisa."

9¾in (24.5cm) long

$2,500-3,200   **L&T**

A Japanese Meiji lacquer box, decorated with landscape and floral panels and fans on a millefleur ground, multiple artist signatures.

This item may have been a diplomatic gift.

4¼in (11cm) wide

$1,900-2,500   **GORL**

A Japanese Meiji black and gilt lacquer box.

8¼in (21cm) high

$950-1,050   **DUK**

A Japanese Edo lacquer kettle and cover.

Nashiji is a technique within lacquerwork. Gold or silver flakes are sprinkled onto a lacquered surface. A layer of Nashiji lacquer is then applied and burnished with charcoal, so that the gold or silver can be seen through the top layer of lacquer.

12in (30.5cm) long

$450-550   **JN**

A pair of Japanese Meiji Shibayama and lacquer vases, with birds and foliage in mother-of-pearl, ivory, and tortoiseshell, each neck and foot with a silver-metal rim.

6in (15cm) high

$2,500-3,200   **JN**

A Japanese Meiji gold lacquer tray, with mother-of-pearl and coral decoration.

11¾in (30cm) wide

$1,150-1,400   **DUK**

A Japanese late Meiji silver-mounted Shibayama gold lacquer tsuba, depicting a courtesan entertaining Daruma, signed "Ryogetsu," with original silk pouch.

A tsuba is a traditional Japanese sword guard.

4in (10cm) wide

$5,500-6,300   **BE**

A Chinese Qing celadon jade snuff bottle, with four-character seal mark "chang yi zi sun" to base.

2½in (6.5cm) high

$7,000-8,000   **WW**

A Chinese white and russet jade snuff bottle, carved with chicks and a poem, the stopper with an apocryphal Qianlong mark.

2½in (6.5cm) wide

$3,200-3,800   **L&T**

A Chinese Qing white jade "cats" snuff bottle.

Tobacco was introduced to China by the Portuguese in the mid-to-late 16thC. It was originally smoked in pipes, but by the late 17thC, the use of snuff and snuff bottles had become a regular part of the social rituals of the upper classes. Snuff bottles became objects of beauty, ways to display social status and wealth.

2¼in (6cm) high

$13,000-15,000   **WW**

A Chinese Qianlong pewter "chilong dragon" snuff bottle.

1736-95   *2in (5cm) high*

$500-650   **WW**

An 18thC to 19thC Chinese gilt-decorated soapstone snuff bottle.

1¾in (4.5cm) high

$1,600-2,000   **WW**

A Chinese Tongzhi copper snuff bottle, cast with a scholar in a landscape, stopper with mother-of-pearl inset, four-character mark.

1862-74   *2¼in (6cm) high*

$1,000-1,150   **WW**

A 19thC Chinese coconut shell snuff bottle, incised with a scholar courting a young lady, the reverse with a poetic stanza, ivory stopper.

3¼in (8cm) high

$2,500-3,200   **L&T**

A Chinese Guangxu parcel-gilt and glass snuff bottle, with a European glass micromosaic, marked.

1875-1908   *1¾in (4.5cm) high*

$650-750   **WW**

A late 19thC Chinese interior-painted rock crystal snuff bottle, some damages.

4¼in (11cm) high

$250-320   **FLD**

A Chinese interior-painted glass snuff bottle, signed "Yu Tian" and dated.

1895   *2½in (6.5cm) high*

$800-950   **WW**

A 19thC to 20thC Chinese pale apple-green jadeite snuff bottle.

2¼in (5.5cm) high

$2,300-2,800   **WW**

A Chinese interior-painted rock crystal snuff bottle, painted with a cockerel and small birds, signed "Ye Zhong Shan," dated.

1912   *2½in (6.5cm) high*

$1,300-1,800   **WW**

A coral table snuff bottle, carved as a vase among flowers, with bird stopper.

3½in (9cm) high

$750-900   **L&T**

A Chinese pale celadon jade snuff bottle, with carved dragons forming the flanges.

3in (7.5cm) high

$750-1,000   **L&T**

A Chinese pale jade snuff bottle and cornelian stopper.

2¼in (6cm) high

$1,900-2,500   **LC**

A Chinese white jade snuff bottle and stopper, with a coral stopper.

2¼in (6cm) high

$1,500-1,900   **LC**

ESSENTIAL REFERENCE—OPIUM

Opium is a very powerful drug that had been used in China for medicinal purposes as early as the 7thC. After the arrival of tobacco in the 17thC, small amounts of opium were often added to tobacco when it was smoked. Opium was eventually smoked on its own.

● Eager for goods to trade with China in exchange for the vast quantities of tea it bought, Great Britain began cultivating opium in India and shipping it to China for sale. This resulted in the widespread recreational use of opium in China.

● In 1729, the smoking of opium was banned in China. In 1800, its cultivation and importation were also banned. However, opium continued to be illegally smuggled into China.

● In 1839, the Chinese authorities ordered 20,000 chests of foreign opium to be destroyed. The British demanded compensation, triggering the First Opium War (1839-42).

● After its defeat, China was forced to hand over Hong Kong Island to the British and allow the British to trade in more ports. After the Second Opium War (1856-60), the sale of opium was legalized. It is thought that, by 1900, several million people in China were addicted to opium.

● Opium played an important role in Chinese social life, and opium pipes were often objects of great beauty. They were exquisitely crafted from bamboo, sugarcane, ivory, or porcelain, sometimes covered in enamel or tortoiseshell, often elaborately decorated and finished with silver.

● A typical pipe has a metal fitting or "saddle" toward one end, to which a detachable bowl is connected, designed to vaporize the opium when held over a lamp.

A Chinese porcelain opium pipe, with redware pottery bowl with a monk, some restoration.

19¾in (50cm) long

$6,500-7,000   FLD

A Chinese opium pipe, with bamboo stem and brass saddle, with three cabochon stones in copper collars with green hardstone ends.

22½in (57cm) long

$650-750   FLD

A Chinese opium pipe, with tortoiseshell overlaid bamboo stem, brass saddle, black terracotta bowl, and enameled collars to ends.

22¾in (58cm) long

$1,300-1,800   FLD

A Chinese opium pipe, with bamboo stem and ivory tips, green glazed pottery bowl and silver saddle.

21¾in (55cm) long

$750-900   FLD

An early 19thC bamboo, ivory, and white metal opium pipe.

24in (61cm) long

$500-650   BE

A Chinese ribbed wood opium pipe, with toad-form silver saddle and green hardstone mouth piece.

24¾in (63cm) long

£10 350   FLD

An early 19thC bamboo, ivory, and white metal opium pipe, decorated with a butterfly.

21½in (54.5cm) long

$500-650   BE

A Chinese opium pipe, with lacquered stem, embossed silver saddle, and cloisonné enameled ends, with signed floral pottery bowl.

21¼in (54cm) long

$750-900   FLD

A Chinese shagreen opium pipe, in the form of a fist, with grayware bowl.

12¼in (31cm) long

$800-950   FLD

A Chinese bone opium pipe, with figures in landscapes, with embossed plated saddle and gray pottery bowl, stamped with symbols and characters.

20in (51cm) long

$190-250   FLD

A Chinese bone opium pipe, with panels of immortals, mounted with a silver saddle, with redware pottery bowl, some damages.

20in (51cm) long

$400-450   FLD

A Chinese Qianlong mottled yellow glass faceted bottle vase, swirled with orange, four-character mark.

6in (15cm) high

$8,000-9,000   **L&T**

An 18thC Chinese Peking glass yellow and red overlay bottle vase, a chilong dragon around the neck.

5¼in (13.5cm) high

$1,600-2,000   **WW**

A glass yellow and red overlay brush pot, with chilong dragons, the tails framing a taotie mask.

4¼in (10.5cm) high

$400-450   **L&T**

A Chinese Peking glass vase, depicting dragons chasing pearls, on wood stand, slither chips to base.

10½in (26.5cm) high

$300-400   **APAR**

A 19thC Chinese Peking glass ermine red bowl, carved with dragons contesting a pearl, small bubble in glass, rim chip ground out.

X-ray fluorescence tests show unusual amounts of lead, arsenic, and iron in this piece.

7¾in (19.5cm) wide

$650-750   **DN**

A Chinese Qing Peking glass vase, carved with bifid-tailed dragons, Qianlong four-character mark, some surface blemishes.

6½in (16.5cm) high

$3,800-4,400   **DN**

A probably 18thC Chinese Peking glass jar, with double mask handles, in overlaid metal with two chilong, one crack, small flake to rim.

3¼in (8cm) high

$1,050-1,200   **DN**

A Chinese Jiaqing Peking glass vase, remnants of gilding to the engraved mark, four-character Jiaqing mark, some nicks and scratches.

1796-1820   7in (18cm) high

$6,500-7,000   **GORL**

A Japanese Meiji gilt-silver filigree and champlevé enamel glass vase, the glass mounted with gilt-silver scrolls with enameled lily, lotus, and wisteria blossoms, signed "Somei," stamped "C.T. Marsh & Co."

11½in (29.5cm) high 39.9oz

$8,000-9,500   **L&T**

A Japanese Edo gold-lacquer four-case inro, with a takamakie ground and nashiji interiors, signed "Koho."

An inro, literally "seal-basket," is a small container hung from the waist in traditional Japanese clothing, consisting of several small sections held together by a chord.

4in (10cm) long

$3,200-3,800 **DUK**

A Japanese Edo gold-lacquer four-case inro, decorated in hiramakie and takamakie with a sage on horseback, a scholar-official on a dragon on the reverse, signed "Koma Kyuhaku."

Hiramakie is a form of decoration in low relief. Takamakie is a form of decoration in bold relief. Both are typically used on lacquer in gold or silver.

3¼in (8.5cm) long

$3,200-3,800 **L&T**

A Japanese Edo five-case lacquer inro, decorated in gold hiramakie on a roiro ground with three cranes.

3¼in (8cm) long

$950-1,050 **L&T**

A Japanese four-case lacquer inro, by Jitokusai Gyokuzan, with a mountain cat among foliage, the reverse with a waterfall, signed and with seal.

3¼in (8.5cm) high

$5,000-5,700 **BE**

An early 19thC Japanese five-case inro, decorated in takamakie and hiramakie, with a lacquered iron ojime and late 18thC stag antler teahouse netsuke.

4in (10cm) long

$3,200-3,800 **FLD**

A mid-19thC Japanese four-case inro, with a crayfish, with a silver pierced dragon ojime and a red lacquer manju chrysanthemum flower netsuke, some damages.

3¼in (8.5cm) long

$3,200-3,800 **FLD**

A Japanese 19thC Japanese Meiji four-case gold lacquer inro, decorated with Mount Fuji, with nashiji interiors.

3¼in (8cm) long

$550-700 **JN**

A Japanese Meiji gold-lacquer four-case inro, the kinji ground decorated in gold takamakie, hiramakie, and kirikane.

Kirikane is a decorative technique where small pieces of gold and silver plate or foil are arranged on lacquer to create a design.

3¾in (9.5cm) high

$1,150-1,500 **L&T**

A late 19thC Japanese three-case wooden inro, probably Keyaki, with a koto in gold takamakie and silver, signed "Jokasai," with a pressed brass toad ojime and manju probably Kyoto late 18thC netsuke.

3¼in (8.5cm) long

$1,500-1,900 **FLD**

A Japanese Edo hardwood netsuke of a mother tiger and cub, possibly by Kokei of Kuwana, faintly signed.

Netsuke are small sculptural objects, typically made of wood or ivory. In traditional Japanese dress, they were attached to the top of the chord of an inro (see page 137) to keep it in place.

1¼in (3cm) high

$3,200-3,800　　PW

A Japanese Edo wood netsuke of a nursing mermaid.

c1790　　*2¼in (5.5cm) long*

$3,200-3,800　　MAB

A Japanese late Edo wood netsuke of Ashinaga and Tenaga, signed "Minzan."

c1820　　*1¾in (4.5cm) high*

$3,800-4,400　　MAB

A Japanese Meiji wood netsuke of Ashinaga and Tenaga, signed "Tomin."

4in (10cm) high

$1,150-1,500　　MAB

Ashinaga and Tenaga are a pair of Yōkai, or spirits, in Japanese mythology. Ashinaga ("long legs") and Tenaga ("long arms") are often shown working together, with Tenaga on the back of Ashinaga, enabling them to catch fish.

A Japanese Meiji carved wood netsuke of a pug, the eyes inlaid with translucent horn, signed "Toyomasa," some wear.

1½in (3.5cm) high

$550-700　　L&T

A Japanese Meiji carved wood netsuke of two playful puppies.

1½in (4cm) high

$700-800　　TOV

A Japanese early Meiji boxwood netsuke of Fukusuke, typically carved with exaggerated head, the eyes inlaid in horn, signed "Shuzan."

c1870　　*2in (5cm) high*

$1,600-2,000　　MAB

A 19thC Japanese wood netsuke of a tanuki, by Masanaga, signed.

A Tanuki is a Japanese raccoon dog.

1¼in (3cm) high

$650-750　　BRI

An early 20thC Japanese boxwood netsuke of three toads on a discarded sandal, signed.

2½in (6.5cm) long

$3,200-3,800　　ROS

An early 20thC Japanese boxwood netsuke of a toad on a straw sandal, signed.

2in (5cm) long

$1,900-2,500　　ROS

A Chinese Qing ground silk suit of ceremonial armor and helmet of a general, the helmet with gold dragons.

Provenance: Formerly the collection of Diana Kearny Powell, Washington, who inherited the suit from her father Colonel William Glasgow Powell, USMC (1871-1955), who participated in the relief of Peking in 1900.

jacket and skirt 59in (150cm) high
$70,000-80,000   WW

An early to mid-19thC Chinese Qing embroidered "dragon" robe/jifu, with bats, "shou" characters, and dragons chasing pearls, some splits, wear, and stains.

The robe would have originally been worn by a Mandarin of the Imperial court. It is possible this robe was not intended to be lined—the embroidery is of high quality and is almost double-sided.

87¾in (223cm) wide
$23,000-28,000   DN

A 19thC Chinese silk "nine dragon" robe/jifu, embroidered with silk and gold thread with cranes, dragons chasing pearls, and other auspicious objects.

82in (208cm) wide
$13,000-18,000   WW

A late Chinese Qing Imperial Manchu noblewoman's embroidered silk court chao gua outer vest, embroidered with five-clawed dragons chasing a pearl, gold braid on edges loose, minor wear.

54¼in (138cm) high
$3,200-3,800   DN

An 18thC Indian talismanic shirt or jama, the entire Qur'an written to front and back in naskh script, some with gilt ground, with star form on the front of each shoulder, opening at the front with tie, plain interior.

45¼in (115cm) wide
$25,000-32,000   ROS

An early 19thC Indian youth's cotton talismanic shirt, inscribed with the entire text of the Qur'an, written in naskh and thuluth script, reverse with foliate motif on a green ground, foliate motifs containing script to chest.

39¼in (99.5cm) high
$32,000-38,000   ROS

The earliest surviving Qur'an jama date from the middle of the Delhi Sultanate (1206-1626), although the tradition of a shirt with protective powers might be much older. They were fashioned from three pieces of cotton cloth stiffened to provide a smooth surface for scribes and illuminators to work. They were covered with the entire text of the Qur'an, plus the asma-al-husna (99 names of God), and the Shahadah (the profession of faith). Jama may have been worn under battle armor or used to protect the Muslim elite against dangers, such as disease and difficult childbirth.

Judith Picks

While the market for Western-style "brown" furniture is slow, Chinese furniture is currently very popular. This is partly because of its timeless quality. The simplicity of design means that Chinese furniture looks and feels at home in modern interiors. Many 19thC or 20thC items bare strong similarities to Ming designs. For example, a closely related stool to this pair has been identified as huanghuali and dated to the Ming dynasty. Huanghuali (literally "yellow flowering pear" wood) is a member of the rosewood family. It is a slow growing tree of relatively small size and therefore extremely rare. The use of huanghuali wood in Chinese furniture is another reason for the market's strength.

A pair of 19thC Chinese hardwood corner-leg stools, the legs terminating in hoof feet and with humpback stretchers.

19¼in (49cm) wide

$38,000-50,000　　WW

CLOSER LOOK—PADOUK THRONE CHAIR

The back of this chair is pierced and carved with prunus blossom and a centered qilin roundel.

It is of a large and unusual size, implying that it was made for a Chinese gentleman of importance, which appeals to the Chinese market today.

The carving throughout is of extremely high quality.

It has square-section legs joined by an elaborate pierced interwoven splat.

A Chinese padouk throne chair.
c1900　　*44½in (113cm) wide*
$15,000-19,000　　HT

A Chinese huanhuali yoke-back armchair, with cane seat.

45¾in (116cm) high

$2,000-2,300　　DUK

A Chinese Qing huanghuali, huamu and jichimu "official's hat" or yoke-back guanmaoyi armchair, with woven cane seat.

37in (94cm) high

$6,500-7,000　　BRI

An early 20thC Chinese hardwood folding horseshoe-back jiaoyi armchair, partly Huanghuali wood, with cash roundel and geometric pattern, the back splat carved with a ruyihead cartouche.

Provenance: Collected by a Scottish businessman while working in Hong Kong in the 1950s and 1960s.

43¼in (110cm) high

$11,000-12,000　　L&T

An early 20thC Chinese red lacquer corner chair with dragon carved arms.

43¼in (110cm) high

$400-500　　BELL

A pair of early to mid-20thC Chinese hardwood horseshoe-back jiaoyi armchairs, partly Huanghuali wood, the back splat with a qilin below a cartouche of a dragon.

44½in (113cm) high

$16,000-18,000　　L&T

A 20thC Chinese huali low-back armchair, the back splat pierced with an openwork ruyihead.

37in (94cm) high

$12,000-14,000　　L&T

A rare 17thC Chinese huanghuali and huamu-inset recessed leg pingtou'an table, the burr wood top set within a mitered mortise-and-tenon frame.

Wood-block prints depict similar tables used in everyday life, for writing, displaying objects, and dining. Burlwood inserted tabletops were highly prized by scholars for the dynamic contrast in the color and grain. Such tables were particularly intended to enhance the display of antiques.

46½in (118cm) high

$32,000-38,000   BRI

A 18thC to 19thC Chinese Qing hardwood corner-leg tiao zhuo table, carved with keyfret, flowers, and kuilong dragons.

66½in (169cm) high

$50,000-63,000   L&T

A 18thC to 19thC Chinese hongmu wood altar table.

49½in (125.5cm) wide

$1,600-2,000   JN

A Chinese late Qing hardwood scroll table.

49½in (126cm) long

$3,800-4,400   ROS

A Chinese late Qing hardwood kang table, the apron carved with auspicious objects.

42¼in (107cm) long

$1,150-1,500   L&T

A Chinese late Qing hardwood table, the frieze carved with archaic ruyi C and S scrolls and bead motifs.

46¾in (119cm) long

$11,000-14,000   TOV

A 19thC Chinese "rosewood" hall table.

100in (254cm) wide

$3,500-4,000   LSK

A 19thC Chinese export lacquer table, decorated with figures and pavilions in a landscape, with later stand, some craquelure and shrinkage.

The panel was probably adapted from a screen.

69¾in (177cm) long

$5,000-5,700   DN

A 19thC Chinese elm faux bamboo altar table.

112in (284.5cm) long

$1,900-2,500   WW

A mid-19thC Chinese Qing huali wood and pink marble tripod table.

31in (79cm) high

$500-650 **L&T**

A Chinese Guangxu huanghuali folding tray-top table, Guangxu marks to hinges, some shrinkage, some repairs.

1875-1908 *31¼in (79.5cm) wide*

$1,800-2,300 **GORL**

A Chinese late Qing hardwood writing desk, with two drawers and galleried upper section, loss to gallery, some shrinkage.

46¾in (119cm) high

$2,800-3,500 **DN**

A Chinese nanmu-inset huanghuali wine table.

39in (99cm) wide

$13,000-18,000 **MOR**

A late 19thC to early 20thC Chinese padouk twin-pedestal desk.

54½in (138.5cm) wide

$750-900 **WW**

A Chinese carved wood altar table, the apron pierced with scrollwork and bats.

74¼in (188.5cm) long

$3,200-3,800 **BE**

A Chinese hardwood table, with white metal leafy brackets.

71¼in (181cm) wide

$7,500-9,000 **MOR**

A Chinese marble-top console table, with a carved and pierced "dragon and carp" frieze, the legs decorated with blossoming branches.

32¼in (82cm) high

$3,200-3,800 **L&T**

A Chinese Qing hardwood display cabinet, carved with dragons, clouds, birds, flowers, and fruiting branches.

70¾in (180cm) high

$19,000-25,000 WW

A probably 18thC Chinese lacquered cabinet on stand, engraved metal mounts and gilt warriors, on a later ebonized base.

18in (45.5cm) wide

$4,400-5,000 LC

A 19thC Chinese softwood display cabinet, carved with figures and warriors in a landscape.

106¾in (271cm) high

$1,500-1,900 TEN

A late 19thC Chinese Qing red lacquer gilt-decorated cabinet.

76in (193cm) high

$400-500 L&T

A late 19thC Chinese hardwood stepped display cabinet, some losses to molding.

32¼in (82cm) wide

$2,800-3,500 APAR

A late 19thC to early 20thC Chinese red lacquer parcel gilt press cupboard.

72½in (184cm) high

$900-1,000 DN

A pair of Chinese Qing huali Ming-style openwork book shelves, carved with stylized dragons.

75¼in (191cm) high

$3,200-3,800 WW

A Chinese rosewood sideboard, carved with dragons and cloud motifs.

74in (188cm) wide

$4,400-5,000   **CAN**

A Chinese hardwood side cabinet, inlaid with mother-of-pearl floral sprays, and figures among pavilions.

43in (109cm) wide

$950-1,050   **DUK**

A Japanese Meiji lacquer display cabinet, Shodana, decorated in gold hiramakie on a roiro ground.

41in (104cm) high

$1,050-1,200   **L&T**

A Japanese Meiji Shibayama wood cabinet, the doors inlaid with figures, mythical beasts, birds, and flowers, on matching stand.

76in (193cm) high

$11,000-12,000   **L&T**

A Japanese Meiji lacquered wood chest, with metal strappings, handles, and lockplates.

44½in (113cm) high

$2,500-3,200   **L&T**

A Japanese Meiji carved softwood shidana.

63¾in (162cm) high

$1,300-1,900   **LSK**

An early to mid-20thC Japanese lacquer cabinet on stand, with gilt figures and temples, several drawers within, on later carved stand.

67in (170cm) high

$5,500-7,000   **L&T**

A 19thC Chinese porcelain and ebonized wood eight-leaf screen, painted with figures in landscapes, flowers, fish, and taotie masks, one panel missing.

53½in (136cm) high

$2,300-2,800

BELL

A late 18thC to early 19thC Chinese wallpaper four-leaf screen, hand-painted with exotic birds and butterflies.

110¼in (280cm) wide

$9,000-10,000

L&T

A Chinese Qing kingfisher feather table screen, depicting a river and village landscape, with poems and seals, on wood stand.

The technique of inlaying feathers is called diancui, meaning "dotting the kingfishers," whereby the feather is cut into shape and attached with glue onto the base. The most expensive and highest-quality works traditionally used feathers imported from Cambodia and it is said that Chinese Imperial demand for kingfisher feathers may have contributed to the wealth of the Khmer Empire.

24¾in (63cm) high

$7,500-8,000

WW

Λ 19thC Chinese late Qing inlaid hardstone four-leaf screen, some losses and cracks.

68in (173cm) high

$5,000-6,300

DN

A 19thC Chinese slate table screen panel, carved with a prunus tree on later legs, hairline crack and scratches.

9¾in (25cm) wide

$5,000-5,700

GORL

A pair of 20thC Chinese jade and hardwood screens, carved with a dignitary and attendants arriving at a pavilion, the reverses with inscriptions in zhuanshu script.

panels 25½in (65cm) high

$2,500-3,800

CHEF

A Chinese painted marble and wood screen, depicting a Taoist myth, the reverse with a poem.

In the myth depicted here, during the Yellow Emperor's battle with Chiyou, another mythical tribal leader, Xuan Nv, a disciple of the Queen Mother of the West, was sent by Heaven, leading the Troop of Thunder to assist the Yellow Emperor, and bestowed various legendary artifacts, books, and maps. With her help, Chiyou and his army could not hold out and were therefore defeated by the Yellow Emperor.

marble 11½in (29cm) high

$1,900-2,500

DN

A 20thC Chinese dinner gong and beater.

41in (104cm) high

$300-350

FLD

THE FURNITURE MARKET

To be perfectly honest, the furniture market has remained virtually unchanged since the last edition of *Miller's Antiques Handbook and Price Guide*. The market has continued to be very polarized; "brown furniture" has continued to fall. Most auctioneers are reporting that the plain utilitarian 18th-century and 19th-century mahogany is proving difficult, if not impossible, to sell. Some dealers are quoting a substantial drop in prices and a general lack of interest. At the other end of the spectrum, furniture that is really top quality, fresh to the market, and "honest," continues to rise in value. It is not just age that determines the value of a piece of furniture—quality, condition, and "eye appeal" are all important factors, too.

The reasons for the decline in value of average, midrange furniture is complex, most of it is due to fashion—this is true for all antiques. I often say, when valuing an item, to apply my CARD principle: Condition, Age, Rarity, and Desirability—and the most important of those is desirability. Younger buyers believe that old mahogany furniture is just not "cool" and does not fit into today's interiors. There is also a lack of really good-quality examples on the market. Another problem is that vendors are reluctant to enter good antique furniture to auction while prices are depressed.

Pieces that are too bulky for modern interiors need to be of exceptional quality to attract buyers. There is no doubt that Georgian, and especially Regency, pieces sell better than their heavy Victorian counterparts.

Also, certain pieces, such as the davenport, Canterbury, and bureau, do not have any real function in today's homes. However, while ordinary "Georgian-Victorian brown" furniture has nose-dived in value, 20th century, especially Mid-Century Modern, furniture has continued its renaissance. Many dealers also record that American buyers are still not visiting in their previous numbers and this has had a dramatic effect on export sales. However, good-quality American furniture is doing well.

So, has the low- to midrange furniture market reached its nadir? Some of the prices achieved at auction are ridiculously low. These pieces are made of solid wood by skilled craftspeople, and not merely fashioned out of MDF (medium-density fiberboard which is, simply, wood fibers, combined with wax and a resin binder). There are some indicators that prices may be beginning to climb slightly. People are coming around to the idea that "antiques are green" and that recycling or upcycling old furniture is more responsible than destroying more of the Amazon jungle. Also, with some prices so low, younger buyers are looking at auctions when furnishing their first apartment or house. With the interest in Scandinavian furniture growing, young buyers are often sourcing mahogany furniture and painting it. I still find it amusing when I see Gustavian furniture described as with "original" paint, which is unlikely—it was made to be repainted.

Sturdy, good-quality, highly functional pieces are excellent value for money. These pieces could well provide good investment potential, because prices should increase when (and if) the economy improves.

Above: A 19thC Italian ebony pietra dura and gilt metal cabinet on stand, opening to a shelved interior.

c1840   *62¼in (158cm) high*

$100,000-130,000   **DUK**

Top Left: A satinwood cream-painted and parcel-gilt console table, in the manner of Robert Adam.

41¾in (106cm) wide

$3,800-4,400   **DUK**

FURNITURE

UK PERIOD	AMERICAN PERIOD	FRENCH PERIOD	GERMAN PERIOD
Elizabethan *Elizabeth I (1558-1603)*		**Renaissance** *(to c1610)*	**Renaissance** *(to c1650)*
Jacobean *James I (1603-25)*			
Carolean *Charles I (1625-49)*	**Early Colonial** *(1620s-1700)*	**Louis XIII** *(1610-43)*	
Cromwellian *Commonwealth (1649-60)*			**Renaissance/ Baroque** *(c1650-1700)*
Restoration *Charles II (1660-85)* *James II (1685-88)*		**Louis XIV** *(1643-1715)*	
William and Mary *(1689-94)*	**William and Mary** *(1690-1720)*		
William III *(1694-1702)*			
Queen Anne *(1702-14)*	**Queen Anne** *(1720-50)*		**Baroque** *(c1700-30)*
Early Georgian *George I (1714-27)* *George II (1727-60)*		**Régence** *(1715-23)*	
	Chippendale *(1750-90)*	**Louis XV** *(1723-74)*	**Rococo** *(c1730-60)*
Late Georgian *George III (1760-1811)*	**Early Federal** *(1790-1810)* *American Directoire (1798-1804)* *American Empire (1804-15)*	**Louis XVI** *(1774-92)*	**Neoclassicism** *(c1760-1800)*
		Directoire *(1792-99)*	**Empire** *(c1800-15)*
		Empire *(1799-1815)*	
Regency *George III (1812-20)*	**Later Federal** *(1810-30)*	**Restauration** *(1815-30)* *Louis XVIII (1814-24)* *Charles X (1824-30)*	**Biedermeier** *(c1815-48)*
George IV *(1820-30)*			
William IV *(1830-37)*		**Louis Phillipe** *(1830-48)*	**Revivale** *(c1830-80)*
Victorian *Victoria (1837-1901)*	**Victorian** *(1840-1900)*	**2nd Empire** *(1848-70)*	
Edwardian *Edward VII (1901-10)*		**3rd Republic** *(1871-1940)*	**Jugendstil** *(c1880-1920)*

A Charles II oak armchair, the arched scroll top carved with flowers and leaves above strapwork panels.

$3,200-3,800
WW

A Charles II carved oak wainscot chair.

44½in (113cm) high

$1,300-1,800
LC

A 17thC carved oak joint armchair, with shaped cresting rail above a decorative panel, some replacements.

43in (109cm) high

$1,050-1,200
PW

A 17thC oak panel-back armchair, with chevron carved top rail.

$1,500-2,000
CHOR

A 17thC carved oak wainscot armchair, with scrollwork top rail over a floral panel.

$1,400-2,000
SWO

A 17thC wainscot armchair, with leafage carved and pierced top rail, and floral carved panel back.

$1,400-2,000
BRI

A late 17thC carved oak armchair, with strapwork paneled back.

42¼in (107cm) deep

$1,500-2,000
SWO

A pair of William and Mary carved walnut armchairs, with lion finials, serpent arms, and a pierced scroll stretcher carved with mythical creatures.

c1690
50½in (128cm) high

$3,800-4,400
DN

An 18thC oak lambing chair.

$1,800-2,300
BRI

FURNITURE

ESSENTIAL REFERENCE—COUNTRY CHAIRS

Country furniture is furniture made by rural craftsmen.

- **The Windsor is a well-known type of country chair, common in Great Britain from the 17thC, and later made by European settlers in North America.**
- **Windsor chairs are characterized by their solid saddle seats, into which are doweled the bow and the turned or rounded spindles and legs.**
- **In Great Britain, they were commonly made of ash, beech, elm, or yew.**
- **In North America, they were commonly made of ash, hickory, oak, pine, or poplar. American examples were often painted.**

An 18thC yew stick-back Windsor armchair, seat repaired.

$700-750   SWO

A late 18thC elm stick-back Windsor armchair.

42¼in (107cm) high

$1,800-2,300   L&T

A mid-18thC ash, elm and fruitwood spindle-back Windsor armchair, later caps, some woodworm.

38¼in (97cm) high

$1,500-2,000   DN

A Philadelphia fan-back Windsor armchair, with carved ears, knuckle band rests, repaired break to one arm, small blowout to crest on leg.
c1790

$1,900-2,500   POOK

A mid-18thC fruitwood and ash Windsor armchair, attributed to John Pitt.

John Pitt (1714-59) was a chair maker and wheelwright based in Slough, England. Windsor chairs attributed to him are typically of comb-back form with four cabriole legs. Surviving English Windsor chairs with cabriole legs are not common and those with four cabriole legs, considered to be the earlier type, are especially rare.

$1,400-1,900   WW

A New England continuous-arm Windsor armchair, some worm holes.
c1790

$1,900-2,500   POOK

A set of six New England sack-back Windsor armchairs, minor repairs.
c1790

$2,800-3,500   POOK

A late 18thC black-painted comb-back Windsor armchair, possibly New Hampshire, some wear.

42in (106.5cm) high

$4,400-5,000   SK

A pair of Philadelphia hoop-back Windsor armchairs, with early written owner's label for "John Broomall," metal bracket securing one leg, one arm support replaced.
c1800

$1,050-1,200   POOK

An early 19thC Scottish Windsor armchair.

46½in (118cm) high

$1,300-1,800   **L&T**

A mid-19thC Nottinghamshire elm and yew Windsor armchair, stamped "F Walker Rockley."

The Rockley workshop was opened in 1823 in the village of Rockley, Nottinghamshire, England, by William Wheatland. Frederick Walker (fl.1823-71) was a long-serving chair maker for Rockley and later took over the workshop.

$650-750   **WHP**

A 19thC yew high-back Windsor armchair, elm saddle seat.

$450-550   **PW**

A matched set of four ash and elm Windsor elbow chairs.

$750-900   **BRI**

A New England painted rod-back Windsor settee, with original floral stenciled crest and red and black graining.

c1820   *77in (195.5cm) wide*

$1,600-2,000   **POOK**

A mid-18thC New England slat-back armchair, painted red with yellow pinstripes and floral patterns on the slats

43¾in (111cm) high

$3,800-4,400   **SK**

A mid-18thC Philadelphia William and Mary ladder-back armchair, with a later blue surface by Peter Deen, some wear.

$1,500-2,000   **POOK**

A set of six 19thC painted plank seat dining chairs, Lancaster County, Pennsylvania, minor wear.

$1,900-2,500   **POOK**

An early 19thC elm comb-back armchair.

36½in (93cm) high

$1,300-1,800   **L&T**

A 19thC fruitwood and elm Mendlesham chair.

$450-500   **LSK**

FURNITURE

A set of six mahogany dining chairs, Portsmouth, New Hampshire.

c1770   *37¾in (96cm) high*

$5,000-5,700   **SK**

A Pennsylvania Chippendale walnut dining chair, some replacements and repairs.

c1770

$3,800-4,400   **POOK**

A set of six 18thC Anglo-Dutch carved walnut and marquetry dining chairs.

Provenance: The Kent Gallery, London, purchased on April 1, 1925, for £420 ($530).

$4,400-5,000   **WW**

Six of a set of 12 George III mahogany dining chairs, including 2 carvers, replacement seat rails.

c1790

$15,000-20,000 the set   **DN**

Two of a set of eight Regency brass-strung mahogany dining chairs, with two carvers.

35in (89cm) high

$3,200-3,800 the set   **GORL**

A set of eight Regency rosewood and brass inlaid dining chairs, the frames stamped "WILKINSON LUDGATE HILL," maker's initials "JM" and model "2801," with later upholstery.

Joshua Wilkinson established a cabinet, upholstery, carpet, and looking-glass (mirror) warehouse in 1766 in Moorfields, London. The company produced well-made pieces conforming to Regency fashions and marked their furniture, usually with the impressed stamp "WILKINSON LUDGATE HILL." The firm continued to trade under different names into the 20thC.

33in (84cm) high

$3,200-3,800   **L&T**

A set of six Regency mahogany dining chairs, with two carvers.

c1820   *19in (48cm) high*

$700-750   **DN**

A set of six Regency mahogany dining chairs.

32in (81cm) high

$1,300-1,900   **L&T**

Three of a set of six late Regency mahogany dining chairs, each with anthemion to bar back, with two carvers.

c1820

$750-900 the set   DN

A set of 12 late Regency rosewood dining chairs, attributed to Gillows, with scroll carved horizontal splats, some rails stamped with workmen's initials "W," "TB," and "GG."

$7,500-9,000   WW

Six of a set of eight William IV mahogany dining chairs, with two carvers.

36¼in (92cm) high

$1,000-1,150 the set   CHEF

A set of 16 William IV mahogany dining chairs, the back rails carved with flowers, with two carvers.

carvers 34¼in (87cm) high

$19,000-25,000   L&T

Six of a set of eight Irish mahogany dining chairs, stamped and labeled "John Dooly & Son Ltd., Dublin," with two carvers.

c1840

$3,200-3,800 the set   SWO

A set of eight early Victorian mahogany dining chairs, the legs ending in brass caps and porcelain casters.

37in (94cm) high

$6,500-7,500   L&T

Six of a set of 14 carved Victorian mahogany dining chairs, by Eadon and Sons, Sheffield, UK, all stamped.

George Eadon was a cabinetmaker, upholsterer, carver, and gilder, working at 23 Newchurch Street, Sheffield, in the mid-19thC.

$7,000-8,000 the set   MEA

A set of six Victorian mahogany balloon-back dining chairs.

$500-650   LSK

Two of a set of 18 Victorian oak dining chairs, with padded scroll backs and serpentine stuffover seats, on tapered, turned, and fluted legs with porcelain casters.

35½in (90cm) high

$3,800-5,000 the set   L&T

A set of ten Victorian mahogany dining chairs, on tapered reeded legs with porcelain casters.
35in (89cm) high
$2,300-2,800　　　**L&T**

Four of a set of eight Victorian mahogany balloon-back dining chairs, with two carvers.
c1870
$1,050-1,200 the set　　　**DN**

Three of a set of twelve 19thC Regency-style hardwood dining chairs, on saber legs.
$1,900-2,500 the set　　　**DN**

A set of six 19thC North Italian parcel gilt polychrome-painted dining chairs.
49¼in (125cm) high
$3,200-3,800　　　**BELL**

A set of twelve 19thC oak and leather dining chairs, in the manner of A.W.N. Pugin.

Augustus Welby Northmore Pugin (1812-52) was an architect, designer, and writer, and a key figure in the Gothic Revival movement. He worked in mediums that included metalwork, wallpaper, stained glass, ceramics, and furniture.
$3,800-5,000　　　**WW**

A set of 12 late 19thC George II-style carved mahogany dining chairs, attributed to R. Strahan of Dublin.
37in (94cm) high
$2,800-3,500　　　**TEN**

A set of eight late 19thC George III-style mahogany dining chairs, possibly Scottish, in the Hepplewhite style, the splats carved with Prince of Wales plumes and shells, with two carvers.
37¼in (94.5cm) high
$3,200-3,800　　　**L&T**

Three of a set of 12 Gothic-style oak framed dining chairs.
43in (109cm) high
$2,500-3,200 the set　　　**CHEF**

A pair of George II walnut side chairs, on cabriole legs ending in claw-and-ball feet, stamped with a coronet and initial "D."

39in (99cm) high

$1,400-1,900   **L&T**

A pair of George I giltwood side chairs, in the manner of James Moore.

$15,000-19,000   **WW**

A walnut side chair, probably Massachusetts.

c1740-60   *40½in (103cm) high*

$5,300-5,800   **SK**

A carved tiger maple side chair, attributed to William Savery, Philadelphia, Pennsylvania.

c1760-85   *40¾in (103.5cm) high*

$3,800-4,400   **SK**

A carved mahogany side chair, Newport, Rhode Island, the crest centering a carved shell above a vasiform splat, refinished.

An identical chair, with original finish, is in Henry Du Pont's bedroom at Winterthur.

c1760   *40in (101.5cm) high*

$5,000-5,700   **SK**

A pair of mahogany side chairs, some wear, repairs, and replacements.

c1750   *38½in (98cm) high*

$1,300-1,900   **DN**

An 18thC Chippendale carved mahogany side chair, some imperfections.

37in (94cm) high

$700-800   **SK**

An early 19thC German giltwood gilt side chair, by Johann Valentin Raab, with anthemion decorated cresting, on carved lion monopodia front legs, with stamp.

Johann Valentin Raab (1777-1839) was a Frankfurt-based chair maker. His principal commissions included furniture supplied for the Schloss in Würzburg c1807-09.

$1,150-1,500   **DN**

A set of six 19thC Italian ebonized and specimen marble inlaid side chairs, Florence, in late 17thC style.

c1860

$8,000-9,500   **DN**

A pair of George II mahogany hall chairs, the backs with pierced Gothic motifs, some woodworm and wear.
c1750   *38½in (98cm) high*
$3,200-3,800   DN

A late George II mahogany hall chair, the scallop-shell back carved with an armorial, probably a Drummond widow or possibly Bassett of Cornwall.
                    38½in (98cm) high
$3,200-3,800   DUK

A set of five George II mahogany sgabello hall chairs, each with a dished seat.

The sgabello chair originated in Renaissance Italy. Typically, the seat is a small wooden slab, supported at front and back by solid boards cut into an ornamental shape. A solid piece of wood forms the back.
$3,800-4,400   WW

A pair of late George III mahogany hall chairs, old repairs to backs.
                    35½in (90cm) high
$2,500-3,200   BELL

A pair of mahogany hall chairs, the backs with painted leopard's head heraldic panel.
c1825
$1,300-1,800   DN

A pair of late George III mahogany hall chairs, the backs carved with a double-headed eagle.
$5,500-7,000   WW

A pair of William IV Gothic Revival oak hall chairs.
c1830   *36¼in (92cm) high*
$8,000-9,000   DN

A mid-to-late 18thC walnut corner chair, Massachusetts.
                    31½in (80cm) high
$2,300-2,800   SK

A 19thC George III corner chair.
                    29½in (75cm) high
$1,150-1,500   DRA

A 17thC oak box stool with hinged top, worm, structure loose, burn marks.

17in (43cm) wide

$2,800-3,500 CHEF

A late 18thC to early 19thC turned birch Windsor stool, possibly northern New England.

According to expert Nancy Goyne Evans, the appearance of birch in this stool more likely places it in northern New England, perhaps Maine, than in Pennsylvania.

25½in (65cm) high

$3,200-3,800 SK

CLOSER LOOK—REGENCY STOOL

This stool is double-sided, with an X-shape frame.

Its rope-twist arms and paw feet are intricately carved, as is the rossette at the center of the frame.

It has a blue silk-covered drop-in seat.

It is in the manner of William Trotter (d.1834), a Scottish cabinetmaker based in Princes Street, Edinburgh, who was highly influenced by Classical Revival style.

A Regency mahogany double-sided stool, in the manner of William Trotter, some wear, iron reinforcing braces.

c1815 *51½in (131cm) wide*

$32,000-38,000 DN

A George III mahogany footstool, with carved eagle head and lion paw supports, with original needlework upholstery.

19in (48.5cm) long

$5,000-5,700 MART

A near pair of Regency rosewood footstools, attributed to William Trotter.

19¼in (49cm) wide

$2,300-2,800 BELL

A mahogany center stool, the frieze with carved flower motif, one stretcher stamped "C. MUNRO."

c1860 *45in (114cm) wide*

$2,300-2,800 DN

A Victorian mahogany center stool.

49½in (126cm) long

$4,400-5,000 L&T

A French 19thC giltwood dressing stool.

$950-1,050 BLEA

A mahogany stool, possibly Irish, with trade label inscribed "FRANK PARTRIDGE WORKS OF ART 26, KING ST., ST. JAMES'S AND NEW YORK."

19in (48cm) wide

$1,900-2,500 WW

FURNITURE

A pair of late 17thC to early 18thC Louis XIV carved walnut armchairs.

47¼in (120cm) high

$5,500-7,000   DN

A pair of Louis XV walnut armchairs, carved with stylized shell work and foliate elements.

c1730   *41¼in (105cm) high*

$9,000-10,000   DN

A Louis XV carved walnut armchair, by Deshayes, carved with stylized shells and anthemion motifs, stamped "SHAYES" and "JME," some restoration.

Louis Deshayes became a master craftsman in 1756. Established on the Rue des Vieux-Augustins, Paris, he was still active at the beginning of the Revolution.

c1750   *43in (109cm) high*

$1,600-2,000   DN

A mid-18thC George III mahogany Gainsborough armchair.

The Gainsborough armchair was popular in England in the 18thC. It was wide in form, with a high back, open sides, upholstered back and seat, and short upholstered arms. These were sometimes known as "French chairs," because designs were often inspired by French Rococo style.

41in (104cm) high

$4,400-5,000   L&T

A George III mahogany Gainsborough or library chair.

39in (99cm) high

$7,000-7,500   SWO

A George III mahogany Gainsborough armchair.

$4,400-5,000   WW

A George III mahogany open armchair, some repairs.

37in (94cm) high

$1,300-1,800   BELL

One of a set of four George III ebonized and painted open armchairs, later cane work, rubbing to ebonizing.

35½in (90cm) high

$3,800-4,400 the set   BELL

A pair of late 18thC George III mahogany wheel-back open armchairs, in the Sheraton manner.

37in (94cm) high

$1,150-1,500   WAD

An inlaid lolling chair, probably North Shore, Massachusetts.
c1000 *46¾in (117.5cm) high*
$11,000-12,000 **SK**

A George III
mahogany
metamorphic library
armchair, attributed
to Gillows, after the
design by Morgan &
Sanders, some wear
and repairs.
36¼in (92cm) high
c1810
$4,400-5,000 **DN**

A pair of Regency Pavilion-
style bamboo armchairs, in the
manner of William Chambers,
some losses.

**The fashion for bamboo
furniture started with the
designs of Sir William Chambers
in 1757. The design of these chairs
show the influence of Chambers, as well as the designs of Brighton
Pavilion by Crace & Co. There was a resurgence of the chinoiserie style
with the creation of Brighton Pavilion by the Prince Regent (later King
George IV) from 1815-22.**

35½in (90cm) high
$2,500-3,200 **CHEF**

A pair of George III mahogany shield-back
armchairs, attributed to Gillows, some
professional restoration.

**This pair of armchairs relates closely
in design to a Gillows drawing of 1786,
for one of a set of ten "Êbriole Armchair" made
for the Conservative statesman Sir Robert Peel.**
c1790 *28¾in (73cm) high*
$5,500-6,500 **DN**

A late 18thC to early 19thC
Russian mahogany and brass inlaid
Neoclassical open armchair, with
carved eagle's head arm supports.
$1,300-1,900 **WW**

A pair of Regency mahogany bergères, some wear and restoration.
c1810 *37in (94cm) high*
$10,00-11,000 **DN**

A pair of Regency ebonised parcel-
gilt lattice-back open armchairs.
33in (84cm) high
$1,600-2,000 **BELL**

A pair of Empire carved mahogany
fauteuils, in the manner of Jacob
Frères.
c1815 *17in (43cm) high*
$5,000-6,300 **DN**

A George IV beechwood bobbin-
turned armchair, on brass casters.
$900-1,000 **WW**

FURNITURE

A George IV oak leather armchair, attributed to Gillows.
42½in (108cm) high
$2,500-3,200   **L&T**

A pair of George IV mahogany open armchairs.
$950-1,050   **WW**

A pair of Victorian satin walnut tub chairs, stamped "J Kerr & Co. 59399."
$950-1,050   **SWO**

A pair of 19thC Italian Baroque iron and brass curule armchairs.
39in (99cm) high
$2,800-3,500   **L&T**

Two of a set of four early 19thC mahogany shield-back open armchairs, in the Hepplewhite taste.
$5,000-5,700 the set BE

Three of a set of five late 19thC Black Forest open armchairs.
39in (99cm) high
$1,300-1,800 the set   **BELL**

ESSENTIAL REFERENCE—GOTHIC REVIVAL

- The Gothic Revival movement emerged in Great Britain in the mid-18thC and reached its height in the late 19thC. It reflected contemporary interest in the medieval period, particularly in the Gothic style of the 12thC.
- Gothic Revival furniture took inspiration from Gothic Revival architecture, using pointed arches, heraldic motifs, and trefoil and quatrefoil shapes.
- Rosewood, oak, or walnut would often be decorated with heavy, intricate carving and finished with dark staining.
- Upholstery was generally in heavy fabrics, such as velvet, leather, or brocade.
- Although primarily associated with English taste, the Gothic Revival style also appeared in France during the reign of Louis Philippe. It is possible that these chairs may be French, because their design closely relates to a chair attributed to Joseph Pierre Francois Jeanselme, an early to mid-19thC French cabinetmaker.

A pair of Victorian Gothic Revival oak armchairs, with lancet, trefoil, and quatrefoil motifs, each with a paper label marked "Great Hall."
c1850   *51¼in (130cm) high*
$6,500-7,500   **DN**

A pair of late 19thC to early 20thC French beech and needlework upholstered armchairs.
35in (89cm) high
$2,300-2,800   **L&T**

A George II and later walnut wing armchair, on cabochon leaf and husk carved cabriole legs and paw feet.

$7,500-9,000   WW

A mid-18thC mahogany framed tub-back armchair, "NORMAN ADAMS" trade label to underside, later upholstery, some repairs.
36¼in (92cm) high
$3,800-4,400   BELL

A George III mahogany wing armchair.
c1770   *43in (109cm) high*
$5,000-5,700   DN

A Philadelphia Chippendale mahogany easy chair, with Marlborough feet, some upholstery removed.
c1780
$5,500-6,500   POOK

A Regency ebonized and brass-mounted bergère, one rear leg replaced.
c1810   *43¼in (110cm) high*
$3,800-4,400   DN

A George IV rosewood library armchair, in the manner of Gillows, with leaf carved scroll arm fronts, above quarter rosettes.
$6,500-7,500   WW

A William IV oak library armchair, carved with acanthus leaves and rope-twist and lappet borders.
$4,400-5,000   WW

A William IV mahogany and buttoned leather upholstered adjustable armchair, in the manner of Robert Daws, some wear, filler plugs to joints.
c1835   *45in (114cm) high*
$2,300-2,800   DN

An early Victorian mahogany library armchair.
$2,300-2,800   WW

FURNITURE

A Victorian scroll-back easy armchair, by William Birch, stamped "WB 81(?)," tatty upholstery, retipping to back legs.

43¼in (110cm) long

$3,200-3,800   **BELL**

A Gothic Revival oak and leather-upholstered reclining armchair, attributed to Charles Bevan for Marsh & Jones.

See Jeremy Cooper, "Victorian and Edwardian Furniture and Interiors," Thames & Hudson, 1987, figure 267, where a related chair designed by Charles Bevan, and manufactured on licence by Marsh & Jones is illustrated.

c1870   *39¼in (100cm) high*

$3,200-3,800   **L&T**

A 19thC satinwood brass-mounted bergère.

35¾in (91cm) high

$1,900-2,500   **L&T**

A pair of early 20thC Howard & Sons leather club armchairs, the rear legs stamped "HOWARD & SONS LTD/BERNERS ST" and numbered "12667/9010" and "13050/9897."

31in (79cm) high

$3,800-5,000   **L&T**

An early 20thC pair of leather upholstered barrel-back wing armchairs.

43in (109cm) high

$4,400-5,000   **L&T**

An early 20thC George II-style walnut framed wing armchair.

42½in (108cm) high

$2,500-3,200   **L&T**

ESSENTIAL REFERENCE—HOWARD & SONS

Howard & Sons began in 1820 when John Howard started trading on Lemon Street, London, as a cabinetmaker.

- **Howard & Sons pieces are of high quality and received much acclaim at the time, winning prizes at the 1862 and 1878 International Exhibitions and the 1900 Paris Exhibition.**
- **In 1866 George Howard patented the "elastic seat," which radically redesigned the interior working of traditional upholstery.**
- **Howard & Sons chairs and sofas typically have a name or number stamped on the back foot, a paper label on the burlap, or a name stamp on the caster.**
- **Howard and Sons ceased trading in 1947. Today, chairs that follow George Howard's patent are sold by Howard Chairs Limited of London.**

A late Victorian walnut and upholstered armchair, by Howard & Sons, one rear leg stamped "7410 6539" and "HOWARD & SONS BERNERS ST."

33in (84cm) high

$5,000-5,700   **DN**

A pair of French Louis XVI-style mahogany and ormolu-mounted bergères, attributed to François Linke.

The chairs were originally part of a suite of furniture that came from a château in the Loire Valley. François Linke (1855-1946) was an important Parisian cabinetmaker of the late 19thC and early 20thC.

c1900

$5,000-5,700   **WW**

A pair of 20thC 18thC-style high wing-back armchairs.

52in (132cm) high

$1,900-2,500   **BELL**

An 18thC Louis XIV walnut sofa, upholstered with 17thC tapestry panels and cushions.

71¾in (182cm) wide

$4,400-5,000   SWO

An early 18thC and later walnut settee.

44¼in (112.5cm) wide

$5,000-6,300   WW

A George II walnut chair-back settee, with tapered cabriole legs with carved claw-and-ball feet, some repairs to needlework.

c1735   *46in (117cm) wide*

$8,000-9,000   DN

ESSENTIAL REFERENCE—GEORGE HEPPLEWHITE

George Hepplewhite (d.1786) was an English cabinetmaker and furniture designer.

- He was originally apprenticed to Robert Gillow of Lancaster and later moved to London, where he opened his own store on Redcross Street.
- His furniture was simple and elegant, typically in Neoclassical style. He often added inlaid and painted decoration to his work.
- He is known for his pattern book, "The Cabinet-maker and Upholsterer's Guide," published posthumously in 1788. It was influential in Europe and North America, and cabinetmakers often used the guide as a trade catalog. It featured many of his designs and simpler versions of designs by Robert Adam, making them more accessible to the wider market.
- No piece has been unequivocally attributed to Hepplewhite or his firm.

A George III Hepplewhite-style mahogany settee.

c1780   *69in (175cm) wide*

$2,300-2,800   SWO

A late 18thC giltwood settee, possibly English, in Louis XV style.

57in (144.5cm) wide

$1,300-1,800   WW

A George III mahogany and upholstered sofa, some scratches, hairline cracks to one leg.

c1790   *75½in (192cm) wide*

$4,400-5,000   DN

A George III mahogany settee.

78¼in (199cm) wide

$5,000-5,700   SWO

An 18thC gilt-framed sofa.

63¾in (162cm) wide

$1,500-1,900   CHEF

A 19thC American Empire revival sofa, the mahogany frame carved with cornucopias, restored.

79in (200.5cm) wide

$1,300-1,800   DRA

A George IV carved mahogany sofa.

93¼in (237cm) wide

$1,400-1,900   L&T

A Regency ebonized and parcel-gilt sofa.

89½in (227cm) long

$3,200-3,800   L&T

A late Regency mahogany scroll-end settee, one rear leg with molding loss, one leg repaired.

67in (170cm) wide

$1,500-2,000   CHEF

An early 19thC mahogany framed sofa.

76in (193cm) wide

$1,900-2,500   PW

An early Victorian rosewood framed sofa.

75½in (192cm) long

$1,900-2,500   L&T

An early Victorian carved mahogany sofa, in modern silk upholstery.

83½in (212cm) long

$1,050-1,200   L&T

A mid-19thC Victorian double-spoon-back mahogany sofa.

67¾in (172cm) wide

$800-950   L&T

A Victorian triple-chair-back sofa, restored.

67¾in (172cm) wide

$1,800-2,300   BELL

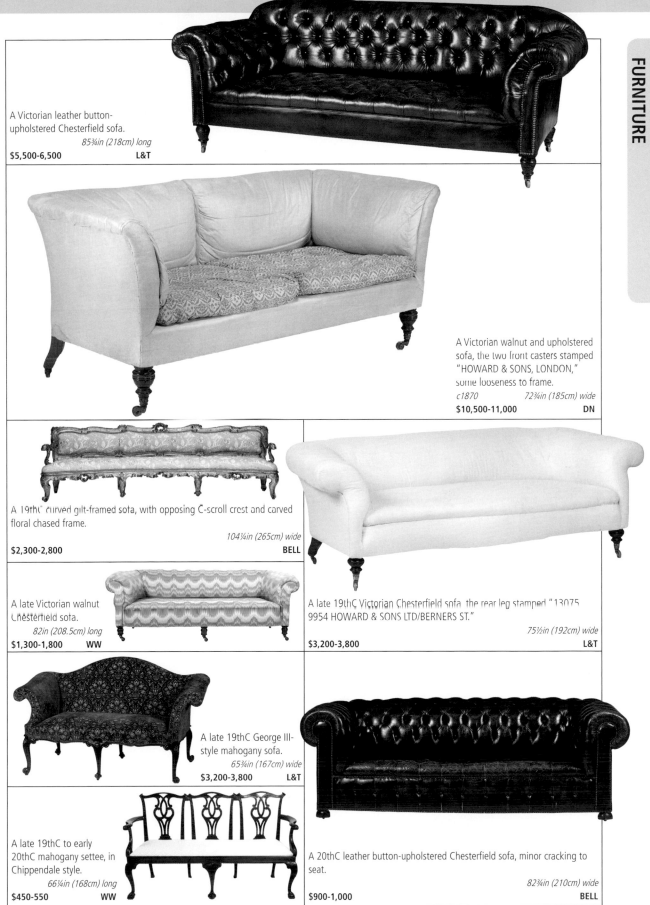

A Victorian leather button-upholstered Chesterfield sofa.

85¾in (218cm) long

$5,500-6,500   **L&T**

A Victorian walnut and upholstered sofa, the two front casters stamped "HOWARD & SONS, LONDON," some looseness to frame.

c1870   *72¾in (185cm) wide*

$10,500-11,000   **DN**

A 19thC curved gilt-framed sofa, with opposing C-scroll crest and carved floral chased frame.

104¼in (265cm) wide

$2,300-2,800   **BELL**

A late Victorian walnut Chesterfield sofa.

82in (208.5cm) long

$1,300-1,800   **WW**

A late 19thC Victorian Chesterfield sofa, the rear leg stamped "13075 9954 HOWARD & SONS LTD/BERNERS ST."

75½in (192cm) wide

$3,200-3,800   **L&T**

A late 19thC George III-style mahogany sofa.

65¾in (167cm) wide

$3,200-3,800   **L&T**

A late 19thC to early 20thC mahogany settee, in Chippendale style.

66¼in (168cm) long

$450-550   **WW**

A 20thC leather button-upholstered Chesterfield sofa, minor cracking to seat.

82¾in (210cm) wide

$900-1,000   **BELL**

FURNITURE

A late Regency rosewood chaise longue.

82in (208cm) long

$800-950   **L&T**

A mid-18thC paneled elm bacon settle, door and cupboards on the reverse, with armrests and small cupboards on the box seat base, some shrinkage and wear.

Bacon settles were a feature of the farmhouse kitchen throughout the 18thC and 19thC. They have always been associated with the hanging of cured sides of bacon, but it seems more probable that the use of these high-back settles was as a hanging space for outdoor clothing, as a display shelf, and as a room divider. The principal living room in a West Country farmhouse was the kitchen, with the entrance directly from the outside and an open fire creating cold drafts. The use of a high-back settle could avert the draft, creating warmth around the hearth.

An early Victorian mahogany chaise longue, the frame decorated with scrolls.

67¾in (172cm) wide

$700-800   **WW**

72in (183cm) high

$3,200-3,800   **CHEF**

An 18thC Dutch Renaissance oak hall bench, the back reinforced.

66¼in (168cm) wide

$3,200-3,800   **CHEF**

A George III oak "Gothick" settle, the back and sides with trefoil-shaped X-form pierced panels.

70in (178cm) long

$13,000-18,000   **L&T**

A pair of Regency or later mahogany window seats, in the manner of Marsh & Tatham.

31½in (80cm) high

$2,000-2,500   **CHEF**

A late 19thC Black Forest bench, the carved plank seat supported by twin carved bears with glass eyes.

"Black Forest" carvings and furniture were once thought to have been made in the Black Forest reigion of Bavaria, Germany, but they were, in fact, mostly produced in Brienz, Switzerland. The craftsman of Brienz carved boxes, clock cases, figures, and furniture from tree trunks. Bears were popular subjects. See page 251.

One of a pair of William IV rosewood window seats.

c1835   52in (132cm) wide

$1,900-2,500 the pair   **DN**

31½in (80cm) wide

$4,400-5,000   **L&T**

A 17thC oak refectory table, on gun barrel ring-turned legs and block feet.

82¾in (210cm) wide

$3,800-4,400   **SWO**

A late 17thC oak three-plank refectory table.

110¼in (280cm) wide

$2,500-3,800   **SWO**

An early 17thC and later oak refectory table, the frieze carved with lunettes.

A refectory table is a long, narrow dining table. They were first used in monasteries in Medieval Europe in the refectory or communal dining room.

103in (216.5cm) long

$3,200-3,800   **WW**

A 17thC and later oak refectory table, the plank top with cleated ends.

109in (277cm) long

$5,500-6,500   **L&T**

An oak refectory table, with associated cleated top.

c1700   *84in (213.5cm) long*

$1,500-2,000   **HT**

An early 18thC Continental joined oak refectory dining table, with a single frieze drawer.

89¼in (227cm) long

$1,500-2,000   **TEN**

An 18thC elm two-plank refectory table, on four gun-barrel legs.

91in (231cm) wide

$1,400-1,900   **CHOR**

An 18thC Georgian oak refectory table, the five-board cleated top above a scroll carved frieze.

81½in (207cm) long

$1,300-1,900   **L&T**

FURNITURE

A William and Mary oak one-drawer gateleg table.

45¼in (115cm) long

$5,500-6,500   SK

A Pennsylvania William and Mary walnut gateleg table, top and brasses replaced.

c1740   *45¾in (116cm) long*

$1,150-1,500   POOK

A George II Irish mahogany drop-leaf table, with plain frieze and cabriole legs with hoof feet.

c1750   *43¼in (110cm) wide*

$1,150-1,500   DN

A George II mahogany drop-leaf dining table, some mildew to underside.

c1760   *48in (122cm) long*

$650-750   POOK

A George II mahogany drop-leaf dining table, possibly Irish.

42¼in (107.5cm) long

$650-750   WW

A George II oak double drop-leaf table, with two frieze drawers.

open 71¼in (181cm) wide

$750-900   SWO

A late 18thC George III oak gateleg table, with a single drawer and opposing dummy drawer.

open 66½in (169cm) long

$1,150-1,500   L&T

A 19thC elm gateleg table on turned supports and stretchered base.

56¾in (144cm) long

$750-900   ECGW

A George III mahogany two-pedestal Cumberland action extending dining table, in the manner of Wilkinson & Sons, some wear.
c1810   *extended 129¼in (328cm) long*
$9,500-10,500   **DN**

A mahogany triple-pedestal dining table, with rosewood crossbanding, some restoration.
c1820   *extended 216½in (550cm) long*
$13,000-15,000   **DN**

An early 19thC Regency mahogany pedestal dining table, the crossbanded tilt top with ebony banding.
71¾in (182cm) diam
$9,000-10,000   **L&T**

A Regency mahogany and brass inlaid twin-pedestal dining table, the frieze with carved rosettes, with two additional leaves.
extended 50½in (128cm) long
$5,500-6,500   **BE**

A George IV mahogany twin-pedestal dining table, with one leaf extension.
111in (282cm) long
$4,400-5,000   **L&T**

An early 19thC three-part mahogany extending dining table, the center section with swiveling top over an ebony inlaid frieze and pull-out ends to support the additional leaves, raised on eight legs, with two pedestal D ends, with four additional leaves.
extended 149½in (380cm) long
$5,000-5,700   **MART**

An early 19thC and later mahogany D-end dining table, with end pedestals and six ring-turned legs, opening with a gateleg action to support final two sections.
155¾in (395.5cm) long
$3,200-3,800   **SWO**

A mid-Victorian mahogany triple-pedestal dining table, with three additional leaves, some restoration and wear.
154¾in (393cm) long
$9,000-10,000   **TEN**

A George III mahogany extending dining table, with kingwood crossbanding, with two D ends, a center section, and four extra leaves.

151½in (385cm) long

$2,800-3,500 **LC**

An early 19thC mahogany extending dining table, with five extra leaves.

190½in (484cm) wide

$18,000-23,000 **SWO**

A Regency mahogany telescopic extending dining table, with three additional leaves and two rounded drop flaps, some scratches and bruising.

86½in (220cm) long

$1,800-2,300 **TEN**

CLOSER LOOK—REGENCY EXTENDING DINING TABLE

This table is in the style of George Bullock (c1778-1818), a sculptor and furniture maker based in Liverpool, celebrated for his impressive craftsmanship and use of exotic woods.

It has four semielliptical additional leaves, each decorated with foliate ebony marquetry, attached with pull-out supports.

The turned feet and shaped plinth and embellished with further floral carving and motifs.

The quality of the craftsmanship is very fine and the condition excellent.

A Regency mahogany circular extending dining table, in the manner of George Bullock.

91¼in (232cm) diam

$80,000-90,000 **DN**

An early 19thC mahogany extending dining table, with concertina action, four additional leaves, restored, some wear.

136¼in (346cm) long

$5,000-6,300 **CHEF**

An early Victorian mahogany extending dining table, with eight leaves.

171¼in (435cm) long

$7,500-8,000 **SWO**

A Victorian Lambs of Manchester figured and bog oak extending dining table, with five extra leaves, stamped on the runner.

Lambs of Manchester was a renowned cabinetmaking firm founded by James Lamb (1816-1903). It won medals at London 1862 Exhibition and the Paris 1867 Exhibition.

extended 169¼in (430cm) long

$3,800-5,000 **BELL**

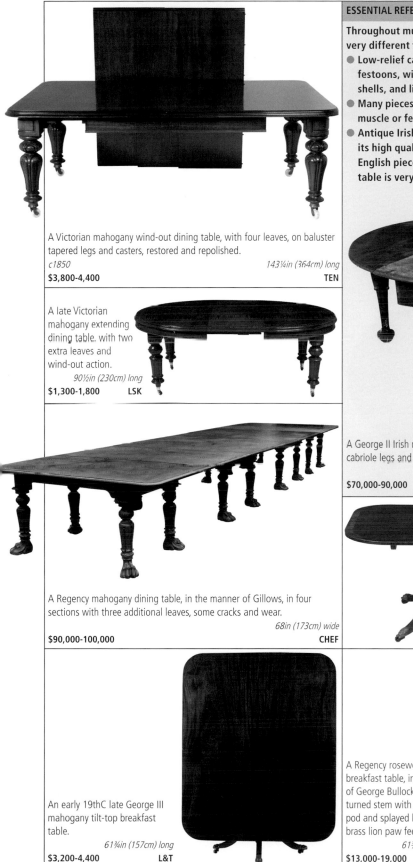

A Victorian mahogany wind-out dining table, with four leaves, on baluster tapered legs and casters, restored and repolished.

c1850   *143¼in (364cm) long*

$3,800-4,400   **TEN**

A late Victorian mahogany extending dining table, with two extra leaves and wind-out action.

90½in (230cm) long

$1,300-1,800   LSK

A Regency mahogany dining table, in the manner of Gillows, in four sections with three additional leaves, some cracks and wear.

68in (173cm) wide

$90,000-100,000   CHEF

ESSENTIAL REFERENCE—IRISH FURNITURE

Throughout much of the 18thC, Irish furniture was stylistically very different from English furniture.

● Low-relief carvings on the aprons of tables included festoons, winged birds, and rosettes. Goblin heads, scallop shells, and lion masks also depicted.

● Many pieces were decorated with animalistic additions, with muscle or fetlock being carved above the paw or claw feet.

● Antique Irish furniture is highly desirable today due to its high quality, and it can often fetch more than similar English pieces. Despite being in need of restoration, this table is very valuable.

A George II Irish mahogany table, on carved lion mask and foliate carved cabriole legs and hairy paw feet, some damages, in need of restoration.

68in (173cm) long

$70,000-90,000   CHEF

A George III mahogany breakfast table, with rosewood banding, on a turned pillar and outswept reeded legs, with lion casters.

c1810   54¼in (138cm) wide

$1,300-1,900   DN

An early 19thC late George III mahogany tilt-top breakfast table.

61¾in (157cm) long

$3,200-4,400   L&T

A Regency rosewood flip-top breakfast table, in the manner of George Bullock, on ring-turned stem with brass-inlaid pod and splayed legs, with cast brass lion paw feet.

61¾in (157cm) long

$13,000-19,000   MEA

FURNITURE

A Regency oak pedestal tilt-top breakfast table.

70¾in (180cm) diam

$10,500-11,000   LSK

A Regency mahogany tilt-top breakfast table, with crossbanded and ebony strung top, on a ring-turned stem and scroll molded splay legs.

56in (142cm) wide

$9,000-9,500   WW

A Regency mahogany pedestal tilt-top breakfast table, with crossbanded and ebony strung top.

c1825   *61in (155cm) long*

$650-750   HAN

A William IV mahogany tilt-top breakfast table, on a ring-turned column to four hipped swept supports.

49½in (125.5cm) diam

$950-1,050   MART

A William IV rosewood snap-top breakfast table.

52½in (133cm) wide

$400-500   BELL

A William IV rosewood tilt-top breakfast table.

51½in (131cm) diam

$550-700   LSK

A William IV rosewood breakfast table.

c1840   *29in (73.5cm) high*

$1,900-2,500   WAD

A Victorian oak tilt-top breakfast table, with crossbanded and ebonized strung top, on a triform stem with applied strapwork decoration and three spiral twist columns.

50in (127cm) diam

$3,200-3,800   WW

A Victorian flame mahogany tilt-top breakfast table, raised on triangular plinth base.

53¼in (135cm) diam

$1,400-1,900   WM

A Regency rosewood and parcel-gilt center table, with gray marble top.
28¼in (72cm) diam
$1,200-1,400 **BLEA**

A Regency rosewood center table, on a faux rosewood turned column, some minor repairs.
49¼in (125cm) diam
$1,900-2,500 **SWO**

A Regency ormolu-mounted rosewood center table, some restoration.
c1815 45½in (115.5cm) diam
$5,000-6,300 **DRA**

CLOSER LOOK—GRAND TOUR TABLE

This table top is inlaid with radiating concentric panels of 112 various marbles and hardstones, including porphyry, malachite, lapis lazuli, harlequin breccia, and alabastro fiorito.

Its centered circular micromosaic panel depicts the Doves of Pliny, with a ribboned campana border.

Specimen marble tops were the ultimate souvenir from the Grand Tour; many were purchased in Italy by young elite travelers and brought back to England.

The Regency base is in the manner of Gillows, with lobed and nulled decoration, a triform base, leaf carved scroll feet, and brass casters.

An early 19thC Italian Roman specimen marble-topped Grand Tour table.
34¾in (88.5cm) diam
$44,000-50,000 **WW**

A George IV specimen marble and mahogany center table, inset with a marble fan motif and black slate border.
30in (76cm) diam
$11,000-14,000 **L&T**

An early 19thC Charles X maplewood table-de-milieu, with Egyptian red porphyry top within a ormolu surround, some damages and losses.
42¼in (107cm) wide
$44,000-50,000 **TEN**

An early Victorian rosewood, satinwood and mahogany parquetry center table, the tilt-top centered by a fan medallion and radiating "tumbling block" veneer panels.
31½in (80cm) diam
$3,200-3,800 **L&T**

A mid-19thC Anglo-Indian rosewood snap-top center table, some losses to fretwork.
53¼in (135cm) wide
$1,050-1,200 **SHAP**

A mid-19thC Anglo-Indian padouk center table, with a foliate carved frieze.
30¾in (78cm) wide
$2,500-3,200 **L&T**

A Sèvres center table, with gilt-metal mounts, the top inset with porcelain panels, the center panel of Louis XVI.

42in (106.5cm) diam

$9,000-10,000 JN

A Napoleon III mahogany, kingwood, burr walnut, and marquetry table-de-milieu, in the Louis XVI style, the drawer applied with mounts in the Weisweiler style.

49½in (126cm) wide

$11,000-12,000 BE

A Victorian carved walnut and marble-mounted center table, the pierced frieze decorated with fruiting branches and armorial shields, one titled "CHABLAIS," some chips and losses.

c1860

59in (150cm) wide

$9,500-10,500 DN

A Victorian walnut snap-top center table.

59in (150cm) long

$2,500-3,200 BELL

A 19thC French boullework marquetry center table, with cut brass inlay on a tortoiseshell ground, with strapwork, leaves, scrolls and winged cherubs.

Boullework is a type of marquetry or inlay developed by the French cabinetmaker André Charles Boulle (1642-1732). It involves veneering furniture with a marquetry of silver, brass, pewter, or tortoiseshell.

58¼in (148cm) wide

$2,300-2,800 WW

A 19thC center table, in 17thC Italian style, the inset marble top within a carved rosette frieze, filled crack to top.

70in (178cm) wide

$3,200-3,800 BELL

A Victorian Gothic revival oak center table, designed by Collier & Plucknett, Warwick, the base designed by John Henry Chamberlain, tabletop possibly a later replacement.

60in (152.5cm) diam

$2,000-2,500 GORL

A 19thC Irish mahogany and marble center table, with four lion monopodia supports, united by platform undertier.

23½in (60cm) diam

$1,150-1,250 BELL

An early 20thC Dresden porcelain center table, the top with panels of figures in 18thC dress, in a gilt-metal and wood frame, the feet joined by a shaped X-stretcher surmounted by a putto.

30¼in (77cm) diam

$11,000-14,000 L&T

An 18thC mahogany drum table, with leather inset top, above four real and four dummy drawers, one handle missing, replaced crossbanding.

35¾in (91cm) diam

$8,000-9,500   **SWO**

A late George III mahogany library table, with later inset writing surface, above four real and four dummy drawers, drawer linings restored, some scratches.

37½in (95cm) wide

$1,800-2,300   **TEN**

A Regency mahogany crossbanded and inlaid revolving drum library table, bordered with ebony lines, with alternate frieze and dummy drawers.

36in (91.5cm) diam

$2,800-3,300   **BE**

An early 19thC Regency mahogany drum table, in the manner of Gillows, with a frieze fitted with four real and four dummy drawers, raised on lotus carved paw feet with brass casters.

50½in (128.5cm) diam

$11,000-14,000   **L&T**

A Regency mahogany library table, in the manner of Gillows.

53in (100cm) long

$1,600-2,300   **CHEF**

A Regency rosewood library table, in the manner of Gillows, with painted inset Grand Tour marble tablet.

53½in (136cm) wide

$13,000-18,000   **CHEF**

A Regency rosewood library table.

101½in (258cm) wide

$4,400-5,700   **L&T**

An early Victorian oak and ebony library table, in the Baroque style.

65¾in (167cm) wide

$6,500-7,500   **L&T**

An early Victorian mahogany drum library table, with six drawers, on a chamfered tapered support and ogee bracket feet.

48¾in (124cm) diam

$800-950   **HAN**

FURNITURE

A George II giltwood console table, with a marble top over a carved frieze, on twisted dolphin supports.

This distinctive table is reminiscent of William Kent's oeuvre. It also relates closely to the designs of Batty Langley and William Jones, published in 1740. The table may originally have had a rectangular plinth base.

49in (124.5cm) wide

$44,000-50,000 DUK

A cream-painted and parcel-gilt console table, in the manner of Robert Adam, the satinwood top painted with a mythological medallion among foliage.

Robert Adam (1728-92) was an influential Neoclassical architect and designer active in the 18thC. He worked alongside his brother James Adam (1730-94).

41¾in (106cm) wide

$3,800-4,400 DUK

A William IV "plum pudding" mahogany marble-topped console table.

70½in (179cm) wide

$2,500-3,200 DUK

A Louis Phillipe mahogany gilt-metal and marble-mounted console table, with serpentine marble top.

c1840 *38½in (98cm) wide*

$800-950 DN

A Victorian mahogany console table, with acanthus leaf carved cabriole front supports with claw feet, with a mirrored back.

63¾in (162cm) long

$2,300-2,800 BE

One of a pair of late 18thC Italian gray painted and parcel-gilt pier tables, with breche violette marble tops above fluted and leaf sprigged frieze, some wear.

46in (117cm) wide

$10,00-11,000 the pair DN

A late 18thC carved silvered wood marble-topped console table, the frieze as two cherubs and a bird of prey, amid flowers and foliage, the hipped cabriole supports with fruit and flowers.

Reputedly, this table originally stood in the "silver room" of Château de Fontainebleau, the favored residence and hunting lodge of the kings of France from the Middle Ages to Napoleon III. The "silver room" may refer to the Boudoir de la Reine, which was Marie Antoinette's bedroom and was lavishly decorated with silvered panels and furniture by the Rousseau brothers in 1786.

39¼in (100cm) wide

$32,000-38,000 LSK

A 19thC carved giltwood console table, of 18thC design, lacking marble top, some replacements and repairs.

63½in (161cm) wide

$2,500-3,200 BELL

A 17thC to 18thC Flemish oak draw-leaf serving table.

70¾in (180cm) wide

$2,500-3,200   **SWO**

An Irish George III mahogany side or serving table, the top with a "plum pudding" centered reserve outlined with boxwood stringing and oblique crossbanding, some repairs to joints.

c1760   *60¼in (153cm) wide*

$9,500-10,500   **DN**

An 18thC and later Continental oak serving table.

56¼in (143cm) wide

$1,500-1,900   **SWO**

A late 18thC George III mahogany and ebony serpentine serving table.

67¼in (171cm) wide

$2,500-3,200   **L&T**

A mahogany and inlaid serving table, of serpentine outline.

c1790   *72½in (184cm) wide*

$3,200-3,800   **DN**

A Regency mahogany serving table, in the manner of Gillows, the top carved with leaves, with three blind frieze drawers.

102¼in (260cm) wide

$7,000-8,000   **CHEF**

An Irish Regency mahogany serving table, by Gillingtons of Dublin, stamped "GILLINGTONS/34251."

61¾in (157cm) wide

$2,500-3,200   **L&T**

A Regency mahogany inverted breakfront serving table.

93in (236cm) long

$2,800-3,500   **L&T**

A George IV rosewood marble-topped decanting table, in the manner of Gillows, on ring-turned and lozenge carved tapered legs.

36in (91.5cm) wide

$6,500-7,500   **WW**

FURNITURE

An early 18thC walnut and cocus wood side table, on bobbin and disk-turned legs.

29¾in (75.5cm) wide

$3,200-3,800   **WW**

A Charles II carved giltwood side table, the top inset with later yellow marble.

This side table was formerly the base of a cabinet on stand.

33¾in (86cm) wide

$4,400-5,700   **WW**

A Sheraton period mahogany, satinwood banded and polychrome decorated demilune side table, probably Irish.

52in (132cm) wide

$1,600-2,300   **LSK**

A Scottish Regency rosewood side table, attributed to William Trotter, Edinburgh.

William Trotter was born into a family of merchants in 1772. He became a member of The Merchant Company in 1797 and, by 1809, was sole proprietor of the firm Young & Trotter. In 1819, he was elected Master of The Merchant Company, and from 1825-27 he was Lord Provost of Edinburgh. Trotter continued to trade from 9 Princes Street until his death in 1833.

35½in (90cm) wide

$3,800-4,400   **L&T**

A Regency mahogany side table, in the manner of Gillows.

c1820   *35¾in (91cm) wide*

$1,150-1,250   **DN**

A French kingwood, ormolu, and marquetry side table.

30in (76cm) wide

$2,300-2,800   **JN**

An early 19thC Dutch walnut marquetry and bone inlaid side table.

29¼in (74cm) wide

$900-1,000   **L&T**

A 19thC Italian carved wood and silvered side table, in the Rococo style, with a faux-marble top, the pierced apron with scrolling acanthus leaves centered by a female mask.

51¼in (130cm) wide

$1,900-2,500   **BE**

A late Regency specimen wood tilt-top occasional table, possibly Isle of Man, Great Britain.

21¼in (54cm) diam

$1,050-1,200 L&T

A George IV burr yew and crossbanded tilt-top occasional table, in the manner of William Trotter, some replacements to veneer, split joint to center.

c1825 *29in (73.5cm) diam*

$1,900-2,500 DN

A Regency septarian nodule inset rosewood occasional table.

c1825 *21¾in (55cm) diam*

$1,300-1,800 WAD

A pair of Victorian black lacquer and parcel-gilt occasional tables, with mother-of-pearl inlay.

c1860 *17¼in (44cm) diam*

$675-750 DN

One of a pair of 19thC Continental Empire-style ash occasional tables, the tops with oak marquetry inlay.

31½in (80cm) diam

$5,000-6,300 the pair DN

A Scottish slate and ebonized wood occasional table, the top painted with a Highland hunt scene, probably after Landseer, on faux bamboo supports.

20in (51cm) diam

$1,900-2,500 WW

A late Victorian walnut and specimen marble-top table.

22¾in (58cm) wide

$3,200-3,800 CHEF

An Edwardian two-tier oval satinwood occasional table, in the manner of Waring and Gillows, with mirror inset panels.

26½in (67cm) wide

$400-450 FLD

An Edwardian nest of four occasional tables, each with whitewood stringing, on spider leg supports and sledge feet, damaged stretcher on smallest table.

max 15in (38cm) wide

$650-750 PW

FURNITURE

- The term "Pembroke table" originated with the Countess of Pembroke, who is said to have ordered the first example of its time.
- Pembroke tables were lightweight, easily movable drop-leaf tables, with one or two drawers, which could be used as a bedside table, or for dining, writing, and serving tea. They were usually on casters for ease of use.
- Sofa tables evolved from the Pembroke table during the later 18thC. They were narrower and longer than Pembroke tables, and were primarily designed to stand behind sofas. Candlesticks or table lamps might be placed upon them.

A late 18thC George III painted satinwood, rosewood, and mahogany harlequin Pembroke table, the top with a spring-released superstructure with drawers and pigeonholes.

42¼in (107cm) wide

$7,000-7,500   **L&T**

A George III rosewood and marquetry inlaid Pembroke table, with tulipwood crossbanding, centered with a satinwood fan patera, on faux fluted square tapered legs and spade feet.

36½in (92.5cm) wide

$2,500-3,200   **WW**

A George III satinwood Pembroke table, with kingwood banding, later painted with Venus and two cherubs, on brass caps and leather roller casters, stamped with workman's initials "IC."

The initials "IC" might relate to Isaac Greenwood, a cabinetmaker for Gillows. In August 1780, he was noted as making "satten wood" Pembroke tables.

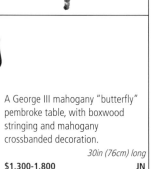

open 37¼in (94.5cm) wide

$1,300-1,800   **WW**

A George III mahogany Pembroke table, with satinwood and tulipwood crossbanding, over a single end drawer and opposing faux drawer.

31in (78.5cm) long

$700-800   **MART**

Gillows of Lancaster was established c1730 by Robert Gillow.

- The firm rapidly established a reputation for supplying high-quality furniture to rich families in Great Britain.
- It is best known for its restrained mahogany furniture, made with superb technical craftsmanship. The mahogany was often imported from the West Indies and Jamaica.
- In 1897, Gillows merged with Waring of Liverpool to become Waring and Gillow. In 1980, Waring and Gillow joined with the cabinetmaking firm Maple & Co. to become Maple, Waring and Gillow, subsequently part of Allied Maples Group Ltd.
- Some Gillows furniture is stamped, but because a large proportion is not, pieces are often attributed to Gillows based on their style and design.

A George III mahogany "butterfly" pembroke table, with boxwood stringing and mahogany crossbanded decoration.

30in (76cm) long

$1,300-1,800   **JN**

A Regency mahogany Pembroke table, by Gillows of Lancaster, the frieze drawers stamped "GILLOWS LANCASTER."

44½in (113cm) wide

$1,300-1,900   **L&T**

A Regency japanned Pembroke table, the top decorated with three figures flying a kite, replacement piece to hinge, casters broken.

$700-800   **SWO**

A 19thC satinwood Pembroke table, painted with stylized floral and foliate motifs, some ring marks, losses, and scratches.

35in (89cm) wide

$1,150-1,250   **ECGW**

A Regency mahogany and satinwood crossbanded sofa table, some damages.

48in (122cm) wide

$700-800   **CHOR**

A Regency mahogany and coromandel sofa table, with ebony line inlay.

38½in (98cm) wide

$2,500-3,200   **L&T**

A late Regency rosewood and brass marquetry sofa table, crossbanded and inlaid with flowers and leaves.

57¼in (145.5cm) wide

$1,900-2,500   **WW**

A George IV rosewood and satinwood crossbanded sofa table, some repairs, split across top.

closed 40½in (103cm) wide

$1,500-1,900   **DN**

A mahogany sofa "dressing" table, with lifting section enclosing a fitted interior, some later replacements.
c1825   *57in (145cm) wide*

$500-650   **DN**

A Regency mahogany satinwood crossbanded and strung sofa table.
c1825   *35½in (90cm) wide*

$800-950   **HAN**

An early 19thC rosewood and inlaid sofa table, bordered with sycamore, ebonized, and brass lines.

extended 48½in (123cm) wide

$900-1,000   **BE**

An 18thC George III mahogany writing table, with gilt tooled leather insert, two frieze drawers to one side, dummy drawers to the others.

50in (127cm) wide

$3,800-4,400   **L&T**

A George III harewood and marquetry lady's writing table, in the manner of John Cobb, with satinwood panels.

27½in (70cm) wide

$1,400-1,900   **WW**

A late George III mahogany writing table, with a leather effect writing surface.
c1810 53½in (136cm) square
$2,000-2,500 MOR

A Regency mahogany specimen marble-topped writing table.
31½in (80cm) wide
$5,000-6,300 CHEF

A George IV mahogany writing table, attributed to Gillows, the top inset with gilt tooled leather.
42¼in (107cm) wide
$1,900-2,500 WW

A Charles X mahogany writing table, with replaced tooled leather inset writing surface, on columnar-turned legs, flat "H"-shaped stretchers, with concealed casters.
c1830 38in (96.5cm) wide
$5,000-5,700 DN

An early to mid-19thC bird's-eye maple writing table, by Gillows, signed "John Mason Jnr," leather top replaced, some slight wear.
42¼in (107cm) wide
$2,300-2,800 TEN

An English walnut writing table, the top inset with gilt tooled leather, the single drawer and front applied with ormolu rose and scroll mounts, the knees with foliate pendants and sides with bearded masks.
c1860 51½in (131cm) wide
$4,400-5,700 MOR

A Victorian satinwood writing table, with a pierced brass gallery with roundel ornament, with a tooled leather inset writing surface.
40¼in (102cm) wide
$1,900-2,500 BE

A late 19thC French tulipwood and ormolu-mounted writing table, in the Louis XV style, possibly by François Linke, with vernis Martin-style decoration, one foot mount detached, wear to one leg.
52¼in (133cm) high
$28,000-35,000 DN

A Louis XV-style ebony and red boullework bureau plat, the scrolled angled legs with applied ormolu mounts, with masks to each side, scrolling sabots and brass casters.
c1900 69in (175.5cm) wide
$13,000-18,000 SWO

An early 18thC Queen Anne burr walnut fold-over card table, opening to a gros- and petit-point panel of a courtly scene, with candle stands and guinea wells.

$14,000-18,000

36¼in (92cm) wide

L&T

A mahogany and mahogany veneer inlaid card table, probably Langley Boardman (1774-1833), Portsmouth, New Hampshire, inlaid with stringing, bellflowers, and panels.

c1807

$10,00-11,000

35¼in (89.5cm) wide

SK

A pair of George III "D" shaped mahogany and inlaid card tables, with satinwood and rosewood crossbanding and boxwood stringing, repolished finish, bowing to top of both, minor restoration, baize replaced.

c1800

$9,500-10,500

36¼in (92cm) wide

DN

A pair of George III French Hepplewhite mahogany fold-over card tables, with urn-carved friezes, on anthemion carved and cabriole legs, some scuffing and sun bleaching, one crack.

$44,000-50,000

36in (91.5cm) wide

GORL

An early to mid-Victorian rosewood and Tunbridgeware fold-over games table, attributed to Edmund Nye.

Edmund Nye worked in Tunbridge Wells, UK, from 1809 until his death in 1863. He was renowned for the high quality of his work, earning Royal patronage from 1836 and exhibiting at the Great Exhibition of 1851.

$4,400-5,000

35¾in (91cm) wide

L&T

A pair of Victorian walnut and marquetry inlaid hinged-top card tables, with labels for "W&A Chapman Ltd. 20-26 North Street Taunton," and "Trevor Page Nos. G20719/G20720."

$2,500-3,800

35in (89cm) wide

LSK

A late Victorian amaranth, kingwood, parquetry, and marquetry fold-over games table.

$4,400-5,700

34in (86.5cm) wide

L&T

A French ormolu-mounted mahogany concertina action card table, by Henry Dasson, repolish starting to split.

1881

$2,500-3,200

33¾in (85.5cm) wide

BELL

An Edwardian mahogany and satinwood crossbanded hinged-top games table, with a roulette wheel flanked by four games counter sections, with baize table opposite.

$2,500-3,200

37in (94cm) wide

GWA

A late 17thC William and Mary oak lowboy.

33in (84cm) wide

$1,050-1,200   **L&T**

A George I walnut lowboy, with veneered and crossbanded top.

26¾in (68cm) wide

$7,500-9,000   **L&T**

An early 18thC featherbanded walnut lowboy, with quarter-veneered top and concave starburst center drawer, on later cabriole legs.

30in (76cm) wide

$11,000-13,000   **GORL**

A Philadelphia Queen Anne walnut dressing table, on cabriole legs with shell carved knees ending in trifid feet.

c1760   *32in (81.5cm) wide*

$27,000-33,000   **POOK**

An 18thC walnut lowboy, fitted three small drawers, later handles, some scratches.

30in (76cm) wide

$900-1,000   **CHEF**

A Chippendale walnut dressing table, Lancaster, Pennsylvania, the thumb-molded top overhanging a case with shell and spandrel carved drawer.

c1770   *38¼in (97cm) wide*

$55,000-60,000   **POOK**

A Regency mahogany and gilt-metal-mounted marble-topped dressing table, the frieze with revolving drawers, maker's stamp "WILKINSON LUDGATE HILL," minor discolouration.

c1820   *61in (155cm) high*

$1,400-1,800   **DN**

A late Regency mahogany dressing table.

44in (112cm) wide

$2,500-3,200   **L&T**

A George IV mahogany dressing table, attributed to Gillows, with reeded edged three-quarter gallery.

47¾in (121cm) wide

$4,400-5,000   **WW**

FURNITURE

A George III mahogany piecrust tea table.
c1765   *30½in (77.5cm) diam*
$950-1,050   **POOK**

A Chippendale walnut tea table, Pennsylvania, some wear to top.
c1770   *32¾in (83cm) wide*
$3,200-3,800   **POOK**

A Chippendale mahogany tea table, Lancaster or Reading, Pennsylvania.
c1775   *33in (84cm) wide*
$16,000-20,000   **POOK**

A 19thC rosewood wine table, by Gillows of Lancaster, stamped "GILLOWS," some old repairs.
19¾in (50cm) wide
$2,500-3,200   **PFR**

A pair of George III mahogany and marquetry fold-over tea tables, inlaid with checker stringing and kingwood banding.
42¼in (107cm) wide
$7,000-7,500   **WW**

An early Victorian mahogany teapoy, in the manner of Gillows, the interior fitted lidded compartments and mixing bowls, one glass bowl broken.
c1840   *29¼in (74cm) high*
$650-750   **DN**

A late Victorian walnut teapoy, the interior fitted with mixing bowls, labelled "ROBERT ROUGH," hinge top loose, lifting and losses to veneer.
28½in (72.5cm) high
$500-650   **DRA**

A late 19thC French Second Empire giltwood, patinated metal, and porcelain-mounted guéridon, the top depicting Napoleon, signed "Seller," enclosed in a border of 12 portrait plaques.
23½in (60cm) diam
$5,000-6,300   **L&T**

An Irish exhibition yew wood carved fold-over tea table, the frieze carved with a harp and shamrock sprays, on an ornate baluster stem, the quadruple pod adorned with shamrock, thistle, and rose, on scroll legs.

This table was an exhibition piece displayed at the Irish International Exhibition, a world fair held in Dublin in 1907. The decision to hold the exhibition was taken at the Irish Industrial Conference in April 1903 and was inspired by a small exhibition in Cork (The Cork International Exhibition) five years earlier, which was intended to improve the trade of Irish goods.
38in (97cm) long
$18,000-23,000   **MEA**

A Federal mahogany, birch and rosewood veneer work table, attributed to Judkins and Senter, Portsmouth, New Hampshire, left rear leg broken and repaired.

c1810-20   *30¾in (78cm) high*

$7,000-7,500   **SK**

A Regency lacquer chinoiserie work table.

24½in (62cm) wide

$500-650   **BELL**

A Louis Philippe burr walnut sewing table.

16½in (42cm) diam

$550-650   **BLEA**

A George III mahogany architect's table, with a baize-lined sliding panel and compartments, including a pivoted quadrant pen drawer, some wear, small crack to top.

c1760   *35¾in (91cm) wide*

$5,000-6,300   **DN**

A 17thC monk's oak tilt-top table, folding back to create a chair, later supports, seat split, later carving.

A monk's table is a dual piece of furniture, designed to save space. When the table is not in use, the top folds back to create a chair or settle. Tables of this type were made in Europe from the 16thC, although it is unclear whether they were actually used by monks.

37in (94cm) wide

$3,800-4,400   **CHOR**

A Regency mahogany horseshoe hunt table, attributed to Gillows, some wear, gouge to front right.

A hunt table is semicircular drinking table, often with grooves for coasters and a well for decanters or unopened bottles. It was used for drinks and refreshments before and after a fox hunt.

67¾in (172cm) wide

$25,000-38,000   **CHOR**

A 19thC Italian Istrian marble table, carved with a top panel of a griffin, the supports carved with winged lion monopedia and acanthus.

78¾in (200cm) wide

$32,000-38,000   **SWO**

A 19thC coromandel lacquer-topped low table, on a later stand, minor chips to stand, decorated refreshed.

59¾in (152cm) wide

$7,500-9,000   **DN**

FURNITURE

A late 17thC oak dresser base, section missing from top, replacement escutcheons and handles.
68in (172.5cm) wide
$750-900   **PW**

A late 17thC oak dresser, on block and turned spiral twist cup and cover supports.
63¼in (160.5cm) wide
$4,400-5,000   **WW**

A joined ash open dresser.
c1700   *82¾in (210cm) long*
$2,300-2,800   **TEN**

A George II oak dresser, with three mahogany banded frieze drawers and an arc d'arbelète apron.
80½in (204.5cm) wide
$2,500-3,200   **WW**

A George III oak dresser base.
c1780   *65¾in (167cm) wide*
$1,400-1,900   **DN**

A late 18thC oak dresser, some shrinkage and veneer losses.
91¾in (233cm) wide
$1,000-1,250   **CHEF**

A 17thC oak dresser.
75½in (192cm) high
$1,150-1,500   **PW**

An early 18thC oak dresser, the plate rack with flared ogee pediment over a pierced arcaded frieze.
76in (193cm) wide
$5,000-5,700   **MART**

A George II oak dresser, the base with a center fretwork arch and planked pot shelf, later support for shelf, replacement brass handles.

80in (203cm) wide

$2,500-3,200 PW

A mid-18thC oak potboard dresser.

72¼in (183.5cm) high

$1,000-1,250 WW

An 18thC oak dresser, loose cornice section on the right hand side, stains on the top surface.

89¾in (228cm) wide

$5,000-5,700 CHEF

An 18thC oak and fruitwood dresser, the plate rack with an arcaded frieze, on later bracket feet.

80in (203cm) high

$3,800-4,400 MART

An 18thC Welsh Swansea Valley potboard dresser, some minor spots, minor undulation.

Dressers flourished from the 17thC, especially in Wales. Those made in South Wales were typically low dressers, with an open rack below a potboard, while North Wales dressers were tall, closed, with boards behind the upper shelves. Some mid-Wales dressers combined the northern and southern forms. Welsh dressers were made to be great showpieces, handed down from generation to generation, and they were often embellished with decorative motifs.

82in (208cm) high

$1,500-2,000 PFR

An 18thC and later oak potboard dresser.

71¼in (181cm) wide

$1,900-2,500 FLD

An 18thC and later oak Welsh Conway Valley dresser.

58¾in (149cm) wide

$900-1,150 WHP

A Georgian elm dresser.

79¼in (201cm) high

$1,150-1,500   **LC**

A late 18thC George III oak potboard dresser base and associated plate rack canopy, some wear, drawers relined, split to frieze.

74in (188cm) high

$1,800-2,500   **DN**

A late 18thC George III oak open potboard dresser, some restoration.

77¼in (196cm) high

$1,800-2,500   **TEN**

A 18thC to 19thC George II-style oak Welsh dresser, possibly composed of earlier elements, backboard replaced.

83in (211cm) high

$1,000-1,500   **DRA**

A late 18thC to early 19thC oak Swansea Valley potboard dresser, some repairs, replacements, losses and cracks.

71¾in (182cm) high

$1,400-1,900   **PFR**

A George III enclosed dresser, some staining, rack possibly associated, base slightly bowed, some repairs.

c1800   *81¼in (206cm) high*

$900-1,150   **TEN**

A mid-19thC George II-style oak Welsh dresser, some repairs and replacements, braces to legs.

78in (198cm) wide

$1,000-1,250   **DRA**

A late 16thC Tuscan walnut side cupboard.

26¾in (68cm) wide

$2,300-2,800 **ROS**

A 17thC joined oak Westmorland Court cupboard, with lunette and guilloché carving, with initials "ID," some decay and splits, repairs to hinges, one later shelf, later locks, dated.

1696 *70¾in (180cm) high*

$1,500-2,000 **TEN**

A late 17thC to early 18thC South German walnut and marquetry cupboard, some wear, some wood lacking to back boards, fabric lining distressed.

87¾in (223cm) high

$5,000-6,300 **DN**

A George I black lacquer and gilt japanned hanging bowfront corner cupboard, attributed to John Belchier, some marks and scratches.

The design bears close relation to an example bearing John Belchier's trade label, and the quality of the decoration supports the attribution. John Belchier (fl.1717-53) owes his high reputation to a distinguished series of bureau cabinets decorated in green or scarlet japanning or veneered with fine cuts of burr walnut.

c1720 41¾in (106cm) high

$7,000-7,500 **DN**

A late 17thC to early 18thC paneled oak tridarn.

74¾in (190cm) high

$3,800-5,000 **SWO**

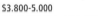

A pair of 18thC French crossbanded kingwood corner cupboards, with shaped Breche d'Alep marble tops, with gilt-metal mounts, marble cracked, bases restored.

32¾in (83cm) wide

$7,000-7,500 **BELL**

A late 18thC painted poplar hanging cupboard, Pennsylvania, front surface worn down.

40in (101.5cm) high

$3,800-4,400 **POOK**

A late 18thC poplar two-part Dutch cupboard, Pennsylvania, with matchstick cornice, panels, and spice drawers, some shrinkage, chips, and cracks, brasses replaced.

83¾in (212.5cm) high

$9,500-10,000 **POOK**

FURNITURE

A George III mahogany floor corner cupboard, swan-neck pediment with key pattern and rosette molding.

87in (221cm) high

$4,400-5,000   **PW**

A George III oak hanging cupboard, on bracket feet.

78¾in (200cm) high

$2,300-2,800   **CHEF**

A painted pine and poplar two-part Dutch cupboard, Lancaster County, Pennsylvania, with faux tiger and crotch-grain decoration, with smoke decorated doors.

c1830   *84¼in (214cm) high*

$48,000-53,000   **POOK**

An early 19thC oak housekeeper's cupboard.

74in (188cm) wide

$2,500-3,200   **BRI**

An early 19thC Canadian painted pine Dutch cupboard.

85½in (217cm) high

$3,800-5,000   **POOK**

An early to mid-19thC North European painted pine press cupboard.

81½in (207cm) wide

$950-1,050   **DN**

A 19thC Northern European painted pine cupboard, locked shut with no key, some wear.

70in (178cm) high

$650-750   **DN**

A 19thC oak and fruitwood marquetry court cupboard, with some late 16thC to early 17thC marquetry panels, some probably German.

63¾in (162cm) high

$2,500-3,800   **WW**

A George II mahogany clothes press, the paneled doors incorporating four false drawer fronts.
c1750   83in (211cm) high
$3,200-3,800   **DN**

An 18thC French oak armoire, with "love-bird" carved cresting, stripped and limed, some warping, some timber loss.
90½in (230cm) high
$2,300-2,800   **CHEF**

A New Jersey Chippendale highly figured walnut linen press.
c1780   83½in (212cm) high
$3,500-4,300   **POOK**

An 18thC Dutch walnut and marquetry kas or armoire, inlaid with fruitwoods, mother-of-pearl, and ivory.
95¼in (242cm) high
$9,000-10,000   **WW**

A George III mahogany linen press, with kingwood banding, the back of the cornice inscribed "S C No. 3."
82¾in (210cm) high
$3,800-5,000   **WW**

A Regency mahogany clothes press, in the manner of George Bullock.
c1815   73¼in (186cm) high
$1,900-2,500   **DN**

A George IV Channel Islands mahogany and satinwood strung clothes press, locks stamped "Threshers, London," warping to inset panels, some replacement stringing, one section of molding detached.
c1825   85¾in (218cm) high
$2,800-3,800   **DN**

A pair of 19thC japanned wardrobes, with chinoiserie decoration, the brass hinges stamped "HORNE PATENT."
72¼in (183.5cm) high
$6,500-7,500   **WW**

A mid-to-late 15thC French oak chest.

81in (206cm) wide

$5,500-7,000   **SWO**

A 16thC Italian walnut cassone, carved with grotesques, birds, and foliate scrolls centered by a profile portrait, with iron handles.

43¾in (111cm) wide

$3,800-4,400   **L&T**

A late 16thC to early 17thC Anglo-German oak and parquetry Nonsuch chest, inlaid with buildings and geometric borders, with iron handles.

Nonsuch chests are thought to have been made in Southwark, London, by émigré German and Dutch cabinetmakers. Their decoration of parquetry spired buildings derive from prints by Hans Vredeman de Vries (1527-1604). They became to be known as "Nonsuch" chests after Henry VIII's palace of Nonsuch, because their decoration was thought, wrongly, to represent that building.

48½in (123cm) wide

$2,500-3,800   **WW**

A walnut cassone, dated.

1644   *58¼in (148cm) wide*

$2,800-3,500   **SWO**

A 17thC Italian walnut cassone.

69¼in (176cm) long

$4,400-5,000   **ECGW**

A late 17thC oak coffer, with bird carved frieze.

50in (127cm) wide

$650-750   **BRI**

An 18thC and later Welsh oak coffer bach.

69in (175.5cm) wide

$750-900   **WW**

An early 18thC North Italian painted cassone.

57in (145cm) long

$1,800-2,300   **BE**

A 19thC black lacquer chest, with chinoiserie decoration, the interior with a later lift-out metal liner.

Provenance: Castletown, Co. Kildare, Ireland, bought c1910 for £9 ($11).

47¾in (121cm) wide

$5,000-6,300   **WW**

A painted dower chest, Pennsylvania, sponge-decoration with star panels, initialed "IHC," dated.

1773   *50in (127cm) wide*

$3,500-4,300   **POOK**

A late 18thC painted pine dower chest, Pennsylvania, with panels of hearts and flowers.

48½in (123cm) wide

$3,800-5,000   **POOK**

A late 18thC paint-decorated blanket chest, New England, some molding replaced.

48in (122cm) wide

$7,500-9,000   **SK**

A late 18thC Chippendale walnut blanket chest, Pennsylvania, with wrought iron hardware and brasses, newer blocking to feet.

46in (117cm) long

$3,500-4,300   **POOK**

A painted pine dower chest, Berks County, Pennsylvania, inscribed "Cadarina Schefern," feet and brasses replaced, dated.

1816   *47¾in (121.5cm) wide*

$5,000-6,300   **POOK**

CLOSER LOOK—PENNSYLVANIA DOWER CHEST

Dower—or hope—chests were given to young girls preparing for marriage and used to store household items, such as embroidery and linens.

Original blue painted grounds are rare and especially sought after, particularly when in excellent condition.

The chest is painted with unicorns, birds, horses, and tulips, with a center ivory star medallion on the top.

The painted soldiers holding tulips on the lower drawers are rare on a chest like this.

A painted pine dower chest, Berks County, Pennsylvania.

c1775   *49in (124.5cm) wide*

$290,000-350,000   **POOK**

A painted pine dower chest, Lebanon County, Pennsylvania, minor wear.

c1815   *41½in (105.5cm) wide*

$11,000-13,000   **POOK**

A painted pine dower chest, Centre County, Pennsylvania, with trees, love birds, and flowers, inscribed "Daniel Houser," repaired breaks to foot facings, hardware replaced, dated.

1817   *47½in (120.5cm) wide*

$20,000-25,000   **POOK**

A Charles II oak chest of drawers, the top drawer not staying closed, minor losses.

c1660   *30in (76cm) wide*

$1,800-2,300   **DN**

A late 18thC William and Mary oak chest of drawers.

40¼in (102cm) wide

$1,900-2,500   **L&T**

A William and Mary oyster veneered chest of drawers, with sycamore crossbanding.

37½in (95cm) wide

$7,500-9,000   **LC**

A late 17thC to early 18thC oyster veneered chest of drawers, with holly banding and stringing.

35in (89cm) wide

$3,800-5,000   **HT**

CLOSER LOOK—STUDDED LEATHER CHEST

This chest is entirely covered in leather, with the exception of the pine back. English leather-covered trunks and chests were produced by coffer-makers, primarily intended for traveling.

The domed top has a coronet and initials "C.R." This may relate to James Brydges, 8th Baron Chandos (1642-1714), or his son, also James Brydges and later 1st Duke of Chandos (1674-1744).

There is extensive studwork decoration on the front, top, and sides, with scrolls, flowers, and borders of hearts.

This piece may have been by William Johnson, who succeeded Richard Pigg Jr. as Royal coffer maker in 1707. The nailing patterns are similar to pieces made for the Royal household.

An early 18thC George I studded leather muniment or traveling chest, with one long and eight short drawers.

There are two notes attached to the interior, one reads: "This chest with drawers is covered in horse-hide: it is possible, but not probable that it was a travelling chest: Mr Percy Macquoid inclines to the opinion it was not: the frame work of the stand and the upper part of the legs indicate that it was not so used: English: about 1640 A:D: Purchased: 1917: cost £65 [$80]." The second references a similar chest, sold by Sotheby's December 6, 1918, now on a later low stand.

40¼in (102.5cm) wide

$15,000-19,000   **SWO**

A Queen Anne olivewood oyster veneered chest of drawers, inlaid with holly banding, on later bracket feet.

40in (101.5cm) wide

$3,200-3,800   **WW**

A Queen Anne walnut chest of drawers, inlaid with stringing, with quarter veneered and crossbanded top.

c1710   *38¼in (97cm) wide*

$5,500-6,500   **DN**

An early 18thC walnut bachelor's chest, the quarter-veneered hinged fold-over top with cross and feather banding.

30in (76cm) wide

$6,500-7,500   **WW**

ESSENTIAL REFERENCE—GILES GRENDY

Giles Grendy was an important furniture maker of the 18thC.

● He was apprenticed in 1709 and, by 1716, was established and taking on his own apprentices.

● He had a workshop in St John's Square, Clerkenwell, London, where he ran a successful, largely export business.

● He made a large selection of furniture, including tables, chairs, mirrors, and case furniture.

● Although it is known that he had a thriving workshop, firm attributions are rare, with little evidence of bills in country house records and few pieces still in existence bearing one of his two trade labels. However, a virtually identical chest to this, bearing the trade label of Giles Grendy, has been previously recorded.

A George II walnut and featherbanded chest of drawers, attributed to Giles Grendey, with molded quarter-veneered top, some old repairs, feet rollers lacking, handles and locks replaced.

c1740   *31½in (80cm) wide*

$32,000-38,000   **DN**

A George II mahogany harlequin bachelor's chest, the fold-over top with a baize surface and a rising secrétaire compartment, the front with three sham drawers, above two real drawers.

28in (71cm) wide

$2,500-3,200   **WW**

A George III mahogany serpentine chest of drawers.

c1760   *37½in (95cm) wide*

$7,000-8,000   **L&T**

A Pennsylvania Queen Anne walnut semitall chest of drawers, with herringbone inlays.

c1760   *38¾in (98.5cm) wide*

$3,800-4,400   **POOK**

A cherry chest of drawers, possibly Litchfield County, Connecticut, with fluted quarter columns and a scalloped skirt, replacement brasses, refinished

c1770   *39¼in (99.5cm) wide*

$6,500-7,500   **POOK**

A Queen Anne cherry chest of drawers, Pennsylvania, some repairs.

c1770   *34½in (87.5cm) wide*

$5,000-6,300   **POOK**

An 18thC Dutch floral marquetry inlaid walnut serpentine chest of drawers.

32¼in (82cm) wide

$1,900-2,500   **BELL**

A late 18thC Dutch floral marquetry inlaid chest of drawers, with later handles, some splits.

35¾in (91cm) wide

$1,900-2,500   **BELL**

FURNITURE

A late 18thC birch chest of drawers, by Joseph Short, Newburyport, Massachusetts, shrinkage crack to left side.

36in (91.5cm) wide

$4,400-5,000 SK

An 18thC George III mahogany serpentine chest of drawers, the drawers with banded inlay.

43¼in (110cm) wide

$3,200-3,800 L&T

An 18thC George III oak and walnut double chest of drawers.

59¾in (152cm) wide

$3,200-3,800 L&T

A George III mahogany gentleman's dressing chest, in the manner of Gillows, inlaid with satinwood banding.

43in (109cm) wide

$6,500-7,500 HAN

A George III figured mahogany bachelor's chest, with a brushing slide, previously refinished, replacement brass fittings, filled shrinkage split.

29¾in (75.5cm) wide

$2,500-3,200 MART

A George III mahogany and crossbanded chest of drawers, the top drawer opening to a sliding panel.

c1800 *36¼in (92cm) wide*

$1,600-2,300 DN

A George III satinwood serpentine chest of drawers, with rosewood banding to top, some damage to veneers, water splash marks.

39in (99cm) wide

$3,800-4,400 CHEF

A George III serpentine mahogany chest of drawers, the top drawer with baize-covered slide with further compartments.

36¼in (92cm) wide

$3,800-5,000 ECGW

A Federal cherry child's chest of drawers, Pennsylvania, chips to one knob and front foot.

c1815 *17¼in (44cm) wide*

$3,200-3,800 POOK

A Sheraton tiger maple chest of drawers, Pennsylvania, with mahogany inlaid stiles, stains to top.
c1820   *42in (106.5cm) wide*
$3,800-5,000   **POOK**

A late Regency Channel Islands mahogany and tulipwood checker-banded chest of drawers, some wear, some replacements to veneers.
c1820   *43¾in (111cm) wide*
$2,500-3,200   **DN**

A late Regency mahogany campaign washstand chest of drawers, the hinged top opening to a mirror and recesses, with tin wash basins.
32¾in (83cm) wide
$2,500-3,800   **L&T**

A painted pine child's chest of drawers, possibly by Lehn, Pennsylvania, minor wear.
c1830   *19in (48.5cm) wide*
$3,200-3,800   **POOK**

An early 19thC Anglo-Chinese teak campaign chest, in two halves, the top incised "H.A."
Campaign chests were chests of drawers designed to be easy to break up or fold for ease for traveling, such as when on military campaigns.
29½in (75cm) wide
$3,800-4,400   **WW**

An early 19thC putty-painted pine blanket chest, New England, the top opening to a well, loose panel, minor paint wear.
38½in (98cm) wide
$3,800-4,400   **SK**

An early 19thC satinwood and mahogany chest of drawers, with crossbanded top, some wear, lined with oak.
46¾in (119cm) wide
$2,300-2,800   **DN**

A poplar chest of drawers, by John Sala, Soap Hollow, Pennsylvania, painted red with stenciled highlights, the sides with black-painted panels with date and initials "LC," "Manufactured By John Sala," minor wear, one scallop repaired to backsplash.
1871   *38in (96.5cm) wide*
$32,000-38,000   **POOK**

A 19thC mahogany serpentine chest of drawers, with brushing slide.
45¾in (116cm) wide
$5,500-6,500   **DUK**

A Louis XV to Louis XVI transitional kingwood marquetry block-front marble-topped commode.

37¾in (96cm) wide

$3,500-4,300   **BE**

A Louis XV kingwood and parquetry bombé commode, with breche violette marble top, the corners and feet mounted with ormolu mounts.

c1730   *52¾in (134cm) wide*

$13,000-18,000   **L&T**

An early-18thC Maltese olivewood and parquetry serpentine commode, with brass swan-neck handles supported by Maltese lions, cracks to veneer.

46in (117cm) wide

$3,200-3,800   **CHOR**

A mid-18thC Austrian walnut parquetry petite commode, with gilt-metal mounts.

21¾in (55cm) wide

$650-750   **L&T**

A Louis XV kingwood, tulip, and ormolu-mounted bombé marble-topped commode, by Leonard Boudin.

c1750

$6,500-7,500   **JN**

A Louis XV kingwood and amaranth marble-topped marquetry commode, with gilt-metal mounts.

31½in (80cm) wide

$1,900-2,500   **L&T**

A Louis XV kingwood, inlaid, and gilt-metal-mounted serpentine bombé marble-topped commode.

51½in (130.5cm) wide

$4,400-5,000   **BE**

A Louis XV serpentine kingwood marble-topped commode.

52in (132cm) wide

$4,400-5,000   **SWO**

An 18thC Sicilian painted and lacquered serpentine commode.

55½in (141cm) wide

$4,400-5,000   **BELL**

An 18thC Italian Neoclassical marquetry inlaid walnut commode, in the manner of Giuseppe Maggiolini, minor warp and losses of veneer, shrinkage splits, woodworm damage.

Giuseppe Maggiolini (1738-1814) was an important cabinetmaker from Milan, Italy. His work is characterized by superb Neoclassical and arabesque marquetry in walnut, olivewood, tulipwood, and sometimes rosewood.

49¼in (125cm) wide

$5,000-5,700   BELL

CLOSER LOOK—NORTH ITALIAN COMMODE

This commode has a pair of short drawers at the top, with a pair of long drawers beneath.

It is decorated with marquetry reserves depicting Neoclassical motifs, such as flowering urns, cornucopia, and scrolling acanthus.

The detail is exquisite throughout.

The style resembles that of influential Milanese Neoclassical cabinetmaker Giuseppe Maggiolini.

One of a pair of North Italian walnut, tulipwood, and marquetry commodes.

c1790

48¾in (124cm) wide

$25,000-32,000 the pair   DN

An 18thC French marquetry marble-topped breakfront commode, ormolu mounts.

37in (94cm) wide

$5,000 5,700   JN

An 18thC French kingwood and ormolu marble-topped commode.

47in (119.5cm) wide

$4,400-5,000   JN

An 18thC Italian marquetry inlaid walnut commode, with mythological figural and foliate scrolling decoration.

46¼in (117.5cm) wide

$6,500-7,500   WAD

A Dutch rosewood and marquetry serpentine commode, some warping to top, losses to veneer, shrinkage gaps.

c1780

39¾in (101cm) wide

$3,200-3,800   DN

A late 18thC George III satinwood and tulipwood commode, with crossbanding and painted floral panels, on trompe-l'oeil square legs, some scratches and splits, losses to veneer.

52¾in (134cm) wide

$5,500-6,500   TEN

A French Directoire mahogany marble-topped commode.

50in (127cm) wide

$1,900-2,500   WW

A late 18thC to early 19thC Portuguese painted chestnut commode.

54¼in (138cm) wide

$5,000-6,300   WW

FURNITURE

A late George III crossbanded satinwood and mahogany bowfront commode.

44½in (113cm) wide

$2,800-3,500   **MOR**

A 19thC Continental painted serpentine commode, some woodworm, splits to joints.

56¼in (143cm) wide

$4,400-5,000   **DN**

A pair of 19thC Italian marquetry inlaid walnut commodes, after Giuseppe Maggiolini, later suede lining, minor warping to veneer.

48¾in (124cm) wide

$9,000-10,000   **BELL**

A 19thC French mahogany, parquetry, and ormolu marble-topped petit commode.

35in (89cm) wide

$1,900-2,500   **JN**

CLOSER LOOK—MALTESE COMMODE

This commode is inlaid with intricate seaweed marquetry panels.

There is a cartouche of a stag and hound at the top and panels of putti on the sides.

It was originally one of a pair owned by William Parnis, an eminent 19thC Maltese lawyer. It was inherited by his younger son and passed down by descent.

Despite some damage and wear, the aesthetic appeal of this piece ensures its value.

A Maltese marquetry commode, on ebonized bun feet, general wear, losses to veneer and inlay, splits to drawer bases.

62½in (159cm) wide

$44,000-50,000   **CHOR**

A 19thC Italian walnut and marquetry commode.

34in (86.5cm) wide

$1,900-2,500   **DUK**

A late 19thC Italian-style marble-topped commode, stamped "Gillows Lancaster."

50¾in (129cm) wide

$1,900-2,500   **LC**

A late 19thC Louis XVI-style marble-topped commode, after Jean-Henri Riesener.

46¾in (119cm) wide

$6,500-7,500   **WW**

A French ormolu-mounted marble-topped kingwood and vernis Martin decorated bombé commode, with a paper label printed "FOREST/ TAPISSERIE/EBENISTERIE/33, rue de Provence/PAR," light scratches.

Maison Forest was a renowned manufacturer and retailer in Paris in the late 19thC.

c1900   *35¾in (91cm) wide*

$6,500-7,500   **BELL**

A Jacobean geometric molded and joined oak chest on stand, with some later additions and restoration.

50¾in (129cm) high

$1,900-2,500   LSK

A 17thC Continental molded and paneled oak chest on stand, 22 drawers within.

54¼in (138cm) high

$5,000-6,300   SWO

CLOSER LOOK—PHILADELPHIA CHIPPENDALE HIGH CHEST

While chests on stands were supplanted by chests on chests in late 18thC England, chests on stands, or high chests, remained fashionable in North America, and were often influenced by Thomas Chippendale's designs.

This high chest has a broken-arch bonnet with applied floral carving.

The center drawer of the lower section is carved with Rococo shell and grasses.

In the United States today, high chests are among the most sought-after pieces of furniture by collectors.

A Philadelphia Chippendale walnut high chest, on cabriole legs with claw-and-ball feet.

c1770   *95in (241.5cm) high*

$23,000-28,000   POOK

A Queen Anne walnut crossbanded chest on stand.

60¼in (153cm) high

$1,500-2,000   L&T

A George I walnut chest on stand, inlaid with stringing, the back with an ivorine inventory label, inscribed "J.G.L.105."

55½in (141cm) high

$5,000-6,300   WW

A mid-18thC red-painted carved cherry high chest, by Elijah Booth, Woodbury, Connecticut, some replacements, some scratches, losses to thumb molding.

$11,000-14,000   SK

A Queen Anne tiger maple high chest, possibly New Jersey, minor repairs and replacements, lacking drops.

c1765   *73in (185.5cm) high*

$14,000-18,000   POOK

A Queen Anne Octorara tall chest, Chester County, Pennsylvania, with removable cabriole legs with lambrequin knees, some lip repairs.

Octorara chests typically stand on short detachable cabriole legs or have ogee feet with bracket cusps. This chest has a combination of both. The name derives from the Octoraro Creek in Pennsylvania.

c1780   *66in (167.5cm) high*

$11,000-12,000   POOK

A George I walnut chest on chest, with cross and feather-banded burr veneered drawers, the lowest drawer with a parquetry inlaid sunburst concave panel.

71½in (181.5cm) high

$11,000-14,000 WW

A George I walnut chest on chest, the lowest drawer with "sunburst" marquetry panel, one handle off.

70in (178cm) high

$6,500-7,500 CHEF

An early 18thC walnut and crossbanded chest on chest, with a molded dentil cornice.

67¾in (172cm) high

$3,800-5,000 BE

A mid-18thC elm chest on chest.

77¼in (196cm) high

$800-950 BELL

A mid-18thC George III mahogany chest on chest, with a blind fret carved frieze.

73½in (187cm) high

$2,800-3,500 L&T

A New England Chippendale maple chest on chest, with a bonnet top and fan-carved drawer.

c1770   *86½in (219.5cm) high*

$5,000-6,300 POOK

An 18thC walnut secrétaire chest on chest, with feather and crossbanding, sunburst inlay to bottom drawer.

42in (106.5cm) high

$1,300-1,600 BRI

A George III oak chest on chest, with pine-lined drawers, some wear and splits, replacement handles.
c1780   *69in (175cm) high*
$900-1,000   **DN**

A late 18thC George III mahogany chest on chest, minor faults to drawers.
70½in (179cm) high
$1,900-2,500   **TEN**

A George III mahogany chest on chest, with a Greek key frieze, the base with brushing slide.
c1790   *73¾in (187cm) high*
$2,300-2,800   **DN**

A George III mahogany chest on chest.
44in (112cm) high
$2,500-3,200   **BRI**

A George III mahogany chest on chest, with applied carved frieze and dentil cornice, on bracket feet.
48in (122cm) wide
$1,900-2,500   **FLD**

A George III mahogany bowfront chest on chest.
c1800   *61½in (156cm) high*
$750-900   **DN**

A 19thC George III mahogany chest on chest.
74½in (189cm) high
$900-1,000   **L&T**

A 19thC figured walnut chest on chest, with brass handles.
66¼in (168cm) high
$1,900-2,500   **ECGW**

A George II burr walnut secrétaire cabinet, the interior with 12 drawers, above a secrétaire drawer fitted with pigeonholes and further drawers.

76½in (194.5cm) high

$6,500-7,500   WW

A mid-18thC early George III mahogany secrétaire cabinet, brass handles on the sides.

79½in (202cm) high

$4,400-5,000   L&T

An 18thC and later secrétaire on chest, with feather and crossbanding, the fall enclosing pigeonholes and marquetry drawers, with a later leather writing surface.

49in (124.5cm) high

$3,800-5,000   WW

A late 18thC painted walnut two-part secrétaire, probably Lancaster County, Pennsylvania.

83½in (212cm) high

$10,000-11,000   POOK

A George III mahogany secrétaire cabinet, the interior with 16 satinwood and rosewood crossbanded drawers, the base with a secrétaire above 6 short drawers.

78¾in (200cm) high

$5,000-6,300   SWO

A Regency fiddleback mahogany and gilt-metal-mounted secrétaire cabinet, in the manner of George Bullock, the fall opening to a leather inset, small drawers and pigeonholes, some marks and wear, some shelves lacking.

A related cabinet design is published in Richard Brown, "The Rudiments of Drawing Cabinet and Upholstery Furniture" (1822), plate XVIII. Brown appears to have copied an unpublished design of George Bullock, who supplied a pair of bookcases of this form for New Longwood, the residence-in-exile of Napoleon.

c1815   *78¾in (200cm) high*

$6,500-7,500   DN

A 19thC Louis XVI-style mahogany, satinwood and parquetry secrétaire à abbatant, in the manner of Jean Henri Riesener, opening to an interior fitted for writing.

Jean-Henri Riesener (1734-1806) was one of the best-known cabinetmakers in France during the reign of Louis XVI.

55½in (141cm) high

$4,400-5,700   L&T

A Victorian pollard oak Wellington secrétaire chest, the second and third drawers fitted as a secrétaire.

51¼in (130cm) high

$4,400-5,000   L&T

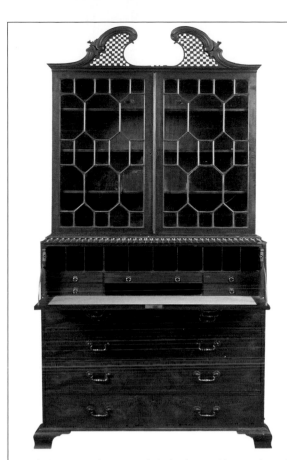

An early George III mahogany secrétaire bookcase, with unusual pagoda molding to base, some molding and beading losses.

90½in (230cm) high

$25,000-32,000 CHEF

A Boston, Massachusetts, Chippendale mahogany secrétaire desk and bookcase, with flame carved finials, rosettes, and center pediment, on an oxbow form base with fan-carved interior.

c1770 *95in (241.5cm) high*

$13,000-18,000 POOK

A late 18thC George III mahogany secrétaire bookcase, with a secrétaire drawer fitted with drawers and pigeonholes.

43¼in (110cm) wide

$2,300-2,800 L&T

A late 18thC George III mahogany and inlay secrétaire bookcase, with a secrétaire drawer fitted with pigeonholes and drawers.

92½in (235cm) high

$3,200-3,800 L&T

A George III mahogany secrétaire bookcase, the secrétaire drawer enclosing an arrangement of drawers and pigeonholes.

c1800 *86½in (220cm) high*

$900-1,000 DN

A 19thC George III mahogany secrétaire bookcase, with a secrétaire drawer opening to pigeonholes and drawers.

91¾in (233cm) high

$1,500-2,300 L&T

A Pennsylvania or Southern Federal walnut secrétaire bookcase, the broken-arch bonnet with star inlaid rosettes, some losses, repairs, and replacements.

c1810 *98½in (250cm) high*

$19,000-25,000 POOK

A Queen Anne walnut bureau bookcase, the interior with drawers and a center cupboard, the fall enclosing drawers and a well compartment, lacking original feet, door mirrors replaced by silk-backed glass.

81¼in (206cm) high

$5,000-6,300   **CHEF**

A George I walnut and burr walnut bureau bookcase, feather and crossbanded, with three adjustable shelves, a pair of candle slides, the stepped interior with pigeonholes and doors, with a sliding well cover and a later leather-lined writing surface.

88in (223.5cm) high

$16,000-20,000   **WW**

A George I walnut bureau bookcase, with mirror doors and a featherbanded fall, the interior with pigeonholes and drawers, later mirror doors, some repairs.

83½in (212cm) high

$2,800-3,500   **TEN**

A pair of early 18thC black lacquer bureau bookcases on stands, the base with fall front.

60in (152.5cm) high

$11,000-15,000   **JN**

An early 18thC slope-front walnut bureau cabinet, the arch-top door panels inlaid with boxwood and ebony string, the interior, with two concave cupboard doors, two secret compartments, and pigeonholed compartment and drawers.

79in (201cm) high

$7,500-9,000   **MEA**

An early 18thC Italian walnut and marquetry bureau bookcase, possibly Genova, the fall revealing a later baize writing surface and eight drawers, with a sliding well cover and two secret drawers.

Provenance: Count Redmond Toler Clayton-Browne Clayton (1863-1937) of the Villa La Punta, Cervara, Santa Margherita, Liguria, Italy.

80in (203cm) high

$3,200-3,800   **WW**

An 18thC Dutch feather-banded figured walnut bureau cabinet, the fall enclosing a stepped and welled interior, restored, hole cut in back section of top.

92½in (235cm) high

$2,500-3,200   **BELL**

A George I walnut and burr walnut bureau cabinet, cross and feather banded, the hinged fall opening to pigeonholes and drawers, on later bracket feet.

76¾in (195cm) high

$5,000-6,300 **WW**

A George II walnut bureau bookcase, shelves and drawers within, losses and wear, replacement feet, back shelves missing.

$2,500-3,200 **SWO**

An 18thC Portuguese painted bureau cabinet, with faux marble and floral decoration, the doors enclosing shelves, the hinged fall revealing pigeonholes and drawers.

80in (203.5cm) high

$9,500-10,500 **WW**

A 19thC Dutch walnut and marquetry bureau bookcase, with allover floral and bird marquetry, in three parts, with associated top.

87¾in (223cm) high

$5,500-7,000 **L&T**

A George II mahogany breakfront library bookcase, with a triangular arched pediment and diamond-shaped glazing bars, the base with paneled cupboards.

97in (246.5cm) high

$32,000-38,000 **DUK**

An 18thC George III mahogany breakfront bookcase, with a broken-arch pediment.

106¾in (271cm) high

$3,200-3,800 **L&T**

A George III and later mahogany secrétaire breakfront library bookcase, the doors with Prince of Wales plumes of feathers, with a sécretaire drawer fitted with pigeonholes and drawers, with satinwood faux-fluted secret pilaster compartments, with a leather-lined writing surface.

130in (330cm) wide

$5,000-6,300 **WW**

A George III mahogany breakfront bookcase.

85½in (217cm) wide

$4,400-5,000 **SWO**

A George III mahogany breakfront library bookcase, in the manner of Thomas Chippendale, some wear and replacements, previously cut in half.

This bookcase relates in design and scale to a pair of bookcases supplied by Thomas Chippendale to Sir Lawrence Dundas (1712-81) for his library at 19 Arlington Street, Piccadilly, London, and for his country seat in Yorkshire Aske Hall in 1764. The Arlington and Aske bookcases, invoiced at £80 and £73 respectively (about $10,300 and $9,500 in today's money), were the most expensive items of furniture on Chippendale's invoice to Sir Lawrence Dundas.

c1780   *149½in (380cm) wide*

$15,000-19,000   DN

A late 18thC George III mahogany breakfront library bookcase, after a design by Thomas Sheraton, with molded cornice and tassel molded frieze.

The designs for the astragal molding on the doors of the present bookcase are taken directly from Thomas Sheraton's "Cabinet-Maker and Upholsterer's Drawing Book," 1791.

124in (315cm) wide

$14,000-17,000   L&T

A George III mahogany breakfront bookcase, with four glazed doors with arched astragals and fabric linings within fluted columns, the base with two paneled doors flanked by two banks of drawers.

137¾in (350cm) wide

$8,000-9,500   SWO

A late George III mahogany library breakfront bookcase, some glaze cracking, scuffs, and splits, some repairs.

96¾in (246cm) wide

$5,000-6,300   TEN

An Irish Regency mahogany and ebony breakfront bookcase, with ebony line inlay, one door stamped "1083."

89in (226cm) high

$12,000-14,000   L&T

An early 19thC Regency rosewood library breakfront bookcase, in the manner of Gillows, some fading, some molding missing, fine splits.

87½in (222cm) wide

$5,000-6,300   TEN

A Regency rosewood dwarf breakfront bookcase.

72½in (184cm) wide

$4,400-5,000   L&T

A Victorian mahogany breakfront library bookcase, with reeded foliate scroll corbels flanking the cupboards.

86in (218.5cm) long

$1,900-2,500 **BE**

CLOSER LOOK—BREAKFRONT BOOKCASE

This bookcase is of exhibition quality in the Sheraton taste.

The dentil molded cornice sits above a frieze inlaid with fluting and flowerheads.

The astragal glazed doors are inlaid with husk trails.

The base has four panel doors, two painted with en grisaille roundels of Classical busts, two inlaid with ribbon-tied garlands and urns.

A late 19thC rosewood, satinwood, mahogany, marquetry ebonized and polychromed breakfront bookcase.

91¾in (233cm) high

$19,000-25,000 **L&T**

A Victorian oak breakfront bookcase, in the Gothic Revival taste, the stepped castellated cornice with pine cone finials, some replacement locks, general wear and fading.

c1880 *120in (305cm) wide*

$5,000-6,300 **DN**

A Regency mahogany "Gothick" bookcase on stand, the astragal and arch molded glazed doors opening to shelves, the stand with a fret molded apron.

81in (206cm) high

$1,500-2,000 **L&T**

An early 19thC red-painted "Harvard" stacking bookcase, probably Massachusetts, some losses and cracks.

102in (259cm) high

$9,000-10,000 **SK**

A Victorian burr oak bookcase.

98½in (250cm) high

$1,300-1,800 **MOR**

A late Victorian oak bookcase, in the manner of A.W.N. Pugin, the frieze decorated with courtly musicians in a landscape.

101¼in (257cm) high

$6,500-7,500 **BE**

An early 19thC satinwood bookcase cabinet, inlaid with ebonized stringing, with detachable Classical pediment.

82in (208.5cm) high

$3,200-3,800 **WW**

A Regency green painted pine bookcase cabinet.

45¾in (116cm) high

$1,300-1,800   **L&T**

A Regency mahogany double-sided bookcase, on a writhen turned pedestal and four molded cabriole legs, carved leaf caps, and brass casters.

27½in (70cm) wide

$1,600-2,000   **MOR**

One of a pair of Regency mahogany waterfall bookcases, on turned feet with brass caps and casters.

c1815   *33in (84cm) wide*

$9,000-10,000 the pair   **DN**

A Regency lacquered, painted, and parcel-gilt waterfall bookcase, the lower cupboard with a reverse-painted glass panel, some wear, chips to paint, gilt rubbed.

c1815   *54in (137cm) high*

$1,300-1,800   **DN**

A Regency simulated rosewood waterfall bookcase cabinet.

c1815   *47¼in (120cm) high*

$800-950   **DN**

An early Victorian marble-topped mahogany glazed bookcase cabinet.

c1840   *52¼in (133cm) wide*

$1,200-1,400   **HAN**

A Victorian marble-topped mahogany and ebonized beaded low bookcase, stamped "Holland & Sons."

64½in (164cm) wide

$5,000-6,300   **BE**

A 19thC Louis XIV-style ormolu-mounted, figured walnut, ebony and ebonized open bookcase, with winding mechanism for retractable silk cover, slight fading.

66½in (169cm) wide

$3,500-4,000   **BELL**

A late 16thC Flemish oak cabinet, carved with strapwork panels and fluted pilasters, the lower section with Romayne head panels, split to one panel.

66½in (169cm) high

$3,200-3,800 SWO

A late 18thC to early 19thC Dutch walnut and floral marquetry domed display cabinet, of canted outline.

85in (216cm) high

$2,300-2,800 BE

CLOSER LOOK—SATINWOOD CABINET

This cabinet of is exhibition quality and in excellent condition.

It may have been made by Holland and Sons, manufacturers to Queen Victoria.

There is inlaid, strung, and crossbanded decoration throughout, and ormolu mounts with intricate foliate details.

The single paneled door is beautifully inlaid in bone and various woods with ribbon-tied musical instruments, scrolling foliage, and geometric motifs.

A mid-18thC satinwood cabinet.

59½in (151cm) high

$32,000-38,000 SWO

A William IV rosewood collector's cabinet, with 30 small drawers behind arched panel doors, flanked by Classical columns.

52¾in (134cm) high

$1,900-2,800 CHEF

A 19thC walnut and floral marquetry bombé cabinet.

79in (200.5cm) high

$2,800-3,500 BRI

An early 19thC dovetail-constructed painted spice cabinet, New England, with 24 named drawers, a drawer replaced, bracket base replaced.

48½in (123cm) high

$7,000-8,000 SK

A 19thC rosewood, tulipwood and ormolu-mounted breakfront cabinet, in the Louis XV style, with inset porcelain panels depicting 18thC figures, some scuffs and veneer losses, one split.

62¼in (158cm) wide

$19,000-25,000 TEN

A late Victorian oak estate cabinet, the top with 15 short drawers with painted labels, the base with labeled cupboard doors opening to a shelved interior.

61in (155cm) high

$2,000-2,500 L&T

A late 19thC Italian ebonized and tortoiseshell display cabinet, with ivory marquetry panels of grotesques, applied with lapis lazuli and hardstone cabouchons.

67¼in (170.5cm) high

$3,200-3,800   WW

A late 19thC French kingwood, parquetry, marquetry, and gilt-metal-mounted breakfront vitrine, the sides with shaped projecting angles headed with sculptured Classical masks.

70¾in (180cm) high

$16,000-19,000   BE

A late 19thC Louis XV-style vernis Martin bombé display cabinet, veneered in kingwood, with five painted panels, with brass mounts.

Vernis Martin was developed by the Martin family, an 18thC French family of artists. The Martins included four brothers, Guillaume, Julien, Robert, and Étienne-Simon, and Robert's son Jean-Alexandre. Vernis Martin was a japanning or lacquer technique designed to imitate East Asian lacquer, used widely in 18thC and early 19thC France.

76in (193cm) high

$7,000-8,000   PW

ESSENTIAL REFERENCE—FRANÇOIS LINKE

François Linke (1855-1946) was an important Parisian cabinetmaker of the late 19thC and early 20thC and one of the key figures of the Louis XVI Revival movement.

- **He was born in Pankraz, in what is now the Czech Republic, and moved to Paris at the age of 20.**
- **By 1881, he had established a workshop in Paris in the Faubourg St. Antoine.**
- **He was soon known for the exceedingly high quality of his craftsmanship, and his impressive ability to work in wood carving, bronze, and marquetry.**
- **He won the gold medal at the Paris Exposition Universelle in 1900.**
- **He took inspiration from Louis XV and XVI furniture, and his work typically includes fine lavish mounts applied to comparatively plain structures of quarter-veneered kingwood or tulipwood.**
- **Pieces by or attributed to François Linke often fetch higher prices than work by earlier cabinetmakers.**

A late 19thC to early 20thC French kingwood vitrine cabinet, in the manner of François Linke.

77¼in (196cm) high

$11,000-14,000   L&T

An early 20thC French kingwood and vernis Martin marble-top display cabinet, the frieze with gilt-metal rams" masks, laurel garlands, and musical trophies.

56¼in (143cm) high

$6,500-7,500   L&T

An Edwardian satinwood standing corner cabinet, with Howard & Sons label.

74¾in (190cm) high

$1,900-2,500   MOR

A 17thC Flemish tortoiseshell and ebony cabinet on stand, possibly Antwerp, with painted scenes from the Life of Christ, the inlaid interior with mirror back, some restoration.

70¾in (180cm) high

$10,000-11,000   CHOR

A William and Mary black japanned cabinet on stand, decorated with chinoiserie pavilions and figures, the interior with 12 drawers, on a later silvered carved stand.

65½in (166.5cm) high

$4,400-5,700   DUK

A William and Mary collector's cabinet on stand, of oyster veneered laburnum wood, on a later inlaid stand.

45¾in (116cm) high

$4,400-5,000 SWO

A William III walnut and crossbanded cabinet on stand, the interior with 11 drawers and a cupboard with 3 further drawers, on later stand, some wear, splits to doors, later handles and hinges.

c1695 *59in (150cm) high*

$2,500-3,200 DN

CLOSER LOOK—ITALIAN CABINET ON STAND

This cabinet has a center pietra dura panel of a parrot among fruit and foliage. Pietra dura is an inlay technique, where semiprecious stones are used in mosaic form to create a picture.

This panel is flanked by metal capped columns and pietra dura simulated drawers within ripple molding.

The lower section has a further panel of parrots, above tapered fluted legs joined by an X-form stretcher.

The quality and condition of the piece are superb.

A 19thC Italian ebony pietra dura and gilt-metal cabinet on stand, opening to reveal a shelved interior.

c1840 *62¼in (158cm) high*

$100,000-130,000 DUK

A late 17thC to early 18thC Continental walnut, rosewood, tortoiseshell and ivory cabinet on stand, Dutch or Flemish, some possible restoration.

47¼in (120cm) wide

$3,200-3,800 DN

An 18thC Dutch rosewood and ebony Baroque cabinet on stand or luiermanskastje, with ripple moldings, floral carving, and three Corinthian capital pilasters.

79¼in (201.5cm) high

$6,500-7,500 WW

An 18thC mahogany Chippendale-style display cabinet, interior worn, some glass cracked.

70½in (179cm) high

$3,800-4,400 SWO

A late 18thC Continental walnut side cabinet, inlaid with marquetry baskets of flowers, interior with five short drawers and single shelf, base with long frieze drawer, on square-section tapered legs with wavy stretchers.

7in (195.5cm) high

$5,000-6,300 PW

A mid-19thC walnut and marquetry inlaid credenza, the top and frieze inlaid with satinwood marquetry, the door with marquetry depicting a musical theme.

A credenza is a long side cabinet with shelves at each end. They were popular in the mid-to-late 19thC.
$5,000-5,700   HAN

A Victorian walnut credenza, the center panel door with satinwood inlay, fronted by turned and fluted pilasters with gilt-metal Corinthian capitals.

78in (198cm) wide
$1,900-2,500   BRI

A Victorian gilt-metal-mounted, marquetry inlaid, figured walnut credenza.

59½in (151cm) wide
$2,000-2,500   BELL

A Victorian gilt-metal-mounted, figured walnut credenza, with ceramic-mounted center panel door.

72in (183cm) wide
$1,500-1,900   BELL

A Victorian figured walnut, marquetry inlaid, and gilt-metal-mounted breakfront credenza, the center paneled door with proud pilasters.

67in (170cm) wide
$2,000-2,500   LSK

A Regency mahogany and marble-topped fitted chiffonier, enclosing three flights of eight drawers.

49¼in (125cm) wide
$2,500-3,200   LSK

An early 19thC Regency rosewood chiffonier, crack to center mirror, small losses to the carved decoration.

48½in (123cm) high
$2,300-2,800   TEN

A William IV mahogany chiffonier.

77¼in (196cm) high
$950-1,050   SWO

A late 17thC to early 18thC Flemish ebony and kingwood cabinet, inlaid with ivory stringing, with geometric paneled decoration, on an associated later ebonized stand.

40½in (103cm) wide

$3,800-4,400 **WW**

CLOSER LOOK—SIDE CABINET

This sideboard has a shaped Carrara marble top, above a frieze decorated with stars and roundels.

It has a hinged lattice door with faux leather book spines, flanked by columns with Egyptian Revival sphinx heads and concave mirrored shelves.

It stands on high-quality carved lion's paw feet.

It is in the manner of James Newton (1773-1821), a prominent Regency cabinetmaker.

One of a pair of Regency rosewood and giltwood side cabinets.

51½in (131cm) wide

$60,000-65,000 the pair **WW**

A Regency rosewood and brass-mounted secrétaire side cabinet, in the manner of Gillows, with a later leather writing surface.

33½in (85cm) wide

$4,400-5,700 **WW**

A Regency rosewood marble-topped side cabinet, with reeded column angles, on turned toupie feet.

37in (94cm) wide

$6,500-7,500 **L&T**

A Regency rosewood and brass inlaid marble-topped side cabinet, the frieze inlaid with cut brass panels, on ebonized turned feet.

50in (127cm) wide

$1,400-1,900 **L&T**

A Regency rosewood and brass inlaid low breakfront side cabinet, with brass inlaid doors and grille inserts lined with silk.

100in (254cm) long

$1,500-2,000 **L&T**

A Regency rosewood and brass inlaid side cabinet, in the manner of John McLean, the frieze with a gilt-metal mount depicting a male mask, the shaped outset corners with female mask mounts, some wear, internal shelf lacking.

c1815 *47¼in (120cm) wide*

$10,000-13,000 **DN**

A William IV marble-topped side cabinet, in the manner of Marsh & Tatham, repaired split to marble, chipping to gilt scrolls, one rosette detached.

73½in (187cm) wide

$4,400-5,000 **BELL**

An early 19thC Anglo-Indian rosewood side cabinet, the doors carved and centered by leaf carved roundels, on carved paw feet.

60¾in (154cm) wide

$6,500-7,500   **L&T**

A pair of mid-19thC kingwood, crossbanded, and gilt-metal-mounted pier cabinets, with applied scagliola panels, the canted angles headed with palmette, foliate, and scroll ornament.

31in (79cm) wide

$9,500-10,500   **BE**

A pair of Napoleon III gilt-metal-mounted premier and contra-partie boullework side cabinets, the protective glass tops scratched and chipped, minor rubbing to ebonizing.

31½in (80cm) wide

$4,400-5,700   **BELL**

A pair of 19thC specimen wood floral marquetry inlaid bowfront corner cabinets.

27½in (70cm) wide

$2,300-2,800   **BELL**

A 19thC French rosewood, harewood and ormolu-mounted glazed standing side cabinet.

53in (134.5cm) wide

$1,400-1,800   **TRI**

A Victorian walnut and tulipwood banded display/side cabinet, with vitrine top above two drawers, some wear.

c1880   *31in (79cm) wide*

$1,300-1,900   **DN**

An early 20thC satinwood vitrine or bijouterie cabinet, on square tapered legs, lacking cross stretcher.

19in (48cm) wide

$1,200-1,400   **FLD**

An early 18thC Queen Anne burr walnut miniature apothecary's cabinet, with a fitted interior, some marks and shrinkage, minor restoration.

20½in (52cm) wide

$6,500-7,500   **DN**

A George II walnut side cabinet, the fold-over top above a frieze drawer, with a fitted interior.

31in (78.5cm) wide

$1,400-2,000   **CHOR**

An early 19thC late George III mahogany and satinwood crossbanded breakfront sideboard, with two inlaid shell medallions, outlined with plain and chequer stringing.

94½in (240cm) wide

$1,300-1,900   **L&T**

A Regency mahogany three-piece sideboard, with ebonized beaded frieze with applied cast bronze leaf and fruit wreaths, raised on a pair of carved, painted, bronze-effect "panther" monopodia, flanked by matching pedestals.

96in (244cm) wide

$8,000-9,500   **SWO**

A 19thC Sheraton-style mahogany and inlaid sideboard, with satinwood crossbanding and marquetry inlays.

66¼in (168cm) wide

$2,300-2,800   **LSK**

A Scottish Regency mahogany sideboard, by James Mein, Kelso, with ebonized decoration, maker's label inside drawer "JAMES MEIN/ CABINET MAKER/KELSO."

The Mein family were cabinetmakers in Kelso, Scotland, c1784-1851. After James Mein the Elder died in 1830, his nephew, also called James Mein, took over the business until it went bankrupt in 1851. Their patrons included the 5th and 6th Dukes of Roxburghe for Floors Castle and the Earl of Haddington for Mellerstain.

c1830   *70in (178cm) wide*

$5,000-6,300   **L&T**

A Mid-Atlantic Sheraton mahogany and tiger maple sideboard, some veneer/inlay repairs.

The Mid-Atlantic region of the United States sits roughly in the middle of the East Coast, located between New England and the South Atlantic states. The region includes Delaware, Maryland, New York, New Jersey, Pennsylvania, Washington, D.C., Virginia, and West Virginia.

c1830   *78in (198cm) wide*

$3,800-4,400   **POOK**

A Gothic Revival Marsh & Jones inlaid oak sideboard, attributed to Charles Bevan.

c1870   *96in (244cm) wide*

$11,000-13,000   **L&T**

A late Victorian oak sideboard, the raised back with a dentil and carved frieze over five leaded glass doors and turned Ionic columns, the base with two paneled doors, one enclosing a cellaret.

106¾in (271cm) wide

$3,200-3,800   **SWO**

A George III mahogany partner's desk, the locks signed "Joseph Brammah," replacement handles, splits to leather top.

c1770   *47¾in (121cm) wide*

$2,800-3,500   **DN**

A George III mahogany pedestal desk.

c1780   *67¾in (172cm) wide*

$950-1,050   **DN**

A George III mahogany pedestal desk.

49¼in (125cm) wide

$2,500-3,200   **HAN**

A George III mahogany four-pedestal partner's desk, inset with a later tooled suede writing surface, with outline moldings, on casters.

43¼in (110cm) wide

$5,000-5,700   **WW**

A Charles X birch and ebonized partner's desk, with later gilt-tooled leather inset, on molded block feet, one small section lacking.

c1830   *61in (155cm) wide*

$1,300-1,900   **DN**

A mid-19thC camphorwood and ebony campaign desk, with fitted inset brass sunken handles, lacking feet, top worn, some losses and splits.

47in (119.5cm) wide

$2,300-2,800   **SWO**

A Victorian brass-bound pollard oak partner's desk, with replacement green skiver, one side sun-bleached, fine cracks to veneers.

63in (160cm) wide

$5,500-6,500   **GORL**

A Victorian oak pedestal desk, by Edwards & Roberts, with later leather top, chips to handles, key missing.

Edwards & Roberts was founded in 1845 and became one of the leading London cabinetmakers of the 19thC, producing high-quality new furniture and also restoring, adapting, and making replicas of earlier English and French pieces. The firm's pieces were typically of Georgian design, often with satinwood marquetry.

54in (137cm) wide

$1,000-1,500   **BELL**

A Victorian mahogany partner's desk.

71¾in (182cm) wide

$2,300-2,800   **L&T**

An early Georgian walnut kneehole desk, veneered with feather banding, with brass drop handles.

31in (78.5cm) wide

$5,000-6,300 HT

A late 19thC lacquer chinoiserie kneehole writing desk, two handles lacking backing screws, center drawer damaged.

51¼in (130cm) wide

$2,300-2,800 BELL

A mid-Victorian mahogany Carlton House desk, polished and restored, drawer linings replaced.

Carlton House desks were developed during the Regency period, and named after the London home of the Prince of Wales (later George IV). They were typically made from mahogany and satinwood, and characterized by a superstructure of drawers and pigeonholes running along the back and sides of the desk.

47¾in (121cm) wide

$3,800-4,400 TEN

A George II mahogany kneehole desk.

35¾in (91.5cm) wide

$1,300-1,900 WW

An 18thC walnut kneehole pedestal desk.

29¼in (74cm) wide

$1,900-2,500 APAR

An 18thC figured walnut veneered kneehole desk, with a pull-out fitted secrétaire, all crossbanded.

33½in (85cm) wide

$1,600-2,300 TRI

A 18thC George III mahogany and inlay roll-top desk, the top enclosing drawers and pigeonholes, with a pull-out ratchet adjusted leather writing surface.

43in (109cm) wide

$3,200-3,800 L&T

A Sheraton revival desk, painted with cherubs, replacement leather top.

40¼in (102cm) wide

$1,900-2,500 CHOR

A late Victorian coromandel banded painted satinwood writing desk, with fitted interior over fold-out writing surface.

24¾in (63cm) wide

$1,900-2,500 BELL

A George III satinwood, mahogany, and ebony bonheur-du-jour.

28¼in (72cm) wide

$2,300-2,800   **L&T**

A Regency rosewood bonheur-du-jour, inlaid with boxwood and brass, with a lidded pen tray and inkwell compartment, the right side with a pull-out sewing frame.

23in (58.5cm) wide

$2,300-2,800   **WW**

A Victorian walnut bonheur-du-jour, on cabriole supports with ormolu mounts.

42in (106.5cm) high

$1,300-1,900   **BRI**

A 19thC French marquetry inlaid gilt-metal-mounted rosewood bonheur-du-jour, restored.

34¾in (88cm) wide

$2,800-3,500   **BELL**

A late Victorian ebonized amboyna, gilt-metal-mounted, and porcelain plaque adorned bonheur-du-jour, lacking feet.

53¼in (135cm) wide

$3,800-5,000   **APAR**

A late 19thC Louis XVI-style tulipwood, satinwood, and purple heart bonheur-du-jour, with Sèvres-style porcelain mounts.

48in (122cm) wide

$2,500-3,200   **TEN**

An Edwardian satinwood, tulipwood banded and polychrome painted bonheur-du-jour.

20in (51cm) wide

$2,500-3,200   **TEN**

A French kingwood brass-mounted bonheur-du-jour, inset with painted porcelain ovals, with a pull-out writing surface.

28in (71cm) wide

$3,200-3,800   **MEA**

An early 18thC oak bureau, on bracket feet.

25in (63.5cm) high

$1,500-2,000   **BRI**

CLOSER LOOK—JAPANNED BUREAU

Japanning was a technique developed in Great Britain in the 17thC to 19thC to imitate imported Asian lacquer.

This bureau is intricately decorated, with floral and figural motifs, and a scene of figures and temples on the slanting front panel.

Beneath are two long drawers, on a separate stand with a pierced frieze, raised on cabriole legs.

An early 18thC George I japanned bureau.

$11,000-12,000

The panel opens to an interior with pigeonholes and drawers, all with further decoration.

27¼in (69cm) wide

L&T

A Chippendale-style carved mahogany block-front slant-lid desk, scratches to left side, replacement feet, some repairs and damages.

39¾in (101cm) wide

$2,800-3,500   **SK**

∧ mid-18thC George III mahogany slant-front bureau, opening to drawers and pigeonholes.

43in (109cm) wide

$2,500-3,800   **L&T**

A late 18thC George III rosewood and padouk bureau.

49¼in (125cm) wide

$1,000-1,150   **DN**

A George III mahogany campaign bureau, in two sections, with pull-out writing surface, fitted with pigeonholes and drawers.

c1770   *34¼in (87cm) wide*

$3,800-5,000   **HAN**

A late 18thC Continental south German or Italian fruitwood and marquetry bureau, with ebonized carved decoration, inlaid with figures with ivory details.

48½in (123.5cm) wide

$1,600-2,300   **WW**

A George III walnut writing bureau, the crossbanded fall opening to a fitted interior with boxwood stringing, replacement brass batwing escutcheons.

35½in (90cm) wide

$650-750 **LSK**

An early 19thC Dutch mahogany and marquetry cylinder bureau, the fall with drawers and pigeonholes, some wear and repairs.

46in (117cm) wide

$1,900-2,500 **DN**

A Regency campaign cylinder-top bureau, with a writing slide and pigeonholes and drawers, brass handles on the sides.

42½in (108cm) high

$2,300-2,800 **L&T**

A 19thC Dutch walnut and marquetry inlaid writing bureau, with a fitted interior with a well.

44in (112cm) wide

$2,500-3,200 **LSK**

A late 19thC Italian cylinder bureau, by Luigi Pasquale (1822-94), with inlaid decoration, with Luigi Pasquale paper label, inscribed "Ricordo sagliano 1880 Pietro Micca."

Pietro Micca became a hero in Turin when he sacrificed his own life for the good of the city in 1706 by blowing up a tunnel with French soldiers about to attack.

1880

$3,800-5,000

34¼in (87cm) wide

APAR

A 19thC Dutch mahogany and marquetry inlaid cylinder bureau, some shrinkage, small veneer losses.

47¼in (120cm) wide

$1,500-2,000 **TEN**

A late 19thC Louis XV-style kingwood bureau-de-dame, the roll top with a vernis Martin panel.

33in (84cm) wide

$800-950 **L&T**

A late 19thC to early 20thC Louis XVI-style mahogany, parquetry, and ormolu-mounted bureau-à-cylindre, Paris, after a model by Jean-Henri Riesener, possibly by François Linke, some interior drawers lacking, wear to writing surface.

42½in (108cm) wide

$9,00011,500 **DN**

ESSENTIAL REFERENCE—DAVENPORTS

The Davenport developed in the late 18thC. It is a type of desk or small writing cabinet.

- **Gillows made a desk of this type for a Captain Davenport in the 1790s, hence the name.**
- **The basic form consisted of a small chest of drawers, with a desk compartment on top, sometimes with pull-out slides to hold papers or finished letters.**
- **Davenports are typically symmetrical, with dummy drawers on one side to match the real ones. The finest examples often have secret drawers.**
- **For most of the 19thC, Davenports were used by women.**
- **Mahogany was the most popular wood for Davenports, but rosewood and burr walnut were also used.**

A George IV rosewood Davenport, by Gillows of Lancaster, opening to reveal four short drawers and a secret dummy drawer, stamped.

20¾in (53cm) wide

$1,000-1,150   **LSK**

An early Victorian mahogany Davenport, stamped "Miles & Edward, 134 Oxford Street London," numbered "40570," some fading and shrinkage.

c1840   *19in (48cm) wide*

$950-1,050   **TEN**

A William IV amboyna and rosewood Davenport, the interior with two drawers, two false drawers, and a secret stationary drawer, replacement locks.

c1835   *22in (56cm) wide*

$1,800-2,300   **DN**

A Victorian walnut piano-top Davenport, with brass grill.

24in (61cm) wide

$1,500-2,300   **JN**

A Victorian figured walnut Davenport, inlaid in satinwood with stringing, with a pop-up stationery compartment.

23in (58.5cm) wide

$750-900   **MOR**

A Victorian walnut Davenport, with jack-in-the-box stationery cabinet.

22in (56cm) wide

$800-950   **LC**

A 19thC figured walnut piano-top Davenport, with fitted interior.

12in (30.5cm) wide

$1,150-1,250   **JN**

A Victorian mahogany Davenport desk.

c1880   *19¾in (50cm) wide*

$550-700   **K&O**

FURNITURE

A Regency rosewood Canterbury.

There are two kinds of Canterbury. The first is an open-topped rack, with partitions for storing sheet music or music books. The second kind is designed to stand by a table at dinner and has partitions to hold cutlery and plates. It is thought that the Canterbury was named after the Archbishop of Canterbury, who commissioned the first example.

18in (46cm) wide

$800-950   L&T

A Regency mahogany Canterbury.

17in (43cm) wide

$900-1,000   CHEF

A Regency rosewood Canterbury.

17¾in (45cm) wide

$800-950   BE

A Regency mahogany Canterbury, the drawer with brass handles.

20¾in (53cm) wide

$950-1,050   DN

A Regency mahogany Canterbury, with ebonized stringing.

c1815   20in (51cm) wide

$550-700   DN

A Regency mahogany Canterbury.

c1820   20in (51cm) wide

$750-900   DN

A Regency mahogany Canterbury.

22in (56cm) wide

$1,300-1,900   L&T

A Victorian burr walnut Canterbury, with a brass gallery.

35¾in (91cm) high

$700-750   SWO

A Victorian rosewood Canterbury.

61in (155cm) wide

$450-500   PW

A mid-Victorian walnut Canterbury.

c1870   22in (56cm) wide

$900-1,000   DN

Judith Picks

This needlework mirror is an exquisite piece. Its designs are worked in colored silks and metal thread. There is a country house in the arch, beneath which are animals, insects, flowers, and trees. The center mirror is flanked with full-length depictions of Charles II and his wife Catherine of Braganz. At the bottom are a lion and unicorn, with further flowers and insects and a center fish pond.

A Charles II silk and walnut needlework mirror, with a center mirror in a molded frame.

26in (66cm) high

$5,000-6,300 **WW**

A Charles II silver mirror, embossed with foliate decoration and putti, the pediment with a female mask.
c1680 *27½in (70cm) high*
$9,000-10,000 **WW**

A Queen Anne and later giltwood pier mirror.
64¾in (164.5cm) high
$5,000-6,300 **WW**

CLOSER LOOK—GEORGE II WALL MIRROR

This mirror has a rocaille and column frame, with exquisitely detailed pierced and carved chinoiserie decoration.

The top is carved with a Chinese man sitting under a leaf canopy hung with bells and flanked with exotic birds.

The edges are carved with leaf branches, supporting brackets for porcelain vases or figures, with rockwork and trellis decoration.

Chinoiserie decoration was popular with some of the most celebrated mid-18thC mirror designers, including Matthias Lock, Thomas Johnson, and John Linnell.

A George II giltwood and carton-pierre wall mirror.
c1755-60 *74½in (189cm) high*
$130,000-180,000 **WW**

One of pair of George III carved giltwood mirrors, in the manner of Matthias Lock, some wear.
c1770 *50½in (128cm) high*
$19,000-25,000 the pair **DN**

An 18thC George III giltwood mirror, with a pierced and carved Rococo frame with "C" scrolls, and shell and acanthus cresting.
56¼in (143cm) high
$2,500-3,200 **L&T**

One of a pair of George III giltwood wall mirrors, some wear and restoration.
c1790 *53¼in (135cm) high*
$20,000-25,000 the pair **DN**

A George III carved giltwood convex wall mirror, with eagle surmount.
c1800 *48½in (123cm) high*
$2,000-2,500 **DN**

A Regency convex mirror, with an eagle finial, the base with fish or serpents.

59¾in (152cm) high

$8,000-9,500 LC

An early to mid-19thC Continental carved giltwood, composition, and cream-painted wall mirror, possibly Scandinavian, some wear.

86¼in (219cm) high

$3,200-3,800 DN

A mid-19thC carved giltwood and gesso wall mirror, in the Chinese Chippendale taste, with an eagle finial.

86½in (220cm) high

$16,000-20,000 WHP

A Victorian Rococo-style carved giltwood mirror.

49¼in (125cm) high

$4,400-5,700 L&T

A 19thC Italian Baroque gilt framed wall mirror, with floral baskets and cornucopia among acanthus sprays, flanked by winged beasts.

Provenance: Formerly the property of Cecil Chubb, the one-time owner of Stonehenge, who gifted the monument to the nation.

145in (368cm) high

$9,000-10,000 BELL

A 19thC George II-style walnut and painted mirror.

58¾in (149cm) high

$650-900 L&T

A 19thC George III-style giltwood wall mirror, in the manner of John Linnell, some wear, losses to silvering

33¾in (86cm) high

$3,200-3,800 DN

A 19thC Italian Venetian blue glass and giltwood wall mirror.

41¾in (106cm) high

$3,800-4,400 WW

A late 19thC George III-style carved giltwood and composition wall mirror.

76in (193cm) high

$3,800-4,400 DN

A Regency giltwood and painted overmantel mirror, the frieze depicting "Love Disarmed."

58¾in (149cm) long

$700-750   **L&T**

A Regency gilt triple overmantel mirror, the frieze depicting Mars in a Chariot, flanked by lyres.

57½in (146cm) wide

$1,600-2,300   **L&T**

An early 19thC rosewood overmantel mirror.

50½in (128.5cm) wide

$950-1,050   **WW**

A Victorian gilt framed overmantel wall mirror, minor chips to gilding, some losses.

86½in (220cm) high

$1,300-1,800   **BELL**

A Victorian giltwood overmantel mirror, in Rococo style, by J. & W. Vokins, the back with a stencil mark inscribed "J & W VOKINS, Carvers & Gilders, To the Royal Family 14 & 16 GREAT PORTLAND, ST. W., LATE 5, JOHN ST., OXFORD ST. & 3 GREAT CASTLE STREET."

50in (127cm) high

$3,800-4,400   **WW**

A Victorian giltwood and gesso overmantel mirror, in Rococo style, with cherubs holding swags of flowers.

60¾in (154.5cm) wide

$750-900   **WW**

A Victorian giltwood and stucco overmantel mirror.

50in (127cm) wide

$500-650   **TRI**

A George III carved giltwood girandole mirror, in the manner of John Bradburn and William France, regilded, some losses, restored break to leaf.

Two almost identical mirrors hang in the gallery of Aske Hall, the Yorkshire estate purchased by Sir Lawrence Dundas, 1st Baronet (1712-81) in 1763 and the present seat of the 4th Marquess of Zetland. These were made for Sir Lawrence in c1764-65 by John Bradburn and William France.

c1765

59in (150cm) high

$44,000-50,000   **DN**

A pair of carved giltwood two-branch girandoles, surmounted by a ho ho bird, some repairs, some small losses, mirror plates tarnished.

47¼in (120cm) high

$9,500-10,500   **TEN**

FURNITURE

A Regency mahogany and ebonized cheval mirror.

"Cheval" is French for "horse." Mirrors of this type were called "cheval" because of their four supporting legs.

65½in (166.5cm) high

$3,800-4,400   WW

A Regency mahogany, brass strung, and gilt-metal-mounted cheval mirror, with lion mask handles, repolished, some discoloration to plate.

c1815   63¾in (162cm) high

$3,800-4,400   DN

A William IV mahogany cheval mirror.

78¾in (200cm) high

$3,800-4,400   L&T

A late 19thC Georgian-style mahogany and satinwood cheval mirror.

91¼in (232cm) high

$1,900-2,500   L&T

An Edwardian mahogany cheval mirror, with Classical blind fret and broken swan-neck pediment, some discolouration.

65in (164cm) high

$750-900   PW

A George IV mahogany and brass inlaid dressing mirror, probably Irish, minor chips and replacements to veneers and moldings, some discoloration.

c1825   20¾in (53cm) high

$1,900-2,500   DN

A late 19thC rosewood and ivory-mounted "skeleton" dressing mirror, with a later oval plate, with label for "HARRIS & SONS, Plymouth/14-9-93."

1893   20¾in (53cm) high

$1,300-1,900   DN

An Edwardian silver-mounted dressing table mirror, by Henry Matthews, Birmingham.

1903   11¼in (28.5cm) high

$2,300-2,800   DN

An 18thC mahogany brass-bound wine cooler.

25¼in (64cm) high

$500-650   **HAN**

A George III mahogany and brass-bound wine cooler, the lid with ax-head handle, with zinc-lined interior.

c1780   *28¼in (72cm) high*

$1,400-1,900   **DN**

An 18thC George III brass-banded mahogany wine cooler, with a metal-lined interior.

21¼in (54cm) high

$1,900-2,500   **L&T**

An 18thC George III mahogany wine cooler, with a lead-lined interior.

27¾in (70cm) high

$1,300-1,800   **L&T**

A George III mahogany wine cooler, with brass banding.

24½in (62cm) high

$800-950   **LC**

A George IV mahogany sarcophagus-form cellaret, with associated gilt-metal lion's paw feet, some damage to hinge.

28¾in (73cm) wide

$1,300-1,800   **BELL**

A George IV mahogany sarcophagus-form wine cooler, some chips, old paper label.

c1825   *35in (89cm) wide*

$1,800-2,300   **DN**

An early 19thC and later mahogany and brass-bound wine cooler, with Gillows-style cast brass lion's mask ring handles.

25¼in (64cm) wide

$900-1,000   **WW**

FURNITURE

A late Victorian ebonized and bone étagère, by Howard & Sons, with bone spindles, stamped "HOWARD & SONS BERNERS STREET."

31in (79cm) high

$4,400-5,000   L&T

An early George III mahogany kettle stand, with piecrust top.

20½in (52cm) high

$8,000-9,000   L&T

A late 18thC and later matched pair of elm and mahogany dumb waiters, possibly Scottish or Isle of Man.

39¼in (100cm) high

$1,600-2,000   DN

A George III mahogany kettle stand, on a turned and wrythen column and tripod base with claw-and-ball feet.

c1790   22in (56cm) high

$3,200-3,800   LC

A Regency mahogany dumb waiter.

41½in (105.5cm) high

$800-950   WW

ESSENTIAL REFERENCE—GERRIT JENSEN

Gerrit Jensen (fl.1680-1715) was of Dutch or Flemish origin. He was known to be working in St Martin's Lane, London, by 1680, and was known as a preeminent "Cabbinet maker and Glasse seller." He was the only cabinetmaker working in England during this period known to have used metal inlays and elaborate "seaweed" or "arabesque" marquetry. His furniture reflects the fashionable French court styles of Pierre Golle, André Charles Boulle, and Daniel Marot.

A pair of William and Mary kingwood, rosewood, and marquetry candle stands, in the manner of Gerrit Jensen.

c1690   35½in (90cm) high

$19,000-25,000   DN

A late 18thC black-painted cherry candle stand, attributed to Nathaniel Dominy V, East Hampton, Long Island, New York.

26in (66cm) high

$1,300-1,900   SK

A Regency mahogany folding dumb waiter, by Gillows, on tapered reeded and turned supports, on four reeded legs with brass caps and casters.

45¼in (115cm) high

$5,500-6,500   L&T

A Regency mahogany whatnot, with four tiers above a Canterbury base, splits and losses to center divider, handles misshapen, drawer lining with glued repairs.

c1815   *65¼in (166cm) high*

$900-1,000   **DN**

A 19thC Irish Killarney yew and marquetry four-tier whatnot.

39¾in (101cm) high

$1,600-2,000   **WW**

A late 18thC Dutch Neoclassical satinwood and coromandel vase stand, with a pierced brass gallery.

19in (48cm) high

$750-900   **L&T**

A George III mahogany dished tray, with center ivory plaque inscribed "Mary Dolby February the 14th 1766."

Presumably, given the date, this tray was given as a Valentine's present.

18½in (47cm) diam

$500-650   **WW**

A late 18thC George III mahogany butler's tray, on a later turned stand.

tray 24in (61cm) wide

$1,400-1,900   **L&T**

A Georgian mahogany butler's tray, on a later stand.

35in (89cm) wide

$950-1,050   **CHEF**

A George III Scottish tray.

22¾in (58cm) wide

$400-500   **CHOR**

A George III mahogany tray, previously mounted.

23in (58.5cm) wide

$550-700   **WW**

A mid-to-late Victorian lacquer and parcel-gilt papier-mâché tray, in the manner of Jennens and Bettridge.

32¾in (83cm) wide

$900-1,000   **DN**

A 17thC oak tester bed, the canopy with a gouged cornice and fluted apron, with later incised foliate lozenge panels.

78¾in (200cm) long

$6,500-7,500   **BE**

A Regency mahogany and brass campaign four-poster bed, by Morgan and Sanders, London, with brass trade plaque, "Patent/Morgan & Sanders Manufacturers/16 & 17 Catherine Street, Strand, London," with modern hangings.

Established in 1800, Thomas Morgan and Joseph Sanders' cabinetmaking firm was one of London's most successful of the early 19thC. Their designs were highly sought after by wealthy patrons, including several members of the Royal Family and Lord Nelson. Today, their pieces are particularly desirable.

95¼in (242cm) high

$9,000-10,000   **L&T**

An early Victorian mahogany tester bed frame, with later headboard, one carved leaf knocked upright, footboard missing, canopy with old splits and cracks.

c1840   *87¾in (223cm) long*

$1,050-1,200   **DN**

A late 19thC to early 20thC Louis XVI-style fruitwood marquetry and parquetry mahogany bedframe, the mounts by Jean Rabiant.

This piece is made after a design by Jean-Henri Riesener (1734-1806) for the commode for La Chambre de Louis XVI à Versailles.

72¾in (185cm) long

$10,000-13,000   **FRE**

An 18thC Dutch polychrome painted and parcel-gilt leather six-leaf screen, in the style of Hondecoeter, some damages.

130in (330cm) wide

$3,200-3,800   **MOR**

An 18thC and later four-leaf room screen, each panel inset with a tapestry panel, with later damask covers to rear of screen.

69in (175cm) high

$3,500-4,000   **DN**

A Victorian and later oak four-leaf room divider, inset with oil landscapes.

52¼in (133cm) high

$750-900   **WHP**

Judith Picks

This screen has an interesting origin. Its velvet panels depict the rose, thistle, and shamrock, the national flowers of England, Scotland, and Ireland, and they were removed from the dais at Delhi, from which Queen Victoria was proclaimed Empress of India in 1877 by the Viceroy of India, Lord Lytton (1831-99). The Dehli Durbar of 1877 was the culmination of transfer of control of much of India from the British East India Company to The Crown.

An ebonized three-leaf screen, with 19thC embroidered velvet panels, hinges discolored.

66¼in (168cm) high

$2,800-3,500   **DN**

A Regency tortoiseshell and ivory tea caddy, with single lidded interior, minor chips.

Tortoiseshell is a material produced from the shells of certain species of tortoise or sea turtle. It was used decoratively on luxury furniture, jewelry, boxes, clocks, and more. Tortoiseshell antiques are controlled by trade rules under the CITIES act.

4¾in (12cm) wide

$750-900   **BELL**

A Regency blonde tortoiseshell and white metal inlaid tea caddy, with an initialed cartouche.

7in (18cm) wide

$650-750   **LSK**

A Regency mother-of-pearl inlaid tortoiseshell tea caddy, with a twin lidded interior, on gilt-metal ball feet.

7½in (19cm) wide

$700-800   **BELL**

A 19thC green tortoiseshell two-division tea caddy, with ivory and pewter stringing, with a monogrammed plaque.

7¼in (18.5cm) wide

$3,200-3,800   **FLD**

Judith Picks

From the 17thC to early 19thC, tea was a luxury in Great Britain. High-quality tea caddies were produced to reflect this. This tea caddy, made of expensive tortoiseshell, is decorated with inlaid mother-of-pearl floral borders and acanthus scrolls. Tea came to Europe from China in the early 17thC and was at first expensive. Drinking tea became an important social pastime in fashionable circles, in part to give hosts the opportunity to display their wealth. Tea was kept in small locked caddies to protect theft or spillage by servants. The mistress of the house would have kept the key.

A Regency inlaid tortoiseshell sarcophagus-form tea caddy.

8in (20.5cm) wide

$1,900-2,500   **L&T**

CLOSER LOOK—TORTOISESHELL TEA CADDY

This tortoiseshell tea caddy is embellished with ivory banding and foliate mother-of-pearl marquetry.

The top has graduated cavetto moldings.

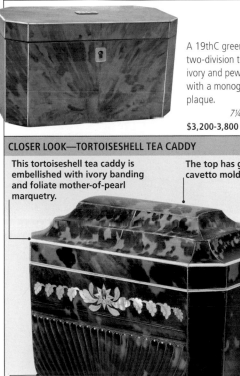

The front is gadrooned. Tortoiseshell can be difficult to manipulate, making this kind of detail hard to achieve.

The interior has twin lidded compartments, with fabric and metal lining.

A George IV or William IV tortoiseshell veneered tea caddy.

c1830   *7in (17.5cm) wide*

$1,500-2,000   **DN**

A late Regency tortoiseshell tea caddy, inlaid with pewter and ivory stringing, the lid with a gold metal plaque initialed "G.P.," the sides with lion masks, ring handles.

9¾in (25cm) wide

$750-900   **WW**

A 19thC tortoiseshell tea caddy, with ivory stringing, with twin lidded compartments, some damages.

6¼in (16cm) long

$650-750   **FLD**

An Edwardian blonde tortoiseshell tea caddy, by Martin Hall & Co., Sheffield, with stylized foliate and scrollwork silver mounts.

1903   *4¼in (11cm) wide*

$1,900-2,500   **BE**

A Regency penwork sarcophagus-form tea caddy, with chinoiserie decoration, later gilt-metal handles and claw-and-ball feet.

9in (23cm) wide

$1,200-1,400   BRI

A Regency penwork sarcophagus-form tea caddy, with chinoiserie decoration, the interior with two lidded compartments.

8in (20.5cm) wide

$1,200-1,400   WW

A Regency penwork sarcophagus-form tea caddy, the interior lid painted with a country house.

7¾in (19.5cm) wide

$800-950   SWO

CLOSER LOOK—MAUCHLINE TEA CADDY

This tea caddy is in excellent condition and comes from the collection of the late John Wright, who was a member of The Mauchline Collectors Club.

Mauchline ware was produced in Mauchline and its surrounding towns in South West Scotland over the 19thC and early 20thC.

The lid, all four sides, and the three interior lidded caddies are decorated in detailed penwork with images of Scottish country houses: Keithock, Stracathro, Burn, Langley Park, Edzell, Findhaven Castle, Dunellar Castle, and the Abbey of Aberbrathwick.

Larger pieces of Mauchline ware tend to fetch good prices, especially if, as here, the subject matter is rare.

A Victorian Mauchline ware sycamore and penwork tea caddy, by C. Stiven, Laurencekirk.

12in (30.5cm) wide

$8,000-9,500   CAN

A Regency penwork sarcophagus-form tea caddy, decorated with exotic figures with a camel and elephant.

9¾in (25cm) wide

$750-900   WW

A George III mahogany and quillwork tea caddy, with lidded interior.

5in (13cm) wide

$550-700   BE

A George III curled paper tea caddy, each panel with stylized flowers.

4¾in (12cm) wide

$1,300-1,800   FLD

A pear-shaped fruitwood tea caddy.

7in (18cm) high

$1,150-1,400   K&O

A melon-shaped fruitwood tea caddy.

6in (15cm) high

$2,000-2,500   K&O

A Georgian painted wood inn two-division tea caddy, with two dormer roof windows, inn sign missing.

10¼in (26cm) high

$1,500-2,300   **JN**

A 19thC painted house tea caddy, with twin lidded compartments with ivory handles, decorated with trellis glazed windows, and a verandah, the back with a stable door.

7¾in (19.5cm) wide

$5,000-6,300   **WW**

A novelty 19thC painted wood Gothic castle tea chest, with lancet windows, painted with shields, with a clock tower compartment for a pocket watch, the interior with two mahogany lidded lift-out canisters and a sugar bowl.

9¾in (24.5cm) high

$1,900-2,500   **WW**

A Georgian painted wood tea caddy, the roof lifting to reveal two tea canisters.

7½in (19cm) long

$1,300-1,900   **JN**

A Georgian painted wood two-division tea caddy, with door, five windows, and creepers growing up the side.

8½in (21.5cm) long

$1,300-1,900   **JN**

A 19thC painted cottage tea caddy, with trellis glazed windows, the foiled interior lacking lid.

6¾in (17cm) high

$1,800-2,300   **WW**

A George III mahogany tea caddy, inlaid with a ribbon and swag, the top with a shell.

5¾in (14.5cm) wide

$500-650   **SWO**

A George III mahogany inlaid tea caddy.

6in (15cm) wide

$650-750   **SWO**

A George III tea caddy, attributed to Henry Clay, with ground Nashiji mother-of-pearl and lacquer finish.

Nashiji is a form of Japanese lacquerwork (see page 132). Henry Clay (d.1812) was an 18thC artist and inventor, known for his Classical-style tea caddies. He was a key figure in Birmingham's jappaning industry and later became the "Japanner in Ordinary to His Majesty and His Royal Highness the Prince of Wales."

A 18thC two-division tea caddy, inlaid with mother-of-pearl ovals depicting "FIDES" (faith), "SPES" (hope), and "CHARITAS" (charity).

8in (20.5cm) high

$5,500-6,500

JN

4¾in (12cm) wide

$1,900-2,500

BELL

A George III yew wood inlaid tea caddy, with boxwood and checker strung.

7¾in (19.5cm) wide

$500-650

SWO

A late 18thC to early 19thC burr elm tea caddy, opening to a single covered compartment and glass bowl, inlaid with the coat of arms for the Coke family.

6¾in (17cm) wide

$750-900

L&T

A Regency rosewood tea caddy, of lyre form, with brass inlaid "strings," hidden drawer to one side.

8¼in (21cm) high

$650-750

LC

An early 19thC cube parquetry tea caddy, inlaid with rosewood, birch, and mahogany, with twin lidded interior.

9¾in (24.5cm) wide

$750-900

WW

A Victorian gilt-brass-mounted walnut tea caddy, the lidded compartments with brass plaques inscribed "BLACK" and "GREEN."

8¾in (22.5cm) wide

$700-800

L&T

A 19thC Irish tea caddy, with figures and deer in landscape, with hunter and dog surmount, with two lidded compartments and mixing bowl.

14½in (37cm) wide

$750-900

BRI

A 19thC Irish Killarney yew and fruitwood marquetry tea chest, the interior with two lift-out lidded canisters and a sugar bowl.

13½in (34.5cm) wide

$450-500

WW

A painted and découpage-decorated dresser box, by Joseph Lehn (1798-1892), Lancaster, Pennsylvania, minor wear.

13¼in (33.5cm) wide

$950-1,050   **POOK**

A mid-19thC painted pine dresser box, by Jacob or Jonas Weber, Lancaster County, Pennsylvania.

4¼in (11cm) wide

$38,000-50,000   **POOK**

A mid-19thC painted pine dresser box, by Jacob or Jonas Weber, Lancaster County, Pennsylvania, inscribed on underside "Made in 1850," some wear.

7½in (19cm) wide

$50,000-63,000   **POOK**

A 19thC rosewood brass-bound gentleman's vanity box, the interior with razors, silver-plated bottles, twin glass ink wells, and a sprung mirror, with dated note.

1846   11in (28cm) long

$450-500   **FLD**

A Victorian rosewood brass-bound traveling toiletry box, fitted with 12 silver-gilt jars and boxes, by Thomas Diller, London, the lock stamped "J. Bramah of 124 Piccadilly," with leather outer case.

1847   14¼in (36cm) wide

$800-950   **LSK**

A Victorian walnut dressing case, fitted with silver-gilt-mounted cut-glass bottles, and boxes, the lids engraved "ED," with a mirror, blotter and lift-out tray with accessories, with marks for "W. & J. MILNE, MAKERS, 126 PRINCES ST./ EDINBURGH."

1860   13½in (34.5cm) wide

$1,900-2,500   **L&T**

A Victorian silver taveling dressing table set, by Thomas Johnson, London, retailed by H. Tooke, Liverpool, initialed, hobnail cut-glass bodies, in a brass-bound walnut case, the cover with a brass cartouche "F.E. Edwards 28 November 1866."

1865   13¼in (33.5cm) long 9⅞oz

$2,500-3,200   **WW**

A 19thC French rosewood brass-bound vanity box, with a mirror, 11 silver-topped bottles, and a lift-out tray of tools, in outer leather case.

11¾in (30cm) long

$1,050-1,200   **FLD**

A George III quillwork decorated sewing box, with later oval embroidered panel with initials "BR," fitted compartments in the interior.

11in (28cm) wide

$450-500   BE

A Napoleonic prisoner of war straw work box, the interior fitted with boxes and drawers.

15in (38cm) wide

$300-400   ECGW

A Regency blond tortoiseshell sewing box, the domed lid divided by pewter lines to an ivory boss.

7¾in (20cm) wide

$400-500   BLEA

A Regency penwork work box, with ivory handles and feet, handwritten label to underside.

11½in (29cm) wide

$1,300-1,900   L&T

A burr ash and steel-studded Palais Royal sewing box, the interior with fitted tray of mother-of-pearl tools, some wear to edges.

The Palais Royal was the area of Paris surrounding the Royal Palace, which in the 18thC and 19thC was known for producing and selling small and elaborate objets d'art, including sewing boxes and tools. Palais Royal pieces are typically of very high quality.

c1830   *7½in (19cm) wide*

$1,000-1,150   BLEA

A 19thC specimen wood inlaid sewing box, the metal inscribed "Presented to Mrs Lawrence by the Scholars attending the Sabbath School of Crossmichael as a token of their gratitude and regard July 1842."

12¼in (31cm) wide

$300-400   WHP

An ebony sewing box, inlaid in cut mother-of-pearl and abalone shell, the interior with letter compartment and tray of sewing tools.

c1860   *14in (35.5cm) wide*

$700-800   BLEA

A Victorian walnut sewing box, marquetry inlaid with a British three-masted ship, the interior fitted with eight Tunbridgeware lidded containers.

14¼in (36cm) wide

$1,150-1,250   BELL

A late 19thC Italian rosewood sewing box, by Luigi Pasquale (1822-94), with ivory, copper, pewter, and specimen wood inlay, enclosing lift out trays, lacking mirror.

9¾in (25cm) wide

$500-650   APAR

A late 17thC to early 18thC Chinese hardwood and engraved paktong mounted writing box, possibly Huanghuali, some losses, staining, and splits.

This box is of the style and form made for the Dutch East India Company.

18½in (47cm) long

$3,200-3,800   BELL

A late 18thC George III tortoiseshell and silver-mounted taveling writing nécessaire, with silver plaque engraved "EM," the interior with two silver-topped glass inkwells, four nibs, and a mechanical pencil, some cracks, feet slightly bent.

3¼in (8cm) wide

$2,500-3,200   CHEF

An early 19thC fiddleback mahogany and satinwood drum or keg shape stationery box, the lid with a leather note and pen holder.

10¾in (27.5cm) high

$750-900   WW

A mid-Victorian coromandel writing box, decorated with an Indian tiger hunt in gilt-metal, abalone shell, and mother-of-pearl, fitted with letter and pen and ink compartments.

16in (40.5cm) wide

$1,600-2,300   TRI

A Victorian Mauchline ware sycamore and penwork writing box, decorated with a castle within woodland, the interior with seven lidded compartments.

12in (30.5cm) wide

$5,000-5,700   CAN

A Victorian walnut and brass-mounted writing box, with a Jasperware plaque, with a fitted interior with stationery compartments, mother-of-pearl tools, and fold-out slope.

17¾in (45cm) wide

$2,300-2,800   LC

An Edwardian mahogany and satinwood writing box, the interior with a leather-lined fold-out writing surface, small drawers and stationery divisions.

14½in (37cm) wide

$300-400   MOR

A Regency rosewood letter box, possibly Irish, with brass plates inscribed "Answer'd, Unanswer'd" and Antrim beneath a coronet.

7½in (19cm) wide

$2,300-2,800   LC

A mid-Victorian red boullework letter box, with fitted interior, bearing a label "Falstaff & Hannaford, Regents Street."

7½in (19cm) wide

$750-800   TRI

A 16thC South German domed-top box, with 273 inlaid pieces, depicting dogs, falcons, rabbits, hares, birds, lions, tortoises, and snails.

The engraved animals are based on designs by Virgil Solis (1514-62).

18½in (47cm) wide

$19,000-25,000   SWO

A late 17thC to early 18thC kingwood strong box or coffre fort, with strapwork brass mounts, with secret drawers to lid.

15¼in (39cm) wide

$3,800-4,400   WW

A needlework raised stumpwork casket, with animals, flowers, and figures, possibly with Charles II and Catherine of Braganza, some sun bleaching, minor staining, some losses.

c1670   *12¼in (31cm) wide*

$15,000-19,000   TEN

A 17thC Indo-Portuguese bone inlaid table cabinet, decorated with micromosaic panels, with fitted drawers, heavy wear throughout, handles missing.

Despite the damage, the intricacy of this table cabinet assures its value.

10¾in (27cm) wide

$7,000-7,500   APAR

An 18thC Georgian shagreen decanter box, fitted with six cut-glass decanters and stoppers, a wine funnel and a wine glass.

10¼in (26cm) wide

$1,500-2,000   L&T

A late George III mahogany box, with rosewood crossbanding, set with Chinese pith paintings of birds.

10in (25.5cm) wide

$1,900-2,500   DUK

A pair of George III mahogany cutlery boxes, banded in tulip wood, and with fitted interiors, some splits, scratches, and blemishes.

$1,400-1,800   CHOR

A George III Neoclassical inlaid mahogany urn-shaped knife or cutlery stand, the later pop-up mechanism damaged.

24½in (62cm) high

$2,300-2,800   BELL

An early 19thC painted poplar dome lid box, by the "Compass Artist," Lancaster County, Pennsylvania, leather handles added and removed from sides, hinges replaced.

16¾in (42.5cm) wide

$28,000-34,000 **POOK**

A 19thC painted poplar dome lid box, by the "Compass Artist," Lancaster County, Pennsylvania, repaired blowout to one hinge.

7½in (19cm) wide

$38,000-44,000 **POOK**

These boxes are part of a group of more than 60 objects that have been attributed to the "Compass Artist." They are attributed to the same artist due to his use of distinctive compass work and freehand decoration.

A painted pine slide-lid box, made for Peter Nehs, by John Drissell (1762-1846), Bucks County, Pennsylvania, inscribed "Ich kam in ein Land da stund geschrieben an der Wand/Sei fromm und ver schwiegen was nicht dein ist das lass liegen."

The inscription translates as "I came to a land where it was written on the wall/Be pious and never hide anything that is not yours, let it lie."

10¾in (27.5cm) long

$19,000-25,000 **POOK**

A mid-19thC painted pine slide-lid box, by Jacob or Jonas Weber, Lancaster County, Pennsylvania, with floral decoration on a dark blue ground, lacking interior dividers.

/in (18cm) wide

$11,000-14,000 **POOK**

A Victorian Howell James & Co. coromandel table casket, pierced Gothic silver mounts, the hinged cover releasing five leather-bound household books.

8¾in (22cm) wide

$1,000-1,150 **HAN**

A Victorian Mauchline ware sycamore and penwork gaming box, decorated with stately homes, the interior with gaming counter compartments and card division packs.

11½in (29cm) wide

$8,000-9,000 **CAN**

A 19thC Italian marquetry box, with interlacing foliate scrolls.

14¼in (36cm) wide

$2,500-3,300 **CHOR**

A late 19thC shagreen jewelry box, with silver mounts, with inset miniature, the silver feet engraved "TW" and "TM" and the date "9.9.91."

1891 5¾in (14.5cm) wide

$2,500-3,200 **DN**

An Indian hardwood and bone inlaid casket.

9¾in (25cm) wide

$1,800-2,300 **SWO**

A 19thC American tôleware tray.

8¾in (22cm) wide

$5,000-6,300   **POOK**

A 19thC American black tôleware coffeepot, some wear.

10¼in (26cm) high

$450-500   **POOK**

A 19thC American black tôleware box, some wear.

9¼in (23.5cm) wide

$300-350   **POOK**

A 19thC tôleware chinoiserie tea canister, later converted into a table lamp.

19½in (49.5cm) high

$1,800-2,300   **WW**

A Victorian Tunbridgeware tea caddy, with a view of Battle Abbey Gatehouse, enclosing a glass mixing bowl and two lidded canisters.

Tunbridgeware is a form of decorative woodware, created by gluing strips of wood together to form a pattern. Various types of wood were used to create colors, including oak, sycamore, maple, and holly. Pieces became popular souvenirs for visitors to Tunbridge, England, in the 18thC and 19thC.

14½in (37cm) long

$1,900-2,500   **TEN**

CLOSER LOOK—AMERICAN TÔLEWARE TRAY

Tôleware refers to items made of tinplated sheet iron or steel, covered in black asphaltum, and then painted; the name comes from the French tôle peinte, meaning "painted sheet."

This tray is in very good condition, with the original decoration still vibrant and in tact.

It was almost certainly made in Pennsylvania.

It is painted red, which is an uncommon and therefore valuable color in American tôleware.

A 19thC American red tôleware bread tray.

10½in (26.5cm) wide

$11,000-14,000   **POOK**

A pair of late Victorian tôleware tea canisters, with Chinese figures and gilt and mother-of-pearl highlights.

29in (73.5cm) high

$3,800-4,400   **WW**

A 19thC Tunbridgeware tea caddy, depicting a church, some cracks and chips, one small repair.

9¾in (25cm) wide

$950-1,050   **ECGW**

A 19thC Tunbridgeware box, the cover with a country house, label verso "W. Childs of Brighton," some scratches, losses, and warping.

9½in (24cm) wide

$750-900   **ECGW**

An 18thC miniature oak chest on chest.

28in (71cm) high

$2,500-3,200 SWO

An early 19thC Continental miniature walnut and line-inlaid bowfront chest of drawers, with bone handles and bun feet.

6¼in (16cm) wide

$1,500-2,000 REEM

An early 19thC miniature mahogany chest of drawers, the top with burr wood veneers.

12½in (32cm) wide

$650-750 L&T

A George III miniature mahogany and crossbanded chest of drawers.

c1820 *16½in (42cm) wide*

$500-650 HAN

A Classical miniature carved mahogany chest of drawers, Ossining, New York, inscribed in graphite on backboard, "To Mifs. Sarah Jane Brewster Presented to her By Her Grand-Father Wm. G. Burr, March 20, 1843 Made at the Sing Sing State Prison."

Sarah Jane Brewster (1839-91) was the daughter of Mary Burr Brewster (1815-59) and W.H. Brewster of Cazenovia, New York. Sarah lived with her grandparents for most of her life. Her grandfather William G. Burr (1790-1860), a cooper by trade, worked at the New York State Auburn Prison and later the Sing Sing Prison as keeper of the cooperage department. He remained in Ossining as an agent for prison-made goods for several years.

1843 *13½in (34.5cm) wide*

$14,000-18,000 FRE

A miniature mahogany chest of drawers, with inlaid stringing.

8¾in (22cm) high

$300-400 SWO

A 19thC miniature painted pine and poplar chest of drawers, Pennsylvania, one knob replaced.

12in (30.5cm) high

$1,150-1,400 POOK

A 19thC miniature painted pine drysink.

21¾in (55cm) wide

$750-900 POOK

A George III mahogany tilt-top apprentice table, on tripod legs.

10½in (26.5cm) high

$1,300-1,900 JN

A mid-19thC miniature fruitwood and parquetry table.

17in (43cm) wide

$400-500 L&T

A Classical miniature carved mahogany sofa, probably Philadelphia, Pennsylvania, retaining early, possibly original upholstery.

c1825 *17½in (44.5cm) long*

$2,500-3,200 FRE

A Federal miniature painted and stenciled Windsor settee.

c1830 *15in (38cm) long*

$1,000-1,150 FRE

A mid-19thC miniature Pennsylvania painted plank seat chair, minor wear.

12½in (32cm) high

$900-1,000 POOK

A 17thC boxwood shoe-form snuff box, with armorial and floral decoration, the sole with a two-masted ship, the sliding lid with a bull's head, dated.

1639   *4in (10cm) long*

$2,500-3,200   **TOV**

A late 18thC Scandinavian maple snuff box, relief carved with an urn and lion.

5in (13cm) long

$950-1,050   **WW**

A late 18thC to early 19thC mahogany frog snuff box, with a pull button opening the spring-loaded head.

3¼in (8cm) long

$2,800-3,500   **TOV**

An early 19thC Stobwasser-type lidded snuff box, painted with bearded figure with Masonic regalia.

3½in (9cm) diam

$500-650   **HAN**

A 19thC wooden fish snuff box, probably Scandinavian.

4¼in (11cm) long

$350-400   **BLEA**

A 19thC treen snuff shoe, with tack, mother-of-pearl, and bone inlay.

5½in (14cm) long

$500-650   **WW**

CLOSER LOOK—NAPOLEONIC SNUFF BOX

This rare snuff box is carved in the form of warship, with gun ports to port and starboard, and cannons and cannon balls at the sides.

The top is carved with a figure of Napoleon, below Napoleon's crest with "N" in a laurel wreath with flags.

SNUFF BOX, CARVED BY ONE OF NAPOLEON'S STAFF, AT LONGWOOD, ST HELENA, 1819.

The figurehead depicts the Merovingian King Childeric I, whom Napoleon believed he was descended from.

It is mounted on a later stained wood plinth, with a gilt plaque inscribed "SNUFF BOX, CARVED BY ONE OF NAPOLEON'S STAFF, AT LONGWOOD, ST. HELENA, 1819." Longwood House was the residence of Napoleon from his exile in 1815 until his death in 1821.

A Napoleonic carved coquilla nut table snuff box.

1819   *6¼in (16cm) long*

$10,000-11,000   **WW**

An early 19thC French carved coquilla nut snuff box, the lid with a coach and horses.

3in (7.5cm) wide

$230-280   **WW**

A 19thC pressed treen snuff box, with Masonic Temple and emblems, tortoiseshell simulated interior.

3¼in (8.5cm) diam

$500-650   **HAN**

A 19thC French pressed burr snuff box, inscribed "Fideite-Amour-Amitie-Pont Les De La Vie," tortoiseshell liner, cracked.

3½in (9cm) diam

$550-600   **BLEA**

A mid-17thC lignum vitae wassail bowl, with a single reeded girdle molding.

The word "wassail" originates from the Anglo-Saxon phrase "waes hael," which means "be in good health." Wassail, a kind of hot mulled punch, was drank in celebration, typically on the Twelfth Night, January 5.

8in (20.5cm) high

$2,500-3,200　　WW

A Charles II lignum vitae wassail bowl, with a later silver rim above reeded bands.

14¼in (36cm) high

$5,000-6,300　　WW

CLOSER LOOK—WASSAIL BOWL

This wassail bowl is of a large and rare size.

The brass plaque bears a coat of arms, possibly that of the White family of Weymouth.

It is dated "1694." It is very unusual for wassail bowls to be dated, which adds to the value.

It is inscribed "Thomas White" and "Bibi Potum et non Defundo," roughly translating as "Drink and do not spill."

A William and Mary lignum vitae wassail bowl, on a ring-turned foot.

15¼in (38.5cm) high

$21,000-25,000　　WW

An 18thC Norwegian Karelian birch peg tankard, with lion thumbpiece and carved rampant lion to lid.

Karelian birch is a distinctive tree growing only in Karelia, a historic region covering parts of Finland, Sweden, and Russia.

9¾in (25cm) high

$850 1,050　　SWO

A Norwegian birch and pine peg tankard, bound in leather strips, with scrolling handle.

6¾in (17cm) high

$300-400　　LC

A 19thC German carved and turned rhinoceros horn goblet, the faceted bowl on a spreading foot and a conforming plinth.

7½in (19cm) high 29⅞oz

$14,000-16,000　　WW

A 19thC treen turned lignum vitae flask, with stopper.

8¾in (22.5cm) high

$300-350　　WW

A treen carved lignum vitae castellated turret spill vase.

6¼in (16cm) high

$200-250　　BE

A carved pine lollipop butter stamp, decorated with tulips, initialed "FC," some wear, dated.

1816   *8¾in (22cm) high*
$3,200-3,800   **POOK**

A 19thC Scottish treen sycamore butter stamp, carved with thistles, a flowerhead and hearts, the handle inscribed "HAYFARM" and "WE FEAR NAE FOE."

                                        9¾in (24.5cm) long
$500-650   **WW**

A 19thC turned and carved eagle butter stamp, some surface loss to center.

4½in (11.5cm) diam
$190-250   **POOK**

An early 19thC carved coquilla nut nutmeg grater, lacking grater.

2¼in (6cm) high
$150-200   **WW**

An 18thC fruitwood knitting stick, carved with Saint George slaying the dragon, with a bone-mounted aperture.

Knitting sticks were commonly found in the households of the British working classes from the 17thC to the 19thC. They were used to mend or make clothes, and were usually carved by hand.

5½in (14cm) long
$2,500-3,200   BLEA

A 19thC treen sailor's nutmeg grater, of whale form, the base with a steel grater.

2¼in (5.5cm) long
$2,800-3,500   **WW**

A Regency treen spoon, possibly Welsh, the handle punch decorated with a heart, inscribed "MADE for MJ," dated.

1816   *7½in (19cm) long*
$1,300-1,800   **WW**

A 19thC hardwood juice press, the brass hinge stamped "Will and Finck S.F. Cal," with bone terminals.

9¾in (25cm) long
$450-500   **BLEA**

A late 18thC boxwood knitting sheath, initialed "R.M.F.B. 1785 19 Sepr A.P."

1785   *8in (20.5cm) long*
$1,500-2,000   **TOV**

A fruitwood knitting stick, of exaggerated scroll form, initialed "JB," mount with brass plate.

9in (23cm) long
$500-550   **BLEA**

A treen "goose wing" sheath, with female figure on one side and geometric and heart decoration on the other, dated.

1714   *8¾in (22.5cm) long*
$300-400   BE

An 18thC carved mahogany pipe tamper, modeled as a sitting dog.

3¼in (8cm) high
$500-550   TOY

A late 18thC to early 19thC handheld fruitwood braid loom, probably Welsh.

6½in (16.5cm) long
$550-600   BLEA

ESSENTIAL REFERENCE—SHAKESPEARE MEDALLION

This medallion is supposedly carved from the mulberry tree that William Shakespeare planted in his garden at New Place in Stratford-on-Avon, England, and was possibly worn by 18thC actor David Garrick when performing in Shakespeare's plays. The owner of New Place in the mid-18thC, Reverend Francis Gastrell, grew annoyed with the quantity of tourists, and in the 1750s felled the tree and later demolished New Place. Objects carved from the mulberry tree first started to appear 1760-70, after Gastrell sold the wood to local carvers and turners, such as Thomas Sharp and George Cooper, who were eager to make souvenirs.

An 18thC carved treen Shakespeare bust medallion, probably of mulberry wood, with a silver mount.

3¼in (8.5cm) diam
$3,200-3,800   WW

A 19thC treen candle box, in the form a northeastern fisherman's house, on brass ball feet, some splitting.

7in (18cm) wide
$3,500-4,000   TEN

A 19thC pair of walnut bellows, relief carved with a horse and rider, with fitted bronze spout.

36½in (93cm) long
$1,150-1,400   MOR

A 19thC artist's pine articulated lay doll, in need of restoration.

12½in (31.5cm) high
$1,200-1,400   LOCK

A pair of 19thC treen Brighton bun taveling candlesticks, with snuffer.

5in (12.5cm) diam
$400-500   WW

A 19thC treen child's rocking chair money box.

6¼in (16cm) high
$180-230   BE

A late 19thC to early 20thC treen pen tray, of two pigs feeding at a trough.

15½in (39.5cm) long
$650-750   WW

An early 18thC yew wood lever nutcracker, probably English, scratch-carved with vases of flowers and hearts.

4½in (11.5cm) long

$1,300-1,800   **TOV**

A George II boxwood treen nutcracker, initialed "SL" with geometric carved decoration, dated.

It is rare to find an authentic date on this kind of boxwood nutcracker.

1739   3in (7.5cm) high

$5,000-6,300   **MAB**

A 19thC carved treen nutcracker, in the form of Mr. Punch.

7¾in (19.5cm) long

$150-200   **FLD**

A 19thC carved oak nutcracker of a bearded figure, stamped "Cop of original now 1874 rotten with age pray preserve this."

7¾in (20cm) high

$1,900-2,500   **FLD**

A 19thC carved wooden novelty nutcracker, modeled as a monkey's head, some surface wear and rubbing.

7¾in (19.5cm) high

$100-130   **FELL**

A late 19thC Swiss Black Forest-style carved walnut figural nutcracker, in the form of a laughing gnome.

10¼in (26cm) high

$180-230   **WW**

A Swiss Black Forest-style carved wood nutcracker, modeled as a bear's head, the grip inscribed "Grindelwald," surface wear and rubbing.

7¾in (19.5cm) high

$190-250   **FELL**

A late 19thC to early 20thC Black Forest carved wood nutcracker, playing music when handle is lifted.

1½in (4cm) high

$750-900   **WW**

A 19thC Black Forest carved bear stick stand, with glass eyes.

43¼in (110cm) high

$3,200-3,800   L&T

A late 19thC Black Forest carved wood group of two bears, the adult about to spank the youngster with a golf club.

14¼in (36cm) high

$2,800-3,500   WW

A late 19thC Black Forest coat hook, the bear holding a hat, skis, and pole, with horn hooks.

15¾in (40cm) high

$3,200-3,800   WW

A pair of late 19thC Bavarian Black Forest seated bear wall brackets.

8¾in (22cm) high

$950-1,050   HANN

A late 19thC to early 20thC Black Forest carved wood bear stick stand, with removable metal drip tray, some damages.

25in (63.5cm) high

$1,000-1,150   FLD

A 19thC Bavarian Black Forest St. Bernard dog.

15¾in (40cm) long

$2,800-3,500   HANN

A rare Bavarian Black Forest tobacco jar and cover, modeled as a hound holding a pipe, his head and back pouch opening to reveal interiors for tobacco.

This is thought to be one of only two known examples of this figure.

19¼in (49cm) high

$14,000-18,000   HANN

A late 19thC Black Forest carved wood wall plaque, depicting dead game, two fish, a heron, and a game bird.

24¾in (63cm) high

$800-950   WW

A late 19thC Black Forest carved wood model of a mountain dog, possibly a St. Bernard, with glass eyes.

9½in (24cm) long

$1,150-1,400   WW

A late 19thC Black Forest chamois group, with distributor's label, "C.D. Schirrmann, 7 Rue Royale Paris."

43¼in (110cm) high

$6,500-7,500   MEA

ESSENTIAL REFERENCE—NOTTINGHAM ALABASTER

Nottingham alabaster was mainly quarried in Tutbury and Chellaston near Nottingham, England. During the 14thC to 16thC, altarpieces and devotional images were incredibly popular at home and abroad, with high demand for carvings from the merchant classes and religious institutions. Many hundreds of English alabasters were exported, with some discovered at Santiago de Compostela in Spain and as far north as Iceland.

A 15thC Nottingham alabaster and polychrome decorated fragment, depicting the Coronation of the Virgin, with gilt highlights.

11¼in (28.5cm) wide

$14,000-18,000   WW

A 16thC South Netherlands oak carving of Saint Martin and a beggar.

22in (56cm) high

$3,200-3,800   GORL

A 17thC Flemish carved oak Entombment group, a small section broken away.

This piece was exhibited in "Treasures from Sussex Houses," in "Bronzino to Boy George," Brighton Museum, England, 1985.

22½in (57cm) high

$11,000-14,000   GORL

A 17thC carved and painted pine and limed wood carving of the Madonna, standing on cherubs" heads.

12in (30.5cm) high

$800-950   SWO

A late 17thC to early 18thC Spanish carved polychrome and parcel-gilt figure of a saint, possibly Francis Xavier.

68¼in (173.5cm) high

$1,300-1,900   L&T

A pair of early 18thC Flemish sculpted limewood models of putti, some cracks, chips, and bangs.

28½in (72.5cm) high

$4,400-5,000   DN

An 18thC and later, possibly Flemish, carved oak figure of Saint George and the dragon.

22¾in (58cm) high

$2,300-2,800   LC

A late 18thC Italian carved and polychromed wood cherub.

22in (56cm) high

$1,500-2,000   L&T

A late 18thC Continental carved wood Corpus Christi, the figure of Christ mounted on a fruitwood crucifix above a skull, some faults and repairs.

26¾in (68cm) high

$1,900-2,500   TOV

An early 20thC carved and painted carousel chariot side panel, by Gustav Dentzel.

31½in (80cm) wide

$1,300-1,800   **POOK**

A carved and painted bird tree with hanging cherries, by David Guilmet.

20½in (52cm) high

$2,800-3,500   **POOK**

A Pennsylvania carved and painted rooster, signed "W. Kinstler," minor wear.

c1900   *23½in (59.5cm) high*

$13,000-18,000   **POOK**

A turned and painted saffron cup, by Joseph Lehn (1798-1892), Lancaster, Pennsylvania.

3in (7.5cm) high

$7,000-7,500   **POOK**

A late 19thC carved and painted carousel figure of a giraffe, attributed to Daniel Muller at the Dentzel Company, Philadelphia.

66in (167.5cm) high

$90,000-110,000   **SK**

A carved and painted bird on stump, by Schtockschnitzler Simmons (fl.1885-1910), southeastern Pennsylvania.

7in (18cm) high

$9,000-10,000   **POOK**

A carved and painted pine eaglet, by Wilhelm Schimmel (1817-90), Cumberland Valley, Pennsylvania, some flakes to talons.

4in (10cm) high

$14,000-18,000   **POOK**

An early 20thC folk art carved and painted sitting dog, found in Zanesville, Ohio.

19½in (49.5cm) high

$3,200-3,800   **POOK**

A 19thC carved and painted carnival target bust, as the head of a woman with black cloth headband, metal plate at base reads "MIETTE."

19¾in (50cm) high

$1,300-1,800   **SK**

CLOCKS

A late 17thC walnut and seaweed marquetry inlaid tall case clock, by John Shaw, Holborn, with brass eight-day five-pillar bell-striking movement, the dial engraved with the Doves of Pliny.

86½in (220cm) high

$11,000-13,000   LSK

A late 17thC walnut and beech marquetry inlaid tall case clock, with eight-day two-train movement, dial signed "Rich: Fennel Kinsington."

86½in (220.5cm) high

$9,500-10,500   PW

ESSENTIAL REFERENCE—WILLIAM CLEMENT

William Clement was one of the leading London clockmakers of the late 17thC.

● **He was born in Rotherhithe and spent his early career as an anchorsmith and blacksmith.**

● **He turned to clockmaking when he moved to Southwark in 1677, and later became Master of the London Clockmakers' Company in 1694.**

● **Clement was one of the earliest makers to apply the anchor escapement to clockwork, making a long pendulum practicable.**

A William and Mary walnut tall case clock, by William Clement, with one-month five-pillar bell-striking movement with anchor escapement, the dial, signed "Gulielmus Clement Londini Fecit."

79¾in (202.5cm) high

$65,000-80,000   WW

A William and Mary tall case clock, by Samuel Watson, signed to dial, the case inlaid with floral and foliate marquetry and ebonized trim.

Samuel Watson (fl.1687-1710) was as an important Coventry and later London clock and watchmaker known for his timekeeping innovations, including the five-minute repeater watch. Over his career, Watson was commissioned by Charles II and by Sir Isaac Newton.

82in (208cm) high

$19,000-23,000   L&T

A William and Mary tall case clock, by John Knibb, Oxford, with eight-day bell-striking movement with recoil anchor escapement and outside countwheel, signed to dial, in a walnut and ebony case with marquetry panels.

John Knibb was born c1650 and was apprenticed c1664 to Joseph Knibb, his older brother, in St Clement. Joseph moved to London in 1670, John took over the Oxford business. He was Mayor of Oxford 1698-99 and 1710-11 and continued making clocks until 1722.

82¾in (210cm) high

$19,000-25,000   WW

A William and Mary walnut, olive wood, and floral marquetry tall case clock, by James Clowes, London, with one-month five-pillar bell-striking movement with outside countwheel and anchor escapement, signed to dial, some restoration to case.

James Clowes (c1643-1705) was born in Astbury, Cheshire, UK, older brother of John (b.1751) and son to James Clowes Sr., a nail maker of Odd Rode. James Clowes Jr. became a Free Brother of The Clockmakers' Company in 1671.

c1690   78½in (199.5cm) high

$19,000-25,000   DN

A tall case clock, by Samuel Barrow, with eight-day bell-striking movement, in a black lacquered case, chinoiserie decoration.

Samuel Barrow, London, was apprenticed in 1688 to John Barrow and became a Freeman of the Clockmakers' Company in 1696, working until c1704.

84¼in (214cm) high

$2,800-3,300   BE

ESSENTIAL REFERENCE—JOSEPH WINDMILLS

Joseph Windmills was one of the finest clockmakers of late 17thC London.

● He was born c1640-50, and joined the Clockmakers' Company as a Free Brother on September 29, 1671.

● In 1699, he was elected as the youngest Warden of Clockmakers' Company, and in 1702 became Master.

● His son Thomas Windmills later went into business with him, and the firm lasted until Thomas's death in 1737.

● Clocks made by the firm were typically signed "Windmills" or "J & T Windmills."

A William III burr walnut and marquetry tall case clock, by Joseph Windmills, London, with one-month bell-striking movement with countwheel and anchor escapement, some replacements to case.
c1695   81in (206cm) high
$28,000-33,000   DN

An early 18thC Queen Anne seaweed marquetry tall case clock, by Robert Pike, London, with eight-day twin-fusee bell-striking movement, the dial signed.
85in (216cm) high
$7,500-9,000   L&T

A Queen Anne walnut eight-day tall case clock, by Lewis Beavan, Bristol, England, with four-pillar bell-striking movement with anchor escapement, signed to dial, columns missing from hood.
c1705   89½in (227.5cm) high
$3,800-4,400   DN

A burr walnut tall case clock, by Joseph Windmills, London, with one-month six-pillar bell-striking movement with anchor escapement and outside countwheel, signed to dial, rebuilt caddy top, later finials, plinth restored.
c1695   89in (226cm) high
$18,000-23,000   TEN

An early 18thC walnut marquetry inlaid tall case clock, by Joseph Windmills, London, with one month bell-striking movement, the dial signed.
87¾in (223cm) high
$13,000-18,000   L&T

A William III walnut and foliate marquetry tall case clock, by John Williamson, Leeds, with twin-train bell-striking movement with internal countwheel, the signed dial.

John Williamson (c1651-1748) was born in Guisley, near Leeds. He trained in London, and gained his freedom of the Worshipful Company of Clockmakers in 1682, before returning the following year to Leeds. The workmanship and quality of his clocks are considered equal to the main London makers of the time.
c1700   82in (208cm) high
$25,000-30,000   BELL

A walnut marquetry inlaid tall case clock, by Richard Rooker (fl.1694-1748), London, with eight-day six-pillar bell-striking movement, signed to dial, some restoration.
72¾in (185cm) high
$15,000-19,000   BE

A George I walnut eight-day tall case clock, by Henry Battercon, London, with five-finned pillar inside rack and bell-striking movement with anchor escapement, signed to dial, some replacements and restoration.

Henry Batterson was born in Waddesdon, Buckinghamshire, in 1676 and apprenticed to William Davison in 1694, transferring to Jonathan Puller in 1696 and gaining his freedom of the Clockmakers' Company in 1701.

c1720   90½in (230cm) high

$7,000-7,500   DN

A burr walnut tall case clock, by John Jefferies, London, with ringed five-pillar eight-day bell-striking movement, signed to dial.

c1730   94½in (240cm) high

$4,400-5,000   SWO

An early to mid-18thC carved oak tall case clock, by Thomas Gorsuch, Salop, Shrewsbury, England, with eight-day two-train bell-striking movement, some damages.

82in (208cm) high

$2,000-2,500   PW

A mid-18thC George II mahogany tall case clock, by Miles Wedred (Wetherhead), Kirkby Lonsdale, the case attributed to Gillows, with eight-day bell-striking movement, the dial with revolving moon phases, engraved "Tempus Fugit."

93¼in (237cm) high

$7,000-8,000   L&T

An 18thC scarlet lacquer and gilt chinoiserie tall case clock, by William Jourdain, London.

96in (244cm) high

$3,800-4,400   BRI

A mahogany tall case clock, case possibly by Gillows, with eight-day four-pillar bell-striking movement with anchor escapement, the dial signed "Finney, Liverpool" and inscribed "The Man is Yet Unborn, Who duly Weighs an hour," some chips and scratches to case.

c1780   101¼in (257cm) high

$4,400-5,000   TEN

A mid-18thC eight-day tall case clock, by Robert Grinling, Yarmouth, in a black japanned chinoiserie case.

$1,900-2,500   CHOR

A late 18thC precision tall case timepiece, with four-finned-pillar eight-day movement with deadbeat duplex escapement regulated by seconds pendulum, in an architectural mahogany case, replacement hands, some wear.

81in (205.5cm) high

$2,500-3,200   DN

A George III mahogany musical tall case clock, by Samuel Deacon, Barton-in-the-Beans for Robotham, Leicester, with eight-day four-pillar triple-train bell-striking movement with anchor escapement, with music train playing seven tunes, the frontplate engraved "S.D.B. 1788," the dial inscribed "ROBOTHAM," the arch painted with an automaton scene of musicians, some wear.

Samuel Deacon (1746-1816) was born in Ratby, Leicestershire, UK. After his apprenticeship, he was employed as a clockmaker's journeyman, later setting up on his own as a clockmaker in the small hamlet of Barton-in-the-Beans.

1788   *98in (249cm) high*
$11,000-14,000   DN

A Chippendale walnut tallcase clock, by George Fix, Reading, Pennsylvania, with eight-day movement, signed to dial, the case with a broken-arch bonnet, some losses and replacements.

This is one of the finest Reading clocks known and remains in remarkable condition.

c1795   *93in (236cm) high*
$25,000-32,000   POOK

A Federal walnut tall case clock, by John Hoff, Lancaster, Pennsylvania, with eight-day movement, the case with line inlay.

c1805   *91½in (232.5cm) high*
$5,500-6,500   POOK

A Regency mahogany tall case clock, with eight-day striking deadbeat movement, the dial signed "Wieland of Walworth," with brass fretwork decoration.

c1810   *81½in (207cm) high*
$7,500-9,000   SWO

An early 19thC American Federal mahogany tall case clock, with painted dial, the case inlaid with an eagle.

90½in (230cm) high
$2,300-2,800   DRA

A Regency mahogany and marquetry inlaid tall case clock, by Davies, North Shields, with twin-train bell-striking movement with anchor escapement, signed to dial, with "rocking ship" automaton to arch, some damages.

89¼in (227cm) high
$3,200-3,800   BELL

An early 19thC mahogany long case regulator, by Edward Smith, Dublin, signed dial, with eight-day six-pillar single-train movement with deadbeat escapement and mercury jar pendulum, crack to plinth, losses to canopy.

Edward Smith worked as a clock manufacturer and brass founder at 34 Jervis Street in Dublin, c1801-58. In 1801 he was appointed Clock Manufacturer to the General Post Office.

92¼in (234cm) high
$5,000-5,700   PW

An early 19thC Scottish tall case clock, by John Donald, Glasgow, the painted dial in a drumhead case above a fluted column trunk and molded panel base.

78in (198cm) high
$3,800-4,400   L&T

An early 19thC Portuguese painted chestnut tall case clock, with eight-day bell-striking birdcage movement, the dial signed "Jeremie Girod Porto e Coruna."

91¾in (233cm) high

$1,300-1,800 WW

A William IV mahogany three-train quarter-striking tall case clock, by Pryor, London, with three-train movement with anchor escapement and internal countwheel, signed to dial.

83in (211cm) high

$2,300-2,800 BELL

A William IV mahogany long case regulator timepiece, by James McCabe, London, with brass eight-day five-pillar movement with deadbeat escapement, jeweled pallets and beat adjustment, with a mercury jar compensated pendulum, signed to dial, numbered "2476," in Gothic carved case.

In 1811, James McCabe inherited his father's clock, chronometer, and watch making business, which had been founded in 1778. James McCabe had been previously apprenticed to Reid and Auld of Edinburgh.

76¾in (195cm) high

$10,000-11,000 WW

A mid-to-late Victorian carved oak long case regulator timepiece, by James McCabe, London, with eight-day six-pillar movement with Harrison's maintaining power and deadbeat escapement, signed to dial and numbered "3330," some shrinkage and losses to veneers.

76½in (194.5cm) high

$13,000-18,000 DN

A mid-19thC French mahogany weight-driven long-duration long case regulator, by Jean-Aimé Jacob, Paris, the case inset with a barometer and two thermometers.

Jean-Aimé Jacob (1793-1871) was apprenticed in 1813 to Pierre Louis Berthoud. By 1825, he had established his own workshop where he styled himself Élève de Breguet. Long-duration year-going regulators were a speciality.

72½in (184cm) high

$11,000-14,000 ECGW

A Victorian walnut long case regulator, the movement attributed to Odber, Birmingham, England, with eight-day movement with deadbeat escapement with split anchor and jeweled pallets, with mercury jar pendulum, signed "Bennett, Torquay" to dial.

Although unsigned, two identical movements have been noted with similar shaped plates and with split anchors, both signed for Odber, Birmingham, with a further floor-standing regulator signed for Reid & Sons, Newcastle-on-Tyne, also housing a near-identical movement. Bennett owned the retail jewelers premises situated in Lower Union Street, Torquay, from their opening in the mid-Victorian period until closing in 1985.

76¾in (195cm) high

$8,000-9,500 BE

A mid-Victorian Reformed Gothic carved oak long case wall regulator timepiece, in the manner of A.W.N. Pugin, with eight-day five double-screwed baluster pillar frosted gilt movement, engraved "ARNOLD & LEWIS, SUCCESSORS TO, I. SIMMONS, WATCH & CLOCK MANUFACTURERS," some wear to case.

Isaac Simmons worked in Manchester c1834-51 and was succeeded by Arnold and Lewis, who continued at the same address until c1905. The movement may have been supplied by James Condliff, Liverpool (fl.c1816-62). The quality of the movement suggests this clock was intended for an important location where great accuracy was required. It may have been the "shop regulator," used to set the times of other clocks made by Simmons, or a clock made specifically for a wealthy private client or business.

85in (216cm) high

$11,000-12,000 DN

A late 17thC basket-top bracket clock, by Edmund Appley, London, with eight-day double-fusee five-pillar bell-striking movement with verge escapement, in an ebonized case with brass filigree work.

Edmund Appley (d.1688) was born in Westmoreland and moved to London, where he was apprenticed in 1670 to Jeffrey Bayley. He became a Freeman of the Clockmakers' Company in 1678.

13in (33cm) high

$8,000-9,500 **BE**

A Charles II or William and Mary ormolu-mounted walnut calendar clock, by John Knibb, Oxford, with eight-day double-fusee movement with verge escapement, signed to backplate and dial.

See page 254 for another John Knibb clock.

c1690 *14½in (37cm) high*

$15,000-19,000 **FRE**

An early to mid-18thC French boullework bracket clock, by Estienne, Paris, with signed bell-striking movement with verge escapement.

46in (117cm) high

$2,500-3,200 **KEY**

A George II ebonized bracket clock, by Samuel Whichcote, London, with twin-fusee movement with verge escapement, with signed backplate.

24in (61cm) high

$5,000-6,300 **DUK**

A George III ormolu-mounted ebonized balloon bracket clock, by Justin Vulliamy, London, with twin-train fusee bell-striking movement converted to anchor escapement, signed to dial, some restoration.

François-Justin Vulliamy (1712-97) was the son of a pastor at Gingins, in the Pays de Vaud region in Switzerland. He emigrated to England in 1730, and in 1743 went into partnership with Benjamin Gray (d.1764). Gray had received a Royal Warrant in 1742, which later passed to Vulliamy. François-Justin Vulliamy's son, Benjamin Vulliamy, was also a prominent clockmaker (see page 265).

c1770 *20¾in (53cm) high*

$5,500-6,500 **BELL**

CLOSER LOOK—RÉGENCE BRACKET CLOCK

Parquetry of this kind is rare in clocks from the late Régence period, when boullework marquetry was more commonly used.

The matching bracket is decorated with an ormolu eagle and a pair of masques de comédie. The masques are identical to a pair found on a Régence bombé commode by Etienne Doirat (1675-1732), suggesting the case and bracket may have been made at Doirat's workshop in Paris.

The dial has a double ring of blue numerals against a white dial, assembled from 25 individual pieces. It was possibly made by Siméon de Ville, who was Roquelon's brother-in-law and l'Emailleur du Roi (the Royal Enameller).

The quality of the individual elements—parquetry, ormolu, enamel, and movement—together make this an exceptional piece.

A Régence ormolu-mounted parquetry kingwood and amaranth bracket clock, by Etienne Roquelon (b.1718), Paris, with eight-day movement with silk suspension and verge escapement, signed to backplate

c1730-40 *41in (104cm) high*

$9,500-10,500 **FRE**

A mid-18thC ebonized bracket clock, by John Hampson, Wrexham, with single-fusee bell-striking movement, signed and numbered "1160."

17¾in (45cm) high

$2,800-3,500 **PW**

A bracket clock, by Samuel Toulmin, London, with eight-day double-fusee movement with verge escapement and pull quarter repeat, in an ebonized bell-top case.

Samuel Toulmin worked in the Strand, London, c1757-83. A number of watches and clocks are signed by him, including a bracket clock in the Virginia Museum, a watch in the China Gelis collection, and a watch in the Guildhall Museum.

21¼in (54cm) high

$4,400-5,700 **BE**

An 18thC six-hour bracket clock, by Charles Goode (fl.1686-1730), London, with two-train fusee bell-striking movement, in olivewood case.

This is a six-hour clock made for the Italian market. The dial is numbered one to six, dividing the day into the quarters to regulate the prayer cycle of monks. In general, such clocks had a single hand, although this one has two. Six-hour clocks were common in 15thC to 17thC Tuscany.

18in (45.5cm) high

$20,000-25,000 **DUK**

An 18thC mahogany double-fusee repeating bracket clock, by Thomas Upjohn, Exon, UK, with two-train bell-striking movement, recently refurbished.

19¾in (50cm) high

$5,500-6,500   ECGW

A late 18thC mahogany bracket clock, by John Hamilton, Glasgow, with double-fusee movement, in Chinese Chippendale-style case.

1780-84   18in (46cm) high

$5,000-5,700   PW

An ebonized chiming bracket clock, by James Tregent, London, with two-train repeater bell-striking movement, on ogee wall bracket.

clock 6½in (16.5cm) high

$11,000-13,000   HT

A George III ebony-cased bracket clock, by Clay, London, quarter chiming, with verge escapement.

c1790

$8,000-9,500   JN

A George III mahogany bell-top bracket clock, by John Davidge, London, with twin-fusee bell-striking movement with anchor escapement, signed to dial.

19¾in (50cm) high

$4,400-5,700   WW

A George III ebonized bracket clock, by John Ward, London, with twin-fusee bell-striking movement with verge escapement, signed to dial.

19½in (49.5cm) high

$4,400-5,700   WW

A George III mahogany bracket clock, by Rolfe, Clerkenwell, with double-fusee bell-striking movement.

15in (38cm) high

$1,500-2,300   HAN

A late Regency mahogany bracket clock, in the manner of Thomas Hope, by James Gorham, Kensington, London, with twin-train bell-striking chain fusee movement with anchor escapement, the dial signed "James Gorham/ KENSINGTON/Clock & Watch Maker/to The Royal Family," door hinges repaired.

c1820   18½in (47cm) high

$2,800-3,500   BELL

An early 19thC Irish bracket clock, by Milton & Sons, Dublin, with triple-fusee bell-striking movement with anchor escapement, in an ebonized case with brass and mother-of-pearl inlay.

19¾in (50cm) high

$5,500-7,000   ECGW

An early 19thC ebonized bracket clock, with three-train fusee movement striking ten chimes, losses to corner frieze.

24½in (62cm) high

$3,200-3,800 **ECGW**

A Victorian mahogany bracket clock, with eight-day triple-fusee bell-striking movement, some wear.

c1840   *20½in (52cm) high*

$2,500-3,200   **DN**

A mahogany musical bracket clock, by Parkinson and Frodsham, Change Alley, London, with eight-day five-pillar bell-striking double-fusee movement.

The Romano-Egyptian-style case to the design of Thomas Hope.

20in (51cm) high

$2,300-2,800   **BE**

A 19thC French tortoiseshell and boullework bracket clock, with eight-day bell-striking movement, stamped "LaGarde a Paris," serial no.3112.

31in (79cm) high

$4,400-5,000   **L&T**

A 19thC French Louis XV-style japanned bracket clock, with eight-day bell-striking movement, serial no.3747, on matching bracket.

26½in (67cm) high

$2,500-3,200   **L&T**

A 19thC mahogany and gilded Gothic bracket clock, with triple-fusee gong-striking movement.

28½in (72.5cm) high

$4,400-5,000   **PW**

A Victorian ormolu-mounted tortoiseshell bracket clock, by J.C. Jennens, London, with triple-train chain fusee bell-striking movement with anchor escapement, signed.

c1880   *22in (56cm) high*

$4,400-5,000   **BELL**

A late 19thC Louis XV boullework ormolu-mounted bracket clock, the movement stamped "Bright, Paris," on matching bracket, some missing inlay, feet loose.

23¼in (59cm) high

$2,500-3,200   **SWO**

An Edwardian mahogany musical gong and bell-striking bracket clock, inscribed "Syd F Stanley, Chancery Lane," with chime selector subsidiary dials.

24in (61cm) high

$3,200-3,800   **SWO**

A French Régence tortoiseshell and ormolu-mounted mantel clock, by Baltazar Martinot, Paris, with eight-day twin-train bell-striking movement.

Baltazar Martinot (1636-1716) came from an important dynasty of Rouen watchmakers. He received his master's degree in watchmaking in Paris in 1660 and became Valet de Chambre-Horloger Ordinaire of the Queen Mother in 1665.

24in (61cm) high

$3,200-3,800   WW

A late 18thC Viennese grande sonnerie mantel clock, with two-day gong-striking movement.

22¾in (58cm) high

$3,200-3,800   BE

A late 18thC Meissen Marcolini porcelain mantel clock, with Swiss four-pillar bell-striking fusee movement with watch-type verge escapement, underglaze blue crossed swords and asterisk mark, some repairs and restoration.

10½in (26.5cm) high

$3,800-4,400   DN

A Louis XVI ormolu and pietra dura mantel clock, with eight-day bell-striking movement.

14in (35.5cm) high

$1,400-1,800   JN

A Regency ormolu and patinated bronze mantel timepiece, with four-pillar eight-day single-chain fusee movement with anchor escapement, replacement hour hand, some wear.

12in (30.5cm) high

$3,200-3,800   DN

A Regency mahogany and brass line inlaid lancet-shaped mantel clock, retailed by John Grant, Fleet Street, London, movement by Handley & Moore, no.3781, with bell-striking twin-train gut fusee movement with anchor escapement.

John Grant (d.1810), an eminent maker, was a member of the Clockmakers' Company by 1781. Handley & Moore, apprenticed to Thwaites, supplied high-quality movements to the trade.

17¼in (44cm) high

$1,900-2,500   BELL

An Empire ormolu mantel clock, by L. Moinet, Paris, with twin-train bell-striking movement with external countwheel, lacking bell, dial chipped.

Louis Moinet (d.1853) was the secrétaire of Abraham-Louis Breguet (1747-1823), founder of Breguet, a watchmakers' company today owned by Swatch.

26¾in (68cm) high

$3,200-3,800   BELL

A late Regency brass-mounted ebonized mantel timepiece, by Finer & Nowland, London (fl.1805-25), with four-pillar chain fusee movement with anchor escapement, repair on the dial, some wear to ebonising.

c1820   *8¾in (22cm) high*

$5,500-6,500   BELL

An early 19thC French Empire gilt and patinated metal mantel clock, with eight-day bell-striking movement.

14½in (37cm) high

$1,900-2,500   L&T

An early 19thC French Empire gilt-metal mantel clock, by Blanc Fils, Palais Royal, with eight-day bell-striking movement.

17¾in (45cm) high

$3,200-3,800   L&T

A gilt bronze mantel clock, by Arnold & Dent, London, the movement numbered "524."

The partnership of Edward J. Dent and John Roger Arnold began in 1830 and lasted ten years. The firm specialized in chronometers, precise clocks, and other instruments. Its clocks are of extremely high quality.

c1835   *24¼in (61.5cm) high*

$6,500-7,500   L&T

A mid-19thC Louis Philippe ormolu striking portico mantel clock, by Destape, Paris, with two-train movement with countwheel.

18½in (47cm) high

$700-800   BELL

A mid-19thC French boullework portico mantel clock, with twin-train bell-striking movement, signed "Laine Paris," numbered "424/72," with visible pendulum.

c1850   *20in (50.5cm) high*

$750-900   MOR

A mid-19thC French gilt bronze and porcelain mantel clock, by Lerolle, Paris, with eight-day bell-striking cylinder movement, numbered "814," with Sèvres-style porcelain dial.

25¼in (64cm) wide

$2,500-3,200   LSK

A carved mahogany pediment, wall or mantel clock, by Sir John Bennett, London, with eight-day chain-fusee movement, backplate stamped "5784," signed to dial.

Sir John Bennett (1814-97) was an eminent clockmaker and watchmaker, the son of watchmaker John Bennett. He was later knighted and became a politician.

21¼in (54cm) high

$1,800-2,300   BE

A mid-19thC Paris porcelain mantel clock, signed "Rey â Paris."

15¾in (40cm) wide

$1,300-1,800   BE

A 19thC Black Forest mantel clock, with brass movement.

24½in (62cm) high

$1,300-1,800   WW

A 19thC Bavarian Black Forest musical mantel clock.

26in (66cm) high

$5,500-6,500   HANN

A 19thC carved oak Black Forest cuckoo mantel clock, some damages.

25¼in (64cm) high

$800-950   FLD

A 19thC French patinated and gilt-bronze mantel clock, by Japy Frères, Paris, with eight-day bell-striking movement, signed, stamped "E.P. LÉPOSÉ/5564."

The firm of Japy Frères et Cie was founded in 1774 by Frederick Japy. The business rapidly expanded and, by 1804, Japy employed 300 people at his factory in Beaucourt. From 1806, he took five of his sons into partnership and the firm expanded, eventually becoming one of the largest makers of clocks in Europe. The business continued into the 20thC but, during the interwar period, it went into decline and closed c1940.

21¼in (54cm) high

$3,200-3,800 **L&T**

A 19thC French marble mantel clock, by Raingo Frères, Paris, with eight-day bell-striking movement with brocket escapement.

Raingo Frères was founded in Paris in 1813 by Belgian Zacharie Joseph Raingo (1775-1847) along with his three brothers. Zacharie's speciality was astronomical clocks. The company also made a variety of clocks, including some for the home of Emperor Napoleon III.

18½in (47cm) high

$1,400-1,800 **PW**

A bronze and ormolu Gothic mantel clock, by Valogne à Paris, with eight-day bell-striking movement with outside countwheel, the backplate stamped "811."

24½in (62cm) high

$1,400-1,800 **BE**

A late 19thC engraved gilt-brass and silver-plated mantel clock, by Howell James & Co., with eight-day bell-striking movement, signed and numbered "1193" on backplate, with Japy Frère Med D'Honn roundel.

19¾in (50cm) high

$1,900-2,500 **DN**

A marble, bronze and ormolul mantel clock, by Marti, Paris, with eight-day bell-striking movement, no.8288, the dial marked "Fd. Viteau, 7 Rue Vivienne."

Samuel Marti was a prolific 19thC French clockmaker, known to be working c1860 at Le Pays de Montbeliard, Paris, making roulant blancs. He joined forces with Japy Frères and Roux in 1863 in order to market their movements to firms such as L'Epée.

19in (48cm) high

$1,500-2,000 **BE**

A French Louis XVI-style ormolu mantel clock, by S. Marti, with twin-train bell-striking movement, no.138.

c1885 *24½in (62cm) high*

$1,500-2,000 **BELL**

A late Victorian walnut Gothic Revival mantel clock, by Dent, London, no.41210, with three-train chain fusee striking movement with anchor escapement.

c1890 *24¾in (63cm) high*

$3,800-4,400 **BELL**

A gilt-metal-mounted ebonized mantel clock, retailed by Wilson, Penrith, with three-train chain fusee bell-striking movement with anchor escapement.

c1890 *29½in (75cm) high*

$3,500-4,000 **BELL**

TABLE 265

CLOCKS

A night-and-day spring table clock, attributed to Joseph Knibb, London, with twin-fusee bell-striking movement with verge escapement and revolving night hour disk set on a pivot, with later dial and ebonized case.

Joseph Knibb (1640-1711) was born in Oxford and apprenticed in Newport Pagnell. He later operated in both Oxford and London. He was elected as a Steward of the Clockmakers' Company in 1684 and Assistant in 1689. He retired in 1697. He was the elder brother of John Knibb (see page 254).

c1675   *16¼in (41.5cm) high*

$12,000-14,000   DN

A George III mahogany musical automata table clock with pull-repeat, by Thomas Hunter Jr., London, with five-pillar three-train fusee movement with verge escapement, some repairs and replacements.

Thomas Hunter Jr. was apprenticed 1734 and became free of the Clockmakers' Company in 1742. He was appointed Warden of the Clockmakers' Company in 1762, and Master in 1765. He died in 1785.

c1760   *19¾in (50cm) high*

$11,000-14,000   BELL

ESSENTIAL REFERENCE—BENJAMIN VULLIAMY

Benjamin Vulliamy was born in 1747 and probably trained by his father, Justin Vulliamy (see page 259). He became the King's Clockmaker by Royal appointment in 1773.

- **He built a regulator for the King's Observatory at Kew, England, which served as the Prime Meridian until Greenwich Royal Observatory took over in 1884.**
- **He is best known for his decorative sculptural timepieces in the Neoclassical taste, created from white marble and Derby biscuit porcelain with fine cast and chased ormolu mounts. As Royal clockmaker, Vulliamy supplied several timepieces of this type to the Royal family, many of which still reside in the Royal collection.**
- **He was succeeded by his son, Benjamin Lewis, who worked from 52 Pall Mall, served as Warden 1821-25 and was appointed Master five times.**

A George III ebonized table clock, by Benjamin Vulliamy, London, no.272, the five-pillar twin-fusee rack and bell-striking movement with half deadbeat escapement and pull-quarter repeat, minor repairs and adjustments, with contemporary wall bracket.

c1796   *25½in (65cm) high*

$25,000-32,000   DN

CLOSER LOOK—JOSEPH WINDMILLS BRACKET CLOCK

This bracket clock contains a four-pillared gut fusee movement with verge escapement, with a pull repeat chiming the hours and quarters on two bells, and a pull chord to chime the alarm.

The brass dial has a silvered chapter ring, with winged cherub spandrels at the corners.

The ebonized case has a pierced basket top, surmounted by a "Quare"-type baluster, and detailed pierced panels at the sides.

It was made by Joseph Windmills, a prominent and highly skilled clockmaker of the 17thC. See page 255 for his tall case clocks.

A late 17thC ebonized table or bracket clock, by Joseph Windmills, London.

15¼in (39cm) high

$30,000-35,000   CA

A George III table clock, by Robert Philp, London, with six-pillar triple-chain fusee movement with verge escapement, chiming a melody, in an ebonized case with Rococo brass mounts, some shrinkage.

Robert Philp worked in London c1740-81. He was a maker of musical and astronomical clocks and watches, known to have supplied clocks sent to China.

c1770   *22in (56cm) high*

$11,000-14,000   DN

A late 18thC George III gilt-brass-mounted mahogany musical table clock, by William Bull (fl.1770-1804), Stratford, with six-pillar triple-chain fusee movement with verge escapement, playing seven melodies, the curtain rising when music plays to reveal a festival scene, minor restoration.

25¼in (64cm) high

$8,000-9,500   DN

A late 18thC ebonized striking table clock, by Robert Dovers, Bath, UK, with three-train fusee bell-striking movement with anchor escapement.

20in (51cm) high

$6,500-7,500   HT

A 19thC Victorian Gothic Revival rosewood regulator table clock, by Charles Frodsham, with balance-wheel fusee movement.

Charles Frodsham (1810-71) was maker of clocks, watches and chronometers. His company was known for making high-quality carriage clocks and time-precision regulator clocks.

18in (46cm) high

$5,000-6,300   L&T

An early to mid-19thC English carriage timepiece, in the manner of Thomas Cole, with eight-day three-pillar single-chain fusee movement with Harrison's maintaining power train with underslung English lever escapement, some wear, replacement foot.

4¼in (11cm) high

$1,900-2,500 DN

A "Goliath" carriage clock, by John Moore & Sons, London, with twin-fusee gong-striking movement, the backplate signed and numbered "13480."

John Moore & Sons of Clerkenwell was located at 38 Clerkenwell Close, c1801-75.

21½in (54.5cm) high

$10,000-11,000 GTH

A Regency Gothic Revival ormolu carriage timepiece, by Dwerrihouse and Fletcher, London, with eight-day four-pillar single-chain fusee movement with vertical English lever escapement, some wear.

John Fletcher was a chronometer maker to the Admiralty. He was a finisher and a springer, meaning he was highly skilled in his work. Later Fletcher bought out Dwerrihouse & Carter of 27 Davies St., Berkeley Square; timepieces signed "Fletcher, late Dwerrihouse & Carter" are also known.

An engraved bell-striking brass carriage clock, by Breguet à Paris, with repeat and alarm, in leather case.

5½in (14cm) high

$5,000-5,700 JN

c1830 *7in (18cm) high*

$3,800-4,400 DN

A mid-19thC French boullework "pendule portative," Moser, Paris, no.8976, with two-train eight-day bell-striking movement with two-plane "chaffcutter" escapement, some damages.

8¼in (21cm) high

$2,500-3,200 DN

A French gilt-brass carriage clock, by Japy Frères, Beaucourt and Paris, with eight-day two-train bell-striking movement with gilt platform lever escapement, stamped to backplate.

c1860 *7¼in (18.5cm) high*

$1,600-2,300 DN

A 19thC brass carriage clock, with two-train eight-day gong-striking movement with repeater.

6½in (16.5cm) high

$1,800-2,300 PW

A 19thC French brass Aesthetic Movement clock, inset with painted pottery panels.

7in (18cm) high

$3,200-3,800 HANN

A mid-to-late 19thC French engraved gilt-brass gorge cased petit sonnerie striking carriage clock, possibly by Drocourt, with eight-day two-train bell-striking movement with silvered platform lever escapement and push-button repeat and alarm, dial lacking alarm hand.

4½in (11.5cm) high

$5,000-6,300 DN

A miniature "Japonesque" enamel carriage timepiece, retailed by Le Roy & Fils, Paris, with eight-day movement with vertical lever escapement, the backplate inscribed.

The firm of "Le Roy & Fils" was founded in Palais Royal, Paris in 1785 by Basille Charles Le Roy. On his death, he left the business to his son, Charles-Louis, who continued producing clocks signed "Le Roy & Fils" until 1845, when the firm was sold to Casimir Halley Desfontaines, later succeeded by his son. The firm continued trading in the hands of various successors well into the 20thC.

c1880   *2¾in (7cm) high*
$3,200-3,800   **DN**

A L'Epée brass repeating carriage clock, with two-train gong-striking movement with visible escapement, mild surface wear.

6in (15.5cm) high
$2,500-3,200   **BELL**

A late 19thC brass and champlevé carriage clock, by Sharman D. Neill, Belfast, with brass eight-day gong-striking movement with repeater, with leather case.

7in (18cm) high
$1,600-2,000   **LC**

A late 19thC French brass and chinoiserie repeating carriage clock, with eight-day gong-striking movement with a lever escapement, the backplate stamped "PATENT SURETY POLLER" and "G.L.," without handle

7in (17.5cm) high
$3,800-4,400   **WW**

A late 19thC brass repeating carriage clock, by Sharman D. Neill, Belfast, with gong-striking movement and visible escapement, with case.

8¼in (21cm) high
$3,200-3,800   **HAN**

A silver-mounted tortoiseshell carriage clock, London, with twin-train movement with push/repeat and lever escapement, the backplate stamped "E G L" and "PARIS No 2655."

1893   *6in (15cm) high*
$1,000-1,150   **BELL**

A French gilt-brass gorge-cased grande and petite sonnerie carriage clock, by Drocourt, no.16290, with platform lever escapement, signed, with leather traveling box, some wear.

Pierre and Alfred Drocourt had a Paris-based business with a factory at Saint Nicolas d'Aliermont. Its carriage clocks are generally of the best quality, and the firm won numerous medals at International Exhibitions in the second half of the 19thC.

c1890   *7in (17.5cm) high*
$12,00-14,000   **BELL**

A French grande and petite sonnerie carriage clock, by Drocourt, no.30089, with twin-train movement with Chinese duplex platform escapement, stamped, with leather travelling case.

c1900   *8in (20.5cm) high*
$9,500-10,500   **BELL**

A French brass and champlevé enamel carriage clock, with twin-barrel gong-striking movement with repeated, with leather carrying case.

1900   *6½in (16.5cm) high*
$3,800-4,400   **HT**

An early 17thC iron-framed lantern clock, with posted countwheel bell-striking movement with verge escapement, some restoration.

15in (38cm) high

$5,500-6,500 **DN**

A rare Charles I "first period" brass lantern clock, with posted bell-striking movement, now with verge escapement, the dial later inscribed "John Harford, Bath, 1658," some replacements and repairs, blackplate missing.

Comparisons with similar clocks suggest this may be the work of Richard Milborne, from the London "first period" of lantern clockmaking. John Harford, active in Bath from c1654, may have acquired and overhauled the clock later, then sold it under his own name.

c1620-30 *15½in (39.5cm) high*

$18,000-23,000 **DN**

A Charles II brass lantern clock, by Edward Webb, Chew Stoke, with posted countwheel bell-striking movement with later anchor escapement, in typical "Chew Valley" frame, some replacements and repairs, alarm lacking.

Edward Webb was a clockmaker active 1678-93 in Chew Stoke, Somerset, England. He was probably the son of Charles Webb, who owned a foundry in Chew Stoke. After his death, he was succeeded by clockmaker Edward Bilbie.

c1680 *15¾in (40cm) high*

$6,500-7,500 **DN**

A Charles II brass lantern clock, London, with posted countwheel bell-striking movement with verge escapement, some wears and repairs, movement converted.

c1670 *15in (38cm) high*

$5,500-6,500 **DN**

A Charles II brass miniature striking lantern clock, by Joseph Knibb, London, with converted verge escapement and alarm train, later handles and latches.

c1670 *9¼in (23.5cm) high*

$6,500-7,500 **BELL**

A William and Mary brass miniature lantern timepiece, by Daniel Parker, Fleet Street, London, the movement with verge escapement and alarm train, some replacements, one foot broken.

9½in (24cm) high

$2,000-2,500 **BELL**

A pyramidical brass skeleton timepiece, by John Pace, Bury St Edmunds, England, no.253, with eighteen-day movement with Graham's deadbeat escapement, under a glass dome.

John Pace (d.1867) lived and worked in Bury St Edmunds. His workshop was at 19 Abbeygate Street. He exhibited a virtually identical skeleton timepiece at the 1851 Great Exhibition.

c1855 *17in (43cm) high*

$5,000-6,300 **BELL**

A brass skeleton clock, with chain-driven movement, under a glass dome, on a walnut base.

19¾in (50cm) high

$1,500-2,000 **LC**

A Victorian brass skeleton clock, by W.E. Vale, Lichfield, with glass display case.

9¾in (24.5cm) high

$500-650 **LOCK**

A George III ormolu, Geneva enamel and paste set automaton timepiece, for the Chinese market, attributed to William Carpenter, with later musical movement, no.33702.

William Carpenter was a member of the Clockmakers' Company 1770-1817, gaining his freedom in 1781. During his working career, he produced many complex automata clocks, often for the Chinese market. The Chinese Emperor Qianlong (1735-95) collected clocks throughout his reign, as had his grandfather, Emperor Kangxi. This resulted in a substantial expansion for English merchants and makers. The missionary Valentine Chalier observed in 1736 that the Chinese Imperial palace contained more than 4,000 clocks.

c1800   *11½in (29cm) high*

$60,000-65,000   **BELL**

A George III brass-cased traveling alarm timepiece, by Thomas Mudge and William Dutton, with 30-hour movement with verge escapement, with later oak bracket.

5¼in (13.5cm) high

$16,000-20,000   **WW**

A mahogany and cherry dwarf clock, Lancaster County, Pennsylvania, with eight-day movement, the dial signed "Geoe. Eby Manheim" above a reverse-painted panel.

Few examples of this form are known.

c1830   *40½in (103cm) high*

$25,000-32,000   **POOK**

CLOSER LOOK—NIGHT CLOCK

This clock is modeled as a Classical vase with lion's head handles and ormolu ornamentation, on a bronze plinth with a large ormolu starburst.

The dial is signed "Bofenschen à Paris," an expert clockmaker and inventor (fl.1780-1813), who worked alongside French horologist Abraham Louis Breguet (1747-1823).

It is an unusual piece, designed to be used both during the day and at night. The vase contains an oil reserve and wick that can be lit at night, which projects the time through an adjustable lens in the reverse.

Despite some wear and untested movement, the rarity of this night clock assures its value.

An early 19thC bronze and ormolu night clock, some scratches to lens, chips to enamel.

20in (51cm) high

$14,000-18,000   **DN**

A rare mid-19thC Black Forest Schild clock, with weight-driven movement, with triple automata and painted dial, with an architectural scene and three men with hammers for the bells.

12in (30.5cm) high

$3,800-4,400   **LSK**

A mid-19thC cast iron Turret clock, by Smith & Sons, St John's Square, Clerkenwell, London, with twin-winding barrels below eight cogs, some damages.

$1,500-1,900   **FLD**

A Black Forest carved wood clock, with Paris eight-day movement.

20in (51cm) wide

$4,400-5,000   **JN**

A Russian "Fabergé" model enamel urn-shaped clock, with Classical enamel portraits below a band with silvered dial, key pattern and scrolled feet.

6in (15cm) high

$3,200-3,800   **JN**

A rare French silver beehive clock, movement by Saudrais A. Nantes, the sides with applied bees, on claw feet.

5in (12.5cm) high

$1,900-2,500   **JN**

A Louis XVI blue porcelain and gilt-metal clock garniture, with eight-day movement, with candelabra.

clock 21in (53.5cm) high

$2,300-2,800   JN

An early 19thC Charles X rouge marble and bronze clock garniture, with eight-day bell-striking movement, with a pair of urns.

clock 20in (50.5cm) high

$1,600-2,000   L&T

A mid-19thC French ormolu and silvered metal clock garniture, with eight-day bell-striking movement, the case in Gothic Revival or troubadour style, with a pair of urns.

clock 19¾in (50cm) high

$1,900-2,500   DN

A Napoleon III Louis XVI-style gilt and patinated bronze clock garniture, by Barbedienne, with Japy Frères eight-day bell-striking drum movement, no.925, with candelabra.

clock 26½in (67.5cm) wide

$5,500-7,000   WW

A Napoleon III Louis XVI-style ormolu and patinated bronze figural clock garniture, by Brulfer, Paris, with eight-day bell-striking movement, with candlesticks.

clock 21¾in (55.5cm) high

$5,000-6,300   WW

A 19thC French ormolu and champlevé enamel mantel clock garniture, by Dufaud, Paris, with candlesticks.

clock 12in (30.5cm) high

$2,500-3,200   GWA

A 19thC French ormolu clock garniture, by Raingo Frères, Paris, with candelabra.

clock 17in (43cm) high

$3,200-3,800   JN

A 19thC French clock marble and ormolu garniture, signed "DROUARD, CALAIS," with candelabra.

clock 32in (81.5cm) high

$3,800-5,000   JN

A mid-to-late 19thC French porcelain Sèvres-style gilt-metal-mounted clock garniture, with eight-day two-train movement, painted with Watteauesque and landscape panels.

clock 24½in (62cm) high

$15,000-19,000   DN

A late 19thC gilt bronze and rouge griotte marble four-glass clock garniture, by Julien Leroy, Paris, with twin-train bell-striking movement, with Cupid-form candelabra.

clock 18in (46cm) high

$3,200-3,800   CA

A late 19thC German Dresden porcelain clock garniture, with brass eight-day striking drum movement, stamped "180248," with associated Berlin candelabra.

clock 23¾in (60.5cm) high

$2,800-3,500   WW

A French "Japonisme" ormolu, bronze, and cloisonné enamel clock garniture, movement no.20176, with cylinder escapement, regilt, hand missing, with candelabra. *c1890*

clock 15¾in (40cm) high

$3,800-5,000   BELL

A late 19thC French gilt bronze and marble clock garniture, after Clodion, with eight-day bell-striking movement, serial no.315872, with candelabra.

clock 15¼in (39cm) high

$4,400-5,000   L&T

A late 19thC gilt bronze and malachite mantel clock garniture, by Moreau, Paris, with twin-train bell-striking movement with outside countwheel, with candelabra.

clock 22½in (57cm) high

$13,000-16,000   CA

A late 19thC brass French mantel clock garniture, with twin-barrel gong-striking movement, with champlevé decoration and a porcelain panel in the style of Boucher, with two urns.

Champlevé is a decorative technique where hollows are made in a metal surface, then filled with coloured enamels.

clock 12¼in (31cm) high

$3,800-5,000   PW

A late 19thC to early 20thC French porcelain and gilt-brass clock garniture, with gong-striking movement, the dial marked "R. STEWART/PARIS," with porcelain urns.

clock 13½in (34.5cm) high

$1,600-2,300   L&T

An 18thC 30-hour striking wall clock, signed "Henry Baker, Malling," with four-posted movement with anchor escapement, with a later wall bracket.

c1750 *11in (28cm) high*

$1,300-1,800 **TEN**

A George III red japanned tavern timepiece, by John Dwerryhouse, London, with recoil anchor escapement, signed.

John Dwerryhouse is recorded as working at 23 Charles Street, Berkeley Square, from 1770 to 1805.

58¼in (148cm) high

$5,000-5,700 **WW**

A Massachusetts Federal lyre-form striking banjo timepiece, by Aaron Willard, Boston, with eight-day striking movement, neck panel replaced.

c1815 *38in (96.5cm) high*

$5,500-6,500 **POOK**

A late 18thC parcel-gilt and chinoiserie tavern timepiece, by William Buckland, Thame, with single-train movement with anchor escapement, some damages.

59in (150cm) high

$3,500-4,000 **BELL**

A Regency mahogany "Norfolk" drop-dial wall timepiece, by Matthew Read (1756-1826), Aylsham, England, with four-pillar movement with anchor escapement, some replacements.

c1820 *49¼in (125cm) high*

$950-1,050 **BELL**

ESSENTIAL REFERENCE—ACT OF PARLIAMENT CLOCKS

Wall clocks for taverns, inns, assembly rooms, and other public buildings were introduced in the 1720s.

- These tavern clocks had large dials, because they were designed to be seen clearly from a distance.
- They are often called Act of Parliament clocks, although this is something of a misnomer.
- In 1797, Prime Minister William Pitt the Younger passed an act introducing a five-shilling duty on clocks.
- The act was repealed a year later due to its negative effect on the clock industry, but it gave rise to the popular misconception that these clocks were put up in taverns for customers who could not afford to own one. In fact, most tavern clocks predate the act.

An Act of Parliament clock, by James Coates, Cirencester, England, with black japanned trunk, some splits to dial, dents and losses.

58in (147.5cm) high

$5,000-5,700 **GORL**

A mahogany wall clock, with eight-day bell-striking movement, the painted dial signed "Upjohn, Exeter."

The Upjohn family were a well-known and prolific family of clockmakers working in both Exeter and London. The Exeter branch of the family included William Upjohn (b.c1754), John Upjohn (b.1771), and his son Robert Wittingham Upjohn (b.1807), who took over from his father as keeper of the Exeter Cathedral clock.

47¼in (120cm) high

$2,500-3,200 **BE**

A Regency mahogany wall timepiece, by Handley and Moore, London, with four-pillar single-fusee movement, in a saltbox-type case, dial refinished, restoration to case.

George Handley and John Moore went into partnership after their former Master, John Thwaites, died in 1800. The business was continued as John Moore and Sons after the death of George Handley. The workshop was known for producing public clocks and supplying movements to other makers, and continued into the early years of the 20thC.

19in (48.5cm) high

$2,300-2,800 **DN**

A Viennese mahogany "Lanterndlur" wall timepiece, by Andreas Alzinger, Vienna, with one-month four-pillar movement with deadbeat escapement, some wear.

c1825 *45¼in (115cm) high*

$4,400-5,000 **DN**

A late Regency to William IV parcel-gilt faux rosewood world-time tavern timepiece, possibly East Anglian School, with four-pillar movement with anchor escapement, loose center panel, crack to trunk, decoration worn.

57½in (146cm) high

$3,800-4,400　　　　BELL

An early 19thC mahogany wall timepiece, by John Draper, Rochford, the brass movement with tapered plates and long pendulum.

45¼in (115cm) high

$2,300-2,800　　　　CHEF

A Viennese inlaid mahogany grande sonnerie Biedermeier wall clock, with four-pillar triple-train gong-striking movement with lenticular bob pendulum, some wear.

c1840　　　　43¼in (110cm) high

$1,800-2,300　　　　DN

An early Victorian mahogany drop-dial wall timepiece, Vulliamy, London, with four-pillar single-fusee movement with half-deadbeat escapement, numbered "1378," the dial signed, with crowned Royal "V.R." cipher, inscribed "POOR LAW COMMISSION," some wear.

This piece seems to have been supplied for use by The Poor Law Commission at Somerset House in c1837, shortly after Victoria had ascended the throne. The Poor Law Commission was a body established after the passing of the Poor Law Amendment Act 1834 to administer poor relief and tackle unemployment and homelessness, generally by placing those unable to provide for themselves in a workhouse.

c1836-37　　　　24in (61cm) high

$11,000-12,000　　　　DN

A Viennese mahogany and boxwood outlined wall regulator, "Dachluhr," by Peter Peuker, Wien, the movement with deadbeat escapement and Harrison's maintaining power.

c1845　　　　34in (86.5cm) high

$2,500-3,200　　　　BELL

A late 19thC Black Forest cuckoo clock, with two-train movement, paper label for Camerer, Kuss & Co., half the door detached, chips and cracks.

15¾in (40cm) high

$900-1,000　　　　BELL

A carved oak cuckoo clock, with eight-day double-fusee gong-striking movement, labeled "Camerer Cuss of 186, Uxbridge Road."

33½in (85cm) high

$2,300-2,800　　　　BE

A late 19thC to early 20thC American perpetual calendar wall clock, by the William L. Gilbert Clock Company.

33½in (85cm) high

$750-900　　　　APAR

A 20thC gold, diamond, and enamel strut clock, by Asprey, London, the engine-turned enamel dial with diamond-inset hands, signed, hallmarked for London.

4¼in (11cm) high

$7,000-7,500　　　　BE

WATCHES

A late 17thC pair-cased pocket watch, by Sam Drossade, London, with crown wheel and verge escapement, with a rotating blue steel disk with moon and sun, some denting and scratching.

This watch has been in a safe for at least 50 years and so is in very good condition for its age.

$9,000-10,000   ECGW

A fusee pocket watch, by Thomas Tompion, London, signed, numbered "4360," in copper case.

1709-13   *2in (5cm) diam 4oz*

$3,800-4,400   GWA

A pair-case pocket watch, by C. Cabrier, London, with verge movement, no.5829, gilt-metal case, some wear.

c1730   *1½in (3.5cm) diam*

$1,200-1,400   HAN

A mid-18thC French yellow metal and rock crystal cased pocket watch, by J.J. Bourdillat, Paris, with chain-driven verge fusee movement, with silver regulator dial.

1¾in (4.5cm) diam 1¾oz

$5,000-6,300   LSK

A George II gold pair-cased pocket watch, by James Chater, London, with single-fusee verge movement, later converted to lever escapement, the case repoussé decorated with "Roman Charity" scene, some dents.

James Chater Sr. was admitted to the Clockmakers' Company 1718, gaining his freedom in 1726. He died in 1762. The layout of the decoration on the outer case bears strong similarities to an example by Augustin Heckel, a German émigré working in London c1715-46.

c1739   *2in (5cm) diam*

$3,200-3,800   DN

A George II triple-cased verge pocket watch, for the Middle Eastern market, by Markwick, Markham, Perigal, London, with single-fusee verge movement with verge escapement and Tompion-type adjustment, marked "R.D." and "12988," in tortoiseshell outer case.

During the second half of the 18thC, the firm Markwick, Markham, Perigal specialized in producing clocks and watches for export to the Middle East. The firm was founded when James Marwick (Jr.) went into partnership with his son-in-law, Robert Markham. After Marwick's death in 1730, the business was continued by Markham and his successors, with Francis Perigal Sr. joining the business in c1750.

c1751   *2½in (6.5cm) diam*

$1,900-2,500   DN

A gold pair-cased open-faced pocket watch, with verge fusee movement, engraved "Jn. Mansfield, London," the back cover chased with the Choice of Hercules, minute hand missing, with leather case.

1762   *2in (5cm) diam 3⅜oz*

$2,300-2,800   DN

A Regency silver cylinder pocket watch, by John Roger Arnold, London, with gilt full-plate single-fusee movement with cylinder escapement with jeweled escape wheel pivots, numbered "3438," the case hallmarked "A.G." over "J.M.," some hairlines and dents.

John Roger Arnold (1769-1840) was the son of the renowned chronometer maker John Arnold. He was apprenticed in 1792 and gained his freedom by 1796. He became Master of the Clockmakers' Company in 1817 and later went into partnership with E.J. Dent.

c1814   *2¼in (5.5cm) diam*

$3,200-3,800   DN

A gold Continental skeletonized quarter repeater Jacquemart automaton pocket watch, with verge movement, some wear, automata mechanism missing.

c1820   *2¼in (5.5cm) wide 4⅜oz*

$4,400-5,000   TEN

An early 19thC Swiss automaton repeater striking pocket watch, with blue enamel and gold crescent moon.

2¼in (5.5cm) diam

$2,500-3,200 HANN

An early 19thC Swiss gold- and enamel-cased fob watch, by G. Henry Valentin, with keywind chain-driven verge fusee movement, the back enamelled.

1½in (4cm) diam 1¾oz

$3,800-5,000 LSK

A pair-case silver pocket watch, with fusee and chain movement with verge escapement, hallmarked London, wear to movement, dent to case.

1847   2¼in (5.5cm) diam

$450-500 FELL

A Victorian lady's black enameled key-wind open-faced fob watch, with gilt cylinder movement, the inner case with "Pigot a Geneve, No 915," movement not working, some damage to case.

1½in (4cm) diam 1⅜oz

$500-550 BELL

A 19thC Swiss gold open faced key-wind musical/repeater pocket watch.

2¼in (6cm) diam 4⅛oz

$3,200-3,800 FLD

A 19thC 18ct gold top-wind fob watch, with enameled case back, signed "ΛLTENLOH Λ BRUXELLES," lacking suspensory loop.

1oz

$700-800 AST

A late 19thC Mensor double-sided open-faced chronograph tachymeter pocket watch.

2¼in (5.5cm) diam

$700-800 LOCK

An 18ct hallmarked half-hunter crown wing pocket watch, by W. Rogers, Liverpool and London.

1888   4⅝oz

$1,900-2,500 FLD

A late 19thC lapis lazuli cased watch, possibly by Hermann Böhm, with verge fusee movement and disk-type regulator, movement not functioning, some wear.

1½in (3.5cm) wide

c1890

$1,300-1,800 DN

An 18ct gold keyless wind half-hunter pocket watch, with three-quarter plate movement and lever escapement, no.30207, engraved "R.C. Oldfield Liverpool," with presentation inscription, hallmarked London, some hairlines.
1891
2in (5cm) diam 3⅞oz
$1,500-2,000   **DN**

An 18ct gold full-hunter pocket watch, by Waltham Mass, with lever movement with bimetallic balance, blued overcoil hairspring, no. "6028383," with presentation inscription, stamped "ROY 18k U.S Assay" and "147224," some scratches, loose glass.

This pocket watch was presented to Captain John Ramsay Gordon from the President of the United States of America for saving lives from a stricken ship of the American Schooner "Frank O Dame" at sea on October 12, 1896.
2in (5cm) diam 3½oz
$3,800-4,400   **TEN**

An 18ct hallmarked open-faced crown wing chronograph pocket watch, by Thomas Russell & Son, Liverpool and Chester.
1897
5oz
$1,800-2,300   **FLD**

A gentleman's 18ct gold-cased open-faced pocket watch, the movement signed "John Bull & Co. 49 High Street Bedford no.28550," hallmarked London.
1897
3⅞oz
$1,500-2,000   **LOCK**

A Cartier diamond-set platinum and rock crystal pendant fob watch, with keyless-wind movement with club-tooth lever escapement, signed to dial, suspending from a bar brooch pin, the bezel initialed "F.J.," French control mark, numbered "9020," with fitted case.
c1915
1½in (4cm) wide
$21,000-25,000   **WW**

An Art Deco lady's Cartier gold and enamel pendant watch, the movement signed "European Clock and Watch Company," dial signed "Cartier" and "Bte S.G.D.E," the gold case with red and black enamel, with a fixed gold and enamel hoop with attached jade rings.
1in (2.5cm) diam
$9,000-10,000   **BOUR**

An 18ct gold top-wind half-hunter pocket watch, the balance cock with diamond end stone, the backplate engraved "The Field," the dial inscribed "J.W. Benson," London.
1920
$1,500-2,000   **HT**

A George V gentleman's 9ct gold-cased half-hunter pocket watch, with 17-jewel keyless movement, the backplate numbered "240627," on a 18ct gold curblink watch chain, on a 9ct gold pendant.
5¾oz
$3,200-3,800   **LSK**

A 9ct gold Waltham USA pocket watch, with 15-jewel movement with damascened plates and lever escapement, numbered "24043334," signed, the case numbered "813385" hallmarked Birmingham, with 9ct Albert chain.
1925
1⅝oz
$1,300-1,800   **ECGW**

A gentleman's Rolex Prince wristwatch, reference no.1490, serial no.28184, with signed manual wind movement, yellow metal case stamped "14k," some wear.

c1926   *1in (2.5cm) high*

$4,000-4,800   **FELL**

A gentleman's Rolex Prince wristwatch, reference no.1490, serial no.07709, with signed manual wind movement, numbered "72210," silver case hallmarked Glasgow, some wear.

1930   *1in (2.5cm) high*

$3,800-5,000   **FELL**

A 1950s gentleman's Rolex Shock Resisting 9ct gold wristwatch, on later 9ct bracelet.

          1¼in (3cm) diam

$1,400-1,800   **HAN**

A Rolex Oyster Perpetual 18ct gold wristwatch, ref.6564, no.385054, with 25-jewel automatic movement, adjusted to five positions and temperature, cal.1030, no.N674293, on a crocodile strap, light wear.

c1958   *1½in (3.5cm) diam*

$3,200-3,800   **DN**

CLOSER LOOK—ROLEX WRISTWATCH

The Rolex Oyster Perpetual Submariner is a desirable model, made famous by being worn by James Bond in the early Bond movies.

It was purchased from A.V. Hewitt in Amersham on November 5, 1965, and is accompanied by its original documentation.

This is a rare variant with orange numerals on the dial.

The watch is in excellent original condition.

A Rolex wristwatch, model no.1023420, serial no.1029/6636, with box.

The sale of this watch made the British auction record for a Rolex Submariner.

$380,000-440,000   **LOCK**

A 1970s gentleman's Rolex Oysterquartz Day-Date wristwatch, model no.19018, ref.6123446, with 18ct gold case and Rolex President bracelet.

          1½in (3.5cm) wide

$5,500-6,500   **BRI**

A gentleman's Rolex Oyster Perpetual GMT-Master bracelet watch, reference no.1675, serial no.3386008, signed automatic caliber 1570, with a signed stainless steel Oyster bracelet with Oysterclasp, with box and papers.

c1973   *1½in (4cm) diam*

$16,000-23,000   **FELL**

A lady's Rolex Oyster Perpetual Datejust bracelet watch, ref.6927, serial no.7563936, signed automatic caliber 2030, with mother-of-pearl dial, with 18ct yellow gold case and President bracelet with folding Crownclasp, some scratches.

c1983   *1in (2.5cm) diam*

$4,400-5,000   **FELL**

A Rolex Oyster Perpetual Day-Date 18ct gold wristwatch, model no.16613, serial no.Z348177, the dial with diamond numerals, integral President 18ct gold bracelet, with two Rolex pouches, minor wear.

          dial 1¼in (3cm) diam

$16,000-23,000   **HAN**

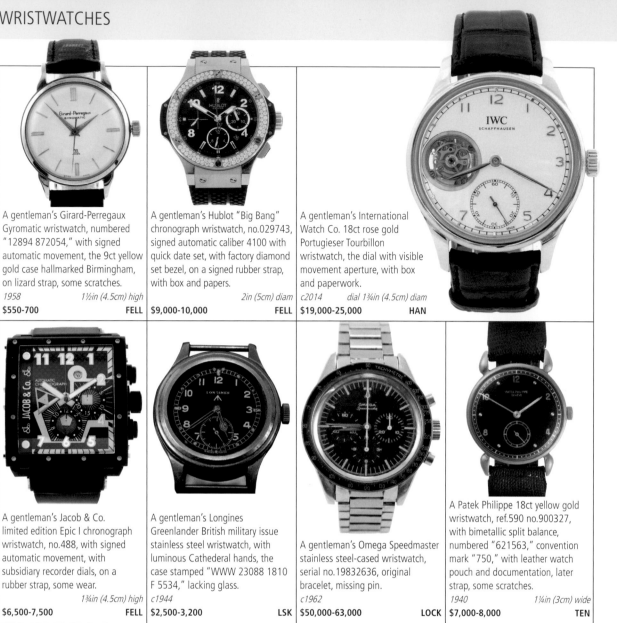

A gentleman's Girard-Perregaux Gyromatic wristwatch, numbered "12894 872054," with signed automatic movement, the 9ct yellow gold case hallmarked Birmingham, on lizard strap, some scratches.

1958   *1½in (4.5cm) high*
$550-700   **FELL**

A gentleman's Hublot "Big Bang" chronograph wristwatch, no.029743, signed automatic caliber 4100 with quick date set, with factory diamond set bezel, on a signed rubber strap, with box and papers.

2in (5cm) diam
$9,000-10,000   **FELL**

A gentleman's International Watch Co. 18ct rose gold Portugieser Tourbillon wristwatch, the dial with visible movement aperture, with box and paperwork.

c2014   dial 1¾in (4.5cm) diam
$19,000-25,000   **HAN**

A gentleman's Jacob & Co. limited edition Epic I chronograph wristwatch, no.488, with signed automatic movement, with subsidiary recorder dials, on a rubber strap, some wear.

1¾in (4.5cm) high
$6,500-7,500   **FELL**

A gentleman's Longines Greenlander British military issue stainless steel wristwatch, with luminous Cathederal hands, the case stamped "WWW 23088 1810 F 5534," lacking glass.

c1944
$2,500-3,200   **LSK**

A gentleman's Omega Speedmaster stainless steel-cased wristwatch, serial no.19832636, original bracelet, missing pin.

c1962
$50,000-63,000   **LOCK**

A Patek Philippe 18ct yellow gold wristwatch, ref.590 no.900327, with bimetallic split balance, numbered "621563," convention mark "750," with leather watch pouch and documentation, later strap, some scratches.

1940   1¼in (3cm) wide
$7,000-8,000   **TEN**

An 18ct gold automatic calendar wristwatch, signed "Universal, Geneve," the cloisonné dial depicting Saudi Arabia, signed and numbered "1666757 100105 3," with convention mark "18k0.750," some wear.

This watch was made to commemorate the forming of Saudi Arabia by King Abdul Al Aziz. Polychrome enamel dials are extremely rare and are usually made to commemorate events or special limited edition series.

c1953   1½in (3.5cm) wide
$7,500-9,000   **TEN**

A gentleman's Vacheron Constantin 18ct gold World Time wristwatch, with box and paperwork, light wear.

c2016   dial 1½in (4cm) diam
$15,000-19,000   **HAN**

A George III mahogany bayonet-tube mercury stick barometer, by Nairne and Blunt, London, with signed vernier scale and spirit thermometer, some wear.

Edward Nairne (1726-1806) and his former apprentice Thomas Blunt (d.1822) collaborated from 1774 until 1793.

c1780   38in (96.5cm) high
$5,000-6,300   DN

A George III mahogany stick barometer, by Cary, London, signed to dial, with vernier scale, light tarnishing.

38¼in (97cm) high
$1,500-2,000   BELL

A Regency mahogany mercury stick barometer, by Alexander Adie, Edinburgh, with brass vernier adjustment screw and signed vernier scale, probably for use in a lighthouse.

Alexander Adie (1774-1858) was apprenticed to his uncle, the eminent Scottish instrument maker John Miller, in 1789. In 1804, Miller and Adie went into partnership after Miller's death in 1815. Adie was particularly interested in meteorological instruments and is perhaps best known as the inventor of the Sympiesometer in 1818. He later took his son into partnership in 1835.

37¼in (94.5cm) high
$4,400-5,000   DN

A George III mahogany cistern tube stick barometer, by Benjamin Martin, London, with hygrometer, and Fahrenheit and Reaumur mercury thermometer, signed.

Benjamin Martin (fl.1756-82) was a prolific writer on the subjects of science, art, and instruments, and launched the monthly "General Magazine of the Arts and Sciences" in 1755. He is thought to have been the first maker to incorporate a hygrometer into a barometer with thermometer and marketed the instrument as a "Triple Weather Glass."

c1760   36½in (93cm) high
$5,000-6,300   DN

A Regency brass-mounted mahogany stick barometer, with silvered hydrometer, signed vernier scale, and Fahrenheit scale mercury tube thermometer, some discolouration.

This barometer is almost certainly by Robert Brettell Bate, who operated in London c1808-47. Bate was celebrated for his nautical instruments including marine barometers and was appointed as "Instrument-maker to Her Majesty's Honourable Boards of Excise and Customs."

c1815   43¾in (111cm) high
$4,400-5,000   DN

A mahogany bowfront stick barometer, by Watkins & Hill, with concealed mercury tube and vernier dial, some cracks, screw missing.

Watkins & Hill are recorded as working at Charing Cross London between 1819-57.

c1830   38½in (98cm) high
$3,200-3,800   TEN

A rosewood bowfront stick barometer, by Alexander Adie & Son, Edinburgh, with pressure vernier dial, signed, crack to pediment, finial loose, vernier knob missing.

c1835-45   41¾in (106cm) high
$5,500-7,000   FELL

A mahogany bowfront stick barometer, with mercury tube, vernier dial, and thermometer box, signed "Dollond, London," some cracks to veneer.

The Dollond family of scientific instrument makers began with Peter Dollond in 1750 and continued until the firm's acquisition by Aitchison in 1913. This barometer would have been made by George Dollond (1774-1856), who continued the business after the death of his uncle, Peter, in 1820. George was instrument-maker to both William IV and Queen Victoria.

c1840   38½in (98cm) high
$2,800-3,500   TEN

A George III mahogany wheel barometer and timepiece, by James Gatty and George Jamison, London, with hydrometer, Fahrenheit scale mercury thermometer, level, and timepiece with eight-day four-pillar single-fusee movement, signed, in triple-strung rosewood crossbanded case.

James Gatty worked in London as a maker of barometers in the late 18thC to early 19thC. He is one of the most sought-after makers of early wheel barometers. George Jamison was a watchmaker and clockmaker working in London and Portsmouth 1786-1810, known for his chronometers and his complex spherical skeleton clocks.

46in (117cm) high

$4,400-5,700   **DN**

A George III inlaid mahogany mercury wheel barometer, by James Gatty, London, with hygrometer, mercury thermometer, spirit level, signed, some repairs and replacements.

c1800   *38¼in (97cm) high*

$1,900-2,500   **DN**

A Louis XV ormolu-mounted kingwood barometer, by Lange de Bourbon, with a wheel barometer and thermometer.

Lange de Bourbon (fl.1750-75) was a notable maker of clocks and barometers, awarded the title of "Machiniste-Faiseur de Baromètre du Roi" before 1757. The form of this barometer, attributed to Claude-Joseph Desgodets, exists in a number of examples by important makers.

c1760   *45½in (115.5cm) high*

$21,000-25,000   **FRE**

A mahogany barometer, by John Hargraves and Thomas Tatham, with quadrant-form semicircular scale, concealed mercury tube, signed and dated.

Similar examples have been found signed "Thomas Hargraves of Settle," possibly a relation of John Hargraves. They must have been working in Settle around the same time, and producing unusual barometers, possibly in the same workplace.

1830   *40¼in (102cm) high*

$3,500-4,000   **TEN**

A Regency mahogany wheel barometer, by John Russell, Falkirk, Scotland, with thermometer scale, barometric pressure dial and lower eglomisé panel.

18½in (47cm) high

$15,000-19,000   **SK**

An Edwardian 15ct gold-cased aneroid pocket barometer and altimeter scale, by Ross, London, inscribed "ROB'T EMMET. MORETON MORRELL, WARWICK, ENG.," hallmarked Chester, England, some wear.

The inscription relates to Robert Emmet, a wealthy American-born banker of Irish heritage born in New York in 1872. He later moved to Warwickshire, England, where he built a substantial re-creation of an Elizabethan manor house called Moreton Paddox at Moreton Morrell.

1907   *2in (5cm) diam*

$750-900   **DN**

CLOSER LOOK—HENRY PYEFINCH BAROMETER

It consists of an angled mercury tube, a thermometer tube, a register dial, and center hygrometer dial.

The center shows a printed "Perpetual Regulation of Time" dial, with apertures for the equation of days of the month, sun rises and sun sets, feast days, Zodiac signs, and high water at London Bridge.

The instruments are housed within a mahogany case with an architectural pediment and turned brass finials.

It is in need of restoration, with a broken thermometer, a cracked mercury tube, and losses on the dial—but the rarity and unusual form of this barometer make it a valuable piece.

A mahogany angle barometer, by H. Pyefinch, in need of restoration.

Henry Pyefinch (fl.1763-90) was an instrument maker based in London. In 1765, in conjunction with Portuguese scientist J.H. de Magellan, he patented an instrument to measure the effect of the weight of the atmosphere and the variations caused by heat and cold.

c1765   *43in (109cm) high*

$15,000-19,000   **TEN**

A barograph, by Negretti & Zambra, London, the clockwork drum mounted on lacquered brass bedplate with signed maker's plate, the atmosphere drums acting on counterweighted pen arm.

A barograph is a barometer used for recording barometric pressure over time by marking changes in atmospheric pressure on a paper chart.

c1920   *19in (48cm) wide*

$2,300-3,000   **CM**

A George III pocket globe, by J. Newton, London, applied with 12 hand-colored printed gores and two polar calottes, in a fishskin case, some damages and losses.

1782 *3in (7.5cm) diam*

$15,000-19,000 **DN**

A George III pocket celestial globe, by John & William Cary, with 12 hand-colored printed gores, marked "NEW CELESTIAL GLOBE by J & W Cary, Strand," with a shagreen case.

3in (7.5cm) diam

$7,500-9,000 **TEN**

A Gilbert and Sons pocket globe, the case decorated with signs of the Zodiac, dated.

1807 *3in (7.5cm) diam*

$3,800-4,400 **PW**

A Regency library table globe, by G. & J. Cary, London, the sphere applied with 12 colored printed gores, trade label "CARY'S, NEW SIX INCH, TERRESTRIAL GLOBE, DRAWN, from the latest AUTHORITIES., London Published by G. & J.Cary, January I, 1824," stand reglued.

1825 *10in (25.5cm) high*

$6,500-7,500 **DN**

A Newton's "New and Improved Terrestrial Table Globe," on a wood stand, split to globe, some surface wear.

12in (30.5cm) diam

$2,500-3,200 **CHOR**

A pair of early Victorian terrestrial and celestial globe, on mahogany stands, labeled "Newton's New and Improved Celestial/Terrestrial globe, manufactured by Newton & Son, Chancery Lane, London," stand engraved "published 1st January 1844."

Founded in 1780 by John Newton, the firm of Newton & Son went on to be among the leading manufacturers of fine globes in the 19thC.

c1844 *globes 12in (30.5cm) diam*

$28,000-33,000 **CHOR**

A Victorian terrestrial library globe, by Cruchley, with 12 gores, inscribed "CRUCHLEY'S NEW TERRESTRIAL GLOBE From the most recent Authorities EXHIBITING THE DISCOVERIES IN EQUATORIAL AFRICA, NORTH POLE, And the new Settlements & Divisions of AUSTRALIA, NEW ZEALAND, CALIFORNIA, TEXAS & c. LONDON G.F. CRUCHLEY MAP SELLER, GLOBE MAKER & PUBLISHER, 81 FLEET STREET," on a mahogany stand, dated.

1869 *36½in (92.5cm) high*

$6,500-7,500 **WW**

A mid-19thC Terrestrial Globe, by J.G. Klinger, Nuremberg, with 12 colored gores and brass pins at the pole, inscribed "The Earth," in original case.

2¼in (6cm) diam

$2,300-2,800 **TEN**

A Kelvin Hughes star globe, set within lacquered brass horizon and meridian rings, in a mahogany case.

1975 *10¾in (27cm) wide*

$550-700 **BELL**

CLOSER LOOK—VARIABLE MICROSCOPE

It comes with a Martin lens, five Lieberkuhn lenses, two high-power lenses, five button-type objective lenses, and a collar for combining objectives to make compound objectives.

As variable microscopes are complex and were not always well-constructed, it is rare to find one in such good condition.

This microscope is signed "Ann and George Adams," referring to the wife and son of George Adams Sr. (c1709-73); Ann Adams and George Adams Jr. (1750-95) traded under this name (1773-75) until George completed his apprenticeship. It is rare to for an instrument of this period to be signed by a woman.

A variable microscope can be used as a simple microscope using just one lens, or as a compound microscope, using many lenses. These were rare in the 18thC, due to their expense.

An Adams variable microscope.
c1773

$140,000-180,000   **FLIN**

A mid-to-late 18thC ptolemaic armillary sphere, probably Italian, with an axis with sun and moon orbits within armillary universe, on a pinewood figure of Atlas, holding articulated models of Saturn and Jupiter, on a Corinthian column.

The number of moons depicted is interesting. Saturn was thought to have five moons between 1684 (when Cassini discovered the fifth) and 1789, when Herschel found two more. Jupiter's four moons were all discovered by Galileo in 1609-10, with no more being found until 1892.

63in (160cm) high

$13,000-18,000   **CM**

A Cuff-type brass microscope, with plano mirror, screw focusing, and brass tilting stand, some repairs, in mahogany case.
c1780

$3,200-3,800   **TEN**

A brass-cased astronomical telescope, by Broadhurst Clarkson & Co., the lens with a two draw eyepiece, stamped "ADVANCED STARBOY, BROADHURST CLARKSON & CO.," in a wood box, with folding tripod stand.
50in (127cm) long

$1,000-1,150   **WW**

An astronomical refracting telescope, by T. Cooke & Sons Ltd., London and York, the main tube with star finder and eyepiece, signed, with original pine box, with performance statement, tripod and accessories.
84in (213.5cm) high

$3,200-3,800   **CM**

A mid-17thC English brass Gunter-pattern horary quadrant, with twin pinhole sight vanes, the apex pierced with a hole for plumb line and engraved with a shadow square annotated 1-10 in both directions and divided into fifths, with a sector arranged as a quarter of an astrolabe for a fixed latitude showing the sky projection between equator and tropics.

Edmund Gunter was born in Hertfordshire in 1581 and studied at Oxford 1600-03, during which time he developed his interest in mathematics and started designing his own instruments. In 1615, he took holy orders. In 1620, he became professor of astronomy at Gresham College. In 1623, he published his work "De Sectore et Radio or The Description and Use of the Sector, the Cross-staffe and other instruments," which included the design of quadrant on which this piece is closely based.

4in (10cm) wide

$2,500-3,800   **DN**

A noon-day cannon dial, probably French, the marble base incised with sundial and latitude 46:50, with lacquered brass fittings.
c1880   *6in (15cm) high*

$1,600-2,300   **CM**

An Edwardian 9ct gold opisometer or map measuring tool, combined with a compass doubling as a magnifying glass, hallmarked for J.C. Vickery, London, in original case.
1908   *3½in (9cm) long 2¼oz*

$1,900-2,500   **MART**

A brass-bound mahogany-cased two-day marine chronometer, by Parkinson & Frodsham, London, no.456, with chain fusee movement with cylindrical ring-turned pillars, with Earnshaw spring detent escapement.

Parkinson & Frodsham was established in 1801 by William James Frodsham (1778-1850) and William Parkinson (d.1842). Their business continued throughout the 19thC at Change Alley, supplying chronometers to the Admiralty and to shipping lines.

c1825   5in (13cm) long
$5,500-6,500   **BELL**

An early 19thC mahogany-cased marine chronometer, by William Cozens, London, no.104, with chain-driven fusee movement, in gimbaled lacquered brass case.

6½in (16.5cm) wide
$3,800-5,000   **LSK**

A two-day brass marine chronometer, the movement with Earnshaw escapement, the dial inscribed "Thomas Adams, Maker to H.R.H. PRINCE ALBERT, 36 Lombard St. London, 3132."

c1860   7in (18cm) wide
$2,500-3,800   **CM**

A brass bound rosewood two-day Royal Observatory Marine Chronometer, by Charles Frodsham, London, no.3169, with signed chain fusee movement with Earnshaw detent escapement, cut bimetallic compensated balance with Airy's bar and Rokeby's side-winding mechanism, engraved with Government arrow.

The Royal Observatory records show that this chronometer was issued to seven HM ships across the late 19thC and early 20thC, before being transferred to the Australian Government in 1921.

c1880-84   7½in (19cm) square
$13,000-18,000   **BELL**

A 19thC rosewood-cased marine chronometer, by Thomas Charles Tidmas, London, no.6576, with chain-driven fusee movement, the case with plaque "Sold by A Baharie, Lawrence Street, Sunderland" and paper label for "George Gowland, Liverpool."

7in (17.5cm) wide
$5,000-6,300   **LSK**

A late 19thC brass-mounted mahogany 2½ days ship's marine chronometer, by John Fletcher, London, no.2130, with silvered metal plaque inscribed "Cork," restored split to top.

7in (17.5cm) wide
$2,500-3,200   **GORL**

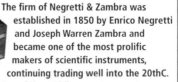

A late 19thC mahogany-cased two-day marine chronometer, by Negretti and Zambra, London, the circular four-pillar single-chain fusee movement with Harrison's maintaining power, Earnshaw-type spring detent escapement, fitted with electrical wiring posts.

The firm of Negretti & Zambra was established in 1850 by Enrico Negretti and Joseph Warren Zambra and became one of the most prolific makers of scientific instruments, continuing trading well into the 20thC. The design of the middle-error temperature compensation to the balance of the present timepiece was developed by Swedish Victor Kullberg, who set up in London c1851 and became one of the finest makers of marine chronometers of the later 19thC.

7in (18cm) wide
$2,500-3,200   **DN**

A two-day Kaisermarine chronometer, by W.G. Ehrlich, Bremerhaven, no.451, the movement with Earnshaw escapement, Uhrig-type balance, and helical balance spring with jeweled detent, with a bowl engraved with Kaisermaine crown and "M," top lid of box missing.

c1886   7½in (19cm) wide
$2,500-3,800   **CM**

A George III mahogany and brass Hadley's navigational octant, possibly by George Adams Sr., London, with inset engraved boxwood diagonal scale divided into 20 arcminutes, with pinhole sight, index arm, and hinged filters.

In 1760, George Adams Sr. was appointed as Mathematical Instrument Maker to King George III, for whom he supplied a vast range of apparatus. A near identical instrument attributed to Adams is illustrated in J.A. Bennett, "The Divided Circle," page 132.

c1770   *8¼in (21cm) long*
$1,800-2,500   **DN**

A vernier octant, by Christopher Johnson, the ivory scale divided to 95 degrees, with brass index arm, pinhole sight, note plate, and pin feet, missing shades, mirrors replaced, dated.

1796   *15½in (39.5cm) radius*
$1,300-1,900   **CM**

A whaling octant, probably by David White Laird, Leith, the ivory scale divided to 100 degrees and stamped "WH" by 50 degrees, the index arm inscribed "James Clark/First Mate Whaling Barque "North of Scotland"/of Peterhead; died at NORTH GREENLAND,/26th July, 1847," pinhole sights, three shades, mirrors and feet, some losses.

The "North of Scotland" was a 297-ton whaling barque built at Sunderland in 1845. It seems James Clark died en route from Iceland on the July 26, 1847, at 46 years old. This octant, with little sign of use, was probably presented to his widow by the owners. It is unknown who the scale divider "WH" is. Only one other similar example exists, which is held by the National Museum of Scotland in Edinburgh, with a maker's label for David White Laird, Leith (fl.1834-51).

c1847   *10½in (26.5cm) radius*
$1,000-1,500   **CM**

A shagreen and card three-draw telescope, by Dollond, London, with polished brass mounts, signed, with dust slides.

c1780   *closed 10½in (26.5cm) long*
$900-1,000   **CM**

A late 18thC Italian card and vellum eight-draw telescope, with turned ivory dividers, with original lenses, the main tube covered in shark skin.

closed 17in (43cm) long
$4,400-5,000   **CM**

A marine telescope, by Carl Zeiss, Jena, the lens numbered "274," the main lens housing Apochromat N2 274, splash cuff, tapered leather-covered main tube, and dust slide, within lined leather tube.

The telescope is believed to have been owned by Grand Admiral Karl Dönitz (1891-1980), who succeeded Erich Raeder as Commander-in-Chief of the Kriegsmarine on January 30, 1943. He quickly developed the infamous "wolf packs" of submarines used to persecute allied convoys. After Hitler's suicide on April 30, 1945, Dönitz was, briefly, chancellor of the crumbling Reich until the arrest of the Flensburg Government on May 23. This telescope may have been given to Dönitz when he was commissioned as an acting sublieutenant in 1913.

c1900-06   *closed 13in (33cm) long*
$2,100-2,500   **CM**

ESSENTIAL REFERENCE—TRACTION TORPEDO

A. Légé & Co. were a firm of scientific instrument makers based in Hatton Garden, London. The idea behind the Traction Torpedo was that several would be hitched to an endless chain within the confines of a harbor or secure area. When not in use, they would settle harmlessly on the seabed, but when needed, the chain was started and the torpedoes rose and "patrolled" the harbor. The accompanying research refers to one other example made of "Delta Metal," which was supposed to be resistant to seawater. Because this one appears to be brass, it may be a working prototype used as a sales pitch to Governments. Their rarity suggests that this complicated and dangerous system was never deployed, perhaps unsurprisingly when the risk to the users' own ships was greater than that of their enemies.

A pair of 7 x 50 Kriegsmarine U-boat binoculars, by Leitz, stamped "BEH" and "459822," with rubberized eyepiece caps, maker's code, and Kriegsmarine mark, dated, in original case.

1944   *10in (25.5cm) high*
$1,800-2,500   **CM**

A Kriegsmarine U-boat brass clock, the dial marked and numbered "15953," with going-barrel movement, backstamped "16725."

8in (20cm) wide
$5,500-6,500   **CM**

A rare A. Légé & Co. patent "traction torpedo," London, constructed in brass panels with adjustable side planes and tail fins, split ballast keel, and explosive plunger.

c1886   *60in (152.5cm) long*
$7,000-7,500   **CM**

Judith Picks

Scrimshaw pieces always need to be examined carefully. There are a lot of fakes on the market, and only about 30 percent of those I see are actually genuine. Look out for later resin reproductions. Be wary of pieces that seem too perfect, that note the name of the ship and the date, because genuine examples with this information are rare. If it seems too good to be true, it probably is.

A sailorwork scrimshaw whale tooth, incised and carved with a whaleboat and school of whales.

c1840   5¾in (14.5cm) high 8¾oz

$650-750   **CM**

A scrimshaw whale's tooth depicting the S.S. "Great Britain."

5in (13cm) high

$550-700   **CM**

A female figurehead, carved from laminated wood with polychrome finish, on base with two thole pins.

c1860   54in (137cm) high

$15,000-19,000   **CM**

A 19thC carved laminated yellow pine figurehead, possibly of Amerigo Vespucci, on an ebonized plinth.

without plinth 59in (150cm) high

$1,900-2,500   **CM**

A late 19thC figurehead, probably from a private steam yacht, modeled as a young lady clutching a flower, restoration to terminus.

64in (162.5cm) high

$25,000-32,000   **CM**

A bell from the Cunard liner R.M.S. "Lucania."

One of a famous pair of late Victorian Cunarders, "Lucania" was built by Fairfield's at Glasgow and launched in 1893. She took the Blue Riband for the fastest Atlantic crossing one month after her maiden voyage. "Lucania's" career was brought to an abrupt end when she caught fire in Liverpool in 1909.

1893   10in (25.5cm) high

$7,500-9,000   **CM**

A brass ship's bell from HMS "Hurst," inscribed with the ship's name, with later threaded suspension loop.

The success of chartered pleasure steamers as minesweepers and submarine hunters in WWI inspired the Admiralty to design and build their own. Hurst was a "Racecourse" Class paddle minesweeper built under the "Emergency War Programme" by Dunlop, Bremner & Co. Also known as the "Ascot" Class, 32 were built. They were lightly armed and manned by a crew of 50. HMS "Hurst" was broken up in 1922.

1916   14in (35.5cm) high

$1,050-1,200   **CM**

A brass and oak mounted model cannon, set on wood from HMS "Victory," the hallmarked silver plaque detailed "H.M.S Victory, piece of one of the planks on which Lord Nelson fell, given to M.L.G on board during repairs to quarter deck."

It is not uncommon to find pieces that are reputedly from the HMS "Victory." Most are worth little, because most are not from the HMS "Victory."This item, deemed genuine by trade and collectors alike, is much more valuable.

6in (15.5cm) wide

$5,000-6,300   **BELL**

A 12-bolt diving helmet, by Siebe Gorman & Co. Ltd., no.19342, with spring return valve telephone port, exhaust, fitted internally with chin buzzer and telephone speaker, finished with remnant tinning.

19in (48.5cm) high

$5,000-6,300   **CM**

A Union Flag, landed with the 3rd Canadian Division at Juno Beach, D-Day, June 6, 1944, carried by "P" Commando Sublieutenant. Alan Dalton R.N., the canvas sleeve stenciled "3YD JACR[?]," some wear.

Sir Alan Dalton C.B.E. D.L. (1923-2006) joined the Royal Navy in April 1943. In September 1943 he was posted to "P" Commando and trained with Force "J" for operation Neptune (the naval element of the Normandy landings). On D-Day, the unit was landed just before 7:30 a.m. and Dalton guided this division of 14,000 men across the beachhead carrying this flag.

68½in (174cm) wide

$48,000-57,000   **CM**

MUSIC BOXES

An early part overture musical box, by Henri Joseph Lecoultre, no.224, exposed controls, playing four airs, professional restoration, with walnut case.

c1826 *12¼in (31cm) wide*

$5,500-6,500 **APAR**

A mid-19thC rosewood key wind musical box, by Nicole Frères, the brass cylinder playing eight operatic airs with original tune sheet, no.32011.

Nicole Frères was established in Geneva, Switzerland, in 1814. The firm made music boxes of an exceptionally high quality, which are highly sought after today.

20½in (52cm) wide

$1,300-1,800 **CHOR**

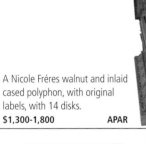

A Nicole Fréres walnut and inlaid cased polyphon, with original labels, with 14 disks.

$1,300-1,800 **APAR**

A late 19thC Swiss amboyna-cased cylinder music box, with change/repeat and stop/start, with six cylinders.

21¼in (54cm) wide

$2,300-2,800 **BELL**

A late 19thC Swiss burr walnut cylinder music box, playing eight airs, with Asian figures drumming on six bells.

case 21¼in (54cm) wide

$2,800-3,500 **BELL**

A late 19thC Swiss marquetry rosewood cylinder music box, six bells with Chinaman drummer and dancing ballerina, imperfection to case.

32in (81.5cm) wide

$2,800-3,500 **POOK**

A 19thC rosewood musical box and matching stand, by Nicole Frères, Geneva, the movement with brass bedplate with twin combs playing six airs on seven cylinders, plus six cylinders and three tune sheets.

box 37in (94cm) wide

$15,000-19,000 **CHOR**

A 19thC German symphonium, in a walnut case, the cover depicting a dancing couple.

18in (46cm) wide

$1,050-1,200 **WM**

A Victorian penny-in-the-slot Sirion polyphon, with 30 disks each playing two tunes, some cracks and chips.

discs 22¾in (57.5cm) diam

$11,000-15,000 **UNI**

A 19thC Swiss rosewood musical box with clock, retailed by Keith Prowse & Co., London, playing ten airs with nine bells, the clock dial, with eight-day bell-striking movement.

28in (71cm) wide

$7,000-8,000   **WW**

A late 19thC Symphonion Rococo walnut disk musical box, with harmony comb arrangement, with 44 disks.

19in (48cm) wide

$2,500-3,200   **SWO**

A late 19thC Mermod Frères rosewood and inlaid 12-air musical box, with cylinder and three pairs of bells, with a Mandarin striking them, with patent number plaque.

25½in (65cm) wide

$1,800-2,300   **APAR**

A bells-in-view musical box, playing ten airs with tune card, in crossbanded rosewood case inlaid with musical instruments on the top and front.

23½in (60cm) wide

$2,500-3,200   **FLD**

A late 19thC probably Swiss tortoiseshell-cased singing bird box, in fitted leather box, split on one corner.

4in (10cm) wide

$2,500-3,200   **APAR**

A late 19thC to early 20thC Swiss tortoiseshell musical singing bird box, retailed by Finnigans, New Bond Street, London, inscribed "TO SARAH FROM Mary + Douglas," the back with a hinged compartment possibly for snuff.

4in (10cm) wide

$2,300-2,800   **WW**

A German silver singing bird box, by Karl Griesbaum, with key.

c1925   *4in (10cm) wide*

$1,900-2,500   **SWO**

A Continental silver bird automaton musical box, in the manner of Karl Griersbaum, stamped "925 Sterling" and "EB," some damages.

4in (10cm) long

$2,500-3,200   **FLD**

A Patek Philippe tortoiseshell, gold, and enamel singing bird music box, several chips, lacking winder, case broken at hinges.

Patek Philippe was founded in Geneva, Switzerland, in 1839. Today, it remains an independent, family-owned watch manufacturer.

3¾in (9.5cm) wide

$20,000-25,000   **POOK**

CLOSER LOOK—JAMES II CANDLESTICKS

These candlesticks have octagonal bases, fluted columns, and shaped drip pans.

They are engraved within feather mantling with the armorial of Burnell of Essex impaling Gybbons of Norfolk, along with another.

They are in exceptional condition for their age, having been stored in a bank vault.

Wooley and Wallis silver specialist Rupert Slingsby described them as "among the best of the best in terms of condition, color, form and marks."

A pair of James II silver candlesticks, maker's mark "TD," probably Thomas Dymock, London.
1685   *9¾in (24.5cm) high 3⅝oz*
$98,000-105,000   **WW**

A pair of George II silver candlesticks, engraved with a cipher, by Abraham Buteux, London.
1730   *6in (15cm) high 21oz*
$7,500-9,000   **WW**

A pair of George II silver candlesticks, with engraved armorials, by James Gould, London.
1737   *7½in (19cm) high 34⅜oz*
$3,200-3,800   **LSK**

A set of four George II cast silver candlesticks, by John White, London, two sticks wobbling.
1738   *8¼in (21cm) high 83oz*
$18,000-23,000   **CHEF**

An Irish George II silver candlestick, by Robert Calderwood, Dublin.
c1740   *9in (23cm) high 19oz*
$1,900-2,500   **ADA**

A pair of mid-18thC Irish silver candlesticks, by Bartholomew Mosse, Dublin.
c1740   *8¼in (21cm) high 29oz*
$3,200-3,800   **WW**

A pair of George II silver candlesticks, each engraved with a crest, scratch weights to base: "N:1 27=17" and "N: 2 28," by John Cafe, London.

John Cafe was a silversmith based in London who specialized in candlesticks. He died in 1757.
1748   *9½in (24cm) high 54oz*
$4,400-5,000   **SWO**

A pair of George II Channel Islands silver Rococo candlesticks, with engraved crest of the Carey family of Guernsey, by Guillaume Henry, Guernsey.

See Frederick Cohen and Nicholas Du Quesne Bird, "Silver in the Channel Islands," Jersey Museums Service, page 43.
8in (20.5cm) high 28¼oz
$32,000-38,000   **MART**

A pair of George II cast silver candlesticks, with engraved crests, by William Grundy, London.
1754   *9½in (24cm) high 43oz*
$2,300-2,800   **FLD**

SILVER & METALWARE

A pair of George II silver table candlesticks, the bases cast with stylized shells, by John Cafe, London.
1755 8¾in (22.5cm) high 36½oz
$5,000-5,700 SWO

A pair of George III silver candlesticks, by John Robinson II, London.
1763 9in (23cm) high 34oz
$3,200-3,800 WW

A pair of George III silver candlesticks, engraved with a crest, by Ebenezer Coker, London.
The crest is that of Beckford, Charlewood, Meade, Nichols, Lovat, Upton, and other families.
1765 10¼in (26cm) high 41¾oz
$3,800-4,400 WW

A pair of George III silver candlesticks, crested to bases, by John Cox, London, general surface wear.
1767 9in (23cm) high 32oz
$3,500-4,000 APAR

A pair of George III silver candlesticks, with two vacant cartouches, maker's mark "I.W," possibly John Welding or James Wiburd, London.
1772 12½in (32cm) high
$2,800-3,500 WW

A pair of George III Channel Islands silver Rococo candlesticks, decorated with shells and anthemion, maker's mark "IA," Guernsey.
c1763-1807 10in (25.5cm) high 42oz
$32,000-38,000 MART

A set of four George III silver candlesticks, by John Schofield, London, some scratches and dents.
1783 11¼in (28.5cm) high 67¾oz
$9,500-10,500 CHOR

A pair of George IV silver five-light candelabra, with Royal arms, by Charles and John Fry II, London.
These candelabra were owned by one of George III's seven sons. However, they could not have been owned by his eldest son, George, who succeeded to the throne as King George IV in 1820, or by fourth son, Edward Duke of Kent, who died in the same year.
1824 29¼in (74cm) high
$60,000-65,000 SWO

A Victorian silver candelabrum centrepiece, the base depicting a fox-hunting scene, the stem decorated with oak leaves, inscribed to base "Presented To John Stapylton Sutton Esq, of Elton Hall in the County of Durham by the Members of the Hurworth & Durham County Hunts and Other Friends in Consideration of His Disinterested Preservation of Foxes," some splits and scratches, Hennell house mark, by Robert Hennell, London.
1853 22½in (57cm) high 197oz
$11,000-14,000 TEN

A set of four Tiffany & Co. silver candlesticks, reproduced from a design by David Willaume in 1739, marked, minor wear.
c1914 9¼in (23.5cm) high 83¼oz
$4,400-5,000 DRA

SILVER & METALWARE

A rare George II Channel Islands silver chamberstick, by Jean Gavey (fl.c1715-75), Jersey.

This is believed to be the only known example of a Channel Islands silver chamberstick in existence. It was probably a special commission from a client who had seen such pieces in England or on the Continent. Contrary to most English examples, it does not feature a fitting for a separate snuffer.

5½in (14cm) diam

$9,000-10,000   **MART**

ESSENTIAL REFERENCE—PAUL STORR

Paul Storr (1771-1844) was one of the greatest silversmiths of his time.
- **He was apprenticed c1785 to Andrew Fogelberg and, by 1796, had started his own shop.**
- **He began working with the firm Rundell and Bridge in 1807, and in 1822 went into partnership with John Mortimer.**
- **Although he held no official title, Storr enjoyed patronage from many important figures of the period, including George III, and carried out commissions from the Duke of Portland and Lord Nelson, among others.**
- **Storr's designs were influenced by Neoclassical decorative styles and ancient Roman silver. His work is known for its superior quality and its high level of craftsmanship.**

A George III silver chamberstick, engraved with an episcopal miter and the badge of a Royal Duke, probably for Frederick, Duke of York and Albany and Bishop of Osnabruck, by Paul Storr, London.

1817   *6¼in (16cm) diam 14oz*

$1,800-2,300   **WW**

A George III silver chamberstick, initialed, by John Carter II, London.

1775   *8⅛oz*

$500-650   **BE**

A pair of George III silver chambersticks, one snuffing cone associated, by Henry Chawner, London.

1794   *16¼oz*

$1,050-1,200   **BELL**

A pair of George III silver chambersticks, probably by John Hutson, London, splits to sconces, repairs to handles.

1797   *25¾oz*

$1,050-1,200   **BELL**

A George III silver chamberstick and scissor snuffers, engraved with a monogram, by William Fountain, London, the scissors unmarked.

1798   *6¼in (16cm) long 9⅞oz*

$500-650   **WW**

A pair of Victorian silver chambersticks, crests of Boughton and Crabtree on the snuffers, by Robert Dicker, London.

1874   *4¾in (12cm) diam 15½oz*

$1,400-1,800   **WW**

A pair of Victorian traveling silver chambersticks, by Wright & Davies, London.

1885   *3¾in (9.5cm) long 6¼oz*

$750-900   **WW**

A Charles II provincial silver chalice, marks worn, probably by Thomas Mangy, York.

c1675 *9¼in (23.5cm) high 13¾oz*

$5,000-5,700 **WW**

A Charles I silver wine cup, scratch initialed "W" over "E*A," maker's mark attributed to Barnabus Gregory, London.

1630 *5in (13cm) high 4oz*

$19,000-25,000 **WW**

A pair of James II silver mugs, with chinoiserie decoration, by Francis Singleton, London.

1688 *3½in (9cm) high 8¾oz*

$7,000-7,500 **WW**

A William and Mary silver chinoiserie mug, the front with an armorial, the base scratch initialed "1695," "A.H" over "A.H," stamped "W.T. ANDREW," maker's mark "IA," probably by John Austin, London.

The shield is that of Hayne of Fryer Wadon, Dorset, England, granted in 1601.

1689 *3½in (9cm) high 6⅛oz*

$8,000-9,500 **WW**

A late 17thC Channel Islands silver wine cup or goblet, inscribed "M.T," "I.B" and "G.O," by Robert Barbedor (fl c1677-1701), Jersey and Guernsey.

c1690 *5½in (14.5cm) high 7⅛oz*

$10,000-11,000 **MART**

A William III silver cup and cover, the underside with scratch weight "36:3," by Pierre Harache, London.

1698 *7in (17.5cm) high 34½oz*

$6,500-7,500 **WW**

A Queen Anne silver mug, with later initials, by John Elston, Exeter.

1709 *3½in (9cm) high 3¾oz*

$1,900-2,500 **WW**

An early George I Britannia Standard silver tumbler cup, engraved with an 18thC cipher, detailed "March 15th 1717," maker's mark indistinct, London, some dents.

1716 *1¾in (4.5cm) high 2oz*

$1,900-2,500 **BELL**

An early 18thC Scottish thistle tot cup, with reeded girdle and engraved armorial shield above, by John Seaton.

1½in (4cm) high 1⅛oz

$5,500-6,500 **L&T**

A George II mug, by Dougal Ged, Edinburgh, Assay Master Archibald Ure.

1734   *3in (7.5cm) high 5oz*

$2,500-3,200   **L&T**

An 18thC Channel Islands silver christening cup, inscribed "a AB don de Son Parain & Mareine Isaac Le Lacheur & Jeanne Bevi 1771," by Guillaume Henry, Guernsey.

This cup was exhibited at the 1978 Channel Islands Silver Exhibition, Guernsey Museum & Art Gallery.

2½in (6cm) high 3⅜oz

$1,200-1,400   **MART**

A pair of George III silver wine goblets, maker's mark rubbed, London, some knocks.

1774   *7¼in (18.5cm) high 14⅜oz*

$750-900   **GORL**

A George III communion cup, engraved "Relief Church Paisley 1785," engraved on opposing side "Drink abundantly o beloved for my blood is drink indeed," by Alexander Gairdner, Edinburgh.

1784   *8¼in (21cm) high 16⅞oz*

$9,000-10,000   **L&T**

A pair of George III silver goblets, engraved with the Wynne crest, by John Wakelin and Robert Garrard, London.

1796   *6in (15cm) high 16oz*

$2,300-2,800   **WW**

A Canadian silver christening mug, inscribed "Matilda G. Faribault, from her affectionate Godfather, Jno. Fraiser, 1st Jan/1832," by Laurent Amiot, Quebec City.

c1820   *2½in (6.5cm) high*

$7,000-7,500   **FRE**

An early Victorian fox-mask stirrup cup, gilt interior, by George Fox, London.

A stirrup cup is a cup of wine or other alcoholic drink offered to someone on horseback who is about to depart on a journey or hunt.

1845   *4¾in (12cm) long 6¾oz*

$6,500-7,500   **LC**

A French silver goblet, maker's mark obscured, export mark, light scratches, in a fitted case.

c1840-79   *4¾in (12cm) high 6¼oz*

$300-400   **DN**

A Victorian silver beaker, the underside stamped "Hunt and Roskell, Late Storr and Mortimer 3183," by John Samuel Hunt, London.

1864   *3½in (9cm) high 5¼oz*

$1,500-1,900   **WW**

A Victorian silver goblet, presentation inscribed, London.

1865   *7¾in (20cm) high 10oz*

$550-650   **BELL**

An early 17thC German embossed and engraved silver-gilt tankard, possibly by Augsburg, some wear and repairs.

11½in (29cm) high 47⅝oz

$19,000-25,000 CHEF

A Charles II silver tankard, with an armorial shield, maker's mark "R.P," London.

1667   6¾in (17cm) high 27⅝oz

$9,000-10,000 WW

A George I silver tankard, the front later initialed, by Richard Bayley, London, some repairs.

1724   7in (18cm) high 25oz

$1,300-1,800 WW

A Philadelphia silver tankard, by Jeremiah Elfreth.

c1750   8½in (21.5cm) high 40½oz

$5,000-6,300 POOK

A George II Channel Islands silver half pint baluster tankard, inscribed "TD LH," by Jean Henry (fl.c1727-83), Guernsey.

c1750   3½in (9cm) high 5¾oz

$3,800-4,400 MART

A George II silver and parcel-gilt tankard, later decorated in the Rococo manner, by William Shaw and William Priest, London.

1756   7¼in (18.5cm) high 22oz

$1,600-2,000 WHP

An 18thC Scandinavian silver peg tankard, the cover with rampant lion and set with a coin, inscribed, maker's mark "PC," dated.

1761   7in (17.5cm) high 19½oz

$2,500-3,800 WW

A George III silver tankard, crested and initialed, by William Turton, London.

1776   7¾in (20cm) high

$1,600-2,000 BE

A George III silver and silver-gilt tankard, inscribed "Presented to Quarter Mast'r Serg't Patrick Sloan, By Lieut Colonel A Borton & the officers of the 9th East Norfolk Reg't, as a token of their esteem & in appreciation of his gallant & meritorious Conduct during a service of 21 Years in the Corps," by Rebecca Emes & Edward Barnard, London.

1814   8¼in (21cm) high 32⅝oz

$3,200-3,800 CHOR

SILVER & METALWARE

An early George II silver miniature or toy bullet teapot, by Micou Melun, Falmouth, with broken wooden handle, some scratches and wear.

c1730   *4¾in (12cm) long 2⅜oz*

$1,500-2,000   **DN**

A George II Scottish silver teapot, ivory spacers to handle, by George Cooper, Aberdeen.

c1735   *6in (15cm) high 19½oz*

$5,000-6,300   **SWO**

A George II bullet teapot, the interior grill pierced, by James Ker, Edinburgh, Assay Master Edward Lothian.

James Ker was an important silver- and goldsmith working in Edinburgh. He entered into partnership with his son-in-law William Dempster as Ker & Dempster, and together they made some of the most important mid-18thC Scottish plate.

1742   *5¾in (14.5cm) high 19⅛oz*

$3,800-5,000   **L&T**

A George II Channel Islands silver teapot, with ebonized wooden handle, by Jean Gavey (fl.c1715-75), Jersey.

8½in (22cm) long 17⅛ oz

$18,000-23,000   **MART**

A late 18thC to early 19thC Scottish teapot, with engraved Classical scrolling border and swagged oval medallions, by Nathaniel Gillet, Aberdeen.

The crest is that of the family of Johnstone, the motto "nunquam non paratus" ("Never unprepared").

9½in (24cm) high 18½oz

$3,200-3,800   **L&T**

A George III silver teapot and stand, with monograms, by Hester Bateman, London, some wear and splits.

Hester Bateman (1709-94), née Needham, was an important 18thC silversmith. After the death of her husband, a gold and silversmith, in 1760, she took over the family business. Her pieces are graceful and refined in shape, with restrained decoration, typically in the form of beaded edges. She was later joined by her sons Peter and Jonathan.

1786   *stand 6¼in (16cm) wide 16½oz*

$1,800-2,300   **GORL**

A George III silver teapot, with ivory finial and wooden handle, by Alice & George Burrows II, London, some hairlines, dent to spout.

1803   *11¼in (28.5cm) long 13⅝oz*

$300-400   **DN**

A George III silver teapot, by Crispin Fuller, London, some light scratches, splits to ivory bands.

1805   *11in (28cm) 18¾oz*

$500-650   **DN**

An American silver teapot, with carved ivory handle, monogrammed, by Gorham and Co., retailed by Mermoid and Jaccards.

c1900   *6in (15.5cm) high 10½oz*

$300-400   **WW**

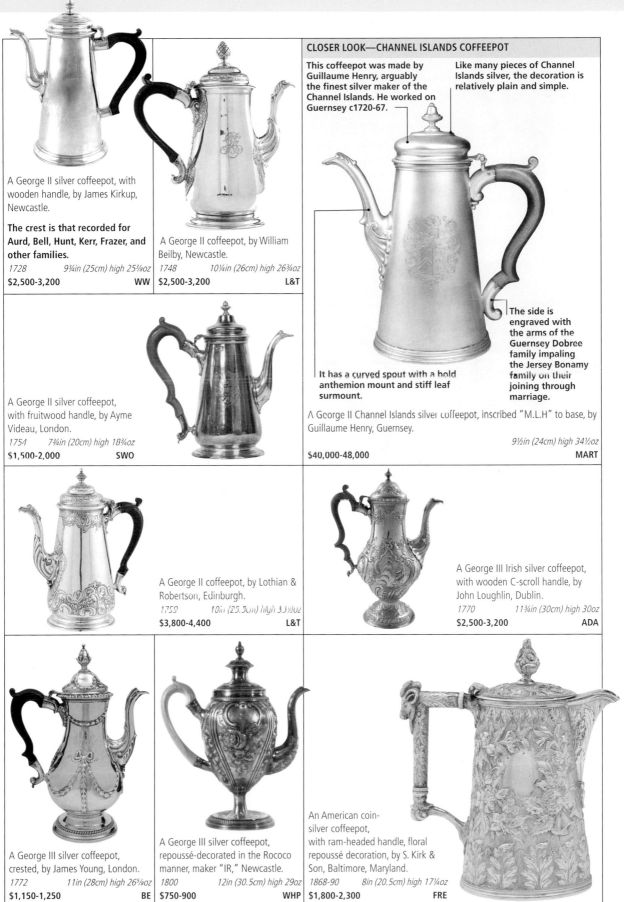

A George II silver coffeepot, with wooden handle, by James Kirkup, Newcastle.

The crest is that recorded for Aurd, Bell, Hunt, Kerr, Frazer, and other families.

1728   *9¾in (25cm) high 25⅜oz*
$2,500-3,200   **WW**

A George II coffeepot, by William Beilby, Newcastle.

1748   *10¼in (26cm) high 26¾oz*
$2,500-3,200   **L&T**

A George II silver coffeepot, with fruitwood handle, by Ayme Videau, London.

1754   *7¾in (20cm) high 18¾oz*
$1,500-2,000   **SWO**

CLOSER LOOK—CHANNEL ISLANDS COFFEEPOT

This coffeepot was made by Guillaume Henry, arguably the finest silver maker of the Channel Islands. He worked on Guernsey c1720-67.

Like many pieces of Channel Islands silver, the decoration is relatively plain and simple.

The side is engraved with the arms of the Guernsey Dobree family impaling the Jersey Bonamy family on their joining through marriage.

It has a curved spout with a bold anthemion mount and stiff leaf surmount.

A George II Channel Islands silver coffeepot, inscribed "M.L.H" to base, by Guillaume Henry, Guernsey.

9½in (24cm) high 34½oz
$40,000-48,000   **MART**

A George II coffeepot, by Lothian & Robertson, Edinburgh.

1759   *10in (25.5cm) high 33½oz*
$3,800-4,400   **L&T**

A George III Irish silver coffeepot, with wooden C-scroll handle, by John Loughlin, Dublin.

1770   *11¾in (30cm) high 30oz*
$2,500-3,200   **ADA**

A George III silver coffeepot, crested, by James Young, London.

1772   *11in (28cm) high 26⅝oz*
$1,150-1,250   **BE**

A George III silver coffeepot, repoussé-decorated in the Rococo manner, maker "IR," Newcastle.

1800   *12in (30.5cm) high 29oz*
$750-900   **WHP**

An American coin-silver coffeepot, with ram-headed handle, floral repoussé decoration, by S. Kirk & Son, Baltimore, Maryland.

1868-90   *8in (20.5cm) high 17¼oz*
$1,800-2,300   **FRE**

A Queen Anne Britannia standard silver chocolate pot, marks rubbed.

10¼in (26cm) high 27⅜oz

$3,200-3,800　　　　CHOR

A Queen Anne silver hot milk pot, engraved with an armorial, the underside with scratch weight "11=14=0," by Thomas Parr I, London.

1713　　7½in (19cm) high 11¼oz

$5,000-6,300　　　　WW

A Queen Anne silver chocolate pot, by Gabriel Sleath, London.

1713　　9½in (24cm) high 23⅞oz

$3,200-3,800　　　　WW

A George II Channel Islands silver covered hot milk pitcher, with boxwood handle and finial, with engraved armorial, by Guillaume Henry, Guernsey.

This piece was inspired by an original design by Paul de Lamerie of London.

c1727　　4½in (11.5cm) high 8⅞oz

$27,000-35,000　　　　MART

A George II silver tea kettle on stand, with lamp, later chased with chinoiserie figures, later inscribed, with raffia covered swing handle, by Daniel Chartier, London, some repairs and losses.

The inscription records the presentation of the kettle in 1873 to Helen Mary "May" (1853-1940), on the occasion of her marriage to Henry Brooks Gaskell (1846-1907) of Kiddington Hall, Oxford. May Gaskell was reputedly the last love of Pre-Raphaelite artist Edward Burne Jones and may possibly have served him tea from this pot.

1743　　　12in (30.5cm) high 56¾oz

$1,800-2,300　　　　BELL

A George II silver kettle on stand, with burner, with leather-bound hinged handle, by George Methuen, London.

1748　　12½in (32cm) high 60oz

$1,900-2,500　　　　WW

A repoussé silver kettle on stand, by J. Charles Edington, some dents.

1831-32　　15¾in (40cm) high 129oz

$5,000-5,700　　　　POOK

A Victorian silver kettle on stand, with 18thC-style Rococo decoration, by Walter Morisse, London, burning lacking.

1849　　without handle 12½in (31.5cm) high 71¼oz

$2,300-2,800　　　　TEN

A matched 1820s tea service, London.
6½in (16.5cm) high 48⅜oz
$900-1,000   **L&T**

A Philadelphia coin-silver tea and coffee
service, in Neoclassical style, inscribed
to underside "Julia C. Mayer, wife of
the Hon. George May Keim of Reading
Pennsylvania From her mother Mrs.
Christopher Mayer of Lancaster 1826,"
by R. & W. Wilson.
c1826
$3,800-5,000

coffeepot 12in (30.5cm) high 118⅝oz
POOK

A William IV silver tea service, chased with
forget-me-not flowers within acanthus panels,
by Robert Hennell, London.
1834   *teapot 11in (28cm) wide 50⅜oz*
$2,300-2,800   **HT**

A Victorian silver
tea set, engraved
with a crest, by Walter
Morrisse, London.

The crest is that of Dod of Edge, Cheshire.
1850   *11¼in (28.5cm) high 48¾oz*
$1,050-1,200   **WW**

A silver tea service, with gilt lining to sugar bowl and milk pitcher, by
Edward & John Barnard, London.
1865   *8¼in (21cm) high 91¾oz*
$2,300-2,800   **L&T**

A silver tea service, with crest engraved cartouches, numbered "5650" and
"5601," teapot and coffeepot impressed "Late Storr & Mortimer," by John
Hunt & Robert Roskell, London, some tarnishing, cracking to spacers.
1870   *11in (28cm) long 82⅛oz*
$5,000-5,700   **FELL**

A Victorian engraved tea and coffee service, the
teapot handle detached but present, by John
Ruddock, Sheffield.
1874   *coffeepot 9¾in (25cm) high 70¾oz*
$1,200-1,400   **LC**

A Victorian silver tea and coffee service, by
Roberts & Belk, Sheffield.
1875   *82⅞oz*
$3,800-4,400   **WAD**

A late Victorian silver bachelor's tea set, by
Mappin & Webb, London.
1890   *22oz*
$950-1,050   **FLD**

SILVER & METALWARE

An early George I silver tea caddy, the base engraved with marriage initials, by John East, London.

1724   *4in (10cm) high 4⅞oz*

$1,500-2,000   **HT**

A George I silver tea caddy, the base inscribed "The Gift of Mr. John Bristol to Madame Martha Carey Wife of Darell Carey J.M.S," by John Newton, London, date letter rubbed.

The inscription relates to the Carey family of Guernsey.

c1730   *5½in (14cm) high 8oz*

$2,300-2,800   **MART**

CLOSER LOOK—SCOTTISH TEA CADDY

Scottish silver tea caddies are exceedingly rare. While the use of tea caddies would have been as common in Scotland as elsewhere in Great Britain, it seems the fashion in Scotland was for wooden caddies, or English makers supplied silver tea caddies to Scotland.

The lid is engraved with a foliate border, with a fruiting bud finial.

This caddy is decorated with an foliate engraved border and a keyhole pendant cartouche with crest and motto within.

The condition and quality are very high.

A rare George III drum tea caddy, by William Kerr, Edinburgh.

1772   *4¾in (12cm) high 1¼oz*

$5,500-7,000   **L&T**

A pair of George II silver tea caddies, with detachable lead liners, by Samuel Taylor, London.

1744   *5¾in (14.5cm) high 19¾oz*

$2,300-2,800   **WW**

A pair of George II silver tea caddies, by Samuel Taylor, London.

1750   *5½in (14cm) high 17½oz*

$2,500-3,200   **TEN**

A pair of George III silver tea caddies, engraved with the Wynne Finch crests, by Lewis Hearne and Francis Butty, London.

1760   *6½in (16.5cm) high 19oz*

$1,600-2,000   **WW**

A pair of early George III silver tea caddies, by Pierre Gillois, London.

1761   *4¾in (12cm) high 13⅝oz*

$2,800-3,500   **MART**

A George III silver tea caddy, by Hester Bateman, London.

1782   *4¼in (11cm) long 9¾oz*

$4,400-5,000   **WW**

A George III silver tea caddy, by Robert Hennell, London, some repairs.

1791   *5¾in (14.5cm) high 12¾oz*

$1,200-1,400   **BELL**

An unusual late 15thC silver-gilt seal-top spoon, probably French, later assayed in London, marked with a tent.

The leopard's head mark in the bowl was used in London 1528-34 and the date letter mark refers to 1530. However, the maker's mark, a tent, is not elsewhere recorded on English silver, suggesting that this spoon was probably made by a Continental craftsman. It was probably made in France c1470 and later submitted for assay in London in 1530.

c1470   6¼in (16cm) long 1¼oz

$9,500-10,500   **WW**

A Henry VIII silver Apostle spoon, "The Master," the reverse prick dot initialed "1628" "I.A" over "R.P," with gilded Apostle finial, maker's mark of a device, possibly a basket, London.

1534   7in (17.5cm) long 1¾oz

$12,000-14,000   **WW**

An Elizabeth I provincial silver seal-top spoon, the reverse scratch initialed "A.D," by John Gladwin and John Utting, Lichfield.

c1580   6in (15.5cm) long 1⅛oz

$7,500-9,000   **WW**

An Elizabeth I provincial lion sejant spoon, by John Avery, Exeter.

c1590   6in (15cm) long ⅞oz

$1,900-2,500   **LC**

A James I silver Apostle spoon, with gilded finial of Saint Mathias, the reverse prick dot initialed, "N.H" over "H.B," over "1621," by William Cawdell, London.

1611   7in (18cm) long 1⅞oz

$6,500-7,000   **WW**

A Charles I silver Apostle spoon, with finial probably of Saint Paul, by Edward Hole, London.

1632   7in (17.5cm) long 1⅝oz

$1,900-2,500   **WW**

A Charles I seal-top spoon, initialed seal "MN," by Benjamin Yates, London.

1637   6in (15cm) long ⅞oz

$800-950   **BE**

A Charles I silver Apostle spoon, with gilded finial of Saint Jude, the reverse prick dot initialed, "G.Y," probably by Thomas Paulson, London.

1637   7in (18cm) long 1⅞oz

$2,800-3,500   **WW**

A Charles II provincial silver Trefid spoon, with a rudimentary rattail, the reverse scratch initialed "T*S," by Marmaduke Best, York.

This is an important York spoon, because it was made to the new design outside of London, indicating the mobility of goldsmiths and journeyman and their desire to produce the latest fashions. The goldsmith had not shaken off the earlier style of spoon making— he struck a mark in the bowl, unusually for a Trefid. You would expect to see a reeded rattail but this spoon has a rudimentary rattail.

1665   7½in (19cm) long 1⅜oz

$2,800-3,500   **WW**

A James II silver Trefid spoon, with a plain rattail, by John King, London.

Interestingly, this spoon has an additional punch containing a crest. Crests are usually engraved on silver, not struck, so the owner must have commissioned this punch for their own silver.

1686   10¼in (26cm) long 3¾oz

$5,000-6,300   **WW**

A pair of late 17thC provincial silver Trefid spoons, with ribbed rattails, prick dot initialed "B" over "I*I," by Thomas Havers, Norwich.

c1689   7½in (19cm) long 3¼oz

$7,500-9,000   **WW**

A William and Mary Sussex silver Trefid spoon, with a ribbed rattail, scratch initialed "E" over "IM" over "WA," by Robert Colegate, Lewes.

c1690 *7¾in (20cm) long 1⅝oz*
$1,800-2,300 **WW**

A William III West Country silver lace-back Trefid spoon, prick dot initialed "T.W" over "W.W" over "1700," by Richard Sweet II, Chard.

c1700 *7¾in (20cm) long 1½oz*
$3,800-5,000 **WW**

A William III silver lace-back Trefid spoon, with foliate scroll decoration, scroll rattail, prick dot initialed "A.N" over "R.T" "April 25 1701," by Richard Sweet III, Honiton.

c1701 *8in (20.5cm) long 1¾oz*
$4,400-5,000 **WW**

A Queen Anne Scottish provincial silver dog-nose spoon, scratch initialed "RG" over "HG" over "Od" over "11 9," by David Dunlop, Canongate.

c1704 *7¾in (19.5cm) long 1¾oz*
$5,500-6,500 **WW**

A Scottish provincial Hanoverian pattern tablespoon, the reverse engraved "WF/SG," with engraved fleur-de-lis rattail, with armorial shield, by John and Francis Brown, Perth.

The working careers of John and his son Francis Brown are somewhat confused. Although recorded in Perth as early as 1724, they appear to have worked in Edinburgh and possibly Elgin as well. No marks have been confidently ascribed to either of these periods and all their work is tied to Perth. The double drop and engraved rattail is also a feature unique to these makers in Scottish silver and shows much closer comparison to Continental European work than British.

7¾in (20cm) long 1⅞oz
$8,000-9,500 **L&T**

A Queen Anne provincial silver Hanoverian pattern basting spoon, by Thomas Robinson, Chester.

1711 *14¼in (36cm) long 5⅝oz*
$2,500-3,200 **WW**

A George II Channel Islands silver Hanoverian pattern soup ladle, marked "PA," for Pierre Amiraux, I, II, and III.

c1740 *12½in (32cm) long 5⅛oz*
$1,200-1,400 **MART**

A George II Irish silver Hanoverian pattern dessert spoon, by George Hodder, Cork.

c1740 *6¾in (17cm) long*
$400-500 **ADA**

A pair of George III Irish provincial bright-cut silver tablespoons, engraved with a crown and leopard's head crest, by William Fitzgerald, Limerick.

c1800 *9½in (24cm) long 4oz*
$3,200-3,800 **ADA**

A George III Irish provincial silver Celtic-point basting spoon, erased terminal, by Maurice Fitzgerald, Limerick.

c1800 *12½in (32cm) long 3⅝oz*
$2,300-2,800 **WW**

A Scottish provincial Fiddle pattern toddy ladle, initialed "B," marks "IPR" and castle turrets, by John and Patrick Riach, Forres.

1825-35 *6½in (16.5cm) long 1¼oz*
$3,500-4,000 **LC**

A George I Irish flagon, with a harp-shaped handle, engraved with a coat of arms, by Thomas Williamson, Dublin.

1718 *12in (30.5cm) high 35¹⁄₂oz*

$9,000-10,000 **LC**

A George II Irish silver cream pitcher, by John Hamilton, Dublin, some repairs and wear.

c1730-40 *4¾in (12cm) high 7³⁄₄oz*

$10,000-11,000 **TEN**

A George II silver beer pitcher, by John Swift, London, engraved with an armorial, with traces of gilding.

The Arms are possibly that of the Duke of Hamilton.

1736 *12¾in (32.5cm) high 59oz*

$9,500-10,500 **WW**

A pair of George II provincial silver sauceboats, with flying dolphin handles, engraved with an armorial and a tiger crest for Dent, initialed "D" over "I.I," by James Kirkup, Newcastle, England, some wear.

1747 *7¾in (19.5cm) long 28¼oz*

$11,000-13,000 **TEN**

A George II silver cream pitcher, inscribed "I.G.L," by Pierre Maingy (fl.c1739-76), Guernsey.

3½in (9cm) high 3⅛oz

$8,000-9,500 **MART**

A mid-to-late 18thC beer pitcher, probably Colonial, crested.

7¼in (18.5cm) high 26oz

$2,500-3,200 **LC**

An Irish provincial silver cream pitcher, stamped "STERLING," by Michael McDermott and Daniel McCarthy, Cork.

c1780 *5in (12.5cm) high 5½oz*

$2,500-3,200 **ADA**

An American coin-silver repoussé water pitcher, by S. Kirk & Son, Baltimore, Maryland.

1868-90 *9in (23cm) high 31¼oz*

$1,900-2,500 **FRE**

A silver cow creamer, with import marks for London, some dents, lid loose.

c1897 *5½in (14cm) 6¼oz*

$1,600-2,000 **BELL**

A Dutch silver goat creamer, with red glass eyes.

1905 *5½in (14cm) long 4⅞oz*

$1,500-2,000 **WW**

A Charles II silver paten, on a raised foot, maker's mark "L.S" crowned, probably by Leonard Sutton, London.

A paten, or diskos, is a small plate, usually made of silver or gold, used to hold Eucharistic bread that is to be consecrated during Mass.

1680   6½in (16.5cm) diam 9⅝oz
$2,500-3,200   WW

A George II silver kettle stand, with an armorial, on three lion paw feet, by George Hindmarsh, London.

The marital arms of Sir Edmund Isham, 6th Baronet (1690-1772) Lamport Hall, Northants, impaling (Elizabeth) Wood.

1732   9¾in (25cm) long 28oz
$7,500-9,000   WW

A George II silver side dish, with an armorial, detailed underneath "No 60 20 = 9," by Paul de Lamerie, London.

1737   9½in (24cm) diam 20oz
$5,000-6,300   BELL

A George II silver strawberry dish, engraved with an armorial, by Christian Hillan, London.

1739   9in (23cm) diam 15oz
$2,900-3,500   WW

A George II Channel Islands silver card waiter, inscribed "M.L.H" to underside, by Guillaume Henry, Guernsey.

7in (18cm) diam 8¾oz
$5,000-5,700   MART

A George III salver, with armorial, by William and Patrick Cunningham, Edinburgh.

The motto reads "leges juraque serva" ("observe the laws").

1802   18in (46cm) diam 84½oz
$3,800-4,400   L&T

A Scottish silver salver, engraved with a coat of arms and motto, Edinburgh.
c1805   20in (51cm) diam 93¾oz
$2,300-2,800   BELL

A George III silver salver, engraved with an armorial, on four foliate shell feet, maker's mark "WS," possibly by William Stroud, London.

1815   24¾in (63cm) diam 223oz
$11,000-12,000   TEN

A set of ten George IV silver-gilt plates, with chased and repoussé Rococo decoration, by Thomas Burwash, London.

1821   9½in (24cm) diam total 186⅞oz
$9,000-10,000   HT

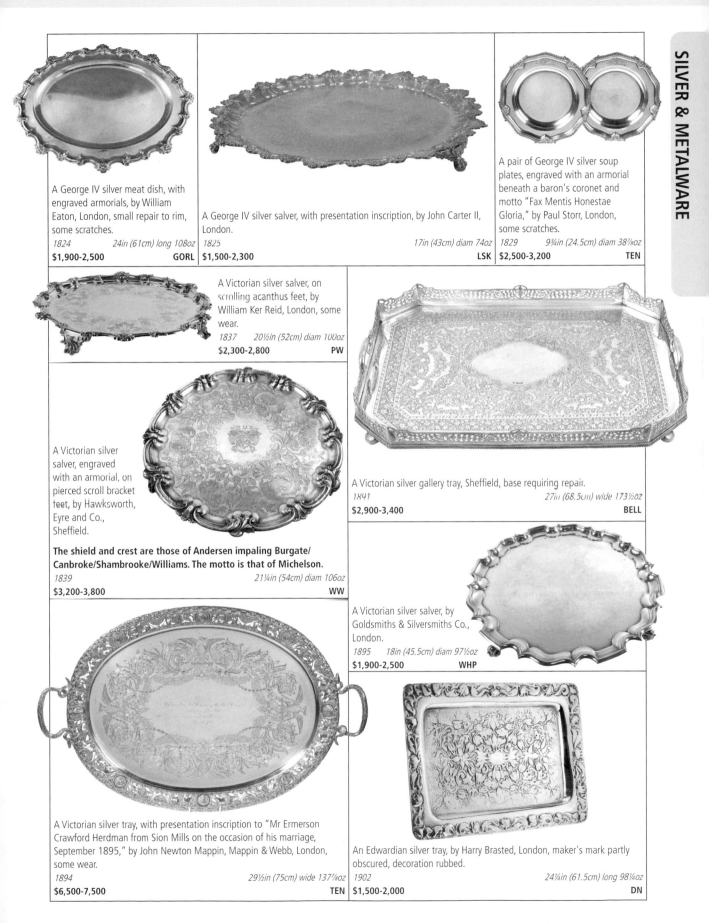

A George IV silver meat dish, with engraved armorials, by William Eaton, London, small repair to rim, some scratches.
1824   24in (61cm) long 108oz
$1,900-2,500   **GORL**

A George IV silver salver, with presentation inscription, by John Carter II, London.
1825   17in (43cm) diam 74oz
$1,500-2,300   **LSK**

A pair of George IV silver soup plates, engraved with an armorial beneath a baron's coronet and motto "Fax Mentis Honestae Gloria," by Paul Storr, London, some scratches.
1829   9¾in (24.5cm) diam 38⅞oz
$2,500-3,200   **TEN**

A Victorian silver salver, on scrolling acanthus feet, by William Ker Reid, London, some wear.
1837   20½in (52cm) diam 100oz
$2,300-2,800   **PW**

A Victorian silver salver, engraved with an armorial, on pierced scroll bracket feet, by Hawksworth, Eyre and Co., Sheffield.

The shield and crest are those of Andersen impaling Burgate/ Canbroke/Shambrooke/Williams. The motto is that of Michelson.
1839   21¼in (54cm) diam 106oz
$3,200-3,800   **WW**

A Victorian silver gallery tray, Sheffield, base requiring repair.
1841   27in (68.5cm) wide 173½oz
$2,900-3,400   **BELL**

A Victorian silver salver, by Goldsmiths & Silversmiths Co., London.
1895   18in (45.5cm) diam 97½oz
$1,900-2,500   **WHP**

A Victorian silver tray, with presentation inscription to "Mr Ermerson Crawford Herdman from Sion Mills on the occasion of his marriage, September 1895," by John Newton Mappin, Mappin & Webb, London, some wear.
1894   29½in (75cm) wide 137⅞oz
$6,500-7,500   **TEN**

An Edwardian silver tray, by Harry Brasted, London, maker's mark partly obscured, decoration rubbed.
1902   24¼in (61.5cm) long 98¼oz
$1,500-2,000   **DN**

SILVER & METALWARE

A Charles II silver porringer and cover, engraved with an armorial, maker's mark "WC," London.

The cover has a later spool-shaped finial with London Assay Office additions hallmarks for 2008 (case number 8566).

1662   7¾in (19.5cm) high 31oz
$9,000-10,000   **WW**

A James II Irish silver porringer and cover, with scroll handles with female heads, by John Phillips, Dublin.

1685-87   7¾in (20cm) high 28½oz
$13,000-15,000   **WW**

A William III silver monteith, the underside with scratch weight "56=0," by Robert Cooper, London.

1701   11in (28cm) diam 55¼oz
$19,000-25,000   **WW**

CLOSER LOOK—QUEEN ANNE MONTIETH

A montieth is a form of large punch bowl, with a notched rim for suspending punch cups.

This example is decorated with foliate strapwork and crests, with lion masque handles.

The collar is detachable and has a scalloped rim applied with cherub heads flanked by rope-twist scrolls.

The foot is inscribed, "Presented to H.J. Hines by the Directors of the Royal Exchange Assurance. 1919." The Royal Exchange Assurance Corporation was a British insurance company operating 1720-1968.

A Queen Anne Britannia silver monteith, by Robert Timbrell and Joseph Bell, London.

1710   11in (28cm) diam 64⅜oz
$15,000-19,000   **FRE**

A rare George I sugar bowl and cover, with engraved crest, by Henry Bethune, Edinburgh.

When compared to the survival of early teapots, the rarity of early sugar bowls becomes much more apparent. Few surviving sugar bowls still have their original cover. This piece was probably part of a matching tea service.

1725   4¾in (12cm) diam 12½oz
$13,000-15,000   **L&T**

A George III soup tureen and cover, on lion's paw feet, engraved with the arms of Cholmeley and Harrison, by William Bennett, London.

1812   17in (43cm) wide 171⅝oz
$6,500-7,500   **HAN**

An early 19thC Maltese silver sugar bowl and cover, maker's mark "GC," possibly for Gaetano Cauchi or Giuseppe Cousin, Captain Sir Alexander Ball period.

Captain Sir Alexander John Ball was a Rear Admiral and close friend of Lord Nelson. He directed the blockade of Malta 1798-1800 and served as Civil Commissioner of the island 1802-09.

1800-09   5¼in (13.5cm) high 8¾oz
$2,300-2,800   **WW**

An American silver tureen and cover, with female bust handles, by Samuel Kirk, Baltimore, Maryland, some dings.

c1828   16¼in (41.5cm) wide 104⅝oz
$9,000-10,000   **POOK**

A William IV graduated set of four silver meat dishes, each engraved with a coat of arms, with Old Sheffield Plate covers, the dishes by John Bridge, London.

The Arms on the dishes are slightly different to those on the covers, but they are both the Arms of Maitland.

1831   max 24in (61cm) long 317oz
$13,000-15,000   **LC**

A Victorian Irish silver soup tureen and cover, with poppy seed handle finial on a bed of poppy leaves, by Patrick Loughlin, Dublin, dent to interior rim.

1838   14¼in (36cm) long 91¾oz
$3,800-5,000   **GORL**

A James II silver lighthouse-form sugar caster, maker's mark "CW," possibly for Caleb Westbrook, London.

1686   *7¾in (19.5cm) high 11oz*
$8,000-9,500   **WW**

A George III silver sugar vase and cover, engraved with the Macaulay crest, by Daniel Smith and Robert Sharp, London.

1787   *7¼in (19.5cm) high 17¾oz*
$2,500-3,200   **WW**

A William and Mary Channel Islands silver lighthouse pepper pot, of Huguenot influenced form, inscribed "E.G" to base, by Abraham Hebert (fl.c1660-1700), Jersey.

4in (10cm) high 2⅛oz
$12,000-14,000   **MART**

A George III Irish silver dish ring, later engraved crest and motto, probably by Michael Homer, Dublin.

The crest is associated with O'Duinne, Doyne, and Dunn of Ireland.

c1785   *7½in (19cm) diam 15¼oz*
$1,600-2,000   **WW**

A late 19thC American silver dish ring, owned by "Boss" Croker, pierced with shamrocks, harps, a round tower, and a wolfhound, with the arms of the Croker family, stamped "Sterling."

Richard "Boss" Welstead Croker (1843-1922), was an Irish-American politician and a leader of New York City's Tammany Hall, a political organization founded in 1789 that later began a center for Democratic politics.

9½oz
$1,200-1,4000   **WHYT**

A George II silver cake basket, the center with an armorial, by Samuel Herbert & Co., London.

The shield is that of Fleetwood.

1751   *14¼in (36cm) long 53¾oz*
$3,800-5,000   **WW**

A pair of Victorian silver fish servers, by Francis Higgins II, London, light scratches.

1865   *knife 13¼in (33.5cm) long 13½oz*
$1,900-2,500   **DN**

A William IV Irish silver Fiddle pattern oversize tongs with rattail bowls, crested and inscribed with monogram, by Philip Weekes, Dublin.

1830   *11¼in (28.5cm) long 10oz*
$9,000-10,000   **ADA**

An set of eighteen early 20thC German silver crowned-cipher knife rests.

30¾oz
$1,900-2,500   **WAD**

A George III silver jockey cap caddy spoon, by Joseph Taylor, Birmingham.

1799   *2in (5cm) long ¼oz*
$550-700   **WW**

A George III silver-mounted shell caddy spoon, engraved with Markham crest, by Matthew Linwood, Birmingham.

c1810   *3in (7.5cm) long*
$700-800   **WW**

A mid-18thC Dutch silver table bell, by Cornelis De Haan, The Hague.

1768   *5¼in (13.5cm) high 10oz*
$9,500-10,500   **WW**

An Elkington & Co. silver-gilt, enamel, and glass Graeco-Pompeian-style three-piece table garniture, with three later glass dishes.

The Graeco-Pompeian service was created for the 1862 International Exhibition in London. It comprised of 13 pieces and was designed by W. Albert Willms (d.1899), who was awarded a medal of artistic merit for it. Willms trained as a modeler and engraver at Klagman, Dieterle, and Constant in Paris, but later relocated to London. In 1857, he became head of Elkington's design studio.

1862   *largest 16in (40.5cm) high 149¾oz*
$14,000-18,000   **BELL**

A George III silver cream bucket, with blue glass liner, by William Plummer, London.

1770   *4¼in (105cm) 2⅜oz*
$1,800-2,300   **WW**

CLOSER LOOK—VICTORIAN SILVER CENTERPIECE

This impressive Victorian centerpiece is modeled as a lady falconer seated on a horse, holding her falcon, about to let it fly.

Beside her stands a cadger, carrying a padded wooden cadge, which is a frame on which birds of preys are carried.

This prize was originally won by William Stuart Sterling Crawfurd (1819-87) who, having a reputation for hosting good horse races, was invited by King William of the Netherlands to bring his horses to Dorn, in the Netherlands, to race them at the King's own club, the Hawking Club.

This is mounted on a wooden base applied with the Dutch Royal coat of arms, inscribed "LOO CHALLENGE CUP 1851" and "CHALLENGE CUP GIVEN BY HM THE KING OF THE NETHERLANDS TO BE WON TWO YEARS IN SUCCESSION BY THE SAME PERSON WON IN 1851 AND 1852, BY MR STIRLING CRAWFURD'S DARKIE."

A Victorian presentation silver centerpiece, by John Samuel Hunt, overstamping another maker, London.

1851   *28in (71cm) high 176oz*
$60,000-65,000   **WW**

A William and Mary silver dog collar, inscribed "Miss R Jenkins, Charlton Hill 1691," minor wear.

3¾in (9.5cm) diam
$3,800-4,400   **TEN**

A George III silver honey skep and stand, by John Emes, London.

A skep is a man-made beehive or basket, used for catching and transporting bees. First, the swarm is shaken off the branch so that they fall into the skep. The skep is then turned upside down, propped on a stone, and transported.

1802   *5½in (14cm) diam 14½oz*
$13,000-15,000   **WW**

A pair of Spanish silver snuffers, Madrid.

1841   *5⅛oz*
$400-500   **WAD**

The must-have reference books for anyone collecting and valuing silver

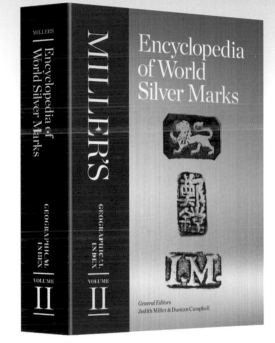

Volume I
provides a visual index
of marks listed by type

Volume II
lists marks by
country of origin

Millers Encyclopedia of World Silver Marks
by Judith Miller and Duncan Campbell
is available from all good book retailers
at $175 US and $200 Canadian

ESSENTIAL REFERENCE—WINE LABELS

Wine labels became popular in the mid-18thC.

- They were generally made of silver or silver-plate, although enamel, pottery, porcelain, and other materials were also used.
- More than 500 silversmiths are recorded as having made wine labels. Intricate examples from the great London makers, such as Paul Storr or Benjamin Smith, are sought after. Labels from the workshop of Hester Bateman are also popular.
- In the 1860s, new British legislation allowed for the sale of single bottles of wine with paper labels. Wine was increasingly served straight from the bottle in which it had been purchased, and wine labels fell largely out of use.

A George III silver wine label, incised "SHERRY," by Hester Bateman, London.

c1775   2¼in (6cm) long ¼oz
$900-1,000   WW

A George III Irish provincial silver armorial wine label, incised "PORT," by John Warner, Cork.

c1790   2¼in (5.5cm) long ¼oz
$550-700   WW

A George III silver armorial wine label, incised "SHERRY," maker's mark worn, London.

1791   3½in (9cm) long 1¼oz
$950-1,050   WW

A George III silver wine label, with mounted Prince of Wales feathers, incised and blackened "FALERNUM," by Peter and Ann Bateman, London.

Peter Bateman was the son of Hester Bateman (see page 294). Ann Bateman was Hester's daughter-in-law, and the widow of another of her sons, Jonathan Bateman.

1792   2in (5cm) long ¼oz
$650-750   WW

A George III silver armorial wine label, incised "SHERRY."

c1795   1½in (4cm) long ⅜oz
$500-650   WW

A pair of George III silver wine labels, incised "HERMITAGE" and "RED CHAMPAGNE," by Paul Storr, London.

1814   2in (5cm) long 2¼oz
$1,900-2,500   WW

A set of six Irish George III silver wine labels, engraved "BAR SAC," "FRONTIGNAN," "CALCAVELLA," "HERMITAGE," "CLARET," and "HOCK," probably by John Townsend, Dublin.

c1809   2¼in (6cm) wide 2⅛oz
$1,900-2,500   GORL

A George III silver armorial elephant wine label, pierced "LISBON," by Edward Farrell, London.

1815   3¼in (8.5cm) long ¾oz
$4,400-5,000   WW

A George III silver wine label, incised "SIRCIAL," by William Bateman, London.

William Bateman was the son of Jonathan and Ann Bateman, and the grandson of Hester Bateman.

1815   2in (5cm) long ¼oz
$700-750   WW

A George III silver-gilt lion's pelt wine label, inscribed "CHAMPAIGN," by Paul Storr, London.
1815 *2¾in (7cm) long 1⅝oz*
$1,300-1,900 **WW**

A George III Scottish rhodium-plated silver wine label, inscribed "To Mrs M. Whytock for HOME MADE WINE from Cal: Hort: Soc 1816," by William Peat, Edinburgh.
1815 *2¾in (7cm) long 1⅛oz*
$400-500 **WW**

A George III silver-gilt armorial wine label, pierced "CLARET," by John Reily, London.

The crest is that of the 6th Earl of Shaftsbury.
c1817 *2¼in (6cm) long ¾oz*
$700-750 **WW**

A pair of George IV silver wine labels, pierced "DANTZIC" and "EAU D'OR," by Philip Rundell, London.
1823 *2in (5cm) long 2oz*
$950-1,050 **WW**

An early 19thC Scottish provincial silver wine label, incised "CURRANT," by William Ferguson, Peterhead.
c1825 *1¾in (4.5cm) long ¼oz*
$1,050-1,200 **WW**

A William IV cast wine label, pierced "MADEIRA," by Paul Storr, London.
1835 *2¼in (5.5cm) long ¾oz*
$800-950 **LC**

A pair of Victorian silver fox wine labels, incised "PORT" and "MADEIRA," by Robert Garrard, London.
1849 *2½in (6.5cm) long 2oz*
$900-1,000 **WW**

A Victorian silver armorial wine label, pierced "SHERRY," by Rawlings and Summers, London.
c1850 *2¼in (6cm) long 1oz*
$450-550 **WW**

A Victorian silver armorial wine label, pierced "SHERRY."
2½in (6.5cm) long
$900-1,000 **WW**

SILVER & METALWARE

A George III silver wine funnel, initialed, by Peter, Ann, and William Bateman, London.

1812   *5in (12.5cm) high 2½oz*
$500-650   **WW**

A George III wine funnel, with cheesecloth ring, by Thomas Paine Dexter, London.

1818   *5½in (14cm) long 6½oz*
$700-750   **LC**

A pair of George III silver armorial wine coolers, the handles numbered "1" and "2," by Paul Storr, London.

The arms are those of Baring, Baron Ashburton.

1795   *8¾in (22.5cm) high 79⅜oz*
$16,000-20,000   **WW**

A rare early Charles II miniature or toy wine taster, maker's mark "WG," London.

1665   *2in (5cm) diam ⅜oz*
$1,900-2,500   LC

A late 17thC Channel Islands silver wine taster, inscribed "E.B" to side, by Robert Barbedor (c1677-1704), Jersey and Guernsey.

4¾in (12cm) long 3¼oz
$9,000-10,000   **MART**

A William IV silver wine funnel, with detachable strainer, by Charles Fox, London.

1833   *5¾in (14.5cm) long 8⅜oz*
$3,800-4,400   **TEN**

A pair of George III silver wine coasters, with turned wooden bases, by J.E. Terrey & Co., London, some nicks, marks rubbed.

1816   *5in (12.5cm) diam 11⅞oz*
$1,500-2,000   **GORL**

A pair of George IV tall silver coasters, engraved with a crest and motto, by Emes and Barnard, London.

The motto and crests are those for Carus-Wilson of Casterton Hall, Westmorland.

1828   *4in (10cm) high 19oz*
$4,400-5,000   **WW**

A Canadian silver wine taster, by Paul Lambert, Quebec.

c1740   *5⅜oz*
$12,000-15,000   **FRE**

A George IV silver brandy pan, by William Sharp, London.

1820   *13in (33cm) long 23oz*
$1,600-2,000   **WW**

ESSENTIAL REFERENCE—SILVER PLATE

The invention of Sheffield plate in the mid-18thC was a key development in the production of silver objects. Silver plate was cheaper and more suitable for mass-produced objects.

- Plating was developed in 1742 by Thomas Bolsover (1704-88) of Sheffield. The process involved fusing copper and silver together under heat, then rolling the fused metals under pressure to produce a sheet of workable metal. This technique was commonly used from the 1770s.
- In 1840, Elkington & Co. took out a patent for electroplating. A metal object (originally copper, later nickel) attached to a positive anode and a block of pure silver attached to a negative anode would both be immersed in a plating bath. An electric current would be passed from positive to negative, resulting in a fine sheet of silver being applied to the object. Electroplating is typically whiter and harsher in appearance than Old Sheffield plate.
- Electroplating ultimately came to replace Old Sheffield plate. The process was safer, and made complex structural ornament and decoration easier to achieve.

A George III Old Sheffield Plate argyle, with a hinged water compartment.

An argyle is a pot used for keeping gravy or sauce warm, first used by the 5th Duke of Argyle. It has an outer liner that can be filled with boiling water via the spout, keeping the gravy within warm while on the table.
c1790   6¼in (16cm) high
$250-320   WW

A Sheffield silver-plated épergne, minor fleabites to glass.
c1810   18in (45.5cm) high
$1,200-1,400   POOK

A George III Old Sheffield Plate ewer, by Matthew Boulton.
c1810   10¾in (27.5cm) high
$230-280   WW

A pair of Old Sheffield Plate wine coolers, engraved with armorials and the motto "Gloria Finis," for the Brooke family, liners present, some wear, copper showing under feet.
c1820/30   11¼in (26cm) high
$2,500-3,200   TEN

An Old Sheffield Plate wine cooler, by Matthew Boulton.
c1820   9½in (24cm) high
$400-500   WAD

A Victorian silver-plated whiskey cask, modeled as a barrel on a cart, with attached bucket, inscribed "Whisky" and "From C R & R R to W W 1st November 1867," under glass dome on stand.
17in (43cm) long
$950-1,050   GWA

A pair of 19thC Sheffield silver-plated two-branch three-light candelabra, by Creswick & Co., Sheffield.
20in (51cm) high
$650-750   MEA

A New York Fireman's silver-plated speaking trumpet, for the Wandowonack Fire Co., Queens County, one dent, dated.
1890   19in (48.5cm) high
$1,600-2,000   POOK

A Victorian electroplated argyle, with interior water compartment, with Wynne Finch crests, by Martin, Hall and Co.
5½in (14cm) high
$300-350   WW

A pair of late 19thC George II-style electroplated candlesticks, probably by James Pinder & Co.
12½in (32cm) high
$400-450   DN

ESSENTIAL REFERENCE—VENETO-SARACENIC

Veneto-Saracenic ware is characterized by the technique of inlaying precious silver, gold, or black compound onto brass within intricate decorative patterns of arabesques and other abstract motifs.

- It was initially made in the Levant and Persia and subsequently manufactured in Northern Italy.
- The patterns are interpretations of Islamic compositions encompassing European motifs, such as curling tendrils, flowers, and knotwork.
- This type of metalwork was much sought after in Europe during the 15thC and 16thC.

A Veneto-Saracenic brass salver, possibly 16thC Venetian, with silver-inlaid decoration.

19¼in (49cm) wide

$5,500-7,000   CHEF

A Dutch bronze mortar, cast with a band reading "Wibrans Tot Amsterdam 1696."

1696   *13¼in (33.5cm) high*

$10,000-11,000   SWO

A pair of pewter trumpet-base candlesticks, marked "B B 1664," possibly for Beza Boston.

1664   *7in (18cm) high*

$1,800-2,300   WW

A late 17thC sheet brass candlestick, initialed "SWM."

17¾in (45cm) high

$5,000-5,700   WW

A George II brass salver, maker's mark "TW."

8¾in (22.5cm) diam

$3,200-3,800   WW

An Edwardian brass eagle floor-standing lectern, by Jones & Willis, with inscription to commemorate the coronation of King Edward VII and Queen Alexandra.

c1902   *70in (178cm) high*

$2,800-3,300   FLD

Judith Picks

This dog collar was worn by Boatswain, the beloved Newfoundland dog of Lord Byron, celebrated poet and leading figure in the Romantic movement. Byron was as much famed for his scandalous behavior as for his literary talent. When told he could not bring a dog to Cambridge University, he brought a bear instead. Indeed, Byron's gamekeeper's widow reported that damage had been done to this very collar "by a Bear which Lord Byron kept for his own amusement and with which Boatswain had many severe encounters." Lord Byron adored Boatswain, for whom he constructed a monument at Newstead Abbey and wrote his "Epitaph to a Dog" after his death in 1808. In this epitaph, Boatswain was said to possess, "Beauty without Vanity,/Strength without Insolence,/Courage without Ferocity,/and all the virtues of Man without his Vices."

An 18thC Italian copper wine cooler, with repoussé decoration, lion's mask ring handles, and lift-out liner.

36¾in (93.5cm) wide

$4,400-5,000   WW

An 18thC Edinburgh pewter flagon.

13½in (34.5cm) high

$750-900   HT

A 19thC copper and brass peat/log bin, with lion mask loop handles.

24¾in (63cm) high

$550-700   L&T

A brass dog collar, engraved "Rt. Honble LORD BYRON," ten teeth missing, minor splitting and wear, in later fitted mahogany display case with engraved plaque, with accompanying documentation.

17¼in (44cm) diam

$21,000-25,000   TEN

A Philadelphia pewter tankard, by Parks Boyd.

c1805   *7½in (19cm) high*
$7,000-7,500   **POOK**

A pewter dish, by Joseph Danforth, Middletown, Connecticut, some dents.

c1785   *13¼in (33.5cm) diam*
$700-750   **POOK**

A pewter basin, by Joseph Danforth Jr., Richmond, Virginia, marked with eagles above "JD."

1807-12   *12in (30.5cm) diam*
$1,200-1,400   **SK**

A pewter flagon, by Boardman & Co., New York.

c1835   *13¾in (35cm) high*
$500-650   **POOK**

A 19thC pewter ciborium, by George Richardson, Cranston, Rhode Island, repair to hinge, crack to body.

A ciborium is a vessel, usually of metal, used in the Christian Church to hold consecrated Eucharistic bread.

6¾in (17cm) wide
$550-650   **POOK**

A copper coffeepot, by Peter Derr (1793-1868), Berks County, Pennsylvania, impressed "P. Derr," some wear.

10in (25.5cm) high
$7,000-8,000   **POOK**

A 19thC Pennsylvania punched tin coffeepot, with floral and heart decoration.

10in (25.5cm) high
$1,300-1,800   **POOK**

A 19thC Pennsylvania punched tin coffeepot, with a gooseneck spout, impressed "Sands."

11in (28cm) high
$2,800-3,500   **POOK**

A 19thC punched tin heart-form cheese strainer, some wear.

15½in (39.5cm) wide
$3,800-4,400   **POOK**

OBJETS DE VERTU

A George III silver vinaigrette, with silver-gilt interior and domed pierced grill, by Thomas Meriton, London.

Vinaigrettes are small boxes used to hold sponges soaked in smelling salts, pleasant smelling oils, perfume, or aromatic vinegar. They were used by Georgian and Victorian ladies and gentlemen to revive faintness and ward off unpleasant odors.

1800

$450-500   FLD

A George III silver patent slide-action vinaigrette, with a push button opening two eyeholes, gilded interior, stamped "Patent," by Daniel May, London.

1801   *1¼in (3cm) long ½oz*

$1,900-2,500   WW

A George IV silver "castle-top" vinaigrette, depicting Abbotsford, maker's mark "T.S.," Birmingham.

1825

$950-1,050   BRI

A George IV gold-mounted citrine vinaigrette.

c1825   *1¼in (3cm) wide*

$2,300-2,800   L&T

A William IV silver-gilt vinaigrette, by Joseph Willmore, Birmingham.

1831   *3½in (9cm) high*

$1,300-1,800   SWO

ESSENTIAL REFERENCE—NATHANIEL MILLS

Nathaniel Mills (1746-1840) registered his first mark as a silversmith, in 1803, as a partner of Mills and Langston. Soon afterward he set up his own workshop in Caroline Street, Birmingham.

- **His son, also called Nathaniel Mills (1811-73), later took over the business.**
- **Both father and son were eager to incorporate new techniques into their work, such as stamping, casting, and engine turning.**
- **The workshop made silver boxes, vinaigrettes, card cases, and snuff boxes. It specialized in "castle-top" pieces, which depicted architectural scenes. Obscure buildings, or rare views of well-known buildings, can attract high prices.**
- **These "castle-top" boxes were sold as souvenirs and the business was successful. Nathaniel Mills the younger died rich, leaving £30,000 (about $2.4 million today) in his will.**

A silver "castle-top" vinaigrette, depicting Balmoral, by Joseph Taylor and John Perry, Birmingham, date letter indistinct.

1¾in (4.5cm) long

$950-1,050   SWO

A Victorian silver purse vinaigrette, by Gervase Wheeler, Birmingham.

1838

$400-500   BRI

A Victorian silver "castle-top" vinaigrette, depicting Abbotsford, the reverse with engraved initials, maker's mark "E.S.," Birmingham.

1841

$750-900   BRI

A Victorian silver "castle-top" vinaigrette, depicting Warwick Castle, by Nathaniel Mills, Birmingham.

1841

$1,000-1,150

An 18ct gold vinaigrette, by John Yapp and John Woodward, Birmingham.
1846   1½in (3.5cm) long
$2,500-3,200   **SWO**

A Victorian silver vinaigrette, depicting a watermill, by Nathaniel Mills, Birmingham.
1846
$650-750   **BRI**

A Victorian silver "castle-top" vinaigrette, depicting Abbotsford House, by Nathaniel Mills, Birmingham.
1848   1½in (4cm) long
$800-950   **FLD**

An S. Mordan and Co. silver-gilt-mounted glass double scent bottle or vinaigrette, stamped "S. Mordan & Co., Makers," with date mark.
1858
$650-750   **FLD**

A Victorian silver vinaigrette, with initials "C.D.," by E. Smith, Birmingham.
1859
$300-400   **BRI**

A Victorian silver combination vinaigrette, modeled as a barrel, by Henry William Dee, London, with associated silver bracelet.
1869   1¼in (3cm) long 2⅛oz
$1,500-2,000   **FELL**

A Victorian silver cornucopia-shaped combination vinaigrette and scent bottle, with suspension chain and amethyst colored cabochon, by S. Mordan and Co., London.
1872   4in (10cm) long 1¾oz
$500-650   **GORL**

A Victorian silver thimble-shaped vinaigrette, of a spider web design, maker's mark "A.D.," London.
1873
$750-900   **BRI**

A Victorian silver whistle vinaigrette, by George Unite, Birmingham.
1875   2½in (6.5cm) long ¾oz
$650-750   **WW**

A Victorian combined vinaigrette and scent bottle, maker's mark "T.J.," London.
1877
$500-650   **BRI**

An Irish Georgian silver table snuff casket, the lids with a crest of a hand and monogram, by Benjamin Stokes, Dublin.

The sign of the hand dexter alludes to the Daly's kinship to the O'Neills of Ulster.

c1750   3¾in (9.5cm) wide 7oz

$7,000-8,000 ADA

A George II to George III Irish silver snuff box, with six compartments, an engraved crest and coat of arms, initialed "EB," maker "S," by Benjamin Stokes, Dublin.

c1760   3in (7.5cm) diam 3½oz

$4,400-5,000 LC

A George III silver-gilt and micromosaic snuff box, by Hockley and Bosworth, London.

1815   3in (7.5cm) long

$7,000-7,500 WW

An early Victorian "castle-top" snuff box, depicting Warwick Castle, by Nathaniel Mills, Birmingham.

1838   2½in (6.5cm) long 1½oz

$1,050-1,200 LC

A silver "castle-top" snuff box, depicting Kenilworth house, by Nathaniel Mills, Birmingham, some wear.

3in (7.5cm) wide 2½oz

$1,000-1,150 PW

CLOSER LOOK—SILVER SNUFF BOX

This is a fine example of a rare "castle-top" snuff box.

The lid is engraved with a view of East Cliff Lodge, Ramsgate, after a watercolor by Turner, apparently painted when Turner visited the house in 1797.

The gilt interior is engraved with the Montefiore crest on the lid.

It was probably a special commission by Sir Moses Haim Montefiore (1784-1885), financier, philanthropist, and President of the Board of Deputies of British Jews 1835-74. He purchased the house in 1830 and lived there with his wife until his death.

A Victorian silver snuff box, by Hilliard & Thomason, Birmingham.

1854   3½in (9cm) long 6½oz

$65,000-80,000 MAB

A George IV silver raised relief "Pedlar" snuff box, engraved with two crests, by John Linnit, London.

The crests are those of Hervey-Bathurst, Baronets of Clarendon Park, Wiltshire.

1825   4in (10cm) long 6¼oz

$2,500-3,800 WW

An early Victorian silver table snuff box, by Nathaniel Mills, Birmingham.

1839   3¼oz

$700-800 HAN

A Victorian Scottish silver thistle-form snuff box, with Cairngorm cover.

2½oz

$400-450 WAD

An 18thC diamond-set, carved quartz and gold-mounted horse's head snuff box, possibly by the widow of the jeweler Louis Buyrette, Berlin.

Similar stone selection, carving, and eye mounts can be seen in a series of dudelsack (German bag pipe) boxes by the jeweler Louis Buyrette.

c1760   *3in (7.5cm) high*

$8,000-9,500   **WW**

A rare 18thC Channel Islands silver-mounted cowrie snuff box, maker's mark "IH," Guernsey, engraved "MSBK," some losses, some small dings to lid, lid hinge loose.

This is believed to be only the second piece of Channel Islands silver mounted with a cowrie shell. The other example is a cowrie shell spoon by Guillaume Henry of Guernsey.

3¼in (8.5cm) long

$2,300-2,800   **MART**

A French enameled gold-mounted and tortoiseshell snuff box, maker's mark indistinct, discharge marks for Eloi Brichard (1756-62) and Paris date letter "T," some cracks and paint loss.

1759-60   *3½in (9cm) wide*

$12,000-14,000   **TEN**

A German enameled gold snuff box, maker's mark "LC," with crowned "K," Hanau, some losses.

c1780   *3¾in (9.5cm) wide 6⅛oz*

$27,000-33,000   **ECGW**

A Regency gold and enamel snuff box.

1¼in (3cm) wide

$900-1,000   **HT**

An early 19thC Swiss 18ct gold and enameled snuff box, maker's mark "S&D," Geneva, some chips and scratches.

c1820   *2¾in (7cm) long 1⅞oz*

$11,000-12,000   **GORL**

A 19thC Continental enameled 20ct gold snuff box, in the manner of Jean Ducrollay, with panels after Francois Boucher, one panel probably a replacement, some wear.

A box of similar design by Ducrollay, with en plein still-life enamels, can be found in the Musee de Louvre, Paris.

3¼in (8cm) wide

$19,000-25,000   **TEN**

A mid-19thC lacquered papier-mâché Freemasons' snuff box, painted with an eye, ear, and padlocked lips alluding to the Freemasons' motto, "Audi, Vide, Tace."

The motto "Audi, Vide, Tace" ("Hear, See, Be Silent") relates to one of the symbols of Masonry that is most understood: secrecy.

4in (10cm) diam

$1,600-2,000   **WW**

A 19thC Italian micromosaic and tortoiseshell snuff box, depicting the falls at Tivoli, some cracking, lifting away from lid, base faded.

3in (7.5cm) diam

$5,500-6,500   **GORL**

An early 18thC Continental gold-mounted tortoiseshell box, set with three semiprecious stones and watercolors.

3½in (9cm) wide

$1,050-1,200   CHOR

A Georgian tortoiseshell étui, modeled as a saddle bag, with inlaid metal decoration.

3in (7.5cm) high

$900-1,000   FELL

A Regency tortoiseshell nécessaire, with ivory banding, fitted a silver thimble and ivory cylindrical case.

4in (10cm) high

$500-650   CHOR

An early 19thC tortoiseshell needle packet box.

2½in (6.5cm) long

$300-350   BLEA

A tortoiseshell and mother-of-pearl étui, with needle card, silver scissors, silver pencil, tape measure, folding knife, scale, stiletto, and thimble, some damages.

c1840   *4¼in (11cm) high*

$300-350   BLEA

A Victorian silver-mounted tortoiseshell playing cards box, by Saunders and Shepherd, Chester, England, with the playing card suits in silver, with a playing card under glass, the interior of set with two whist markers.

1897

4in (10cm) long

$500-650   WW

An early 20thC tortoiseshell piqué needle case.

$200-250   FELL

An inlaid tortoiseshell miniature box.

$500-650   SWO

A George V silver and tortoiseshell ring box, by Kemp Brothers, Birmingham.

1918   *7in (18cm) wide*

$250-320   TRI

A probably late 17thC silver quill case or toothpick case.
3¼in (8cm) long ¾oz
$400-500 WW

A George III silver toothpick box, the velvet-lined interior lacking mirror, by Samuel Pemberton, Birmingham.
1786 *3¼in (8.5cm) long 1⅛oz*
$1,400-1,800 WW

A George III gold-mounted tortoiseshell toothpick box, velvet-lined, with mirror.
c1800 *3½in (9cm) long*
$550-650 WW

A George III silver toothpick box, by Samuel Pemberton, Birmingham.
1800 *2¾in (7cm) long ¾oz*
$400-500 WW

A George III 18ct gold toothpick box, by Alexander J. Strahan, London.
1805 *40oz*
$1,500-1,900 SWO

A George III velvet-lined gold-mounted tortoiseshell toothpick box, with a center carved ivory landscape scene, probably by Stephany and Dresch, in fitted case.
c1790 *4in (10cm) long*
$1,300-1,800 WW

A George III gold-mounted silver toothpick box, set with an image of a dog.
c1790 *3½in (9cm) long 1¾oz*
$800-900 WW

A George III silver filigree toothpick box, velvet-lined, with mirror.
c1790-1800 *3¼in (8cm) long ⅞oz*
$450-500 WW

A George III silver-mounted shaqreen toothpick box, velvet-lined, with mirror.
c1800 *4in (10cm) long*
$650-750 WW

A 19thC gold-mounted rock crystal toothpick box, the coach door initialed "WR."
c1830-35 *2¾in (7cm) long*
$1,200-1,400 WW

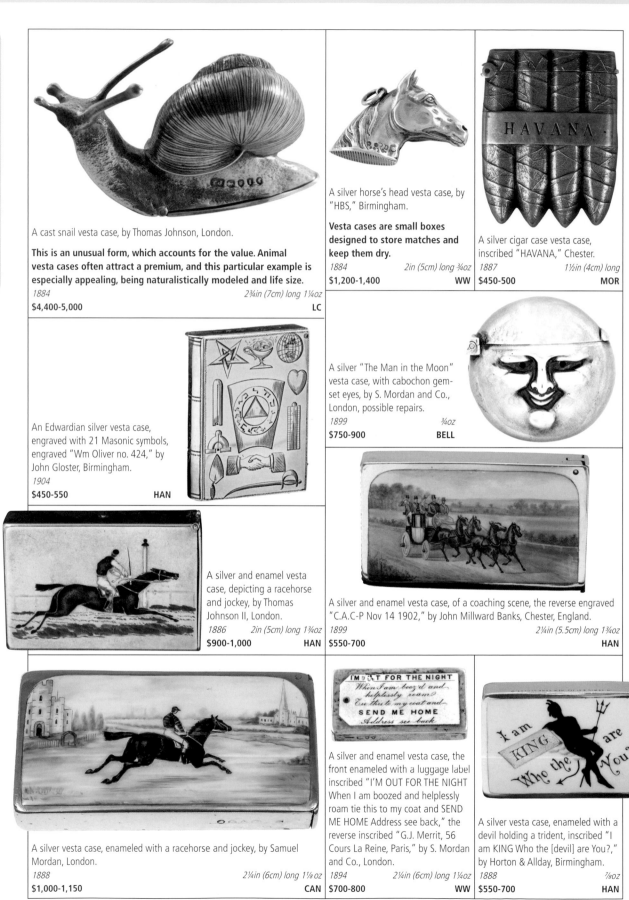

A cast snail vesta case, by Thomas Johnson, London.

This is an unusual form, which accounts for the value. Animal vesta cases often attract a premium, and this particular example is especially appealing, being naturalistically modeled and life size.

1884   *2¾in (7cm) long 1¼oz*
$4,400-5,000   **LC**

A silver horse's head vesta case, by "HBS," Birmingham.

Vesta cases are small boxes designed to store matches and keep them dry.

1884   *2in (5cm) long ¾oz*
$1,200-1,400   **WW**

A silver cigar case vesta case, inscribed "HAVANA," Chester.

1887   *1½in (4cm) long*
$450-500   **MOR**

An Edwardian silver vesta case, engraved with 21 Masonic symbols, engraved "Wm Oliver no. 424," by John Gloster, Birmingham.

1904
$450-550   **HAN**

A silver "The Man in the Moon" vesta case, with cabochon gem-set eyes, by S. Mordan and Co., London, possible repairs.

1899   *¾oz*
$750-900   **BELL**

A silver and enamel vesta case, depicting a racehorse and jockey, by Thomas Johnson II, London.

1886   *2in (5cm) long 1¾oz*
$900-1,000   **HAN**

A silver and enamel vesta case, of a coaching scene, the reverse engraved "C.A.C-P Nov 14 1902," by John Millward Banks, Chester, England.

1899   *2¼in (5.5cm) long 1¾oz*
$550-700   **HAN**

A silver vesta case, enameled with a racehorse and jockey, by Samuel Mordan, London.

1888   *2¼in (6cm) long 1⅛oz*
$1,000-1,150   **CAN**

A silver and enamel vesta case, the front enameled with a luggage label inscribed "I'M OUT FOR THE NIGHT When I am boozed and helplessly roam tie this to my coat and SEND ME HOME Address see back," the reverse inscribed "G.J. Merrit, 56 Cours La Reine, Paris," by S. Mordan and Co., London.

1894   *2¼in (6cm) long 1¼oz*
$700-800   **WW**

A silver vesta case, enameled with a devil holding a trident, inscribed "I am KING Who the [devil] are You?," by Horton & Allday, Birmingham.

1888   *⅞oz*
$550-700   **HAN**

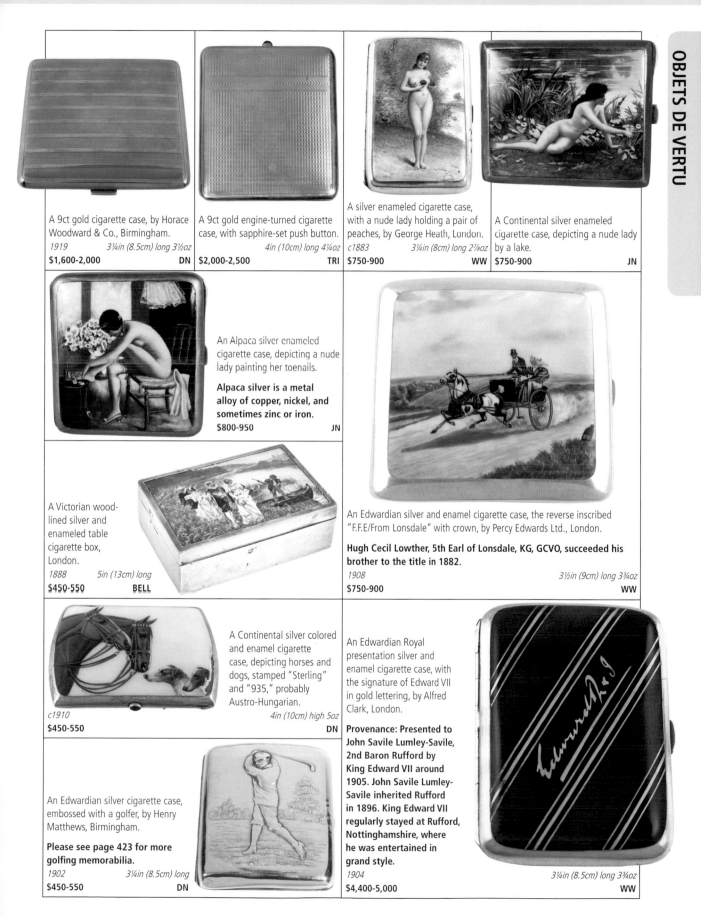

A 9ct gold cigarette case, by Horace Woodward & Co., Birmingham.
1919 *3¼in (8.5cm) long 3½oz*
$1,600-2,000 DN

A 9ct gold engine-turned cigarette case, with sapphire-set push button.
4in (10cm) long 4¼oz
$2,000-2,500 TRI

A silver enameled cigarette case, with a nude lady holding a pair of peaches, by George Heath, London.
c1883 *3¼in (8cm) long 2⅞oz*
$750-900 WW

A Continental silver enameled cigarette case, depicting a nude lady by a lake.
$750-900 JN

An Alpaca silver enameled cigarette case, depicting a nude lady painting her toenails.
Alpaca silver is a metal alloy of copper, nickel, and sometimes zinc or iron.
$800-950 JN

A Victorian wood-lined silver and enameled table cigarette box, London.
1888 *5in (13cm) long*
$450-550 BELL

An Edwardian silver and enamel cigarette case, the reverse inscribed "F.F.E/From Lonsdale" with crown, by Percy Edwards Ltd., London.
Hugh Cecil Lowther, 5th Earl of Lonsdale, KG, GCVO, succeeded his brother to the title in 1882.
1908 *3½in (9cm) long 3¾oz*
$750-900 WW

A Continental silver colored and enamel cigarette case, depicting horses and dogs, stamped "Sterling" and "935," probably Austro-Hungarian.
c1910 *4in (10cm) high 5oz*
$450-550 DN

An Edwardian silver cigarette case, embossed with a golfer, by Henry Matthews, Birmingham.
Please see page 423 for more golfing memorabilia.
1902 *3¼in (8.5cm) long*
$450-550 DN

An Edwardian Royal presentation silver and enamel cigarette case, with the signature of Edward VII in gold lettering, by Alfred Clark, London.
Provenance: Presented to John Savile Lumley-Savile, 2nd Baron Rufford by King Edward VII around 1905. John Savile Lumley-Savile inherited Rufford in 1896. King Edward VII regularly stayed at Rufford, Nottinghamshire, where he was entertained in grand style.
1904 *3¼in (8.5cm) long 3¾oz*
$4,400-5,000 WW

A rare London enamel snuff box, with the coat of arms for the Hippesley family, the sides with Meissen-style landscapes, with gilt-metal mounts.

The crest and the first quarter of the shield are those of Toby Ipsley of Hambleton in Rutland, granted in 1681.

c1740-45   *2½in (6.5cm) long*

$3,800-4,400   **WW**

A mid-to-late 18thC German enamel, painted with Meissen-style puce scenes, the interior lid with figures around a statue of Neptune.

3in (7.5cm) long

$3,800-4,400   **WW**

A Birmingham or South Staffordshire enamel gilt-metal-mounted lion snuff box, the lid with a hunter chasing a leopard.

c1760   *4¼in (11cm) long*

$4,400-5,000   **WW**

A Birmingham enamel snuff box, painted with figures, the interior with a portrait of the actress, Mrs. Mary Brooks (nèe L'Hereux), with gilt-metal mounts.

The source for the portrait of Mrs. Brooks is a mezzotint by Richard Houston, after Thomas Worlidge. Mary L'Hereux married the Irish engraver, John Brooks, in 1756. He was made bankrupt three years later. Mrs. Brooks turned to acting in order to support herself and her three children.

1760-65   *3¼in (8cm) long*

$2,800-3,500   **WW**

A Birmingham enamel shoe snuff box.

c1760-70   *4in (10cm) long*

$1,000-1,150   **WW**

A Birmingham or South Staffordshire enamel snuff box, painted with a drunk and his bare-breasted companion, the base after a Robert Hancock print, with gilt-metal mounts.

c1765-70   *3½in (9cm) long*

$2,300-2,800   **WW**

CLOSER LOOK—BATTERSEA ENAMEL SNUFF BOX

Pictorial enamels emerged at a factory in Battersea, London, in the mid-18thC and are highly collectible today.

The lid is printed in sepia with a scene of soldiers attacking the Trojan horse.

The sides and base have panels of shells and floral motifs on a diaper ground.

The lid's interior has a portrait of a Chancellor of the Exchequer. Given the date, and the similarly to a 1754 print by John Hinton, it seems probable that the portrait is of Henry Pelham. However, it also bears similarities to Sir Robert Walpole or Henry Boyle.

A Battersea enamel snuff box.

c1750-55   *3¼in (8.5cm) long*

$4,400-5,000   **WW**

Judith Picks

The Jacobites were the supporters of King James II, usurped by William and Mary in 1688 in the Glorious Revolution. Later, it became a general term for those who favored the restoration of the Stuart dynasty, including supporters of both James Francis Edward Stuart, James II's son, nicknamed the Old Pretender, and of his son Charles Edward Stuart, nicknamed Bonnie Prince Charlie or the Young Pretender. The portrait on this box of Bonnie Prince Charlie is after one by Sir Robert Strange. This box is unusual in its brazen display of the Prince's likeness. Such portraits would typically be concealed on the interior lid of a box to protect its owner from accusations of treason.

A Birmingham enamel snuff box, of Jacobite interest, painted with a portrait of Bonnie Prince Charlie, reserved on ground of flags and other military motifs, the sides with Classical ruins and Italianate landscapes.

c1760   *3½in (9cm) long*

$1,150-1,500   **WW**

A Birmingham or South Staffordshire enamel bonbonnière, modeled as two dogs fighting over a game bird.
c1760-65   *3in (7.5cm) long*
$2,300-2,800   **WW**

A Birmingham or South Staffordshire enamel swan bonbonnière.
c1760-70   *3in (7.5cm) long*
$2,300-2,800   **WW**

A late 18thC Bilston enamel boxing match patch box, titled "Set To."
c1770   *1¾in (4.5cm) wide*
$1,500-1,900   **HAN**

An English enamel patch box, probably Bilston, inscribed "God Bless the United States" to lid, paper label for "D M & P Manheim, New York and London."
c1770-80   *1¾in (4.5cm) wide*
$5,000-6,300   **WW**

A Bilston enamel patch box, inscribed "Great Washington to Thee We owe our Liberty," with internal mirror, paper label for "D M & P Manheim, New York and London."
c1780   *1¾in (4.5cm) wide*
$3,200-3,000   **WW**

An early 19thC enamel patch box, probably South Staffordshire, printed with a portrait of Admiral Nelson, titled "Nelson & Victory," with interior mirror.
                    2in (5cm) long
$1,900-2,500   **KEY**

A Battersea enamel portrait plaque, depicting Maria Gunning, Countess of Coventry, in a metal frame.

This image of Maria Gunning is copied from Jean-Etienne Liotard's 1749 painting of her in Turkish costume. Maria Gunning was a celebrated beauty of the 18thC, so much so that she was once mobbed in Hyde Park, London. Against her husband's advice, she wore heavy makeup despite her young age, which contributed to her death at the age of 27 from lead and mercury poisoning.
c1760   *4¼in (10.5cm) high*
$2,800-3,500   **WW**

An oval enamel plaque, printed with a portrait of General Clinton.

General Clinton was British Commander-in-Chief in North America during the American Revolutionary War. Clinton laid siege to the city of Charleston in 1780, forcing the surrender of the city in May 1780.
c1780   *3in (7.5cm) long*
$2,300-2,800   **KEY**

A South Staffordshire enamel wine funnel, with gilt-metal mounts.
c1770   *4¼in (11cm) high*
$3,800-5,000   **WW**

A French Empire enamel perfume bottle and stopper, with silver cap and base.
                    2½in (6.5cm) high
$1,500-2,000   **JN**

ESSENTIAL REFERENCE—CARD CASES

From the late 18thC to the early 20thC, calling cards were used in polite society to announce the arrival of a visitor, to request a visit, or as a gesture in place of an actual social call.

- On making a first visit to a new acquaintance, it was good etiquette to leave a card with a servant and then depart. If a card was sent in return, a visit could be attempted next time.
- When visiting a friend, a lady or gentleman would present their card to the servant at the door. If the master or mistress of the house was "at home"—here meaning not only in the house but at leisure to receive visitors—the visitor would be invited in. If not, their card would be left to show that they had called.
- Both ladies and gentlemen would have carried cards with them when making social calls. Young unmarried ladies sometimes held a joint card with their mothers, but husbands and wives typically had separate cards.
- Card cases were made from tortoiseshell, mother-of-pearl, ivory, silver, and other metals.
- Silver "castle-top" card cases, depicting buildings of note, often castles, cathedrals, and country houses, are among the finest.
- Desirable makers of silver card cases include Edward Smith, Taylor & Perry, Joseph Wilmore, and Nathaniel Mills.

A William IV silver "castle-top" card case, depicting Newstead Abbey, the reverse with a medallion of Lord Byron, by Taylor and Perry, Birmingham.

1836   *3¾in (9.5cm) long 2¼oz*
$1,300-1,800   **WW**

An early Victorian silver card case, by Joseph Willmore, Birmingham, William IV duty mark, cover loose.

1838   *3¾in (9.5cm) long*
$450-500   **DN**

A Victorian silver "castle-top" card case, depicting Lincoln Cathedral and Windsor Castle, by Joseph Willmore, Birmingham.

1844   *4in (10cm) long 2¾oz*
$1,900-2,500   **WW**

A Victorian silver engraved "castle-top" card case, depicting Bar Gate, Southampton, by Nathaniel Mills, Birmingham.

1843   *4in (10cm) long 2¼oz*
$3,800-4,400   **WW**

A Victorian silver-gilt "castle-top" card case, with Melrose Abbey, by Nathaniel MIlls, Birmingham.

1845   *3½in (9cm) high 1¾oz*
$2,800-3,500   **HAN**

A rare Victorian silver "castle-top" card case, depicting St Michael's Mount with the Royal yacht "The Victoria and Albert," by George Bower and Son, Birmingham.

Queen Victoria and Prince Albert visited St Michael's Mount on September 6, 1846.

1846 4¼in (10.5cm) long 2¼oz
$6,500-7,500   **WW**

A Victorian silver card case, engraved with the Scott monument, Edinburgh, minor dent, maker's mark "FM," Birmingham.

1847   *4in (10cm) long*
$400-450   **CHOR**

A Victorian silver "castle-top" card case, depicting St Paul's Cathedral, by Nathaniel Mills, Birmingham.

1844   *4in (10cm) long 2⅜oz*
$1,600-2,000   **WW**

A Victorian silver "castle-top" card case, depicting Jenny Lind in Bellini's "La Sonnambula," by Edward Smith, Birmingham. **Johanna Maria Lind (1820-87), better known as Jenny Lind, was a Swedish opera singer, often known as the "Swedish Nightingale." Lind gave her first performance in London on May 4, 1847.**
1848   *4¼in (10.5cm) long 2⅜oz*
$1,150-1,400   **WW**

A Victorian silver "castle-top" card case, depicting Kensington Palace, by Nathaniel Mills, Birmingham.
1848   *3½in (9cm) long 1⅞oz*
$1,600-2,000   **WW**

A Victorian silver "castle-top" card case, depicting King's College Cambridge, by Nathaniel Mills, Birmingham.
1853   *4in (10cm) long 2¼oz*
$2,300-2,800   **WW**

A Victorian silver "castle-top" card case, depicting the Crystal Palace, by Nathaniel Mills, Birmingham.
1853   *4in (10cm) long 2⅛oz*
$2,300-2,800   **WW**

A Victorian silver "castle-top" card case, depicting Balmoral, the reverse with similar decoration and inscribed "F.Wright, 1893," by Alfred Taylor, Birmingham.
1861   *4in (10cm) long 2⅝oz*
$1,050-1,200   **WW**

A rare Victorian Irish silver "castle-top" card case, depicting Dun Laoghaire harbor, the reverse with a crest and inscribed "From Schriber and Sons 1864," by John Schriber, Dublin.

The cartouche is engraved with a viscount's coronet ensigning the crest of Menteith of Scotland and Hodge(s) and Hodgekins of England, but is absent from official Irish records.
1863   *4in (10cm) long 2¼oz*
$15,000-19,000   **WW**

A mid-19thC Victorian gem-painted tortoiseshell card case, depicting the Scott Monument, Edinburgh, with ivory edging.
4in (10cm) long
$160-200   **DN**

A Victorian pressed tortoiseshell and pewter strung card case, depicting York Minster to each side.
4in (10cm) long
$190-250   **DN**

A Victorian painted papier-mâché card case, with ivory edging, hinge slightly loose, crazing crack.
4¼in (11cm) long
$190-250   **DN**

A James II silver tubular nutmeg grater, maker's mark worn, London.

Nutmeg has been valued for its medicinal properties since medieval times. It gained popularity in the 18thC. After the Napoleonic Wars, when Great Britain gained control of Run Island, then the world's sole source of nutmeg, it became increasingly affordable.

1686   2¼in (6cm) long ¾oz
$1,900-2,500   **WW**

A William and Mary to William III silver nutmeg grater, the base cover opening to a compartment, by Thomas Kedden.

c1690-1700   2¾in (7cm) long ⅞oz
$1,300-1,800   **WW**

A William and Mary to William III silver tear-drop nutmeg grater, maker's mark "I.A," London.

c1690-1700 1½in (4cm) long ¾oz
$2,300-2,800   **WW**

A Continental silver urn-shaped nutmeg grater, with pull-out grater.

c1740   2in (5cm) high ¾oz
$500-550   **WW**

A George III silver nutmeg grater, initialed "A.H.," by Thomas Willmore, Birmingham.

1798
$500-550   **BRI**

A George III silver-gilt nutmeg grater, monogrammed, by Joseph Taylor, Birmingham.

1799   1½in (4cm) high ⅝oz
$650-700   **WW**

A George III silver novelty egg-shaped nutmeg grater, lacking interior, by Samuel Merriton II, London.

1810   1½in (4cm) long
$300-400   **LSK**

A George IV silver nutmeg grater, with a crest, by Nathaniel Mills, Birmingham, lacking date letter.

c1825   1⅛oz
$500-550   **HAN**

A silver nutmeg grater, with initialed cartouche, by Hilliard & Thomason, Birmingham.

1855   1½in (4cm) long ⅝oz
$700-750   **WW**

A Victorian pear-form silver nutmeg grater, by Hilliard & Thomason, Birmingham.

1856   1½in (4cm) long ¾oz
$3,800-4,400   **WW**

A Victorian silver walnut nutmeg grater, with silver-gilt interior, by Jane Brownett, London.

Jane Brownett was a smallworker, chiefly making silver vesta cases, boxes, tongs, purses, and novelties. She took over her husband Abraham Brownett's silver workshop in London after his death in 1867. He had previously been half of the partnership Brownett & Rose formed c1858.

1886   1½in (4cm) long 1¼oz
$1,500-2,000   **WW**

A Victorian 10ct gold pencil, modeled as a salmon, by S. Mordan and Co., retailed by Leuchars and Son.

Sampson Mordan (1790-1843) was a British silversmith. In 1822, along with his associate Joseph Isaac Hawkins, he patented the first mechanical pencil. The partnership dissolved in 1837, after which Mordan continued to sell his pencils and other metalware under the name S. Mordan and Co.

2¼in (6cm) long ¼oz

$950-1,050   WW

A Victorian silver "supersize" mechanical pencil, engraved 'Xmas 1881," by S. Mordan and Co., retailed by Jones of Paris and London.

1881   closed 5½in (14cm) long

$800-950   WW

A silver and gold four-stage telescopic pencil, with design registration number, by S. Mordan and Co. for Hamilton and Co., Calcutta.

designed 1881   1¼in (3cm) closed ½oz

$650-750   WW

A Victorian silver hand bell pencil.

closed 1½in (3.5cm) long ⅛oz

$900-1,000   WW

A silver watering can inkwell and pen, the pull-out telescopic spout forming the pen, by S. Mordan and Co., London.

1878   4¼in (10cm) high

$1,500-2,000   WW

A pair of silver menu card holders, by John Harris, London.

1853   2¼in (6cm) long 4¼oz

$550-700   WW

CLOSER LOOK—NOVELTY MUSTARD POT

This mustard pot and spoon is cast and chased in the form of a Hussars or Royal Artillery busby.

It is inscribed with the motto "I Am Ready."

It was manufactured by Elkington & Co., a metalware company founded by George Richard Elkington in Birmingham in 1801.

It is engraved with the Scottish family crest of Fraser and Maxwell.

A set of four Edwardian silver and enamel game bird menu card holders, by S. Mordan and Co., Chester, in retailer's case from Austin & William, Conduit Street, London, some scratches.

1908   1½in (3.5cm) high

$3,200-3,800   TEN

An Edwardian silver mustard pot and spoon, missing glass liner.

1910   4½in (11.5cm) high 6¼oz

$5,000-5,700   DN

A Kate Greenaway napkin ring, showing a girl teaching children their alphabets, by Simpson, Hall, Miller & Co.

This is the only known figural napkin ring with three Kate Greenaway figures.

3½in (9cm) high

$2,300-2,800   MORP

A silver cat pepperette, by James Barclay Hennell, London, Design Registration mark for 1895.

1881   *3in (7.5cm) high 3¼oz*

$1,400-1,800   **DN**

A silver partridge pepper pot, by R.H.H., Sheffield.

1925   *3¾in (9.5cm) high 4⅜oz*

$950-1,050   **WW**

A Mappin & Webb silver-plated military-themed cruet set, raised on ball feet, one detached but present.

7in (18cm) wide

$450-500   **LOCK**

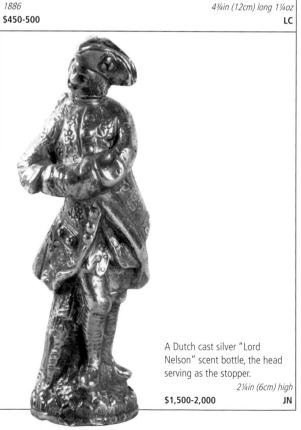

An engraved posy holder, by George Unite, Birmingham.

1886   *4¾in (12cm) long 1¼oz*

$450-500   **LC**

An engraved cast silver-gilt horn-form posy holder, with coat of arms and motto "SIT PRUDENTIA" below "WASHINGTON HIBBERT," by Samuel Rudduck and Jachariah Jennings, London.

1829   *4¼in (11cm) long 4oz*

$1,300-1,800   **LC**

A Victorian silver-mounted green hard-stone scent bottle, the center with a harp, the reverse with a shamrock, Queen's Duty head mark.

2¼in (5.5cm) long

$450-550   **WW**

A Victorian silver-mounted glass owl scent bottle, with glass eyes, repaired scratch, by S. Mordan and Co., London.

1894   *3¼in (8cm) long*

$700-800   **WW**

A Dutch cast silver "Lord Nelson" scent bottle, the head serving as the stopper.

2¼in (6cm) high

$1,500-2,000   **JN**

A silver amatory spice box, with "MALGRE LAVIE," the base with a ho ho bird beneath "A LA GUERRE ET A LA PAIS" (at war and peace), maker's mark "T.T," London.

c1690   *1½in (4cm) long ⅞oz*
$3,200-3,800   **LC**

An 18thC silver spice box, later dot engraved "PL 1781."

3¼in (8cm) wide 3⅛oz
$700-800   **L&T**

A silver stamp moistener, with the face of David Lloyd George, by William Hutton & Sons Ltd., Sheffield, some wear.

1912   *3in (7.5cm) high 2¾oz*
$400-450   **FELL**

A silver apple corer, monogrammed, by Hampston, Prince and Cattles, York.

c1800   *6in (15cm) long 1¼oz*
$900-1,000   **WW**

A silver-gilt and gold filigree traveling mirror, with velvet lining.

c1680-90   *3½in (9cm) long*
$2,500-3,200   **WW**

A rhinoceros silver box, by John Septimus Beresford, London.

1879   *4¼in (11cm) long 5½oz*
$3,800-4,400   **GORL**

A silver regimental-style dragon table cigar lighter, by Synyer & Beddoes, Birmingham, some dents.

1923   *5½in (14cm) long 6⅛oz*
$800-950   **DN**

A late 18thC Dutch silver pocket corkscrew, with later Dutch tax mark.

3¼in (8cm) long
$550-700   **WW**

A George III silver pocket corkscrew, by Joseph Taylor, Birmingham.

c1800   *3½in (9cm) long*
$400-450   **WW**

A 19thC bone-handled steel twin-pillar rack and pinion corkscrew, in the manner of Lund, stamped "Patent," lacks brush.

closed 6in (15cm) high
$800-900   **FLD**

OBJETS DE VERTU

ESSENTIAL REFERENCE—FANS

Folding fans were developed in China and Japan and came to Europe in the early 16thC. They were commonly used from the 17thC to early 20thC.

● While some antique fans have struggled in recent years, the market is improving for rare fans in good condition.

● Chinese fans are often sought after. While chiefly associated with export trade, Chinese fans also had their place in the Qing court.

● Classic brisé fans are popular, as are European fans depicting scenes of great interest or by key designers, such as Frances Houghton or Jules Donzel.

A George III engraved and hand-colored imaginary map paper fan, the "LAND OF MATRIMONY," with islands "ENCHANTED," "Coquet," and "Divorce," with the "OCEAN OF LOVE" and the "Bay of Repentance," printed by T. Pike, King Street, Bloomsbury, with wooden guards and sticks.

1788   *9¼in (23.5cm) long*

$2,500-3,200   **WW**

A French single paper leaf fan, by Jules Donzel, depicting a newly married couple departing a church, with mother-of-pearl sticks and guards, signed "Donzel," in card box labeled "F. Noble Jones."

Donzel was one of the most fashionable 19thC fan painters, one of three members of the family whose designs were sought by the top Paris makers, including Duvelleroy and Keys. This fan was carried by Queen Mary at the Wedding of Princess Victorian Louise of Prussia and Prince Ernest Augustus of Cumberland, Berlin, May 24, 1913.

c1880   *13in (33cm) wide*

$2,300-2,800   **SAS**

A late 19thC French ostrich feather fan, with tortoiseshell sticks and a rose-cut diamond-set monogram, in original silk covered box, retailed by Buissot.

$1,300-1,800   **REEM**

A Chinese harbor scene fan, the wooden sticks lacquered.

c1840-60   *guards 11in (28cm) long*

$3,200-3,800   **TEN**

A mid-19thC Chinese Canton tortoiseshell brisé fan.

9in (23cm) high

$1,800-2,500   **MAB**

A 19thC Chinese lacquer brisé fan, gilded and painted with equestrian figures and attendants.

7¾in (19.5cm) high

$1,600-2,000   **MAB**

A mid-19thC Chinese carved tortoiseshell Mandarin fan, the sticks and guards elaborately carved, in original box.

guards 10¾in (27cm) long

$5,500-6,500   **TEN**

A late 19thC Chinese tortoiseshell brisé fan.

7¾in (19.5cm) high

$2,500-3,200   **MAB**

CLOSER LOOK—CHINESE REPUBLIC PERIOD FAN

This Chinese paper fan depicts a European girl and a hound in a garden.

It is in the style of Lang Shining, otherwise known as Giuseppe Castiglione (1688-1766). Castiglione was an 18thC Jesuit who took the name Lang Shining while in China.

It was made in the Chinese Republic period (1912-49), but is apocryphally dated the 22nd year of Qianlong's reign, 1757, with a poem composed by Emperor Qianlong and signed "Yu Minzhong" (1714-79).

The extreme fine quality of painting on this piece ensures its value.

An ink and color on paper fan.

20¾in (52.5cm) wide

$15,000-19,000   **L&T**

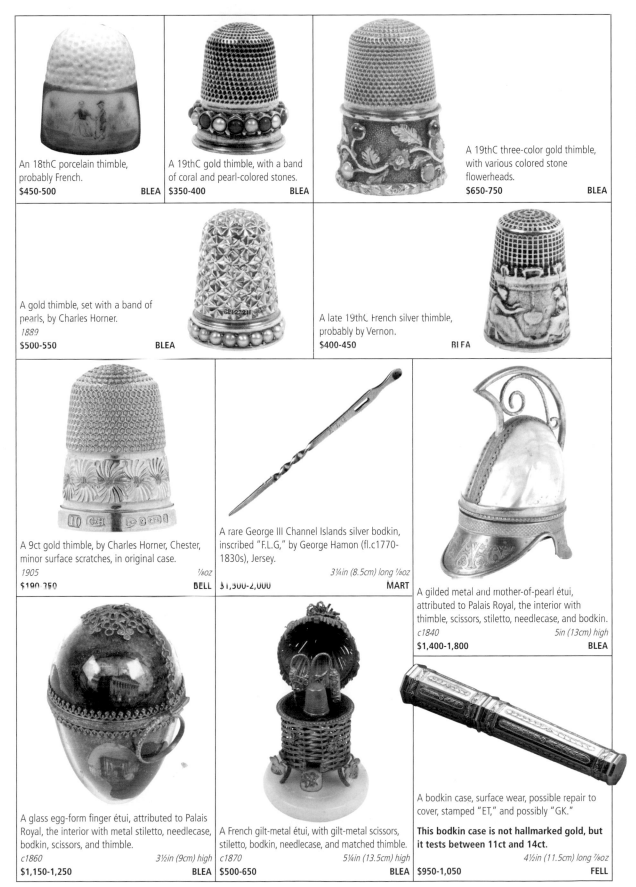

An 18thC porcelain thimble, probably French.
$450-500 BLEA

A 19thC gold thimble, with a band of coral and pearl-colored stones.
$350-400 BLEA

A 19thC three-color gold thimble, with various colored stone flowerheads.
$650-750 BLEA

A gold thimble, set with a band of pearls, by Charles Horner.
1889
$500-550 BLEA

A late 19thC French silver thimble, probably by Vernon.
$400-450 BI FA

A 9ct gold thimble, by Charles Horner, Chester, minor surface scratches, in original case.
1905 *⅛oz*
$190-250 BELL

A rare George III Channel Islands silver bodkin, inscribed "F.L.G," by George Hamon (fl.c1770-1830s), Jersey.
3¼in (8.5cm) long ⅛oz
$1,500-2,000 MART

A gilded metal and mother-of-pearl étui, attributed to Palais Royal, the interior with thimble, scissors, stiletto, needlecase, and bodkin.
c1840 *5in (13cm) high*
$1,400-1,800 BLEA

A glass egg-form finger étui, attributed to Palais Royal, the interior with metal stiletto, needlecase, bodkin, scissors, and thimble.
c1860 *3½in (9cm) high*
$1,150-1,250 BLEA

A French gilt-metal étui, with gilt-metal scissors, stiletto, bodkin, needlecase, and matched thimble.
c1870 *5¼in (13.5cm) high*
$500-650 BLEA

A bodkin case, surface wear, possible repair to cover, stamped "ET," and possibly "GK."
This bodkin case is not hallmarked gold, but it tests between 11ct and 14ct.
4½in (11.5cm) long ⅞oz
$950-1,050 FELL

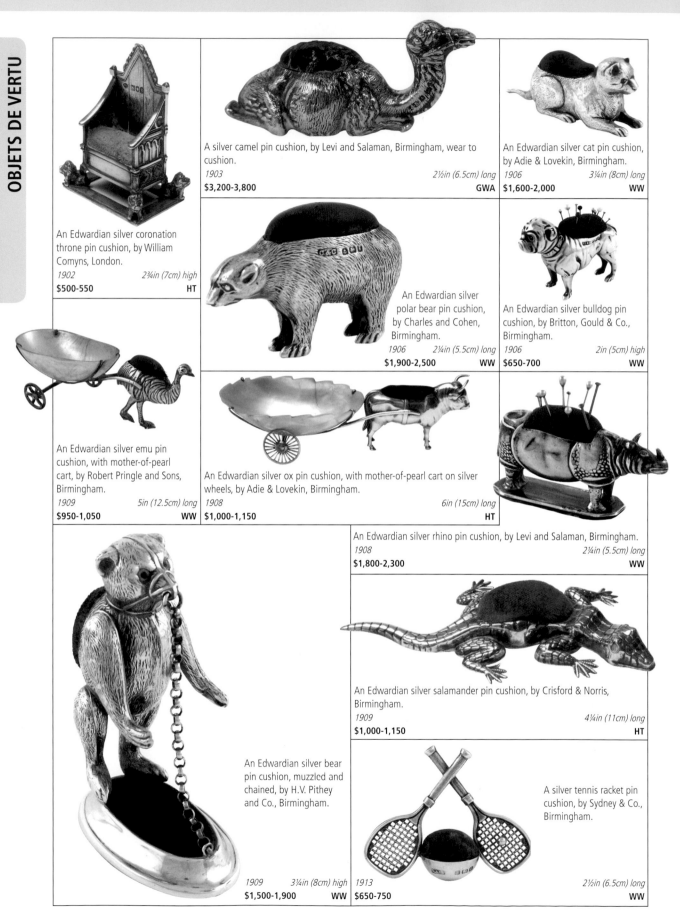

An Edwardian silver coronation throne pin cushion, by William Comyns, London.
1902 *2¾in (7cm) high*
$500-550 HT

A silver camel pin cushion, by Levi and Salaman, Birmingham, wear to cushion.
1903 *2½in (6.5cm) long*
$3,200-3,800 GWA

An Edwardian silver cat pin cushion, by Adie & Lovekin, Birmingham.
1906 *3¼in (8cm) long*
$1,600-2,000 WW

An Edwardian silver polar bear pin cushion, by Charles and Cohen, Birmingham.
1906 *2¼in (5.5cm) long*
$1,900-2,500 WW

An Edwardian silver bulldog pin cushion, by Britton, Gould & Co., Birmingham.
1906 *2in (5cm) high*
$650-700 WW

An Edwardian silver emu pin cushion, with mother-of-pearl cart, by Robert Pringle and Sons, Birmingham.
1909 *5in (12.5cm) long*
$950-1,050 WW

An Edwardian silver ox pin cushion, with mother-of-pearl cart on silver wheels, by Adie & Lovekin, Birmingham.
1908 *6in (15cm) long*
$1,000-1,150 HT

An Edwardian silver rhino pin cushion, by Levi and Salaman, Birmingham.
1908 *2¼in (5.5cm) long*
$1,800-2,300 WW

An Edwardian silver salamander pin cushion, by Crisford & Norris, Birmingham.
1909 *4¼in (11cm) long*
$1,000-1,150 HT

An Edwardian silver bear pin cushion, muzzled and chained, by H.V. Pithey and Co., Birmingham.
1909 *3¼in (8cm) high*
$1,500-1,900 WW

A silver tennis racket pin cushion, by Sydney & Co., Birmingham.
1913 *2½in (6.5cm) long*
$650-750 WW

A gold and malacca walking stick, possibly French, marks obscured, split at end of the stick, dated.

1781 *36¾in (93.5cm) long*

$900-1,000 DN

A 19thC whalebone sailor's walking cane, the handle inset with abalone, the stem carved with diamond and spiral twist decoration.

37½in (95.5cm) long

$1,300-1,900 WW

A 19thC Dresden porcelain and yellow-metal-mounted malacca cane, brass ferrule, some wear.

39¾in (101cm) long

$650-700 DN

CLOSER LOOK WHALEBONE CANE

This rare scrimshaw whalebone walking cane is impressively decorated and clearly made by a master craftsman.

The shaft is unusual, carved with panels of spiraled, rope twist, and crosshatched patterns. The pommel is carved as a Turk's head knot.

This cane is particularly desirable because of its various tortoiseshell inlays on the handle.

Canes of this type were typically worked from the jawbone of a whale by American and European sailors and sold in the port cities.

A mid-19thC scrimshaw walking cane.

36¼in (92cm) long

$25,000-32,000 EBA

One of a pair of late 19thC Indian white metal choba staffs, with tiger head terminals, probably of Indian silver.

Provenance: Formerly owned and brought back from India by Sir James Thompson (1940-29), Governor of Madras 1904.

23½in (60cm) long

$5,000-5,700 the pair BELL

A probably Viennese cased rock crystal and amethyst parasol or entoutcas handle, with gold and enamel mounts, in a fitted Vickery case, in the manner of Anton Wildhack, lacking original tips.

An entoutcas (French for "in any case') is a combined parasol and umbrella. The firm of J.C. Vickery was founded around 1890 by John Collard Vickery. By 1913, Vickery was listed as a goldsmith, silversmith, jeweler, dressing case and fitted traveling bag manufacturer, watch and clock importer, with Royal Warrants from the King and Queen of the United Kingdom, the King of Spain, the King and Queen of Denmark, the Queen of Norway, and the King of Sweden.

c1900 *13½in (34.5cm) long*

$2,500-3,200 BELL

A silver and Connemara marble mounted bog oak cane, by Rent and Parker, sponsor's mark B&P, Birmingham.

c1893 *13in (33cm) long*

$1,900-2,500 WHYT

A silver dog's head handle walking stick, with ebony tapered shaft, by "W.S," London.

1887 *35in (89cm) long*

$450-500 SWO

An American patriotic carved cane, by Thomas Jefferson Craddock, with the achievements of Thomas Jefferson, minor wear.

Craddock served in the 5th Virginia cavalry of the Confederate States under the leadership of Thomas L. Rosser.

c1890 *36in (91.5cm) long*

$800-950 POOK

An early 20thC 18ct gold hare's head cane handle, with ruby eyes, French assay marks.

2¾in (7cm) long 1⅛oz

$3,800-4,400 FELL

An early to mid-20thC Dunhill Aquarium table lighter, reg. no.737418, maker's mark to base, decorated with fish among seaweed, with plated mounts.

4in (10cm) wide

$2,500-3,200   **ROS**

A 1950s Dunhill Aquarium table lighter, by Ben Shillingford, decorated with fish among seaweed, with gilt-metal fittings.

3¾in (9.5cm) wide

$5,000-5,700   **HAN**

A Dunhill "Aquarium" table lighter, with Perspex panels with tropical fish, with silvered mounts, stamped marks, "Reg. No. 737418," some scuffing.

4in (10cm) wide

$4,400-5,000   **SWO**

A Dunhill "Aquarium" table lighter, the Perspex panels with tropical fish amid waterweed, with silvered metal fittings, stamped with patent number "143752."

2¾in (7cm) high

$1,300-1,800   **SWO**

A Dunhill Aquarium table lighter, by Ben Shillingford, reg. no.737418, the Perspex panels with tropical fish.

4in (10cm) wide

$3,800-4,400   **HAN**

A 1950s Dunhill Aquarium table cigarette casket, by Ben Shillingford, the lid inset with a Perspex plaque with fish among seaweed, Dunhill label on the cedar-lined interior.

8¼in (21cm) wide

$5,000-5,700   **HAN**

An Art Deco silver-gilt Dunhill "Unique" cigarette lighter, with a 15-jewel Swiss watch movement, London import marks, numbered "1581," marked "Pat No 143752," some wear, movement not working.

1926   *1¾in (4.5cm) high*

$1,300-1,800   **ECGW**

A Dunhill 9ct gold cigarette lighter, Birmingham.

1949   *2¼in (5.5cm) long*

$1,000-1,150   **FELL**

A Dunhill lighter, stamped "Dunhill U.S. Pat 2102108, Outer Jacket 14K Gold."

2in (5cm) long

$300-400   **LOCK**

A Dunhill Namiki maki-e lacquer desk pen, fish and sea plants within a powder gilt ground, six character signature, nib marked "Medium Dunhill Namiki 3 Made in Japan."
c1930
$1,900-2,500   **HAN**

A limited edition Montblanc "Skeleton Antoni Gaudi" fountain pen, no.109/128, with overlay reminiscent of the Casa Batllo, stamped "Au750," the nib stamped "18K."
$9,000-10,000   **DN**

A limited edition Montblanc "Year Of The Golden Dragon" fountain pen, no.479/888, the Meissen porcelain hand painted with a dragon, the nib stamped "18K," with box and papers.
2000
$4,400-5,000   **DN**

A Dunhill Namiki maki-e fountain pen, the black urushi ground with gold dust togidashi maki-e, with taka maki-e foliage, signed "Namiki" in Kanji, with a red Kao, no.3 nib stamped "14ct," with lever filling system.
c1935
$8,000-9,000   **DN**

A limited edition Montblanc "Great Characters Mahatma Gandhi" fountain pen, no.199/241, stamped "Au750," the nib stamped "18K," with box and papers.
2009
$11,000-13,000   **DN**

A limited edition Montblanc "Skeleton Genghis Khan" fountain pen, no.20/35, with overlay resembling Mongol armor, stamped "pt950," the nib stamped "Au750."
$20,000-25,000   **DN**

A Parker Duofold Giant 125th Anniversary gold and diamond fountain pen, limited edition no.4/125, the nib stamped "18K," in a Parker display box with a gold-plated pen holder and ink bottle.
issued 2013
$15,000-19,000   **DN**

A Pelikan maki-e/Raden Sunlight M1000 lacquer and abalone shell fountain pen, limited edition no.165/300, the medium nib stamped "18C-750," piston filling system, with a Pelikan box, certificate, leaflet, and outer card packaging.
$5,500-6,500   **DN**

A Platinum Autumn maki-e fountain pen, by Rosui, the cap and barrel with togidashi and takamaki-e autumnal landscape, the nib stamped "14K," with a lever filling system, signed, with red kao mark.
c1930   *5½in (14cm) long*
$3,200-3,800   **DN**

A Waterman 452 fountain pen, BHR with silver overlay, engraved name.
c1920
$300-400   **HAN**

OBJETS DE VERTU

A George III Blue John Neoclassical -shape vase, on a Blue John and white marble pedestal on a slate plinth, lacking finial, some repairs.

Blue John is a semi-precious material found in Derbyshire, which was used in 18thC France and England to manufacture decorative urns and other objects.

c1780   *14¼in (36cm) high*
$5,500-6,500   **DN**

A George III Blue John campana urn, on a black marble plinth.

8¾in (22.5cm) high
$6,500-7,000   **WW**

A George III Blue John campana urn vase, on a black marble base.

11¾in (30cm) high
$4,400-5,000   **HAN**

A pair of late George III or Regency Blue John and fluorspar urns, the marble bases possibly replacements, one urn chipped, one urn glued.

9½in (24cm) high
$5,000-5,700   **DN**

A probably late 17thC German silver-gilt-mounted moss agate cup and cover, crack to cover.

4¼in (11cm) high
$8,000-9,000   **BE**

An 18thC gold-mounted green agate egg, French or English, inscribed "DIEU VOUS BENIT" (God bless you), push button diamond opening.

2¼in (5.5cm) long
$3,800-4,400   **WW**

A late 18thC agate and gilt-metal-mounted nécessaire, with paste clasp, with scissors and pencil, metal mount loose, cover cracked.

4in (10cm) long
$800-900   **CHEF**

A 19thC gilt-metal-mounted porphyry urn vase, some scratches.

9¼in (23.5cm) high
$1,900-2,500   **TEN**

A French Mellerio dits Meller 18ct gold and enamel scent bottle, the cover set with a cabochon ruby and sapphire, engraved "Mellerio R. Paix 9," in a Masis Joaillier box, wear to enamel.

c1880   *2¾in (7cm) high 2⅜oz*
$4,400-5,000   **DN**

A silver-gilt and enamel throne salt cellar, maker's mark of Savikov, unknown assay master, Moscow.

This is possibly not by Sazikov.

1895   *3¼in (8.5cm) high 4¼oz*

$1,900-2,500   **WW**

A silver-gilt and enamel box, set with colored stones, by Feodor Ruckert, Moscow.

Feodor Ruckert was one of Fabergé's workmasters. He specialized in cloisonné enamel for the Moscow workshop and also worked independently for himself and for other retailers.

1908-17   *3½in (9cm) long 5⅞oz*

$13,000-15,000   **WW**

An Art Nouveau-style silver cloisonné pocket cigarette case, maker's mark, second Kokoshnik mark.

c1910   *4in (10cm) wide 7⅛oz*

$1,800-2,300   **HAN**

A silver and enamel kovsh, with date marks and French import marks.

A kovsh is a traditional oval-shaped drinking vessel or ladle, used to serve and drink mead from as early as the 10thC.

1896-1908   *5¼in (13.5cm) long*

$3,200-3,800   **WW**

A silver and enamel kovsh, with enamel landscape scene, with allover enamel patterns and cabochon stones, mark head "88."

9in (23cm) long 34oz

$11,000-12,000   **JN**

An enamel kovsh, with champlevé enamel and cabochon stones.

5in (12.5cm) long

$800-950   **JN**

A silver-gilt and enamel box, with eagle motif, cabochon, rubies, and diamonds, stamped "A.H.88," in leather fitted case.

3½in (9cm) long

$5,000-6,300   **JN**

A Fabergé-style enamel frame, set with seed pearls and cabochon sapphires.

4½in (11.5cm) high

$2,300-2,800   **JN**

ESSENTIAL REFERENCE—FABERGÉ

Fabergé was founded in St. Petersburg in 1842 by Gustav Fabergé, a goldsmith of French extract. The business was later taken over by his two sons, Peter Carl and Agathon Fabergé.

- **It produced a wide range of items, including cigarette cases, boxes, mantel clocks, picture frames, animal sculptures, flower carvings, and jewelry. It is best known for its jeweled enamel Easter eggs.**
- **Carl Fabergé attracted the attention of Czar Alexander III in 1882 at the Pan-Russian Exhibition in Moscow. From 1885, the House of Fabergé held the title of "Supplier to the Court of His Imperial Majesty."**
- **Fabergé work was renowned for its innovation and beauty.**
- **At its height, Fabergé employed nearly 500 people, including talented craftsmen, such as Michael Perchin, Henrik Wigstrom, Feodor Ruckert, and Erik Kollin.**
- **Fabergé was forced to close in Russia in 1918 following the Revolution.**

A Fabergé silver-gilt and enamel hinge-lidded cigarette box, engraved "L.C.O March 1st 1936," by Albert Holmström (1876-1925), detailed "88," "Fabergé" in Cyrillic, enamel losses throughout, with Cartier case.

3in (7.5cm) long 3oz

$5,500-7,000   **BELL**

An early 19thC silver pug dog snuff box, with later red eyes, unknown maker's mark, assay master Nikolay Dubrovin, Moscow.

c1830   *2¾in (7cm) long 1⅜oz*

$1,000-1,150   **WW**

A silver and silver-gilt cheroot case, the back depicting the Kremlin, maker's mark possibly for Fyedor Verkovsyev or Verkhovtsev, assay master "A.C," Moscow, some wear.

1853   *5¼in (13.5cm) long 6⅛oz*

$1,600-2,000   **FELL**

A silver and niello work cheroot case, with locking mechanism, the base with a view of the Kremlin, assay master Viktor Savinkov, Moscow.

1865   *4¼in (10.5cm) 4⅝oz*

$450-550   **WW**

A pair of silver beakers, maker's mark "HJ," assay master Nicholai Bubrovin, Moscow, 84 zolotniki, some light scratches.

A zolotnik was a small Russian unit of weight, used from the 10thC to the 20thC. One zolotnik is equal to approximately ⅛ oz.

1839   *3in (7.5cm) high 5⅞oz*

$1,200-1,400   **DN**

A silver tankard, niello-decorated with four panels, depicting the Kremlin, with inscription, assay master Viktor Vasilyevich Savinsky, Moscow, some wear.

1862   *5in (13cm) high 16oz*

$3,200-3,800   **APAR**

A Fabergé silver snail, by Henrik Wigstrom, St. Petersburg, import marks for London 1911, importer's mark of Charles Fabergé, 91 zolotnik.

This snail was probably modeled as the handle of a hard-stone paperweight and is now lacking its stone base.

c1908   *4in (10cm) long 3⅞oz*

$6,500-7,500   **WW**

A Fabergé silver egg, with gold thumbpiece set with a sapphire, by Henrik Wigstrom, Fabergé.

2½in (6.5cm) long 2½oz

$6,500-7,500   **WW**

A Fabergé silver box, with a frieze of Imperial eagles, marked "K Fabergé," Moscow.

6¾in (17cm) long 27oz

$9,000-10,000   **SWO**

A Fabergé silver paper knife, with rose quartz terminal, mounted with a cabochon garnet in gold collet, signed "ÔÀÁÂÐÆÅ," maker's mark "AR" for work master Anna Ringe, and 88 zolotnik with kokoshnik.

8¼in (21cm) long

$2,500-3,200   **WW**

A late 16thC egg tempera, gold leaf, gesso, and wood pane "Virgin of Tenderness" or "Eleusa" icon, two insert splints on the back.

An "Eleusa" icon is a type of icon showing the infant Jesus Christ nestled against the Virgin Mary's cheek. "Eleusa" means "tenderness or showing mercy."

17½in (44.5cm) high

$9,000-10,000 SHP

An 18thC triptych icon, polychrome and gold leaf iconography, wire hinges.

A triptych is a picture on three panels, typically hinged together and used as an altarpiece.

6¾in (17cm) high

$2,500-3,200 HAN

An 18thC Russian School painted and gilded quadripartite icon, of "The Pokrov," "The Procession of the Icon, Moscow," "The Exaltation of the True Cross," and "The Installation of the Girdle of the Mother of God."

12½in (32cm) high

$1,900-2,500 WW

An early 19thC Moscow School egg tempera, gold leaf, gesso, and wood portable iconostasis, consisting of 15 panels, the top row depicting Old Testament forefathers, the second depicting prophets paying homage to the Virgin of Znamenie, the third depicting feasts of the Orthodox Church, the lowest row depicting Jesus Christ flanked by Mary, John the Baptist, archangels, and several saints.

Provenance: Acquired through inheritance by the descendants of Alexander Ivanovich Nelidov (1835-1910), Russian Ambassador to Turkey, Italy, and France.

extended 55in (139.5cm) wide

$15,000-19,000 SHP

A 19thC icon, "The Mother and Child," with gilt-metal and silver oklad and walnut frame.

An oklad is a metal cover protecting an icon, usually made of gilt or silvered metal.

12¼in (31cm) high

$950-1,050 REEM

A mid-19thC icon, depicting Christ, with silver oklad, maker unknown, assay master "AC," possibly A. Suyechin, Moscow, pre-Kokoshnik mark.

1868 *12¼in (31cm) high*

$700-800 GWA

A "Madonna and Child" icon, with silver oklad, stamped marks, in later glazed case.

1883-84 *12¼in (31cm) high*

$1,000-1,150 SWO

An icon, depicting Christ Pantocrator.

14in (35.5cm) high

$1,600-2,000 CLAR

A traveling silver triptych icon, depicting Saint George and the Dragon, with a king and queen on each side, dated.

1889 *3¾in (9.5cm) long*

$1,500-2,000 JN

A pair of Imperial Porcelain Factory figures of Ottoman Janissaries, modeled after Meissen originals, blue cipher marks, some losses and chips, one hand reglued.

The Imperial Porcelain Factory of St. Petersburg was established in 1744, first under Dmitri Vinogradov and later under J.G. Müller. After the 1917 Revolution, the factory was taken over by the state.

c1770   *6¼in (16cm) high*

$5,000-5,700   **BELL**

A 19thC porcelain Kamchatka woman, possibly by Imperial Porcelain Factory, from the "Peoples of Russia" series, titled in French and Cyrillic.

8¾in (22cm) high

$11,000-12,000   **GYM**

A 19thC porcelain Laplander, possibly by Imperial Porcelain Factory, from the "Peoples of Russian" series, titled in French and Cyrillic.

$21,000-25,000   **GYM**

A 19thC porcelain Barbarian lady, possibly by Imperial Porcelain Factory, from the "Peoples of Russia" series, titled "Femme Barabien" in French and Cyrillic.

8¾in (22cm) high

$10,000-11,000   **GYM**

A Gardner porcelain peasant street vendor, impressed mark, restored to neck, hat, and basket.

In 1766, English entrepreneur Francis Gardner opened a porcelain factory in Verbilki, near Moscow, with the permission of Catherine the Great. The factory traded as Gardner until 1892, when it was acquired by M.S. Kusnetov and then known as Kusnetsov Brothers until its closure in 1917.

c1830   *7in (18cm) high*

$1,500-2,000   **DN**

A Gardner porcelain berry picker, impressed "4," professional restoration.

c1830-40   *8¼in (21cm) high*

$3,200-3,800   **BE**

An Imperial Porcelain Factory figure of a masked lady, some chips and flaking.

c1840   *5in (13cm) high*

$4,400-5,000   **PW**

An early to mid-19thC Gardner porcelain desk stand, modeled as a kneeling peasant, the logs on his back forming an inkwell and pounce pot, impressed factory marks and "8," lacking cover.

5in (13cm) high

$5,500-6,500   **BE**

A mid-19thC Moscow biscuit porcelain figure, of a Russian peasant breaking a hole in the ice, impressed mark, some losses, glued repairs to arms.

9¾in (25cm) high

$1,500-2,000   **DN**

A late 19thC Imperial Porcelain Factory presentation Easter egg, with the cipher of Alexander III (1845-94).

4½in (11.5cm) high

$3,200-3,800 WW

CLOSER LOOK—RAPHAEL SERVICE OYSTER DISHES

These oyster dishes were made at the Imperial Porcelain Factory in St. Petersburg and are part of the Raphael Service.

They are painted with Classical figures on a red ground, within radiating panels of Classical ornament, with heraldic devices painted on the handles.

A late 19thC to early 20thC Imperial Porcelain Factory presentation Easter egg, gilded with the monogram of Empress Maria Feodorovna (1847-1928).

Maria Feodorovna was born Princess Dagmar of Denmark. She had been engaged to the heir apparent, Nicholas Alexandrovich, at the time of his death from meningitis in 1865. She married the future Alexander III the following year. The couple were crowned in Moscow in 1883.

4¾in (12cm) high

$4,400-5,000 WW

The Raphael Service was commissioned by Alexander III in 1883 for the Tsarskoselsky Palace and was inspired by Raphael's frescoes in the Loggias of the Vatican. The decoration was so extensive that the service was not completed until 1903.

The condition of these dishes is excellent. They have been carefully stowed in a cupboard for almost 90 years, having been acquired by an engineer from Blackburn in the 1920s while on a trade mission to Russia.

A set of three oyster dishes, dated.

1900-02 *5¾in (14.5cm) wide*

$28,000-35,000 TEN

An Imperial Porcelain Factory vase, painted with hazel tree branches, printed factory mark, impressed numeral "1," dated.

1909 *9½in (24cm) high*

$2,800-3,500 BELL

A 19thC carved cornelian bulldog's head cane handle, with tiger's eye eyes and a gold strap collar inset with a diamond, struck "H.W," possibly for Henrik Wigstrom, with "56" control marks.

1¾oz

$1,900-2,500 BE

A pair of late 19thC silver-mounted cut-glass monogrammed claret pitchers, by Shanks and Co., Moscow, with mythical dolphin scroll handles.

1890 *10¼in (26cm) high*

$4,400-5,000 WW

A Fabergé hardstone frame, the chalcedony frame with ten cabochon rubies set in the internal white enamel striated border, workmaster's initials "A" for Karl Armfelt, 88 zolotnik, inventory no.14351, some cracks, in hollywood box, with Imperial eagle over the Fabergé mark.

3¼in (8cm) high

$38,000-44,000 WW

A Fabergé-style cut glass caviar bowl, with silver and enamel lid with sturgeon handle.

4½in (11.5cm) diam

$1,900-2,500 JN

A Fabergé-style green jade box and cover, with diamond-set gold initials.

2¾in (7cm) diam

$2,300-2,800 JN

A Queen Anne heavy baluster wine glass.
c1710   *6in (15cm) high*
$2,300-2,800   **ROS**

A teared balustroid stemmed wine glass.
c1720-30   *7¼in (18.5cm) high*
$900-1,000   **WAD**

A George I baluster wine glass, with trumpet bowl, above ball knop and triple annulated knop, with teared hollow baluster knop.
c1725   *6in (15cm) high*
$1,500-2,000   **ROS**

A George II wine glass, with teared trumpet bowl, above triple angulated knop, true baluster, and inverted baluster knop.
c1735   *7¾in (19.5cm) high*
$1,150-1,250   **ROS**

A Dutch armorial alliance wine glass, engraved in the manner of Willem Otto Robart, with a coat of arms and motto, the reverse with clasped hands and inscription.
c1740   *7½in (19cm) high*
$4,400-5,000   **TEN**

A set of eight mid-18thC plain stemmed engraved wine glasses.
                    7in (18cm) high
$4,400-5,000   **WAD**

CLOSER LOOK—JACOBITE WINE GLASS

The Jacobites were the supporters of King James II, usurped by William and Mary in 1688. Later, it became a general term for those who favored the restoration of the Stuart dynasty.

This glass is engraved with a rose, representing James Francis Edward Stuart, Prince of Wales, James II's son (nicknamed the Old Pretender); and with two rose buds, representing James' sons, Charles Edward Stuart (nicknamed Bonnie Prince Charlie or the Young Pretender) and Henry Benedict Stuart.

It is also engraved with an oak leaf, a symbol of the Stuart family.

It is inscribed with the Latin word "Fiat," meaning "Let it come to pass."

A Jacobite knopped air twist-stemmed wine glass, tiny chips.
c1750   *6¾in (17cm) high*
$1,050-1,200   **WAD**

A George II Beilby wine glass, the bowl enameled and gilded, above opaque double series twist stem, on conical foot.

The Beilby siblings, William, Richard, and Mary, were all skilled glass decorators, working for various factories in the Newcastle area. Their glassware is characterized by its painted white and colored enamel decoration, and it was produced over a short period around 1760. Only a handful of pieces are signed, and many are attributed to the Beilby family on account of their style and quality.
c1750-60   *6in (15.5cm) high*
$6,500-7,000   **ROS**

A mid-18thC teared bobbin knopped wine glass.
                    7½in (19cm) high
$3,200-3,800   **WAD**

A mid-18thC teared knop air twist-composite stemmed wine glass.

7½in (19cm) high

$950-1,050   **WAD**

A rare blue twist wine glass, one small chip.

1760-70   *6½in (16.5cm) high*

$3,800-4,400   **WAD**

An engraved red color twist-stemmed wine glass.

c1760-80   *5¼in (13.5cm) high*

$2,800-3,500   **WAD**

A color twist wine glass, minor surface scratching.

c1765   *6in (15cm) high*

$1,500-1,900   **TEN**

An 18thC Continental friendship wine glass, engraved with two soldiers, inscribed "AMITIE."

6¾in (17cm) high

$3,800-4,400   **DUK**

A Georgian "Britannia" engraved wine glass, on a facet-cut stem and conical foot.

c1780   *6in (15cm) high*

$1,200-1,400   **L&T**

A Dutch armorial wine glass, engraved with arms of Delfland within a Dutch fence border on a beaded knop and baluster stem with air tear.

Delfland is the name of a Dutch water board. The use of a Dutch fence to encircle the armorial is also recorded on a large 18thC wall chart depicting numerous coats of arms of officials of the Delfland water board.

c1780 9¼in (23.5cm) high

$4,400-5,000   **TEN**

A mid-18thC knopped hollow inverted baluster-stemmed sweetmeat or champagne glass.

6in (15.5cm) high

$750-900   **WAD**

An engraved air twist-stemmed sweetmeat or champagne glass.

c1750-60   *6in (15.5cm) high*

$650-750   **WAD**

An opaque twist-stemmed sweetmeat or champagne glass.

c1760-70   *7in (17.5cm) high*

$650-750   **WAD**

A teared heavy baluster-stemmed glass goblet.
c1710   *7¼in (18.5cm) high*
$3,800-4,400   **WAD**

A Queen Anne heavy baluster drinking glass, with conical bowl, knopped stem, and spreading double foot.
c1710   *5¾in (14.5cm) high*
$1,000-1,150   **ROS**

A Queen Anne heavy baluster glass, with conical bowl above a teared angular knop, with a basal true baluster knop.
c1710   *7in (17.5cm) high*
$3,800-4,400   **ROS**

A teared balustroid-stemmed glass goblet.
c1720-30   *7in (18cm) high*
$900-1,000   **WAD**

A mid-18thC enameled ale glass, on a straight enamel twist stem, on a spreading foot.
7¼in (18.5cm) high
$550-700   **L&T**

A mid-18thC knopped air twist-stemmed glass goblet, tiny chip.
7½in (19cm) high
$450-500   **WAD**

A rare red, white, and blue color twist-stemmed glass goblet.
c1760   *7¾in (20cm) high*
$13,000-15,000   **WAD**

A honeycomb-molded opaque twist-stemmed glass goblet.
c1760-80   *7½in (19cm) high*
$500-650   **WAD**

A George III cordial glass, with funnel bowl above a double series opaque twist stem.
c1775   *7in (17.5cm) high*
$1,150-1,400   **ROS**

A 19thC millefiori and engraved glass rummer, on an air twist stem and star cut foot.
6¼in (16cm) high
$4,400-5,000   **DUK**

A 17thC wine bottle, with applied stag's head seal, string rim.

The seal on this bottle was previously uncataloged. It seems likely that the bottle has Cornish associations, perhaps with the Bolitho family. The surface of the glass shows signs of burial, and the family history suggests it was found by chance on the West Penwith moors.

c1665-70   *8¾in (22cm) high*
$13,000-18,000   **BKA**

Judith Picks

A Yorkshire collector bought this wine bottle for just £30 ($38) at Doncaster Antiques Fair in early 2018. Its exceptional condition led him to think it was a replica of an antique bottle, and it was only several days later that its true authenticity was established. It represents a late 17thC "European" shaft and globe transitional form. Its most distinctive features are characteristic of the shaft and globe type, but it has a relatively squat shape and shorter neck, indicative of the emergence of the onion style of bottle dominant in the early 18thC. It is unusual in more than its shape, being green with a gray tinge in color, with thick walls manufactured of high-quality glass.

A rare English transitional shaft and globe wine bottle, with "GR" seal, dated.
1682   *6½in (16.5cm) high*
$25,000-32,000   **BBR**

A James II "sack" onion bottle, label on reverse.

It is believed this bottle belonged to the famous pirate Samuel White, who spent his time in Burma.

7½in (19cm) high
$1,500-2,000   **JN**

A late 17thC to early 18thC onion bottle, with an applied bladed lip, initialed "WG."

6in (15cm) high
$500-650   **FLD**

An early 18thC sealed onion mallet wine bottle, with kick-in base, the seal initialed "P/HA."
6¾in (17cm) high
$2,500-3,200   **WW**

An 18thC Alpine liquor bottle, with optical honeycomb decor and tin screw cap.
6in (15cm) high
$3,800-4,400   FIS

A 19thC Ricketts-style bottle, with "RHC 1815" seal.

The seal refers to Richard Hall Clarke of Bridwell, Devon.

1815   *11in (28cm) high*
$180-230   **FLD**

An English apple green glass wrythen bottle.
c1850   *10¼in (26cm) high*
$500-650   **DN**

A Victorian painted glass carboy, depicting the "Cutty Sark" and another clipper.
26¾in (68cm) high
$450-550   **L&T**

GLASS

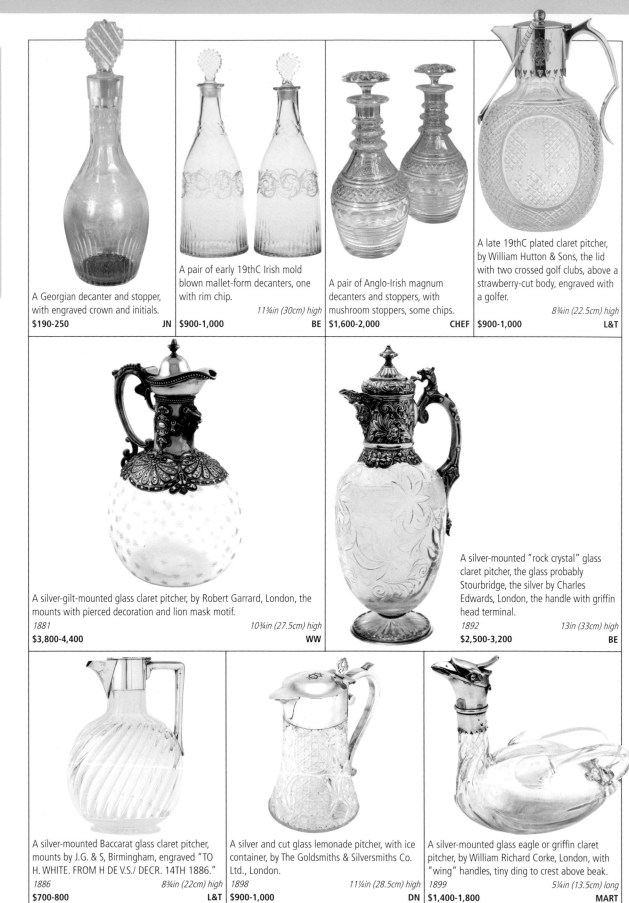

A Georgian decanter and stopper, with engraved crown and initials.

$190-250   **JN**

A pair of early 19thC Irish mold blown mallet-form decanters, one with rim chip.

11¾in (30cm) high

$900-1,000   **BE**

A pair of Anglo-Irish magnum decanters and stoppers, with mushroom stoppers, some chips.

$1,600-2,000   **CHEF**

A late 19thC plated claret pitcher, by William Hutton & Sons, the lid with two crossed golf clubs, above a strawberry-cut body, engraved with a golfer.

8¾in (22.5cm) high

$900-1,000   **L&T**

A silver-gilt-mounted glass claret pitcher, by Robert Garrard, London, the mounts with pierced decoration and lion mask motif.

1881   *10¾in (27.5cm) high*

$3,800-4,400   **WW**

A silver-mounted "rock crystal" glass claret pitcher, the glass probably Stourbridge, the silver by Charles Edwards, London, the handle with griffin head terminal.

1892   *13in (33cm) high*

$2,500-3,200   **BE**

A silver-mounted Baccarat glass claret pitcher, mounts by J.G. & S, Birmingham, engraved "TO H. WHITE. FROM H DE V.S./ DECR. 14TH 1886."

1886   *8¾in (22cm) high*

$700-800   **L&T**

A silver and cut glass lemonade pitcher, with ice container, by The Goldsmiths & Silversmiths Co. Ltd., London.

1898   *11¼in (28.5cm) high*

$900-1,000   **DN**

A silver-mounted glass eagle or griffin claret pitcher, by William Richard Corke, London, with "wing" handles, tiny ding to crest above beak.

1899   *5¼in (13.5cm) long*

$1,400-1,800   **MART**

A 15thC German glass krautstrunk or beaker, with applied drops of glass.

4¼in (11cm) high

$20,000-25,000   **FIS**

A 16thC German marbled red glass mug, with spun sprawling foot.

4¼in (11cm) high

$2,500-3,200   **FIS**

An Austrian mug, by Anton Kothgasser, painted with a pair of birds, inscribed "insèparable," the rim painted in gold.

c1820   4¼in (10.5cm) high

$2,300-2,800   **FIS**

A Czech Lithyalin cup, by Friedrich Egermann, with gilt medallions and Gothic panels, gold marks to base.

Lithyalin is a type of opaque glass made to resemble semiprecious stones. It was developed by Friedrich Egermann.

c1830   4¼in (11cm) high

$13,000-18,000   **FIS**

A mid-to-late 19thC Bohemian glass goblet and cover, engraved with deer in a forest, some chips, cover possibly associated.

21¾in (55.3cm) high

$2,500-3,200   **DN**

A pair of 19thC Bohemian glass and gilt candlestick lusters, with floral and portrait panels, lacking lusters, some losses.

11¾in (30cm) high

$1,600-2,000   **MART**

A pair of late 19thC Bohemian opaline glass vases.

14¾in (37.5cm) high

$2,500-3,200   **ROS**

A pair of late 19thC Bohemian or Beykoz glass enameled bottles and stoppers, for the Eastern market, some chips.

16½in (42cm) high

$3,800-4,400   **DN**

A pair of late 19thC-style Bohemian campana urns, decorated with panels of foliate gilding.

14½in (36.5cm) high

$1,900-2,500   **ROS**

A pair of Regency cut glass urns and covers.

11¼in (28.5cm) high

$650-750 **L&T**

A pair of Irish glass lidded jars, some scattered chips.

11½in (29cm) high

$500-550 **CHOR**

An Irish glass navette-shaped pedestal bowl, some chips.

10½in (26.5cm) high

$650-750 **CHOR**

A pair of Irish lidded bowls, with diamond cuts, some chips.

11½in (29cm) high

$500-650 **CHOR**

A pair of early 19thC Roman micromosaic plaques, of the tomb of Caecilia Metella and of a ruined temple, possibly The Temple of Saturn, some running splits.

Micromosaics are a type of mosaic created from tiny fragments of glass, called tesserae.

2½in (6.5cm) diam

$9,500-10,500 **TEN**

A mid-19thC Italian micromosaic panel of the Roman Forum, in the manner of Domenico Moglia, some scuffing, some wear to frame.

14½in (37cm) wide

$9,500-10,500 **BELL**

A 19thC New England Glass Company ruffled plated amberina glass bowl.

c1818-78 *2½in (6.5cm) high*

$1,900-2,500 **LHA**

A 19thC glass bell-shaped font/ vessel, gilt highlighted.

This vessel is thought to be the base of an 18thC Mughal hookah pipe, which increases the interest and value.

7in (18cm) high

$5,000-5,700 **TRI**

A turquoise glass jewelry casket, possibly Palais Royal or Moser, minor losses.

5in (13cm) high

$900-1,000 **FELL**

A stained glass panel, some panels cracked, dated.

1536 *18¼in (46.5cm) high*

$1,050-1,200 **CHOR**

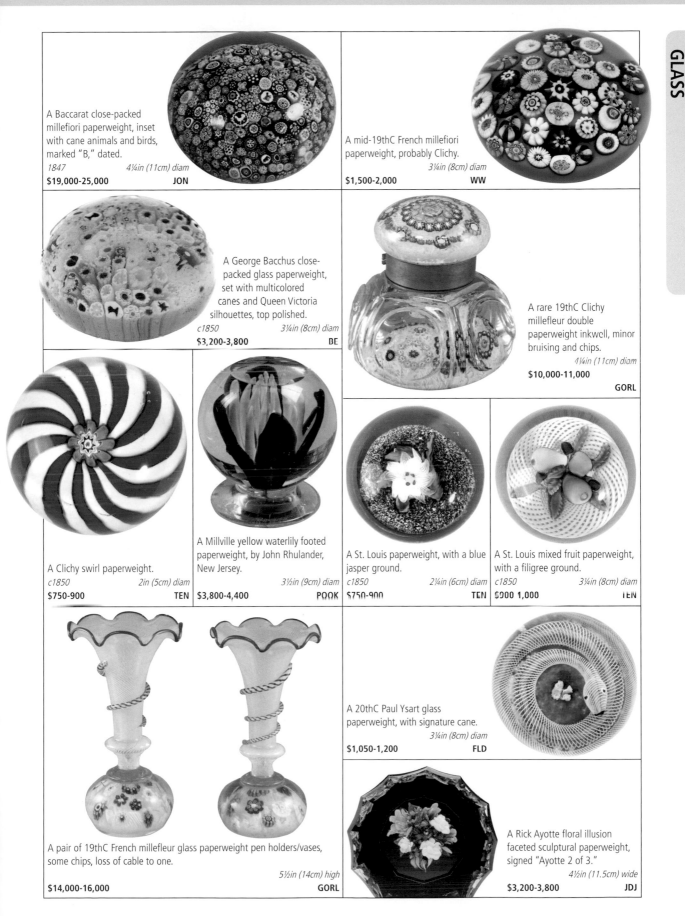

A Baccarat close-packed millefiori paperweight, inset with cane animals and birds, marked "B," dated.
1847   *4¼in (11cm) diam*
$19,000-25,000   **JON**

A mid-19thC French millefiori paperweight, probably Clichy.
3¼in (8cm) diam
$1,500-2,000   **WW**

A George Bacchus close-packed glass paperweight, set with multicolored canes and Queen Victoria silhouettes, top polished.
c1850   *3¼in (8cm) diam*
$3,200-3,800   **BE**

A rare 19thC Clichy millefleur double paperweight inkwell, minor bruising and chips.
4¼in (11cm) diam
$10,000-11,000
GORL

A Clichy swirl paperweight.
c1850   *2in (5cm) diam*
$750-900   **TEN**

A Millville yellow waterlily footed paperweight, by John Rhulander, New Jersey.
3½in (9cm) diam
$3,800-4,400   **POOK**

A St. Louis paperweight, with a blue jasper ground.
c1850   *2¼in (6cm) diam*
$750-900   **TEN**

A St. Louis mixed fruit paperweight, with a filigree ground.
c1850   *3¼in (8cm) diam*
$900-1,000   **TEN**

A pair of 19thC French millefleur glass paperweight pen holders/vases, some chips, loss of cable to one.
5½in (14cm) high
$14,000-16,000
GORL

A 20thC Paul Ysart glass paperweight, with signature cane.
3¼in (8cm) diam
$1,050-1,200   **FLD**

A Rick Ayotte floral illusion faceted sculptural paperweight, signed "Ayotte 2 of 3."
4½in (11.5cm) wide
$3,200-3,800   **JDJ**

LIGHTING

A pair of Regency gilt and cold-painted bronze candelabra, by Cheney, with griffin monopodia and lion's paw feet.

11½in (29cm) high

$2,300-2,800   **WW**

A pair of mid-19thC ormolu candelabra, with bronze putto support on white marble and gilt-metal base, both cherubs with holes, probably once for electrification.

42¼in (107cm) high

$25,000-32,000   **CHOR**

A pair of Napoleon III ormolu figural candelabra, attributed to Raingo Frères, inscribed "Raingo 11 Vieux," stamped "RG."

The firm of Raingo Frères was founded by four brothers in Paris in 1813. It was initially known for its fine-quality clocks but, by the 1840s, it also made bronzes and finely cast ormolu mounts. By 1860, it had carried out commissions for Napoleon III.

44in (112cm) high

$15,000-19,000   **WW**

A pair of 19thC Empire-style gilt and patinated bronze candelabra, in the manner of Martin-Guillaume Biennais.

25¾in (65.5cm) high

$3,200-3,800   **WW**

A pair of 19thC six-light candelabra, supported by a bronze putto on a white marble column.

24½in (62cm) high

$2,000-2,500   **CHOR**

A pair of late 19thC ormolu and malachite four-light candelabra.

12¼in (31cm) high

$1,900-2,500   **WW**

A pair of French patinated bronze and gilt-bronze candelabra, by Henri Picard (1840-90), signed, stamped "Victor Paillard."

Henri Picard (1840-90) famously supplied works to Emperor Napoleon III of France.

38in (96.5cm) high

$16,000-20,000   **JN**

A pair of 19thC gilt-metal nine-light candelabra, some rubbing.

34½in (87.5cm) high

$5,000-5,700   **CHOR**

A pair of early 20thC French gilt-metal and glass candelabra, attributed to Maison Bagues.

26½in (67cm) high

$5,500-6,500   **WW**

An 18thC Dutch brass 12-light chandelier.

25¼in (64cm) wide

$1,800-2,300 **WW**

A 19thC French ormolu and cut glass Louis XVI-style 12-branch chandelier.

By repute, originally owned by Princess Caroline Murat (1833-1902), Great Niece of Napoleon Bonaparte and granddaughter of Joachim Murat, King of Naples. She lived and died at Redisham Hall after marrying John Lewis Garden, whose family owned it.

56in (142cm) high

$3,200-3,800 **HALL**

A 19thC French Sèvres porcelain ormolu-mounted six-light chandelier.

45in (114.5cm) high

$1,500-2,000 **WAD**

An early to mid-Victorian cut glass six-light waterfall chandelier, attributed to F. & C. Osler.

55in (140.5cm) high

$3,200-3,800 **L&T**

A 19thC brass lantern, lacking three glass panels.

35½in (90cm) high

$2,500-3,200 **DN**

A 19thC Georgian-style brass hall lantern.

34¾in (88cm) high

$1,150-1,400 **L&T**

A 19thC gilt-metal framed hall lantern, with colored glass panels.

$700-800 **FLD**

A late 19thC ormolu hall lantern.

36¾in (93.5cm) high

$2,500-3,200 **WW**

A Louis XIV-style bronze hall lantern.

23½in (60cm) high

$6,500-7,500 **CHOR**

A Regency-style gilt and patinated brass hall lantern.

34¼in (87cm) high

$8,000-9,500 **DN**

A pair of Victorian patinated bronze figural gas lamps, by R.W. Winfield & Co., Birmingham, the supports cast as Native Americans, with Victorian lozenge marks, dated.

R.W. Winfield & Co. were prominent 19thC metalware producers. They exhibited at both the Great Exhibition of 1851, and again at the International Exhibition of 1862. The design registry at Kew holds the design and illustration for these lamps, confirming that they were produced by Winfield and registered in the summer of 1866.

1866   *21¾in (55cm) high*

$1,600-2,300   L&T

A 19thC Venetian carved, polychromed, and gilt blackamoor torchère.

78¼in (199cm) high

$2,300-2,800   L&T

A late Victorian silver-plated Corinthian column pedestal oil lamp, by Walker & Hall.

35¼in (89.5cm) high

$500-650   LSK

An Edwardian silver Hinks Patent Corinthian column pedestal oil lamp, by Walker & Hall, base by Hawksworth, Eyre & Co., Sheffield.

1907   *26¾in (68cm) high*

$1,300-1,800   APAR

A pair of early 20thC Venetian polychrome-decorated carved pine blackamoor torchères.

74in (188cm) high

$5,000-6,300   WW

A Regency ormolu ceiling light, attributed to William Collins, previously fitted for gas, now for electricity.

36½in (93cm) high

$1,500-2,000   L&T

A French wrought iron, brass, and glazed three-light electrolier.

c1900   *27½in (70cm) wide*

$1,600-2,000   DN

A set of four early 20thC Louis XV-style gilt-metal wall lights, wired for electricity.

19¼in (49cm) high

$1,150-1,400   L&T

A pair of 19thC glass and gilt-metal twin-branch table lights.

27½in (70cm) high

$5,000-5,700   BE

An 18thC silver-topped gold, diamond, and polychrome enamel "Carnival Mask" locket ring, with gold lettering reading "SOVS LE MASQVE LA VERITE."

⅛oz

$6,500-7,000 LHA

A George III garnet-set gold suite of jewelry, in fitted Payne & Son case.

necklace 16½in (42cm) long

$7,500-9,000 WW

A Georgian gold and garnet bracelet.

7½in (19cm) long

$2,300-2,800 LC

A Georgian diamond and blue enameled marquise-shape brooch pin, one diamond lacking, damages to enamel.

c1800-20 1in (2.5cm) long

$2,300-2,800 HAN

A Regency gold brooch pin, set with a pearl, emerald, amethyst, chrysolite, and emerald (PEACE), the reverse engraved "Watier's 1 July 1814."

This brooch pin was made to commemorate a victory of the Duke of Wellington over Napoleon in 1814. (In fact, the war was far from over, and the Battle of Waterloo was fought the following year). John Watier was a favorite chef of the Prince Regent, and he was chosen to organize a masked ball held in Burlington House on July 1, 1814, in celebration. This brooch pin would have probably been presented to a lady guest to celebrate the occasion.

1814 1¼in (3cm) wide

$2,500-3,200 WW

A late Georgian gold mourning ring, comprising a white skeleton, on woven hair.

size O½ ⅛oz

$2,800-3,500 FELL

A rare 18ct gold enamel memorial ring, for Lord Byron, inscribed "Byron," with "In Memory Of" in gilt script, the inner band engraved "Died 19 April 1824 Aged 36."

There are believed to be only two other recorded examples of Lord Byron memorial rings of this type.

size O½

$15,000-19,000 TEN

CLOSER LOOK—FRENCH 1789 PENDANT

This pendant was made in May 1789 to commemorate Louis XVI's return to Paris from Versailles to summon the Estates General.

The Royal blue guilloché enamel is mounted with gold decoration and inscribed "1789" in the center.

Around the outside, the pendant is inscribed "Redeunt Saturnia Regna" (the kingdom of Saturn returns). The reverse is inscribed "Rejouissons nous Le Roi nous est renou" (We are pleased the King is returned).

This item's connection to the French Revolution adds to its interest and value.

An 18thC French pendant, on a 9ct gold neckchain.

2¼in (5.5cm) diam

$4,400-5,000 LC

A late Georgian gold micromosaic necklace, with panels depicting Classical ruins.

17¼in (44cm) long 1⅞oz

$5,000-6,300 FELL

Judith Picks

Items linked to Lord Nelson are generally very desirable, and this ring is particularly special. It was given to Admiral Sir Benjamin Hallowell Carew by Admiral Lord Nelson. Hallowell was born near Boston in 1760 and was the only American member of Nelson's "Band of Brothers." His career spanned the American Revolutionary Wars, the French Revolutionary Wars, and the Napoleonic Wars. This ring differs significantly in design from the well-known group of 58 enameled rings made by John Salter in 1806 and given to every admiral and post-captain who fought at the Battle of Trafalgar. It is a unique piece, and its existence highlights the strong bond between Nelson and Hallowell.

The carved yellow gold memorial Nelson-Hallowell ring, containing a woven lock of Nelson's hair, engraved "Lord Nelson OBT. 21st Oct. 1805 A47."

¾in (2cm) diam

$32,000-38,000 DUK

JEWELRY

A mid-19thC gold-filigree-mounted shell cameo pendant brooch pin, some chips and losses, later hinge and pin.

2½in (6.5cm) wide

$800-950   **BELL**

A Victorian 15ct gold-mounted shell cameo brooch pin, some scratches, needs resetting.

2½in (6.5cm) high ¾oz

$650-750   **PW**

ESSENTIAL REFERENCE—MOURNING JEWELRY

The Victorians took mourning etiquette very seriously.

- Queen Victorian spent much of her reign in mourning for her husband, setting a trend for strict mourning among her subjects.
- Victorian mourning jewelry was typically dark in color. It included gold and silver brooch pins enameled in black, or pieces made of tortoiseshell or jet.
- Where Georgian mourning jewelry was often morbid in design, featuring grave-digging tools, skulls, and skeletons (see page 353), Victorian mourning jewelry used softer imagery, such as angels, clouds, and Classics motifs.
- Pieces of mourning jewelry often contain space to keep a lock of hair of the dead.

A 19thC gold-mounted sardonyx cameo brooch pin, probably Julius Caesar, some wear.

2in (5cm) long ⅝oz

$1,900-2,500   **FELL**

A Victorian gold and stained green tiger's eye brooch pin, later pin.

c1870   1in (2.5cm) long

$400-450   **DN**

A Victorian mourning carved hardstone cameo pendant brooch pin, with rose or pear-cut 2.7ct diamonds, empty hair chamber on reverse.

3½in (9cm) long 1oz

$2,500-3,200   **DRA**

A Victorian pearl and diamond crescent moon brooch pin.

1in (2.5cm) wide 0.6ct

$950-1,050   **GWA**

A Victorian diamond crescent and star brooch pin, one diamond missing, in original case.

1¼in (3cm) wide ¼oz

$2,300-2,800   **BELL**

A Victorian enameled fox head hand-painted brooch pin, with 18ct yellow gold bezel surround, the reverse inscribed "W.B. Ford. 1871," hairline cracks.

1½in (4cm) wide

$550-700   **HAN**

A Victorian pearl and diamond-set 15ct gold star brooch pin.

1½in (4cm) diam

$750-900   **PW**

A Victorian enamel, seed pearl, and diamond heart-shaped brooch pin or pendant, inscribed "FP, 10th June 1897," in period leather case.

¾in (2cm) long

$1,300-1,800   **CHEF**

An early Victorian diamond brooch pin, the diamonds set in gold-backed silver.

c1840   2¼in (5.5cm) long ⅝oz 11.75ct

$9,000-10,000 DN

A mid-Victorian gold chimera brooch pin, French assay marks, surface scratches.

c1870   1in (2.5cm) diam ⅜oz

$900-1,000 FELL

A Victorian yellow metal, emerald, and diamond set brooch pin, by Garrard & Co., in original box.

1½in (4cm) wide ¼oz

$550-700 LSK

A Victorian Etruscan Revival gem-set yellow gold brooch pin, attributed to Marchesini, French import mark, with S.J. Shrubsole invoice and box.

c1875   1½in (4cm) wide ½oz

$1,400-1,800 DRA

A late Victorian turquoise and diamond flowerhead brooch pin, in silver and gold.

1¼in (3cm) diam

$2,300-2,800 WW

A late Victorian rose gold and 3ct diamond snowflake pendant/brooch pin, containing 17 old European cut diamonds, stamp "PAT.88."

¼oz

$3,800-4,400 LHA

ESSENTIAL REFERENCE—GIULIANO FAMILY

Carlo Giuliano Sr. arrived in London c1860 and established a workshop in Frith St., initially making jewelry for other retailers.

- In 1874 he opened his own outlet.
- He made jewelry in the Renaissance, Greek, and Etruscan styles, always with a high level of craftsmanship.
- His sons, Carlo Jr. and Arthur, joined him in the business and continued after his death in 1895 until Arthur's death in 1914.
- Although this brooch pin is not signed, the design, execution, and high quality of the piece are characteristic of the Giuliano workshop, and the Giuliano box was clearly made for this pin.

A Victorian diamond arrow brooch pin, in silver and gold.

2¼in (6cm) long

$1,000-1,150 LC

A Victorian diamond, ruby, and enamel heart brooch pin, in silver and gold, numbered "1722."

1¾in (4.5cm) long

$450-500 ECGW

An enamel and diamond quatrefoil brooch pin, by Carlo and Arthur Giuliano, some losses to enamel, in original case.

1in (2.5cm) wide

$1,600-2,300 CHEF

A late Victorian Child & Child gold, enamel, and 1.5ct diamond brooch pin, with maker's mark, some solder repairs, some chips to enamel.

Child & Child opened in Seville Street in Knightsbridge, London, in 1880. The firm closed in 1916.

2¼in (5.5cm) long ¼oz

$2,500-3,200 FELL

JEWELRY

A Victorian 6ct diamond and 14ct gold crescent brooch pin, detachable hinged pin.

2¾in (7cm) long ½oz

$3,800-4,400   HAN

A 19thC gold, sapphire, and diamond crescent brooch pin.

2½in (6.5cm) long ¼oz

$1,500-1,900   BE

A Victorian gold and topaz brooch pin.

2¼in (5.5cm) wide

$950-1,050   LC

An early Victorian gold turquoise sentimental brooch pin, minor dents and one chip, with case.

3¼in (8cm) long ⅜oz

$1,000-1,250   FELL

A Victorian moonstone, ruby, and diamond heart and bow brooch pin.

1in (2.5cm) long

$750-900   HAN

A Victorian ruby, pearl, and diamond dragonfly brooch pin, with center 1.9ct diamond, in silver and gold.

2¾in (7cm) wide

$10,000-11,000   WW

A Victorian diamond-set garland-style drop bow brooch pin, in yellow gold-backed silver.

2¼in (6cm) long

$2,300-2,800   HAN

Judith Picks

This brooch pin is believed to have belonged to Victoria, Duchess of Kent (formerly Princess Victoria of Saxe-Coburg-Saalfeld), who, upon her death in 1861, left her jewelry to her daughter, Queen Victoria. The pin was later gifted by Queen Victoria to her youngest daughter, Princess Beatrice of the United Kingdom (later Princess Henry of Battenberg) on the event of her 14th birthday, April 14, 1871. Princess Beatrice (1857-1944) was the youngest of Queen Victoria's nine children. Affectionately called "Baby" by her mother, she stayed at her side until the Queen's death on January 22, 1901.

A Victorian turquoise and 1.25ct diamond brooch pin, inscribed "Had belonged to dear grandmama V. From Mama V.R. 14th April 1871. To Beatrice."

3in (7.5cm) long ½oz

$11,000-14,000   TEN

A late 19thC 0.81ct emerald and diamond anchor brooch pin, some surface scratches, some abrasion to emerald, with case.

2¼in (5.5cm) long ⅝oz

$6,500-7,500   FELL

A late Victorian sapphire and 5ct diamond openwork brooch pin, some replacement gems.

2¼in (5.5cm) high ½oz

$3,200-3,800   FELL

An early Victorian gold aquamarine cross pendant/brooch pin, with cannetille surrounds, with a late Victorian gold rope-twist chain.
pendant 2¾in (7cm) long ½oz
$3,200-3,800   FELL

A mid-Victorian 17ct diamond floral necklace, some wear, in Collingwood case.
6¼in (16cm) long 1¼oz
$18,000-23,000   FELL

A mid-Victorian 18ct gold, split pearl, enamel and gem-set snake necklace, some wear, small dent to snake head.
17¾in (45cm) long 1⅛oz
$3,800-4,400   FELL

A Victorian gem-set snake necklace, the snake's mouth forming the clasp and holding its own tail, in later snake print box.

Snake necklaces or chains, made of interlocking gold links to simulate scales, were fashionable from the 1840s. Collectors aim to buy them in excellent condition, becaause they are difficult and expensive to repair.
14½in (37cm) long ¾oz
$3,200-3,800   CHEF

A Victorian pink topaz and gold parure, in Bright & Sons case.
necklace 15¾in (40cm) long
$23,000-28,000   LC

A 19thC micromosaic "animal head" necklet, in gold openwork mounts.
15in (38cm) long
$3,200-3,800   LC

A Victorian Renaissance Revival ruby and emerald pendant, by John Brogden, in N. Bloom & Sons box.
c1880   pendant 3¼in (8.5cm) long
$5,000-5,700   DN

A Renaissance Revival yellow gold, sapphire, diamond, and enamel pendant, by Edward Tessier, London, with fitted box signed "EDWARD TESSIER 26. NEW BOND ST LONDON."

This item is accompanied by an American Gemological Laboratories sapphire identification and origin certificate, no.1089852, dated February 1, 2018, stating Mineral Type: Natural Corundum, Variety: Sapphire, Origin: Ceylon (Sri Lanka).
2¼in (6cm) high ⅜oz
$23,000-28,000   LHA

A Victorian banded agate suite, the brooch pin with a glazed locket back containing hairwork, some wear, in fitted case.
necklace 20in (51cm) long
$6,500-7,000   TEN

A late Victorian diamond and cultured pearl pendant necklace, with "Savage, 41 High Street, Kensington W." case.
$4,200-4,400   BELL

A late Victorian garnet, pearl, and diamond pendant.
1¼in (3cm) diam
$2,300-2,800   LC

A Victorian bangle, with panels of Jupiter, Mars, and Mercury, with pin clasp, light wear.
1½in (3.5cm) diam 1⅞oz
$6,500-7,000   TEN

A Victorian diamond, turquoise, and gold bangle, with fitted box.

The stone section can be detached, allowing it to be worn as a brooch pin or pendant.
$5,500-6,500   LC

A Victorian gold and 18ct garnet slide bracelet, some rubbing.
c1880
2¾in (7cm) long 1oz
$2,500-3,200   ECGW

A late Victorian, gold, opal, and diamond carved-head hinged bangle.
c1890
2¼in (6cm) wide ⅝oz
$2,300-2,800   SWO

A Victorian 18ct gold banded agate and black enameled mourning ring, detailed "In Memory Of" and "James Dimond Obt 4th Septr 1845," London.
1845
size J ¼oz
$550-700   BELL

An early Victorian half pearl and emerald cluster ring, one claw missing, one replacement pearl.
c1850
size R½
$450-500   DN

ESSENTIAL REFERENCE—ETRUSCAN REVIVAL

The Etruscan civilization resided in parts of ancient Italy from the 8thC BC to the 3rdC BC, when it was absorbed into the Roman Republic.

- In the early 19thC, original Etruscan jewelry was unearthed in tombs outside Rome, including wrought golden earrings and necklaces.
- This led to a trend for Victorian Etruscan Revival jewelry, inspired by Etruscan designs.
- Etruscan Revival jewelry typically makes use of gold and some semiprecious stones, often with intricate filigree or granulation.

A late Victorian diamond, ruby, and 18ct gold ring, some wear.
c1890
size N
$750-800   DN

A gentleman's 18ct gold signet ring, set with a bloodstone engraved with a coat of arms, Chester.
1891
size V
$950-1,050   WW

A pair of Victorian diamond ear pendants, with later screw fittings.
1in (2.5cm) long
$4,000-4,800   DN

A pair of Victorian Etruscan Revival pendant earrings.
2¾in (7cm) long ⅜oz
$1,500-2,000   TEN

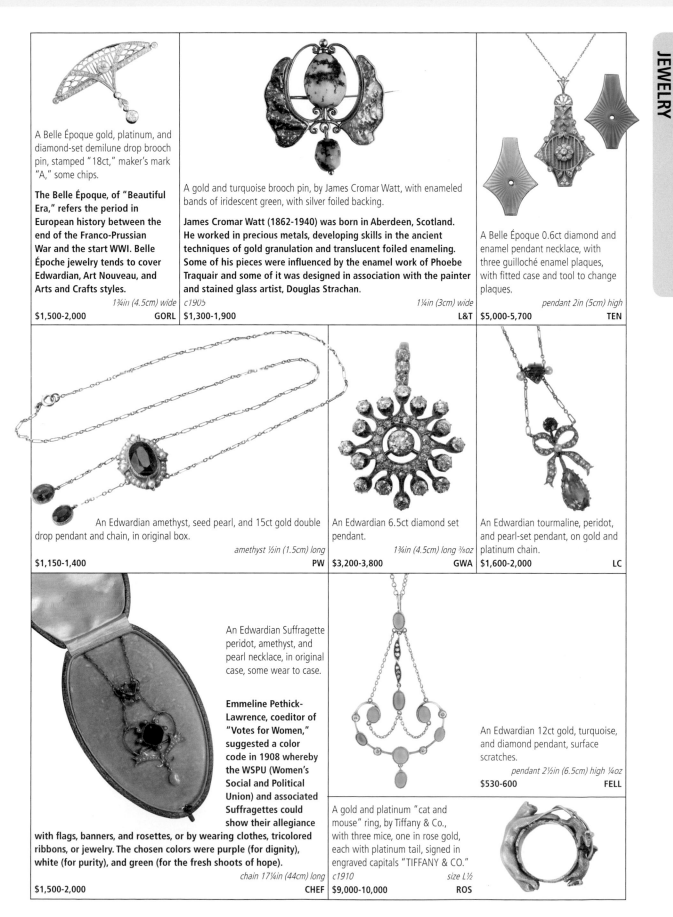

A Belle Époque gold, platinum, and diamond-set demilune drop brooch pin, stamped "18ct," maker's mark "A," some chips.

The Belle Époque, of "Beautiful Era," refers the period in European history between the end of the Franco-Prussian War and the start WWI. Belle Époche jewelry tends to cover Edwardian, Art Nouveau, and Arts and Crafts styles.

1¾in (4.5cm) wide

$1,500-2,000   **GORL**

A gold and turquoise brooch pin, by James Cromar Watt, with enameled bands of iridescent green, with silver foiled backing.

James Cromar Watt (1862-1940) was born in Aberdeen, Scotland. He worked in precious metals, developing skills in the ancient techniques of gold granulation and translucent foiled enameling. Some of his pieces were influenced by the enamel work of Phoebe Traquair and some of it was designed in association with the painter and stained glass artist, Douglas Strachan.

c1905   *1¼in (3cm) wide*

$1,300-1,900   **L&T**

A Belle Époque 0.6ct diamond and enamel pendant necklace, with three guilloché enamel plaques, with fitted case and tool to change plaques.

pendant 2in (5cm) high

$5,000-5,700   **TEN**

An Edwardian amethyst, seed pearl, and 15ct gold double drop pendant and chain, in original box.

amethyst ½in (1.5cm) long

$1,150-1,400   **PW**

An Edwardian 6.5ct diamond set pendant.

1¾in (4.5cm) long ³⁄₈oz

$3,200-3,800   **GWA**

An Edwardian tourmaline, peridot, and pearl-set pendant, on gold and platinum chain.

$1,600-2,000   **LC**

An Edwardian Suffragette peridot, amethyst, and pearl necklace, in original case, some wear to case.

Emmeline Pethick-Lawrence, coeditor of "Votes for Women," suggested a color code in 1908 whereby the WSPU (Women's Social and Political Union) and associated Suffragettes could show their allegiance with flags, banners, and rosettes, or by wearing clothes, tricolored ribbons, or jewelry. The chosen colors were purple (for dignity), white (for purity), and green (for the fresh shoots of hope).

chain 17¼in (44cm) long

$1,500-2,000   **CHEF**

An Edwardian 12ct gold, turquoise, and diamond pendant, surface scratches.

pendant 2½in (6.5cm) high ¼oz

$530-600   **FELL**

A gold and platinum "cat and mouse" ring, by Tiffany & Co., with three mice, one in rose gold, each with platinum tail, signed in engraved capitals "TIFFANY & CO."

c1910   *size L½*

$9,000-10,000   **ROS**

An Art Nouveau 15ct gold, ruby, pearl, and opal necklace, stamped "15ct," minor wear.

15½in (39.5cm) long ⅜oz

$1,000-1,150   **FELL**

An early 20thC Continental Art Nouveau gold moonstone and seed pearl necklace.

16¼in (41.5cm) long ¾oz

$1,300-1,800   **FELL**

An early 20thC Murrle Bennett & Co. silver opal necklace.

17¾in (45cm) long ¼oz

$1,500-2,000   **FELL**

A Russian Art Nouveau amethyst and demantoid garnet pendant necklace, stamped "56 zolotnik gold" (14ct gold) with a Kazan regional mark.

pendant 2¼in (5.5cm) high ½oz

$1,800-2,500   **TEN**

An Art Nouveau garnet and diamond pendant, in platinum and gold.

pendant 1½in (4cm) long

$1,900-2,500   **WW**

An Art Nouveau enamel, diamond, and pearl pendant, by Child & Child.

2¾in (7cm) high

$1,900-2,500   **TEN**

An Art Nouveau Krementz amethyst, diamond, freshwater pearl, enamel, and 14ct yellow-gold pendant-brooch pin, marked, Newark, New Jersey.

1½in (4cm) high ⅜oz

$1,300-1,800   **CLAR**

A gold, diamond, and red gem-set and plique-à-jour enameled brooch pin.

2in (5cm) wide ⅜oz

$800-950   **BELL**

A late 19thC Art Nouveau plique-à-jour diamond, enamel, pearl, and yellow-gold pendant brooch pin, some losses to enamel.

2½in (6.5cm) long

$2,300-2,800   **PW**

An Art Nouveau diamond scroll brooch pin, in silver on gold.

1½in (4cm) wide

$1,600-2,300   **WW**

A Riker Brothers Art Nouveau yellow gold bangle bracelet, with embossed pattern of dragons and Celtic scroll, with Riker cipher.

c1912   *7½in (19cm) diam ⅝oz*

$3,800-4,400   **DRA**

An Arts and Crafts white metal, moonstone, and cabochon brooch pin, attributed to Sibyl Dunlop.

c1925   *2in (5cm) wide*

$500-650   L&T

An Arts and Crafts sterling silver and enamel pendant, by James Fenton, Birmingham, some chips.

1908   *1½in (4cm) long*

$400-500   SWO

A Wiener Werkstätte silver and opal brooch pin, designed by Josef Hoffmann, marked "JH" and "WW."

Wiener Werkstätte was an artistic community and organization established by Koloman Moser and Josef Hoffmann in Vienna in 1903. It had much in common with the English Arts and Crafts movement.

1905-10   *2½in (6.5cm) wide*

$19,000-25,000   QU

A cabochon, sapphire, enamel, and gem-set pendant, by H.G. Murphy, in pierced yellow gold setting, on a gold chain, in original box.

This pendant sold for a record price for the maker.

pendant 1½in (4cm) wide

$90,000-100,000   WW

An Arts and Crafts Murrle Bennett & Co. "Tree of Life" silver and enamel pendant, on silver link chain, stamped "MB" and "950."

1¼in (3cm) wide

$900-1,000   DUK

An Arts and Crafts Murrle Bennett & Co. silver and enamel pendant, stamped "MB" and "950."

1½in (3.5cm) wide

$650-750   DUK

An Arts and Crafts silver, gold, and opal necklace, attributed to Dorrie Nossiter, some surface wear, later brooch pin fittings.

Similarly designed pieces have also been attributed to Sybil Dunlop.

pendant 2¼in (6cm) high ½oz

$1,900-2,500   FELL

An Arts and Crafts gem-set silver brooch pin, attributed to Dorrie Nossiter, set with moonstone, lapis lazuli, chalcedony cabochons, and circular-cut garnets.

Dorrie Nossiter (1893-1977) trained at the School of Art in Birmingham and went on to produce jewelry. Her work is rarely signed and is easily confused with that of her friend Sibyl Dunlop, who worked in a similar style.

1½in (3.5cm) long

$1,500-2,000   WW

CLOSER LOOK—PHOEBE ANNA TRAQUAIR BROOCH PIN

This brooch pin is attributed to illustrator, painter, and embroiderer Phoebe Anna Traquair (1852-1936), the first woman to be elected to the Royal Scottish Academy.

It depicts a slumbering figure attended by two angels, one playing an instrument.

It has a bead and cord border mount.

The enamel bears similarities to Traquair's enamel panel, "The Dream" from 1909, and the frame bears similarities to her "The Awakening" pendant from 1903.

A silver and chrysoprase pendant necklace, attributed to Omar Ramsden.

2¾in (7cm) long

$1,300-1,800   WW

A cloisonné enamel pendant necklace, by Harold Stabler.

1¾in (4.5cm) high

$1,050-1,200   WW

An Arts and Crafts enamel and silver brooch pin, attributed to Phoebe Anna Traquair.

c1909   *2in (5cm) wide*

$8,000-9,000   GTH

A gem-set Cartier "Fruit Bowl" brooch pin, with black onyx, calibré-cut emeralds, sapphires, and a ruby, inventory number to reverse "3577," in fitted case.

$23,000-28,000   WW

An Art Deco platinum sapphire and diamond bow brooch pin.

2¾in (7cm) wide

$4,400-5,000   FLD

An Art Deco diamond brooch pin.

2in (5cm) long

$2,300-2,800   CHOR

An Art Deco 3.25ct diamond double-clip brooch pin, set with round brilliant-cut, eight-cut, and baguette-cut diamonds, one pin deficient.

2in (5cm) wide ½oz

$2,300-2,800   TEN

An Art Deco emerald and 3.6ct diamond bar brooch pin, some gaps between diamonds and settings.

3¼in (8cm) long ⅜oz

$2,500-3,200   TEN

An Art Deco jade and 0.15ct diamond brooch pin, one jade loose.

2¼in (5.5cm) long ¼oz

$1,150-1,500   TEN

An Art Deco onyx and diamond bow brooch pin, with center old brilliant-cut 0.4ct diamond.

c1920   *2in (5cm) long*

$450-550   DN

An Art Deco carved jadeite and brilliant-cut diamond panel brooch pin, with platinum brooch pin fittings.

2¼in (5.5cm) long

$1,900-2,500   PW

A French Art Deco brooch pin, set with carved black onyx and circular-cut diamonds in white gold, French control marks, in fitted Bolin box.

1½in (4cm) wide

$5,000-5,700   WW

An Art Deco cultured pearl and diamond flowerhead cluster pendant/brooch pin, the platinum openwork setting with 114 round old-cut diamonds.

1½in (4cm) diam

$3,200-3,800   HAN

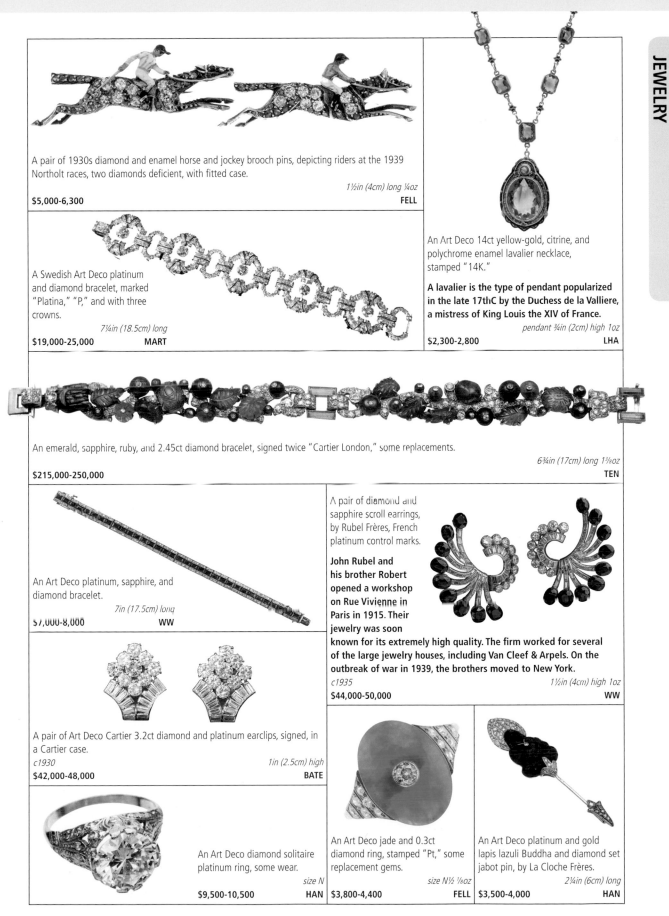

A pair of 1930s diamond and enamel horse and jockey brooch pins, depicting riders at the 1939 Northolt races, two diamonds deficient, with fitted case.

1½in (4cm) long ¼oz

$5,000-6,300　　**FELL**

A Swedish Art Deco platinum and diamond bracelet, marked "Platina," "P," and with three crowns.

7¼in (18.5cm) long

$19,000-25,000　　**MART**

An Art Deco 14ct yellow-gold, citrine, and polychrome enamel lavalier necklace, stamped "14K."

A lavalier is the type of pendant popularized in the late 17thC by the Duchess de la Valliere, a mistress of King Louis the XIV of France.

pendant ¾in (2cm) high 1oz

$2,300-2,800　　**LHA**

An emerald, sapphire, ruby, and 2.45ct diamond bracelet, signed twice "Cartier London," some replacements.

6¾in (17cm) long 1⅜oz

$215,000-250,000　　**TEN**

An Art Deco platinum, sapphire, and diamond bracelet.

7in (17.5cm) long

$7,000-8,000　　**WW**

A pair of diamond and sapphire scroll earrings, by Rubel Frères, French platinum control marks.

John Rubel and his brother Robert opened a workshop on Rue Vivienne in Paris in 1915. Their jewelry was soon known for its extremely high quality. The firm worked for several of the large jewelry houses, including Van Cleef & Arpels. On the outbreak of war in 1939, the brothers moved to New York.

c1935　　*1½in (4cm) high 1oz*

$44,000-50,000　　**WW**

A pair of Art Deco Cartier 3.2ct diamond and platinum earclips, signed, in a Cartier case.

c1930　　*1in (2.5cm) high*

$42,000-48,000　　**BATE**

An Art Deco diamond solitaire platinum ring, some wear.

size N

$9,500-10,500　　**HAN**

An Art Deco jade and 0.3ct diamond ring, stamped "Pt," some replacement gems.

size N½ ⅛oz

$3,800-4,400　　**FELL**

An Art Deco platinum and gold lapis lazuli Buddha and diamond set jabot pin, by La Cloche Frères.

2¼in (6cm) long

$3,500-4,000　　**HAN**

JEWELRY

A Chanel vintage gold-tone "Matelassé" cuff bangle, signed, some hairlines and scratches.

c1981-85   *2¼in (6cm) diam*

$450-500   **FELL**

A coral ring, by Gerda Flöckinger, set in yellow precious metal in the form of a crown, marked "G F."

Gerda Flöckinger is a preeminent mid-20thC jeweler. She was born in Austria in 1927 and moved to England as a child. She started her jewelry business in 1956 and, in 1971, became the first contemporary jeweler to have a solo exhibition at the Victoria and Albert Museum.

size L-M

$2,500-3,200   **CHEF**

A silver Georg Jensen "Continuity" ring, designed by Vivianna Torun, model no.443, stamped "925S," "443," "Torun," hallmarked "GJLD," import mark for London, surface wear.

1969   *size O 1in (2.5cm) wide ¼oz*

$300-450   **TEN**

A pair of 1960s Kutchinsky 18ct gold 0.45ct diamond and turquoise earrings, signed, hallmarks for London, some wear.

1965   *¾in (2cm) diam ⅝oz*

$3,200-3,800   **FELL**

A 1950s Tiffany & Co. 14ct yellow gold, moonstone, ruby, and diamond flower pin, in original box.

3in (7.5cm) long ⅝oz

$1,900-2,500   **POOK**

A Georg Jensen silver brooch pin, designed by Arno Malinowski, model no.318, stamped "STERLING," "DENMARK," "318," hallmarked "GJLD," import mark for London, surface wear.

1964   *1½in (4cm) square ¾oz*

$1,000-1,150   **TEN**

A 1970s Tiffany & Co. diamond, ruby, emerald, and sapphire set clip, signed "Tiffany & Co.," surface scratches, one gem deficient.

3in (7.5cm) long 1oz

$5,500-6,500   **FELL**

A mid-20thC 22-25ct diamond bracelet, French assay marks, surface scratches.

7¼in (18.5cm) long 2⅜oz

$20,000-25,000   **FELL**

A mid-20thC yellow gold, sapphire, and diamond S-scroll brooch pin.

1½in (4cm) long

$750-900   **MART**

A 1950s 10ct diamond and 14ct white gold floral brooch pin, Austrian marks.

2¾in (7cm) high ½oz

$3,500-4,000   **ECGW**

An early 1970s 14ct gold retro tanzanite ring, with bark textured design in the style of Andrew Grima.

Tanzanite was discovered as a new gem in 1967.

size M ½oz

$1,800-2,300   **GWA**

A Jakob Bengal chrome-plated metal and red plastic necklace.

1932 *17in (43cm) long*

$550-700 **GRV**

A pair of 1960s Marcel Boucher gold-plated metal and enamel cuff bracelets.

2¼in (6cm) diam

$300-450 **GRV**

A 1980s Chanel gold-plated metal necklace.

16½in (42cm) long

$950-1,050 **GRV**

A pair of 1980s Chanel gold-plated metal earrings.

2¾in (7cm) long

$500-650 **GRV**

A 1970s Ciner gold-plated metal, rhinestone, glass, and cream enamel bangle.

2¼in (6cm) diam

$250-320 **GRV**

A 1960s pair of Coppola e Toppo gold-tone metal and rhinestone earrings.

1½in (3.5cm) diam

$500-650 **GRV**

A 1950s Christian Dior gold vermeil-plated and multicolored rhinestone necklace, brooch pin and earrings set, designed by Mitchel Maer.

necklace 16½in (42cm) long

$1,300-1,900 **GRV**

A pair of Christian Dior rhodium-plated metal and rhinestone earrings.

1968 *1¾in (4.5cm) long*

$450-550 **GRV**

A 1930s Theodor Fahrner silver-gilt bracelet.

7½in (19cm) long

$700-800 **GRV**

A pair of 1960s Gripoix turquoise poured glass, rhinestone, and gold-plated metal earrings.

1½in (4cm) diam

$700-750 **GRV**

JEWELRY

A pair of 1950s Miriam Haskell gilt-metal, pink glass, faux pearl, and rhinestone earrings.

2½in (6.5cm) long

$400-500   **GRV**

A 1960s Jomaz emerald green glass and rhinestone, rhodium-plated bracelet.

7¾in (19.5cm) long

$450-550   **GRV**

ESSENTIAL REFERENCE—JOSEFF OF HOLLYWOOD

Eugene Joseff (1905-48) was a prominent 1930s costume jewelry designer and the founder of Joseph of Hollywood.

● He began his career in an advertising agency in Chicago, before moving to Los Angeles to train as a jewelry designer.

● From 1931, he made costume jewelry pieces for Hollywood movies, renting his work to the studios to allow for potential rehire. He worked in a huge range of styles, creating pieces for popular movies, such as "The Wizard of Oz," "Gone with the Wind," and "Casablanca."

● In 1935, he founded Joseff of Hollywood and opened a store, Sunset Jewelry, where he sold replicas of movie originals.

● His pieces were often large to ensure they could be seen on screen. Another key feature was the use of semimat "Russian gold" plating, which he developed to prevent reflections from studio lighting.

● Eugene Joseff died in a plane crash in 1948. The company was continued by his widow and is still family-run today.

A 1940s Joseff of Hollywood Egyptian Revival Scarab necklace, with three turquoise scarabs set on "Russian gold" mounts and chain, signed "Joseff Hollywood."

9¾in (25cm) long

$700-800   **PC**

A 1940s Joseff of Hollywood Pinwheel necklace, bracelet, and earring set, in "Russian gold," necklace and bracelet signed "Joseff Hollywood," earrings signed "Joseff."

necklace 10¾in (27.5cm) long fastened

$650-750   **PC**

A 1950s Joseff of Hollywood "Russian Gold Plate" necklace.

17¾in (45cm) long

$550-700   **GRV**

A 1950s Joseff of Hollywood "Russian Gold Plate" and rhinestone bangle.

2¾in (7cm) diam

$500-650   **GRV**

A Knoll and Pregizer sterling silver, black enamel, and rhinestone brooch pin.

2in (5cm) long

$650-750   **GRV**

A 1950s Matisse copper and enamel necklace and earrings set.

necklace 17¾in (45cm) long

$190-250   **GRV**

A 1920s Bohemian Egyptian Revival necklace, possibly by Max Neiger, with Jablonec Bohemian green and red glass, unsigned.

8½in (21.5cm) long fastened

$190-250   **PC**

A 1960s Henry Perichon silver and purple poured-glass brooch pin.

3¼in (8cm) long

$450-550 GRV

A 1950s Elsa Schiaparelli gold-tone metal, turquoise glass, and rhinestone bracelet.

7in (18cm) long

$450-500 GRV

ESSENTIAL REFERENCE—TRIFARI

Trifari is probably the best-known costume jewelry manufacturer.

● It was founded in New York in 1912 by Italian Gustavo Trifari (1883-1952), who was soon joined by Leo Krussman and Karl Fishel.

● Trifari produced a range of high-quality costume jewelry, supplying pieces to various Hollywood and Broadway productions.

● After Alfred Phillipe joined as head designer in 1930, it became the United States' second largest costume jewelry firm. Phillipe's designs were very popular in the 1930s to 1950s, especially his "Crown" pins and "Jelly Bellies."

● Trifari was sold to Hallmark Jewelry Co. in 1975 and to Liz Claiborne, Inc. in 2000.

A 1950s Roger Scemama silver-gilt and rhinestone necklace and earrings set.

necklace 14½in (37cm) long

$1,000-1,150 GRV

A 1940s Trifari gold vermeil and rhinestone necklace.

15¾in (40cm) long

$450-500 GRV

A 1940s Trifari gold vermeil, sapphire rhinestone, and enamel bracelet and earrings set.

bracelet 6¼in (16cm) long

$400-500 GRV

A figural Peacock Trifari Moghul "Jewels of India" brooch pin, designed by Alfred Philippe, with green melon carved "Jello Mold" stone, signed crown "Trifari Pat, Pend."

designed 1949 2in (5cm) long

$400-500 PC

An early 1950s Trifari turquoise molded-glass necklace, in the shape of a chrysanthemum, signed "Trifari."

9½in (24cm) long

$300-400 PC

An early 1950s Trifari necklace and bracelet, signed "Trifari Pat, Pend."

necklace 8¾in (22cm) long

$300-450 PC

A 1930s German-patented (DRGM) black Bakelite, rhinestone, and silver tone metal necklace and bracelet.

necklace 16¼in (41cm) long

$750-900 GRV

A mid-18thC and later carved giltwood chimney piece, in the manner of Matthias Locke, with statuary marble slips and plinths, jambs restored.

69in (175cm) wide

$15,000-19,000   **CHEF**

An 18thC painted carved wood chimney piece, to a design by Robert Adam, with replacement stone slips.

This chimney piece is comparable in design and size to two drawings of chimney pieces executed by Robert Adam for the Adelphi buildings in London, built 1768-72 and demolished in the early 1930s.

84½in (214.5cm) wide

$7,000-8,000   **CHEF**

A George III pine and gesso decorated chimney piece, with acanthus detail, the main frieze centered by a dancing putti.

c1790   58¾in (149cm) high

$1,150-1,500   **DN**

A late 18thC marble statuary chimney piece, the frieze depicting the Vestal Virgins, some losses.

The Vestal Virgins in ancient Rome were priestesses of Vesta, Goddess of the Hearth.

63¾in (162cm) wide

$25,000-32,000   **CHEF**

A George III carved pine chimney piece.

78¼in (199cm) wide

$2,500-3,200   **WW**

A George III carved and giltwood chimney piece, possibly by Thomas Johnson, with statuary marble slips.

64in (162.5cm) wide

$15,000-19,000   **CHEF**

A 19thC George II-style pine and gesso fire surround.

76¾in (195cm) wide

$2,300-2,800   **L&T**

A 19thC oak and burr oak fire surround, in the Palladian style.

90½in (230cm) wide

$1,150-1,500   **L&T**

A northern French Henri IV cast iron fireback, cast with Saint Hubertus, cast with the legend, "Frilo.c. de Witri," dated.

Saint Hubertus or Hubert (c656-727) became Bishop of Liège in 708 AD. He was venerated during the Middle Ages, being patron saint of hunters, mathematicians, opticians, and metalworkers, and was sometimes known as the Apostle of the Ardennes.

1570   *30¼in (77cm) wide*
$5,000-6,300   **DN**

An 18thC cast iron and steel serpentine fire grate, in the manner of Robert Adam.

30¾in (78cm) wide
$2,500-3,200   **CHEF**

A Regency cast iron fire grate, in the manner of George Bullock (1777-1818).

38¼in (97cm) wide
$1,900-2,500   **CHEF**

An early 19thC cast iron Sarcophagus fire grate, in the manner of George Bullock.

33in (84cm) wide
$3,200-3,800   **CHEF**

A Gothic Revival John Hardman & Co. wrought and cast iron fire basket and dogs, by A.W.N. Pugin (1812-52).

c1850   *51½in (131cm) wide*
$3,800-5,000   **L&T**

A 19thC cast iron fire grate, by Thomas Elsleyin, after a design by Thomas Chippendale.

35in (89cm) wide
$4,400-5,000   **CHEF**

A George III pierced steel fender.

48in (122cm) wide
$700-800   **SWO**

A Regency gilt-brass fender.

63¾in (162cm) wide
$1,900-2,500   **L&T**

A late Victorian brass club fender.

54¾in (139cm) wide
$2,300-2,800   **WW**

A late 19thC to early 20thC brass fender, in late 18thC French taste, some wear, one sphinx wing restored.

63¾in (162cm) wide
$3,200-3,800   **DN**

A leather fire bucket, inscribed "J. Fogg/No 3.," minor wear to paint, dated.

1823   *11in (28cm) high*

$2,500-3,200   **WHIT**

A painted leather fire bucket, by John Fenno, Boston, Massachusetts, inscribed "NOBIS VICINISQUE/ JOHN HARBACH," maker's mark "I.FENNO," some scratches, dated.

1790   *12½in (32cm) high*

$2,800-3,500   **SK**

A 19thC navette-shaped mahogany and brass-mounted peat bucket.

14½in (37cm) high

$750-900   **WW**

A Victorian painted leather fire bucket, with the Royal coat of arms, with a later leather handle.

11½in (29cm) diam

$550-700   **L&T**

A pair of Philadelphia Chippendale brass andirons.

c1780   *19½in (49.5cm) high*

$10,000-11,000   **POOK**

A pair of 19thC Louis XV-style gilt and patinated bronze chenets.

21½in (54.5cm) high

$1,150-1,250   **WW**

A set of early 19thC Georgian brass fire tools.

tongs 30¾in (78cm) long

$400-500   **L&T**

A set of early 19thC English steel fire irons, some wear.

28in (71cm) long

$1,900-2,500   **DN**

An 18thC carved and painted fire screen, designed as an Elizabethan woman, in-painting in breaks at the arm.

47in (119.5cm) high

$3,800-4,400   **SK**

A Victorian painted cast iron garden seat, with wooden splats.

68in (172.5cm) long

$1,500-2,000　　　　JN

A Victorian painted cast iron "oak, twigg and serpent" garden bench.

52in (132cm) long

$1,300-1,900　　　　L&T

A Victorian Coalbrookdale-type cast iron garden seat, with wooden slatted seat.

67¾in (172cm) long

$2,800-3,500　　　　BE

A Victorian Coalbrookdale fern-pattern garden bench.

71¾in (182cm) wide

$1,000-1,150　　　　CHEF

One of a pair of Coalbrookdale-style cast iron and pierced garden benches.

67in (170cm) wide

$2,500-3,200 the pair　　　　MEA

A 19thC botanical pattern rustic garden bench.

50in (127cm) wide

$1,400-1,800　　　　PW

A late 19thC cast iron "oak and ivy" pattern garden seat, attributed to Coalbrookdale, with slatted wood seat.

The original design, no.119253, was registered and patented by the Coalbrookdale Iron Foundry at the Public Record office on March 8, 1859, and is seat no.30 in their 1875 Castings Catalogue. It was designed by the sculptor John Bell, one of Coalbrookdale's principal designers.

59¾in (152cm) wide

$3,800-5,000　　　　DN

A late 19thC French cast iron garden seat, probably Val D'Osne foundry, with Gothic Revival decoration.

The design for this bench is illustrated in the 1858 Barbezat & Cie's Founderies du Val d'Osne catalogue, under "Bancs de Jardin," plate 251. However, this pattern is also included in other publications as being of slightly earlier, English design; Himmelheber has it as being a production of James Yates at his Effingham Works in Rotherham, c1840. The later 19thC dating of this bench would suggest that the French foundry house is a more probable candidate.

48½in (123cm) wide

$6,500-7,500　　　　DN

A Victorian Coalbrookdale-type cast iron garden armchair, decorated with Gothic designs, with wooden slatted seat.

$300-400　　　　BE

ARCHITECTURAL ANTIQUES

A pair of 19thC Scottish Garnkirk "fireclay" urns on stands, one with script date "12/10/41."

35½in (90cm) high

$1,900-2,500   L&T

A late 19thC pair of Scottish Garnkirk "fireclay" garden urns and pedestals, stamped "GARNKIRK."

33¾in (86cm) high

$2,500-3,200   L&T

A pair of 20thC sculpted limestone garden urns, some scuffs.

48¾in (124cm) high

$25,000-32,000   DN

A pair of 20thC carved limestone garden urns.

54¼in (138cm) high

$9,500-10,500   DN

A pedestal horse trough, made to imitate white marble, some wear.

55in (139.5cm) long

$750-900   JN

A pair of lead garden urns, with cast cherub masks.

19in (48cm) high

$1,600-2,300   BE

A 19thC painted cast iron garden fountain, on a limestone base, repainted, some wear.

c1880   *67¾in (172cm) high*

$14,000-18,000   DN

A bronze fountain of a cherub, sitting on a dolphin playing a flute, signed "A Rhind," dated.

The Rhinds were an important 19thC family of sculptors from Edinburgh, notably John, William Birnie and J. Massey. A. Rhind is unrecorded, but believed to be a member of the family.

1926   *35in (89cm) high*

$3,200-3,800   CHEF

An early 20thC painted metal and carved limestone mounted armillary sphere, with internal copper register of Roman numerals, repainted, some wear, plinth associated.

66¼in (168cm) high

$4,000-4,800   DN

A late 17thC to early 18thC carved marble bust of a Classical lady, possibly Diana.

32¼in (82cm) high

$2,500-3,800   WW

Judith Picks

Robert of Baston was a Carmelite monk known for his verses and songs. It is said that he was taken by the kings Edward I and Edward II on their military campaigns to Scotland, where he was captured by Robert the Bruce and forced to write and sing verses about the defeat of his own countrymen in return for his release. This is the event that is depicted in this sculpture.

The sculptor, Robert Forrest (1789-1852), was a successful stonemason from Carluke, Lanarkshire. His most famous

work is the statue of Lord Melville that tops the column in St Andrew Square, Edinburgh. He often sculpted historical and literary figures.

A carved sandstone group, "King Robert the Bruce and the Monk of Baston," by Robert Forrest of Carluke (1789-1852).

c1830   *118in (300cm) wide*

$11,000-12,000   L&T

A mid-19thC Scottish fireclay figure of Fidelity, by Grangemouth Coal Co., stamped.

The Grangemouth Coal Company was established in 1839 and by the midcentury they were operating the Grangemouth Brickworks, manufacturing fireclay bricks and ornamental pottery. They displayed at the Great Exhibition in 1851, and it is believed this model of "Fidelity" was shown there. The company ceased trading in 1912.

49¼in (125cm) high

$5,000-6,300   L&T

A 19thC Scottish carved marble Classical figure, by Lawrence Macdonald (1799-1878), signed.

46¾in (119cm) high

$19,000-25,000   HANN

A life-size statue of Hebe.

84in (213.5cm) high

$1,300-1,900   JN

A marble figural group of "The Three Graces."

90½in (230cm) high

$5,000-5,700   SWO

A rare set of four early 20thC Bromsgrove Guild lead figures of "The Seasons," modeled by Walter Gilbert, Winter with molded mark.

The Bromsgrove Guild of Applied Arts was established in 1884 by Walter Gilbert, initially producing decorative ironwork but later producing bronze and lead work as well as wood and stone carvings. By 1908, they had established a retail outlet in Victoria Street, London, as a result of their most famous commission, the iron and bronze gates outside Buckingham Palace.

42½in (108cm) high

$38,000-44,000   TEN

A bronzed metal garden fountain, modeled as a cherub supporting a shell, some dirt.

42¼in (107cm) high

$550-700   CHOR

A bronzed resin figure of Peter Pan, after the model in Kensington Gardens, London, by George Frampton, incised "EM."

50½in (128cm) high

$2,500-3,200   HALL

A pair of 17thC to 18thC Scottish carved limestone lions.

37½in (95cm) high

$3,800-5,000   **L&T**

A pair of 19thC Scottish "fireclay" lions, by Brown's of Ferguslie Park, stamped "R. Brown & Son/Ferguslie/Paisley."

41¾in (106cm) long

$1,900-2,500   **L&T**

A 19thC stone figure of a lion.

41¼in (105cm) high

$3,800-5,000   **L&T**

A pair of early 20thC composition stone lion figures.

24in (61cm) wide

$650-750   **L&T**

A pair of 19thC Scottish cast iron lions, Carron Foundry, Falkirk.

44in (112cm) long

$3,800-5,000   **L&T**

A pair of 20thC sculpted limestone lions, in the manner of Antonio Canova (Venetian, 1757-1822).

The original lions upon which these are based were sculpted in marble by Canova in 1792 for the tomb of Pope Clement XIII in St. Peter's in Rome. The lions were greatly admired, and therefore copied from the start. One well-known pair that was cast in bronze from Canova's original works in 1860 now adorns the front of the Corcoran Gallery of Art in Washington, D.C.

67¼in (171cm) long

$44,000-50,000   **DN**

A pair of Philadelphia wood and perot cast iron Newfoundland dog garden figures.

These are the only pair known to exist and retain an excellent painted surface.

c1857-78   *65in (165cm) long*

$60,000-65,000   **POOK**

A pair of early 20thC stone figures of dogs, after a model by Henri Alfred Marie Jacquemart.

60¼in (153cm) high

$5,000-6,300   **L&T**

A late 19thC Continental stone composition model of an owl.

59in (150cm) high

$8,000-9,000   **DN**

A Victorian granite dog kennel.

26in (66cm) wide

$1,900-2,500   **L&T**

A 19thC Harris & Co. swell-bodied copper weathervane, of a Native American Indian, depicting Massasoit the great Wampanoag chief, retaining old yellow painted and verdigris surface.

35in (89cm) high

$23,000-28,000   **POOK**

A molded and painted sheet copper Goddess of Liberty weathervane, by Cushing & White, Waltham, Massachusetts, some wear and solder repairs.

c1865-75   *38½in (98cm) high*

$25,000-32,000   **SK**

A 19thC full-bodied copper horse and sulky weathervane, purportedly by Dan Patch, reverse cleaned.

72in (183cm) wide

$16,000-23,000   **POOK**

A late 19thC molded copper "Smuggler" running horse weathervane.

31in (78.5cm) long

$3,800-5,000   **SK**

A swell-bodied leaping stag weathervane, attributed to L.D. Cushing & Co. Massachusetts, with old verdigris and gilt surface.

c1875   *27in (68.5cm) wide*

$19,000-25,000   **POOK**

A 19thC swell-bodied copper setter weathervane, with old gilt over verdigris surface.

31½in (80cm) wide

$5,000-5,700   **POOK**

A 19thC swell-bodied copper rooster weathervane, with old yellow over verdigris surface, old repaired bullet hole.

28¼in (72cm) high

$4,400-5,000   **POOK**

A 19thC swell-bodied copper lamb weathervane, possibly Fiske, with cast zinc head retaining old verdigris surface, ears and bar replaced.

27½in (70cm) wide

$19,000-25,000   **POOK**

A 19thC swell-bodied copper whale weathervane, some repaired bullet holes.

36in (91.5cm) long

$32,000-38,000   **POOK**

A Bidjar handwoven wool palace-size oriental rug.

Bidjar is in North West Persia.

216in (548.5cm) long

$1,600-2,000 WHIT

A Bidjar carpet.

c1910 *239¾in (609cm) long*

$11,000-12,000 SWO

A Bokhara carpet, the madder field decorated with foliate and geometric motifs.

Bokhara is in the North East of the Persian Empire.

149½in (380cm) long

$1,900-2,500 DN

A Heriz Tabriz silk pictorial rug, decorated with trees, animals, figures, and portrait bust spandrels, heavy corrosion to the browns.

The weavers of Heriz, or Heris, in Northwest Persia, were famous for their large wool-piled carpets, made with strong dyes. In the late 19thC, fine silk carpets were also produced on a cottage industry basis. Production had mainly ceased by 1900.

c1880 *71¼in (181cm) long*

$6,500-7,500 WW

A Heriz "Tree of Life" rug, some dirt and errors.

86¾in (220cm) long

$1,900-2,500 BELL

An early 20thC Heriz rug, the blue ground with herati field, some losses.

139in (353cm) long

$1,800-2,300 WES

CLOSER LOOK—ISFAHAN SOUF PRAYER RUG

Isfahan, in Central Persia, was a center for rug and carpet making in the 17thC. After 200 years of decline, production was reintroduced by weavers brought in from Kashan in the 1920s.

The top of the rug depicts a mihrab, the niche in the wall of a mosque that shows the direction to Mecca.

The flat woven field is embellished with piled palmettes and scrolling vines, bordered by piles of pictorial cartouches between guard stripes.

The condition is good and the colors vibrant.

An early to mid-20thC Mamoury Isfahan carpet, signature to one end.

111in (282cm) long

$3,800-4,400 L&T

An Isfahan rug, with signature "by order of Sadegh, Seirafian, Esfahan, Iran," some wear, one repair.

66¼in (168.5cm) long

$5,000-6,300 DN

An Isfahan silk Souf prayer rug.

c1920 *76¾in (195cm) long*

$13,000-18,000 LC

ESSENTIAL REFERENCE—KASHAN RUGS

Kashan, in Central Persia, was the center of rug and carpet making in the 16thC and 17thC. Production declined in the 18thC, but the late 19thC saw a reintroduction of traditional craftsmanship.

- Late 19thC and early 20thC Kashan weavings are typically of very high quality, woven using a cotton foundation with a Persian knot.
- Silk rugs were made alongside wool-piled ones. These were often of prayer format and made in large quantities in the 1920s.
- There are two terms loosely used to describe fine late 19thC to early 20thC Kashans: Kurk, referring to the quality of the wool, and Mohtasham, probably the name of a master weaver who owned workshops in the city.

A wool Kashan Mohtasham rug.

c1880   *80in (203cm) long*

$15,000-19,000   FRE

A late 19thC to early 20thC Kashan Mohtasham carpet.

122in (310cm) long

$7,000-7,500   L&T

An antique Kirman scenic carpet.

92in (233.5cm) long

$4,400-5,000   CLAR

A Kashan carpet, the indigo field of scrolling vines around a cusped pole medallion.

c1930   *162¼in (412cm) long*

$3,800-5,000   TEN

A Khorassan carpet, some wear, losses and repairs.

The Khorassan province is in the North East of Persia.

161½in (410cm) long

$3,200-3,800   DN

A Kirman Laver carpet, the ivory field with a floral faceted medallion, some fading and dirt.

Kirman, or Kerman, carpets, are named after the city and province of Kirman in Southeast Persia. It has been a major center for the production of carpets since the 15thC. The regional wool, Carmania wool, from which these carpets are made, is of very high quality.

111in (282cm) wide

$2,300-2,800   BELL

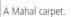

An early 20thC Kashan silk souf carpet, frayed at borders, some staining.

125½in (319cm) long

$9,500-10,500   CHOR

A Mahal carpet.

The term Mahal is used to describe rugs and carpets from a particular region in North West Persia. The name probably derives from the village of Mahallat.

141¾in (360cm) long

$6,500-7,000   DN

A Mahal carpet, the red ground with scrolling foliage.

c1900   *275½in (700cm) long*

$8,000-9,000   SWO

A late 19thC to early 20thC Meshed carpet, East Persia.

Meshed is in North East Persia.

164½in (418cm) long

$650-750   L&T

A Nain carpet, the ivory field of scrolling vines and palmettes around a sky blue pole medallion.

The town of Nain is in Central Persia.

c1970   *225½in (573cm) long*

$7,500-9,000   TEN

A Qum Erami silk carpet.

Qum, also Ghom or Kum, is in Central Persia.

$7,500-9,000   DN

A mid-20thC Qum Rug.

$1,900-2,500   WAD

A late 19thC to early 20thC Sarouk Fereghan rug.

Rugs and carpets were made in and around the village of Sarouk, in West Persia, in the second half of the 19thC and the early 20thC. Production was on a cottage industry basis, so designs and styles vary considerably. Center medallions framed by spandrels were a common motif.

78¾in (200cm) long

$1,300-1,800   L&T

An early 20thC Sarouk rug, some losses and alterations.

270in (686cm) long

$1,900-2,500   WES

A Serapi carpet, some wear and losses.

Serapi rugs were woven in the mountains of Northwest Persia on a family and small workshop basis. They were woven almost exclusively by women. They are named after the town of Serab, from which these carpets were traded.

c1900   *144in (366cm) long*

$2,800-3,500   POOK

A Sultanabad carpet, some staining and light wear.

Sultanabad is in West Persia.

c1930   *141¾in (360cm) long*

$2,300-2,800   TEN

ESSENTIAL REFERENCE—TABRIZ CARPETS

Tabriz is an important weaving center in Northwest Persia.

- Tabriz was one of the world's major cities from the 11thC. In the 13thC, it became capital of the Mongol Empire. It soon became an important weaving center and, by the 16thC, was one of the leading producers of carpets in the East.
- Weaving declined in the 18thC, but in the late 19thC was reestablished on a workshop basis.
- Tabriz weavers often copied or adapted designs from other areas. They chiefly made room-size carpets, although smaller rugs were also produced.
- Their late 19thC to early 20thC pieces are typically soft red, cream, and indigo.

A late 19thC to early 20thC Tabriz "Hadji Jalili" carpet.

137in (348cm) long

$1,500-2,000   L&T

An early 20thC Tabriz carpet, worn overall, some rebinding, fringes cut short.

128¼in (326cm) long

$1,800-2,300   DN

A 1940s Tabriz carpet, the sky blue field of Shah Abass design.

171¾in (436cm) long

$3,200-3,800   TEN

A part-silk Sino Tabriz carpet.

125in (317.5cm) long

$3,200-3,800   CLAR

A Tabriz carpet, some wear, some replacement binding, losses to tassels.

152in (386cm) long

$6,500-7,500   DN

A late 19thC Ziegler carpet.

Ziegler and Co., of Manchester, England, established a carpet manufactory in Sultanabad, West Persia, in 1883. The firm aimed to combine traditional 16thC and 17thC Persian carpet design with Western tastes, employing both major designers from Western department stores and local artisans in Sultanabad.

275½in (700cm) long

$7,000-7,500   L&T

A late 19thC Ziegler carpet.

151½in (385cm) long

$7,500-9,000   L&T

A Persian silk "Tree of Life" rug, "Ex Liberty."

84in (213.5cm) long

$1,900-2,500   JN

A Northwest Persian runner, some repairs.

c1920   *144in (366cm) long*

$1,300-1,600   POOK

A mid-to-late 19thC Akstafa rug, Southwest Caucasus, with horse and riders with Akstafa peacocks.

102in (259cm) long

$5,000-6,300   **WW**

A late 19thC Kuba rug, East Caucasus.

62¼in (158cm) long

$950-1,050   **MART**

An early 20thC Lenkoran rug, South East Caucasus.

112½in (286cm) long

$500-650   **WW**

A Shirvan prayer rug, repairs to sides.

c1920   *64in (162.5cm) long*

$750-900   **POOK**

A late 19thC Seychour rug, East Caucasus, in a traditional Eastern design of stylized gul motifs within a Western-style floral border.

$7,500-9,000   **PW**

A late 19thC Soumac carpet.

157½in (400cm) long

$1,600-2,000   **L&T**

A late 19thC Caucasian runner, the indigo field surrounded by tribal and zoomorphic devices.

128in (325cm) long

$950-1,050   **LC**

A Caucasian carpet.

c1910   *110in (279.5cm) long*

$1,900-2,500   **POOK**

An early 20thC prayer rug, South Caucasus, possibly dated "1912."

$800-950   **WAD**

A Mahal carpet.

179¼in (455cm) long

$3,800-5,000 SWO

An early 20thC Anatolian kelim.

119in (302cm) long

$900-1,000 L&T

A late 19thC Anatolian rug, in Gendje style.

62¼in (158cm) long

$650-750 WW

An Anatolian Kayseri rug.

c1920

$1,600-2,300 WAD

A Turkoman carpet.

c1910 *132in (335.5cm) long*

$1,600-2,300 POOK

A late 19thC Ushak carpet, West Anatolia, in two sections.

Ushak was a center of carpet production in the 16thC and 17thC, best known for its "star" and medallion carpets. In the late 19thC and early 20thC, Ushak had a resurgence of carpet making, often supplying pieces for export to Europe and North America.

169¼in (430cm) long

$1,300-1,900 L&T

An early 20thC Ushak runner, Anatolia, made from two runners.

270in (686cm) long

$3,200-3,800 WW

An Ushak carpet, the pale field decorated with geometric and stylized foliate motifs, losses to tassels, some areas of possible repair.

225¼in (572cm) long

$12,000-14,000 DN

An Ushak green ground carpet, damages and losses to borders.

145¾in (370cm) long

$4,400-5,700 CHEF

A 19thC American hooked rug, minor fraying, old repairs, mounted.

75in (190.5cm) wide

$7,000-8,000   POOK

A 19thC French Savonnerie Empire-style carpet, with center fan medallion and a Classical twin griffin flaming athenienne.

193in (490cm) wide

$19,000-25,000   WW

An Aubusson tapestry carpet, some fading, exterior border trimmed, later backing.

152in (386cm) long

$2,300-2,800   BELL

An Agra carpet, India.
c1930-50   191¼in (486cm) long

$5,000-6,300   WW

A pair of Agra runners, Central/North India.
c1880   267¾in (680cm) long

$28,000-35,000   LC

An Amritsar carpet, Punjab, Northwest India.
c1880   185in (470cm) long

$19,000-25,000   LC

A 1930s to 1940s Irish wool carpet, by Dun Emer Guild Ltd., Dublin.

144¾in (367.5cm) wide

$3,800-5,000   MEA

A Celtic "hunting" wool carpet, designed by George Bain (1881-1968) for Quayle and Tranter Ltd., Kidderminster.

George Bain was born in Scrabster in Northern Scotland and single-handedly revived interest in Celtic and Insular art. His book, "Celtic Art: The Methods of Construction," was published in 1951.

143¾in (365cm) wide

$3,200-4,400   SWO

A Spanish carpet, probably Madrid, inscribed "MD," dated.
1954   136½in (347cm) long

$2,500-3,200   L&T

A New Jersey "Broderie Perse" quilt, with 156 squares with chintz appliqués, inscribed "Trenton N.J.," with names from the Vallette, Coleman, McNeely, and Aitken families, some light staining, dated.

1843   *103in (261.5cm) wide*

$12,000-14,000   **POOK**

A mid-19thC child's appliqué album quilt, inscribed "Elizabeth Walker," probably reduced in size, some staining, in acrylic case.

48in (122cm) long

$4,400-5,000   **POOK**

A mid-19thC appliqué "Rose of Sharon" quilt.

78½in (199.5cm) wide

$2,000-2,500   **FRE**

A pieced and tied child's quilt, possibly New York State, with printed cotton and wool pieces, with appliqué figure of an African-American child, signed "Ida Murphy."

c1870   *53¾in (136.5cm) wide*

$3,200-4,400   **FRE**

An appliqué album quilt, signed "Mrs. Catherine Tyson," scattered staining, dated.

1857   *84in (213.5cm) square*

$2,300-2,800   **POOK**

A 19thC pieced "Bar and Star" quilt, probably Orange County, NY, with 18thC copperplate-printed linen and printed cotton patches.

The 18thC linen came from the wedding dress fabric of Abbie "Nabby" Forsyth, who married Daniel Greenleaf, October 3, 1791, in Norwich, Connecticut.

87½in (222.5cm) wide

$1,500-2,000   **FRE**

A late 19thC appliqué "Whig Rose" quilt, minor stains.

88in (223.5cm) wide

$500-650   **POOK**

A late 19thC pieced quilt, with potted tulips.

84in (213.5cm) wide

$500-550   **POOK**

A late 19thC Pennsylvania floral appliqué quilt, minor staining.

91in (231cm) long

$700-750   **POOK**

An early 20thC Hawaiian "Ku'u Hae Aloha" or "Flag" quilt, with Hawaiian flags and coat of arms, some stains and fading.

93in (236cm) long

$7,500-9,000 SK

Judith Picks

This quilt, "Scenes from American Life," was made by Mrs. Cecil White, Hartford, Connecticut. It is incredibly detailed and is composed of 55 vignettes, depicting figures engaged in various pursuits, including a bartender serving his customers, a rodeo star, tennis players, golfers, baseball players, a billiards scene, farming scenes, a fiddle player, dancers, swimmers, weddings, men in uniform, a man getting his shoes shined, and many more scenes. The quilt is bordered by touring cars, pickup trucks, and steam trains. The rich social history depicted on this quilt makes it an especially interesting piece.

A pieced and appliqué folk art quilt, "Scenes of American Life."

c1925-30 *77in (195.5cm) long*

$60,000-65,000 SK

An appliqué cockscomb quilt, minor staining.

c1900 *75in (190.5cm) long*

$550-700 POOK

A pieced memorial quilt, inscribed "This quilt was made 5/2 1907 by Mary R. Fisher 87 years old for remembrance to John R. Shaner the tailor," some staining.

1907 *80in (203cm) wide*

$1,000-1,150 POOK

A Tennessee State Fair First Prize quilt, silk and velvet star variant with triangle outer border, some losses and fraying.

1909 *83in (211cm) long*

$650-750 POOK

An early 20thC pieced alphabet quilt, mounted, light stains.

79in (200.5cm) long

$900-1,000 POOK

A 20thC Hawaiian floral quilt, with floral appliqué.

82in (208.5cm) long

$1,050-1,200 SK

A Mennonite "Trip Around the World, Sunshine and Shadow" quilt, Elmira, Waterloo County, Ontario.

c1940-50 *87in (221cm) wide*

$450-500 SK

CLOSER LOOK—BRUSSELS TAPESTRY

This important Brussels tapestry comes from the "History of Venus" series. It depicts Venus disclosing to Diomedes the conduct of his wife Aegialia, with figures and trees in the foreground, the ocean and Cupid on an elephant behind.

It is probably after Bernard van Orley and may be from the workshop of Guasparo di Bartolommeo Papini, after Alessandro Allori.

The scene is within a naturalistic border woven with animals, bunches of fruit, birds, and flowers.

It is in good condition considering its age, with well-preserved colors.

A mid-16thC Brussels mythological tapestry, from the "History of Venus" series.

256in (650cm) wide

$100,000-100,000

SWO

An 19thC Aubusson tapestry panel, some restoration, rebacked.

90in (228.5cm) high

$2,500-3,200

CHEF

A 17thC to 18thC Brussels verdure tapestry.

106in (269cm) wide

$9,500-10,500

BRI

A mid-16thC Brussels mythological tapestry, after Bernard van Orley, "Venus saves Aeneas from the wrath of Diomedes," from the "History of Venus" series.

154¼in (392cm) wide

$50,000-57,000

SWO

A mid-18thC Brussels Teniers tapestry, of the Kermesse, with groups of peasants making merry outside an inn, in picture frame border with the Brussels town mark in the selvedge.

This version of the Kermesse is attributed by H.C. Marillier in his "Handbook to the Teniers Tapestries" to the Van der Borcht brothers, Pierre (fl.1712-63) and François (fl.1720-65).

213¾in (543cm) wide

$13,000-19,000

SWO

A late 17thC tapestry panel, emblematic of fall, Mortlake or Hatton Garden, London, from the "Mortlake Months" series woven with a vineyard scene.

The "Mortlake Months" series was probably based on the Brussels suite of "The Months," by Gilles de Leyniers

109¾in (279cm) high

$23,000-28,000

SWO

A mid-18thC Brussels tapestry, in Rococo style, after Jean-Antoine Watteau's "La Partie carrée."

This tapestry in the fête galante style depicts figures in a stagelike setting in the manner of Jean-Antoine Watteau's celebrated painting "La Partie carrée" of c1713. The figure of Pierrot is an almost exact copy.

56¼in (397cm) wide

$5,500-7,000

WW

TEXTILES

A 16thC Flemish historical tapestry, "The Story of Julius Caesar," depicting the "Enthronement of Caesar and Cleopatra," from the "Story of Julius Caesar and Cleopatra" series.

133½in (339cm) high

$25,000-32,000   **SWO**

A 17thC Franco-Flemish tapestry depicting soldiery in Roman-style armor and a horse, with later borders and rebacked.

62¼in (158cm) high

$7,500-9,000   **DN**

A mid-17thC Flemish tapestry, possibly depicting the story of Daphne "from Ovid Metamorphoses."

129½in (329cm) wide

$4,400-5,000   **GWA**

An early 17thC Florentine allegorical tapestry, emblematic of Winter, after Alessandro Allori.

161in (409cm) wide

$90,000-100,000   **SWO**

A late 17thC to early 18thC Flemish "verdure" tapestry panel.

84¼in (214cm) high

$2,300-2,800   **DUK**

A late 17thC verdure tapestry, woven in wools, some fading and dirty, old repairs, and possible alternations.

102¼in (260cm) high

$1,900-2,500   **BELL**

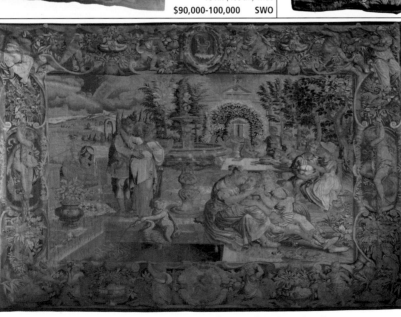

An early 17thC Florentine allegorical tapestry, emblematic of Spring, after Alessandro Allori.

192¼in (488cm) wide

$110,000-130,000   **SWO**

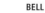

An 18thC verdure tapestry.

135¾in (345cm) high

$3,200-3,800   **WW**

A mid-17thC English embroidered panel, worked in silk and wool on a silk satin ground, framed and glazed.

15in (38cm) wide

$1,150-1,400 HT

A Charles II raised needlework portrait of a family, in later ebonized glazed frame.

20in (51cm) wide

$4,400-5,000 SW

A silk and silver thread needlework picture, by Mary Sibley, depicting the Sibley sisters, the verso stating that "all three were with child and that Mary was the daughter of Mr Cresnard of Earlscone (Earls Colne) Essex and married George Sibley gent of Westham, Essex, who was the son of Nathan Sibley, Deputy of Coleman Street ward of London," in later glazed frame.

The figures in this picture were directly taken from Wenceslaus Hollar's (1607-77) fashion plate etchings, "Theatrum Mulierum." The center figure is a direct copy of Mulier Generosa Anglica.

1670 *7in (18cm) wide*

$7,500-9,000 WW

A late 17thC Charles II embroidered beadwork panel, worked on white silk, in original japanned frame, some tears and stains to corners.

22¾in (58cm) wide

$9,000-10,000 DN

A late 17thC English stump work picture, depicting Adam and Eve in the Garden of Eden, framed.

14½in (37cm) wide

$4,400-5,700 SWO

A late 17thC embroidered panel.

24½in (62cm) wide

$1,300-1,800 SWO

An 18thC early Georgian needlepoint wall hanging, worked in gros and petit point, some restitching.

102¼in (260cm) high

$5,500-6,500 GORL

An 18thC woolwork of a shepherd and shepherdess, framed, under glass.

4¼in (11cm) wide

$5,500-7,000 CHEF

A band sampler, with acorns above flowers, pairs of hands reaching for hearts and a thistle, all above "Jane How ... Her Sampler," with pine frame, some fading, dated.

1654 *32¾in (83cm) high*

$3,200-3,800 CHEF

A Charles II "boxer" band needlework sampler, in later gilt frame.

32¾in (83.5cm) high

$1,300-1,800 WW

A Georgian sampler, by Frances Tydeman.

17in (43cm) high

$400-500 LC

A Regency needlework sampler, by M. Watt, inscribed "M. WATT 1810," in later glazed ebonized frame.

8½in (21.5cm) high

$300-400 WW

A George IV needlework sampler, by Mary Simpson, worked with Adam and Eve, with a verse, inscribed, in later glazed mahogany frame, dated.

1828 *26in (66cm) wide*

$650-750 WW

An early 19thC Georgian silk and needlework sampler, with an alphabet above the names "HENRY MACKENZIE" and "PANUEL GRANT" and a verse, with the author's name "MARGARET MACKENZIE," in an ebonized frame.

This sampler is thought to have been worked by the daughter of Henry Mackenzie (1745-1831), the author of the novel "The Man of Feeling," and to have been bought from Cullen House previously.

15in (38cm) high

$9,500-10,500 L&T

A Pennsylvania silk-on-linen sampler, by Rose Abbott, allover toning, dated.

1829 *17in (43cm) high*

$2,500-3,200 POOK

A silk-on-linen house sampler, by Sarah Ann Rundell, minor staining, dated.

1828 *16½in (42cm) high*

$950-1,050 POOK

A Pennsylvania silk-on-linen sampler, by Elizabeth Cooper, a few tack holes and toning to edges, dated.

1831 *21¾in (55cm) high*

$1,300-1,800 POOK

CLOSER LOOK—17THC VELVET JERKIN

The jerkin was a garment worn to protect the doublet worn below, and to provide extra warmth and protection.

This example is made of the finest Italian crimson velvet and must have belonged to a man of great wealth and importance.

It has silk at the shoulder wings and hem, adorned with gold and silver thread braids. The collar is interlined with heavy buckram.

Few specimens of late 16thC or early 17thC costume survive, making this an especially rare find.

A short-waisted velvet jerkin, the shoulder interlined with linen, with silver-gilt wrapped acorn-shaped buttons, with purpose-made mount.

c1610-25   chest 40¼in (102cm) wide

$90,000-100,000   **KT**

A Gabrielle Chanel couture crêpe romain "little black dress," with sequinned fringes, the bolero edged with beaded and sequinned fronds, lacking shoulder fringes.

This design was illustrated in French and American Vogue between April and June 1926, notably worn by the Marquise de Jaucourt and modeled by Marion Morehouse.

1926   34in (86.5cm) bust

$10,000-11,000   **KT**

CLOSER LOOK—AVANT GARDE ROBE

This robe is an extraordinary example of British avant garde clothing made on the eve of World War I.

It was designed by Percy Wyndham Lewis (1882-1957), a writer, painter, critic, and cofounder of the avant garde Vorticist movement in art.

It is decorated with stylized foxes, fish, swans, and kneeling figures.

The fabric may have been among the textiles produced by the Bloomsbury Group's Omega Workshops, although another similar printed panel of this design was attributed to the Rebel Art Centre, a short-lived workshop set up in 1914 after Lewis and several Omega artists had quarreled with the Bloomsbury set.

An embroidered and block-printed silk robe.

c1914   52in (132cm) long

$44,000-50,000   **MAL**

A French caraco bodice, of early 1760s brocade, woven with lacy ribbon trails, plumes, and bouquets, with boned front closure.

c1780

$1,900-2,500   **KT**

A rare 1820s young man's brown wool double-breasted tailcoat, with stiffened collar, composition buttons, with short tails with pockets.

32in (81.5cm) chest

$6,500-7,500   **KT**

A striped silk gauze dress, with empire-line bodice and puffed sleeves, satin rouleaux edging, and appliquéd flowers.

c1825   30in (76cm) bust

$5,000-6,300   **KT**

A Lucile Ltd. bridal gown, of silk and sheer chiffon, edged and trimmed with pearl beads and fringing, with small lace pouch, labeled "17 West 38th St, New York."

Lucile traded from 17 West 36th Street between 1910-12. This was the wedding dress of Eugenie Ward Root Riley (1889-1974), granddaughter of multimillionaire landowner Andrew Ward, worn on her marriage to army officer James Wilson Riley of South Carolina.

1912   32in (81cm) bust

$5,500-6,500   **KT**

A Carven couture embroidered and beaded white organza dress.

1948-50   20in (51cm) waist

$32,000-38,000   **KT**

A Thea Porter muslin "gypsy" dress, edged with gold braid, woven lily label.

1969-71   size 10

$8,000-9,500   **KT**

TEXTILES

A pair of English doeskin gloves, with embroidered ivory satin gauntlets, edged in silver lace, lined in salmon pink silk, inked "R.A.C Eshott, 1778."

Provenance: Gifted to Rebecca Ann Colt of Eshott Hall, near Morpeth, Cumbria, England. In 1778, Rebecca's husband Thomas Carr was created High Sheriff of the county and, for the inaugural procession, he commissioned richly embroidered robes and saddle cloths and carried these 17thC gloves.

c1630-40   11¾in (30cm) long
$6,500-7,500   KT

A pair of silver lace and ivory satin lady's shoes, adorned with silver bobbin lace and silver strip passementerie.

c1720-30   10¼in (26cm) long
$38,000-44,000   KT

A 1930s Jean Patou black wool felt hat, with two large cartwheels of monkey fur, colobus satanas, with center velvet coils, labeled.

22in (56cm) diam
$1,050-1,200   KT

Judith Picks

It is widely believed that the Votes for Women sash was first seen at the Women's Sunday demonstration held on June 21, 1908, in Hyde Park, London. The Editor of "Votes for Woman" magazine, Emmeline Pethick-Lawrence, encouraged supporters to attend the demonstration dressed in their best white dress, to ensure the sash was clearly visible and show the world that they were respectable and to defuse fears of violence. The sash was created by the Women's Social and Political Union and is thought to have been designed by Sylvia Pankhurst, Emmeline Pankhurst's daughter. It is probable that the sashes were sold at department stores. Selfridges in London certainly stocked a range of dresses, brooch pins, ribbons, hats, and drapery in suffrage colors.

An early 20thC woven "Votes for Women" sash, printed with black letters with green and purple stripes, the original hook-and-eye fastening stamped "Nicklin's."

$5,500-6,500   FLD

A Hermès "Cosmos" scarf, designed by Philippe Ledoux, one pull to fabric.

issued 1964   35½in (90cm) wide
$500-650   FELL

A Hermès "Wedgwood" scarf, designed by Philippe Ledoux, minor water marks.

designed 1974   35¾in (91cm) wide
$450-550   FELL

A Hermès "Republique Francaise Liberte Egalite Fraternite" scarf, designed by Joachim Metz, signed, minor marks.

This scarf was designed to commemorate the bicentenary of the French Revolution.

issued 1989   35½in (90cm) square
$300-400   FELL

A Hermès cashmere and silk shawl, "Brides de Gala" pattern, designed by Hugo Grygkar, some snags and pulls, some spots.

55in (140cm) square
$700-800   LHA

A Chanel silk and wool shawl, with the Chanel motif throughout, with label.

48½in (123cm) wide
$1,000-1,150   DN

An Aspinal of London pebble leather and calf "Buffalo" cabin bag, with brass hardware, on two wheels, with dust bag.

18in (46cm) wide

$500-650   **DN**

An Asprey ostrich leather "Darcy Belgravia" handbag, with alligator skin accents and silver-tone hardware.

14¾in (37.5cm) wide

$3,800-5,000   **FELL**

A Berluti alligator leather "Deux Jours" briefcase, some wear, lacking shoulder strap.

15¾in (40cm) wide

$3,200-3,800   **FELL**

A Berluti "Venezia" leather weekend bag, the zippered interior with two compartments and a zipper compartment, blind stamped "Berluti."

13½in (34cm) wide

$800-900   **DN**

A Cartier vintage "Happy Birthday Bordeaux" handbag, with dust bag and box.

11in (28cm) wide

$1,000-1,150   **FELL**

An early 1990s Cartier alligator skin "Pantere" handbag and coin purse, with gold-tone hardware, with maker's dust bag.

11½in (29cm) wide

$1,300-1,900   **FELL**

A Céline "Micro Luggage" leather handbag, with red leather trim, expandable side wing, and red leather-lined interior.

10¼in (26cm) wide

$1,600-2,000   **FELL**

A Chanel vintage lambskin leather purse, serial no.1708055, with gold-tone hardware and maker's signature CC turn-lock front fastening, minor wear.

Chanel was founded in France in 1910 by Coco Chanel, and today continues to create high-end clothing, jewelry, and perfume.

c1989-91   *8¾in (22cm) wide*

$1,500-2,000   **FELL**

A vintage Chanel "Maxi Classic Flap" quilted lambskin leather purse, serial no.3061509, with gold-tone hardware and CC logo, turn-lock fastening, some scuffs, hairlines to hardware.

c1994-96   *13¼in (33.5cm) wide*

$2,500-3,200   **FELL**

A Chanel tricolor "Gabrielle Hobo" bag, from the Fall/Winter 2017 Collection.

10¾in (27.5cm) wide

$2,800-3,500   **FELL**

A Chanel quilted leather shoulder bag, with gilt clasp and chain, stamped serial number, with original dust bag.

9¾in (25cm) wide

$1,000-1,150   **CHEF**

TEXTILES

A Christian Dior "Lady Dior" lizard skin purse, with gold-tone hardware, some light scratches and scuffing, with maker's care guide, authenticity card, dust bag, and associated box.

9½in (24cm) wide

$2,500-3,200   **FELL**

A Christian Dior "Mini Micro-Cannage Diorama Flap" perforated calfskin leather exterior purse, serial no.13.BO.0155, with silver-tone hardware, minor abrasion to base corners, with maker's dust bag.

27in (18cm) wide

$1,300-1,800   **FELL**

ESSENTIAL REFERENCE—HERMÈS

Hermès is one of the top brands of handbags and purses.

- **It was founded in 1837 by Thierry Hermès. It originally specialized in horse saddles and carriage fittings. It produced its first handbags and purses in 1922.**
- **Its famous bags include the "Kelly," designed in the 1930s and later used by Grace Kelly; the "Birkin," designed for actress Jane Birkin in 1984; and the "Evelyne," designed for a casual everyday look.**
- **Vintage and new Hermès handbags are often sought after today. The world record for a Hermès handbag was a Hermès Birkin, which sold for £253,700 ($319,660) at Christie's in 2017. Another Hermès Birkin sold for £163,500 ($206,000) at Christie's in 2018.**
- **Condition has a significant effect on value, as does the material the bag is made of.**

A Gucci "Positano" hobo bag, serial no.155563 200047, with maker's monogram canvas exterior and red leather trim, with twilly scarf woven through grommet holes, with maker's dust bag.

Gucci was founded by Guccio Gucci in Florence, Italy, in 1921. The firm originally specialized in leather riding gear and luggage and later added handbags and clothing to its list of products.

14¼in (26cm) wide

$300-400   **FELL**

A Gucci "Soho" grained leather purse, serial no.308983 520981, with gold-tone hardware, quilted interlocking "GG" logo, light wear, with maker's dust bag and maintenance guide.

11in (28cm) wide

$750-900   **FELL**

A 1930s Hermès of Paris crocodile handbag, fully stamped "Hermes Paris, 24FG St Honore," wear to metalwork, light rubbing, with a later Hermes slip case.

10½in (26.5cm) wide

$4,000-4,800   **GORL**

A Hermès niloticus crocodile sellier "Kelly" handbag, with gold-tone hardware, stamped "Hermès," with "H" blindstamp, some wear, with dust bag.

2004   *12½in (32cm) wide*

$10,000-11,000   **LHA**

A Gucci "GG Marmont" quilted leather purse, with "GG" snap closure, the interior with a zippered compartment.

9¾in (25cm) wide

$1,200-1,400   **DN**

An Hermès "Chocolate Taurillon Clemence Jypsiere" bag, with palladium hardware, stamped "Hermès, with "N" blindstamp, with box and dust bag.

2010   *11in (28cm) wide*

$2,800-3,500   **LHA**

An Hermès "Epsom Evelyne TPM" handbag, with silver and palladium hardware, stamped "Hermès," with "JO" blindstamp, with box and dust bag.

2011   *7in (18cm) high*

$1,900-2,500   **LHA**

A Hermès "Birkin 35" ostrich leather handbag, gold-tone turn lock fastening, padlock, clochette, and key, minor wear, with maker's dust bag, box, and rain cover.

13¾in (35cm) wide

$12,000-14,000   **FELL**

A Hèrmes Porosus Crocodile Kelly 35 handbag, with gold-tone hardware, with padlock and two keys.

14in (35.5cm) wide

$15,000-19,000 FELL

A limited edition Mulberry "Beaded Bayswater" chocolate brown and oak Darwin leather handbag, serial no.063348, with antique brass hardware, oak leather handles and trim, and maker's signature postman's lock fastening, signs of use.

14¼in (36cm) wide

A Hermès "Blue Jean Birkin 35" pebbled leather handbag, with gold-tone turn lock fastening, feet scuffed, with maker's care guide, rain protector, dust bag, and box.

13¾in (35cm) wide

$13,000-16,000 FELL

$650-750 FELL

A Prada "Saffiano" leather handbag, the satin interior with two pockets and two zippered compartments, with Prada dust bag.

11¾in (30cm) wide

$550-700 DN

A Louis Vuitton "Idylle Neverfull MM" handbag, serial no.CA0182.

The Monogram Idylle (previously Mini Lin) Canvas Collection is a newer line that sports a lighter canvas, made of 58 percent cotton, 24 percent linen, and 18 percent polyamide.

18in (46cm) wide

A Mulberry Bayswater oak leather handbag, with brass clasp and padlock, with original retail tag.

11¼in (36cm) wide

$650-750 CHEF

$1,050-1,200 FELL

A Louis Vuitton "Monogram Empreinte Artsy MM" monogram embossed calfskin leather handbag, serial no.CA0165, with gold-tone hardware, some scratches, with maker's dust bag.

15¼in (39cm) wide

$1,800-2,500 FELL

A Louis Vuitton "Capucine MM" taurillon leather handbag, serial no.AH1105, with orange coated edges, maker's initials, with silver-tone hardware.

14¼in (36cm) wide

$2,800-3,500 FELL

A Louis Vuitton "Monogram Carryall" coated canvas and leather soft multipurpose bag, with two side pockets, a padlock, and a name tag.

16½in (42cm) wide

$1,000-1,150 DN

A Louis Vuitton "Monogram Vernis Alma BB" monogram embossed patent leather handbag, serial no.MI2110, some faint marks and hairlines.

c2010 *9in (23cm) wide*

$1,050-1,200 FELL

An early 20thC Maison Goyard fitted gown trunk, in black "Goyardine" printed canvas, monogrammed "M.A.K./PHILADELPHIA" with various shipping labels, labeled "GOYARDAINE."

43½in (110.5cm) wide

$9,000-10,000   **FRE**

An Edwardian leather traveling trunk, in hide with brass stud reinforced corners and strap banding, stenciled "J.F. CHRISTIE," stamped "LECKIE GRAHAM & CO./ MANUFACTURERS/GLASGOW."

33in (84cm) wide

$900-1,000   **L&T**

A Hermès leather-bound canvas suitcase, with stamped brass furniture and bosses, opening to a void, cotton-lined interior with two leather straps.

c1935   *31¾in (80.5cm) wide*

$1,900-2,500   **L&T**

A Louis Vuitton Damier steamer trunk, serial no.N31640, stenciled "E.B.K/Salem/Mass/u.s.a," locks stamped "0132," with brass handles, some wear.

c1890

$7,500-9,000   **WES**

A Louis Vuitton wardrobe steamer trunk, serial no.350391, retailed by Marshall Field & Company, Chicago, monogrammed and stenciled "M.McC.," locks stamped "041545," tears, wear, and abrasions.

c1914   *44½in (113cm) high*

$5,500-6,500   **WES**

Judith Picks

Louis Vuitton (1821-92) opened his first store in 1854 and had his first great success with the "Trianon" trunk in 1858. This trunk was waterproof, canvas-covered, and airtight, meaning that, unlike previous trunks, it did not need to have a sloped top to let water run off it. Instead, it was a more practical and stackable shape. To combat reproductions by rivals, Vuitton introduced beige-and-brown striped canvas in 1876, followed in 1888 by its checkered "Damier" pattern and in 1896 by the "LV" monogram fabric. From 1932, it also produced handbags, its first being the "Noe" and the "Speedy."

Louis Vuitton trunks remain highly collectible today. The only problem with them is that, when full, you really need a servant to help you carry them! They are exceptionally heavy and now are usually used for decorative or storage purposes, not for travel.

A Louis Vuitton traveling trunk, with brass mounts, wooded slats, and "LV" fabric, with interior label for "149 New Bond Street, London," stamped "192993," lacking internal tray.

43½in (110.5cm) wide

$7,000-7,500   **GORL**

A Louis Vuitton case, no.1074290, Paris, with brass corners, hinges, and lock, no.290909, the interior with lift-out clothes holder, with outer cover.

29in (73.5cm) long

$3,800-4,400   **JN**

A 1990s Louis Vuitton monogrammed leather shoe trunk/suitcase, with 12 interior compartments, labeled "Ave. Marceau 78 Paris, Nice. 2 Ave de Suède," numbered "938217."

23½in (60cm) long

$2,500-3,200   **KT**

A Louis Vuitton traveling jewelry case, with brass locks, no.1252027, opening to a velvet interior with lift-out jewelry tray, serial no.1051049.

13½in (34cm) long

$5,000-6,300   **JN**

ESSENTIAL REFERENCE—JOSE DE ACOSTA

The "Naturall and Morall Historie of the East and West Indies," originally "Historia Natural y Moral," established Jose de Acosta's reputation as an enthusiastic observer capable of relating detailed and realistic descriptions of the New World. Acosta was a Spanish Jesuit who first traveled to the Americas in 1570. In addition to notes on the natural history of the places he visited, including Peru, Panama, and Mexico, he describes Incan and Aztec customs and natural geographical features, such as tides, lakes, rivers, and mineral resources. He also established several universities in South America, where native languages were carefully studied and recorded, and was responsible for bringing a printing press to Peru in the 1570s.

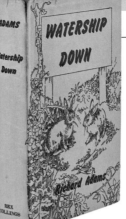

Adams, Richard, "Watership Down," first edition, published by Rex Collings, London, 8vo, ownership signature on endpaper.

This copy contains a compliments slip from the Ministry of Agriculture, Fisheries and Food, where Adams worked at the time of writing. Rex Collings was a one-man publishing outfit who took on "Watership Down" in 1972 and printed 2,500 copies. He said to a friend at the time, "I've just taken on a novel about rabbits, one of them with extrasensory perception. Do you think I'm mad?" The book was a success and was later republished by Penguin.
1972
$650-750　　　　　　　　　　　　　　L&T

Acosta, Jose de (1540-1600), "Naturall and Morall Historie of the East and West Indies," first English edition, printed by Val Sims for Edward Blount and William Aspley, London, quarto, minor staining to leaves.
1604　　　*7¼in (18.5cm) high*
$16,000-20,000　　　　　　SK

Barrie, J.M., "Peter Pan in Kensington Gardens.," first edition, illustrated by Arthur Rackham, published by Hodder & Stoughton, London, small 4to, 50 color plates, some rubbing and splitting.
1906
$650-750　　　　　　　L&T

Bemelmans, Ludwig, "Madeline," first edition, illustrated by Bemelmans, published by Simon and Schuster, New York, 4to, some wear.
1939
$1,500-2,000　　　　SWA

Borges, Jorge Luis, "El jardin de senderos que se bifurcan" ("The Garden of Forking Paths"), first edition, published by Sur, Buenos Aires, 8vo, signed and dated to half title by Borges.
1942
$5,000-6,300　　　　　　　FRE

Bradbury, Ray, "Fahrenheit 451," limited edition no.145/200, illustrated by Joe Muganini, published by Ballantine, New York, 8vo, signed by Bradbury, with first trade edition dust jacket with mild wear.

This limited edition of "Fahrenheit 451" is bound in Johns-Manville Quinterra, an asbestos material that is especially resistant to fire—the idea being that this book, unlike so many within the novel, cannot be burned.
1953
$9,000-10,000　　　SWA

Brooke, Rupert, "The Collected Poems," published by Sidgwick and Jackson, London, 8vo, binding by Sybil Pye, with her stamped monogram date for 1944.

Sybil Pye recorded her bindings, this being no.136 (See Marianne Tidcombe, "Women Bookbinders 1880-1920").
1918
$2,800-3,500　　　GORL

Carroll, Lewis, "Alice's Adventures in Wonderland," illustrated by John Tenniel, second (first published) edition, published by Macmillan and Co., 8vo, spine torn, split, some losses, old ink signature "Lizzie" to back matter.

Due to Tenniel's dissatisfaction with the printing of the illustrations, the original first edition was recalled before sale. This issue was the first published edition.
1866
$3,800-5,000　　　　　BELL

BOOKS & MAPS

Cervantes, Saavedra, Miguel de (1547-1616) "The History of the Most Renowned Don Quixote of Mancha: and His Trusty Squire Sancho Pancha," English translation by John Phillips (1631-1706), published by Thomas Hodgkin, London, some stains and tears.

1687   *12in (30.5cm) high*

$4,400-5,000   **SK**

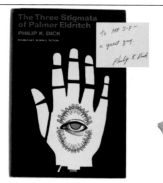

Dick, Philip K., "The Three Stigmata of Palmer Eldritch," first edition, published by Doubleday & Company, Garden City, 8vo, inscribed by Dick "To MR S-F-/a great guy/Philip K. Dick," some rubbing to spine.

1965

$16,000-20,000   **SWA**

Donne, John (1572-1631), "Pseudo-Martyr," first edition, printed by William Stansby for Walter Burre, London, quarto, in a custom phase box.

After Henry VIII led the British people into the Protestant religion, his citizens struggled with Royal allegiances and religious conscience. In "Pseudo-Martyr," Donne, himself a converted Catholic, advises British Roman Catholics to take the Oath of Allegiance to James I. This was Donne's first appearance in print; he later made his name as a poet.

1610   *8¾in (22cm) high*

$21,000-25,000   **SK**

Christie, Agatha, "The Mysterious Affair at Styles," first edition, published by John Lane, The Bodley Head, London, in quarter morocco solander box.

Agatha Christie (1890-1976) was one of the best-loved and best-selling crime writers of the 20thC and remains incredibly popular today. "The Mysterious Affair at Styles" was her first book and the debut of Hercule Poirot.

1921

$5,500-6,500   **KEY**

Dickens, Charles, "The Personal History of David Copperfield," first edition in original 19/20 parts, published by Bradbury & Evans, London, in a morocco backed box, with 40 engraved plates, some repairs.

1849-50   *8¾in (22cm) high*

$3,200-3,800   **DOY**

Dostoevsky, Fyodor, "The Brothers Karamazov," first English edition, translated by Constance Garnett, published by William Heinemann, London, 8vo, joints weak, some wear.

The original book was published in Russian in 1880.

1912

$6,500-7,500   **L&T**

Collodi, Carlo, "The Story of a Puppet or The Adventures of Pinocchio," first English edition, illustrated by Enrico Mazzanti, published by T. Fisher Unwin, made for The Children's Library.

1892

$2,500-3,200   **CHOR**

Dickinson, Emily, "Poems Second Series," first edition, first issue (one of 960 copies), published by Roberts Brothers, Boston, edited by T.W. Higginson and Mabel Loomis Todd, some rubbing, spine darkened.

1891   *7in (18cm) high*

$1,900-2,500   **DOY**

Doyle, Sir Arthur Conan, "The Hound of the Baskervilles," first edition, illustrated in 16 plates by Sidney Paget, 8vo, some rubbing.

1902

$1,150-1,400   **BLO**

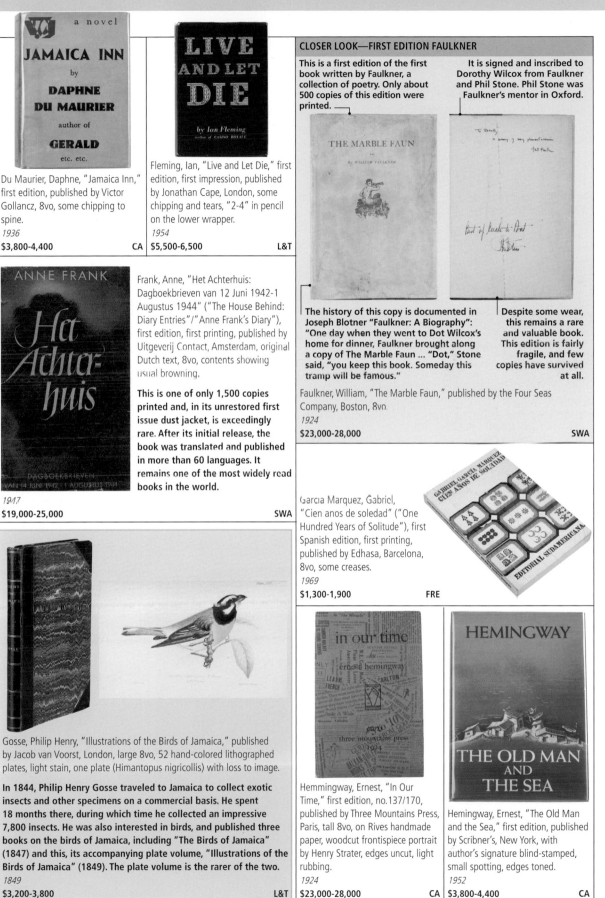

Du Maurier, Daphne, "Jamaica Inn," first edition, published by Victor Gollancz, 8vo, some chipping to spine.
1936
$3,800-4,400   CA

Fleming, Ian, "Live and Let Die," first edition, first impression, published by Jonathan Cape, London, some chipping and tears, "2-4" in pencil on the lower wrapper.
1954
$5,500-6,500   L&T

CLOSER LOOK—FIRST EDITION FAULKNER

This is a first edition of the first book written by Faulkner, a collection of poetry. Only about 500 copies of this edition were printed.

It is signed and inscribed to Dorothy Wilcox from Faulkner and Phil Stone. Phil Stone was Faulkner's mentor in Oxford.

The history of this copy is documented in Joseph Blotner "Faulkner: A Biography": "One day when they went to Dot Wilcox's home for dinner, Faulkner brought along a copy of The Marble Faun ... "Dot," Stone said, "you keep this book. Someday this tramp will be famous."

Despite some wear, this remains a rare and valuable book. This edition is fairly fragile, and few copies have survived at all.

Faulkner, William, "The Marble Faun," published by the Four Seas Company, Boston, 8vo.
1924
$23,000-28,000   SWA

Frank, Anne, "Het Achterhuis: Dagboekbrieven van 12 Juni 1942-1 Augustus 1944" ("The House Behind: Diary Entries"/"Anne Frank's Diary"), first edition, first printing, published by Uitgeverij Contact, Amsterdam, original Dutch text, 8vo, contents showing usual browning.

This is one of only 1,500 copies printed and, in its unrestored first issue dust jacket, is exceedingly rare. After its initial release, the book was translated and published in more than 60 languages. It remains one of the most widely read books in the world.
1947
$19,000-25,000   SWA

Garcia Marquez, Gabriel, "Cien anos de soledad" ("One Hundred Years of Solitude"), first Spanish edition, first printing, published by Edhasa, Barcelona, 8vo, some creases.
1969
$1,300-1,900   FRE

Gosse, Philip Henry, "Illustrations of the Birds of Jamaica," published by Jacob van Voorst, London, large 8vo, 52 hand-colored lithographed plates, light stain, one plate (Himantopus nigricollis) with loss to image.

In 1844, Philip Henry Gosse traveled to Jamaica to collect exotic insects and other specimens on a commercial basis. He spent 18 months there, during which time he collected an impressive 7,800 insects. He was also interested in birds, and published three books on the birds of Jamaica, including "The Birds of Jamaica" (1847) and this, its accompanying plate volume, "Illustrations of the Birds of Jamaica" (1849). The plate volume is the rarer of the two.
1849
$3,200-3,800   L&T

Hemmingway, Ernest, "In Our Time," first edition, no.137/170, published by Three Mountains Press, Paris, tall 8vo, on Rives handmade paper, woodcut frontispiece portrait by Henry Strater, edges uncut, light rubbing.
1924
$23,000-28,000   CA

Hemingway, Ernest, "The Old Man and the Sea," first edition, published by Scribner's, New York, with author's signature blind-stamped, small spotting, edges toned.
1952
$3,800-4,400   CA

Jardine, Sir William, and Selby, Prideaux John, "Illustrations of Ornithology," first edition, published by W.H. Lizars, Edinburgh, and Longman, Rees and Co., London, 4vo, volumes 1-3, with 149 engraved plates, some hand colored.
1826-35
$4,400-5,000   **L&T**

Joyce, James, "Haveth Childers Everywhere: Fragment from Work in Progress," first edition, no.38/100 (of 685 copies) published by Henry Babou and Jack Kahane and The Fountain Press, Paris and New York, 4to, signed in pencil by James Joyce, in box.

This is the second book installment of Works in Progress, the gradually unfolding development of "Finnegans Wake," which further unfolded into the revised text of the eventual full book publication in 1939.
1930
$6,500-7,500   **FRE**

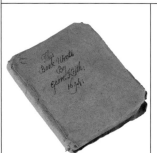

Keith, George, "Truth Advanced in the Correction of Many Gross & Hurtful Errors," published by William Bradford, New York, 4to, 18thC sewn wrappers over original wrapper, some worming causing losses.

This is one of the earliest books printed in New York.
1694
$32,000-38,000   **FRE**

Kerouac, Jack, "On the Road," first edition, first printing, published by Viking, New York.
1957   *8¼in (21cm) high*
$1,800-2,300   **DOY**

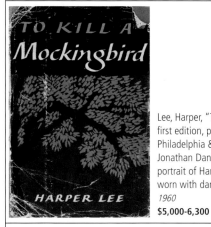

Lee, Harper, "To Kill a Mockingbird," first edition, published by Lippincott, Philadelphia & New York, 8vo, with Jonathan Daniels blurb and Capote portrait of Harper Lee, dust jacket worn with damp staining.
1960
$5,000-6,300   **SWA**

London, Jack, "The Call of the Wild," first edition, first issue, illustrated by Philip R. Goodwin and Charles Livingston Bull, published by The Macmillan Company, New York, 8vo, inscribed by the author on the half title "Yours for the Revolution, Jack London, Glen Ellen, Feb. 22, 1911."
1903
$3,800-4,400   **SWA**

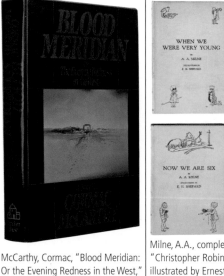

McCarthy, Cormac, "Blood Meridian: Or the Evening Redness in the West," first edition, first printing, published by Random House, New York.
1985
$1,600-2,000   **DOY**

Milne, A.A., complete set of four "Christopher Robin" first editions, illustrated by Ernest H. Shepard, published by Methuen, London, 8vo, all but the last title signed by Milne.
1924-28
$11,000-15,000   **SWA**

Milton, John (1608-74), "Paradise Lost: A Poem in Ten Books," first edition, printed by S. Simmons, London, quarto, trimmed close, marginal loss to one text leaf, tooled in blind.

1669   6¾in (17cm) high

$14,000-18,000   **SK**

Montgomery, L.M., "Anne of Green Gables," first edition, first impression, illustrated in eight plates by M.A. and W.A.J. Claus, published by L.C. Page & Company, Boston, 8vo, two owner's signatures at front.

1908

$3,800-5,000   **SWA**

Potter, Beatrix, "The Tale of Peter Rabbit," first trade edition, published by Frederick Warne, 16mo, color frontispiece and 30 color plates, some light rubbing and staining.

In 1901, Strangeways privately printed 250 copies of "The Tale of Peter Rabbit." Due to the book's success, it was then taken on by Frederick Warne, who printed "The Tale of Peter Rabbit" in color in 1902. The 1901 Strangeways edition is rarer than the 1902 trade edition, and therefore more valuable. See "Miller's Antiques Handbook & Price Guide 2018-2019," page 397, for an example worth $25,000-32,000.

1902

$800-950   **BLO**

Steinbeck, John, "Of Mice and Men," first edition, first issue, published by Covici-Friede, New York, 8vo.

1937

$1,500-2,000   **SWA**

Sharpe, R. Bowdler, "Monograph of the Paradiseidae, or Birds of Paradise, and Ptilonorhynchidae, or Bower-Birds," first edition, published by H. Sotheran, London, 8 parts in 2 volumes, 79 hand-colored lithographic plates by W. Hart after Hart, J. Gould, and J.G. Keulemans.

1891-98

$35,000-40,000   **L&T**

Stanley, Henry M., "How I Found Livingstone, Travels, Adventures and Discoveries in Central Africa," first edition, published by Sampson Low, London, 8vo, 5 maps and 28 plates.

1872

$950-1,050   **L&T**

Sendak, Maurice, "Where the Wild Things Are," first issue with scarce original dust jacket, published by Harper & Row, New York, oblong 8vo, signed and inscribed by Sendak with an original early full-length drawing of Max.

Provenance: Ex-collection playwright, choreographer, friend of Sendak, and fellow children's book author and illustrator, William Archibald, with his ownership signature on the half title.

1963

$15,000-19,000   **SWA**

Stoker, Bram, "Dracula," first edition, first issue, published by Archibald Constable, Westminster, 8vo, spine darkened, scattered soiling, closed tear to title repaired.

1897

$13,000-18,000   **SWA**

Stowe, Harriet Beecher, "Uncle Tom's Cabin, or, Negro Life in the Slave States of America," first English edition, published by C.H. Clarke, London, 8vo, 40 full-page illustrations, tissue guards, light spotting.
1852
$500-650   LC

Tolkien, J.R.R. "The Lord of the Rings," first editions, published by Allen & Unwin, London, octavo, in three volumes, each volume with a map illustrated by the author, with lslip of paper inscribed "If you would like a signature for "The Lord of the Rings," you can stick this in with my good wishes. J.R.R.Tolkien 20/6/73."
1954-55   *8¾in (22.5cm) high*
$8,000-9,500   WHYT

Tolkien, J.R.R., "The Hobbit, or There and Back Again," second impression, published by George Alen & Unwin Ltd., London, 8vo.
1937
$2,300-2,800   L&T

Tolstoy, Leo, "War and Peace," first edition, 8vo, Moscow, six parts in four vols, some wear and repair, with later morocco backed boards.
1868-69
$3,800-5,000   CHEF

Twain, Mark, "The Adventures of Huckleberry Finn," first edition, earliest available issue, published by Charles L. Webster, New York.
1885   *8½in (21.5cm) high*
$7,500-9,000   DOY

Wells, H.G., "Kipps: The Story of a Simple Soul," first edition, first printing, published by Macmillan and Co., split inside spine, discoloration to jacket, creased end flap.
1905
$7,000-8,000   CUTW

Yeats, W.B., "The Winding Stair and Other Poems," first edition, published by Macmillan and Co., London, 8vo, cloth to a design by Sturge Moore, some fading, book plate and early owner's inscription.

This edition differs considerably to the work of the same name published in New York in 1929.
1933
$700-800   L&T

Wells, H.G., "The War in the Air," first edition, published by George Bell and Sons, with a story removed from "The Strand" Magazine 1909 by H.G. Wells "My First Aeroplane (Alauda Magna)," page ends foxed.
1908
$11,000-14,000   CUTW

Wells, H.G., "Bealby," first edition, published by Methuen & Co., printer's date "25/11/14," advertisement leaflets dated "Spring 1915."
1915
$1,900-2,500   CUTW

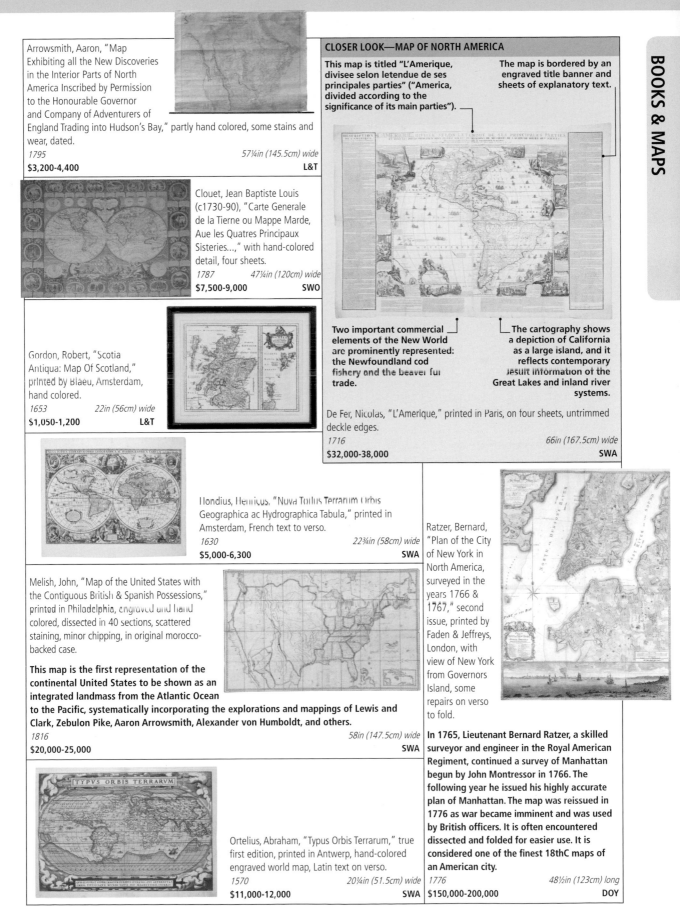

Arrowsmith, Aaron, "Map Exhibiting all the New Discoveries in the Interior Parts of North America Inscribed by Permission to the Honourable Governor and Company of Adventurers of England Trading into Hudson's Bay," partly hand colored, some stains and wear, dated.
1795   *57¼in (145.5cm) wide*
$3,200-4,400   **L&T**

Clouet, Jean Baptiste Louis (c1730-90), "Carte Generale de la Tierne ou Mappe Marde, Aue les Quatres Principaux Sisteries...," with hand-colored detail, four sheets.
1787   *47¼in (120cm) wide*
$7,500-9,000   **SWO**

Gordon, Robert, "Scotia Antiqua: Map Of Scotland," printed by Blaeu, Amsterdam, hand colored.
1653   *22in (56cm) wide*
$1,050-1,200   **L&T**

Hondius, Henricus, "Nova Totius Terrarum Orbis Geographica ac Hydrographica Tabula," printed in Amsterdam, French text to verso.
1630   *22¾in (58cm) wide*
$5,000-6,300   **SWA**

Melish, John, "Map of the United States with the Contiguous British & Spanish Possessions," printed in Philadelphia, engraved and hand colored, dissected in 40 sections, scattered staining, minor chipping, in original morocco-backed case.

This map is the first representation of the continental United States to be shown as an integrated landmass from the Atlantic Ocean to the Pacific, systematically incorporating the explorations and mappings of Lewis and Clark, Zebulon Pike, Aaron Arrowsmith, Alexander von Humboldt, and others.
1816   *58in (147.5cm) wide*
$20,000-25,000
                    SWA

Ortelius, Abraham, "Typus Orbis Terrarum," true first edition, printed in Antwerp, hand-colored engraved world map, Latin text on verso.
1570   *20¼in (51.5cm) wide*
$11,000-12,000   **SWA**

CLOSER LOOK—MAP OF NORTH AMERICA

This map is titled "L'Amerique, divisee selon letendue de ses principales parties" ("America, divided according to the significance of its main parties").

The map is bordered by an engraved title banner and sheets of explanatory text.

Two important commercial elements of the New World are prominently represented: the Newfoundland cod fishery and the beaver fur trade.

The cartography shows a depiction of California as a large island, and it reflects contemporary Jesuit information of the Great Lakes and inland river systems.

De Fer, Nicolas, "L'Amerique," printed in Paris, on four sheets, untrimmed deckle edges.
1716   *66in (167.5cm) wide*
$32,000-38,000
                    SWA

Ratzer, Bernard, "Plan of the City of New York in North America, surveyed in the years 1766 & 1767," second issue, printed by Faden & Jeffreys, London, with view of New York from Governors Island, some repairs on verso to fold.

In 1765, Lieutenant Bernard Ratzer, a skilled surveyor and engineer in the Royal American Regiment, continued a survey of Manhattan begun by John Montressor in 1766. The following year he issued his highly accurate plan of Manhattan. The map was reissued in 1776 as war became imminent and was used by British officers. It is often encountered dissected and folded for easier use. It is considered one of the finest 18thC maps of an American city.
1776   *48½in (123cm) long*
$150,000-200,000   **DOY**

Saxton, Christopher and Speed, John, "The Kingdome of England," hand colored, engraved by Abraham Goos for Bassett and Chiswell, inaccurately dated "1646."

c1676   *21in (53.5cm) wide*
$550-700   **CHEF**

Sayer, Robert, "North American Map," printed in London, hand colored in outline, signed "Robert Sayer, Versailles, 20 Jan 1783," some tears.

1786   *47¼in (120cm) wide*
$1,800-2,300   **L&T**

Schedel, Hartmann "World map," extracted from the Liber Chronicaru, published by A. Koberger, Nuremberg, with Latin text, the reverse with 14 wood engravings, with some tape, small marginal losses, minor staining.

Based upon Ptolemy, and produced the year that Columbus announced his discovery of America, Schedel's map omits Scandinavia, southern Africa, and the Far East. The Indian Ocean is depicted as a landlocked sea.

1493   *22¼in (56.5cm) wide*
$7,000-7,500   **DOY**

ESSENTIAL REFERENCE—JOHN SPEED

John Speed (c1552-1629) is arguably the most famous English cartographer. He was also a historian.

- **He was the son of a tailor, was brought up to carry on the family trade, and became a member of the Merchant Taylors' Company in 1580.**
- **Within the guild he came to the notice of Sir Fulk Greville, under whose patronage he was ultimately able to leave tailoring to pursue his history writing and mapmaking.**
- **In 1611, his first great work of history, "The History of Great Britain under the Conquests of ye Romans, Saxons, Danes and Normans," was published.**

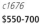

Speed, John, "Cambridgeshire described with the devision of the hundreds," published by Sudbury and Humble, hand colored and engraved, some surface wear.

The shields around the edge are of Cambridge Colleges.

c1611   *20½in (52cm) wide*
$950-1,050   **CHEF**

Speed, John, "Map of the World," sold by George Humble, hand-colored copper engraving, with allegorical figures representing the four elements, diagrams of "Heavens and Elements," with illustrations of eclipses and celestial hemispheres, portraits of circumnavigators including Sir Francis Drake, framed.

22in (56cm) wide
$7,500-9,000   **HAN**

Speed, John, "The Invasions of England and Ireland," engraved by Cornelius Danckerts for George Humble.

c1627   *20¾in (53cm) wide*
$900-1,000   **CHEF**

Speed, John, "Cornwall," published by Bassett & Chiswell, engraved by Jodocus Hondius, with hand coloring, English text verso with woodcut initial by William Godbid.

1676   *15¼in (38.5cm) wide*
$1,050-1,200   **BLO**

Speed, John, "Britain as it was devided in the tyme of the Englishe Saxons," published by Sudbury and Humble, hand-colored copper engraving, English text to verso, framed and glazed.

20½in (52cm) wide
$1,800-2,300   **HAN**

Walton, Robert, "A New and Accurat Map of the World Drawne According to ye Truest Descriptions Latest Discoveries & Best Observations yt Have Beene Made by English or Strangers," printed in London.

This is an exceptionally fine example of this scarce English world map, often mistaken for the very similar geography and design of John Speed.

1659   *22in (56cm) wide*
$6,500-7,500   **SWA**

CLOSER LOOK—18THC WOODEN DOLL

This is a rare 18thC turned, carved, and painted wooden doll.

She has a detailed face, with inset dark glass eyes, stitched brows, eyelashes, and a wool wig.

She wears full formal evening dress, with wired skirt hoops, short shift, linen petticoat, knitted silk stockings, brocade shoes, and a cream silk brocade open robe, with a pearl choker around her neck.

She carries a glass bell and watch key, an enameled watch set, and silk gauze cap with pearls, artificial flowers, and silk ribbons.

An English 18thC wooden doll, with stuffed cotton arms and white painted legs, slight wear to face, some fingers missing.

Provenance: Purchased by Isabella Byne (1745-97), a reverend's daughter who married into the wealthy Carr family, probably as a gift for her daughters.

13in (33cm) high

$38,000-44,000   SAS

An 18thC turned and carved painted wooden doll, with stuffed wool wig, with stuffed cotton arms and wood hands, in original silk robe, missing one lower leg and two fingertips, some wear.

24in (61cm) high

$7,500-9,000   SAS

A George II wooden doll, "Ursula," with painted gesso-covered face and remains of wig, in silk quilted dress, minor loss to gesso, lower leg loose.

It is written on the back of the torso that "Ursula" belonged to Grace Marshall, London, 1752.

c1752   *28in (71cm) high*

$7,500-9,000   C&T

A carved and painted wooden doll, with gesso-covered head, with cloth and kid leather arms and legs, in a later silk gown, arms lacking stuffing, some repair to legs.

c1770   *29in (73.5cm) high*

$2,300-2,800   C&T

A late 18thC fully jointed carved wooden doll, in early 19thC dress, some losses.

30in (76cm) high

$4,400-5,000   WHP

An Autoperipatetikos walking china head doll, with concealed clockwork.

patented 1862   *9½in (24cm) high*

$950-1,050   BE

A late 18thC wooden doll, with gesso-covered and painted head and neck, with remnants of original wig.

Prices for these early dolls reached a zenith several decades ago which in general they rarely reach today; but exceptions such as this rare doll do occur.

21in (52cm) high

$19,000-25,000   BER

A German china shoulder-head doll, with glass eyes, on a cloth body with leather forearms and period clothing.

28in (72cm) high

$2,500-3,200   BER

TOYS & MODELS

ESSENTIAL REFERENCE—BRU JEUNE & CIE

Bru Jeune & Cie (1866-83) was founded in Paris by Léon Casimir Bru.

- Bru dolls characteristically have fixed paperweight eyes and closed mouths.
- As well as fashion dolls, the firm made some novelties, including crying or laughing dolls and dolls with revolving heads.
- Dolls are typically marked "Déposé" and "Bru Jne & Cie" or "Bru Jne." Some dolls may also be marked with a letter (A-M), which relates to the doll's size.

A Bru Bébé bisque shoulder-head doll, with paperweight eyes and old mohair wig, on a kid body with bisque forearms, paper label to body, bisque incised "Bru Jne 6," fingers restored.

18in (45.5cm) high

$19,000-25,000   **BER**

A fashion bisque socket-head doll, attributed to Bru, with glass eyes and "Mona Lisa" smile, on a kid body, in a wool walking dress with lace trim, the head incised "A."

The "A" model is the smallest known Bru doll; as the letters of the alphabet progress, the height of the model grows.

12in (30.5cm) high

$2,300-2,800   **MORP**

ESSENTIAL REFERENCE—JUMEAU

Jumeau (1842-99) was founded at Montreuil-sur-Bois by Pierre François Jumeau.

- The firm's dolls typically have large fixed paperweight eyes, swivel heads, pierced ears, and closed mouths.
- Early Jumeau dolls are marked with only a number; later dolls, made after Pierre's son Emile Jumeau took over the company in 1875, are sometimes marked with a red check mark on the head.
- Jumeau dolls are known for their elegant, fashionable outfits, and a surviving doll with its original wardrobe is very collectible.
- Jumeau remains one of the most sought-after doll makers internationally.

A Jumeau bisque head doll, with fixed glass eyes and mohair wig, on composition jointed limbs and body, in silk dress, the body stamped with maker's name.

c1870   *15in (38cm) high*

$5,000-5,700   **HT**

A Bru Bébé bisque socket-head doll, with hand-blown glass eyes and human hair wig, on wood and composition jointed body, in original chemise, the head incised "Bru Jne 5," some play wear, with extra clothes and accessories.

Provenance: Originally owned by Ruth Colby (b.1893) of 74 Clinton Avenue, Montclair, New Jersey, USA. It is rare to find an all-original doll with clear provenance and documentation.

16in (40.5cm) high

$13,000-19,000   **MORP**

A 1890s French "Eden Bébé" bisque head doll, with glass eyes and later wig, on original French jointed wood and composition body, incised "Eden Bébé Paris."

20in (51cm) high

$1,500-1,900   **MORP**

A shy-faced Gauthier Bébé, with glass eyes and replacement wig, on original French wood and composition body, recostumed, the head incised "F.G.8," some paint touch-ups.

20in (51cm) high

$2,000-2,500   **MORP**

A 1870s "French fashion" bisque shoulder-head doll, probably by Gautlier, with glass eyes, swivel head, and human hair wig, on leather body, with period clothing, head incised "4."

15¼in (39cm) high

$1,150-1,500   **BER**

A French pressed bisque shoulder-head doll, probably Jumeau, with mohair wig, two fingers chipped, firing crack behind ear.

17¼in (44cm) high

$3,200-3,800   **SAS**

A Jumeau "Triste" bisque socket-head doll, with distinctive "longface" and mohair wig, on wood and composition body, head incised "14," body stamped "Jemeau Medaille D'Or Paris," some paint wear.

29½in (75cm) high

$9,500-10,500   **MORP**

A Kammer & Reinhardt 117 "Mein Liebling" bisque head character doll, with glass eyes, on an articulated German wood and composition body, recostumed, incised "A&*R 117 58."

The body, although German and of the same age as the doll, is not a style normally associated with a Kammer & Reinhardt doll.

23½in (59.5cm) high

$1,150-1,400 MORP

A Kammer & Reinhardt bisque head toddler doll, with glass flirty eyes and mohair wig, marked "K & R SIMON & HALBIG 126."

32in (81.5cm) high

$700-750 HT

A bisque socket-head "AT" doll, attributed to Kestner, with glass sleep eyes and mohair wig, on a wood and composition Sonneberg-type body, in silk dress and later bonnet, impressed "9."

This doll is believed to have been made by Kestner, and it is referred to by collectors as the "AT" Kestner, because it somewhat resembles the French doll marked "AT."

15in (38cm) high

$4,400-5,000 MORP

A Leopold Lambert automata, with Tete Jumeau bisque head, with original clothes and accessories, with gilt-metal lorgnette and composition legs, with key wind and stop/start lever, head marked "Depose Tete Jumeau," missing one fingertip.

c1890 *18in (45.5cm) high*

$3,200-3,800 C&T

An Armand Marseille Chinese bisque head boy doll, marked "AM 350."

17in (43cm) high

$500-650 HT

A Petit & DuMontier Bébé bisque socket-head doll, with paperweight eyes, on original French wood and composition jointed body with metal hands, incised "P 5 D."

26in (66cm) high

$3,800-5,000 MORP

A Schoenau & Hoffmeister bisque head doll, in original underclothes, later dress, marked "S PB H 1906 No.15."

36in (91.5cm) high

$750-900 HAN

An S.F.B.J. bisque head character boy doll, marked "S.F.B.J. 226 PARIS."

The Société Française de Fabrication de Bébés et Jouets, or S.F.B.J., was formed in the late 19thC and continued to make dolls until the early 1960s.

19in (48.5cm) high

$650-750 HT

A Simon & Halbig bisque head doll, with glass sleeping eyes, marked "SH 1079 DEP 7."

17½in (44.5cm) high

$750-900 HT

An 1890s Jules Steiner Bébé doll, on fullyjointed body, the head incised "A. 25," backstamped "Le Parisien FIre SGD.G 15," the body stamped "Le Parisien Bébé Steiner Paris," retouching to fingers.

23in (58.5cm) high

$1,900-2,500 MORP

A Bliss paper lithograph on wood church, with 23 scripture blocks, some damage to turrets.

21¼in (54cm) high

$750-900   POOK

A G. & J. Lines No.33 dollhouse, with widow's walk, opening to four rooms and two hallways, repainted and repapered.

c1909   *32½in (82.5cm) high*

$450-500   SAS

A wooden dollhouse, probably by G. & J. Lines, opening to six rooms, with fireplaces and a working elevator, refurbished, some replacements.

41in (104cm) high

$500-650   SAS

A mid-19thC Silber and Fleming-style painted and papered wood dollhouse, opening to four rooms.

25½in (65cm) high

$300-400   HT

A Tri-ang wooden dollhouse, with tinplate windows and cardboard shutters, the rooms with original papers and fireplaces, electrically lit.

42in (106.5cm) wide

$1,300-1,900   SAS

An 1870s Silber and Fleming box-back dollhouse, opening to four papered rooms with furniture, on later wood stand, some paint loss and cracks.

39¾in (101cm) high

$500-650   C&T

A Dutch wooden dollhouse.

43in (109cm) wide

$550-650   MORP

A Georgian-style dollhouse, opening to eight rooms, electrically lit, fully furnished, and with a family of dolls, signed and dated, with original "deeds" or bill of sale.

This is an impressive dollhouse, with a high level of detail: some of the artworks on the wall are miniature reproductions of famous works; there are tiny black-and-white photographs situated around the house; and even some birds can be found nesting beneath the fascia.

1979   *72in (183cm) high*

$1,050-1,200   EBA

ESSENTIAL REFERENCE—STEIFF BEARS

Steiff is one of the best-known and most collectible makers of teddy bears and other soft toys.

- Steiff was founded in 1880 by Margarete Steiff (1847-1909) in Giengen, south Germany.
- Her nephew Richard Steiff (1877-1939) joined the company in 1897. Together, they created the first soft toy bear with jointed arms and legs, the "Steiff Bär 55 PB." This was an immediate success, and in 1903 alone Steiff sold more than 12,000 bears.
- Early Steiff bears typically have long, curved arms, slim ankles, large oval feet, and a hump at the top of their backs. Those made after 1904 have a button in one ear. Pre-World War I bears tend to have shoe-button eyes; later bears have glass eyes.
- Although the market has softened in recent years, early 20thC Steiff bears in good condition can sell for high prices.

An early Steiff apricot mohair "rod" teddy bear, with shoe-button eyes, with mohair loss, leather nose possibly replaced.

20in (51cm) high

$11,000-12,000   **BER**

An early Steiff gold plush mohair teddy bear, with mohair wear and loss, restorations to pads, wrists and ankles reinforced.

23½in (60cm) high

$7,000-7,500   **BER**

An early Steiff apricot mohair teddy bear, with swivel head and jointed limbs, with inoperative squeaker, blank ear button, some thinning.

c1906   14in (35.5cm) high

$3,200-3,800   **SAS**

A Steiff straw-stuffed center-seam cinnamon mohair teddy bear, ear button, wear to mohair, repairs to pads.

Cinnamon-colored Steiff bears are popular with collectors but are rarely found in very good condition, because they age more rapidly due to the dye used.

c1909   24in (61cm) high

$2,500-3,200   **C&T**

A Steiff mohair teddy bear, with inoperative growler and FF button, some thinning.

c1909   16in (40.5cm) high

$3,200-3,800   **SAS**

A Steiff straw-stuffed center-seam mohair teddy bear, with swivel head, jointed at shoulders and hips, ear button, some wear.

c1909   16in (41cm) high

$2,000-2,500   **C&T**

A Steiff straw-filled plush teddy bear, with swivel joints, black button eyes, and felt pads.

c1910   12½in (32cm) high

$1,000-1,150   **HT**

A Steiff mohair teddy bear, with swivel head and jointed limbs, inoperative growler, small hole to right pad.

c1910   18¾in (47.5cm) high

$4,00-4,800   **SAS**

An early Steiff blonde teddy bear, with shoe-button eyes and original paw pads, blank ear button, probably originally white.

12½in (32cm) high

$1,050-1,200   **BER**

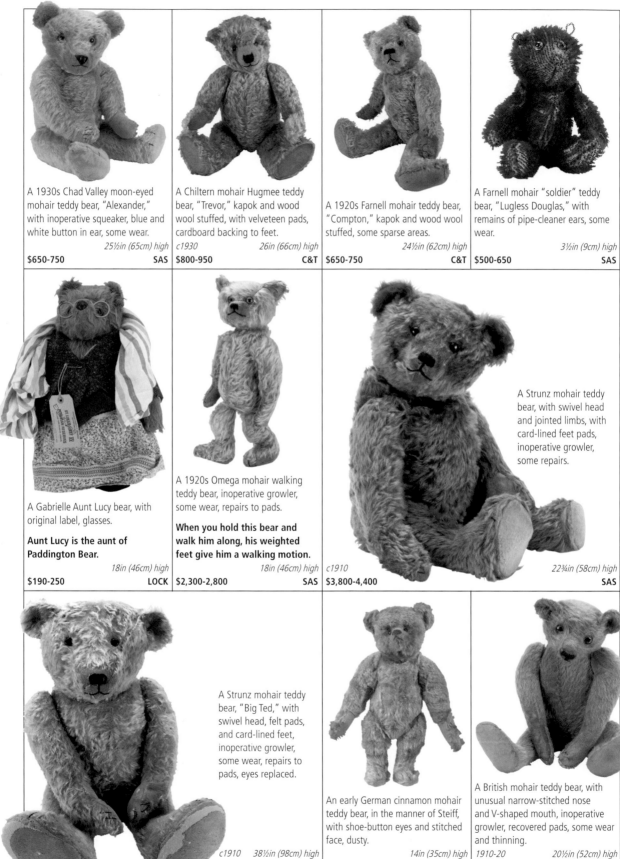

A 1930s Chad Valley moon-eyed mohair teddy bear, "Alexander," with inoperative squeaker, blue and white button in ear, some wear.

25½in (65cm) high

$650-750   **SAS**

A Chiltern mohair Hugmee teddy bear, "Trevor," kapok and wood wool stuffed, with velveteen pads, cardboard backing to feet.

c1930   *26in (66cm) high*

$800-950   **C&T**

A 1920s Farnell mohair teddy bear, "Compton," kapok and wood wool stuffed, some sparse areas.

24½in (62cm) high

$650-750   **C&T**

A Farnell mohair "soldier" teddy bear, "Lugless Douglas," with remains of pipe-cleaner ears, some wear.

3½in (9cm) high

$500-650   **SAS**

A Gabrielle Aunt Lucy bear, with original label, glasses.

Aunt Lucy is the aunt of Paddington Bear.

18in (46cm) high

$190-250   **LOCK**

A 1920s Omega mohair walking teddy bear, inoperative growler, some wear, repairs to pads.

When you hold this bear and walk him along, his weighted feet give him a walking motion.

18in (46cm) high

$2,300-2,800   **SAS**

A Strunz mohair teddy bear, with swivel head and jointed limbs, with card-lined feet pads, inoperative growler, some repairs.

c1910   *22¾in (58cm) high*

$3,800-4,400   **SAS**

A Strunz mohair teddy bear, "Big Ted," with swivel head, felt pads, and card-lined feet, inoperative growler, some wear, repairs to pads, eyes replaced.

c1910   *38½in (98cm) high*

$2,500-3,200   **SAS**

An early German cinnamon mohair teddy bear, in the manner of Steiff, with shoe-button eyes and stitched face, dusty.

14in (35cm) high

$1,300-1,900   **BER**

A British mohair teddy bear, with unusual narrow-stitched nose and V-shaped mouth, inoperative growler, recovered pads, some wear and thinning.

1910-20   *20½in (52cm) high*

$700-800   **SAS**

An early 20thC Bing Werke tinplate open-top limousine, printed "B W Made in Bavaria," some damages.

Bing was founded by brothers Ignatz and Adolf Bing in 1863. It made toy boats, cars, and trains.

12½in (32cm) long

$1,150-1,250 FLD

A German Carette lithographed tin limousine, with rubber tires and seated chauffeur.

c1910 12½in (32cm) long

$3,200-3,800 BER

A Gunthermann tinplate clockwork car, modeled after "Bluebird," in original box, with key.

Major Sir Malcolm Campbell MBE (1885-1948) was a British racing motorist and journalist, who gained the land speed record on land and water during the 1920s and 1930s using various vehicles called "Bluebird."

19¾in (50cm) long

$2,300-2,800 LC

A clockwork-driven Gunthermann 8-man racing scull, in lithographed tin, some touch-ups.

29in (73.5cm) long

$15,000-19,000 BER

A Märklin Jolanda painted tin clockwork riverboat, with original rigging, anchor-wheeled cradle and American flag, some small touch ups.

29in (73.5cm) long

$50,000-57,000 POOK

A Märklin hand-painted tinplate revolving castle fort, some restoration.

Märklin was founded in Göppingen, Germany, in 1856, by Theodor Friedrich Wilhelm Märklin. It produced boats, trains, horse-drawn vehicles, and more, and it soon became a world leader in toy production.

21in (53.5cm) wide

$5,000-5,700 BER

A Rock & Graner tin toy omnibus, painted with destinations, "Kew Gardens, Sloane St., Chelsea, Brompton," with a pair of carved and painted wooden horses, coachman, and driver, incomplete, in a cardboard box with mail label.

Rock & Graner (1813-1904), Göppingen, Germany, were the premier toy maker of their time. They made a variety of omnibuses for different world cities. This model was made in the 1860s and mailed in 1901 from a French lady in Manchester, England, to a Miss J.B. Wright in Biggleswade, in a box inscribed "Not to be opened." Despite some damage, it is a remarkable survivor.

15¼in (39cm) long

$38,000-44,000 SWO

A near mint Japanese "Tremendous Mike" lithographed tin clockwork robot, made by Aoshin Shoten, boxed.

9in (23cm) long

$14,000-18,000 BER

Judith Picks

This toy is very rare, because it was made as a gift for only the best customers. It was one of the most complicated toys made in the 19thC. It features a lithographed tin clown sitting at an easel, sketching. The crank-operated mechanism is controlled by a double cam that can be changed to draw different designs. The cams or disks that come with the toy paint four alternative scenes: one man profile to left, two men profile to right, one with a top hat, one with a parrot.

A mechanical toy, by Phillip Vielmetter Mechanische Werkstätten, Berlin.

1885 5in (13cm) wide

$7,000-7,500 BER

A near mint Corgi Toys "The Riviera" Gift Set, no.31.

The Corgi Toys range of die-cast models was launched by the Mettoy company in 1956.
$400-450   W&W

A yellow Corgi Toys No.406S LandRover 109WB, minor play wear, in original box.
$1,300-1,800   LSK

A near mint Corgi Toys No.490 Volkswagen "breakdown" truck, in original box.
$1,500-2,000   LSK

A Corgi Toys "JAMES BOND'S ASTON MARTIN DB5," no.261, with one bandit figure and "secret instructions" envelope.
$250-320   LSK

A near mint Corgi Toys Promotional Commer "HAMMONDS" van, with "HAMMONDS" paper label, in original box, numbered "462" in pen on end flaps.
$455-500   LSK

A mint Corgi Toys "The Green Hornet's Black Beauty," no.268, in original box.
$400-500   W&W

A near mint Dinky Toys prewar No.22B closed sports coupe, "Hornby series" cast to underside.
$1,050-1,200   LSK

A near mint Dinky Toys No. 504 Foden 14-ton tanker, in original box.
$1,050-1,200   LSK

A near mint Dinky Toys No.919 guy van, in original box.
$1,050-1,200   LSK

A French Dinky no.881 "Pinder" GMC circus truck, with animals in the trailer, in original box with packing piece.
$650-750   LSK

An Austin "Junior Forty Pathfinder" Grand Prix Racer pedal car.
c1950
$4,400-5,000   **CUTW**

A Gendron Buick pedal car, overpainted, windshield probably replaced.
56in (142cm) long
$15,000-19,000   **BER**

A clockwork-driven Hans Eberl Limousine.
c1910   *11in (28cm) long*
$2,800-3,500   **DEN**

An Ives "Flying Artillery" horse-drawn caisson.
22in (56cm) long
$7,500-8,000   **BER**

A cast iron William Shimer
& Son police wagon, Freemansburg,
Pennsylvania, restored.
c1900   *21in (53.5cm) long*
$2,300-2,800   **MORP**

A pristine Structo motor dispatch
truck.
9¼in (23.5cm) long
$3,800-4,400   **BER**

A 1920s American Nat'l Buick Juvenile Auto Line pedal car, some
accessories replaced.
42in (106.5cm) long
$7,000-7,500   **BER**

An Arcade cast iron
white moving van,
sporadic paint loss.
13in (33cm) long
$1,900-2,500   **POOK**

A near mint Hubley HFD fire engine pumper truck, with original nickel-
plated boiler, number plate "7292," with original decal at rear.
c1932   *21in (53.5cm) long*
$3,800-4,400   **BER**

A Citroen hand-painted clockwork "Au Louvre" delivery van, hand crank
to start the engine, windshield reattached to body, rear doors repainted.
15in (38cm) long
$50,000-57,000   **BER**

A Britains Set 60 1st Bombay Lancers Display, first issue, some paint chips, in "Sons of Our Empire" label box.

This piece is fresh to the market, having been recently found in an attic. Vectis specialist Simon Clark has said, "It is very rare to find a set of this age in 'untouched' condition still contained in its original box."

1896
$18,000-23,000   **VEC**

A Doll Company hand-painted electric lighthouse, the top section spinning, the base with "Doll Co." badge, some repainting.

13in (33cm) long
$7,000-7,500   **BER**

A Martin "Bobby" English clockwork policeman, left hand replaced.

c1901   *7in (18cm) high*
$9,000-10,000   **BER**

An early Britains toy, "The Walking Elephant," three wheels missing.

1885
$5,000-5,700   **C&T**

An Ives hand-painted walking Santa figure, with original clothing.

9½in (24cm) high
$3,800-4,400   **BER**

A Britains set no.1439, "The Roundabout," a merry-go-round driven by a spinning syroscopic wheel, in original box.

C&T Auction's expert James Opie described this roundabout as "the most perfect example I have ever had the pleasure to twirl."

1936
$9,000-10,000   **C&T**

A Marklin hand-painted Churchbury Train Station.

13in (33cm) long
$38,000-44,000   **BER**

CLOSER LOOK—MECHANICAL BANK

This rare cast iron mechanical bank is modeled as a barrel with a painted lead goat on top.

It was made by the firm of J. & E. Stevens & Co. and promotes the Germania Exchange Bank.

It is activated by placing a coin on the goat's tail and turning the faucet, allowing the figure to deposit the coin and seemingly present the depositor with a stein of beer.

It is in largely original unrestored condition and the barrel is painted in scarcer colors.

A Martin "Le Cake-Walk!!!!," paint enhancement to face.

The winners of this dance competition won a cake, hence the name of the dance.

c1903   *8in (20.5cm) long*
$9,500-10,500   **BER**

A Martin model, "Le Gymnaste," leaning back and forth when activated, working his way down the bars.

c1905   *14½in (37cm) long*
$18,000-23,000   **BER**

An 1880s J. & E. Stevens & Co. mechanical bank, tin trap replaced.
$50,000-57,000   **BER**

A 19thC boxed Jaques Staunton chess set, one king stamped "Jaques London," labeled "The Staunton Chess-Men, Two Prize Medals Awarded 1861, Jaques & Son, London," some losses and damages.

king 11½in (29cm) high

$3,200-3,800   **HAN**

A 20thC Venetian chess set, by Piero Benzoni, the onyx and marble top with a silvered-gilt border, the chess pieces of silver plate and gold plate.

$950-1,050   **CHOR**

A rosewood games compendium, with a Staunton pattern boxwood and ebonized chess set, checkers, dominoes, cribbage board, playing cards, a boxwood tumbler, and dice.

1869   *13in (33cm) wide*

$900-1,000   **BE**

A 19thC set of carved agate dominoes, probably Italian, in a leather case.

1¾in (4.5cm) wide

$300-400   **WW**

A Victorian walnut games compendium, with satin birch veneered interior, with ivory games boards and pieces for backgammon, chess, cribbage, checkers, dominoes, and whist, with dice, markers, counters, and playing cards.

14½in (37cm) wide

$3,200-3,800   **WW**

A 19thC board game, "Amusement in English History," by William Sallis, London, hand-colored lithographs mounted on folding linen sheet, in publisher's cloth on boards

Each lithograph depicts a monarch and an event during their reign up to the wedding of Queen Victoria. It is possible that this originally came with cards, although these are no longer present.

c1840   *25¼in (64cm) wide*

$300-400   **LSK**

A 19thC French Loysel's Patent Chivalric Game of Tournoy, with a roulette-type spinning wheel, scoring dial, two balls, 24 pottery playing pieces, and instruction booklet, in a walnut case.

$500-650   **LC**

A set of Charles Hodges "Astronomical" playing cards, by Stopforth & Sons, London, with 52 hand-colored engraved cards with duty card, rubbed at corners, lettering slightly faded, some foxing to cards, in a Morocco leather case with instruction book.

c1827

$6,500-7,500   **CHOR**

A part set of playing cards from the card game "Panko or Votes for Women: The Great Card Game Suffragists v Anti-Suffragists," by Peter Gurney of London, comprising 38 illustrated cards.

This game was sold by the Women's Social and Political Union at its stores, as well as by independent merchants, to raise funds for the cause. The cards show various scenes of Women's Suffrage, with one depicting Wallace Dunlop, one of the first hunger strikers, and another depicting Christabel Pankhurst holding a Votes for Women scroll.

c1910

$190-250   **FLD**

A Victorian-type safety rocking horse, by Ian Armstrong of Durham, of layered pine construction.

$450-500   WHP

An F.H. Ayres carved and painted wooden trestle rocking horse, with original leather saddle and tack, horsehair tail and mane, with gold "F.H. Ayres" transfer.

42¼in (107.5cm) wide

$650-750   SAS

A J. Collinson carved and painted wooden trestle rocking horse, remains of horsehair mane and tail, some paint lifting.

44¾in (113.5cm) long

$250-320   SAS

A Lines Bros. carved and painted wooden trestle rocking horse, cast "LL & Bros" into metalwork, some wear.

44in (112cm) long

$450-500   SAS

A carved and painted wooden trestle rocking horse, No.2, for Selfridges, with original leather saddle and tack, with horsehair tail and mane, stenciled "2 SELFRIDGE," some wear.

32in (81.5cm) long

$700-750   SAS

A Stevenson Bros. rocking horse, with Elizabeth II hallmarked silver plaque, two replaced sections to upper right legs, cracks to left legs, minor chips to body.

45¾in (116cm) high

$900-1,000   APAR

A rocking horse, by H. Wakefield Boston, with walnut and mahogany turned stand, incised monogram and "44" to underside.

41¾in (106cm) high

$1,900-2,500   PW

An Edwardian rocking horse.

This rocking horse was on long-term loan to the historic building preservation organization National Trust for Scotland, which displayed it in the children's nursery at Kellie Castle, Fife.

80in (203cm) long

$3,200-3,800   L&T

A late 19thC French Velocipede horse tricycle, with cast iron head, with hand-peddled chain mechanism causing the back wheels to turn, repainted.

32½in (82.5cm) long

$500-650   SAS

A Bassett-Lowke maroon LMS C/W "Precurser" 4-4-2 tank loco No.6810.
$400-500   **LSK**

A near mint early German Bing hand-painted stream-type 0-gauge engine and tender, with bell and stacks, marked "GBN" and "O/35."

This was made for the American market. The cow catcher at the front, for pushing objects on the tracks out of the way, resembles American trains rather than European.
engine 8½in (21.5cm) long
$15,000-19,000   **MORP**

A Hornby "Princess Elizabeth" loco and tender 20V AC, some chips, light corrosion.
1938
$1,500-2,000   **LSK**

A mint Lee Marsh Model Company 0-gauge finescale 2-rail electric tender locomotive, British Railways Princess Royal Class 4-6-2 "Princess Beatrice" RN 46209, boxed with instruction manual.
$3,800-4,400   **W&W**

A Märklin 1-gauge hand painted clockwork outline locomotive, for the American market, cow catcher reattached, bell and smoke stack restored.
10in (25.5cm) long
$2,800-3,500   **BER**

A Märklin 0-gauge Schlitz Beer Car, with script advertising, "Schlitz THE BEER THAT MADE MILWAUKEE FAMOUS," some discoloration.
6½in (16.5cm) long
$23,000-28,000   **BER**

A Märklin Gotthard 1-gauge hand-painted electric locomotive, with dual engines and cast iron trucks, one handrail missing, two steps bent.
16in (40.5cm) long
$2,300-2,800   **BER**

A Wrenn W2269X British Railways green Rebuilt Bulleid 4-6-2, no.34053, "SIR KEITH PARK," no.61044, packer no.3.

Only 270 of this model were made.
$500-650   **LSK**

A Voltamp #2115 Interurban trolley car, probably original first series, with factory-installed auto-reverse, with headlight bulb.
c1907-12
18in (45.5cm) long
$19,000-25,000   **BER**

A near mint limited edition Wrenn W2417 British Railways green Castle Class 4-6-0, no.5034, "CORFE CASTLE," no.143 of a limited edition of 250, no.330892, packer no.2.
$650-750   **LSK**

An exhibition-quality model of a 7¼in-gauge Great Western Railway Grange Class 4-6-0 locomotive and tender, no.6860 "Aberporth Grange," built by David Aitken, with copper boiler.

100in (254cm) long

$90,000-110,000   DN

An exhibition-quality 5in-gauge model of the British Railways Standard Class 9F 2-10-0 tender locomotive No.92024, built by B.G. Aldred, to the Attilio Franco and Piero Crosti boiler design.

The British Railways BR Standard Class 9F 2-10-0 is a class of steam locomotive designed for British Railways by Robert Riddles. The Class 9F was the last in a series of standardized locomotive classes designed for British Railways during the 1950s, and was intended for use on fast, heavy freight trains over long distances. It was one of the most powerful steam locomotive types ever constructed in Great Britain.

70¾in (180cm) long

$32,000-38,000   DN

A 10¼in-gauge model of the London Midland Scottish No.6100 "Royal Scot" tender locomotive, built with Bassett Lowke castings.

The locomotive with the Royal Scot Train was exhibited at the Century of Progress Exposition, Chicago, 1933, and made a tour of the United States and Canada.

148¾in (378cm) long

$32,000-38,000   DN

A rare 7¼in-gauge model of a London and Northwestern Railway 4-4-0 tender locomotive No.2663, "George the Fifth," with copper boiler no.87189 built by Swindon Boilers.

This model was built from Bassett Lowke castings c1912 and rebuilt by R. Fenwick in the 1980s to early 1990s.

84¼in (214cm) long

$25,000-32,000   DN

An exhibition-quality 5in-gauge model of a 4-4-0 Great Western Railway "Armstrong" No.7 tender locomotive, based on the original design by William Dean, with copper boiler.

William Dean (1840-1905), designer of the original full-size locomotive, was the second son of Henry Dean, manager of the Hawes soap factory in New Cross, London. William went on to become Chief Locomotive Engineer for the Great Western Railway from 1877 until his retirement in 1902.

81in (206cm) long

$11,000-14,000   DN

A live steam 7¼in gauge 2-6-4 Stainer class 4P boiler tank engine, with two outside cylinders, Walschaerts gear, 3 manometers marked "BRUCE ENGINEERING," the loco mounted on a wheeled "HANDY HEIGHT PRODUCTS" scissor jack.

$19,000-25,000   LSK

ESSENTIAL REFERENCE—CURLY LAWRENCE

The initials on the locomotive, LBSC, once stood for the London Brighton & South Coast railway, but in this case refer to the pen name of the designer, Curly Lawrence (1883-1967), who worked for the LSBC company. He was born William Mathieson and changed his name to Lillian Lawrence in 1902. He was known to school chums as "Dolly" and to friends as "Curly." He was a married man, an open cross-dresser, and a skilled live-steam model engineer. He created some controversy over his view that scale locomotives should be powered like the real thing, with coal-fired multi fire-tube boilers instead of spirit-fueled water-tube boilers.

A 3½in live steam locomotive and tender, "LBSC Betty," 2-6-2, constructed by T. Head, built to a design by Curly Lawrence.

47¼in (120cm) long

$28,000-33,000   CHT

An exhibition-quality 5in-gauge model of a Great Central Railway Robinson Class 11F "Director" 4-4-0 tender locomotive No.505, "Ypres," built by Steam Age, paintwork by Louis Raper of Failsworth.

1973   *62½in (159cm) long*

$13,000-18,000   DN

A 5in-gauge model of a LMS 2-6-0 Hughes Crab locomotive and tender, no.2874, built by Thomas Tegg of Reading.

Thomas Tedd won silver at the Model Engineer Exhibition in 2008. The LMS Hughes Crab or Horwich Mogul was a mixed class 2-6-0 designed by George Hughes and was built 1926-32. No.2874 was built at Crewe.

1994   *48in (122cm) long*

$20,000-25,000   SHEF

An exhibition-quality built 5in-gauge model of a Great Western Railway 4-4-0 "Bulldog" tender locomotive, no.3433, built by Bob Wilkinson, with copper boiler.

60¼in (153cm) long

$15,000-20,000   DN

A 19thC model steamboat, with boiler and steam plant, with brass fittings.

41¾in (106cm) long

$9,500-10,500

WW

A builder's model of the cargo vessel S.S. "Knottingley."

The steel screw cargo steamer "Knottingley" was built by John Crown & Sons Ltd. at Sunderland, England, and completed in June 1907. She sailed for the Wetherall Steamship Company, the Cambo Shipping Co., Davidson's of Aberdeen, the Antwerp Shipping & Bunkering Co., and the Brabo Steamship Co., before being torpedoed and sunk by a German E-boat on July 26, 1940.

1907 *70in (178cm) long*

$3,200-3,800

CM

A live steam-powered model launch, fitted with mahogany-lagged boiler to single cylinder engine, with flywheel.

c1910 *51in (129.5cm) long*

$1,400-1,900

CM

A builder's model of the S.S. "Clan Malcolm," built by Craig, Taylor & Co., Stockton, for Clan line.

The "Clan Malcolm" was completed in April 1917 and survived World War I. She was wrecked on passage from London to the Clyde on September 25, 1935.

1917 *88in (223.5cm) long*

$15,000-19,000

CM

A Marklin "Battleship Sankt Georg" model, with replacement lifeboats and canes, some touching up, areas of masts reattached.

There is only one other known example of this model in existence.

1919-21 *28in (71cm) long*

$190,000-250,000

BER

A builder's model for the "Suez Canal Radial Cutter Suction Dredger Kadruka," built by William Simons & Co. Ltd., Renfrew, for the Egyptian government.

1930 *65in (165cm) long*

$5,000-6,300

CM

A builder's model for the twin-screw motor yacht and "little ship" "Wilna" R.T.Y.C., latter H.M.S. "Aisha," built by Cochrane & Sons Ltd., Selby, modeled by C. Crawford & Sons, Sunderland.

"Wilna" R.T.Y.C. was designed by Norman Hart and purchased by W.H. Collins in 1934 for £14,400 (about $920,000 today). By 1939, he had ordered a larger replacement and "Wilna" was sold to the Royal Navy, renamed H.M.S. "Aisha," and deployed on harbor patrol and later in the rescue missions to Dunkirk.

1934 *32in (81.5cm) long*

$5,000-6,300

CM

A model of the Lowestoft steam drifter "Diana" LT 593, built by Gordon Drew of Highnam Gloucestershire, fitted with gas-fired Cheddar Proteus live steam plant, the hull constructed from copper stakes with brass ribs and riveted copper plate.

58¼in (148cm) long

$4,400-5,000

DN

An exhibition-quality ramin, pine, and mahogany model of a steam launch, "Henry," built by Peter Arnott, with vertical live steam boiler designed by K.N. Harris, with Stuart Turner D10 steam engine.

54¼in (138cm) long

$6,500-7,500

DN

A Cliff Bastin red Arsenal 1930 FA Cup Final jersey, by Bukta, dated.

In 1930, Arsenal won the first major honor in their history with victory in the FA Cup Final, beating Huddersfield Town 2-0. Arsenal now have the most FA Cup wins of any team with a total of 13 victories.
$28,000-33,000 GBA

A Joe Mercer old gold Arsenal No.6 1950 FA Cup Final shirt, by Hope Brothers/Solus Sports, the badge dated.

Arsenal and Liverpool both generally wore red, so they had to change shirt color for the 1950 FA Cup Final. Both teams' change shirt colors were white, so a decision was made by a coin toss. Liverpool played in white, and Arsenal in old gold. Arsenal continued to use the old gold as an alternative change kit throughout the 1950s.
1949-50
$15,000-20,000 GBA

CLOSER LOOK—1909 FA CUP FINAL SHIRT

This shirt was worn during the 1909 FA Cup Final by Bob Hardy, Bristol City's inside right.

The shirt, made by Harris's Sports Depot, Bristol, has a cloth badge with silkwork City Arms of Bristol.

The match was Bristol City vs. Manchester United, at Crystal Palace. Manchester United, appearing in their first FA Cup Final, won the match 1-0. It was the only occasion that Bristol City has played in a FA Cup Final.

Both teams normally wore red shirts so, prior to the final, the FA issued orders for uniform changes. United wore white shirts and City wore

A Bristol City 1909 FA Cup Final shirt.
$19,000-25,000 GBA

A Bobby Moore England 1966 World Cup tracksuit, by Umbro, the reverse lettered "ENGLAND," some mud marks, sold with certificate of authenticity.
1966
$11,000-12,000 GBA

A Terry Paine red England No.19 1966 World Cup Final jersey, by Umbro, with three lions badge.

Terry Paine would have worn this jersey in the 1966 World Cup Final had he been selected to play by manager Alf Ramsey. If he had been selected to play and had worn this shirt, it would be worth even more, roughly $50,000-75,000.
$18,000-23,000 GBA

A FIFA Centenary 1904-2004 jersey, signed by the top 125 players in the world as of 2004, limited edition no.8/10, sold with certificate of authentication.
$5,500-7,000 GBA

A Johnny Holt England international cap, awarded for four successive appearances vs. Scotland 1891-94, the purple cap inscribed "1891-2-3-4."

Johnny Holt was born April 10, 1865 in Church, Lancashire. He joined Everton as a center half in the very first season of the Football League in 1888.
$3,800-4,400 GBA

A Thomas Low Scotland vs. England Junior international cap, inscribed 'S v E, 1896.'

This match was played at Perry Bar, Birmingham. Scotland won 4-1, although some reports have it at 4-0. The scorers were J. McGill and Low.
1896
$300-400 GBA

A Joe Mercer international cap, with "F.A." crest, inscribed "ENGLAND v SCOTLAND," dated.

This was Mercer's second appearance for England, who beat Scotland 2-1 at Hampden Park.
1938-39
$2,800-3,300 GBA

A Roberto Carlos signed pair of Nike Zoom soccer boots, inscribed "R. CARLOS," in display case.
15¾in (40cm) long
$450-550 GBA

A Billy Dunlop Football League Division One Championship 15ct gold and enamel medal, inscribed "LIVERPOOL FOOTBALL CLUB," the reverse inscribed "LEAGUE CHAMPIONSHIP, SEASON 1900-1901, W. DUNLOP, BACK."

This was the first occasion that Liverpool FC won the Football League Division One Championship title. The Scottish left-back Billy Dunlop played for Liverpool FC 1894-1909.

1901

$12,000-14,000   GBA

A Blackburn Rovers 9ct gold and enamel soccer medal, inscribed "BLACKBURN ROVERS FOOTBALL CLUB," hallmarked.

1905

$700-800   GBA

A Billy Wooldridge 15ct gold FA Cup winner's medal, inscribed "THE FOOTBALL ASSOCIATION, WOLVERHAMPTON WANDERERS F.C., ENGLISH CUP, WINNERS, 1907-8, W.T. WOOLDRIDGE, CAPTAIN," cased.

The 1908 FA Cup Final was played at the Crystal Palace. Wolverhampton Wanderers defeated Newcastle United 3-1. The Cup was lifted by the Wolverhampton Wanderers's captain Billy Wooldridge.

1908

$12,000-14,000   GBA

A Patsy Gallacher Scottish Football League Championship 9ct gold and enamel winner's medal, inscribed "SCOTTISH FOOTBALL LEAGUE, CHAMPIONSHIP, 1918-19, WON BY, CELTIC F.C., PAT, GALLACHER."

Patrick "Patsy" Gallacher (1891-1953) was an Irish soccer player who played at inside right for Celtic. In this season, Celtic won the Scottish Football League from their great rivals Rangers by just one point.

1919

$2,500-3,200   GBA

A Cliff Bastin Football League Division One Championship 9ct gold winner's medal, inscribed "THE FOOTBALL LEAGUE, CHAMPIONS, DIVISION 1, ARSENAL F.C., C. BASTIN," dated, in fitted case.

Cliff Bastin was a winger for Arsenal, who won the 1932-33 Football League Division One Title with a total of 58 points, four clear of Aston Villa.

1932-33

$11,000-14,000   GBA

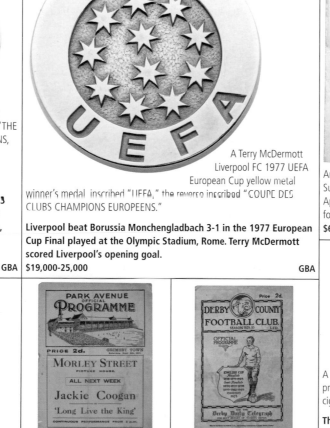

A Terry McDermott Liverpool FC 1977 UEFA European Cup yellow metal winner's medal, inscribed "UEFA," the reverse inscribed "COUPE DES CLUBS CHAMPIONS EUROPEENS."

Liverpool beat Borussia Monchengladbach 3-1 in the 1977 European Cup Final played at the Olympic Stadium, Rome. Terry McDermott scored Liverpool's opening goal.

$19,000-25,000   GBA

An FA Cup Final Aston Villa vs. Sunderland program, Crystal Palace April 19, 1913, heavy horizontal fold, splitting at the spine.

$6,500-7,500   GBA

A 1954 World Cup Korea vs. Turkey program, with cigarette sticker and cigarette flyer.

This is the rarest program issued at the 1954 World Cup, for the Korea vs. Turkey match, played in front of only 4,000 people in Lausanne on June 20, 1954.

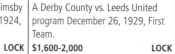

A Manchester United vs. West Bromwich Albion program, Div 1, January 15, 1921.

$1,400-1,800   LOCK

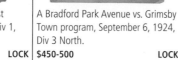

A Bradford Park Avenue vs. Grimsby Town program, September 6, 1924, Div 3 North.

$450-500   LOCK

A Derby County vs. Leeds United program December 26, 1929, First Team.

$1,600-2,000   LOCK

$1,400-1,900   GBA

An early 20thC Hardy Brothers Ltd. "Perfect" trout reel, damage to foot.

3¼in (8.5cm) diam

$300-400   CHEF

A Hardy Brothers Ltd. "Perfect Mk II" drum fly reel, in original box.

3¾in (9.5cm) diam

$650-750   CHEF

A Hardy Brothers Ltd. "Perfect" reel.

c1960   *3¾in (9.5cm) diam*

$450-500   CHEF

An early 20thC Hardy Brothers Ltd. brass-faced "Perfect" fly reel 4," with Turk's head locking screw and rod-in-hand trademark.

$1,500-1,900   CHEF

A Hardy Brothers Ltd. "Perfect" fishing reel, with brass foot, rim tension adjuster, and Bakelite winder, marked, in original box.

2¾in (7cm) diam

$500-650   LC

A Hardy Brothers Ltd. "Perfect" fishing reel, with brass foot and rim tension adjuster, signs of use, with leather pouch, marked.

3¼in (8cm) diam

$300-400   LC

A carved wood and painted half-block model pike, by Charles Farlow & Co., mounted on a mahogany plaque, the verso with a handwritten label, "Caught by J.M. Morgan, in the Oare? near the Maddocks?, Aldworth spinning with a afriat on crocodile tackle weight 19lbs, 1907, Yorkshire September," with Farlow stencil stamp.

49½in (125.5cm) wide

$9,000-10,000   WW

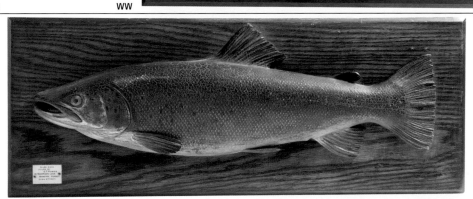

A George V carved and painted wood half-block trout, by Rowland Ward, mounted on oak, with ivory plaque inscribed "6 LBS 6 OZS, KILLED BY G.T. HAWKES IN SHERMAN'S LOCK AVINGTON, KENNET JUNE 6TH 1917," the verso with trade labels, numbered "1503."

28in (71cm) long

$10,000-11,000   WW

A George V carved wood and painted half-block model trout, by Hardy Brothers Ltd., on an oak board, inscribed "MOTE POOL, BLACKWATER, Co. MEATH. WEIGHT 6½ lbs, LENGTH 22½INS, GIRTH 15½."

29in (73.5cm) wide

$4,400-5,700   WW

A Paris Olympic Games winner's medal plaque, designed by F. Vernon, inscribed "CONCOURS DE TIR AUX PIGEONS," reverse inscribed "REPUBLIQUE FRANCAISE, PARIS 1900, EXPOSITION UNIVERSELLE."

1900

$1,200-1,400 GBA

A London 1908 Olympic Games silver prize medal, won by the Canadian athlete Garfield MacDonald for the Hop Step and Jump (Triple Jump).

$4,400-5,700 GBA

A rare St. Moritz Winter Olympic Games gold prize winner's medal, designed by Arnold Hunerwadel, the reverse inscribed "II JEUX OLYMPIQUES D'HIVER, ST MORITZ, 1928," in original box.

The original recipient of this medal is unknown.

1928 *2in (5cm) diam*

$38,000-38,000 GBA

A Squaw Valley Winter Olympic Games bronze participant's medal.

1960 *2in (5cm) diam*

$650-750 GBA

A rare London 1908 Olympic Games Comite D'Honneur bronze and blue enamel badge, the reverse numbered "30."

$11,000-13,000 GBA

An Antwerp Olympic Games gold prize winner's medal, designed by Josue Dupon, minted by Cossemans of Brussels.

The gold plating on the Antwerp 1920 medals was very thin. The IOC later dictated that all gold winner's medals should have at least 6 grams of gold plating to prevent the type of rubbing that occurred with the 1920 medal. The original recipient of this winner's medal is unknown.

1920

$15,000-19,000 GBA

An aluminum alloy London Olympic Games bearer's torch, designed by Ralph Lavers, inscribed "XIVth OLYMPIAD, 1948, OLYMPIA TO LONDON, WITH THANKS TO THE BEARER."

1948

$5,000-6,300 GBA

CLOSER LOOK—WINTER OLYMPICS GOLD MEDAL

The "gold" medal is made of silver-gilt and was designed by Scott Given/Axiom Design.

The obverse has an organic shape, resembling Utah River rock, with an athlete holding a torch, breaking, over the Olympic Rings, inscribed "OLYMPIC WINTER GAMES, LIGHT THE FIRE WITHIN."

The reverse depicts the Greek Goddess Nike and an image of hockey, with the inscription "SALT LAKE 2002, MEN'S ICE HOCKEY."

The base of the ribbon loop has the Roman numeral XIX, signifying the 19th Winter Olympic Games.

A Salt Lake City Winter Olympic Games gold prize medal, awarded to a member of the Canadian men's ice hockey team, in original case.

The Canadian men's ice hockey team beat the US team 5-2 in the final.

2002 *3¼in (8.5cm) diam 18¼oz*

$100,000-110,000 GBA

A bronzed aluminum Rome 1960 Olympic Games bearer's torch, designed by Professor Maiure.

The design of this torch was based on drawings of torches on ancient Etruscan ceramics.

15½in (39.5cm) high

$3,800-5,000 GBA

A blackened aluminum alloy and stainless steel Tokyo Olympic Games bearer's torch, inscribed "XVIII OLYMPIAD TOKYO 1964."

25½in (65cm) high

$5,000-6,300 GBA

A Babe Ruth signed William Harridge American League baseball, with letters of authenticity from PSA/DNA, JSA and SGC.

This baseball was signed on September 12, 1947, at the Hotel Statler in Boston, where the Babe was a guest speaker. It was gifted to a guest at the American Legion Junior Baseball Scholarship banquet.

1947

$38,000-44,000   **MORP**

A Louisville Slugger baseball bat, made for President Gerald R. Ford, signed by the President and by 40 members of the Baseball Hall of Fame.

1974-77

$3,200-3,800   **POOK**

A pair of 1950s Cassius Clay leather amateur training gloves, manufactured by Post, initialed "C.C." inside, stamped "Columbia Gym" inside.

These were discovered in the attic of Cassius Clay's trainer Joe Martin. They were used during the time that Joe Martin was his trainer at the Columbia Gym.

$4,400-5,000   **MORP**

A 1958 Cassius Clay Louisville Golden Gloves Championship Medal.

1¾in (4.5cm) high

$2,500-3,800   **MORP**

A pair of Muhammad Ali Winning S.S. FP-800 boxing gloves, the right-hand glove signed on the inside wrist by Muhammad Ali, the outside signed by Joe Bugner and inscribed "K.L., 1.7.75," the left-hand glove signed on the outside by Muhammad Ali, with a signed letter of provenance, dated.

These gloves were worn by Ali in the World Heavyweight Championship bout vs. Joe Bugner in Kuala Lumpur, June 30, 1975.

1975   *10oz*

$70,000-80,000   **GBA**

A World Championship cricket bat, by Gray Nicholls, signed with team signatures of Australia, England, West Indies, New Zealand, India, Pakistan, and Sri Lanka.

1985

$800-950   **MM**

A unique hand-built Graeme Obree bike frame, used by Obree during various time trials, built by Obree using Reynolds 653, silver soldered using cut down lugs and joining pieces for lightness.

Graeme Obree rode this at Donington Park motor racing circuit in 2009 at the BikerRader.

2006   *45⅞oz*

$5,500-6,500   **GWA**

A yellow-metal and enamel Hour Record medal, the obverse inscribed "Record Du Monde De L'Heure, Graeme Obree," the reverse inscribed "Bordeaux (Fra) 27 April 1994, 52km 713," in fitted case.

These are rare as sporting medals go. Only holders of the One Hour Record receive them.

$1,400-1,900   **GWA**

An unnamed featherie golf ball, some stitches partly undone.

$1,150-1,500   **MM**

A guttie golf ball hammer, with circular face and wide chisel, with leather sheepskin grip.

c1860   *9in (23cm) high*

$450-500   **MM**

An Osmond's patent automaton golf club caddie, with maker's brass plaque, original leather handles, some damages, leather belt strap needs replacing.

c1893   *12½in (32cm) long*

$450-500   **MM**

A rare 17thC to 18thC left-handed spur-toed golf club, the hand-forged iron head with dished face set on an ash shaft, some pitting and light rust.

Purchased in the 1950s for 10 shillings and purportedly previously purchased from a cellar clearance in Leven, Fife, Scotland.

42½in (108cm) long

$40,000-48,000　　GORL

An early R. Forgan St Andrews golden thornwood play club, with Forgan block crown stamp mark and Prince of Wales Feathers on the head.

c1860　　head 5½in (14cm) long

$2,500-3,200　　MM

An R. Davidson Montrose stained beech wood putter, with most of the original hide grip.

Robert Davidson Montrose was a notable early club maker from 1825-70.

c1860　　head 5½in (14cm) long

$1,400-1,800　　MM

A rare R.B. (Buff) Wilson St Andrews A1 No Hosel Patent putting cleek.

c1900

$1,400-1,800　　MM

A rare Browns patent perforated rake iron wry neck putter, lacking grip.

c1904

$1,150-1,500　　MM

A Mika Hakkinen signed and worn late 1999 West McLaren-Mercedes Formula 1 racesuit, with Hakkinen's "Flying Finn" signature, "Hakkinen M, 07/10/99, Ref 037."

In October 1999, Mika Hakkinen became only the seventh driver ever to win back-to-back F1 World Championships.

$7,500-9,000　　GBA

A Ludo Stuart 1920s match-worn Scotland international rugby shirt.

Ludovic "Ludo" Mair Stuart (1902-57) made his Scotland international debut vs. France at Inverleith on January 20, 1923. His final appearance was at Twickenham vs. England March 15, 1930.

$950-1,050　　GBA

ESSENTIAL REFERENCE—REAL TENNIS

Real tennis, or courte paume, is the original indoor racket sport from which the modern game of lawn tennis is descended. Rackets and balls were typically made by the maître-paumiers, often professional players or proprietors of the 200-plus courts in and around Paris. As the best available, these were sold to English players. Tison, a well-known maître-palmier, was born in the 1740s and was still active, although elderly, in the 1820s.

A set of four lopsided real tennis rackets, by Tison, with ash frames and trebled gut stringing.

26½in (67cm) long

$21,000-28,000　　SWO

A Kyran Bracken team-signed England No.20 shirt, from the Rugby World Cup match vs. Georgia, Perth October 12, 2003, inscribed "KYRAN BRACKEN."

2003

$1,400-1,800　　GBA

A Roger Federer signed tennis racket.

$400-500　　GBA

A Bamana wood mask, West Africa, with six horn crest, mounted.

30¼in (77cm) high

$1,400-1,800　　　**L&T**

A Royal Bamileke or Bamum carved wood head, Cameroon, with glass beads and cowry shells attached with mud cement, with buffalo horns and snarling leopard to crown.

Despite its size and weight, this head would have probably been worn during important ceremonies. The face probably represents the Fon or tribal chief. The buffalo horns represent power.

37½in (95cm) high

$1,050-1,200　　　**MART**

A Bushongo painted carved wood mask, Central Congo, with beads and shells, with fabric crown.

Collected c1898-1920 by Major Ian Kelsey. This mask would have been worn at secret military society rites.

7½in (19cm) high

$1,050-1,200　　　**WHYT**

An Ejagham hide-covered Janus helmet mask, Nigeria, with two faces, the lighter with symbols, including unity and hatred.

The Ejagham, or Ekoi, people, come from southeast Nigeria and southwest Cameroon. They are best known for their impressive headdresses and masks.

17¾in (45cm) high

$7,000-8,000　　　**WW**

A Dan carved wood mask, Liberia/Ivory Coast, with hinged jaw.

9½in (24cm) high

$2,900-3,500　　　**SK**

A Dogon carved wood walu antelope mask, Mali, encrustations throughout.

16½in (42cm) high

$3,200-3,800　　　**L&T**

A Kuba carved wood lion mask, Congo, with grass mane.

Collected c1898-1920 by Major Ian Kelsey.

13in (33cm) high

$800-950　　　**WHYT**

A Suku carved wood helmet mask, Democratic Republic of the Congo, with animal crest and geometric designs.

16½in (42cm) high

$2,500-3,200　　　**SK**

A Songye carved wood shield, Democratic Republic of the Congo, with relief-carved Kifwebe masks.

25in (63.5cm) high

$5,000-6,300　　　**SK**

A pair of male and female Yoruba Ibeji figures, Nigeria.

10¾in (27.5cm) high

$3,800-5,000 WW

A Benin bronze leopard, Nigeria, with dot and ring decoration, the head with barred teeth and raised whiskers.

19in (48cm) high

$23,000-28,000 WW

A Duala carved wood stool, Cameroon, with a pierced frieze supported by figures.

21¾in (55.5cm) wide

$700-800 WW

A Jimma carved wood chair, Ethiopia.

38¾in (98.5cm) high

$900-1,000 L&T

A mid-to-late 19thC North Nguni carved wood headrest, Southern Africa, in animal form.

This headrest is part of a wider group of items carved by Zulu speakers in the vicinity of Port Natal. The craftsmen created items both for elite African and Western colonial clients. The majority of other pieces produced were vessels, making this headrest even more unique and valuable

10¾in (27cm) long

$80,000-90,000 L&T

ESSENTIAL REFERENCE—FANTE ASAFO FLAGS

From the 17thC, the Fante groups that inhabited the southwest coast of modern-day Ghana formed military and political units known as "asafo."

- **The name derives from "sa", meaning "war," and "fo," meaning "people."**
- **Each unit developed elaborate traditions of visual art. Among the most striking are flags such as these.**
- **These flags comprised of bold naive imagery appliquéd onto a cotton background, and they commonly depict indigenous proverbs that relate closely to the commissioning Asafo group.**
- **With the British conquest of the region in 1856, many Asafo groups incorporated versions of the Union Jack into the flag to enhance the power of the imagery.**

A Songye carved wood headrest, Democratic Republic of the Congo, with beadwork and a face mask.

5½in (14cm) high

$2,100-2,800 L&T

A Senufo carved wood staff, West Africa, with head-to-head female figures and an avian form at the top.

An early 20thC Fante Asafo cotton appliqué flag, "If we can tame the leopard, what chance have you mere animals?," Ghana, framed by John Jones.

In this flag, an Asafo company is boasting of its military prowess and taunting a rival group. Some Asafo companies had a woman's auxiliary headed by female officers.

An early 20thC Fante Asafo cotton appliqué flag, "We can defend our sacred trees from all predators," Ghana, framed by John Jones.

Certain trees were considered sacred by the Fante and were protected as shrines.

A late 19thC Zulu rhinoceros horn knobkerrie, South Africa.

22½in (57cm) long

56in (142cm) high

$18,000-23,000 SK

$5,000-5,700 WW

70¾in (179.5cm) wide

$1,900-2,500 L&T

67½in (171.5cm) wide

$5,000-6,300 L&T

An Ipiutak walrus ivory carving of a bear, Point Hope, Northwest Alaska.
c600-800   *3½in (9cm) long*
$1,600-2,000   **SK**

An Eskimo Punuk period shaman's torso figure, St. Lawrence Island, Alaska.
800-1400   *2¼in (5.5cm) high*
$1,000-1,150   **SK**

A mid-to-late 19thC Athabascan double-volute copper dagger, Alaska, remnant cloth and leather wrapping on handle.
11½in (29cm) long
$1,900-2,500   **SK**

A mid-19thC Tsimshian carved wood shaman's rattle, with incised and painted thunderbirds, with two native repairs.

The Tsimshian are an indigenous people of the Pacific Northwest Coast. Their communities are mostly in coastal British Columbia and far southern Alaska.
12in (30.5cm) long
$20,000-32,000   **SK**

A late 19thC Eskimo sheep horn spoon, with domestic and hunting scenes.
11in (28cm) long
$2,800-3,500   **SK**

A 19thC Eskimo Arctic walrus ivory bow drill, with incised decoration.
19in (48.5cm) long
$5,000-6,300   **WW**

A 1890s Eskimo carved musk ox jawbone cribbage board, engraved with scenes of hunting and fishing.
13¾in (35cm) long
$1,150-1,400   **SK**

ESSENTIAL REFERENCE—ESKIMO AND INUIT

The term "Inuit," meaning "the people," refers to the indigenous groups residing in the Arctic regions of Alaska, Canada, and Greenland. It replaced the term "Eskimo" from the mid-20thC; tribal art and antiques from pre-c1950 are usually referred to as Eskimo, and those from post-c1950 are referred to as Inuit. The term "Eskimo" was dropped from usage because it is considered offensive. However, the word "Inuit" is not a precise synonym, nor a fully accepted term. Many groups prefer to use their own tribal names, and several groups once called Eskimo, such as the Yupik people of Canada, are not Inuit and have no such word in their language.

An Eskimo mask, Point Hope, Alaska, with bone inlay eyes.

Collected in the 1920s in the Point Hope area.
c1900   *9½in (24cm) high*
$3,500-4,000   **SK**

An early 20thC Eskimo baleen lidded basket, carved walrus tusk handle.
2¾in (7cm) high
$750-900   **SK**

An Alaskan Inuit whalebone snow goggle, with carved eye slits and rounded nose bridge, mounted.
5½in (14cm) wide
$1,300-1,800   **L&T**

A stone and wood animal spirit umiak, by Abraham Apakark Anghik, Salt Spring Island, carried on the back of Sedna, the goddess of the sea.

An umiak is a type of boat used by the Yupik and Inuit peoples, chiefly for transport as opposed to hunting or fishing.

24in (61cm) wide

$20,000-25,000 **WAD**

CLOSER LOOK—SHAMAN WITH OPPOSING FACES

This was made by Karoo Ashevak, a talented Inuit artist who became highly popular c1972. He is considered one of the very best Inuit sculptors.

Ashevak died in a house fire in 1974 at the age of 34, leaving behind him only about 250 works.

The rarity of his work, his originality, and his skill together increase the value of his work.

Shamans are thought to bridge the earthly and spiritual world, and the two sides of this sculpture represent this duality. With its intricate details and whimsical, distorted figure, this is a good example of Ashevak's characteristic style.

A bone, stone, and ivory carving, "Shaman with Opposing Faces," by Karoo Ashevak (1940-74), E4-196, Spence Bay/Taloyoak.

c1973

15in (38cm) high

70,000-80,000 **WAD**

A stone carving, "Winged Shaman," by Barnabus Arnasungaaq (1924-2017), E2-213, Baker Lake/Qamani'tuaq.

Arnasungaaq was an important influence on the community of carvers in Baker Lake and one of the eldest from the original group in this region.

9½in (24cm) high

$2,500-3,800 **WAD**

A stone carving, "Bird of Spring," by Abraham Etungat, R.C.A. (1911-99), E7-809, Cape Dorset/Kinngait, signed in syllabics.

Etungat's original small soapstone carving of "Bird of Spring" was reproduced in a 7ft (2.1m) tall bronze for the Devonian Foundation. The bronze is now displayed in public areas in cities across Canada, including Halifax, Calgary, Vancouver, and Toronto.

20in (51cm) high

$9,000-10,000 **WAD**

A stone falcon, by Kenojuak Ashevak, C.C., R.C.A. (1927-2013).

14½in (37cm) high

$2,800-3,500 **WAD**

A stone carving, "Composition," by Abraham Etungat, R.C.A. (1911-99), E7-809, Cape Dorset/Kinngait, signed in syllabics.

Etungat is most famous for his grand birds with raised wings. He started out working small scale, gradually building up to the larger works and incorporating humans and other animals.

23in (58.5cm) high

$4,400-5,000 **WAD**

A 1970s stone carving, "Man with His Dog" by Osuitok Ipeelee, R.C.A. (1923-2005), E7-1154, Cape Dorset/Kinngait, signed in syllabics.

22½in (57cm) high

$3,800-5,000 **WAD**

A stone carving, "Standing Figure," by John Kavik (1897-1993), E2-290, Rankin Inlet/Kangiqliniq, signed in syllabics.

19in (48.5cm) high

$11,000-12,000 **WAD**

A stone carving, "Bashful Walrus," by Kananginak Pootoogook, R.C.A. (1935-2010), E7-1168, Cape Dorset/Kinngait, signed in syllabics.

13in (33cm) high

$5,000-6,300   **WAD**

A stone carving, "Strutting Polar Bear," by Pauta Saila, R.C.A. (1916-2009), E7-990, Cape Dorset/Kinngait, signed in Roman and syllabics.

Pauta Saila was one of the first Inuk artists to develop a distinctive, personally unique style. Although he worked on a wide variety of subjects, his dancing bears are particularly significant, because polar bears are important shamanistic creatures, embodied spirit helpers of Inuit culture.

c1970   *10in (25.5cm) high*

$11,000-12,000   **WAD**

A stone carving, "Mother Nursing Her Child," by Isa Aqiattusuk Smiler (1921-86), E9-706, Port Harrison/Inukjuak, signed in syllabics with disk number inscribed.

c1968   *8in (20.5cm) high*

$3,800-5,000   **WAD**

A stone carving, "Dogs Defending Their Pack," by Qavaroak Tunnillie (1928-93).

23in (58.5cm) high

$2,500-3,200   **WAD**

A late 1980s stone, antler, and musk ox horn carving, "Shaman With Spirits," by Judas Ullulaq (1937-99), signed in syllabics, Gjoa Haven/Uqsuqtuuq.

Like his brothers, Charlie Ugyuk and Nelson Takkiruq, Judas Ullulaq's work offers a level of creativity and individuality. He worked expertly in stone and bone, and strongly influenced the next generation of artists in the region.

12in (30.5cm) high

$11,000-12,000   **WAD**

A sealskin stencil, "Birds Over the Sun," by Kenojuak Ashevak, C.C., R.C.A. (1927-2013).

20in (51cm) wide

$2,500-3,200   **WAD**

A thread and embroidery floss stroud, by Essie Oonark, O.C., R.C.A. (1906-85), E2-384, Baker Lake/Qamani'tuaq, signed in syllabics.

Provenance: The York Downs Golf and Country Club Collection of Art, Unionville, Ontario. This work was displayed in the dining room from opening day in 1971 until c1990.

c1970   *60in (152.5cm) high*

$20,000-32,000   **WAD**

A framed stonecut picture, "Bird Spirits" by Napatchie Pootoogook (1938-2002), E7-1104, Cape Dorset/Kinngait, no.22/50.

1960   *20½in (52cm) high*

$1,800-2,300   **WAD**

A framed stonecut picture, "Animal Whalers II," by Pudlo Pudlat (1916-92).

20in (51cm) high

$3,200-3,800   **WAD**

A late 19thC Apache beaded hide doll with baby carrier, with tin cone and beaded detail.

11½in (29cm) high

$9,000-10,000   **SK**

Late 19thC Blackfeet beaded buffalo hide double saddlebags, with three brass bells.

112in (284.5cm) long

$4,000-4,800   **SK**

A late 19thC Blackfeet mountain sheep hide and ermine skin headdress, with red trade cloth brow band, the horns covered in silk ribbons.

25in (63.5cm) long

$40,000-48,000   **SK**

A late 19thC Blackfeet felt and ermine skin headdress, decorated with an animal tail, with carved wood horns.

28in (71cm) long

$23,000-28,000   **SK**

A Blackfeet buckskin, canvas, cloth, and beaded rifle case, the inside edge inscribed "BBI.73.PD."

Collected in Montana, c1940.

40½in (103cm) long

$1,600-2,000   **WW**

1930s Cherokee beaded hide moccasins, black-dyed buckskin with velvet cuffs, remnant silk edging on the cuffs, heels restored.

9in (23cm) long

$13,000-18,000   **SK**

19thC Cheyenne hide moccasins, with buffalo rawhide soles, beaded with classic Cheyenne designs and a single thunderbird.

10in (25.5cm) long

$3,800-4,400   **SK**

A rare Plains Cree quill-decorated hide horse crupper, buckskin decorated using six porcupine quill techniques, the fringe with black pony beads.

c1840   24in (61cm) long

$28,000-33,000   **SK**

A 1870s Crow buffalo hide mirror bag, beaded with classic Crow designs, the fringe with white pony beads.

23in (58.5cm) long

$11,000-14,000   **SK**

A Hopi polychrome carved wood katsina, Shalako Mana.

A katsina, or kachina, is a spirit being in the religious reliefs of the Pueblo people, including the Hopi, Zuni, Hopi-Tewa, and certain Keresan tribes.

6½in (16.5cm) high

$3,200-3,800   **SK**

A late 18thC Huron hide pouch, with porcupine quillwork, moose hair embroidery, and a border of metal cones with tufts of deer hair.

9¼in (23.5cm) wide

$65,000-80,000   SK

1870s Lakota beaded buffalo hide moccasins.

10in (25.5cm) long

$2,500-3,200   SK

A Northeast beaded cloth bag, of Wabanaki type, possibly Mi'kmaa.

c1870   6¼in (16cm) high

$1,500-2,000   SK

A late 19thC Lakota beaded cloth and hide doll.

12in (30.5cm) high

$7,500-9,000   SK

A 1870s Lakota beaded buffalo hide cradle, lined with printed cotton, the rawhide tab fringed with bugle beads and brass hawkbells.

24½in (62cm) high

$5,500-7,000   SK

A late 19thC Lakota parfleche box, with green trade cloth trim.

15in (38cm) long

$3,200-3,800   SK

ESSENTIAL REFERENCE—WINTER COUNT

A Winter Count is a pictorial record of events, kept by various North American peoples. This Count covers the years 1786-87 to 1876-77, and was made by Bo-i-de (the Flame, or the Blaze), a Dakota Sioux living 18 miles south of Fort Sully, Dakota Territory. An interpretation of the pictographs can be found in the fourth annual report of the Bureau of Ethnology, 1882-83. This particular Winter Count may have been obtained from Lieutenant H.T. Reed, who was stationed at Fort Sully in 1876. Reed was assisting Garrick Mallery in locating and interpreting Winter Counts. Mallery's studies were published in the fourth annual report of the Bureau of Ethnology, 1882-83.

A Navajo child's wearing blanket, woven on a three-ply wool warp, minor wool loss.

54in (137cm) long

$44,000-50,000   SK

An early 20thC Nez Perce beaded hide woman's dress, fringed with bugle beads and cowrie shells.

49in (124.5cm) long

$4,400-5,000   SK

An 1870s Sioux Winter Count painted on muslin, by Bo-i-de.

43in (109cm) high

$20,000-32,000   SK

A late 19thC Sioux running horse effigy catlinite pipe bowl, rich patina of use.

10½in (26.5cm) long

$23,000-28,000 SK

A late 19thC Sioux painted buffalo hide dance shield, painted with a deer head, penciled "Standing Rock Agency, Fort Yates, N.D. July 4, 1900."

19in (48.5cm) diam

$18,000-23,000 SK

1870s Sioux beaded and quilled hide moccasins, the bifurcated tongues with tin cone and horsehair danglers, minor quill loss.

10½in (26.5cm) long

$2,500-3,200 SK

An 1870s Ute beaded hide tail bag, red ocher pigment overall.

8in (20.5cm) long

$3,200-3,800 SK

Late 19thC Ute beaded hide woman's high-top moccasins, fringed along the sides.

18½in (47cm) high

$5,500-6,500 SK

A mid-to-late 19thC Eastern Plains or Prairie tack-decorated ball-headed club.

27½in (70cm) long

$13,000-18,000 SK

An early to mid 19thC Western Great Lakes puzzle stem pipe, with shell and brass crescent decoration, the black stone bowl with lead and catlinite inlay, old repair.

Collected by James Taylor, an Englishman who emigrated to Canada in 1852.

37½in (95.5cm) long

$14,000-18,000 SK

A late 19thC Plains wood society staff, with cloth-covered crook and fringe, dark patina.

60½in (153.5cm) long

$13,000-18,000 SK

A mid-to-late 19thC Plains or Prairie carved wood grass dance whistle, formed as a bird head.

22½in (57cm) long

$7,000-8,000 SK

A mid-to-late Plains grizzly bear claw necklace, buffalo hide wrapped, rich patina.

claws max 4in (10cm) long

$23,000-28,000 SK

A 19thC Micmac quilled birch bark box, minor quill loss.

The Micmac, or Mi'kmaq, people are indigenous to Canada's Atlantic Provinces, the Gaspé Peninsula of Quebec, and the northeastern region of Maine.

5½in (14cm) diam

$950-1,050   **SK**

A Panamint coiled basketry bowl, eastern California, woven with geometric design.

c1900   *14½in (37cm) diam*

$4,000-4,800   **SK**

A Pima basketry olla, southern Arizona, with a vertical cross and ladder design, stitch loss.

16½in (42cm) high

$1,150-1,250   **SK**

A miniature Pomo basket, California, woven with geometric patterns and two figures, feather detail.

4½in (11.5cm) long

$1,200-1,400   **SK**

An early 20thC miniature Tlingit lidded basket, nick to rim.

The Tlingit people are indigenous to the Pacific Northwest Coast of North America.

2¼in (5.5cm) diam

$950-1,050   **SK**

A late 19thC to early 20thC Yokuts basketry olla, California, woven with a geometric design and "rattlesnake" band.

14in (35.5cm) diam

$12,000-14,000   **SK**

A 1920s Acoma pottery jar, New Mexico.

13¾in (35cm) diam

$5,500-7,000   **SK**

A late 19thC Pueblo pottery bowl, flake to rim, surface abrasions.

The Pueblo people are indigenous to the Southwestern United States.

13in (33cm) diam

$800-950   **POOK**

An early 20thC Hopi pottery canteen, northeastern Arizona, with an avian pattern, some chips.

8½in (21.5cm) diam

$5,000-5,700   **SK**

A Zuni frog jar, with relief-molded frogs and painted butterflies.

The Zuni people are indigenous to the Zuni River Valley in New Mexico.

c1900   *12½in (32cm) diam*

$3,200-3,800   **SK**

A mid-to-late 19thC Maori carved and notched wood tewhatewha fighting staff, attributed to Patoromu Tamatea.

Patoromu Tamatea was a prominent and prolific master carver around Lake Rotoiti in 1850-70 and carved various works, including model canoes, paddles, house gable boards, and wall slabs. He was also reported to have tattooed women.

59¼in (150.5cm) long
$7,500-9,000   **WW**

A late 19thC Maori carved wood and haliotis shell ceremonial paddle, the blade with three tiki figures, with a tiki head terminal.

61½in (156.5cm) long
$15,000-18,000   **WW**

An early 19thC Maori wood paddle hoe, with carved decoration.

Collected by Thomas Laslett (1811-87).

55¾in (141.5cm) long
$9,000-10,000   **WW**

A Maori taiaha or staff, one eye socket inlaid with original paua shell, the others replaced with mother-of-pearl.

65½in (166.5cm) long
$3,200-3,800   **BRI**

A Maori carved wood and haliotis shell walking stick, with five tiki figures, the handle with a tiki terminal.

Presented to Joseph Manning in 1898 as recognition for his saving a Maori boy from drowning in the waters of Lake Rotoiti in the North Island of New Zealand.

35¼in (89.5cm) long
$3,200-3,800   **WW**

A Maori cane, carved as a standing chief, with haliotis shell decoration and inset gold plaque to finial with motto "Ready Aye Ready."

33½in (85cm) long
$3,200-3,800   **WW**

A rare possibly 18thC Maori wooden hand club, carved with a face, the back with a sharp edge.

10¾in (27.5cm) long
$5,000-5,700   **WW**

A 19thC or earlier wooden Maori canoe bailer, with low relief open work frontal crest representing an abstract face.

Provenance: By descent from the Family of John Williams. John Williams (1796-1839) was an English missionary active in the South Pacific. Most of his missionary work was successful, but in November 1839, while visiting the island of Erromango, Vanuatu, John Williams and fellow missionary James Harris were killed and eaten by cannibals. In December 2009, descendants of John and Mary Williams traveled to Erromango for a ceremony of reconciliation. To mark the occasion, Dillons Bay was renamed Williams Bay.

17¼in (44cm) high
$12,000-14,000   **DUK**

An early to mid-19thC Maori carved wood treasure box or "Waku Huia," with projecting tiki heads.

19½in (49.5cm) long
$13,000-19,000   **SK**

An early 19thC Maori heru mapara or small comb, the wooden teeth lashed together with flax fiber.

Maori men followed the Polynesian custom of wearing their hair long and tying it in a large topknot. Feathers were stuck into the topknot by their quills, the tail feathers of the huia, black with white tips, being regarded as the most valuable. Combs were also stuck in the hair for decoration.

6in (15cm) long

$1,900-2,500   JN

A Maori matau paua shell, bone, feather, and fiber pä kahawai or fish hook.

Pä kahawai are trolling lures designed to attract and hook large surface-feeding fish, such as kahawai (sea trout). Adapted from Polynesian trolling lures, pä kahawai are composite lures typically constructed using a ground and shaped paua shell lure set in a wooden shank with a bone barb attached at the base and bound tightly with muka (flax fiber) cord.

4½in (11.5cm) long

$1,300-1,800   JN

A pair of 19thC Maori carved horn scrimshaw powder flasks, one depicting and inscribed "William King and his Wife," tattooed with Tâ moko and holding a war club and with mythical sea scenes, the other with scenes of Dancers.

Wiremu Kingi, also called Te Rangitake, or William King, was born in Manukorihi, New Zealand, in 1795 and died in Kaingaru in 1882. He was a Maori chief whose opposition to the colonial government's purchase of tribal lands led to the First Taranaki War (1860-61). He inspired the Maoris' resistance throughout the 1860s to European colonization of New Zealand's North Island.

12in (30.5cm) long

$5,500-6,500   JN

A pair of Maori wood, abalone shell, and bone hei matau carvings or fish hooks.

Although these could be functional items, they were also worn as pendants for safekeeping and were often treasured family heirlooms. They represented strength, good luck, and safe travel across the water.

$2,500-3,200   HAN

CLOSER LOOK—HEI-TIKI

Hei-tiki are traditional pendants carved by the Maori.

Like many hei-tiki, this example is made of green nephrite, with haliotis shell eyes. Nephrite is a very hard stone and would have been difficult to work.

It is in the form of a human fetus, symbolizing fertility. Hei-tiki were typically worn by women and handed down from generation to generation.

Hei-tiki are greatly sought after by collectors today, and when in good condition, can fetch high prices.

A 18thC to 19thC hei-tiki pendant, New Zealand.

5in (13cm) high

$44,000-50,000   WW

A 19thC Maori hei-tiki pendant, nephrite with red sealing wax, the top with attachment piercing.

4in (10cm) high

$32,000-38,000   WW

A Fiji waseisei necklace, split sperm whale teeth, with 30 curved tusks with faceted tops, on a stand.

longest tusk 5in (12.5cm) long

$15,000-19,000   WW

A 19thC Fijian dui carved tribal club, the handle flaring in the shape of a fan, old bangs and scuffs.

The dui/fan club was used by warriors to deliver blows with a sharp edge.

32in (81.5cm) long

$2,800-3,500   MART

A 19thC Fijian wood ula or throwing club, inlaid in bone with a star and moon motifs.

The grip may possibly have been the work of a Maori carver working in Fiji.

17¼in (44cm) long

$5,000-6,300   DUK

A Fijian carved wood and fiber gunstock club, the name "Sailósa" written near the base, mounted.

33¾in (86cm) high

$1,300-1,900   L&T

An early 20thC South Sea Islands fighting staff, possibly Fijian.

39¾in (101cm) long

$2,500-3,200   HT

A Fijian pineapple or totokia club, with large toothed and spurred striking head.

34in (86.5cm) long

$3,800-4,400   BRI

A Kanak wood club, Vanuatu, with a root head.

26¾in (68cm) long

$2,300-2,800   WW

An Asmat ancestor figure, Buepis Village, Casuarinen Coast, Western Papua, Indonesia.

67in (170cm) high

$18,000-25,000   WW

An early 19thC Austral Islands carved wood paddle, Polynesia, carved with ten dancing girls.

Collected by Thomas Laslett (1811-87).

46½in (118cm) long

$10,000-11,000   WW

A Lake Sentani wood standing female figure, Papua New Guinea.

30in (76cm) high

$60,000-65,000   WW

A Lardil Aborigine cermonial dance headdress, Mornington Island, Queensland, bark wrapped in spun human hair, emu feather crest.

20in (51cm) high

$1,500-2,000   BRI

A Papua New Guinea Gulf gope board, with a mask surrounded by leaf designs, with charred areas.

61in (155cm) high

$5,000-6,300   WW

A Solomon Islands carved shell and wood barava funeral post, with fiber binding.

30½in (77.5cm) high

$5,000-6,300   WW

A Tikopia shell necklace, Solomon Islands, with a center double hook and 12 single hooks.

19in (48cm) long

$8,000-9,500   WW

An 19thC Aboriginal wood, resin and fiber woomera spear-thrower, Western Australia, with remains of red ocher, with a textured back.

Collected by Arthur Allen (1874-1967).

The Indigenous population of Australia is composed of two groups: the mainland Aboriginal people and Torres Strait Islanders. The Torres Strait Islanders live in northern Queensland on the islands between Australia and Papua New Guinea. The Aboriginal people reside mostly in Queensland and New South Wales, along the Murray River. Aboriginal antiques are currently on the rise in value.

27¼in (69cm) long

$900-1,000　　　WW

A 19thC Aboriginal wood club, Murray River, South East Australia, with bands of "peckwork" decoration, with incised hatching to the grip.

Collected by Arthur Allen (1874-1967).

28½in (72.5cm) long

$1,800-2,500　　　WW

A 19thC Aboriginal throwing club.

25in (63.5cm) long

$450-550　　　JN

A 19thC Aboriginal wood narrow shield, New South Wales, Australia, with possum tooth relief-carved wavy linear decoration with a line of lozenges with red ocher and with diaper filled lozenges.

Collected by Arthur Allen (1874-1967).

32¼in (82cm) long

$20,000-32,000　　　WW

An Aboriginal paddle-shaped club, decorated with panels of plain and wavy lines, some old repairs.

31in (79cm) long

$1,300-1,800　　　MOR

An Aboriginal nail club, Queensland, the head with band of metal flanked by clusters of horseshoe nails.

27¼in (69cm) long

$1,300-1,800　　　CHOR

An Aboriginal carved wood broad shield, decorated with rhythmical iterations of interlocking diamonds and waved lines.

43¾in (111cm) high

$8,000-9,000　　　L&T

An Aboriginal wood shield, decorated with stone carved zigzag pattern, the reverse with an integral handle, mounted.

28¾in (73cm) high

$2,800-3,500　　　L&T

An Aboriginal bicornual basket, Jawun, Queensland, Australia, lawyer cane with traces of red ocher decoration.

13½in (34cm) high

$10,000-11,000　　　WW

A near pair of Saxon long wheel-lock holster pistols, by Hans Stockman, Dresden, stamped "HS," with decorative marks.

These pistols are almost identical to other examples made for the Electoral Guard. They were almost certainly made for the Trabantenleibgarde of the Prince Elector Christian II. Hans Stockman is recorded working in Dresden from 1590 until his death in 1639. He became a master of the gunmaker's guild in 1603 and Burger of Dresden in 1605.

c1610

barrel 19in (48cm) long

$34,000-38,000   TDM

A rare 17thC Scottish left-handed snaphaunce belt pistol, with steel stock and with rams horn butt, the four-stage barrel with fluted breech and faceted muzzle with reeded sections dividing, dated.

1648

19in (48cm) long

$13,000-18,000   L&T

A pair of 30-bore silver-mounted flintlock dueling pistols, by John Manton, London, no. 1921, with exceptionally elaborate silver mounts en rocaille, perhaps unfired, in original mahogany case.

These pistols belong to a group of only four known examples by John Manton with silver mounts made by Michael Barnett. They were probably made for Francis Ingram Seymour-Conway (1743-1822), 2nd Marquess of Hertford. What remains of the crest would reinforce this attribution, and they have been associated with a Marquess of Hertford since the early 20thC.

1790-91

15in (38cm) long

$78,000-90,000   TDM

ESSENTIAL REFERENCE—ROBERT WOGDON

Robert Wogdon (1737-1813) was a renowned Georgian gunmaker.

● He was apprenticed in Lincolnshire to Irish gunmaker Edward Newton. He later moved to London, where he worked first on Cockspur Street and later at Haymarket.

● In 1794, he went into partnership with John Barton, forming Wogdon & Barton.

● Wogdon's dueling pistols were famous for their high quality and precision. He tuned his barrels to ensure they were accurate at 12 paces, resulting in more deaths from duels than previously.

● Wogdon pistols were used in the famous duel between prominent American politicians Aaron Burr and Alexander Hamilton in 1804. Wogdon pistols were so well-known that duels were sometimes known as "Wogdon affairs."

A cased pair of 22-bore flintlock dueling pistols, by Wogdon, single set triggers, some age splits to case.

c1785

15in (38cm) long

$18,000-25,000   W&W

A flintlock dueling pistol, by Wogdon & Barton, London, signed, the cock possibly replaced, crack to lock.

c1800

15in (38cm) long

$1,050-1,200   LOCK

A 54-bore flintlock four-barreled "duck's foot" pistol, with four turn-off cannon barrels, false rifling, signed "LAUGHER & SON," cleaned, not functional.

c1805

$5,500-6,500   HOLT

A Highland flintlock dress pistol, by Christie, signed lock, fitted with matching cock and sliding bolt safety, Tower Private proof marks, iron reblued.

John Christie is recorded working in the Small Gun Office, the Tower of London 1794-1830.

c1820

barrell 7¼in (18.5cm) long

$9,500-10,500   TDM

An early 19thC flintlock pistol, by Harding, the barrel stamped "J. Harding, Borough, London, No. 308," with proof marks, engraved "For His Majesty's Mail Coaches."

James Harding is recorded as "Gunmaker to General Post Office," in Blackman Street, Borough between 1810-33.

14½in (37cm) long

$3,800-5,000   SWO

A double-barreled 16-bore percussion holster pistol, by Westley Richards, the barrels engraved "Westley Richards, 170 New Bond St, London," one hammer spur missing.

c1850

12½in (32cm) long

$1,800-2,300   W&W

ARMS & ARMOR

A 9mm French model 1854 pin-fire rifled pistol, by Treuille de Beaulieu for the "Cent Gardes" of Napoleon III.

The "Cent Gardes" were an elite cavalry squadron created by Napoleon III. The contract for their firearms was awarded to Baron Antoine Hector Thésée Treuille de Beaulieu (1809-86), a French General and Captain Inspector of the Châtellerault manufactory.

c1854   11½in (29cm) long

$13,000-18,000   **TDM**

A DB side-by-side 38-bore percussion boxlock pistol, signed "Steward, Yarmouth," B'ham proved.

9in (23cm) long

$950-1,050   **W&W**

A double-barreled 28-bore percussion holster pistol.

13½in (34.5cm) long

$1,000-1,150   **W&W**

A Bergman no.5/1897 self-loading pistol, no.396, stamped "Pistolet Bergman/Patent Brevete S.G.D.G.."

The Bergman model 1897 underwent trials by both the Swiss and British military before being ultimately rejected. Around 800 pistols of this type are believed to have been made, most of which went to commercial customers.

barrel 3in (7.5cm) long

$18,000-23,000   **TDM**

A cased .41 rimfire over-under engraved derringer pistol, serial no.605, mother-of-pearl grips and spur trigger, in case.

c1888-1912   barrel 3in (7.5cm) long

$8,000-9,500   **HOLT**

A rare 7mm over-and-under 20-shot double-action pin-fire volley revolver, no.1226, by Lefaucheux, France, later chromed finish.

c1870   5in (12.5cm) long

$2,500-3,800   **TDM**

An American Smith and Wesson .44 calibre Russian model no.3.6 shot revolver, serial no.25,887, top barrel flat with patents and Springfield address.

1880   barrel 5in (12.5cm) long

$2,500-3,200   **LOCK**

CLOSER LOOK—U.S. MODEL 1911A1 PISTOL

Only 500 of the U.S. Model 1911A1 semiautomatic pistols were made, under Educational Order W-ORD-396. These were issued mainly to U.S. Army Air Corps squadrons.

The pistol is stamped "S. MFG. CO./ELIZABETH, N.J.,U.S.A.," "UNITED STATES PROPERTY/ M1911 A1 U.S.ARMY" with serial number "NoS800221." It carries a "JKC" inspection mark and "P" proofmark.

This is the finest condition known example of this model.

It is accompanied by a 2010 letter giving the gun's history. 1st Lieutenant Charles H. Clark of the Army Air Corps recovered it from a crash scene in 1943 when on a rescue mission.

A U.S. Model 1911A1 semiautomatic pistol, manufactured by the Singer Manufacturing Co.

1940

$320,000-380,000   **ROCK**

A cased 54 bore Irish six-shot percussion pepperbox revolver, by William & John Rigby, Dublin, no.10718, signed and inscribed "Dublin," perhaps unfired, in original case.

1855   barrel 3¾in (9.5cm) long

$42,000-50,000   **TDM**

An early 5-shot 80-bore 1st type Kerr's Patent single-action percussion revolver, marked to the Sussex Artillery Volunteers, some scuffing.

$2,300-2,800   **W&W**

A late 18thC flintlock blunderbuss, the lock signed "Bond," stamped "EC" to stock, some scratches, locking mechanism not functional.

29in (73.5cm) long

$1,600-2,000   **GORL**

An American 40-bore Jennings pattern percussion rifle, converted from flintlock, barrel stamped "12," inscribed "New York."

Isaiah Jennings invented his all-metal breech-loading rifle in New York in 1818. Relatively few examples survive.

c1830   *32¾in (83cm) long*

$7,000-8,000   **TDM**

A 2nd Model 1853 percussion Artillery carbine, with two folding leaf rearsights and bayonet bar at the muzzle, the buttplate tang engraved "V/MxA3/ 411" (Middlesex Artillery Volunteers).

1853   *40in (101.5cm) long*

$1,000-1,250   **W&W**

A presentation Maynard patent first model Saddle Ring Sporting single shot rifle/shotgun, with a .50 caliber rifled barrel and a .55 caliber smoothbore barrel, in case.

1857   *26in (66cm) long*

$7,000-8,000   **POOK**

A cased semismooth bore top lever hammerless boxlock ejector rook rifle, by Holland & Holland, no.21308.

42in (106.5cm) long

$4,000-4,800   **W&W**

CLOSER LOOK —JAMES PURDEY AND SONS RIFLE

This rifle is possibly unique, and may be the only best-quality 8-bore produced by James Purdey and Sons.

It has dovetailed fine 3-stripe Damascus barrels, made by A. Meers.

The metal is decorated with fine scroll and bouquet engraving, probably by J. Lucas, the head engraver at Purdey's.

It has bores with 17-groove Enfield-type rifling, and a marbled and figured full pistol grip Circassian walnut buttstock.

A James Purdey and Sons hammer underlever 8-bore rifle, engraved "J. Purdey & Sons, Audley House, South Audley Street, London," stamped "AM," refurbished, most likely by the factory, some minor pits, in oak and leather Purdey case, with steel bullet mold, striker keys, cleaning rod, and other accessories.

barrels 24in (61cm) long

$70,000-80,000   **JDJ**

A three-band Enfield percussion rifle, the unlined lock marked with crowned "VR" and "1861 Enfield," later date stamped "4/1883," the barrel and barrel bands pitted and refinished.

55in (139.5cm) long

$1,150-1,400   **W&W**

A WCF Winchester Model 1885 single shot falling block volunteer rifle, no.64136.

1893   *43½in (110.5cm) long*

$1,500-2,000   **W&W**

A Martini Henry Mark IV rifle, serial no.4884, the frame marked with crown over "VR/Enfield/1886/IV/1," various Nepalese marks, some minor pitting and bruising, dated.

1908   *49½in (125.5cm) long*

$700-800   **W&W**

A New England cherry drop stock flint lock fowler.

60½in (153.5cm) long

$6,500-7,500   **NA**

ARMS & ARMOR

A Brunswick State two-hand processional sword of the Guard of Julius, Duke of Brunswick and Lüneburg in Wolfenbüttel (1528-89), no.235, dated.

Provenance: The Brunswick Ducal Zeughaus, Wolfenbüttel. Duke Julius of Brunswick-Wolfenbüttel (1528-89) inherited the title following the death of his two older brothers in battle. The swords from his Ducal Guard are all numbered and may be divided into two series, one dated 1573 and the other 1574.

1573   *52¾in (134cm) long*
$21,000-25,000   **TDM**

A late 16thC North European basket-hilted military backsword.
blade 33¼in (84.5cm) long
$6,500-7,500   **TDM**

An 18thC and earlier Scottish basket hilted broadsword, The Cameron Family Sword, the basket of Stirling form, blade inscribed "Yis Suerd was brukyt be Ht Cameron at ye Batttailly off Stirling Bryg MCCXCVII and Bannockburn MCCCXIIIII & Feili Melle," with further plaque engraved "Yis Thrusande Claiffoff Metell gud aeft Tynt 3 hits Shynn in Saxonys Blud."

The tradition of remounting historic family blades is well recorded, in part due to the early 19thC fashion for the Scottish revival fueled by Sir Walter Scott. This blade unusually predates that fashion. Repute suggests that it was remounted in the early 18thC to be taken to Jacobite risings.

38½in (98cm) long
$11,000-13,000   **L&T**

Judith Picks

This sword tells an interesting story. The blade was made in the early 17thC, probably in Germany before being transported to Scotland to be hilted. The basket hilt is applied with silver mounts depicting Jacobite symbols and mottos. Some of these date from the early 17thC, some from c1707 around the time of the Act of Union. The mounts include Classical medallions, Saint Andrew on the cross, and several thistles. The knuckle guard is inscribed, "Prosperity to Schotland, No union, God save ye Kings James VIII." The misspelling of Scotland can be seen on other swords of German manufacture. Together, this suggests that this sword belonged to a Scottish family of high status who were very public in their support of the Jacobite cause. The sword's motto would have been clearly, and controversially, displayed when it was worn at the side or drawn in action.

An early 17thC silver-mounted Scottish basket-hilted sword.
c1620   *blade 40¼in (102cm) long*
$20,000-32,000   **L&T**

A late 18thC French small sword, with tapered German blade, with inscription "Me Fecit Solingen" (Solingen made me), silver hilt close-plated with gold, face decorated in blue and white enamels, some dents, some enamel losses.
28¾in (73cm) long
$6,500-7,500   **TDM**

A 1796-pattern heavy cavalry trooper's sword, marked "Osborn" and "E/19," some wear.
blade 34½in (87.5cm) long
$3,200-3,800   **W&W**

An 18thC to early 19thC Talwar or Indian sword, with iron hilt quillons and recurved knuckle guard with monsterhead finial.
32in (81.5cm) long
$3,200-3,800   **TDM**

An 18thC to early 19thC Tibetan sword, silver hilt with chased decoration.
blade 25½in (65.5cm) long
$5,000-6,300   **TDM**

An early 19thC military officer's basket hilted sword, by Prosser, London, engraved "Prosser."
37½in (95cm) long
$1,800-2,300   **L&T**

A George IV presentation sword of the Honourable Artillery Company, of 1796 light cavalry style, inscribed "Capt General, His Most Gracious Majesty Geo IVth. Colonel, HRH Prince Augustus Frederick, Duke of Sussex."

blade 32in (81.5cm) long

$1,300-1,900　　　　　　W&W

An early to mid-19thC Indian shamshir, with earlier Persian curved single-edge blade of watered steel, some wear.

32¼in (82cm) long

$11,000-12,000　　　　　　TDM

An early 19thC French sidearm, with prominent cockerel's head pommel, hilt loose.

blade 23in (58.5cm) long

$450-500　　　　　　W&W

A Japanese Shinto tachi, the blade decorated with a horimono of a dragon and a figure holding a tsurugi, marked "Kato Tsunatoshi on orders of Fujiwara Teifuku/ On a day of the second month Tenpo eight [1837]" on the reserve, "On the 27th day of the tenth month of the same year at Senju Yamakado Yazaemon [cut through] a head and into the earthenmound below."

Kato Tsunatoshi (d.1863), real name Kato Hachiro, originally came from Dewa's Yonezawa and was a student of Suishinshi Masahide. He moved to Edo during the Bunsei era (1818-30). He also worked under the pseudonym Chojusai.

23½in (59.5cm) long

$6,500-7,500　　　　　　WHYT

A Belgian French style cavalry NCO's sword, marked "Manufacture d'Armes de l'Etat à Liège" on backstrap, dated.

1844　　　　　　*36in (91.5cm) long*

$400-500　　　　　　W&W

A 19thC Turkish yataghan sword.

31½in (80cm) long

$2,300-2,800　　　　　　HT

A German Imperial Damascus honor sword, by A. Werth, Solingen, inscribed "The Officers corps of the Hussars regiment No7 of the King To the Heir Prince Zu Bentheim as a friendly memory," stamped maker's marks.

41in (104cm) long

$7,500-9,000　　　　　　PSA

A late 19thC Indian tulwar sword, the iron hilt with elephant's head pommel and tiger knucklebow, inlaid with gold and fitted with gems.

blade 30¼in (77cm) long

$11,000-12,000　　　　　　GORL

A George V 18th Hussars mameluke-hilted officer's sword.

blade 31¼in (79.5cm) long

$2,500-3,200　　　　　　TDM

A Wilkinson 1822-pattern sword, as issued to the "Blue Hussars."

The Blue Hussars, officially called the Mounted Escort, were a ceremonial unit of the Irish Army established in 1932. It escorted the President of Ireland on state occasions, most famously to and from presidential inaugurations between 1938, when the first president took office, and 1948, when the Escort was disbanded. This sword lacks any serial number, signifying that it was supplied under contract.

c1932-48

$1,300-1,900　　　　　　WHYT

A medieval dagger, possibly Italian, in excavated condition.

c1470-90   blade 12in (30.5cm) long

$3,800-4,400   **TDM**

A composite left-hand dagger, probably French, with iron hilt decorated with cherubic figures and a Classical warrior, with later grip.

c1660   10in (25.5cm) long

$5,000-5,700   **TDM**

An English plug bayonet, stamped with a King's head mark, the mark of the London Cutler's Company and a copper-lined "T" mark, inscribed "God Save King William & Mary" and "Nicholas Arnold 1690," dated.

Bayonets with inscriptions relating to King William and Queen Mary are notably rare. The mark is probably that of Gyles Lyndesy who became Free of the Cutler's Company in 1673.

1690   11½in (29cm) long

$11,000-14,000   **TDM**

An 18thC Indian katar or dagger.

9¾in (25cm) long

$2,500-3,200   **TDM**

An early to mid-19thC Indian dagger kard, with earlier Persian watered single-edge blade, some losses, in its wooden silk-covered scabbard.

7½in (19cm) long

$6,500-7,500   **TDM**

A late 18thC Indian khanjar or dagger, with carved green jade hilt.

blade 8¾in (22cm) long

$15,000-19,000   **TDM**

A Third Reich Teno Subordinate's hewer, the blade with Original Eickhorn and Teno marks, the throat mount numbered "2871."

$1,600-2,300   W&W

A Japanese dagger or aikuchi, with kaku-mune blade, small copper tsuba.

9½in (24cm) long

$700-750   **TDM**

A Victorian dirk, Edinburgh, with bi-knife and fork.

1896   17in (43cm) long

$1,300-1,900   L&T

A Gordon Highlanders officer's dirk and sgian dubh, by R. & H.B. Kirkwood, Edinburgh.

A Scottish dirk is the ceremonial weapon of the Highland Cathairean (warrior), worn by officers, pipers, and drummers of Scottish Highland regiments. A sgian-dubh is a small, single-edge knife worn on the leg as part of traditional Scottish Highland dress.

1906   dirk 11¾in (30cm) long

$7,000-8,000   L&T

A 1st Lanarkshire Militia officer's dirk, the handle with silver studs, mounted with crystal, the scabbard set with bi-knife (inscribed "John Sellars') and fork.

17¼in (44cm) long

$2,500-3,200   L&T

A South German burgonet, some pitting.

c1560-70 9¼in (23.5cm) high

$2,500-3,200 **TDM**

A miter cap of the Grenadier Company, The Queen's Own Regiment of Foot, bearing a Georgian crown, "GR" on Garter with motto, professionally restored, with related documents.

1727-43 14in (35.5cm) high

$1,900-2,500 **W&W**

An officer's white metal helmet of the Montgomeryshire Yeomanry Cavalry, back peak cracked, lining replaced.

$650-750 **W&W**

A Victorian 1847-pattern officer's "Albert" helmet, of the 1st King's Dragoon Guards, some dents and rubbing, plume replaced.

The initials on the headband of this helmet appear to be those of Major Walter Clopton Wingfield, who served with the King's Dragoon Guards 1851-61, and is credited with the invention of Lawn Tennis.

$7,000-7,500 **TDM**

A 19thC miter cap of the Prussian 1st Garde Regtiment, frontplate bearing the Prussian eagle and motto "Pro Gloria et Patria" and "FR," with owner's name "Barthel" and "9. Ky 1. Garde-Regt.Z.F," some moth holes.

15in (38cm) high

$2,300-2,800 **W&W**

A Sussex Yeomanry officer's helmet, with star helmet plate inscribed "Sussex Yeomanry."

post-1902

$4,400-5,000 **W&W**

A Royal Irish Constabulary helmet, inscribed "Con, Primrose" and "JP 60943."

1902

$1,900-2,500 **WHYT**

A Life Guards Other Ranks, lining leather damaged.

post-1902

$1,000-1,150 **W&W**

A World War I Brodie's Patent steel helmet.

$1,200-1,400 **W&W**

A Life Guards Other Ranks helmet, unissued.

post-1953

$1,300-1,800 **W&W**

An officer's tall blue cloth shako, of The Royal Dockyard Battalion, trade label of "Wilkinson & Son London," small tar stain, in its tin case.

$5,500-7,000 **W&W**

A 2nd Edinburgh Rifles Volunteer Corps black cloth officer's helmet, inscribed "Hill Bros military outfitters London."

$2,100-2,500 **L&T**

A pair of mid-16thC fingered gauntlets, probably German, with later leather finger linings.

11¾in (30cm) long

$2,500-3,800   SWO

A North European cuirassier's breastplate, in the late "peascod" fashion, lightly patinated overall.

c1610   *14in (35.5cm) high*

$1,000-1,150   TDM

A set of 19thC cap-a-pie field armor, with etched decoration in the mid-to-late 16thC Italian style, mounted on a wood stand and accompanied by a sword.

$13,000-19,000   TDM

ESSENTIAL REFERENCE—JACKS OF PLATE

Jacks of plates, sometimes referred to as coats of plate, were a uniquely British piece of armor, especially common in North England and Scotland.

- They ceased to be manufactured at the end of the 16thC, although they were used into the 17thC.
- Jacks of plate were once commonly used, but are also extremely fragile. Only 16 known complete jacks of plates survive worldwide today.
- This one formed part of a collection assembled sometime after 1765 at Worden Hall, Lancashire, by Sir William Farington (c1704-81).

An English jack of plate, the iron plates secured by stitches of crossbow twine, the outer fabric discolored and worn.

c1580-90   *28¼in (72cm) high*

$10,000-11,000   TDM

A Georgian Irish officer's gilt gorget, of the Royal Castlewellan Yeoman Infantry, engraved with crowned pre-1801 Royal Arms.

Castlewellan is in County Down, Northern Ireland. The unit was raised in October 1796, under Captain Commandant Richard, 2nd Earl of Annesley.

$3,500-4,000   W&W

A 19thC Turkish cavalry helmet, breastplate, and backplate.

These were worn by someone of officer class in the Sudanese War.

$1,150-1,400   W&W

An early 19thC silver officer's gorget, inscribed "GIII Rex IX Regt.," soldered repair.

5½in (14cm) diam

$4,400-5,000   MART

A Scots Guards Captain's tunic, with gilt bullion embroidery, with 24 gilt King's Crown regimental buttons by Robbins.

post-1902

$500-650   W&W

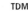

A set of composite 16thC and early 17thC cap-a-pie field armor, mainly Italian, with etched and gilt 19thC decoration.

The decoration of this armor was probably inspired by that of an Italian armor made for Count Annabile Capodilista c1620, which was purchased for the Tower of London Armories in 1840.

$32,000-38,000   TDM

A World War I P/PH gas helmet, with two mica eyepieces, with exhaust valve with its metal tube and composite mouth piece.

This early gas mask was introduced in July 1915 to replace the "Hypo" helmet. The flannel was dipped in sodium phenolate and glycerin. Later, in October 1915, Hexamine was added for protection against phosgene. This altered the nomenclature to "P.H. Helmet" (Phenate Hexamine).

$2,000-2,500   LOCK

A 17thC German signaling cannon, on wooden field-type carriage.

42in (106.5cm) long

$1,900-2,500　　W&W

An 18thC stone bow, with red walnut frame and steel detail, inscribed "H.W. Mortimer & Son, 89, Fleet St, London" and "Gun Makers to His Majesty."

28¾in (73cm) long

$5,000-6,300　　APAR

A rare 1814-issue Georgian color of No.15 Company, 2nd Battalion, the Coldstream Guards, with painted decoration of St. Edward's Crown above the Company symbol (Carolingian crown), "EGYPT," the Sphinx between laurel sprays, "BARROSA," a bugle horn, "PENINSULA" and "WATERLOO," further inscribed "LINCELLES" and "TALAVERA," "XV" in the canton, restored.

This color was recently discovered in near-relic condition and has been expertly restored to museum quality. The 1814-issue color was used until the next issue in 1821.

c1814-21　　　　　　*76½in (194.5cm) wide*

$20,000-25,000　　TDM

A George III painted hardwood truncheon, marked with crown, Royal cipher, and "Fauxhall."

The land where Vauxhall, London, is now located was acquired in the 1230s by a Frenchman named Falkes de Breaute. Over time, the area has been known as Faukeshall, Fauxhall, Fox Hall, Fulke's Hall, Fawkyhall, Faux Well and ultimately Vauxhall, when Vauxhall Gardens opened in 1785.

27½in (70cm) high

$500-650　　CHEF

A Civil War Era 35-star American flag.

1863-65　　*54in (137cm) long*

$3,800-4,400　　NA

A George V painted brass side drum of the 1st Battalion Coldstream Guards.

$500-650　　W&W

An officer's gilt shoulder belt plate of the 13th 1st Somersetshire Prince Albert's Regiment of Light Infantry, some wear.

pre-1855

$1,050-1,200　　W&W

A Victorian officer's full dress embroidered sabretache of the 21st Hussars, bearing crown, "VR" cipher and "21/H" roundel, minor moth traces.

12in (30.5cm) high

$2,300-2,800　　W&W

ESSENTIAL REFERENCE—NEMA CIPHER MACHINE

During World War II, the Swiss Army used a modified version of the German-made commercial Enigma model K machine.

- **Although Switzerland was neutral in WWII, many agents and diplomatic missions operated on Swiss soil, and both the allied forces and the Germans learned how to decode Swiss Enigma K traffic. After this, Switzerland started the development of their own improved machine, which they called Nema. The first machines entered service in 1947.**
- **A total of 640 were built by the Swiss manufacturer Zellweger AG. Three versions were in circulation, which can be discriminated by their serial numbers. TD100-199 were made for the Foreign Office, TD200-419 were training machines, and TD420-740 were operational machines.**
- **Operational machines differ from the training machines, because they have two additional wheels stored inside the top lid and can be recognized by the label on the outer case saying that it should only be released in case of war. Because this is numbered TD610, it is an operational machine.**

A Nema Cipher machine, serial no.TD610, with four double-bearing rotors and two single rotors, including red reflectors, with instruction manual and booklet.

c1948

$4,400-5,000　　CHEF

A pair of German Third Reich Kriegsmarine U-boat binoculars, by Zeiss, stamped "7 x 50 48285 blc," some wear.

$950-1,050　　LSK

An officer's gilt and silver-plated shako plate of the 98th Regiment.
1822-29
$1,500-2,000 W&W

A Naval General Service medal, marked "Navarino."
1848
$1,500-2,000 W&W

A Military General Service Medal, awarded to John Wilkinson 7th Foot, with bars for Toulouse, Orthes, Pyrenees, Vittoria, Salamanca, Badajoz, Albuhera, and Talavera, replacement ribbon, wear to ribbon and clasp.
$3,200-3,800 APAR

An officer's silver glengarry badge of the Argyll & Sutherland Highlanders, marked "Meyer & Mortimer. London," hallmarked "HT," Edinburgh, brooch pin.
1914
$500-650 W&W

A World War I Other Ranks bronzed hat badge, of the 67th Bendigo Infantry, by Stokes & Sons Melbourne.
$500-550 W&W

An Easter Rising Medal, for Kathleen Clarke.

Kathleen Clarke (1878-1972) was one of the founding members of Cumann na mBan, an Irish republican women's paramilitary organization founded in 1914. She was selected by the Irish Republican Brotherhood to be made acquainted with the plans for the 1916 Easter Rising, in case of the death or arrest of all its leaders. The day after the Rising ended, Kathleen founded what became the Irish Volunteers Dependants and National Aid Association to provide support to families who had lost people in the Rising. She later became the first female Lord Mayor of Dublin.
1916
$16,000-20,000 WHYT

An East India Company silver medal for military service in the Third Mysore War.

The Third Anglo–Mysore War (1790–92) was a conflict in South India between the Kingdom of Mysore and the East India Company and its allies, including the Maratha Empire and the Nizam of Hyderabad. This medal was awarded to the higher ranks of native Indian troops: the Jemadars and Serangs.
1791-92   1¾in (4.5cm) diam
$3,200-3,800 WHYT

A Seringapatam Medal 1799 (Honourable East India Company), English version in silver.
2in (5cm) diam
$1,300-1,800 LOCK

A Canada General Service medal, with bars for Fenian Raids of 1866 and 1870, named "850 Pte W Piggott 1/RB," from Woolwich, Kent, with copy medal roll.
1899
$1,000-1,150 LOCK

A 1st pattern bronzed hat badge, of the Australia Commonwealth Horse.
$1,300-1,800 W&W

An Other Ranks white metal hat badge, of the 6th Australian Light Horse.
$450-500 W&W

An Imperial Russian officer's and silver-plated star helmet plate of the 3rd Regiment.
$500-550 W&W

An Egyptian Naqada II period carved breccia stone bird vessel.
3500-3200 BC
$7,000-7,500   **TL**

An Egyptian 19th Dynasty Hapi canopic jar, New Kingdom, the lid with a human face representing the son of Horus Hapi, with hieroglyphic text, placing the vessel under the protection of Nephthys and Hapi.
1292-1189 BC 14in (35.5cm) high 346oz
$18,000-23,000   **TL**

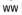

An Egyptian late Dynastic to Ptolemaic period wood sarcophagus mask.
c700-30 BC   *23in (58.5cm) high*
$6,500-7,500   **WW**

An Egyptian Late Period molded faience Shabti for Ankh-hor, with hieroglyphs for Ankh-hor, Governor of Upper Egypt.

A Shabti is a figure in the form of a mummy, placed in an ancient Eygptian tomb. It was believed that Shabtis would work for and assist those they were buried with in the afterlife.

640-570 BC   *4in (10cm) high*
$3,200-3,800   **L&T**

A 4th-3rdC BC bronze figure of Horus.
                               5in (13cm) high
$6,500-7,500   **SWO**

An Egyptian Ptolemaic period cartonnage gilt mummy mask, depicting the Four Sons of Horus with mummifom bodies before Osiris, wearing Atef crown.
332-330 BC
$9,000-10,000   **TL**

A 4th-1stC BC Greek Hellenistic silver kantharos.
4¾in (12cm) wide 4oz
$4,400-5,000   **TL**

A 4th-3rdC BC Greek marble head of a youth, scuffed and worn, nose broken off.
                               4¼in (11cm) high
$2,500-3,200   **DN**

A 1stC BC Greek Hellenistic rock crystal flask.
                               1¾in (4.5cm) high
$3,200-3,800   **TL**

A 1stC BC-3rdC AD Romano-Egyptian gold coiled snake bracelet.

3½in (9cm) long 1½oz

$11,000-12,000 TL

A Roman redware wine flaggon.

AD 100 7½in (19cm) high 19⅞oz

$200-250 LOCK

A 3rd-4thC AD Roman "Apotheosis of Hercules" mosaic center panel, some reconstitution.

Hercules (Greek Herakles) was an important demigod and hero in the Classical world, around whom a major cult developed during the Roman Empire. He was the son of Jupiter (Greek Zeus) and the mortal Alcmene, famous for his strength and guile. This mosaic depicts Hercules being taken to Mount Olympus to take his place among the Immortals after his death.

4in (10cm) diam

$8,000-9,500 TL

A 1stC AD Roman onion-form glass bottle, probably Alexandria.

5in (12.5cm) high

$550-650 HALL

A 5thC AD or later Roman oinochoe, body formed as the head of a boy, the neck with dolphins, handle with putto playing a syrinx.

In Etruria, bronze and terra-cotta wine jars, known as oinochoes, olpes, and kantharol, were often modeled as human heads. This vessel is a later Roman version and would have been used to serve guests at a symposium (Roman commissatio), the part of banquet after the meal dedicated to drinking, music, dancing, recitals, and conversation, which was a key Hellenic—and later, Roman—social institution.

12¾in (32.5cm) high 7¾oz

$9,000-10,000 TL

A 2ndC AD pink sandstone Kushan head of a Jina, Mathura region, Northern India.

11½in (29cm) high

$50,000-63,000 MAB

An Ancient Indus Valley terra-cotta painted zebu bull.

c3000-2200 BC

$650-750 LOCK

A Colima pottery dog.

c100 BC-AD 250 11¾in (30cm) long

$1,050-1,200 SK

A Pre-Columbian Olmec-style jade ceremonial celt, the blade form mimicking the early Mesoamerican agricultural ax, likely depicting a Yucatan chief.

A celt is a prehistoric tool, similar to an adze or an ax-head, used for felling trees or shaping wood. Ceremonial celts were also made.

14in (35.5cm) high

$19,000-27,000 CLAR

A carved rosewood square piano, by Schomacker & Co., Philadelphia.

Provenance indicates, this piano was played by Swedish opera singer Jenny Lind.

patented 1848   *89½in (227.5cm) wide*

$32,000-38,000   **FRE**

A late 19thC satinwood grand piano, by F. Kaim & Sohn Kirchheim-Stuttgart, painted with Neoclassical scenes, in need of retuning.

71¾in (182cm) long

$8,000-9,500   **BELL**

A late 19thC to early 20thC double manual polychromed harpsichord.

82¼in (209cm) long

$3,200-3,800   **L&T**

A maple cello, by Johann Antes Bethlehem, Pennsylvania, top of scroll broken off, some damages, dated.

Johann Antes Bethlehem (1740–1811) is widely regarded as the first bowed string instrument maker in North America. Few examples of his work survive, including a violin at the Moravian Historical Society Nazareth and a viola in the Lititz Congregation Collection. This item may be the earliest American-made cello still in existence.

1763

$21,000-25,000   **POOK**

An early 19thC violin, stamped "PERRY, DUBLIN."

14¼in (36cm) long

$5,000-6,300   **SWO**

A French violin, by Jean Baptiste Vuillaume, Paris, labeled "Jean Baptiste Vuillaume a Paris, Rue Croix des Petits Champs," numbered "1660."

Vuillaume's internal numbers "1660" are closer to the date 1845 than 1840, as quoted by W.E.Hill & Sons in 1917. It is possible that they did not have access to the full chronology of the Vuillaume numbers at that time.

c1845   *14¼in (36cm) long*

$140,000-180,000   **BRO**

A harp, by Sebastian and Pierre Erard, London, engraved "Sebastian and Pierre Erard Patent No. 5698, 18 Great Marlborough Street, London."

Sebastian Erard (1752-1855) was born in Strasbourg and moved to Paris to work as a musical instrument maker. He was later joined in business by his nephew Pierre. Due to the turmoil of the French Revolution, he later moved to London. The firm was based at Great Marlborough Street c1790-1902.

$3,800-5,000   **BRO**

An Anglo Concertina, by Charles Jeffries, London, with 30 nickel keys, six-fold black bellows.

6in (15cm) diam

$5,000-6,300   **BRO**

A two-keyed boxwood oboe, by Thomas Cahusac, London, with silver keys.

c1785   *22½in (57cm) long*

$1,900-2,500   **GHOU**

An eight-keyed rosewood flute, by Rudall & Rose, London, with silver mounts and keys.

c1830   *22½in (57cm) long*

$3,800-5,000   **GHOU**

A French ten-string yew guitar, by Jean Henri Naderman (1734-99), restoration to inlay, some cracks, replacement pegs.

c1772   *17¼in (43.5cm) long*

$6,500-7,500   **BELL**

A 19thC parlor guitar, labeled "Panormo 1827, 26 High Street, Bloomsbury, London, No 878," with ebony 18-fret finger board.

$5,000-6,300   **BRI**

A C.F. Martin and Co. Nazareth PA 000-28 natural acoustic guitar, serial no.72249.

1939   *39in (99cm) high*

$19,000-25,000   **CLAR**

A U.S.-made Fender Stratocaster electric guitar, serial no.9xxx9, with rosewood fretboard neck stamp "JAN 63," pencil date "63," in soft case, with CITIES certificate.

1963

$19,000-25,000   **GHOU**

A Gibson ES-335 semihollow body electric guitar, made in the United States, serial no.A2xxx0 FON T4xxx5, with rosewood fretboard, working electrics, some alterations made for Bigsby tailpiece since removed, with CITIES certificate.

1958

$20,000-25,000   **GHOU**

A Guild D-55NT rosewood and ebony acoustic guitar, made in the United States, serial no.173299, in original case.

Provenance: Christie's, 1999. In the auction listing, Eric Clapton said that he had used this guitar for writing and recording. Lee Dickson recalls that Clapton had owned this guitar since the late 1970s.

1978

$32,000-38,000   **GHOU**

A mid-1960s Wandre Blue Jeans electric guitar, made in Italy, in a vintage Stone Case Company case, with letter of provenance from Zoot Money.

Jimi Hendrix never used this guitar in a gig, but it was the first guitar he ever played in England. In September 1966, Jimi Hendrix arrived at Heathrow Airport from New York with his manager Chas Chandler. They went to Zoot Money's apartment in London, where Chas asked if Zoot knew anyone with a left-handed guitar that Jimi could borrow for a gig. While discussing who to call, Jimi played around on this guitar.

$11,000-13,000   **GHOU**

A George Formby (1904-61) Gibson concert banjolele, serial no.132.

21¾in (55cm) long

$44,000-50,000   **HAN**

A Raffele Calace & Son of Naples mother-of-pearl and tortoiseshell-inlaid mandolin, labeled within, some splits.

24¾in (63cm) long

$900-1,000   **APAR**

DECORATIVE ARTS MARKET

Like many areas of collecting, Decorative Arts pieces have seen a rise in sales and prices of high-end items, and stagnation of mid- to low-end goods.

Many Doulton wares are now simply now considered unfashionable. Demand for the Royal Doulton figures has fallen dramatically and only the prototypes, limited production, and rare "colorways," or palettes, are fetching good money. In addition, demand for works by the Barlows, Eliza Simmance, and Frank Butler has been sluggish. The opposite is true of the Doulton pieces with experimental glazes—especially anything unusual that is lustered or flambéd.

Martin Brothers continue to be strong sellers in the current marketplace. A rare Martin Brothers salt-glazed stoneware grinning grotesque crab, at Phillips Design sale in New York in December 2018 sold for $220,000 (plus a buyer's premium of 25 percent, see page 474). And that same month, Waddington's in Toronto had the most exciting sale of nearly 100 pieces of Martin Brothers work from a private collection—my friend Bill Kime drove across Canada to pick up this collection, which included a small flock of Wally birds.

Moorcroft and Clarice Cliff will command high prices if the pattern and shape are rare, but the more common patterns are stagnant in the market. Wedgwood Fairyland lustre ceramics continue to be on a roll, particularly in the United States, Canada, and Australia—rare patterns, unusual colorways, and experimental or trial pieces are highly contested.

The Ohio School, meanwhile, including Rookwood and Roseville, has had a quiet year, with few exciting pieces coming onto the market. George Ohr continues to excite, but few exceptional pieces come on the market.

Silver from 20th century has continued to sell well, especially pieces by Charles Robert Ashbee and Omar Ramsden, as have rare and unusual Liberty pieces, particularly those designed by Archibald Knox.

In Art Nouveau glass, it is the big names that continue to sell: Lalique, Gallé, Tiffany, Loetz, and Daum.

Bronze and ivory figures by Demêtre Chiparus, Bruno Zach, and Ferdinand Preiss perform well if they are rare, iconic, and exceptional. Although bidders based in the United States and Japan could not take part because of import restrictions on ivory, enough dealers and collectors from other countries are still collecting these figures.

As David Rago, of leading auction house Rago, says, "As for decorative objects, such as ceramics and glass, we are seeing less fall-off on older work, and continued interest in pretty much all postwar glass, from 1950s Italian to high-end contemporary. One exception here has been the market for Tiffany glass and lighting which, in the past two years, has shown a resurgence. Oddly enough, early 20th century ceramics are drawing more attention than much of the postwar work, though that is a more recent trend and has yet to really play itself out.'

The sale of early 20th century furniture has been unremarkable, although when something fresh and with very good provenance appears on the market, so do the collectors—Charles Rennie Mackintosh continues to have a strong following.

Top Left: A Lenci figure, "Primo Romanzo," by Helen Konig Scavini, restoration to hand, reglued finger.

9¾in (25cm) high

$7,000-8,000   **WW**

Above: A bronze sculpture, "The Rattlesnake," by Frederic S. Remington (1861-1909), inscribed "Copyright Frederic Remington, ROMAN BRONZE WORKS INC. N-Y-" and "No. 69," some dirt and surface wear.

24in (61cm) high EST:

$100,000-200,000   **LHA**

CLOSER LOOK—"ANGLO-PERSIAN" VASE

This vase was painted by Leonard King with a Persian-inspired design. Leonard King is one of Burmantofts most sought-after decorators.

It has been painted in an Iznik palette of blue, green, eggplant, and yellow.

Each side is decorated with a varying design of a peacock amid foliage.

Its value is increased by its excellent condition.

A Burmantofts Faience "Anglo-Persian" vase, model no.DS9-94, impressed and painted marks.

14¼in (36cm) high

$11,000-14,000　　　　　　**WW**

A Burmantofts Faience "Anglo-Persian" Poseidon charger, by Leonard King, model no.606, impressed marks, painted marks, "LK" monogram, minor firing faults, and glaze crackling.

18¼in (46.5cm) diam

$7,000-7,500　　　　**WW**

A Burmantofts Faience "Anglo-Persian" floor vase, by Leonard King, model no.164.

Burmantofts Faience Pottery was founded by James Holroyd in 1881 as a side project to his company Wilcocks and continued production until 1904. Its art pottery was strongly influenced by the Aesthetic movement.

21in (53.5cm) high

$2,000-2,500　　　　**WW**

A rare Burmantofts Faience wall charger, by Leonard King, painted with a fantastical beast, impressed maker's marks "BURMANTOFTS/FAIENCE" and with artist's monogram "LK."

c1880　　　15½in (39.5cm) diam

$3,200-4,400　　　　**L&T**

A Burmantofts Faience charger, by William Neatby, impressed marks, painted "Wm J Neatby," dated.

1887　　　15½in (39.5cm) diam

$5,000-6,300　　　　**WW**

A Burmantofts Faience "Partie-Color" jardinière designed, by Joseph Walmsley, model no.2227, impressed and painted marks, minor glaze chips.

9¾in (24.5cm) high

$2,300-2,800　　　　**WW**

A Burmantofts Faience "Partie-Color" jardinière and stand, model no.2115-2116, impressed marks, hairline crack, some chips.

37½in (95cm) high

$5,500-7,000　　　　**WW**

A Burmantofts Faience "Dragon" vase, model no.896, impressed marks.

13½in (34cm) high

$2,500-3,200　　　　**WW**

A Burmantofts Faience sitting dog, model no.1991, impressed marks, professional restoration to ears.

5½in (14cm) high

$500-650　　　　**WW**

A Burmantofts Faience grotesque spoon warmer, model no.1907, impressed marks, minor glaze frits.

6in (15cm) high

$800-950　　　　**WW**

A 1930s Carlton Ware ice bucket, "Crested Bird" and "Water Lily" patterns, printed script mark.

8in (20.5cm) high

$300-350 **FLD**

A 1930s Carlton Ware pedestal gondola, "Explosion" pattern, printed script mark.

13½in (34cm) long

$650-750 **FLD**

A 1930s Carlton Ware footed bowl, "Melange" pattern, printed script mark.

12¼in (31cm) long

$300-400 **FLD**

A rare Carlton Ware coffee service, no.3765, "Red Devil" pattern, with printed and painted marks.

c1933

coffee pot 8in (20.5cm) high

$4,400-5,000 **L&T**

A pair of 1920s Wiltshaw and Robinson Carlton Ware rouleau-shaped vases, "Tutankhamun" pattern, printed mark, Egyptian mark.

10¾in (27.5cm) high

$950-1,050 **FLD**

A 1930s Carlton Ware goblet-form vase, "Wagon Wheels" pattern, printed script mark.

4½in (11.5cm) high

$300-400 **FLD**

A Carlton Ware "Flower and Falling Leaf" charger, printed mark, numbered "1/1369" and "3948."

12½in (32cm) diam

$450-500 **MOR**

A Carlton Ware Guinness toucan and pint glass wall appliqué, impressed "GA2492."

7in (18cm) high

$1,500-2,000 **GORL**

A Carlton Ware Guinness lamp base, printed around base, "If he can say as you can Guinness is good for you How grand to be a Toucan Just think what Toucan do," printed mark, overall crazing.

9½in (24cm) high

$300-400 **PW**

A Clarice Cliff shape 469 "Liner" vase, "Brown Alton" pattern, "Bizarre" mark.

c1933   *8¼in (21cm) high*

$2,300-2,800   **FLD**

A Clarice Cliff shape 356 vase, "Applique Avignon" pattern, "APPLIQUE" and "Bizarre" marks.

It comes with the original price label of 15/6, which is £46.86, or $59,04, in today's money, when the average annual wage was the equivalent of $9,979.18.

c1930   *6¾in (17cm) high*

$2,800-3,800   **FLD**

ESSENTIAL REFERENCE—CLARICE CLIFF

Clarice Cliff (1899-1972) was an important Art Deco ceramics designer.

● She started at A.J. Wilkinson in 1916 as an enameler and, by the mid-1920s, Wilkinson had given her her own studio, Newport Pottery.

● Her "Bizarre" range was launched in 1927 and her "Fantasque" range followed shortly afterward.

● Her tableware, vases, and other items were covered with bold designs, hand painted in thickly applied bright colors. The designs were painted by a group of dedicated decorators, mostly women, who become known as the "Bizarre Girls."

● The demand for Clarice Cliff remains strong, with rare shapes, such as "Yo-Yo" vases, and rare patterns, such as the "Applique" range or "May Avenue," being especially desirable.

CLOSER LOOK—"APPLIQUE BIRD OF PARADISE" WALL

This dish-form wall plaque is hand painted with the "Applique Bird of Paradise" pattern.

Patterns in the "Applique" range are rare and highly sought after.

This plaque is only the second example ever to be discovered, being one of only four pieces known to exist in this pattern.

It was given as a wedding present in 1931 and has been handed down by family descent ever since.

A Clarice Cliff wall plaque, hand painted "Applique" and "Bizarre" marks.

c1931   *13½in (34cm) wide*

$13,000-18,000   **FLD**

A Clarice Cliff dish-form plate, "Orange Applique Lucerne" pattern, "APPLIQUE" and "Bizarre" marks.

c1930   *9in (23cm) wide*

$3,200-3,800   **FLD**

A Clarice Cliff Bizarre "Mei Ping" vase, "Applique Red Tree" pattern, printed and painted marks.

6in (15.5cm) high

$3,800-4,400   **WW**

A Clarice Cliff shape 402 "Conical" biscuit box/cookie jar and cover, "Blue Autumn" pattern, "FANTASQUE" and "Bizarre" marks.

c1930   *7¾in (20cm) high*

$3,800-4,400   **FLD**

A Clarice Cliff "Conical" teapot, "Blue Autumn" pattern, "FANTASQUE" and "Bizarre" marks.

c1930   *5½in (14cm) high*

$1,800-2,300   **FLD**

A Clarice Cliff "Conical" coffeepot, "Comets" pattern.

c1930   *7½in (19cm) high*

$1,300-1,800   **FLD**

A Clarice Cliff "Mr Duck" egg cup set, "Crocus" pattern, various marks.

c1930

$650-750   **FLD**

A Clarice Cliff "Archaic" range vase, "Cubist" pattern, "Fantasque" mark, marked "Replica. Temple of Luxor. Thebes. Capital of the large columns. 1250 BC."
c1929   7in (18cm) high
$1,900-2,500   FLD

A Clarice Cliff "Lotus" pitcher, "Double V" pattern, "Bizarre" mark.
c1929   11¾in (30cm) high
$2,500-3,200   FLD

A Clarice Cliff Bizarre shape 358 vase, "Green Erin" pattern, printed factory marks.
                      8in (20.5cm) high
$1,500-2,000   WW

A Clarice Cliff Bizarre "Isis" vase, "Football" pattern, printed factory marks.
                      9¾in (24.5cm) high
$5,000-6,300   WW

A Clarice Cliff "Globe" tea set for six, "Forest Glen" pattern, printed factory marks, hairlines to two cups, date mark.
1936
$3,800-5,000
                      teapot 5in (12.5cm) high
                                       WW

A Clarice Cliff "Lotus" pitcher, "Honolulu" pattern, "Bizarre" mark.
c1933   11½in (29.5cm) high
$2,800-3,500   FLD

A Clarice Cliff Fantasque Bizarre wall charger, "House and Bridge" pattern, printed factory marks.
                      16½in (42cm) wide
$9,000-10,000   WW

A Clarice Cliff Bizarre shape 362 vase, "House and Bridge" pattern, printed factory marks.
                      8¼in (21cm) high
$2,300-2,800   WW

A Clarice Cliff shape 379 "Yo-Yo" vase, "Inspiration Floral" or "Daisy" pattern, "Inspiration Bizarre" mark, restored.
c1930   8¾in (22.5cm) high
$2,500-3,200   FLD

A pair of Clarice Cliff novelty bird bookends, "Inspiration L'Oiseau" pattern, "INSPIRATION" and "Bizarre" marks.
c1930   7in (18cm) high
$1,150-1,400   FLD

A Clarice Cliff shape 280 vase, "Inspiration Persian," "INSPIRATION" mark.
c1930 6in (15.5cm) high
$950-1,050 **FLD**

A Clarice Cliff shape 370 "Globe" vase, "Jonquil" pattern, "Bizarre" mark.
c1935 6in (15cm) high
$800-950 **FLD**

A Clarice Cliff "Hereford" shape biscuit/cookie barrel, "Latona Knight Errant" pattern, "LATONA" and "Bizarre" marks.
c1930 6¼in (16cm) high
$1,500-2,000 **FLD**

A Clarice Cliff shape 363 vase, "Latona Orchid" pattern, "LATONA" and "Bizarre" marks.
c1929 6¼in (16cm) high
$2,300-2,800 **FLD**

A Clarice Cliff pedestal almond dish, "Luxor" pattern, "Bizarre" mark.
c1929 3½in (9cm) wide
$1,050-1,200 **FLD**

A Clarice Cliff Bizarre "Daffodil" preserve pot and cover, "May Avenue" pattern, printed marks.
5in (13cm) high
$3,200-3,800 **WW**

A Clarice Cliff Bizarre charger, "Moonlight" pattern, printed marks.
18in (45.5cm) high
$5,000-5,700 **WW**

A Clarice Cliff Bizarre "Isis" vase, "Oranges & Lemons" pattern, printed marks.
9¾in (24.5cm) high
$2,300-2,800 **WW**

A Clarice Cliff "Isis" vase, "Poplars" pattern, printed marks, light scratching.
11¾in (30cm) high
$1,900-2,500 **CHEF**

A Clarice Cliff Bizarre "Mei Ping" vase, "Red Cafe" pattern, printed marks, "Sevi Guatelli" paper label.
8¾in (22.5cm) high
$11,000-14,000 **WW**

A Clarice Cliff shape 370 "Globe" vase, "Summerhouse" pattern, "FANTASQUE" and "Bizarre" marks.
c1931 *5½in (14cm) high*
$3,500-4,000 **FLD**

A pair of Clarice Cliff "Teddy Bear" novelty bookends, "Sunburst" pattern, "Bizarre" mark.
c1930
$3,200-3,800 **FLD**

A Clarice Cliff Bizarre "Lotus" pitcher, "Sunray" pattern, printed marks.
11½in (29cm) high
$5,000-5,700 **WW**

A Clarice Cliff "Holborn" fruit bowl, "Sunspots" pattern, "Bizarre" mark.
c1931 *8¼in (21cm) wide*
$1,500-2,000 **FLD**

A Clarice Cliff Bizarre "Mei Ping" vase, "Tennis" pattern, printed mark, professional restoration to the base rim.
12¼in (31cm) high
$5,000-6,300 **WW**

A rare full set of Wilkinson and Clarice Cliff "Allied Commanders of the First World War" Toby jugs/pitchers, designed by Sir F. Carruthers Gould, marked, some crazing, chips and minor wear.

These were issued in limited editions 1915-19.
$9,000-10,000 **WM**

A Clarice Cliff dish-form charger, "Pastel/Seven Color Trees & House" pattern, "Fantasque" mark, restored.
c1930 *16½in (42cm) wide*
$3,800-5,000 **FLD**

A Clarice Cliff "Tolphin" shape pitcher and wash bowl, "Umbrellas & Rain" pattern, "Fantasque" mark.
c1929
$2,800-3,500 **FLD**

A rare Clarice Cliff Bizarre "Grotesque Mask," designed by Ron Birks, in a "Clouvre" glaze, printed marks, minor professional restoration.

Ron Birks was the son of Lawrence Birks, who worked for Minton. He studied modeling and hand painting as an apprentice of Clarice Cliff. It is probable that he modeled this and other "Grotesque Masks" himself, under the supervision of Clarice Cliff.

11¼in (28.5cm) high
$6,500-7,000 **WW**

A rare Clarice Cliff Bizarre "Age of Jazz" table centerpiece, model no.434, printed marks.
8½in (21.5cm) diam
$24,000-28,000 **WW**

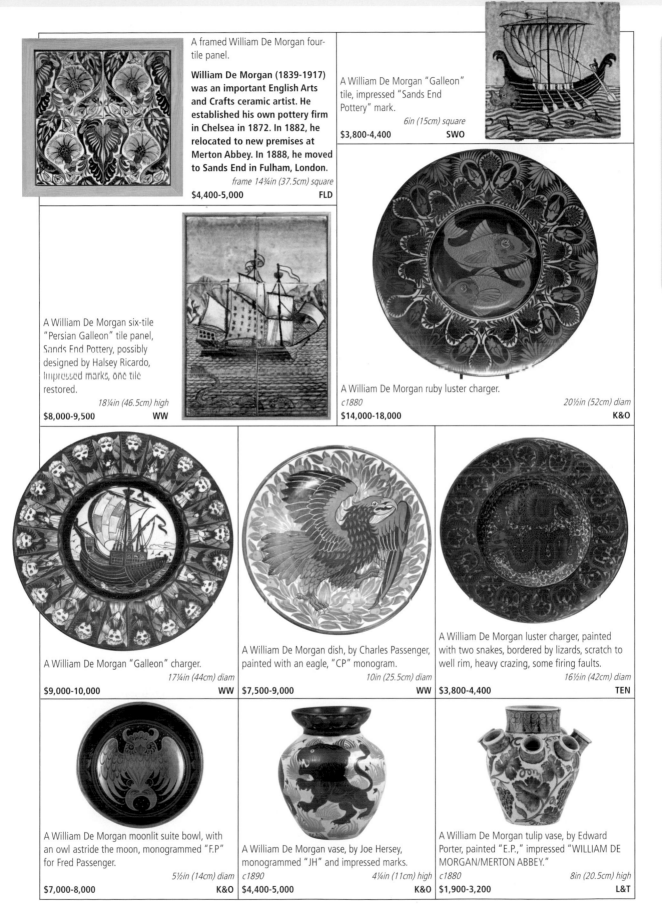

A framed William De Morgan four-tile panel.

William De Morgan (1839-1917) was an important English Arts and Crafts ceramic artist. He established his own pottery firm in Chelsea in 1872. In 1882, he relocated to new premises at Merton Abbey. In 1888, he moved to Sands End in Fulham, London.

frame 14¾in (37.5cm) square

$4,400-5,000 FLD

A William De Morgan "Galleon" tile, impressed "Sands End Pottery" mark.

6in (15cm) square

$3,800-4,400 SWO

A William De Morgan six-tile "Persian Galleon" tile panel, Sands End Pottery, possibly designed by Halsey Ricardo, impressed marks, one tile restored.

18¼in (46.5cm) high

$8,000-9,500 WW

A William De Morgan ruby luster charger.

c1880 *20½in (52cm) diam*

$14,000-18,000 K&O

A William De Morgan "Galleon" charger.

17¼in (44cm) diam

$9,000-10,000 WW

A William De Morgan dish, by Charles Passenger, painted with an eagle, "CP" monogram.

10in (25.5cm) diam

$7,500-9,000 WW

A William De Morgan luster charger, painted with two snakes, bordered by lizards, scratch to well rim, heavy crazing, some firing faults.

16½in (42cm) diam

$3,800-4,400 TEN

A William De Morgan moonlit suite bowl, with an owl astride the moon, monogrammed "F.P" for Fred Passenger.

5½in (14cm) diam

$7,000-8,000 K&O

A William De Morgan vase, by Joe Hersey, monogrammed "JH" and impressed marks.

c1890 *4¼in (11cm) high*

$4,400-5,000 K&O

A William De Morgan tulip vase, by Edward Porter, painted "E.P.," impressed "WILLIAM DE MORGAN/MERTON ABBEY."

c1880 *8in (20.5cm) high*

$1,900-3,200 L&T

ESSENTIAL REFERENCE—DOULTON

The Doulton Factory was founded in 1815 by John Doulton in Lambeth, London. It focused first on everyday stoneware and drainpipes before turning to decorative wares from the early 1870s.

- Key designers of late 19thC and early 20thC Doulton include the Tinworth brothers and the Barlow siblings. The company also worked closely with the Lambeth School of Art, and many of Doulton's Art Nouveau pieces were designed by students there.
- In 1901, Doulton received a Royal warrant. It later became known as Royal Doulton.
- Doulton began producing figurines in the 1880s, first under George Tinworth and later until Charles Noke. From 1912, all figurines were assigned an "HN" number.

A Doulton Lambeth stoneware two-tile panel, by Hannah Barlow, impressed mark, incised monogram, dated.
1874   *each 8¾in (22cm) square*
$1,500-2,000   WW

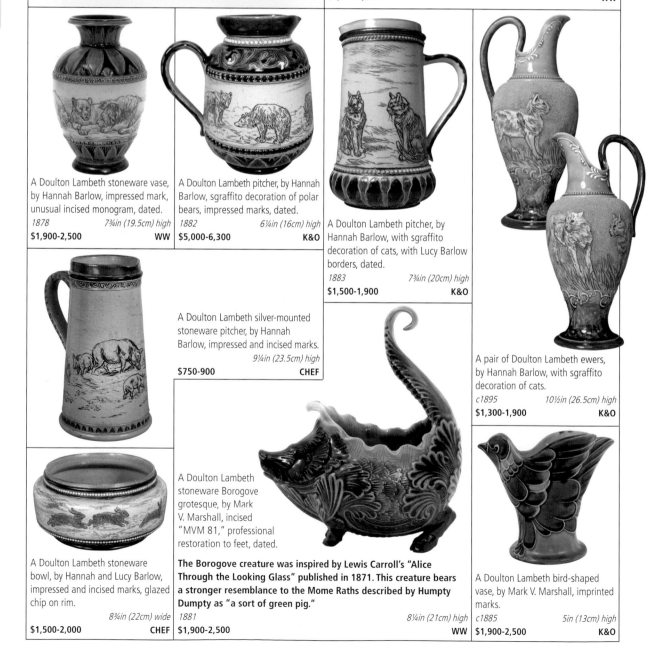

A Doulton Lambeth stoneware vase, by Hannah Barlow, impressed mark, unusual incised monogram, dated.
1878   *7¾in (19.5cm) high*
$1,900-2,500   WW

A Doulton Lambeth pitcher, by Hannah Barlow, sgraffito decoration of polar bears, impressed marks, dated.
1882   *6¼in (16cm) high*
$5,000-6,300   K&O

A Doulton Lambeth pitcher, by Hannah Barlow, with sgraffito decoration of cats, with Lucy Barlow borders, dated.
1883   *7¾in (20cm) high*
$1,500-1,900   K&O

A Doulton Lambeth silver-mounted stoneware pitcher, by Hannah Barlow, impressed and incised marks.
9¼in (23.5cm) high
$750-900   CHEF

A pair of Doulton Lambeth ewers, by Hannah Barlow, with sgraffito decoration of cats.
c1895   *10½in (26.5cm) high*
$1,300-1,900   K&O

A Doulton Lambeth stoneware bowl, by Hannah and Lucy Barlow, impressed and incised marks, glazed chip on rim.
8¾in (22cm) wide
$1,500-2,000   CHEF

A Doulton Lambeth stoneware Borogove grotesque, by Mark V. Marshall, incised "MVM 81," professional restoration to feet, dated.

The Borogove creature was inspired by Lewis Carroll's "Alice Through the Looking Glass" published in 1871. This creature bears a stronger resemblance to the Mome Raths described by Humpty Dumpty as "a sort of green pig."
1881   *8¼in (21cm) high*
$1,900-2,500   WW

A Doulton Lambeth bird-shaped vase, by Mark V. Marshall, imprinted marks.
c1885   *5in (13cm) high*
$1,900-2,500   K&O

A Doulton Lambeth stoneware bear cruet set, the design attributed to Mark V. Marshall, with silver mounts by John Grinshell & Sons, impressed marks, stamped "JG&S," Birmingham.

1899   *2¾in (7cm) high*

$900-1,000   **WW**

A Doulton Lambeth stoneware vase, by Elisa Simmance, impressed mark, incised artist's monogram.

19½in (49.5cm) high

$2,300-2,800   **WW**

A Doulton Lambeth stoneware "Mouse Musician" menu holder, by George Tinworth, impressed mark and incised monogram, minor restoration, date mark.

George Tinworth (1843-1913) trained at Lambeth School of Art and began his career at Doulton's Lambeth factory in 1866. He became one of their more significant modelers and potters, known especially for his stoneware mouse figures, which predate the HN series by several decades.

1885   *3½in (9cm) high*

$2,300-2,800   **WW**

A possibly unique Doulton Lambeth figural group, by George Tinworth, artist's monogram, some firing cracks.

Provenance: Acquired by Margaret Bryan (1884-1977) who worked at the Lambeth factory. The piece has many similarities to Tinworth's model "The Football Srimmage," modeled in 1876 and displayed at the Royal Academy in 1877 and the Paris Exhibition of 1878.

c1900   *6in (15.5cm) high*

$7,000-8,000   **CHEF**

A Doulton Lambeth "School Board" group, by George Tinworth, signed "GT" at the rear, impressed marks.

3½in (9cm) high

$3,200-3,800   **K&O**

A pair of Doulton Lambeth "Seaweed" vases, by George Tinworth.

11in (28cm) high

$550-650   **WHP**

A pair of Doulton Burslem vases, by George White, with Classical scenes, one titled "Spring," with backstamps, marked "Luscian ware."

In 1877, Doulton purchased an interest in a factory in Burslem, North Staffordshire. By 1882 it had fully acquired the factory. The Burslem works focused on bone china and porcelain, in contrast to the Lambeth works that chiefly produced stoneware.

36½in (93cm) wide

$13,000-15,000   **K&O**

A Doulton Burslem hand-painted vase, by R. Holdcroft, printed marks.

c1920   *9¾in (25cm) high*

$2,800-3,500   **K&O**

A late Victorian Doulton Burslem Aesthetic movement tea service, marks to base.

$650-750   **WM**

CLOSER LOOK—FISHERWOMEN

This is a rare and unusually large figural group, designed by Charles Noke.

It is decorated in a purple and red colorway, the center figure with a checked headscarf and polka-dot shawl.

This piece was issued c1917, just four years after the release of the first HN series figure. Many of these early figures had a short run and were produced, or even decorated, to order, making them especially rare.

Although the market for Royal Doulton figures is at a low ebb, rare figures such as this can fetch high prices.

A Royal Doulton group, "Fisherwomen" or "Waiting for the Boats" or "Looking for the Boats," no.HN80, with maker's marks and designer's name.
c1917　　　　　　　　*11¾in (30cm) high*
$11,000-12,000　　　　　　　　**TEAR**

A Royal Doulton "Double Jester" figurine, designed by Charles Noke, no.HN365, titled on base "Two Heads Are Better Than One," some restoration to pillar.
issued 1920-38　　17in (43cm) high
$9,500-10,500　　　　**JN**

A Royal Doulton "Butterfly" figure, designed by Leslie Harradine, no.HN720.
issued 1925-40　　6½in (16.5cm) high
$650-750　　　　**K&O**

A Royal Doulton "Irish Colleen" figurine, designed by Leslie Harradine, no.HN767, marks, some damages.
issued 1925-36　　6½in (16.5cm) high
$650-750　　　　**FLD**

A Royal Doulton "Lady Jester" figurine, designed by Leslie Harradine, no.HN1285, some restoration.
issued 1928-38
$900-1,000　　　　**WM**

A Royal Doulton "Two a Penny" figure, by Leslie Harradine, no.HN1359, restoration to neck.
$2,800-3,500　　　　**PSA**

A Royal Doulton "The Bather" figure, by Leslie Harradine, no.HN1708, hairlines on base and dress.
issued 1935-38　　7¾in (20cm) high
$900-1,000　　　　**WM**

A Royal Doulton prestige "Jack Point" figure, designed Charles Noke, no.HN3925, from a limited edition of 85, printed marks, with certificate.
17in (43cm) high
$1,900-2,500　　**K&O**

A Royal Doulton prestige "The Duke Of Wellington" figure, no.HN5745, from a limited edition of 50, boxed with certificate signed by Michael Doulton.
$3,500-4,000　　　　**PSA**

A 1950s Royal Doulton prototype cleaning maid figurine, designed by Mary Nichol, impressed "1865" on base.
8¼in (21cm) high
$2,300-2,800　　　　**PSA**

A Royal Doulton prototype earthenware Viking figure, impressed "1513," marked "Potted by Doulton & Co.," some restoration.
9¾in (25cm) high
$1,900-2,500　　　　**PSA**

A Royal Doulton Titanian ware figure, "Blighty," by E.W. Light, printed mark, impressed "Blighty."

Royal Doulton's Titanian glaze was developed in 1915 and was made with a titanium oxide, resulting in blue, gray, and green colors. Examples of Titanian ware are rare and often unique.

11½in (29cm) high

$3,200-3,800   WW

A Royal Doulton Bunnykins "Blue Band" set, comprising a drummer no.DB89, drum major no.DB90, cymbal no.DB88, trumpeter no.DB87, and sousaphone no.DB86, from a limited edition of 250.

$1,150-1,400   PSA

A 1920s Royal Doulton Chang ware vase, by Charles Noke and Harry Nixon, signed, with stamp, impressed "5229," light scratches.

8½in (21.5cm) high

$4,400-5,000   DRA

A Royal Doulton Chang flambé vase, by Charles Noke, with marks, light surface wear.

8¼in (21cm) high

$1,150-1,400   APAR

A Royal Doulton decanter box, with a Sung glaze plaque of "The Alchemist" by Charles Noke, fixed for wall mounting, with two glass decanters.

15¾in (40cm) high

$9,000-10,000   K&O

A Royal Doulton miniature Sung moon flask vase, by Charles Noke and Harry Nixon, no.201, signed "Sung."

3¼in (8.5cm) high

$1,500-1,800   HAN

A Royal Doulton prototype "The Fisherman" character jug/pitcher, printed marks.

7in (18cm) high

$4,400-5,000   K&O

A large Royal Doulton prototype flambé character jug/pitcher, "Maori."

$4,400-5,700   K&O

A Royal Doulton prototype "Nelson Mandela" character jug/pitcher, marked "Pascoe & Co, prototype" to base.

$4,400-5,700   K&O

A Royal Doulton "Jan Van Riebeek" loving cup, from a limited edition of 300.

10½in (26.5cm) high

$1,900-2,500   PSA

A Fulper "Vasekraft" flambé earthenware lamp base, "Vasekraft" stamp, "PATENT PENDING U.S. AND CANADA," in need of rewiring.

Fulper was a pottery based in Flemington, New Jersey. It moved from utilitarian stoneware to art pottery in the early 20thC.

c1908   *8¾in (22cm) high*
$900-1,000   DRA

A 1910s Fulper "Cattail" vase, "Verte Antique" glaze, vertical ink stamp, burst glaze bubble on rim, minor grinding chip to base.

12¾in (32.5cm) high
$5,000-5,700   DRA

A 1910s Fulper "Vasekraft" vessel, "Mission Matte" glaze, ink stamp, fleck on rim, grinding flakes to base.

12¼in (31cm) high
$6,500-7,500   DRA

A 1910s Fulper "Venetian Blue" vase, rectangular ink stamp, some scratches, minor grinding flakes.

12½in (32cm) high
$1,300-1,900   DRA

A 1910s-20s Fulper vase, "Leopard Skin Crystalline" glaze, racetrack mark, grinding chips on base.

17in (43cm) high
$800-950   DRA

A Fulper vase, with blue flambé over a mat purple glaze, raised racetrack mark, minor grinding chip, light scratches.

15in (38cm) high
$1,200-1,400   DRA

Judith Picks

"Copperdust Crystalline" is arguably Fulper's best glaze. It was either used on only their best and rarest forms or cost double the usual amount to put on a more common form. Pieces in the form of this vase are typically finished with the "Copperdust Crystalline" glaze. This is a particularly strong example, with even and deep firing. It is in perfect condition, which further increases its value.

A Fulper "Artichoke" vase, vertical incised mark, some burst glaze bubbles.

c1920   *8½in (21.5cm) high*
$1,500-2,000   DRA

A Fulper vase, "Chinese Blue" and ivory flambé glaze, vertical incised mark, some burst glaze bubbles.

c1920   *6¼in (16cm) high*
$650-750   DRA

A rare Fulper vase, "Copperdust Crystalline" glaze, vertical raised mark.

c1920   *11in (28cm) high*
$10,000-11,000   DRA

A Goldscheider terra-cotta figure, impressed "FRIEDRICH GOLDSCHEIDER/ WIEN/REPRODUCTION RESERVEE/1890/10/19," signature "HANIROFF."

c1890   11½in (29cm) high

$3,200-3,800   L&T

A late 19thC Goldscheider earthenware figure, impressed marks.

38½in (98cm) high

$950-1,050   HT

A Goldscheider terra-cotta of a boy, signed "Perigot," mark, numbered "3338 3 67."

30in (76cm) high

$1,150-1,400   JN

A Goldscheider lady in a kimono, by Stephan Dakon, no.6071, fully marked.

15¾in (40cm) high

$3,500-4,000   K&O

A Goldscheider ballerina, by Stefan Dakon, no.6361, with facsimile signature, impressed "6361," overall crazing.

10¾in (27cm) wide

$550-650   PW

A Goldscheider dancer, by Stephan Dakon, no.6930, fully marked.

16½in (42cm) high

$2,300-2,800   K&O

A Goldscheider lady, by Stefan Dakon, no.8083, fully marked.

c1930   13¼in (33.5cm) high

$950-1,050   L&T

A Goldscheider dancer, possibly by Claire Herczeg, no.8399, with paper label, printed marks, impressed "8399/72/31," left hand restored.

c1930   16¼in (41.5cm) high

$1,500-1,900   BELL

A Goldscheider woman, by Claire Herczeg, no.8241, fully marked.

15in (38cm) high

$2,300-2,800   K&O

A Goldscheider figure, "The Captured Bird," by Josef Lorenzl, no.5230, fully marked.

18¾in (47.5cm) high

$5,000-6,300   K&O

A Goldscheider lady, "The Cabaret," by Josef Lorenzl, no.5523, fully marked.

12½in (32cm) high

$2,000-2,500   K&O

A Goldscheider "Mephistopheles," by Josef Lorenzl, no.5537, fully marked.
14½in (37cm) high
$3,200-3,800 **K&O**

A Goldscheider "Columbine," by Josef Lorenzl, no.5778, fully marked.
18in (46cm) high
$5,500-6,500 **K&O**

A Goldscheider woman in pajamas, by Josef Lorenzl, no.5780, fully marked.
15in (38cm) high
$3,200-3,800 **K&O**

A Goldscheider "Butterfly" dancer, by Josef Lorenzl, no.6022, fully marked, professional restoration to ankles and hem.
11in (28cm) high
$1,600-2,000 **WW**

A Goldscheider lady with a Pekinese, by Josef Lorenzl, no.6812, fully marked.
11½in (29cm) high
$1,800-2,300 **K&O**

A Goldscheider nude with a German Shepherd, by Josef Lorenzl, no.7041, fully marked.
14½in (37cm) high
$2,000-2,500 **K&O**

An early Goldscheider nude, "Fascination," by Wihelm Thomasch, made by R. Spuller, no.5060, with eagle standard crest and artist's monogram, fully marked.
19in (48cm) high
$3,800-5,000 **K&O**

A Goldscheider girl, by Claire Weiss, no.6507, impressed signature, marked "GOLDSCHEIDER/ WEIN/6507/52."
c1920 *13in (33cm) high*
$800-950 **L&T**

A Goldscheider lady with borzoi, by Claire Weiss, no.7367, fully marked.
16¾in (42.5cm) high
$2,300-2,800 **K&O**

A Goldscheider earthenware figure, "The Egyptian Dancer," no.5281, black printed mark, impressed "5281/905," some glaze bubbles.
18½in (47cm) high
$3,200-3,800 **DN**

A Goldscheider group of dancers, no.5975, possibly based on the Dolly Sisters, impressed "5975/401/19," marked "Made in Austria," crazing to glaze.
15¾in (40cm) high
$5,500-7,000 **GORL**

A Goldscheider figure of a lady, no.8474, fully marked.
13in (33cm) high
$1,800-2,300 **K&O**

ESSENTIAL REFERENCE—GRUEBY FAIENCE COMPANY

The Grueby Faience Company was established in 1894 by William Henry Grueby in Revere, Massachusetts. It produced architectural tiles and art pottery.

● Its art pottery was inspired by the mat glazes of French pottery and the simplicity of Japanese ceramics.

● Vessels were typically of organic forms, with stylized foliate designs. The majority of pieces were glazed in mat cucumber green.

● Grueby pottery and tiles were popular in the late 19thC and early 20thC and partnered with Tiffany Studios to produce lamp bases.

● The firm began to struggle against increasing mass-market competition and declared bankruptcy in 1909, before finally closing in 1920.

A Grueby vase, by Ruth Erickson, circular "Pottery" stamp, incised "RE," small bruises and flecks.
c1905   5¾in (14.5cm) wide
$3,200-3,800   DRA

A Grueby gourd-shaped vase, by George P. Kendrick, circular "Pottery" stamp and "34."
c1905   12in (30.5cm) high
$34,000-40,000   DRA

A Grueby vase or lamp base, by Wilhelmina Post, circular "Faience" stamp and "WP 4-18-," drilled for lamp.
c1900   12½in (32cm) high
$5,000-6,300   DRA

A Grueby five-handled vase, by Wilhelmina Post and Norma Pierce, circular "Pottery" stamp, incised "WP/145" with Pierce cipher, professionally repaired chips.
c1905   8½in (21.5cm) high
$7,500-9,000   DRA

A Grueby five-handled vase, by Wilhelmina Post, circular pottery stamp, incised "WP," some chips.
c1905   11in (28cm) high
$5,500-7,000   DRA

A 1900s Grueby cuerda seca tile, framed, some chips on back, flecks at front.

In the cuerda seca ("dry cord" in Spanish) technique, thin bands of waxy resin are used to separate different colored glazes during firing.
6¾in (17cm) wide
$2,500-3,200   DRA

A Grueby vase, circular "Pottery" stamp, incised "ER," some hairlines.
c1905   10½in (26.5cm) high
$4,400-5,000   DRA

A Grueby vase, with irises, the circular stamp partly glazed over, incised "ER."
c1905   11¼in (28.5cm) high
$6,500-7,500   DRA

A Grueby vase, with carved irises, circular "Pottery" stamp, incised "N," some small flecks and chips.
c1905   12¼in (31cm) high
$6,500-7,500   DRA

A framed 1910s Grueby cuerda seca ship tile.
6in (15cm) square
$2,800-3,500   DRA

ESSENTIAL REFERENCE—LENCI

The Lenci factory was founded in Turin, Italy, in 1919 by Helen (Elena) Konig Scavini (1886-1974) and her husband Enrico.

● The name, "Lenci" is thought to be a corruption of Helen Konig Scavini's nickname, "Helenchen" or "Lenchen." It is also an acronym of the company's motto "Ludus Est Nobis Constanter Industria" ("Play is Our Constant Work").

● The factory began as a maker of felt dolls, adding earthenware and ceramics figures to its range in 1928.

● Many of the figures were designed by Helen Konig Scavini herself, but Lenci also worked with other designers, such as Giovanni Grande (1887-1937), Abele Jacopi (1882-1957), Mario Sturani (1906-78), and Sandro Vacchetti (1889-1976).

● Konig Scavini's expressive figures perfectly capture the Art Deco style. Her designs were much admired, including by Walt Disney, who allegedly tried to persuade her to work for him.

● The company was taken over in 1937 and ceramic production ceased in 1964.

A Lenci figure, "Primo Romanzo," by Helen Konig Scavini, painted "Lenci" marks and "K" on base, restoration to hand, reglued finger.
9¾in (25cm) high
$7,000-8,000   **WW**

A Lenci figure, "Nella O Nasin" or "Janetti," by Helen Konig Scavini, painted "Lenci" marks, professional restorations.
15¼in (39cm) high
$11,000-14,000   **WW**

A 1930s Lenci glazed earthenware "Sul Mondo" sculpture, Italy, by Mario Sturani and Helen Konig Scavini, signed "Lenci MADE IN ITALY TORINO" with artists" initials, impressed "500," minor dark scuffs.
19in (48.5cm) high
$9,000-10,000
DRA

A Lenci ceramic group of a siren and infant riding a tortoise, by Helen Konig Scavini, signed "Lenci Torino 3-1937—XV MADE IN ITALY" and intialed "K."
1937   *18in (45.5cm) diam*
$4,400-5,000   **DOY**

A 1930s Lenci center bowl, by Helen Konig Scavini, "Nuda con Uccellino su Piatto," Italy, signed "Lenci Made in Italy," professional restoration to bird.
16in (40.5cm) high
$1,500-2,000   **DRA**

A Lenci figure, "Madonna del Vento," painted factory marks, minor chips.
16¼in (41cm) high
$1,300-1,800   **WW**

A Lenci figure of the Madonna, by Paola Bologna, painted marks and date.
1931   *8¾in (22cm) high*
$300-400   **HAN**

A Lenci wall mask, "Maschera Con Nodo," by Helen Konig Scavini, painted marks, "Lenci Torino Italy."
c1930   *10¾in (27.5cm) long*
$2,500-3,200   **K&O**

A Lenci wall mask, "Testa," by Helen Konig Scavini, painted marks, minor professional restoration to tip of scarf.
11½in (29cm) long
$500-650   **WW**

A mid-19thC Minton majolica "Lychees" teapot and cover, impressed "1349/ MINTON" with indistinct date cipher.

Minton were the first English factory to produce majolica, inspired in part by Italian Renaissance maiolica (see page 56-57). Minton's majolica pieces impressed the public at the Great Exhibition of 1851 in London and went on to be very successful.

5in (12.5cm) high

$3,800-4,400   **L&T**

A Minton majolica game pie dish and cover, the cover molded with dead game, with metal liner, impressed date marks, some chips.
c1870   *13in (33cm) wide*
$300 400   **CHEF**

A Minton majolica desk stand, with a hound, grotesque masks, two pen trays, and spaces for an inkwell and pounce pot, impressed "Mintons 1930," some small repairs, with date code.
1876
$2,500-3,200   **BE**

Judith Picks

Paul Comolera (1818-97) was a prominent French sculptor who traveled to work in Stoke-on-Trent in the 1870s to avoid political upheaval in France. He is recorded as working at Minton 1873-76, during which time he produced some of the factory's finest animal models. These were typically covered with a majolica glaze of rich bright colors inspired by the palette of Renaissance maiolica. Some of these, such as his heron and peacock, are well known. Others, such as this stick stand, are very rarely seen. Despite many chips, the rarity of the stand makes it a valuable piece.

A Minton majolica stick stand, modeled by Paul Comolera, depicting a deer beside a tree trunk, the base impressed "2077" and "P Comoler," severe chipping, back right leg missing, one ear detached.
33in (84cm) high
$20,000 32,000   **DEN**

A majolica oyster stand, in the manner of Minton, some damages throughout.
12in (30.5cm) high
$650-750   **WHP**

A George Jones majolica teapot and cover, modeled as a cockerel, some restoration.
c1875   *11in (28cm) wide*
$3,800-5,000   **WW**

A George Jones majolica pitcher, in the Aesthetic manner, impressed mark, old repair to spout, minor frits.
c1870
$450-550   **HAN**

A George Jones majolica cheese dome and stand, with cow finial, impressed "GJ" monogram, some restoration.
c1875   *10¾in (27cm) high*
$700-800   **WW**

A George Jones & Son majolica teapot and cover, with monkey handle and floral finial, molded registration diamond, restoration to spout.
c1875   *9½in (24cm) wide*
$650-750   **WW**

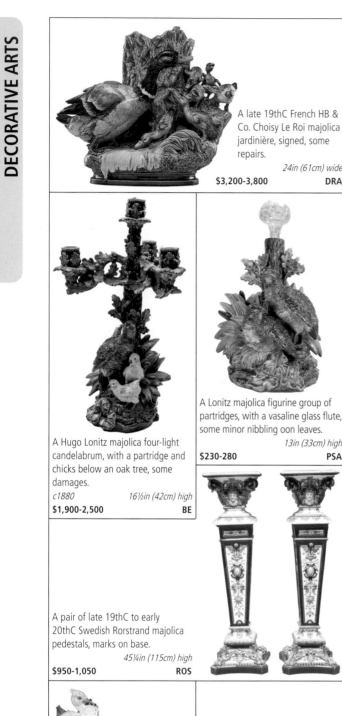

A late 19thC French HB & Co. Choisy Le Roi majolica jardinière, signed, some repairs.

24in (61cm) wide

$3,200-3,800 DRA

A Hugo Lonitz majolica mirror, double fish mark.

c1880 *21in (53.5cm) high*

$1,000-1,250 DRA

A Hugo Lonitz majolica four-light candelabrum, with a partridge and chicks below an oak tree, some damages.

c1880 *16½in (42cm) high*

$1,900-2,500 BE

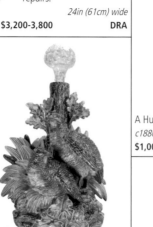

A Lonitz majolica figurine group of partridges, with a vasaline glass flute, some minor nibbling oon leaves.

13in (33cm) high

$230-280 PSA

A late 19thC to early 20thC Jérôme Massier majolica wishing well, modeled with musical frogs, painted "JMF Vallauris" mark, minor damages.

Wells of this type are more commonly seen with songbirds in place of the frogs and are made in several sizes. This one is unusually large.

28¼in (71.5cm) high

$5,000-5,700 WW

A pair of late 19thC to early 20thC Swedish Rorstrand majolica pedestals, marks on base.

45¼in (115cm) high

$950-1,050 ROS

A 19thC majolica pottery heron stick stand, possibly Sarreguemines, some chips and cracks.

48in (122cm) high

$1,900-2,500 CHEF

A early 20thC Cantagalli majolica pedestal basket vase, decorated with Renaissance-style cherubs, and a grotesque griffin, labeled "The gift of her Majesty Queen Victoria to Susan, Duchess of Roxburghe."

20in (51cm) high

$3,800-4,400 FLD

A French majolica group of a Turkish man and woman.

30in (76cm) high

$1,900-2,500 JN

A Martin Brothers stoneware bird tobacco jar, incised "R.W. Martin/ London & Southall," restored, dated.

1880 — *9in (23cm) high*

$23,000-28,000 — **WAD**

A Martin Brothers stoneware bird jar and cover, by Robert Wallace Martin, incised "R W Martin London" to tail feathers, "R.W Martin London & Southall" to head, minor frit chips, dated.

1884 — *13in (33cm) high*

$32,000-38,000 — **WW**

A Martin Brothers grotesque bird, signed "R.W. Martin and Bros London & Southall," dated.

1887 — *8¾in (22cm) high*

$18,000-25,000 — **K&O**

A Martin Brothers stoneware bird tobacco jar, on an ebonized wood base, incised "R.W. Martin & Bros./London & Southall," restored, dated.

1895 — *12½in (32cm) high*

$20,000-25,000 — **WAD**

Judith Picks

Brothers Robert, Edwin, Charles, and Walter Martin began making pottery at their family home in 1873 before setting up in a disused soap works in Southall in 1877. Production continued until 1923.

The brothers handcrafted unusual designs from salt-glazed stoneware. Each had a different role: Robert modeled the figures; Walter threw the pots; Edwin was the decorator, and Charles ran the shop in Holborn. He was known to hide his favorite pots under the floorboards to stop them from being bought.

The creations of the Martin brothers are eccentric and unique, and this tobacco jar is no exception. It is formed as a highly characterised bird, with a large beak and spotted plumage. Waddington auctioneer Bill Kime drove for ten days across Canada in order to bring this item and the collection it belonged to safely to the auction house for sale.

A Martin Brothers stoneware bird tobacco jar, with spotted plumage, incised "R.W. Martin & Bros. London & Southall," dated.

1907 — *8½in (21.5cm) high*

$38,000-44,000 — **WAD**

A Martin Brothers salt-glazed stoneware bird tobacco jar, incised "Martin Bros. London + Southall," dated.

1897 — *10in (25.5cm) high*

$20,000-32,000 — **DRA**

A Martin Brothers stoneware bird jar and cover, by Robert Wallace Martin, incised "R W Martin & Bros London & Southall," dated.

1904 — *10¼in (26cm) high*

$19,000-25,000 — **WW**

A Martin Brothers stoneware bird tobacco jar and cover, by Robert Wallace Martin, incised "R.W. Martin Bros, London, Southall," dated.

1907 — *12½in (31.5cm) high*

$32,000-38,000 — **HALL**

A Martin Brothers stoneware bird jar and cover, by Robert Wallace Martin, on later ebonized base, incised "R W Martin & Bros Southall," dated.

1913 — *7¼in (18.5cm) high*

$14,000-18,000 — **HALL**

A Martin Brothers stoneware bird tobacco jar, on an ebonized wood base, incised "R.W. Martin & Bros., London & Southall," dated.

1914   *9in (23cm) high*

$23,000-28,000   **WAD**

A Martin Brothers salt-glazed stoneware creature tobacco jar, by Robert W. Martin, incised "R.W. Martin + Brothers London," some professional restoration, dated.

1888   *7½in (19cm) high*

$16,000-20,000   **DRA**

A Martin Brothers salt-glazed stoneware grinning grotesque crab, incised "RW Martin + Brothers/ London/6.80 and RW MARTIN," dated.

This was a world record price for a piece of Martin Brothers.

1880   *8 1/8in (21cm) wide*

$320,000-380,000   **PHI**

A Martin Brothers stoneware face pitcher, with a smiling face on each side, incised "R.W. Martin & Bros./ London & Southall," dated.

1897   *9½in (24cm) high*

$7,000-8,000   **WAD**

A Martin Brothers stoneware tobacco jar with cover, by Robert Wallace Martin, with a bemused man's face on each side, the cover formed as a nightcap, repairs, incised "RWM, R.W. Martin & Bros./ London & Southall," dated.

1911   *7¼in (18.5cm) high*

$7,500-9,000   **WAD**

A Martin Brothers stoneware bat wall pocket, incised "R.W. Martin/ Southall."

c1880   *5in (12.5cm) high*

$3,200-3,800   **WAD**

A Martin Brothers stoneware figure of Will Childerhouse, "The Norwich Bellman," inscribed "THE NORWICH BELLMAN 1891," incised "R.W. Martin & Bros. London & Southall," dated.

1900   *6½in (16.5cm) high*

$7,500-9,000   **WAD**

A Martin Brothers stoneware pawn chess piece, modeled as a bust of a soldier in armor, incised "R.W. Martin & Bros., London & Southall," dated.

1902   *3¼in (8cm) high*

$3,200-3,800   **WAD**

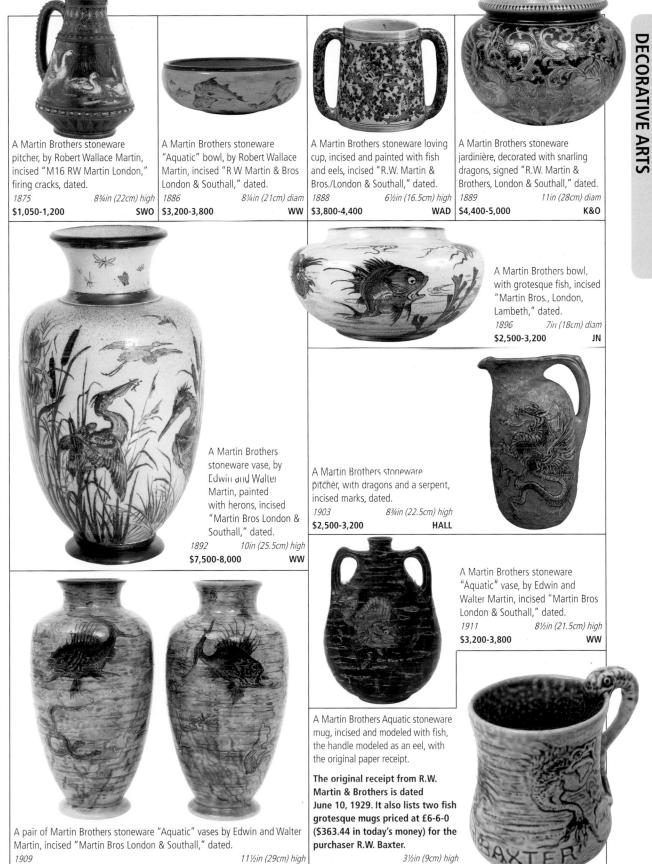

A Martin Brothers stoneware pitcher, by Robert Wallace Martin, incised "M16 RW Martin London," firing cracks, dated.

1875   *8¾in (22cm) high*

$1,050-1,200   **SWO**

A Martin Brothers stoneware "Aquatic" bowl, by Robert Wallace Martin, incised "R W Martin & Bros London & Southall," dated.

1886   *8¼in (21cm) diam*

$3,200-3,800   **WW**

A Martin Brothers stoneware loving cup, incised and painted with fish and eels, incised "R.W. Martin & Bros./London & Southall," dated.

1888   *6½in (16.5cm) high*

$3,800-4,400   **WAD**

A Martin Brothers stoneware jardinière, decorated with snarling dragons, signed "R.W. Martin & Brothers, London & Southall," dated.

1889   *11in (28cm) diam*

$4,400-5,000   **K&O**

A Martin Brothers bowl, with grotesque fish, incised "Martin Bros., London, Lambeth," dated.

1896   *7in (18cm) diam*

$2,500-3,200   **JN**

A Martin Brothers stoneware vase, by Edwin and Walter Martin, painted with herons, incised "Martin Bros London & Southall," dated.

1892   *10in (25.5cm) high*

$7,500-8,000   **WW**

A Martin Brothers stoneware pitcher, with dragons and a serpent, incised marks, dated.

1903   *8¾in (22.5cm) high*

$2,500-3,200   **HALL**

A Martin Brothers stoneware "Aquatic" vase, by Edwin and Walter Martin, incised "Martin Bros London & Southall," dated.

1911   *8½in (21.5cm) high*

$3,200-3,800   **WW**

A pair of Martin Brothers stoneware "Aquatic" vases by Edwin and Walter Martin, incised "Martin Bros London & Southall," dated.

1909   *11½in (29cm) high*

$13,000-19,000   **WW**

A Martin Brothers Aquatic stoneware mug, incised and modeled with fish, the handle modeled as an eel, with the original paper receipt.

The original receipt from R.W. Martin & Brothers is dated June 10, 1929. It also lists two fish grotesque mugs priced at £6-6-0 ($363.44 in today's money) for the purchaser R.W. Baxter.

3½in (9cm) high

$1,150-1,500   **WW**

A pair of late 19thC to early 20thC Minton pâte-sur-pâte vases, by Alboin Birks, on wood bases.

7¾in (19.5cm) high

$5,500-7,000   **PSA**

A late 19thC to early 20thC Minton pâte-sur-pâte vase and cover, on wood base.

Pâte-sur-pâte is a technique where a relief design is created on an unfired vessel by brushing on successive layers of white slip.

vase 9½in (24cm) high

$4,400-5,000   **PSA**

A pair of Minton pâte-sur-pâte pedestal vases, by Albion Birks.

10¾in (27cm) high

$1,500-1,900   **HAN**

A Minton Secessionist plate, with stylised flowering water lilies, printed and impressed marks, crazing, date code.

1910   *15in (38cm) diam*

$1,400-1,800   **SWO**

An Aesthetic movement Minton art pottery charger, printed and impressed marks, painted "LG 42."

c1882   *17in (43cm) diam*

$300-400   **HAN**

A Mintons Aesthetic movement tripod vase, in the Japonesque manner imitating bronze, impressed marks, date code.

1889   *7½in (19cm) high*

$400-500   **BE**

A Minton lidded box, with a Royal Persian turquoise glaze and dragon finial, with Chinese-style decoration, impressed marks, "Minton 1625" and date code.

1872   *12in (30.5cm) high*

$1,600-2,000   **LC**

A set of four Minton's dust pressed tiles, designed by Christopher Dresser, impressed marks, repair to corner of one.

each 8in (20.5cm) square

$800-950   **WW**

A set of four Minton Hollins & Co. two-tile panels, designed by Daniel Cottier, depicting Amor, Mars, Fama, and Fortuna, impressed marks, some damages.

Provenance: Cairndhu House, Helensburgh, Scotland, dining room fireplace. Cairndhu was built in 1871 to designs by William Leiper with the interior design of stained glass and decorative work designed by Daniel Cottier (1838-91).

16¼in (41cm) high

$9,500-10,500   **WW**

An Art Nouveau Minton's plaque, designed by Léon V. Solon, impressed marks and date code, minor chips on corners.

1898   *18in (45.5cm) high*

$4,400-5,000   **WW**

ESSENTIAL REFERENCE—MOORCROFT

Moorcroft was an important 20thC art pottery company.

● **William Moorcroft (1872-1945) began his career at James Macintyre & Co. in Staffordshire in 1897. He was soon running the Macintyre's art pottery studio.**

● **He founded W. Moorcroft Ltd. in 1913. The firm collaborated with Liberty of London and other major retailers. In 1928, William Moorcroft was appointed "Potter to H.M. The Queen."**

● **Moorcroft designs were produced through distinctive tube lining, where outlines of a pattern were piped onto the surface, leaving a low relief outline design that was later filled with colored glaze.**

● **On William Moorcroft's death, his son Walter took over the company. Today, it continues to operate from the factory where it was founded more than 100 years ago.**

A Moorcroft Macintyre "Florian" ware plaque, "Daffodil" pattern, printed mark and painted "M909," painted "W. Moorcroft/des," tiny glaze chip.
c1900
$900-1,000   WAD

A Moorcroft Macintyre miniature vase, "Eighteenth Century" pattern, printed factory mark, painted green monogram.
2½in (6.5cm) high
$400-500   WW

A Moorcroft Macintyre "Florian" ware vase, "Lilac" pattern.
12in (30.5cm) high
$1,150-1,250   PSA

A Moorcroft Macintyre vase, "Pansy" pattern, painted green signature and retailer's mark for Townsend & Co., Newcastle.
c1904-13   *11½in (29cm) high*
$4,400-5,000   BE

A pair of Moorcroft Macintyre "Florian" ware vases, "Iris" pattern, brown Macintyre backstamps, one signed in green "W Moorcroft Des," the other "WM des."
c1898-1906   *11½in (24.5cm) high*
$3,200-3,800   BE

A Moorcroft Macintyre chamberstick, "Poppy" pattern, printed "Macintyre" mark, "Rd. No. 401753" and retailer's mark for Stoner & Co., painted signature "W. Moorcroft/des."
c1904-13
$450-500   WAD

A Moorcroft Macintyre vase, "Scale" pattern, painted marks "W. Moorcroft/Liberty & Co./London-Paris" in green.
c1907   *8in (20.5cm) high*
$3,200-3,800   WAD

A Moorcroft Macintyre "Florian" ware vase, "Violets and Butterfies" pattern, printed "Florian" mark in brown and painted signature "W. Moorcroft/des."
c1900   *8¾in (22cm) high*
$1,000-1,150   WAD

A Moorcroft Macintyre vase, "Wisteria" pattern, printed factory mark, painted green signature, dated.
1913   *8in (20.5cm) high*
$3,800-4,400   WW

A Moorcroft Macintyre silver overlaid teapot, "Claremont" pattern, printed "Rd. No. 420081," painted signature and "8644," cover flange restored, minor loss.
c1905   *6¾in (17cm) high*
$1,900-2,500   WAD

A Moorcroft vase, "Chrysanthemum" or "Revived Cornflower" pattern, painted green signature.

10in (25.5cm) high

$1,900-2,500   **WW**

A Moorcroft vase, "Chrysanthemum" or "Revived Cornflower" pattern, painted green signature, impressed marks, fine stress line to rim.

10¾in (27.5cm) high

$2,300-2,800   **WW**

A Moorcroft vase, "Flambé Claremont" pattern, impressed factory mark, painted signature.

7¾in (19.5cm) high

$2,500-3,200   **WW**

A Moorcroft flambé jar and cover, "Claremont Toadstool" pattern, impressed factory marks and blue painted signature.

c1930   11in (28cm) high

$3,200-3,800   **TEN**

A Moorcroft trumpet-shaped vase, "Dawn" pattern, with flambé luster glaze, impressed mark and blue signature.

9in (23cm) high

$5,500-6,500   **BRI**

An early 20thC Moorcroft vase, "Eventide" pattern, printed "Liberty" mark, impressed "148."

9in (23cm) high

$7,000-7,500   **HT**

A Moorcroft vase, "Eventide" pattern, stamped "MOORCROFT MADE IN ENGLAND with green signature," some scratches.

1918-26   10½in (26.5cm) high

$3,200-3,800   **DRA**

A Moorcroft mat salt glaze vase, "Fish" pattern, underglaze blue signature.

c1928   7¾in (20cm) high

$2,800-3,800   **HAN**

A Moorcroft coffee service, "Hazeldene" pattern, impressed Burslem marks, painted signature in green, minor crack to handle.

c1914-16   9¾in (25cm) high

$2,500-3,200   **WAD**

A Moorcroft vase, "Hazeldene" pattern, painted green signature, printed "Liberty" mark.

6in (15.5cm) high

$2,500-3,200   **WW**

A Moorcroft vase, "Moonlit Blue" pattern, impressed factory mark, painted green signature.

8½in (21.5cm) high

$2,800-3,800 WW

CLOSER LOOK—MOORCROFT TEA SET

This is an unusual Moorcroft tea set, created for Shreve and Company in San Francisco.

Each piece is mounted with silver flowers, with silver handles and rims.

It is tube lined with a green variation of the "Peacock Feather" pattern.

It is incised "W Moorcroft Shreve & Company, San Francisco" on the teapot, and inscribed 'W Moorcroft' on the sucrier and milk pitcher.

A Moorcroft tea set, some crazing, firing crack on teapot, chip on spout.

teapot 6½in (16.5cm) high

$9,000-10,000 SWO

A Moorcroft vase, "Black Peacock Feather" pattern, impressed factory marks, professional restoration to rim.

c1918   *6¼in (16cm) high*

$1,900-2,500 WW

A Moorcroft jardinière, "Persian" pattern, impressed marks, painted green signature.

6½in (16.5cm) high

$2,500-3,200 WW

A Moorcroft squad vase, "Pomegranate" pattern, impressed mark and underglaze green signature.

c1915-18   *7in (18cm) high*

$2,000-2,500 HAN

A Moorcroft "Burslem" vase, "Poppy" pattern.

13in (33cm) high

$5,000-6,300 PSA

A Moorcroft vase, "Tall Trees Landscape" pattern, impressed marks, painted green signature, bruise on foot rim.

9¼in (23.5cm) high

$1,600-2,000 WW

A Moorcroft vase, "Protea" pattern, impressed marks, painted blue signature.

8in (20.5cm) high

$7,500-8,000 WW

A Moorcroft footed bowl, "Waratah" pattern, painted blue signature.

8¾in (22cm) diam

$10,000-11,000 WW

A Newcomb College vase, by Henrietta Bailey (1874-1950), with poppy pods, marked "NC/BO19/HB/JM/Q," remnants of paper label, small fleck on base.

Newcombe College was a woman's art school founded in New Orleans in 1886. Under the tuition of their art professors, its students produced a range of impressive Arts and Crafts pottery until production ceased in 1940. Early pieces from the 1900s, such as this one, are rarer and typically more valuable than later 1920s and 30s pieces.

1907   *9¼in (23.5cm) high*
$19,000-25,000   **DRA**

A Newcomb College bowl, by Mary W. Butler (1873-1937), marked "NC/CD39/MWB/VS," remnants of original paper label, tight lines to rim, stilt pulls to foot.
1908   *10½in (26.5cm) wide*
$8,000-9,000   **DRA**

A Newcomb College vase, by Sadie Irvine (1887-1970), with poppies, marked "NC/SI/OB96/JM," scuffs to body.
1924   *9in (23cm) high*
$2,500-3,200   **DRA**

A Newcomb College scenic vase, by Sadie Irvine, marked "NC/JM/327/SL56/SI."
1930   *5¾in (14.5cm) high*
$2,500-3,200   **DRA**

A Newcomb College vase, by Sara Bloom Levy, marked "NC/BP45/SLB/Q/JM."
1907   *4¾in (12cm) high*
$5,000-5,700   **DRA**

A Newcomb College Transitional vase, by Cynthia P. Littlejohn (d.1959), marked "NC/FQ67/JM/CL/7," the stand with incised "I" in circle.
1913   *8½in (21.5cm) high*
$3,800-4,400   **DRA**

A Newcomb College Transitional chamberstick, by Anna Frances Simpson (1880-1930), incised "SILENTLY ONE BY ONE IN THE INFINITE MEADOWS OF HEAVEN BLOSSOMED THE LOVELY STARS THE FORGET-ME-NOTS OF THE ANGELS," marked "NC/AFS/DK87."
1909   *5in (13cm) wide*
$2,000-2,500   **DRA**

A Newcomb College plate, by Anna Frances Simpson, marked "NC/AFS/FZ81/JM/B," tight hairline and light wear.
1913   *8¾in (22cm) diam*
$1,300-1,800   **DRA**

A Newcomb College scenic vase, by Anna Frances Simpson, marked "NC/150/JM/OC36/FS" with partial paper label.
1924   *10¾in (27.5cm) high*
$7,000-8,000   **DRA**

A Newcomb College lidded jar, by Anna Frances Simpson, marked "NC/SG67/242/JH/AFS," bruise on foot.
1930   *6in (15cm) high*
$2,300-2,800   **DRA**

ESSENTIAL REFERENCE—GEORGE OHR

George Ohr (1857-1918) was an art potter known for his eccentric behavior and highly unusual pieces.

● He was born in Biloxi, Mississippi, where he worked first as a blacksmith, then a file cutter, then a tinker, and then a sailor. In 1879, his childhood friend Joseph Meyer invited him to New Orleans to learn pottery.

● Once back in Mississippi, Ohr dug his own clay from the banks of the Tchoutacabouffa River. With great skill he shaped, and then misshaped, his vessels, folding, denting, crumpling, twisting, and squashing his pots into unique forms.

● Ohr did not confine his eccentricity to unconventional pottery. He called his pots "mud babies" and his workshop the "Pot-Ohr-E." He referred to himself as George Ohr M.D. (mud dauber), George Ohr P.M. (pot maker), "The Unequaled Variety Potter," the "Pot-Ohr," and the "Mad Potter of Biloxi."

● The work of George Ohr is now celebrated and displayed at the Ohr-O'Keefe Museum of Art in Biloxi, Mississippi, designed by architect Frank Gehry.

A George Ohr vase, with ruffled rim and in-body twist, stamped "GEO. E. OHR BILOXI, MISS.," a few chips/flecks oon ruffles.
1895-96   *4¼in (11cm) high*
$5,500-6,500   **DRA**

A George Ohr teapot, with ear handle, stamped "G.E. OHR, Biloxi, Miss."
1897-1900   *8in (20.5cm) wide*
$3,800-4,400   **DRA**

A George Ohr vase, with ribbon handles, raspberry, green, and gunmetal glaze, stamped "G.E. OHR, Biloxi, Miss."
1897-1900   *7¾in (20cm) high*
$60,000-65,000   **DRA**

A George Ohr vase, with in-body twist, speckled and sponged-on ocher, brown, and green glaze, stamped "GEO. E. OHR BILOXI MISS."
1895-96   *6½in (16.5cm) high*
$11,000-12,000   **DRA**

A George Ohr pitcher, with ear handle, stamped "G.E. OHR, Biloxi, Miss."
1897-1900
$16,000-20,000   **DRA**

A George Ohr crumpled vase, stamped "G.E. OHR Biloxi, Miss."
1897-1900   *5in (12.5cm) high*
$12,000-14,000   **DRA**

A George Ohr mug, with ear-shaped handles, gunmetal glaze, glazed-over script signature.
1898-1910   *6in (15.5cm) high*
$7,000-7,500   **DRA**

A George Ohr hat novelty, stamped "G.E. OHR, BILOXI."
1895-96   *4in (10cm) wide*
$8,000-9,000   **DRA**

A George Ohr pitcher, with ear handle, stamped "G.E. OHR, Biloxi, Miss."
1897-1900   *6¾in (17cm) high*
$16,000-20,000   **DRA**

A George Ohr vase, mahogany and gunmetal glaze, stamped "G.E. OHR Biloxi, Miss.," some abrasions.
1897-1900   *6in (15cm) high*
$5,000-5,700   **DRA**

A George Ohr vase, with folded rim, stamped "G.E. OHR, Biloxi, Miss.."
1897-1900   *5½in (14cm) high*
$4,400-5,000   **DRA**

A Pilkington's Lancastrian luster vase, "Apollo," by Gordon Forsyth (1879-1952), inscribed "Apollo," with artist's cipher, impressed factory monogram, "2471/IX/ENGLAND" and date cipher.

This impressive vase is one of the largest pieces ever produced by the factory in luster glazes.

1909   *21¼in (54cm) high*
$60,000-65,000   **L&T**

A Pilkington's Lancastrian vase, by Gordon Forsyth, impressed factory mark, painted artist cipher, date code.
1911   *10¾in (27cm) high*
$4,400-5,000   **WW**

A Pilkington's Lancastrian vase, by Gordon Forsyth, impressed marks, painted artist cipher, date code.
1909   *14½in (37cm) high*
$5,000-6,300   **WW**

CLOSER LOOK—PILKINGTON'S LANCASTRIAN VASE

This vase was designed by Gordon Forsyth, a talented Scottish ceramic designer who worked at Pilkington's c1906-20.

The vase has interesting provenance, from Edward Fielden Pilkington and thence by descent. It was probably a gift from his father, Pilkington's founder Charles Pilkington.

It is an unusually large piece, possibly made for an exhibition.

It is painted with panels of young ladies walking in woodland landscapes.

A Pilkington's Lancastrian vase, impressed marks, painted artist cipher, date code.
1913   *19in (48cm) high*
$23,000-28,000   **WW**

A Pilkington's Lancastrian luster charger, "St. George & The Dragon," designed by Walter Crane, decorated by Richard Joyce (1873-1931), inscribed "CHEVALIER SANS PEUR ET SANS REPROCHE" (the fearless and blameless knight), with date cipher.
1910   *19in (48.5cm) diam*
$50,000-57,000   **L&T**

A Pilkington's Lancastrian luster vase, by Richard Joyce, impressed and painted marks, some crazing, date marks.
1910   *11in (28cm) high*
$11,000-12,000   **DN**

A Pilkington's Lancastrian luster vase, signed "Richard Joyce," date cipher.
1910   *9in (23cm) high*
$3,800-4,400   **K&O**

A Pilkington's Lancastrian luster vase, by Richard Joyce, no.3055, monogram and date cipher.
1913   *6½in (16.5cm) high*
$2,300-2,800   **HAN**

A Pilkington's Lancastrian vase, by William S. Mycock, impressed factory mark, painted artist cipher, date code.
1912   *4½in (11.5cm) high*
$2,300-2,800   **WW**

A Pilkington's Lancastrian dust-pressed "Viking Ship" tile, designed by C.F.A. Voysey, impressed "P" mark, minor glaze frits to edges.
6in (15.5cm) square
$2,800-3,500   **WW**

A Carter's Poole Pottery luster vase, probably designed by Owen Carter, incised "Carter's Poole," dated.
1904   *15in (38cm) high*
$2,300-2,800   **WW**

A Carter's Poole Pottery luster vase, probably designed by Owen Carter, small chip to base rim.
                          7½in (19cm) high
$2,300-2,800   **WW**

A Carter & Company Poole Pottery luster bowl, decorated by Lily Gilham, impressed "Carter's Poole" mark.
                    10¾in (27cm) diam
$1,300-1,800   **WW**

A Carter Stabler & Adams Poole Pottery "Persian Deer" vase, designed by Truda Adams, painted by Margaret Holder, shape no.911, pattern SK, impressed marks, painted marks and artist monogram.
                    8½in (21.5cm) high
$700-800   **WW**

A Carter Stabler and Adams Poole Pottery red earthenware shape number 621/NT vase, designed by Truda Adams, impressed and painted marks.
                    10½in (26.5cm) high
$190-250   **SHEF**

A Carter Stabler and Adams Poole Pottery red earthenware vase, painted by Truda Rivers, pattern ZA, with stylized leaves and flowers.
1922-32   *10¾in (27cm) high*
$190-250   **SHEF**

A Carter Stabler and Adams Poole Pottery red earthenware vase, painted by Ann Hatchard, pattern ZB, impressed and painted marks.
1918-36   *11¼in (28.5cm) high*
$700-750   **SHEF**

A Poole Pottery shape 966 vase, by Ruth Pavely, pattern BR, impressed and incised marks, painted artist cipher.
                    9¾in (24.5cm) high
$750-900   **WW**

A Carter Stabler Adams Poole Pottery vase, impressed pottery marks.
1921-24   *10¼in (26cm) high*
$250-320   **ROS**

ESSENTIAL REFERENCE—ROOKWOOD

Rookwood was founded in 1880 in Cincinnati, Ohio, by Maria Longworth Nichols Storer. It began as a hobby, but soon became one of the most important art potteries in the country.

● Different glazes were used by Rookwood throughout its history. The "Standard" glaze was introduced in 1884. The "Iris," "Sea Green," and "Aerial Blue" glazes were introduced in 1894. The "Vellum" glaze was introduced in 1904.

● Rookwood pieces are marked with a flame logo, and several numbers and letters, ciphers for the year of production, the piece's shape, its glaze, and its artist.

● Rookwood suffered during the Depression. It filed for bankruptcy in 1941, and has changed ownership many times since.

A Rookwood "Vellum" vase, by Lenore Asbury (1866-1933), flame mark, "XXX/904C/V/L.A."
1930   *12in (30.5cm) high*
$4,400-5,000   **DRA**

A Rookwood "Green Vellum" vase, by Sallie Coyne (1876-1939), flame mark, "VIII/904E/SEC/GV," fine crazing.
1908   *7¼in (18.5cm) high*
$1,600-2,000   **DRA**

A Rookwood "Banded Iris Glaze" vase, by Sallie Coyne, flame mark, "X/907DD/SEC," some crazing.
1910   *10¼in (26cm) high*
$1,800-2,300   **DRA**

A Rookwood special-order "Iris Glaze" vase, by Edward T. Hurley (1869-1950), flame mark, "III/S1611A" artist's signature, minor underglaze imperfection.
1903   *19in (48.5cm) high*
$5,500-6,500   **DRA**

A Rookwood winter scenic "Vellum" vase, by Edward T. Hurley, with flame mark and "XV/1660A/V/ETH," fine crazing.
1915   *16½in (42cm) high*
$5,000-5,700   **DRA**

A Rookwood "Jewel Porcelain" vase, by Edward T. Hurley, flame mark, "XXV/ETH/2818," missing lid, crazing, burst glaze bubbles.
1925   *17¼in (44cm) high*
$3,800-4,400   **DRA**

A Rookwood "Black Iris" vase, by Sara Sax (1870-1949); flame mark, "III/905BB/SX/W," minor crazing, some scratches.
1903   *13in (33cm) high*
$3,800-5,000   **DRA**

A Rookwood "French Red" vase, by Sara Sax, with peacock feathers, flame mark, "XXII/2247C/SX," minor scratches.
1922   *13½in (34cm) high*
$15,000-19,000   **DRA**

A Rookwood "Ivory Jewel Porcelain" vase, by Sara Sax, flame mark, "XXVII/927D/SX," scratches, one area of abrasions.
1927   *9in (23cm) high*
$1,150-1,400   **DRA**

A Rookwood "Iris Glaze" vase, by Carl Schmidt (1885-1969), flame mark, "IIII/S1745/W" and artist's cipher.

1904   *3½in (34cm) high*

$7,000-7,500   **DRA**

A Rookwood "Iris" glaze vase, by Carl Schmidt, flame mark, "VII/905C/W/CS," some scratches.

1907   *10in (25.5cm) high*

$3,500-4,000   **DRA**

A Rookwood "Iris Glaze" vase, by Carl Schmidt, flame mark, "XI/CS/950D/W," some crazing, tiny burst glaze bubbles, faint scratches.

1911   *8in (20.5cm) high*

$4,400-5,000   **DRA**

A Rookwood "Marine Scenic Vellum" vase, by Carl Schmidt, flame mark, "XXIV/1358C/V," artist's cipher, some bubbles.

1924   *10¾in (27.5cm) high*

$2,500-3,200   **DRA**

A Rookwood "Standard Glaze" American Indian portrait vase, "Lone Elk Sioux," by Adeliza Sehon (d.1902), with flame mark, "I/904D/ADS/Lone Elk Sioux," original retailer label, some crazing.

1901   *8in (20.5cm) high*

$4,400-5,000   **DRA**

A Rookwood "Iris" glaze vase, by Kataro Shirayamadani (1865-1948), flame mark, "VI/907D," artist's cipher, some crazing, some scratches.

1906   *10¼in (26cm) high*

$5,000-6,300   **DRA**

A Rookwood "Double Vellum" vase, by Kataro Shirayamadani, flame mark, "XXXIII/S," artist's cipher.

1933   *7½in (19cm) high*

$900-1,000   **DRA**

A Rookwood "Iris" glaze vase, by Harriet Wilcox (1869-1943), flame mark, "I/531E/HEW," some crazing.

1901   *5½in (14cm) high*

$700-800   **DRA**

A Rookwood carved mat production vase, flame mark, date, and model, some glaze flecks.

1902   *10in (25.5cm) high*

$700-800   **DRA**

A rare Roseville "Rozane Olympic" hydria, "The Hours Taking the Horses from Juno's Car," marked "ROZANE OLYMPIC POTTERY" with title.

Roseville was founded in Zanesville, Ohio, in 1890 and was closed in 1954.

c1910   *14in (35.5cm) high*
$5,000-5,700   **DRA**

A rare Roseville "Della Robbia" volute krater, body incised "G.B.," professional restoration to chip.

c1910   *17½in (44.5cm) high*
$5,500-6,500   **DRA**

A Roseville mat green jardinière and pedestal, two hairlines.

c1910   *12in (30.5cm) high*
$1,000-1,150   **DRA**

A Roseville "Mostique" jardinière with pedestal.

1915   *10in (25.5cm) high*
$1,050-1,200   **DRA**

A Roseville "Sunflower" jardinière and pedestal, bruise on interior rim.

1925   *10in (25.5cm) high*
$1,150-1,250   **DRA**

A Roseville "Sunflower" vase.

1930   *10in (25.5cm) high*
$750-900   **DRA**

A 1930s Roseville experimental "Nasturtium" vase, small chip and hairline on base.

8in (20.5cm) high
$650-750   **DRA**

A Roseville "Pine Cone" jardinière and pedestal, stamped.

1935   *29in (73.5cm) high*
$800-950   **DRA**

A Roseville "Pine Cone" umbrella stand, raised mark.

1935   *20in (51cm) high*
$1,050-1,200   **DRA**

ESSENTIAL REFERENCE—RUSKIN

Ruskin pottery was founded in Birmingham in 1897-98 by Edward Richard Taylor and his son William Howson Taylor.

- Howson Taylor experimented with a number of techniques, creating revolutionary glazes, including metallic luster glazes and unusual sang-de-boeuf glazes. Some glazes were graduations of two colors, others textured multicolored patterns. His glazes were leadless and the decoration was hand painted.
- The factory struggled in the Depression and finally closed in 1935. Before its closure, the formulae for every glaze was destroyed to ensure that Howson Taylor's work could never be replicated.
- Ruskin pieces are currently on the rise in value, especially those with interesting glazes.

An early 20thC Ruskin Pottery globe and shaft vase, with a mottled and streaked green soufflé glaze, impressed marks.

1911   *10¼in (26cm) high*
$1,050-1,200   **FLD**

A Ruskin Pottery vase, with a speckled blue soufflé glaze, impressed marks.

1916   *13¾in (35cm) high*
$500-650   **FLD**

A Ruskin Pottery high-fired stoneware vase, by William Howson Taylor, purple glaze with turquoise and mint spots, impressed marks, dated.

1906   *7¾in (20cm) high*
$3,800-4,400   **WW**

A 1920s Ruskin Pottery vase, in mottled lavender over a sang-de-boeuf glaze, impressed "Ruskin, England."

            13¾in (35cm) high
$5,500-6,500   **HT**

A Ruskin Pottery high-fired vase, in speckled sang-de-boeuf glaze, impressed marks, dated.

1906   *5in (13cm) high*
$800-950   **K&O**

A Ruskin Pottery vase, in an iridescent kingfisher blue-type luster glaze, impressed marks, dated.

1922   *6in (15cm) high*
$550-650   **FLD**

A Ruskin Pottery high-fired barrel vase, with a red and lavender glaze with copper green spotting, the rim and handles with sang-de-boeuf spotting, impressed marks, dated.

1933   *9¾in (25cm) high*
$1,500-1,900   **FLD**

A Ruskin Pottery high-fired vase, in sang-de-beouf with lavender sweeping and copper spotting glaze, impressed marks, incised 'W. Howson Taylor" and "THIN."

            15¾in (40cm) high
$3,800-4,400   **FLD**

A Ruskin Pottery high-fired vase, shape no.1921, with a mottled purple glaze with the odd pale blue spot, impressed marks on base, minor firing imperfections.

            8¾in (22.5cm) high
$1,300-1,800   **PW**

A Van Briggle vase, with spider and Native American symbols, incised "AA VAN BRIGGLE 1902 III/15," glaze bubbles, minor scuffs.
1902   *5in (12.5cm) high*
$2,500-3,200   **DRA**

A Van Briggle vase, with geese, marked 'AA VAN BRIGGLGE/1903/III/B/5," tiny burst glaze bubbles.
1903   *7in (18cm) high*
$9,000-10,000   **DRA**

A Van Briggle vase, incised "AA VAN BRIGGLE 1903 III/181," some peppering.
1903   *4¾in (12cm) high*
$2,300-2,800   **DRA**

A Van Briggle vase, with Virginia creepers, marked "AA Van Briggle/1904/V/164," scuffs and metal transfer marks.
1904   *8in (20.5cm) high*
$2,500-3,200   **DRA**

A Van Briggle peacock-feather vase, marked "AA VAN BRIGGLE 1904/V/104," burst glaze bubbles, crazing to base.
1904   *11in (28cm) high*
$3,200-3,800   **DRA**

A Van Briggle vase, with tulips, marked "AA VAN BRIGGLE," numbered "68," dated.
1905   *7½in (19cm) high*
$1,300-1,800   **DRA**

A Van Briggle bowl, marked "AA Van Briggle/1905/387."
1905   *11in (28cm) wide*
$1,500-2,000   **DRA**

A Van Briggle gourd vase, signed "AA VAN BRIGGLE/VX/1905/319."
1905   *5in (13cm) high*
$700-800   **DRA**

A Van Briggle vase, incised "AA VAN BRIGGLE COLORADO SPRINGS."
1908-11   *9¼in (23.5cm) high*
$3,800-4,400   **DRA**

A 1910s Van Briggle copper-clad vase, marked "AA Van Briggle Colo Spgs 690."
6¾in (17cm) high
$1,900-2,500   **DRA**

ESSENTIAL REFERENCE—FAIRYLAND LUSTRE

Wedgwood's distinctive Fairyland lustre range was designed by Daisy Makeig-Jones (1881-1945) from 1915-29.

● Makeig-Jones studied at Torquay School of Art, before becoming a tableware painter and designer at Wedgwood in 1909.

● She decorated her Fairyland lustre series with colorful scenes of fantastical lands and magical kingdoms, featuring goblins, sprites, spirits, and other supernatural beings.

● These wares were very popular during and just after WWI, but had fallen out of fashion by the late 1920s.

● Today, they are valued by collectors, with the rarer patterns fetching high values.

A 1930s Wedgwood Fairyland lustre bowl, "Gargoyle" pattern on exterior, "Bird in a Hoop, Rainbow Landscape" on interior, green mark, inscribed "Z496F."

7½in (19cm) wide

$3,800-4,400 HT

A Wedgwood Fairyland lustre Malfrey vase and cover, "Ghostly Wood" pattern, with Portland vase in gold, incised "Shape No. 2312," pattern no.Z4968.

This vase comes with its original receipt, dated "January 27, 1926," which increases its value.

c1926 *13in (33cm) high*

$34,000-38,000 SWO

A Wedgwood Fairyland lustre charger, "Ghostly Wood" pattern, no.Z4968, printed "Wedgwood" mark to base.

15¼in (38.5cm) diam

$23,000-32,000 WW

A pair of Wedgwood Fairyland lustre porcelain vases, "Butterfly Woman" pattern, no.Z4968, with mythical creatures and winged maidens within trees.

9½in (24cm) high

$10,000-11,000 HANN

A 1920s Wedgwood Fairyland lustre bowl, "Geisha" or "Angels" pattern, no.Z4968, Portland Vase mark.

6½in (16.5cm) diam

$3,200-3,800 FLD

A Wedgwood Fairyland lustre shape 2046 vase, "Ghostly Wood" pattern, printed gilt Portland Vase factory mark, painted "Z4968/i," incised "2046," some firing faults.

15¼in (38.5cm) high

$9,500-10,500 TEN

A Wedgwood Fairyland lustre vase, "Goblin" pattern, with Portland Vase mark and "Wedgwood Made in England."

7in (18cm) high

$11,000-14,000 JDJ

A Wedgwood "Flame Daventry" lustre vase, pattern no.Z5413, gilt marks.

Provenance: Ann Makeing-Jones, direct descendant of Josiah Wedgwood I, niece of Daisy Makeing-Jones.

c1926 *7¾in (20cm) high*

$1,900-2,500 HAN

A Wedgwood Fairyland lustre bowl, "Jumping Faun" and "Garden of Paradise" patterns, printed marks, some rubbing to gilt, some crazing.

8in (20.5cm) diam

$2,300-2,800 PW

A Wedgwood Fairyland flame lustre vase, "Pillars" pattern, printed marks.

c1925   *14¼in (36cm) high*

$5,500-7,000   **K&O**

A pair of Wedgwood Fairyland coral and bronze lustre vases with covers, "Rainbow" pattern, no.Z5349, marked.

9in (23cm) high

$3,800-5,000   **HAN**

A Wedgwood Fairyland lustre vase, "Sycamore Tree with Feng Hwang and Bridge" pattern, no.Z5360, gilt marks.

8in (20.5cm) high

$2,000-2,500   **HAN**

A Wedgwood Fairyland lustre plate, "Thumbelina" pattern, with a "Twyford" border, with Portland vase mark "Wedgwood Made in England."

10½in (26.5cm) diam

$6,500-7,500   **JDJ**

A pair of Wedgwood Fairyland lustre shape 3177 vases, "Torches" pattern, the foot and rim interior with "Flaming Wheel" pattern, gold Portland Vase mark and painted "Z4968," one with glued sections on rim.

11½in (29cm) high

$6,500-7,500   **BE**

A pair of Wedgwood shape 3150 vases, "Willow" pattern, no.Z5228, gold-printed marks, black enameled pattern.

8in (20.5cm) high

$3,500-4,400   **GORL**

A Wedgwood Fairyland lustre "K'ang Hsi" bowl, "Woodland Bridge" pattern to exterior, "Garden of Paradise" pattern to interior, highlighted in gilt, printed, and painted marks.

7in (18cm) diam

$2,500-3,800   **WW**

A Wedgwood Fairyland lustre pedestal bowl, "Woodland Bridge" pattern, no.Z4968, printed and painted marks.

7¾in (20cm) diam

$3,200-3,800   **DUK**

A 1920s Wedgwood Fairyland lustre bowl, "Woodland Elves VII—Toadstool" pattern on exterior, "Fairy in a Cage" pattern on interior, "WEDGWOOD ENGLAND" gilt stamp, marked "Z4968," fleck on foot ring, some scratches.

9½in (24cm) wide

$2,800-3,500   **DRA**

A set of Wedgwood Jasperware chess pieces, based on the figures from Macbeth, chip on the blue bishop.

Wedgwood chess sets can fetch high values, because they have an appeal beyond pottery collectors. This set was first designed by John Flaxman in the late 18thC and reproduced from the original mold.

max 4¼in (11cm) high

$3,800-5,000   **PSA**

A Wedgwood "Taurus Bull," by Arnold Machin.

designed c1957   *14¼in (36cm) long*

$200-250   **HAN**

A Wedgwood Pottery vase, by Keith Murray, model no.3820, covered in a "Moonstone" mat white glaze, impressed, printed marks, and facsimile signature.

6¾in (17cm) high

$500-650   **WW**

A Wedgwood mat green vase, by Keith Murray, "KM" monogram.

9in (23cm) high

$300-400   **HAN**

A Wedgwood "Boat Race" bowl, by Eric Ravilious, limited edition no.7/250, boxed with book on Ravilious's designs.

This bowl was originally designed in 1937, then reissued 1986 to mark 50th anniversary of Ravilious's first employment by Wedgwood in 1936.

1986   *12in (30.5cm) diam*

$750-900   **CHOR**

A Wedgwood Pottery vase, by Keith Murray, shape no.3805, printed factory mark, "KM" monogram, minor professional restoration to base rim.

11in (28cm) high

$400-500   **WW**

A Wedgwood bachelor's nine-piece tea set, "Afternoon Tea" pattern, by Eric Ravilious (1903-42), printed marks, minor scratches.

designed 1937   *teapot 6½in (16.5cm) wide*

$4,400-5,000   **GORL**

A Wedgwood King Edward VIII 1937 coronation mug, by Eric Ravilious, model no.CL.6203, printed and painted factory marks.

4¼in (10.5cm) high

$1,300-1,900   **WW**

A Wedgwood turquoise glazed bowl, by Norman Wilson, with moonstone glaze on exterior, impressed and printed "NW."

8¼in (21cm) diam

$150-200   **HAN**

A Weller "Fru-Russett" vase, with eagle, rooster, and hen, signed "Flickens," incised "Weller," some chips and scuffs.

Weller Pottery was founded by Samuel A. Weller (1851-1925) in Fultonham, Ohio, in 1872. The company relocated to Zanesville in 1888. It originally produced tiles and plain pots, before launching its first art pottery line in 1893. Production continued until shortly after the end of World War II.

c1905   6in (15cm) high
$8,000-9,500   DRA

A Weller "Fru-Russett" vase, with nude male and grapevines, body incised "E. Pickens," the base incised "Weller," chip under rim, minor efflorescence.

c1905   18in (45.5cm) high
$7,000-8,000   DRA

A Weller "Dickensware" umbrella stand, by Edward Abel (1868-1937), stamped, etched signature, two chips on inner rim, some minor scratches.

26in (66cm) high
$800-950   DRA

A Weller pitcher, by Jacques Sicard (1863-1925), glazed-over marks.
1903-17   10in (25.5cm) high
$2,000-2,500   DRA

A Weller vase, by Jacques Sicard, base signed "WELLER SICARD."
1903-17   15in (38cm) high
$2,000-2,500   DRA

A Weller pitcher, by Jacques Sicard, with maiden and grape clusters, signed "Sicard Weller," minor glaze flakes.
1903-17   22½in (57cm) high
$3,200-3,800   DRA

A Weller floor vase, by Jacques Sicard, signed, base stamped "WELLER," minor abrasions.
1903-17   23in (58.5cm) high
$5,000-6,300   DRA

A Weller Hudson floor vase, by Hester Pillsbury, signed, manufacturer stamp on base, some scuffs.
1917-34   27in (68.5cm) high
$5,000-6,300   DRA

A Weller Hudson floor vase, by Hester Pillsbury, signed, incised manufacturer mark on base, some glaze losses.
1917-34   24½in (62cm) high
$1,900-2,500   DRA

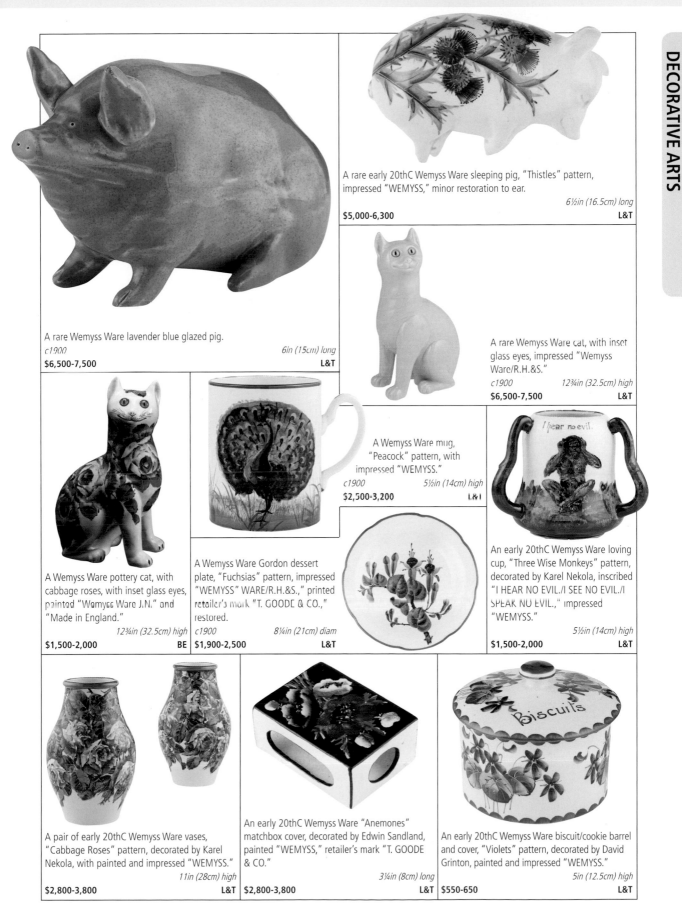

A rare early 20thC Wemyss Ware sleeping pig, "Thistles" pattern, impressed "WEMYSS," minor restoration to ear.

6½in (16.5cm) long

$5,000-6,300 L&T

A rare Wemyss Ware lavender blue glazed pig.
c1900   *6in (15cm) long*
$6,500-7,500 L&T

A rare Wemyss Ware cat, with inset glass eyes, impressed "Wemyss Ware/R.H.&S."
c1900   *12¾in (32.5cm) high*
$6,500-7,500 L&T

A Wemyss Ware pottery cat, with cabbage roses, with inset glass eyes, painted "Wemyss Ware J.N." and "Made in England."
12¾in (32.5cm) high
$1,500-2,000 BE

A Wemyss Ware mug, "Peacock" pattern, with impressed "WEMYSS."
c1900   *5½in (14cm) high*
$2,500-3,200 L&T

A Wemyss Ware Gordon dessert plate, "Fuchsias" pattern, impressed "WEMYSS" WARE/R.H.&S.," printed retailer's mark "T. GOODE & CO.," restored.
c1900   *8¼in (21cm) diam*
$1,900-2,500 L&T

An early 20thC Wemyss Ware loving cup, "Three Wise Monkeys" pattern, decorated by Karel Nekola, inscribed "I HEAR NO EVIL./I SEE NO EVIL./I SPEAK NO EVIL.," impressed "WEMYSS."
5½in (14cm) high
$1,500-2,000 L&T

A pair of early 20thC Wemyss Ware vases, "Cabbage Roses" pattern, decorated by Karel Nekola, with painted and impressed "WEMYSS."
11in (28cm) high
$2,800-3,800 L&T

An early 20thC Wemyss Ware "Anemones" matchbox cover, decorated by Edwin Sandland, painted "WEMYSS," retailer's mark "T. GOODE & CO."
3¼in (8cm) long
$2,800-3,800 L&T

An early 20thC Wemyss Ware biscuit/cookie barrel and cover, "Violets" pattern, decorated by David Grinton, painted and impressed "WEMYSS."
5in (12.5cm) high
$550-650 L&T

ESSENTIAL REFERENCE—ZSOLNAY

The Zsolnay factory in Pecs, southwest Hungary, was founded in 1853.

● In 1885, it acquired the Fischer factory, which had been founded in 1867 and manufactured similar ceramics. Both companies looked to the Persian and Chinese for influence in their designs.

● From the 1890s, Zsolnay developed an eosin process to produce iridescent porcelain.

● They also manufactured frost-resistant ceramics used for buildings, which were particularly popular during the Art Nouveau period, producing ornate roof tiles, such as on St. Matthais Church in Budapest.

● The company was nationalized under Communism, but it regained its independence in 1982 and continues to manufacture porcelain today.

A pair of 19thC Zsolnay vases, with painted and gilded arabesque designs, pattern no.1027, rubbing to gilding.

23½in (60cm) high

$15,000-20,000   **B&H**

A Zsolnay ceramic vase, by Julia Zsolnay (1856-1950), with gilt detailing, printed underglaze blue spire mark, impressed "877."

c1883   *16¼in (41cm) high*

$3,200-3,800   **ROS**

A Zsolnay eosin-glazed vessel, with lizards and cut-out rim, five churches mark, "6436/M," original paper price tag, some scratches.

c1900   *11½in (29cm) wide*

$32,000-38,000   **DRA**

A Zsolnay eosin-glazed vase, with bird skulls, five churches mark, stamped "6157/26/36," professional restoration to one chip.

c1900   *7¾in (20cm) high*

$8,000-9,500   **DRA**

A Zsolnay eosin-glazed tulip-shaped vase, five churches mark, impressed "6174/M," small touch-ups and wear to foot.

c1900   *6¾in (17cm) high*

$3,200-3,800   **DRA**

A Zsolnay eosin-glazed vase, with water lilies and reeds, five churches mark, impressed "6009/M/22," some scratches.

c1900   *11in (28cm) high*

$13,000-18,000   **DRA**

A Zsolnay eosin-glazed vase, five churches mark, impressed "M/5994/23," some grinding flakes, short scratches.

c1900   *13in (33cm) high*

$15,000-20,000   **DRA**

A Zsolnay eosin-glazed vase, five churches mark, impressed "7300," professional restoration.

c1904   *19in (48.5cm) high*

$6,500-7,500   **DRA**

An early 20thC Zsolnay eosin-glazed vase, with a lobster and coral, five churches mark, impressed "M 6177 23," some damages.

Despite the damage, the appearance and look of this vase assures its value. Fieldings' expert Will Farmer said of this vase: "Collectors of different ceramics react differently to damage... the Hungarians put much less weight on the condition of Zsolnay than on the look and rarity of an object."

9¾in (25cm) high

$7,500-9,000   **FLD**

An Arequipa vase, by Frederick H. Rhead, blue pot under tree mark, marked "AREQUIPA CALIFORNIA/1912/506A," grinding chip on base.
1912   6¼in (16cm) high
$90,000-110,000   DRA

CLOSER LOOK—RENÉ BUTHAUD VASE

This vase is the work of French Art Deco ceramicist René Buthaud (1886-1986).

He was heavily influenced by African tribal art, as is reflected in this vase.

One side is incised and glazed with a woman holding a bowl.

The reserve is decorated with a styliszd crocodile and fish.

An Art Deco ceramic vase and cover, painted "RB" monogram on base.
c1925   23¾in (60.5cm) high
$44,000-50,000   ROS

An Arequipa vase, by Frederick H. Rhead (1880-1942), blue pot under tree mark.
c1911-13   5in (12.5cm) wide
$32,000-38,000   DRA

An Ault vase, designed by Christopher Dresser, shape 319, feint impressed facsimile signature.
11½in (29cm) high
$350-430   PW

A Boch Frères Keramis urn, by Charles Catteau (1880-1966), with African farm scene, with "Ch. Catteau" stamp, "BOCH FRERES KERAMIS MADE IN BELGIUM" wolf stamp, impressed "1297," signed "D.2299," minor scuffs to body
designed 1937   14½in (37cm) high
$5,000-6,300   DRA

A Boch Frères Keramis glazed earthenware vase, decorated with penguins, circular black "BOCH FRERES" stamp, signed "D1104," minor scratches.
designed 1927   11¾in (30cm) high
$1,800-2,300   DRA

An Dutch Art Nouveau Brantjes Faience De Purmerend vase, no.1077, painted with a bird of prey, painted and signed marks.
14in (35.5cm) high
$1,500-2,000   DUK

A Cantagalli pottery Iznik charger, painted cockerel mark, minor glaze loss to rim.
15½in (39.5cm) diam
$3,500-4,000   WW

DECORATIVE ARTS

Judith Picks

The "Jazz" series began in 1921, when Eleanor Roosevelt commissioned Cowan to make a punch bowl for her husband, Franklin D. Roosevelt, then governor of New York, later president of the country. She liked the bowl so much that she immediately ordered two more. Because the design was very much admired, Cowan produced a small series of similar bowls. Cowan's pieces epitomize American Art Deco style.

A Cowan glazed earthenware "Jazz" bowl, by Viktor Schreckengost (1906-2008), artist's signature, base stamped "COWAN," professional restoration to chips.
1931   *13¾in (35cm) diam*
$15,000-19,000   **DRA**

A Paul Dachsel vase, Turn-Teplitz, Bohemia, restored drill hole to base.
c1905   *15¾in (40cm) high*
$1,500-2,000   **DRA**

A French oxblood and turquoise glazed stoneware vase, by Pierre-Adrien Dalpayrat (1844-1910), signed, minor grinding chips.
c1900   *11½in (29cm) high*
$5,000-6,300   **DRA**

A glazed stoneware vase, by Pierre-Adrien Dalpayrat, with partial oxblood glaze, incised "Dalpayrat," impressed "717," some touch-ups.
c1900   *10¾in (27.5cm) high*
$1,500-2,000   **DRA**

A Della Robbia bowl, by Annie Smith, inscribed "Au Revoir," dated.
1896   *10½in (26.5cm) diam*
$700-800   **PW**

A Della Robbia two-tile panel, designed by Ford Madox Brown, by Emily Margaret Wood, incised and painted marks, "EMW" monogram, incised "3/98."

The panel has a paper label on the reverse stating that the figure is Archangel Michael, designed by Ford Madox Brown for Morris & Co. and made by his pupil Harold Rathbone at the Della Robbia Pottery. It is actually from Ford Madox Brown's design of Gideon for a stained-glass window by Morris & Co. at St Martins on the Hill, Scarborough. The window depicts Joshua, Saint Michael, and Gideon and was designed in 1862.
c1898   *panel 27½in (70cm) high*
$10,000-11,000   **WW**

A Della Robbia Pottery candlestick, by Marian de Caluwe, painted "DR," "MdeC," and "5," incised "241," with X cipher.
14¾in (37.5cm) high
$11,000-14,000   **WW**

An Etling Art Deco group of children, by Marcel Guillard and Alexandre Kelety, marked, paper retail label, some crazing.
9¾in (24.5cm) high
$650-750   **BELL**

A pair of Gallé faience vases, inscribed "E. Gallé a Nancy," some chips, wear to gilding.
c1900   *8¾in (22cm) high*
$450-550   **BELL**

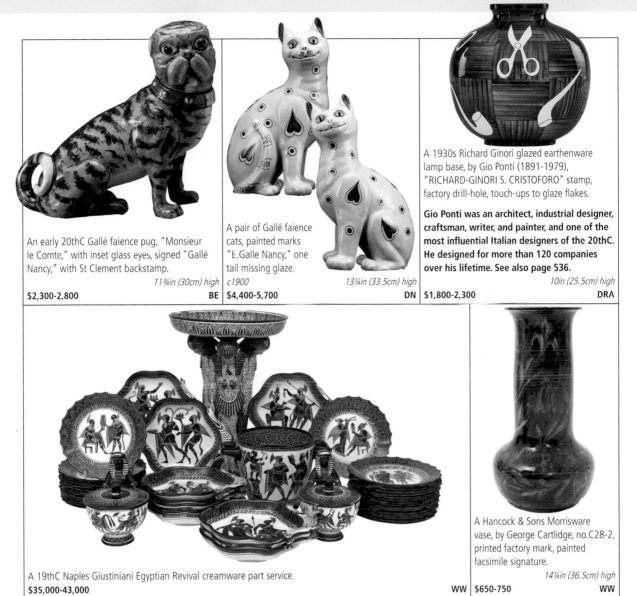

An early 20thC Gallé faience pug, "Monsieur le Comte," with inset glass eyes, signed "Gallé Nancy," with St Clement backstamp.

11¾in (30cm) high

$2,300-2,800   BE

A pair of Gallé faience cats, painted marks "E.Galle Nancy," one tail missing glaze.

c1900   *13¼in (33.5cm) high*

$4,400-5,700   DN

A 1930s Richard Ginori glazed earthenware lamp base, by Gio Ponti (1891-1979), "RICHARD-GINORI S. CRISTOFORO" stamp, factory drill-hole, touch-ups to glaze flakes.

Gio Ponti was an architect, industrial designer, craftsman, writer, and painter, and one of the most influential Italian designers of the 20thC. He designed for more than 120 companies over his lifetime. See also page 536.

10in (25.5cm) high

$1,800-2,300   DRA

A 19thC Naples Giustiniani Egyptian Revival creamware part service.

$35,000-43,000   WW

A Hancock & Sons Morrisware vase, by George Cartlidge, no.C28-2, printed factory mark, painted facsimile signature.

14¼in (36.5cm) high

$650-750   WW

A Hancock & Sons Morrisware vase, by George Cartlidge, no.C27-28, printed and painted marks, facsimile signature.

12¼in (31cm) high

$500-650   WW

A German Karlsruhe enamel-decorated faience vase, by Max Laeuger (1864-1952), tube lined with leaves, marks "PROF. LAUGER" and "Karlsruhe," deaccession number, tight interior hairline, chip on base.

post-1916   *13½in (34cm) high*

$2,000-2,500   DRA

A Langenzersdorfer Keramik earthenware model, "Arrogance," by Eduard Klabena, signed "EK, 114."

c1913-14   *10¾in (27cm) high*

$7,500-9,000   QU

A glazed earthenware vase, by Émile Lenoble, with stamp mark, signed in red "1926.25."

c1930   *11½in (29cm) high*

$3,800-5,000   DOY

A 1930s Longwy glazed earthenware "Atlas" vase, by Maurice-Paul Chevallier (1892-1987), titled, with marks, flaw on inner rim in the making, crazing lines on interior.

15in (38cm) high

$4,400-5,000   DRA

A 1920s Marblehead vase, by Arthur Baggs (1886-1947) and Sarah Tutt (1859-1947), stamped ship mark "MP," incised "AB/T."

4½in (11.5cm) wide

$1,900-2,500   DRA

CLOSER LOOK—MAW & CO. VASE

Maw & Co. of Jackfield, Shropshire, UK, was best known for its mass production of earthenware tiles and architectural ceramics. Arts and Crafts pieces, such as this vase, were a real departure for the firm.

It is painted with dolphins and scenes from the Odyssey, and finished in a distinctive iridescent ruby glaze.

The vase, designed by Walter Crane, is formed as a galley with a swan-head prow and fish tail stern.

This example is in perfect condition.

A Maw & Co. vase, signed.
c1889   *9¼in (23.5cm) high*

$13,000-15,000   K&O

An early 20thC Marblehead vase, by Arthur Hennessey and Sarah Tutt, stamped ship mark "MP," signed "HT."

3½in (9cm) high

$1,600-2,300   DRA

A Clement Massier vase, by M. Alexandy, marked and signed.

12½in (32cm) high

$1,900-2,500   CHEF

A Maw & Co. dust-pressed tile, by Walter Crane, "Vesper," from the Times of the Day series, monogrammed "WC."

8in (20.5cm) square

$400-450   FLD

A French glazed and gilt stoneware vase, by Jean Mayodon (1893-1967), impressed "MJ," "Rouard" retailer paper label, minor rim chips, losses to gilding.

c1940   *14¼in (36cm) high*

$5,000-5,700   DRA

A Merrimac vase, some restoration, flecks on edges of feathers.

The Merrimac Pottery Company was founded in Newburyport, Massachusetts, by Thomas Nickerson in 1902. The company made garden pottery, art pottery, and reproductions of Roman pottery, and it was known for its luster, crackled, and mat glazes. The pottery burned down in 1908.

c1905   *7¾in (20cm) high*

$3,800-4,400   DRA

A Merrimac vase, with crystalline glaze, incised "M/III," some flakes.

c1905   *5in (12.5cm) high*

$3,200-3,800   DRA

A Bernard Moore flambé temple jar and cover, the lid with Chinese symbol, signed and monogram "HL."

12½in (32cm) high

$2,800-3,500   HAN

A faience pottery pug, probably made by Mitterteich, Max Emanuel & Co., with glass eyes.

These dogs and cats are often referred to as Mosanic Pottery. Mosanic Pottery was a trade mark used by Max Emanuel & Co. for products made exclusively for the London store.

c1900   *11¾in (30cm) high*

$350-400   TEN

An early 20thC Gallé-style white pottery cat, probably by Mosanic/Max Emanuel & Co., with glass eyes.

13in (33cm) high

$500-650   BE

A 1900s Norse Pottery vase, with modeled lizard, stamped "Norse/25," some scuffs and scratches.

The Norse Pottery Works was based in Edgerton, Wisconsin. It operated c1903-13, run by Danish immigrant potters Louis Ipson and Thorwald Samson. They took inspiration from ancient Scandinavian artifacts.

12in (30.5cm) high

$1,300-1,800   DRA

A North Dakota School of Mines vase, by Julia Mattson, Grand Forks, North Dakota, blue "NDSM" stamp, incised "JM 466."

1930   *4½in (11.5cm) diam*

$1,500-2,000   DRA

A North Dakota School of Mines glazed earthenware vase, by Margaret Cable, blue "NDSM" stamp, signed "MKC 1917/#41."

1917   *8½in (21.5cm) high*

$9,000-10,000   DRA

A rare Redlands Pottery burnished earthenware covered jar, with lizard, marked.

c1905   *3in (7.5cm) wide*

$10,000-11,000   DRA

A 1900s porcelain vase, by Adelaide Robineau (1865-1929), with crystalline glaze, carved "AR 4 III/X."

2½in (6.5cm) high

$5,000-6,300   DRA

A Rorstrand glazed earthenware floor vase, by Alf Wallander (1862-1914), triple crown mark, marked "A. WALLANDER/99," minor scratches.

This was possibly an exhibition piece.

c1899   *29½in (75cm) high*

$5,000-6,300   DRA

An early 20thC Rosenthal figurine, marked "Ferd Liebermann."

14¼in (36cm) high

$1,300-1,800　　　　**PSA**

A pair of Royal Dux Bohemia porcelain figures, by Edward Eichler, pink triangle, the male impressed "1183," the female "1184."

max 31in (79cm) high

$500-650　　　　**BE**

A Royal Dux dancing girl, by Elly Strobach, with pink triangle, impressed and printed marks.

c1925　　*11¾in (30cm) high*

$750-900　　　　**BELL**

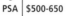

A Royal Dux porcelain figure, pink triangle mark, impressed "CZECHOSLOVAKIA/3268/2."

c1930　*12¼in (31cm) high*

$1,300-1,900　　　　**L&T**

An Art Deco Royal Dux group, no.3046, red triangle mark, impressed marks.

14½in (37cm) high

$650-750　　　　**DUK**

A 1930s Royal Worcester figurine, "Bubbles," by Freda Doughty, modeled as a young girl holding up a glass bubble with a basket of bubbles by her side, puce mark with date code, painted title.

1938　*7in (18cm) high*

$300-400　　　　**FLD**

An Art Nouveau Rozenburg eggshell porcelain vase, painted by S. Schellink, printed factory marks, painted marks, and artist's cipher.

3¼in (8cm) high

$2,300-2,800　　　　**WW**

An Art Nouveau Rozenburg eggshell porcelain plate, painted by S. Schellink, printed factory mark, painted marks, artist's cipher.

6½in (16.5cm) diam

$2,500-3,200　　　　**WW**

Judith Picks

Saturday Evening Girls pieces, such as this, sprung from a club founded in Boston, Massachusetts, in 1899 by librarian Edith Guerrier. Guerrier wanted to educate poor young women in the liberal arts and provide them with a safe and skilled way of earning a living. With the help of Helen Storrow and Edith Brown, by 1908 the Saturday Evening Club had become the Paul Revere Pottery Club.

The pieces made by the Saturday Evening Girls are, like this vase, simple and elegant in design, often making use of natural imagery. Patterns were applied with cuerda seca (Spanish for "dry cord"), a method using thin lines of grease to prevent colored glazes from running into one another.

A Saturday Evening Girls vase, Paul Revere stamp "DECEMBER 1930 SR," marked "BSE," some misses to glaze.

1930　*13½in (34.5cm) high*

$18,000-25,000　　　　**DRA**

A Saturday Evening Girls vase, by Fannie Levine, signed and dated.

1921   *8¼in (21cm) high*

$7,000-8,000   **DRA**

A Teco reticulated vase, stamped "TECO."

The American Terra Cotta Tile and Ceramic Company, or Teco, was founded in 1881 and based in Terra Cotta, Illinois.

c1905   *11¾in (30cm) high*

$5,500-7,000   **DRA**

A rare Teco vase, by Fritz Albert (1865-1940), stamped "TECO," professionally repaired break near top of one leaf, minor scuffs.

c1910   *14in (35.5cm) high*

$38,000-44,000   **DRA**

A Teco vase, in a rare semimat green crystalline glaze, stamped "TECO," restoration to one petal.

c1910   *12in (30.5cm) high*

$3,200-3,800   **DRA**

A Teco blue lobed vase, stamped "TECO," glaze fleck, short line on rim.

c1910   *9in (23cm) high*

$1,000-1,150   **DRA**

A Tiffany Studios Favrile pottery vase, incised "LCT," minor dark scuffs.

1904-19   *12¼in (31cm) high*

$9,500-10,500   **DRA**

A Charles Vyse model of a Pekingese dog, in tenmoku brown glaze, incised "Charles Vyse Chelsea."

                                  6¾in (17cm) wide

$2,800-3,300   **WW**

A Chelsea pottery figure, "The Tulip Woman," by Charles Vyse, initialed, marked "Chelsea," some losses, the base stained, some crazing, dated.

1921   *10¾in (27.5cm) high*

$500-650   **CHEF**

An Art Deco Wilkinson vase, by John Butler, "Tahiti foam" pattern, signed, with painted and printed marks, some crazing.

                                 14¼in (36cm) high

$400-500   **BELL**

DECORATIVE ARTS

A vessel, by Michael Cardew (1901-83), marks for Cardew and St Ives pottery.

This piece was made when Cardew was working with Bernard Leach.

c1922   8¼in (21cm) high

$1,600-2,000   **CHOR**

A tin-glazed Wenford Bridge pottery plate, by Michael Cardew, impressed seal marks.

9¾in (25cm) diam

$750-900   **WW**

A pair of Compton Pottery garden urns, designed by Archibald Knox (1864-1933), for Liberty & Co., mark, one missing a handle, large chips to rims.

c1900   29½in (75cm) wide

$2,800-3,500   **GORL**

A Compton Pottery terra-cotta jardinière, designed by Archibald Knox, for Liberty & Co.

c1905   23¾in (60.5cm) high

$1,150-1,400   **ROS**

The Compton Pottery was an Arts Guild founded in the village of Compton, England, in 1900 by Mary Watts (1849-1938). Its work was stocked by Liberty & Co. After the death of its founder, the Guild continued until 1956.

A slab-built vase, by Shoji Hamada (1894-1978), wax-resist decorated in tenmoku over pale celadon.

7¾in (19.5cm) high

$5,000-6,300   **WW**

A St Ives Pottery stoneware "Leaping Salmon" vase, by Bernard Leach (1887-1979), painted in tenmoku on a gray glaze, impressed seal marks.

11½in (29.5cm) high

$12,000-14,000   **WW**

A St Ives Pottery plate, by Bernard Leach, painted in blue and tenmoku on a celadon ground, with tenmoku rim, impressed seal mark and painted "BL" monogram.

10¾in (27cm) diam

$2,500-3,800   **WW**

A St Ives Pottery stoneware slab vase, by Bernard Leach (1887-1979), with tenmoku glaze, impressed "BL" and "Leach Pottery" seals under foot.

7¾in (20cm) high

$2,800-3,500   **L&T**

A stoneware "Aulos," by William Staite Murray (1881-1962), impressed seal mark, painted "MA2," museum repair to one handle.

10¾in (27.5cm) high

$1,800-2,300   **WW**

A stoneware vase, by Katherine Pleydell-Bouverie (1895-1985), impressed seal mark.

8½in (21.5cm) high

$1,150-1,400   **WW**

A pâte-de-verre glass "Parma Violets" pattern vase, by Gabriel Argy-Rousseau, signed, "FRANCE" on base.

Gabriel Argy-Rousseau (1885-1953) was a prominent glass artist and founder of the Société Anonyme des Pâtes de Verre d'Argy-Rousseau. The firm produced a range of Art Nouveau and Art Deco pieces, many using the technique of pâte-de-verre.

introduced 1918   *6in (15cm) high*
$6,500-7,500   **CHEF**

A pâte-de-verre glass vase, by Gabriel Argy-Rousseau, molded mark "G. ARGY-ROUSSEAU."

c1920   *7¾in (19.5cm) high*
$2,300-2,800   **L&T**

A liqueur glass, by Gabriel Argy-Rousseau, signed "Argy-Rousseau."

1922   *2¼in (5.5cm) high*
$950-1,000   **ROS**

A small pâte-de-cristal "Blackberries" bowl, by Gabriel Argy-Rousseau, signed "G Argy-Rousseau."

c1914   *4in (10cm) diam*
$800-950   **ROS**

A pâte-de-verre vase, by Gabriel Argy-Rousseau, with molded prunus blossoms, signed "G. Argy-Rousseau" and "5487."

6½in (16.5cm) high
$5,500-6,500   **MORP**

A pâte-de-verre glass bowl, by Gabriel Argy-Rousseau, signed in the mold.

introduced 1925   *4in (10cm) wide*
$1,500-2,000   **CHEF**

A pâte-de-verre glass bowl, by Gabriel Argy-Rousseau, signed, some damages.

c1927   *8¼in (21cm) wide*
$1,600-2,000   **FLD**

An enameled glass bowl, by Gabriel Argy Rousseau, decorated with deer, gilt signature, some scratches and wear.

7¾in (19.5cm) wide
$1,300-1,800   **CHEF**

A pâte-de-verre "fleur ouverte" ashtray, by Gabriel Argy-Rousseau, with dark grey fusions, signed "G. ARGY-ROUSSEAU."

1924   *3¾in (9.5cm) diam*
$1,900-2,500   **QU**

A pâte-de-verre "Edelweiss" pendant, by Gabriel Argy-Rousseau, marked "G.A.R," with three holes for cord and tassel.

1924   *2¾in (7cm) high*
$1,500-2,000   **QU**

ESSENTIAL REFERENCE—DAUM

The Daum glassworks was founded in 1878 in Nancy, France, by Jean Daum. His sons Auguste and Antonin Daum took over the factory in 1890s. Daum is still active today.

- The brothers focused on art glass, introducing their cameo glasswares at the Chicago World Fair in 1893. Cameo glass is a technique where multiple layers of glass are carved to achieve a design in low relief.
- Alongside cameo glass, the Daum brothers used a range of techniques, including acid etching, wheel turning, pâte de verre (where crushed glass is packed into molds and fused in a kiln) and "intercalaire" (where powdered glass is sealed between layers of glass).
- The Daum brothers were inspired by the Art Nouveau and later Art Deco movements, and they combined these influences with natural imagery and Asian and Far Eastern inspiration. They were also greatly influenced by the work of Émile Gallé.

A Daum "Pluviose" or "Une pluie" vase, by Henri Bergé, etched with birches in the rain, signed "DAUM NANCY" with Cross of Lorraine.
1900   *3¼in (8.5cm) high*
$4,400-5,000   **QU**

A Daum enameled glass vase, with winter landscape, signed.
c1905   *4¾in (12cm) high*
$2,300-2,800   **K&O**

A Daum "Neige, Corbeaux" vase, with a winter landscape with ravens, signed "Daum Nancy" with Cross of Lorraine.
1905   *4½in (11.5cm) high*
$7,000-8,000   **QU**

A Daum "Winter Scene" vase, with a cameo and enamel scene, signed "Daum Nancy" with Cross of Lorraine.
14½in (37cm) high
$8,000-9,500   **JDJ**

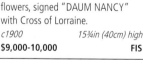

A Daum "Iris et Papillon" vase, with silver mounts, signed "Daum Nancy" with Cross of Lorraine, with Head of Minerva and maker's mark.
1893   *8½in (21.5cm) high*
$3,200-3,800   **QU**

A Daum vase, etched with datura flowers, signed "DAUM NANCY" with Cross of Lorraine.
c1900   *15¾in (40cm) high*
$9,000-10,000   **FIS**

A Daum cameo and enameled "Blackbird" vase, etched "Daum Nancy" with Cross of Lorraine.
6¼in (16cm) high
$12,000-14,000   **MORP**

A rare Daum "Corbeau et Grenouille" (raven and frog) cameo vase, signed "Daum Nancy" with Cross of Lorraine.
14in (35.5cm) high
$15,000-19,000   **JDJ**

A Daum vase, with lady's slipper orchids, spider webs, and bees, acid etched "DAUM NANCY" with Cross of Lorraine, minor losses to gilding, one fleck to rim.
c1900   *21in (53.5cm) high*
$8,000-9,000   **DRA**

An early 20thC Daum cameo vase, with dogwood blossoms, signed in cameo, some bubbles.
7¾in (20cm) high
$1,050-1,200   **DRA**

An early 20thC Daum acid-etched vase, wheel-carved signature, chip on inner rim.

7in (18cm) high

$7,500-9,000   DRA

A Daum vase, etched in relief, signed "DAUM NANCY FRANCE" with Cross of Lorraine.

c1910   19in (48cm) high

$6,500-7,500   FIS

CLOSER LOOK—DAUM "CROCUS" VASE

This Daum vase is an unusual shape.

The colors of the vase shift from mottled purple to yellow to lavender.

It is wheel carved with purple cameo leaves and stems.

The design is over a martelé (hammered) textured background.

A Daum "Crocus" vase, signed in the cameo "Daum Nancy" with Cross of Lorraine.

12in (30.5cm) high

$19,000-25,000   MORP

An early 20thC Daum acid-etched cameo vase, signed in cameo.

3in (7.5cm) high

$1,300-1,800   DRA

A Daum vase, etched in flat relief with primroses, etched "DAUM NANCY FRANCE" with Cross of Lorraine.

c1910-15   11in (28cm) high

$7,000-8,000   FIS

A Daum vase, etched with tobacco plants, signed "DAUM NANCY" with Cross of Lorraine, etched "73."

c1914   12½in (32cm) high

$4,400-5,700   FIS

A Daum cameo glass "Geranium" vase, etched signature "Daum/ Nancy" with the Cross of Lorraine.

8in (20.5cm) high

$5,000-6,300   CLAR

A Daum "Libellules et Renoncules Jaunes" vase, by Henri Bergé and Ernest Schneider, signed "DAUM NANCY" with Cross of Lorraine.

c1904   7¾in (20cm) high

$10,000-11,000   QU

A late 19thC Daum pitcher, acid etched, gilded, and enameled internally with nightshade, gilt signature, minor losses to gilding.

5½in (14cm) high

$3,800-4,400   DRA

A Daum acid-etched cameo glass "Mushroom" pitcher, etched with maker's mark.

c1900   5¼in (13.5cm) high

$7,500-8,000   CA

ESSENTIAL REFERENCE—ÉMILE GALLÉ

Émile Gallé (1846-1904) was an important Art Nouveau glass designer.

- He was born in Nancy, France, and studied botany, chemistry, philosophy, art and glassmaking before joining his father's factory.
- He founded his own studio in 1873. Early works were usually clear glass with gilded or enameled decoration.
- In 1878, Gallé visited the International Exhibition in Paris and was impressed by the cameo glass of English makers Joseph Locke and John Northwood. He switched his own focus to cameo glass, with great success.
- His factory continued after his death in 1904, run by his widow and son-in-law until 1936.

A Gallé "Indien" vase, signed "E. Gallé Nancy."
c1875   7½in (19cm) diam
$5,500-7,000   QU

A Gallé "Cerfeuil hérisse" vase, with etched, painted, and enameled decoration, signed "E. Gallé Nancy."
c1889-95   5in (12.5cm) high
$5,000-6,300   QU

A late 19thC Gallé vase, enameled with purple irises, enamel signature.
c1890   8in (20.5cm) high
$3,200-3,800   FLD

A Gallé vase, marbled in brown, black, and violet, with algae, shells, and sea life engraved in relief.
c1895   11in (28cm) high
$44,000-50,000   FIS

A late 19thC Gallé bud vase, acid etched, enameled and martelé decorated, etched signature.
               5½in (14cm) high
$4,400-5,000   DRA

A pair of late 19thC Gallé Japonesque bottles, enameled and gilded, foot of one reduced, minor flecks to stoppers.
               8¾in (22cm) high
$20,000-32,000   DRA

A late 19thC Gallé cameo glass vase, acid etched and enameled, ornate floral etched signature "Émile Gallé Pour bonheur."
               6in (15cm) high
$11,000-12,000   DRA

A late 19thC to early 20thC Gallé cameo vase, acid etched and fire polished with an aquatic scene, signed in cameo, tiny flecks to rim.
               9½in (24cm) high
$9,500-10,500   DRA

A Gallé vase, inscribed "LES ARBRES SE PARLENT TOUT BAS" (the trees speak to each other), signed "Gallé."

The quote is from Victor Hugo's poem "Aux Arbres."
c1900   18in (46cm) high
$5,500-7,000   QU

A Gallé vase, with marquetry crocus flowers and stems, with etched Asian-style signature "Gallé" and "Etude," some stress lines.

8½in (21.5cm) high

$11,000-13,000   **MORP**

An early 20thC Gallé cameo vase, acid etched with roses, signed in cameo.

14½in (37cm) high

$1,300-1,800   **DRA**

An early 20thC Gallé oleander acid-etched cameo vase, signed in cameo, minor scuffs, metal transfer marks.

18in (45.5cm) high

$5,000-6,300   **DRA**

An early 20thC Gallé cameo vase, acid etched with poppies, signed in cameo, some scuffs.

24¾in (63cm) high

$11,000-13,000   **DRA**

A 1920s Gallé "Le Lac de Côme le Soir" (Lake Como at Night) vase, signed "Gallé."

14in (35.5cm) high

$20,000-32,000   **QU**

A 1920s Gallé lemon-yellow soufflé vase, with plums and leafy branches, signed.

12½in (32cm) high

$9,000-10,000   **FIS**

A Gallé cameo Japanese cherry blossom vase, signed with ornate Asian-style signature "Gallé."

15in (38cm) high

$5,500-7,000   **JDJ**

A Gallé boat-shaped cameo vase, signed "Gallé."

7½in (19cm) long

$2,500-3,200   **JDJ**

A Gallé tulip-shaped bowl, acid etched, fire polished, and gilded, gilt signature to base, some losses to gilding.

c1900   *8¼in (21cm) wide*

$8,000-9,500   **DRA**

A Lalique clear and frosted electric blue glass "Perruches" vase, no.876, etched "R. Lalique France," some flecks.

designed 1919   10in (25.5cm) high
$14,000-18,000   **DRA**

A Lalique cased glass "Poissons" vase, molded "R. LALIQUE," etched "R. Lalique FRANCE," minor bubbles, some flecks and chips.

designed 1921   10in (25.5cm) wide
$13,000-18,000   **DRA**

A Lalique clear and frosted glass "Acanthes" vase, etched "R. Lalique France," some bubbles.

designed 1921   11¼in (28.5cm) high
$12,000-14,000   **DRA**

A Lalique cased glass "Druide" vase, etched "R. Lalique France No.937," rim uneven, residue to interior.

designed 1924   7¾in (20cm) wide
$4,400-5,000   **DRA**

CLOSER LOOK—"MARTIN-PÊCHEURS"

This vase is molded with birds among stylized foliage.

It is made of blue-violet glass, with a white patina.

"Martin-Pêcheurs" is the French term for Kingfisher.

This is one of only two known examples in this color.

A Lalique glass "Martin-Pêcheurs" vase, no.920, molded "R. LALIQUE," some nicks.

designed 1923   9½in (24cm) high
$20,000-32,000   **DRA**

A Lalique amber glass "Sophorai" vase, with white patina, etched "R. Lalique France No.977," some burst bubbles.

designed 1926   9½in (24cm) high
$11,000-14,000   **DRA**

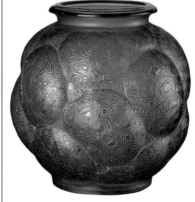

A rare Lalique Alexandrite glass "Tortues" vase, no.966, molded "R. Lalique," stenciled "R. LALIQUE FRANCE," flecks to base.

designed 1926   10½in (26.5cm) high
$32,000-38,000   **DRA**

A Lalique "Salmonides" vase, with blue-gray patina, acid stamped "R. LALIQUE FRANCE."

designed 1928   11½in (29cm) high
$19,000-25,000   **DRA**

A Lalique glass "Milan" vase, acid stamped "R. LALIQUE," some scratches near base.

designed 1929   11¼in (28.5cm) high
$15,000-19,000   **DRA**

A Lalique cased glass "Espalion" vase, etched "R. Lalique mark" and numbered "996."

7in (18cm) high
$6,500-7,500   **CHEF**

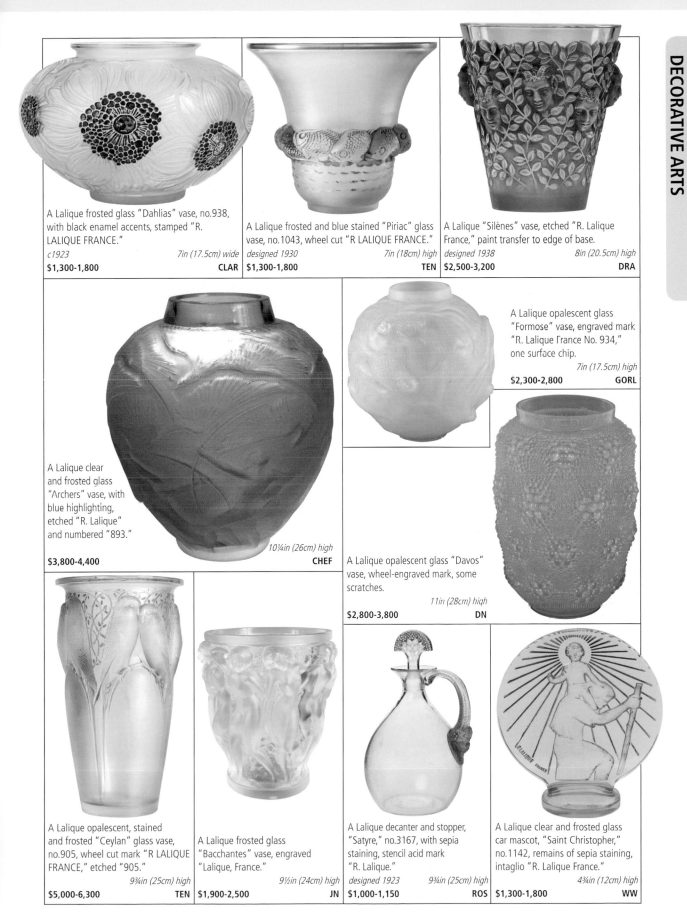

A Lalique frosted glass "Dahlias" vase, no.938, with black enamel accents, stamped "R. LALIQUE FRANCE."
c1923   *7in (17.5cm) wide*
$1,300-1,800   **CLAR**

A Lalique frosted and blue stained "Piriac" glass vase, no.1043, wheel cut "R LALIQUE FRANCE."
designed 1930   *7in (18cm) high*
$1,300-1,800   **TEN**

A Lalique "Silènes" vase, etched "R. Lalique France," paint transfer to edge of base.
designed 1938   *8in (20.5cm) high*
$2,500-3,200   **DRA**

A Lalique clear and frosted glass "Archers" vase, with blue highlighting, etched "R. Lalique" and numbered "893."
10¼in (26cm) high
$3,800-4,400   **CHEF**

A Lalique opalescent glass "Formose" vase, engraved mark "R. Lalique France No. 934," one surface chip.
7in (17.5cm) high
$2,300-2,800   **GORL**

A Lalique opalescent glass "Davos" vase, wheel-engraved mark, some scratches.
11in (28cm) high
$2,800-3,800   **DN**

A Lalique opalescent, stained and frosted "Ceylan" glass vase, no.905, wheel cut mark "R LALIQUE FRANCE," etched "905."
9¾in (25cm) high
$5,000-6,300   **TEN**

A Lalique frosted glass "Bacchantes" vase, engraved "Lalique, France."
9½in (24cm) high
$1,900-2,500   **JN**

A Lalique decanter and stopper, "Satyre," no.3167, with sepia staining, stencil acid mark "R. Lalique."
designed 1923   *9¾in (25cm) high*
$1,000-1,150   **ROS**

A Lalique clear and frosted glass car mascot, "Saint Christopher," no.1142, remains of sepia staining, intaglio "R. Lalique France."
4¾in (12cm) high
$1,300-1,800   **WW**

ESSENTIAL REFERENCE—LOETZ

Loetz was a significant 19thC and early 20thC Bohemian glass manufacturer.

- In 1852, a glassworks factory in Klostermühle, Bohemia, was acquired by Susanne Loetz, widow of the glassmaker Johann Loetz. The factory became known as Loetz Witwe (Loetz Widow) and later just as Loetz.
- In 1879, it was taken over by Max Ritter von Spaun, whose innovative ideas and strong team of designers made Loetz one of Central Europe's largest glassmakers by the turn of the century.
- Many Loetz pieces use iridescence and Art Nouveau decoration.
- The factory closed in 1947.

A Loetz red to cream vase, enameled with blooming dogwood, enameler's marks to base.
c1888   *9in (23cm) high*
$550-650   **M&DM**

A pair of early Loetz blue opal pieced top vases, with floral enamel and gilding.
c1890   *9in (23cm) high*
$750-900   **M&DM**

A pair of Loetz "Octopus" vase, "Federzeichnung" pattern with gilded tracery, inscribed "Patent" to base, losses to gilding.
c1887   *6¼in (16cm) high*
$2,500-3,200   **POOK**

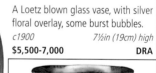

A Loetz "Rubin Phaenomen Gre 8100" vase, with iridescence, engraved to base "Loetz Austria."
1899   *6¾in (17cm) high*
$11,000-12,000   **FIS**

A Loetz blown glass vase, with silver floral overlay, some burst bubbles.
c1900   *7½in (19cm) high*
$5,500-7,000   **DRA**

A Loetz "Papillon" (butterfly wing) vase, made for Max Emanuel, London, after a design by Christopher Dresser.
c1900   *6in (15cm) high*
$400-500   **M&DM**

A Loetz "Phaenomen Gre 2/450" vase, in rare pink or "rosalin" color variant, etched "Loetz Austria" to base, tiny burst bubble.
c1900   *7in (18cm) high*
$5,000-6,300   **DRA**

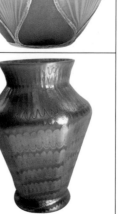

A Loetz candia (gold-green) "Phaenomen" vase, no.7506, signed "Loetz Austria."
c1900   *7½in (19cm) high*
$2,300-2,800   **M&DM**

A Loetz "Phaenomen" vase, with iridescent decoration, signed "Loetz Austria."
    9½in (24cm) high
$13,000-15,000   **MORP**

A Loetz "Cytisus" vase, with wavy band pattern and iridescent oil spots, unsigned.
c1902   7¾in (20cm) high
$4,400-5,000   JDJ

A Loetz "Cytisus" green, pink, and red iridescent vase.
1902   14¼in (36.5cm) high
$2,500-3,200   FIS

An early 20thC Loetz iridescent glass vase, etched "Loetz Austria."
          8¾in (22cm) high
$700-800   LSK

A Loetz "Titania" vase, with green metallic threads between two layers of glass, fleabite to rim.
c1907   7½in (19cm) high
$1,900-2,500   MORP

A Loetz "Titania Perl" vase attributed to Otto Prutscher (1880-1949).
c1908   7in (18cm) high
$5,000-6,300   DRA

A Loetz vase, designed by Josef Hoffmann, overlaid etched violet floral decoration on a blue opal ground.
c1911   8in (20.5cm) high
$27,000-38,000   FIS

A Loetz vase, designed by Adolf Beckert, painted by Franz Wilms, enameled with a peacock design.
1911   11in (28cm) high
$5,000-6,300   FIS

A Loetz vase, etched with a hazelnut branch, etched "Velez."
c1925   8¾in (22.5cm) high
$1,600-2,300   FIS

A Loetz red on uranium green cameo panel rose vase.
c1925   7in (18cm) high
$1,500-1,900   M&DM

A pair of Loetz "Blau an Kamelienrot" vases.

This is a newly discovered Loetz design.
c1925   11in (28cm) high
$2,850-3,500   M&DM

A Monart "Paisley Shawl" glass vase, shape C, with slight iridescence, remains of paper label "V.C.55."

8¾in (22.5cm) high

$1,000-1,150   **ROS**

A Monart cased "Cloisonné" glass vase, shape C.

7¼in (18.5cm) high

$650-750   **ROS**

A Monart vase, shape GA, size VI.

c1935   *6in (15cm) high*

$400-500   **M&DM**

A Monart glass vase, with mottled green graduating to blue with purple whorls and aventurine inclusions.

9¾in (25cm) high

$500-650   **WW**

A Monart vase, shape N, size VI.

c1935   *9in (23cm) high*

$500-650   **M&DM**

A Monart vase, shape OE, size VI.

c1935   *9in (23cm) high*

$450-550   **M&DM**

A 1930s Monart glass vase, in red and blue mottled glass with bubble inclusions, with maker's label and label for the "Parkington Collection/427/Christie's."

10¼in (26cm) high

$1,300-1,800   **L&T**

A Monart "Paisley Shawl" bowl, shape MC, size III.

c1935   *13in (33cm) diam*

$1,000-1,150   **M&DM**

A 1930s Monart glass vase, "Stoneware" pattern, with a luster sheen, with a label for "The Parkington Collection/429/ Christie's."

9¾in (24.5cm) high

$800-950   **L&T**

A Monart glass decanter with stopper and five glasses, printed "Monart" label, all marked "QC-XI."

decanter 11¼in (28.5cm) high

$1,050-1,200   **ROS**

A Moser green to clear "cut out" intaglio cut vase, with poppies and irises.

c1905   *13in (33cm) high*

$2,300-2,800   **M&DM**

An early 20thC Moser marquetry vase, wheel-carved cameo glass, etched manufacturer and artist marks, some flecks and chips.

6½in (16.5cm) high

$1,000-1,150   **DRA**

A 1920s Moser glass vase, with a gilt Oroplastic band of Classical figures, etched mark, scratches to base.

10½in (26.5cm) high

$300-400   **DN**

A Moser "Alexandrit" vase, designed by Heinrich Hussmann, signed "Moser Alexandrit."

c1929   *13in (33cm) high*

$650-750   **M&DM**

A Moser "Lion Hunt" vase, by Gustav Moser-Millot, signed "Moser," with original "Moser-Millot" shop label.

This vase was designed for the Paris 1937 Exhibition and available after exclusively from the Paris Moser shop.

c1937   *10in (25.5cm) high*

$1,000-1,250   **M&DM**

A Moser "Alexandrit" decanter and stopper, signed "Moser Alexandrit"

Alexandrit is a type of glass used by Moser where the color changes depending on light, shifting from purple to blue.

c1929

$650-750   **M&DM**

A Moser "Alexandrit" decanter and stopper, designed by Heinrich Hussmann, signed "Moser Alexandrit."

c1929   *14in (35.5cm) high*

$650-750   **M&DM**

A 1930s Moser glass decanter, with a facet-cut spire stopper, acid marked.

17¾in (45cm) high

$300-400   **FLD**

A set of eight Moser green to clear wine glasses, enameled and applied jewels.

1897   *5in (12.5cm) high*

$1,300-1,500   **M&DM**

ESSENTIAL REFERENCE—ERCOLE BAROVIER

Ercole Barovier (1889-1974) joined his father's company, Artisti Barovier, in 1919 at the age of 30, giving up a career as a physician to focus on art glass.

● He became artistic director of the firm in 1926 and took over management in 1936. After the company's merger with Ferro-Toso in 1942, he remained artistic director until 1972.

● Over his career, he experimented with original and innovative methods, inventing new formulas and dies and perfecting new techniques to create impressive works of art glass.

● His memorable pieces included murine vessels, his 1929 "Primavera" series, his 1930s "Crepuscolo" and "Marina Gemmata" series, and his 1940s organic textured shapes in thick-walled glass.

An Artisti Barovier "Murrine Applicate" vase, cristallo sfumato glass with applied polychrome murrine, signed "AB" with murrine.
c1918-19   *11¾in (30cm) high*
$65,000-80,000   **WRI**

An Artisti Barovier "Murrine Floreali" vase, internally decorated glass with rose and leaf murrine and polychrome threads.
c1920   *11½in (29cm) high*
$32,000-38,000   **WRI**

A Ferro Toso Barovier "Crepuscolo" glass vase, by Ercole Barovier, with iron wool inclusions.
1935-36   *14in (35.5cm) high*
$9,000-10,000   **QU**

A Ferro Toso Barovier "Medusa" vase, by Ercole Barovier, of iridized glass with applications.
1938   *18in (46cm) high*
$24,000-30,000   **WRI**

A Barovier & Toso "Oriente" vase, by Ercole Barovier, cased glass with fused colored ribbons and dark purple on burst gold foil.
c1940   *11in (28cm) high*
$15,000-19,000   **QU**

A Barovier, Toso & Co. "Lenti" vase, by Ercole Barovier, with semi-spherical applications and gold leaf.
1940   *9¾in (25cm) wide*
$15,000-20,000   **WRI**

A Vetreria Artistica Barovier & C. "Crepuscolo" vase, by Ercole Barovier, model no. 14038, with metal inclusions.
c1940   *11½in (29cm) high*
$6,500-7,500   **PHI**

A Barovier & Toso "A Stelle" vase, by Ercole Barovier.
1942   *14¾in (37.5cm) high*
$5,500-7,000   **QU**

A Barovier Seguso Ferro "Incamiciato" vase, with applied collar and foot with gold leaf.
c1938   *14¼in (36cm) high*
$18,000-23,000   **WRI**

A Fratelli Toso vase, with multicolored melted murrins, the surface stained with acid.

c1910　　　7in (18cm) high

$400-500　　　FIS

A monumental incamiciato vase, by C. Maschio, with applied silver leaf and ribbed pasta di vetro handle.

1932　　　16¼in (41cm) high

$16,000-20,000　　　WRI

ESSENTIAL REFERENCE—VENINI & C.

Venini & C. was an important Murano glassworks throughout the 20thC. Today, it is owned by the Damiani Group.

- It was founded in 1921 as Cappellin Venini & C. by Milanese lawyer Paolo Venini and antiques dealer Cappellin. Cappellin left the company a few years later.
- After much success in the 1920s-30s, Venini & C. went on to become one of the leading postwar Italian glassworks.
- Its important designers included Vittorio Zecchin (1878-1947), Gio Ponti (1891-1979), Naopoleone Martnuzzi (1892-1977), Tomaso Buzzi (1900-81), and Carlo Scarpa (1906-78).

A Venini & C. ribbed pink and clear glass "Diamante" vase, by Paolo Venini, acid stamped "venini murano MADE IN ITALY."

1934-36　　　5in (12.5cm) high

$900-1,000　　　QU

A Venini & C. "Laguna" glass bowl, by Tomaso Buzzi.

1932-33　　　9½in (24cm) diam

$15,000-20,000　　　WRI

A Venini & C. "Soffiato" vase, by Napoleone Martinuzzi, model 3044, acid stamped "Venini Murano" and "C.V.M." with a crown.

c1925-26　　　8½in (21.5cm) diam

$9,000-10,000　　　WRI

A Fratelli Toso "Rosso e Nero" vase, incamiciato glass with silver leaf.

c1930　　　7¼in (18.5cm) high

$7,500-9,000　　　WRI

A Venini & C. "Sommerso a Bollicine" vase, by Carlo Scarpa, with burst gold foil and air bubbles, acid stamped "venini murano."

c1934-36　　　6in (15cm) wide

$4,400-5,700　　　QU

A Venini & C. bubbly "Pulegoso" vase, by Napoleone Martinuzzi, acid stamped "venini murano."

c1930　　　14¾in (37.5cm) high

$8,000-9,500　　　QU

A Venini & C. "A Bolle" bowl, by Carlo Scarpa, acid stamped "venini murano."

c1934　　　14½in (37cm) wide

$550-650　　　QU

A Venini & C. "Corroso" cased glass vase, by Carlo Scarpa, acid stamped "venini murano."

c1936   *11½in (29cm) high*

$15,000-20,000   **QU**

A Venini & C. "Murrina del Serpente" bowl, by Carlo Scarpa, maker's decal "VENINI S.A. MURANO."

1940   *13in (33cm) long*

$11,000-14,000   **QU**

A rare Venini & C. "Inciso Velato" vase, by Carlo Scarpa, model 3791.

1940   *12¾in (32.5cm) high*

$110,000-140,000

WRI

A Venini & C. "Battuto Bicolore" vase, by Carlo Scarpa, acid stamped "venini murano ITALIA."

c1940   *4¼in (11cm) high*

$16,000-23,000   **QU**

A Venini & C. "A Macchie" bowl, by Carlo Scarpa, acid stamped "venini murano ITALIA."

c1942   *11in (28cm) long*

$6,500-7,500   **QU**

A Venini & C. "A Fili" vase, by Carlo Scarpa, model no.4540, with a fili and a fasce decoration, light iridization, acid etched "venini/murano/ITALIA."

c1942   *7in (18cm) high*

$50,000-63,000   **PHI**

A Venini & C. "Soffiato" vase, by Vittorio Zecchin, model 1998.

c1925-26   *13in (33cm) high*

$13,000-18,000   **WRI**

A Venini & C. "Amethyst Soffiato" vase, by Vittorio Zecchin, model 1867, signed "Venini Murano."

c1928   *16¼in (41.5cm) high*

$24,000-28,000   **WRI**

A Zecchin-Martinuzzi "Rosso e Nero" vase, by Napoleone Martinuzzi.

c1932   *11¾in (30cm) high*

$11,000-12,000   **WRI**

A Charles Schneider "Cherries" vase, etched in relief.

Charles Schneider (1881-1953) and his brother Ernest (1877-1937) were raised in Nancy, France. Both brothers worked for Daum before founding the Schneider Glassworks in 1917 in Epinay-sur-Seine.

1918-21   *18in (45.5cm) high*
$1,500-2,000   **FIS**

A Charles Schneider vase, in cased mottled glass with applied jade glass decoration, etched signature with amphora mark.

1918-25   *6in (15cm) diam*
$500-650   **DRA**

A Charles Schneider glass floor vase, etched signature and paper label, some light scratches.

1918-30   *18¾in (47.5cm) high*
$650-750   **DRA**

A Charles Schneider amphora vase, Epinay-Sur-Seine, signed, light scratches.

1918-30   *12in (30.5cm) high*
$650-750   **DRA**

An Art Deco Schneider glass and wrought iron vase, internally decorated, acid stamped "SCHNEIDER" to glass, metal etched "FRANCE," small bruise.

18in (45.5cm) wide
$900-1,000   **DRA**

A 1920s Charles Schneider marbled glass shouldered vase, Epinay-Sur-Seine, signed.

12¼in (31cm) high
$500-650   **DRA**

A Schneider "Le Verre Français" cameo glass vase, acid etched, inset with maker's candy-cane mark.

"Le Verre Français" was a line of art glass made by Schneider Glassworks c1918-32.

c1925   *19½in (49.5cm) high*
$750-900   **ROS**

A Schneider "Le Verre Français" cameo glass vase, acid etched with "Lauriers" motif, signed, small filled hole near base.

c1930   *19in (48.5cm) high*
$500-650   **DRA**

A Schneider "Le Verre Français" cameo glass vase, overlaid and acid etched, signed.

c1930   *25½in (65cm) high*
$1,000-1,150   **ROS**

A Schneider "Le Verre Français" "Poissons" vase, with cameo fish and aquatic plants, on acid-textured frosted background, with internal controlled bubbles, signed "Charder Le Verre Francais."

5½in (14cm) high
$13,000-18,000   **JDJ**

A late 19thC Stevens & Williams cameo glass vase, cut with convolvulus and a butterfly.

Stevens & Williams was established in Stourbridge, England, in 1847. In the early 1880s, under manager John Northwood and designer Frederick Carder, Stevens & Williams created new art glass ranges. It received a Royal Warrant in 1919 and changed its name to Royal Brierley. The firm closed in the 1990s. This item was a wedding gift from the management of Stevens & Williams to Marion Jenkins, who was a designer at the factory.

7¼in (18.5cm) high

$2,800-3,500   FLD

A late 19thC Stevens & Williams Rockingham crystal glass bottle vase, with internal gold aventurine flecked decoration.

13¾in (35cm) high

$950-1,050   FLD

A late 19thC Stevens & Williams "Verre De Soie" glass vase.

8¾in (22.5cm) high

$500-650   FLD

A late 19thC Stevens & Williams "Osiris" glass vase, acid marked "PATENT."

6in (15cm) high

$1,500-2,000   FLD

A 1930s Stevens & Williams crystal glass vase, pattern no.65332.

12¼in (31cm) high

$500-550   FLD

An early 20thC Stevens & Williams glass claret pitcher, intaglio cut with arched motifs, with silver-plated mounts.

9¾in (25cm) high

$500-650   FLD

An early 20thC Stevens & Williams sleeve-form decanter, crystal cut with "Whisky."

8¼in (21cm) high

$400-500   FLD

An early 20thC Stevens & Williams liqueur glass, intaglio cut with a floral band in a mat and polished finish.

4in (10cm) high

$400-500   FLD

A 1920s Stevens & Williams hock glass, pattern no.53008, intaglio cut with fruiting grapevines.

8¼in (21cm) high

$950-1,050   FLD

A late 19thC Thomas Webb & Sons gem cameo glass vase, by George Woodall, impressed mark, chip to foot rim.

Thomas Webb & Sons was founded in 1837 in Stourbridge by Thomas Webb. On his death, it was taken over by his son. Thomas Webb & Sons was known for its rock crystal-style glass and cameo pieces. The firm was bought by Crown House Ltd. in 1964 and later became part of the Coloroll group. The factory closed in 1990.

8¼in (21cm) high

$20,000-32,000   DRA

A Thomas Webb cameo glass vase, cut with flowering plants.

c1880-90   3½in (9cm) high

$1,900-2,500   WW

A Thomas Webb & Sons cameo glass vase, wheel carved with flowers and insects, white opaque interior.

c1890   12in (30.5cm) high

$2,500-3,200   DUK

A Thomas Webb & Sons cameo glass vase, wheel carved with ferns.

c1890   6½in (16.5cm) high

$800-950   DUK

A Thomas Webb & Sons cameo glass vase, wheel carved with tree blossoms and butterflies, acid-etched crescent mark to base.

c1890   11in (28cm) high

$1,600-2,000   DUK

A Thomas Webb & Sons cameo glass vase, wheel carved with jasmine blossoms and butterflies, acid-etched mark to base.

c1890

$1,050-1,200   DUK

8¾in (22.5cm) high

A Thomas Webb & Sons cameo glass vase, wheel carved with flowers and insects.

c1890   8¾in (22cm) high

$1,500-2,000   DUK

A late 19thC Thomas Webb and Sons miniature ewer, intaglio cut with ferns and insects.

5¼in (13.5cm) high

$1,200-1,400   FLD

A Thomas Webb cameo pink and white scent bottle, with flowers and butterfly, with silver top hallmarked for Birmingham.

1888   2½in (6.5cm) high

$1,900-2,500   JN

A Thomas Webb & Co. cameo yellow glass scent bottle, with silver cover hallmarked for London.

1884   6in (15cm) long

$1,200-1,400   SWO

An early 20thC Thomas Webb & Sons hock glass, acid marked.

7¼in (18.5cm) high

$190-250   FLD

A late 19thC Tiffany Studios Favrile glass vase, etched "TGC," one burst bubble on rim, residue to interior.

4in (10cm) wide

$2,500-3,800   **DRA**

A Tiffany Favrile presentation vase, with gold and blue iridescent finish, engraved "G Y Tiffany Feby 15th 1898 Lewis C Tiffany."

7¾in (20cm) high

$7,000-8,000   **MORP**

A Tiffany Studios Favrile glass floriform vase, etched "L.C. Tiffany-Favrile W4399," some flaws in the making.

c1905   *17¼in (44cm) high*

$6,500-7,500   **DRA**

A Tiffany Studios floriform vase, etched "L.C.T. 521A," some bubbles.

c1906   *9½in (24cm) high*

$2,500-3,200   **DRA**

A Tiffany Favrile glass calyx floriform vase, engraved "L.C.T. Y7779."

c1905   *19½in (49.5cm) high*

$2,500-3,800   **DOY**

A Tiffany Studios gold Favrile blown glass "Jack-in-the-Pulpit" vase, etched "L.C.T. 4000A," remnants of paper label, minor tool marks near top.

"Jack-in-the-Pulpit" vases were inspired by the American woodland flower Arisaema triphyllum.

c1906   *15¾in (40cm) high*

$3,800-5,000   **DRA**

A pair of early 20thC Tiffany Studios Favrile glass vases, marked, some bubbles in making of, light wear to bases.

13½in (34.5cm) high

$1,600-2,300   **DRA**

A Tiffany Favrile iridescent glass vase, signed "L.C Tiffany Favrile 1811."

c1910   *10½in (26.5cm) high*

$500-650   **ROS**

CLOSER LOOK—TIFFANY STUDIOS VASE

This vase is made of Favrile glass; Favrile was Tiffany's trade name for its iridescent wares, derived from "fabrile," an old English word for "handmade."

It has an unusual and asymetical shape and design.

It is made of blown and applied glass and aventurine, and decorated with a design of leaves and vines.

It is a rare and possibly experimental piece, which increases the value.

A Tiffany Studios vase, etched "L.C. Tiffany Favrile 4570E."

c1910   *6½in (16.5cm) high*

$11,000-12,000   **DRA**

A Tiffany green Favrile vase, with applied gold iridescent collar, signed "L.C. Tiffany—Favrile 163 G."

10in (25.5cm) high

$4,000-4,800   **MORP**

A Tiffany Favrile vase, with iridescent swirl decoration, signed "L.C. Tiffany—Favrile E8432."

8¾in (22cm) high

$3,800-5,000   **MORP**

An early 20thC Tiffany Studios acid-etched blown glass Favrile bud vase, on gilt bronze base, base stamped "TIFFANY STUDIOS NEW YORK 711."

14in (35.5cm) high

$1,800-2,300   **DRA**

An early 20thC Tiffany Studios special-order blown glass Favrile vase, etched "LCT o8787," small burst bubble.

7in (18cm) high

$1,600-2,300   **DRA**

A Tiffany Studios Favrile ruffled compote, etched "1529 1259M L.C. Tiffany-Favrile."

c1918   *6in (15cm) wide*

$1,900-2,500   **DRA**

An early 20thC Tiffany Studios patinated bronze, Favrile glass, and mother-of-pearl Mosaic trivet.

7½in (19cm) diam

$16,000-23,000   **DRA**

A Tiffany Studios blown glass "Cypriote" vase, etched "4989N L.C. Tiffany-Inc. Favrile."

c1919   *4in (10cm) high*

$11,000-12,000   **DRA**

A Tiffany Studios paperweight vase, internally decorated with crocuses, etched "964V L.C.T. Favrile."

c1927   *4in (10cm) high*

$9,500-10,500   **DRA**

A Tiffany cameo vase, with cameo leaves and gold iridescent glass insert, vase signed "L.C.T. 1014B," insert signed "L.C.T. Y6406."

8½in (21.5cm) high

$7,500-9,000   **JDJ**

A pair of Baccarat vases, etched with fuchsias on a uranium glass base, signed "E, BOURGEOIS PARIS DEPOSÈ."

In 1862, Émile Bourgeois founded a glassware store in Paris. He did not allow those who supplied him with glassware to sell it under their own names in his store. Glass exists from Baccarat, Muller Frères, and Caranza that is marked solely with the retailer's "BOURGEOIS" signature.

c1900   *13¾in (35cm) high*
$3,800-4,400   **FIS**

A Baccarat polychrome enamel acid-cut vase.
c1895   *8in (20.5cm) high*
$1,150-1,400   **M&DM**

A James Couper & Sons "Clutha" glass vase, designed by Christopher Dresser (1834-1904).
c1880   *7½in (19cm) high*
$650-750   **L&T**

A pair of James Couper & Sons "Clutha" glass bottle vases, with aventurine and milky trailed inclusions.
c1900   *5in (13cm) high*
$800-950   **L&T**

A Bergun & Schverer cameo vase, with wheel-carved and Martele-carved decoration, signed "Verrerie D'Art De Lorraine B S& Co. Depose."
8½in (21.5cm) high
$5,500-7,000   **MORP**

A D'Argental cameo vase, by Paul Nicolas, signed "D'Argental," with Cross of Lorraine.

St. Louis launched its D'Argental cameo range in c1918, inspired by the success of other firms, such as Gallé and Daum. Its main designer was Paul Nicolas (1875-1952), a former protégé of Émile Gallé. The range continued until the mid-1920s.

12in (30.5cm) high
$2,500-3,200   **M&DM**

A D'Argental vase, by Paul Nicolas, etched "d'Argental."
c1919-25   *6in (15.5cm) high*
$900-1,000   **FIS**

A D'Argental vase, decorated with a Lake Como-like scene, signed "D'Argental."
21½in (54.5cm) high
$1,900-2,500   **JDJ**

A 1920s Degue cameo glass vase, sandblasted glass, signed in cameo, etched "Made in France."
15in (38cm) high
$1,500-2,000   **DRA**

An early 20thC Durand threaded glass vase, some losses to threading.

Durand glass was produced at the Vineland Glass Co. in Vineland, New Jersey, and was funded by French-born glassmaker Victor Durand Jr. (1870-1931). After Durand's death, Vineland merged with the Kimble Glass Co. and art glass production ceased.

8½in (21.5cm) high
$300-450   **DRA**

An Art Deco Etling opalescent glass figure of a seminude dancer, model no.50, on chrome plinth, molded mark "Etling France 50," etched "60852," nick on base.

8¾in (22cm) high
$1,800-2,300   GORL

A Harrach Japonaise vase, enameled with Asian cartouche.

The Harrach family took over a glassworks in Harrochow, Bohemia, in the early 18thC. By 1900, the firm had become a pioneer for Art Nouveau glass. The Harrach glassworks are still in production today.
c1890   14in (35.5cm) high
$750-900   M&DM

A Harrarch iridized and enameled "Rubinglaser" vase.

This design was first shown at the Paris 1900 exhibition.
c1900   12in (30.5cm) wide
$1,500-1,900   M&DM

A Harrach gilded vase, depicting branches and birds.
c1900   5in (13cm) wide
$400-500   M&DM

A set of six Harrach tango cocktail glasses.
c1925   7in (18cm) high
$750-900   M&DM

A Fritz Heckert purple on brick brown iridized vase, designed by Otto Thamm.
c1900   5in (12.5cm) high
$400-500   M&DM

A Joh, Oertel & Co. covered glass box, designed by the Haida school, enameled with vases and flowers.
c1915   7in (17.5cm) high
$1,300-1,900   FIS

A pair of Kralik ball vases, marked in silver "Made in Czechoslovakia."

These were made for the American market. Wilhelm Kralik Söhne was an important Bohemian art glass producer active in the late 19thC and early 20thC.
c1930   8in (20.5cm) high
$1,150-1,400   M&DM

A pair of Kralik ball vases.
c1930   8in (20.5cm) high
$1,150-1,400
M&DM

A Kralik cameo vase, with a landscape scene.
c1935   11in (28cm) high
$750-950   M&DM

A Kralik cameo vase, with a landscape scene.
c1935   6in (15cm) wide
$500-750   M&DM

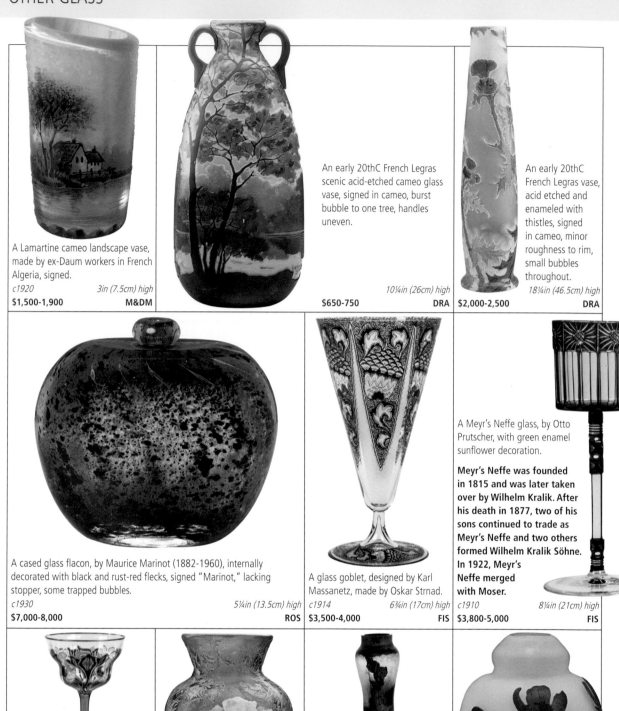

A Lamartine cameo landscape vase, made by ex-Daum workers in French Algeria, signed.

c1920   3in (7.5cm) high
$1,500-1,900   M&DM

An early 20thC French Legras scenic acid-etched cameo glass vase, signed in cameo, burst bubble to one tree, handles uneven.

                    10¼in (26cm) high
$650-750   DRA

An early 20thC French Legras vase, acid etched and enameled with thistles, signed in cameo, minor roughness to rim, small bubbles throughout.

                  18¼in (46.5cm) high
$2,000-2,500   DRA

A cased glass flacon, by Maurice Marinot (1882-1960), internally decorated with black and rust-red flecks, signed "Marinot," lacking stopper, some trapped bubbles.

c1930   5¼in (13.5cm) high
$7,000-8,000   ROS

A glass goblet, designed by Karl Massanetz, made by Oskar Strnad.

c1914   6¾in (17cm) high
$3,500-4,000   FIS

A Meyr's Neffe glass, by Otto Prutscher, with green enamel sunflower decoration.

Meyr's Neffe was founded in 1815 and was later taken over by Wilhelm Kralik. After his death in 1877, two of his sons continued to trade as Meyr's Neffe and two others formed Wilhelm Kralik Söhne. In 1922, Meyr's Neffe merged with Moser.

c1910   8¼in (21cm) high
$3,800-5,000   FIS

A Meyr's Neffe green and colorless wine glass, base marked "547."

c1910   7¾in (20cm) high
$650-750   FIS

An early 20thC Mont Joye twisting vase, gilt glass, enameled and acid etched with poppies.

                  11¼in (28.5cm) high
$550-650   DRA

A Muller Croismare acid-etched glass "Fluogravure" vase, signed "Muller Croismare."

c1910   6¾in (17cm) high
$650-750   ROS

An early 20thC Muller Frères cameo glass vase, acid etched internally with poppies, signed in cameo, polished chip to inner rim, some metal transfer marks.

                  5¾in (14.5cm) high
$500-650   DRA

An early 20thC Muller Frères acid-etched cameo vase, with boar hunting scene, signed "Muller Frès Lunéville" in cameo, some minor flecks.

10¾in (27.5cm) high

$3,200-3,800   DRA

An early 20thC Muller Frères acid-etched cameo glass vase, signed.

16in (40.5cm) high

$750-900   DRA

A rare Phoenix Consolidated Cubist "Ruba Rombic" vase, in topaz, designed by Reubin Haley.

c1928-32   *7in (18cm) high*

$1,500-1,900   M&DM

A Portieux Vallerysthal vase, etched with chestnut leaves and flowers, etched "Vallerysthal."

c1895-1900   *13¾in (35cm) high*

$6,500-7,000   FIS

A set of eight drinking glasses, by Thomas Graham Jackson (1835-1924), for James Powell & Sons.

Laurence W. Hodson, who owned these, was an art collector and a patron of William Morris and other leading artists of the English Arts and Crafts movement.

c1870   *6in (15cm) high*

$700-800   L&T

An early 20thC Quezal glass vase, etched "QUEZAL II."

Quezal was founded in 1901 by former Tiffany employees Thomas Johnson and Martin Bach. It ceased production in 1925.

11in (28cm) high

$1,900-2,500   DRA

An early 20thC Quezal glass pulled-feather vase, etched "QUEZAL 1000," some imperfections on the rim.

7½in (19cm) high

$900-1,000   DRA

A Verrerie De Sèvres acid-etched and fire-polished cameo glass vase, with silver-plated mounts, etched "VS" on the base, dent to rim, wear to mounts.

c1900   *8in (20.5cm) high*

$1,150-1,400   DRA

A Fachschule Steinschönau vase.

This vase was made for the 1925 Paris World Fair.

1925   *11½in (29cm) high*

$7,000-7,500   FIS

A 1920s Steuben "Plum Jade" acid-etched cased glass vase, with lotus flowers, minor polishing near base.

6¾in (17cm) wide

$2,300-2,800   DRA

DECORATIVE ARTS

An early 20thC Steuben blue blown glass "Aurene" vase, etched "Aurene 2683," some scratches.

12in (30.5cm) high

$2,800-3,500 DRA

A Val Saint Lambert vase, inscribed "VSL."

c1906-07 *23½in (60cm) high*
$3,800-4,400 FIS

A 1920s Amalric Walter "Libellule" pâte-de-verre "vide poches" (empty pocket), by Henri Bergé, signed "AWALTER NANCY," "HBergé."

6¾in (17cm) long
$3,500-4,000 QU

A pair of Amalric Walter relief-molded glass dolphin bookends, by Auguste Houillon (1885-1954), signed in mold "A Walter, Nancy, A Houillon," some chips, pencil marks to back, "400," "£2-10-0 Pair."

$2,300-2,800 SWO

An enameled glass pitcher, by Hannah Walton, painted with a mermaid, signed with initials "HW."

Hannah Walton (1863-1940) trained at the Glasgow School of Art and exhibited at the 1888 Glasgow International Exhibition. She shared a studio with her sisters Helen and Constance; all three worked painting and enameling ceramics and glass.

c1900 *6in (15.5cm) high*
$1,500-2,000 L&T

An early 20thC Steuben gold blown glass "Aurene" vase, on wood stand, etched "AURENE 2412," scuffs and scratches.

8in (20.5cm) high
$500-650 DRA

A Val Saint Lambert red over clear "Seurat" vase, shallow foot rim chip.

Val Saint Lambert was founded in 1826 in Belgium and is still operational today.

c1930 *12in (30.5cm) high*
$2,300-2,800 DN

A Val Saint Lambert cut glass vase, in "Topaz" and "Bleu Francais," acid-etched mark.

c1930 *6in (15cm) high*
$2,300-2,800 DN

CLOSER LOOK—"APHRODITE RISING FROM THE WAVES"

The cameo glass plaque is cased in opal over blue over red.

This design is bordered with a triple line, with six arched panels with a seashell motif.

It is carved with the nude figure of Aphrodite rising from crashing waves, her legs submerged in the water, surrounded by seagulls. Aphrodite was a subject favored by Woodall, featuring in variations across a number of plaques and vases.

It was made by George Woodall in c1920, although he had first designed the plaque when working for Thomas Webb & Sons in the 1870s.

A cameo glass plaque, "Aphrodite Rising from the Waves," by George Woodall, signed.

c1920 *8¼in (21cm) diam*
$14,000-18,000 FLD

A Victorian Aesthetic breakfront oak side cabinet, possibly designed by Charles Bevan for Marsh Jones & Cribb.

Charles Bevan (fl. 1865-83) was a furniture designer and manufacturer based in London. He made several designs for Marsh & Jones of Leeds, including a suite of furniture for Titus Salt. He took his son George Alfred into partnership from 1872.

71in (180.5cm) high

$1,300-1,800   **HT**

An Aesthetic movement Collinson & Lock ebonized and painted side cabinet, by Thomas Edward Collcutt.

Thomas Edward Collcutt (1840-1924) was an architect and furniture designer who gained international acclaim for his black ebonized furniture designs for the firm Collinson & Lock. He also designed Wakefield Town Hall, the Imperial Institute in South Kensington, London, and Lloyd's Register building.

c1871   *94½in (240cm) high*

$7,000-8,000   **DN**

CLOSER LOOK—AESTHETIC MOVEMENT CHAIR

This chair has swept arms formed as quarter wheels with turned spindles.

There is a line drawing of this model in "William Watt catalog Art Furniture from Designs by EW. Godwin," 1877. A chair of this type was also included in Watt's display at the 1878 Exposition Universelle in Paris.

Although it is only marked "8513," other chairs of this type carry enamel trade labels for the firm William Watt and a Patent Office Design Registry mark for November 14, 1876. Watt produced furniture by a number of leading designers of the time.

Despite some wear and the poor condition of the fabric, the rarity and the connection with William Watt and E.W. Godwin make this a desirable chair.

A Victorian Aesthetic movement ebonized framed armchair, by William Watt, after the original design by Edward William Godwin (1833-86).

c1877

$70,000-80,000   **MAI**

An Aesthetic Lamb of Manchester inlaid coromandel and rosewood occasional table, by Charles Edward Hoston, the top with copper, brass, and shell inlaid foliate design, stamped "J. Lamb Manchester 51600," minor fire damage, split on one lobe.

26in (66cm) high

$15,000-20,000   **GORL**

A late 19thC Anglo-Japanese carved hardwood padouk cabinet, with Aesthetic-style floral, lunette and medallion decoration in the manner of Thomas Jeckyll, old shippers label of "Crews & Son, Exmouth" to rear.

60¼in (153cm) high

$3,800-4,400   **FELL**

A stained wood, copper, bone, and inlaid metal throne chair, by Carlo Bugatti (1856-1940), with a vellum circular back and seat.

c1900   *57in (145cm) high*

$7,500-9,000   **SWO**

An ebonized, walnut inlaid, and brass and pewter mounted corner chair, by Carlo Bugatti, some damage, later upholstery.

$1,500-1,900   **BE**

A Gallé carved nutwood writing desk, with inlaid wood design, signed.

1905-15   *46¼in (117.5cm) high*

$21,000-25,000   **QU**

DECORATIVE ARTS

An oak settee, by Sidney Barnsley.

Sidney Barnsley (1865-1926) was an important Arts and Crafts architect and furniture maker. In the workshop he shared with his brother Ernest and friend Ernest Gimson, he made chests, cabinets, tables, and other pieces, combining rural carpentry techniques with sophisticated design.

86in (218cm) wide

$50,000-63,000   LC

A walnut dressing table, by Edward Barnsley, with ebonized wood handles.

59in (150cm) high

$2,300-2,800   WW

A Heal's oak sideboard or compactum, ivorine disk on one door, one shrinkage crack, some wear and scratches.

Heal's opened their first store in 1810. By the end of the 19thC, it was one of the best-known furniture suppliers in London, and it is still operational today.

c1910   51¼in (130cm) wide

$2,500-3,200   CHEF

A pair of Heal's oak settles, ivorine plaques on reverse, previous repairs.

The checkered motif of inlaid pewter and ebony on this piece was used by Heals in their furniture exhibited at the 1900 Paris Exhibition.

c1900-10   40¼in (102cm) high

$1,900-2,500   CHEF

A J.S. Henry mahogany and inlaid secrétaire, by George Montague Ellwood (1875-1955), the slatted back with two cupboards enclosing a marquetry-inlaid fall.

c1900   73½in (187cm) high

$4,400-5,700   L&T

A Liberty & Co. oak corner cupboard, with patinated metal, applied ivorine label.

77½in (197cm) high

$1,050-1,200   WW

A Liberty & Co. walnut "Thebes" stool.

c1900   13½in (34.5cm) wide

$1,000-1,150   CHEF

A pair of beech and elm laboratory stools, attributed to Charles Rennie Mackintosh (1868-1928) for Queen Margaret Medical College, Glasgow.

Queen Margaret Medical College was the sole women's-only college of its type in the UK at the time.

1894   27¼in (69cm) high

$5,000-6,300   TEN

Judith Picks

This armchair was designed for the men's Billiards and Smoking Rooms at Miss Cranston's Argyle Street Tea Rooms in Glasgow. In 1898, early in his career, Scottish architect Charles Rennie Mackintosh (1868-1928) was commissioned by entrepreneur Catherine Cranston to furnish her new tearooms. Designer George Walton worked with him, designing the interiors while Mackintosh was in charge of the furnishings.

Mackintosh's designs are bold, simple, and distinctive, combining strong Scottish vernacular design with English Arts & Crafts. He produced three types of seating for the Billiards and Smoking Rooms of the tearoom: a prominent ladder-back armchair, a stool, and this chair, a cube-shaped tub armchair. Its construction is traditional, but its form is unusual; it has broad panels of sawn wood stripped of decoration, a solid box shape and curved aprons, and subtle detailing under the arms and back.

The Argyle Tea Rooms closed in 1920, and much of the furniture was dispersed. This armchair came into the possession of established Glasgow restaurateur William Smith, whose daughter passed it to a friend as a gift.

A Glasgow stained oak armchair, by Charles Rennie Mackintosh.

1898   33in (84cm) high

$145,000-150,000   L&T

A Morris & Co. oak sideboard, stamped "MORRIS & Co/449 OXFORD St" and "no.693," some wear.

79½in (202cm) wide

$5,500-7,000   **DN**

A Morris & Co. walnut refectory table, by George Washington Jack (1855-1931).

c1890   90¼in (229cm) long

$16,000-20,000   **L&T**

A Morris & Co. mahogany table, by George Washington Jack, stamped "MORRIS & CO./449 OXFORD ST/W/1000."

c1895   30in (76cm) diam

$15,000-20,000   **L&T**

A Thompson of Kilburn "Mouseman" oak panel-back armchair, carved in relief with a mouse.

c1940

$5,000-6,300   **MOR**

Judith Picks

This armchair was made by Morris & Co., the decorative arts and furnishings company founded by William Morris in 1861. It was designed by Philip Webb (1831-1915), a close friend of Morris's and the designer of his home, Red House.

Morris & Co.'s reclining armchair was one of the firm's popular designs and was available both in this black finish and in mahogany. The c1912 Morris & Co. illustrated catalog shows that loose covers could be supplied either in "Utrecht Velvet" or in chintz (printed cotton). The commercial success of the design encouraged other firms, notably Liberty & Co. of London and Gustav Stickley in the United States, to produce their own versions.

A Morris & Co. ebonized walnut ladder-back open reclining armchair, by Philip Webb, with five adjustable settings.

26½in (67cm) wide

$9,500-10,500   **LSK**

ROBERT "MOUSEMAN" THOMPSON

Robert Thompson (1876-1955) was a Yorkshire cabinetmaker and important figure in the Arts and Crafts movement.

● His distinctive furniture was made from plain English oak, then shaped with an adze to give the wood a rippled surface.

● Each piece was embellished with a carved mouse. The mouse signature supposedly came from Thompson's description of himself in his early career as being "as poor as a church mouse" and led to him and his furniture being referred to as "Mouseman."

● Several of the craftsmen who trained under Thompson went on to set up on their own, using similar carved animals to sign their work. These included Peter "Rabbitman" Heap and Graham "Swanman" Duncalf.

● The firm Mouseman continues to make handmade furniture today.

A Robert "Mouseman" Thompson oak tallboy, with iron disk hinges and latch, carved with a mouse.

c1928   48½in (123cm) high

$16,000-20,000   **MOR**

A Robert "Mouseman" Thompson oak dresser, the center carcass carved "H" and "1930," the sides with "mouse" signatures.

The Robert Thompson ledger for 1930 notes "Lieut. Col. A.J. Horlick c/o Horlicks Ltd., Slough Buckinghamshire Dresser as sketch submitted 6'0 long x 7" high app £45- -."

83in (211cm) high

$60,000-75,000   **SWO**

A Robert "Mouseman" Thompson monk's armchair, centered with a carved "H" for Horlick, mouse signature on front right leg.

The Robert Thompson ledger for 1939 "1939, Dec 12, 'One Monks chair' £8/8/."

$7,000-8,000   **SWO**

A Robert "Mouseman" Thompson oak refectory table, carved inscription "D.D JOAN 1921-1926, MARY, DIANA, ANGELA, HELEN AND BRIDGET WESTMACOTT 1947-1964," with carved mouse.

72in (183cm) long

$1,900-2,500   **TEN**

DECORATIVE ARTS

A Peter "Rabbitman" Heap oak sideboard, some sun staining to top.

72in (183cm) wide

$2,100-2,500 PW

An oak hay rake dining table, by Gordon Russell, stamped "Gordon Russell Ltd."

c1930 *66¼in (168cm) wide*

$5,000-6,300 DN

A high-back oak armchair, by Mackay Hugh Baillie Scott (1865-1945).

c1895 *47¼in (120cm) high*

$2,300-2,800 L&T

A walnut table, by Mackay Hugh Baillie Scott.

1898 *27in (68.5cm) high*

$3,800-5,000 ROS

A Shapland & Petter oak bookcase cabinet, the door with a stenciled panel inscribed "MY LADIES GARDEN."

Shapland & Petter was a cabinetmaking firm based in Barnstaple, Devon, founded in 1854. The firm continued into the 20thC and was taken over by the LS Group in 1999.

c1900 *87½in (222cm) wide*

$6,500-7,500 L&T

A Shapland & Petter inlaid mahogany cabinet, with marquetry decoration in specimen woods and mother-of-pearl, the locks stamped "S&P/B."

c1900 *51¾in (131.5cm) high*

$7,000-8,000 L&T

A Shapland & Petter oak settle, the back with inset copper panel, "Welcome ever Smiles."

The inscription "Welcome Ever Smiles" is taken from Shakespeare's "Troilus and Cressida."

42¼in (107cm) long

$8,000-9,500 BE

A Shapland & Petter oak stand, designed by William Cowie.

c1905 *80¼in (204cm) high*

$1,900-2,500 TDG

An Arts and Crafts oak bookcase, with Art Nouveau-style script motto "IT'S GUID TO BE MERRY AND WISE," with repoussé copper and leaded glass.

The motto is a quote of Robert Burns, from "Here's a Health to Them That's Awa." This style of furniture is often associated with Liberty & Co., who may have retailed this piece.

c1905 *78in (198cm) high*

$3,800-4,400 TDG

ESSENTIAL REFERENCE—GUSTAV STICKLEY

Gustav Stickley (1858-1942) was a designer and furniture maker who was one of the leading figures of the American Arts and Crafts movement.

● He learned furniture making from his uncle, the owner of a Pennsylvania chair factory. After leaving his uncle's factory, he founded the Stickley Brothers Chair Co. with his brothers Albert and Charles in 1883. It became the largest manufacturer in the state during the 1890s.

● Gustav Stickley founded his own company in 1898, after leaving Stickley Brothers.

● He was strongly influenced by William Morris, but while the English Arts and Crafts movement focused on hand-crafting, Gustav Stickley used machines to create his new and original designs. His work was a radical departure from 19thC American furniture.

● The firm was a great success in the first decade of the 20thC but, by 1915, it was overstretched and Gustav Stickley filed for bankruptcy.

A rare early Gustav Stickley mitered-mullion bookcase, with red decal, lightly cleaned, minor sun fading.

c1901   *56in (142cm) high*
$9,500-10,500   **DRA**

c1940   *40½in (103cm) wide*
$11,000-12,000   **DRA**

A Gustav Stickley bride's chest, with iron hardware, large red decal, some chips, some wear.

A Gustav Stickley and Harvey Ellis bookcase/cabinet, with large red decal, minor staining and fading, one glass crack.

Harvey Ellis (1852-1904) was an architect and painter. He spent the last months of his life working as an architect and designer for Gustav Stickley.

c1903   *68½in (174cm) wide*
$50,000-63,000   **DRA**

A Gustav Stickley and Harvey Ellis bookcase, remnants of paper label, red decal, some staining, missing metal keyhole liners.

c1910   *54in (137cm) wide*
$7,000-8,000   **DRA**

A 1910s Gustav Stickley sideboard, branded, refinished, some filled chips, veneer repairs to doors.

56in (142cm) wide
$3,800-5,000   **DRA**

A Gustav Stickley bow-arm Morris chair, with early red decal, light wear and minor stains, possible burn to front.

c1901   *38½in (98cm) high*
$9,000-10,000   **DRA**

A Gustav Stickley high-back spindle bench, with red decal, old overcoat to original finish, later artificial rush to seat.

c1905   *48½in (123cm) high*
$6,500-7,500   **DRA**

An early 20thC Gustav Stickley settle, no.222, red decal, some edge wear, some wear to cushion and pillows.

80in (203cm) wide
$6,500-7,500   **DRA**

A Gustav Stickley spindled loveseat, red decal, original spring cushion, minor edge wear.

c1910   *50in (127cm) long*
$6,500-7,500   **DRA**

DECORATIVE ARTS

A Gustav Stickley leather-top hexagonal library table, with red decal, remnants of paper label, some wear to leather, two metal brackets stabilizing the top.

c1903   *55in (139.5cm) wide*
$18,000-23,000   **DRA**

A Gustav Stickley and Grueby 12-tile table, with paper label, crack to one tile, minor edge wear.

c1905   *26in (66cm) high*
$14,000-18,000   **DRA**

An L. & J.G. Stickley bookcase, with handcraft decal, one darkened gouge to front left side, minor wear.

Leopold and John George Stickley, brothers of Gustav Stickley, established a new furniture business in Fayetteville in 1902. They initially used the trademark "Onondaga Shops." L. & J.G. Stickley continued after Leopold's and John George's death; it was acquired by Alfred Audi in the 1970s and continues to make furniture today as Stickley, Audi & Co.

c1908   *55¼in (140.5cm) high*
$3,200-4,400   **DRA**

An L. & J.G. Stickley Onondaga Shops flat-arm Morris chair, some dints and wear, crazing to original leather.

c1902-07   *42in (106.5cm) high*
$2,500-3,800   **DRA**

An L.& J.G. Stickley quartersawn oak rocking Morris chair.

38in (96.5cm) high
$2,800-3,500   **CLAR**

An L. & J.G. Stickley Onondaga Shops settle, minor edge wear.

c1902-07   *76in (193cm) wide*
$3,800-5,000   **DRA**

An L. & J.G. Stickley copper-top drink stand, with "The Work Of..." decal, some fading, some chips.

c1912   *28½in (72.5cm) high*
$1,400-1,800   **DRA**

An L. & J.G. Stickley server, branded, some wear.

c1920   *44in (112cm) wide*
$2,000-2,500   **DRA**

An L. & J.G. Stickley twin bed, handcraft decal, side rails replaced.

c1905   *79in (200.5cm) long*
$1,300-1,800   **DRA**

An L. & J.G. Stickley shoe-foot drop-leaf table, with "The Work Of..." decal, light overcoat to original finish.
c1912   *open 42in (106.5cm) diam*
$1,600-2,000   DRA

An L. & J.G. Stickley trestle table, some fading, scratches, and wear, replaced screws.
c1912-18   *60in (152.5cm) long*
$2,300-2,800   **DRA**

A 1910s Stickley Brothers china cabinet, "Quaint" metal label, some darkened damage to front right foot.

The Stickley family consisted of five brothers, all of whom worked as furniture makers. In 1883, Albert, Gustav, and Charles Stickley founded the Stickley Brothers Chair Company in Binghampton, New York. In 1891, Albert moved to Grand Rapids to work with his brother John George; Gustav also soon left, while Charles stayed in Binghampton. The Grand Rapids company was renamed Stickley Brothers, and Albert and John George continued to work together until John George moved to New York on his marriage, where he worked with his brother Leopold as L. & J.G. Stickley.

68¼in (173.5cm) high
DRA

A Stickley Brothers china cabinet, no.8446, with original hammered hardware, with adjustable shelves.
55½in (141cm) high
$1,600-2,000   **CLAR**

A Stickley Brothers quartersawn oak single drawer server, with "Quaint" metal tag, some seam separations.

Some Stickley Brothers pieces were marked with a metal tag reading "Quaint" or "Quaint Furniture." The brothers used this term to define and describe their furniture, and as a way to uniquely brand their work to distinguish it from their brother Gustav Stickley's.
c1910   *34in (86.5cm) wide*
$700-800   **DRA**

A Stickley Brothers sideboard, branded, "Quaint" decal, stenciled numbers, some wear.
c1910-15   *50in (127cm) wide*
$950-1,050   **DRA**

An early 20thC Stickley Brothers server, with copper strap hardware, some replaced pull, some filled chips, damage to veneer, some losses.
54in (137cm) wide
$9,000-10,000   **DRA**

A Stickley Brothers Mission oak "Morris" armchair, with leather cushions.
c1910   *37in (94cm) high*
$1,900-2,500   **L&T**

A Stickley Brothers side table, with "Quaint" metal label, some wear to partial overcoat over original finish.
c1910   *28in (71cm) high*
$3,200-3,800   **DRA**

DECORATIVE ARTS

A Grand Rapids Furniture Co. quartersawn oak library table, with integrated book shelves, dark stains to top.

38in (96.5cm) wide

$550-650   DRA

A Jamestown Furniture Co. stained oak hall chair, in the style of Charles Rohlfs, with polychrome pyrography, chip to one front leg.

c1915   *56in (142cm) high*

$1,000-1,500   DRA

A Limbert sideboard, metal label, dent to center door, seam separations on left side.

c1910   *57in (145cm) wide*

$4,400-5,000   DRA

A Limbert dining table, no.403, some edge wear, extensive wear to top.

Limbert Furniture was founded in 1894 in Grand Rapids, Michigan, by Charles P. Limbert. The factory produced furniture until its closure in 1944.

c1903   *50in (127cm) wide*

$5,000-6,300   DRA

A 1900s Charles Rohlfs tall-back chairs, "R" cipher to each, loose joinery, wear to replaced seats, repair to one chair.

Charles Rohlfs (1853-1936) was an important designer and furniture maker working in Buffalo, New York. He was influenced by the Art Nouveau and Aesthetic movements.

53in (134.5cm) high

$6,500-7,500   DRA

A rare Charles Rohlfs oversize chestnut sofa, carved signature, professional repair to rail, dated.

1904   *111in (282cm) wide*

$27,000-38,000   DRA

A Charles Rohlfs carved library table, with carved signature and date, some sun fading.

1900   *48in (122cm) wide*

$13,000-18,000   DRA

A Roycroft quartersawn oak and leather tall chair, with brass tacks.

Roycroft was a community of artists and craftsmen based near Buffalo, New York, in the late 19thC and early 20thC.

c1915   *41in (104cm) high*

$900-1,000   DRA

An early 20thC Shop of the Crafters inlaid cabinet, water damage to base, straps replaced.

The Shop of the Crafters was owned by Oscar Onken and specialized in Mission furniture in the Arts and Craft style. It was in business 1904-20 and was based in Cincinnati, Ohio.

63¼in (160.5cm) high

$2,300-2,800   DRA

A Bath Cabinet Makers Ltd. walnut and coromandel wood chest, by Charles A. Richter (1876-1945), marked "BCM/1928/C.A. RICHTER," stamped "19826/9769/2."

1928   *55in (140cm) high*

$7,000-8,000   **L&T**

CLOSER LOOK—ART DECO DRESSING TABLE

This dressing table was designed by George Betjemann and Sons Macassar and retailed by Asprey.

It is made of ebony, with ivory and chrome details.

The hinged top has a triptych fold-out mirror, and the base has two swivel compartments.

It comes with a fitted glass, shagreen, and ivory-mounted toilet set, including hallmarked brushes and scent bottles.

An ebony fitted dressing table, marked "Asprey" and "GB&S London."

1928-29   *closed 33¾in (86cm) wide*

$15,000-19,000   **WW**

A pair of leather, fabric, and bronze-covered wood armchairs, by Paul Dupré-Lafon, with certificate of authenticity.

c1929   *37½in (95.5cm) wide*

$110,000-150,000   **PHI**

A 1930s-50s Epstein Brothers console sideboard, in maple and burr maple veneers, with original twin-tone handles.

58¾in (149cm) wide

$3,800-4,400   **TDG**

A 1930s Epstein Brothers lounge suite, in cloud, with wrap-around figured walnut veneers, reupholstered in faux suede.

sofa 70in (178cm) wide

$16,000-19,000   **TDG**

A 1930s Epstein six-seater dining suite, with bird's-eye maple veneers, restored and reupholstered in faux suede.

table 72in (183cm) long

$9,500-10,500   **TDG**

An Heal's Art Deco demilune walnut desk, with a center locking mechanism, ivorine label.

57in (144.5cm) wide

$5,000-6,300   **SWO**

A 1930s Art Deco burr walnut sideboard, with macassar ebony banding, labeled "A H Holden, Hammersmith School of Arts and Crafts."

54¼in (138cm) wide

$3,200-3,800   **TDG**

A 1930s French amboyna, mahogany, and silk upholstery club chair, by Jules Leleu (1883-1961), impressed "LELEU PARIS," refinished, reupholstered.

28½in (72.5cm) high

$2,500-3,200   **DRA**

An Art Deco figured walnut pedestal desk, in the manner of Jules Leleu, with ivory handles and escutcheon plates, with bronze sledge feet.

63¼in (160.5cm) wide

$4,400-5,000   **CHOR**

A Charlotte Perriand "en forme" desk, with carved solid pine base and top, aluminum and pine drawer blocks.

designed c1939, made c1943   *90½in (230cm) wide*

$760,000-880,000   **ARTC**

A Giordano Chiesa coffee table, designed by Gio Ponti, with ash wood base.

c1940   *43¼in (110cm) diam*

$20,000-23,000   **CA**

A rare coffee table, designed by Gio Ponti, made from East Indian rosewood-veneered wood, walnut-veneered wood, walnut, brass, and glass, with a certificate of expertise from the Gio Ponti Archives.

c1940   *33½in (85cm) long*

$50,000-57,000   **PHI**

A Isokon painted plywood "Penguin Donkey" bookcase, designed by Egon Riss (1901-64).

23¼in (59cm) wide

$2,300-2,800   **SWO**

A 1930s Art Deco rosewood and upholstery club chair, by Eugene Schoen, USA/England, impressed "Hungate Schmieg and Kotzian" mark, refinished, and reupholstered.

29in (73.5cm) wide

$1,300-1,900   **DRA**

An Art Deco walnut rocket-form display cabinet.

40¼in (102cm) wide

$1,000-1,150   **SWO**

A 1930s Art Deco cocktail cabinet, in figured walnut veneers, the interior fitted and mirrored with light.

61½in (156cm) high

$4,400-5,700   **TDG**

A pair of 1950s Artek birch-veneered plywood "Paimio" armchairs, designed by Alvar Aalto, Finland, model no.41.

designed 1931-32   *26in (66cm) high*

$15,000-20,000   **PHI**

A set of four pine and steel garden chairs, by Alvar Aalto (1898-1976), Finland, unmarked, some scuffs and scratches.

c1938   *35½in (90cm) high*

$10,000-11,000   **DRA**

A rare pair of walnut, cane and fabric armchairs, by Paolo Buffa, with a certificate of expertise from the Paolo Buffa Archive.

c1940   *30¼in (77cm) wide*

$90,000-100,000   **PHI**

A rare 1940s Johnson Furniture Co. teak, birch, leather, and brass ameoba desk, by Paul Frankl (1886-1958), refinished, some veneer sanded through.

The chest of drawers and desk can be used separately or together.

66in (167.5cm) long

$5,000-6,300   **DRA**

A Cebaso nickel-plated, tubular steel, chrome-plated, and auburn iron yarn "8239" armchair, designed by Erich Dieckmann.

Erich Dieckmann (1896-1944) is among the most important German designers of the Bauhaus, and his tubular steel furniture takes a special position in the context of European tubular steel design of the prewar era.

c1931   *36¼in (92cm) long*

$32,000-38,000   **QU**

A pair of 1940s model H-269 bentwood and upholstery armchairs, by Jindrich Halabala (1903-78), Czechoslovakia.

28½in (72.5cm) high

$3,200-3,800   **ROS**

A 1930s Troy Sunshade Co. chromed steel and upholstery adjustable lounge chair and ottoman, designed by Gilbert Rohde (1894-1944), minor wear.

chair 39in (99cm) wide

$2,500-3,200   **DRA**

A pair of 1930s Troy Sunshade chromed steel and vinyl lounge chairs, by Gilbert Rohde, sticker label on one.

29½in (75cm) high

$7,500-9,000   **DRA**

A pair of 1980s Knoll International bronze and leather "Barcelona" chairs, designed by Ludwig Mies Van Der Rohe (1886-1969).

designed 1929   *31in (78.5cm) high*

$5,500-7,000   **DRA**

DECORATIVE ARTS

Two embroidered panels, by Walter Crane (1845-1915), with period frames.

These panels, with their complex composition inspired by historical design, was probably exhibited as part of the Royal School of Art Needlework's section at the Philadelphia Exposition of 1876.

c1876   max 56¾in (144cm) high
$5,000-6,300   L&T

A pair of Morris & Co. "Bird" pattern wool curtains, by William Morris (1834-96), jacquard-woven woollen double cloth, lined with Morris & Co. "Cray" pattern block-printed cotton fabric.
designed c1884, made c1890
141in (358cm) long
$6,500-7,500   L&T

A Morris & Co. Arts and Crafts embroidered panel, later framed and glazed.

This is a previously unrecorded design for Morris & Co. Worked with their silks and with the same techniques, the design demonstrates the characteristic sophisticated style of the company.
c1895   47¼in (120cm) high
$4,400-5,000   L&T

An Alexander Morton & Co. Donegal carpet, by Gavin Morton and G.K. Robertson.

Donegal carpets are a kind of wool carpets produced in Killybegs, a town in County Donegal, Ireland. Alexander Morton (1844-1923) opened several carpet factories in Donegal in the late 1890s.
c1900   273¼in (694cm) long
$9,500-10,500   L&T

Judith Picks

John Henry Dearle (1859-1932) began his career with Morris & Co. in 1878 as a shop assistant. Morris recognized his potential and, by 1890, he was Head Designer. Under the guidance of May Morris, William Morris's daughter and a skilled embroiderer, Dearle produced a series of portières featuring some of his most recognizable designs. While much of Morris's early embroidery work features repeating patterns, in "Acanthus," Dearle used a center motif that grounds the piece, surrounded by interlocking vines and swirls of colored flowers.

A Morris & Co. "Acanthus," embroidered portière, designed by John Henry Dearle, silk embroidery on linen with green cotton backing, labeled "MORRIS & COMPANY/449 OXFORD STREET/LONDON. W."
c1890   94½in (240cm) high
$38,000-44,000   L&T

An early "Stjärnor på rödt" (stars on red) rug, by Märta Måås-Fjetterström, handwoven wool on a linen warp, hand stitched at a later date with designer's intials "MMF."
1913-19   161½in (410cm) long
$32,000-38,000   PHI

A blue marine rug, by Eileen Gray, cleaned.
designed 1920s-30s   137½in (349.5cm) wide
$1,900-2,500   DRA

An Art Deco hand-knotted wool carpet.
c1930   118in (300cm) diam
$3,800-4,400   ROS

A brass mantel clock, by W.A.S. Benson, with French drum movement.

This rare design is depicted in Ian Hamerton's "W.A.S. Benson," Antiques Collectors" Club, page 102.

10in (25.5cm) high

$8,000-9,000 SWO

A Martin Brothers stoneware clock case, of architectural form, supported by two dragons, numbered "27," inscribed "R.W. Martin/London," dated.

See pages 473-475 for more Martin Brothers.

1875 *10½in (26.5cm) high*

$2,500-3,800 WAD

A Burmantoft Faience mantel clock, model no.1429, modeled in relief with a lioness and cubs, impressed "W.A.," minor glaze loss and frits.

See page 454 for more Burmantofts.

10¼in (26cm) high

$1,500-1,900 WW

A Moorcroft mantel timepiece, with "Made for Liberty & Co" mark and green "W. Moorcroft" signature, some crazing, brass bezel tarnished.

See pages 477-479 for more Moorcroft.

c1910 *5½in (14cm) high*

$1,900-2,500 GORL

An Art Nouveau James Fenton & Co. silver and enamel mantel clock, with arched oak case, stamped maker's mark, hallmarked Birmingham.

1906 *6¼in (16cm) high*

$650-750 L&T

A Liberty & Co. silver "Cymric" mantle clock, designed by Archibald Knox (1864-1933), hallmarked "L&CO," Birmingam.

See page 549 for more Liberty & Co.

1902 *3¾in (9.5cm) high*

$10,000-11,000 LOCK

A Liberty & Co. pewter, enamel, copper, and glass "Tudric" clock, by Archibald Knox, stamped "TUDRIC MADE IN ENGLAND 0629," minor dents.

c1903-14 *7¼in (18.5cm) high*

$4,400-5,000 DRA

A Liberty & Co. pewter and enameled "Tudric" mantel timepiece, in Art Nouveau style, within a planished and cast stylized tree, numbered "0557."

7½in (19cm) high

$4,400-5,000 HAN

A Robert "Mouseman" Thompson English oak mantel clock, with spring-driven movement, the stepped case simulating bricks, with two carved mice, movement not working, small reglued chip at one corner, some water marks.

See page 529 for more Mouseman.

12in (30.5cm) wide

$3,500-4,000 TEN

A 1920s Art Deco J. Chaumet & Cie 18ct red enameled yellow-gold retractable purse timepiece, movement by Vacheron Constantin, stamped indistinctly "Bte S.G.B.G 12045," dial marked "J. Chaumet & Cie Paris Londres," enamel restored to reverse.

1½in (4cm) wide
$3,200-3,800 HAN

A Stevenson Manufacturing Bakelite, glass, and printed paper clock and kitchen timer, by Isamu Noguchi (1904-88), La Porte, Indiana, some scuffs and scratches.

c1932 *6in (15cm) high*
$650-750 DRA

A Lalique "Le Jour et La Nuit" clock, in smoky topaz glass and enameled metal, acid stamped "R. LALIQUE," reenameled metal base.

designed 1926 *15¾in (40cm) high*
$32,000-38,000 DRA

A French silver clock compendium, retailed by Tiffany and Co., Paris, with ivory numbering, barometer, and thermometer, later inscribed to base.

c1920 *2¼in (6cm) high*
$1,900-2,500 WW

A 1940s Art Deco Vitascope Industries Ltd. Bakelite clock, the Odeon-style case with a viewing window with three masted sailing ship automaton.

13in (33cm) high
$650-750 FLD

A 1920s Art Deco E. Mathey-Tissot silver and enamel travel clock, 11-jewel movement striking on a gong, with lapis lazuli feet and button, the case marked "Sterling" and "No.12179," in original case.

Provenance: This piece was given by the Duke and Duchess of Windsor to their butler, Alan Fisher (1930-2006). Fisher worked for the Windsors from 1954 at their French retreat Le Moulin de la Tuilerie at Gif-sur-Yvette and their Parisian home in the Bois de Boulogne.

3½in (9cm) high
$10,000-11,000 HAN

A Continental Secessionist silvered metal mantel clock, in the style of W.M.F.

17½in (44.5cm) high
$1,900-2,500 WW

An early 20thC French Art Deco onyx and marble mantel clock, with eight-day time and strike movement, gilt bronze trim.

26in (66cm) wide
$500-650 DRA

An early 20thC French Art Deco onyx and marble mantel clock.

21in (53.5cm) wide
$400-500 DRA

An Art Deco chinoiserie walnut-cased mantel clock.

c1930 *14in (35.5cm) wide*
$550-650 L&T

A Philippe-Joseph Brocard enameled glass mosque lamp, with naskh inscription, signed "Brocard."

Philippe-Joseph Brocard was initially a glass restorer and later created his own pieces. He is credited with rediscovering the techniques of glass enameling that would inspire Art Nouveau designers, such as Émile Gallé and Daum. Brocard's mosque lamps were shown at the International Exhibition in London in 1871.

7in (17.5cm) long

$2,500-3,800   WW

A Loetz chandelier, with an iridescent blown shade, on brass chains and ceiling cap, shallow flake on fitter.

40in (101.5cm) high

$3,200-3,800   JDJ

An Arts and Crafts glass and patinated brass five-light hanging fixture, with Loetz-style shades, fixture marked "UNO," some chips.

17¾in (45cm) diam

$1,000-1,150   DRA

A pair of 20thC colored glass and repoussé brass dish lights, one pane cracked.

53¼in (135cm) diam

$2,500-3,200   SWO

An Arts and Crafts ironwork lamp, in the manner of Edward Spencer for Artificers Guild, with Monart glass bowl, no.VIII of 70a, paper label.

50¾in (129cm) high

$900-1,000   DUK

A Siot-Decauville gilded bronze table light, "La danse, la Loïe Fuller," by Larche Raoul, made for the Paris World Fair, signed, foundry mark "SIOT-DECAUVILLE FONDEUR."

1900   18in (45.5cm) high

$38,000-44,000   QU

An Art Nouveau patinated bronze table lamp, "La Voie Lactee" (the Milky Way), by Leo Laporte-Blairsy (1865-1923), with a cased blue glass shade probably made by Daum, signed.

An example of this spectacular bronze lamp was exhibited at the Salon of the Societe des Artistes Francais in 1904.

16¼in (41.5cm) high

$38,000-44,000   WW

A bronze "Daphne" table light, by Emil Thomasson, signed, reelectrified.

c1902   11½in (29cm) high

$2,500-3,200   QU

A Daum cameo grapevine table lamp, with hammered iron collar and three-armed spider, signed, base signed "DNF" with Cross of Lorraine, rewired.

14½in (37cm) high

$6,500-7,000   JDJ

A Daum cameo glass table lamp, signed, some surface rust to metal, light marks to glass.

c1910   19¾in (50cm) high

$5,000-6,300   CHEF

A Daum "Verre de Jade" table lamp, on wrought-iron foot.

1918-25   19¾in (50cm) high

$3,800-4,400   QU

A 1930s Daum and Edgar Brandt patinated wrought iron and glass chandelier, metal stamped "FRANCE E. BRANDT," shades signed "DAUM NANCY FRANCE" with Cross of Lorraine.

35in (89cm) high

$7,000-7,500   DRA

CLOSER LOOK—GALLÉ "CLEMATIS" LAMP

This model is the largest of the lamps that Gallé made and is extremely rare.

It is decorated with blue clematis flowers and olive-green leaves and stems, set against a rich yellow background.

The three-armed spider support has stylized Art Nouveau scarab beetles at the tips.

Cameo lamps are generally popular, because the light from within will perfectly display the decoration.

A Gallé cameo glass "Clematis" lamp, signed "Galle" in cameo.

31in (78.5cm) high

$190,000-250,000   MORP

An early 20thC Gallé painted metal and acid-etched cameo glass clematis plafonnier, signed, some bubbles around rim, replacement metal components.

24in (61cm) high

$5,500-7,000   DRA

An early 20thC Gallé cameo lamp, acid etched with flowers, signed, some scuffs to base.

17¼in (44cm) high

$5,500-6,500   DRA

A Le Verre Francais cameo glass table lamp, signed, some dimpling to surface in the making.

17in (43cm) high

$4,400-5,000   JDJ

A Le Verre Francais "Monnaie du Pape" table lamp, etched "Le Verre Francais," fleabite to rim, rewired.

17in (43cm) high

$3,800-4,400   JDJ

A French molded glass and chrome-plated metal ceiling light.

c1930   *37¾in (96cm) high*

$3,200-3,800   **QU**

A 1930s Lalique glass plaffonier, "Lausanne" pattern, no.2479, molded mark, with chains and fixings.

15in (38cm) wide

$3,200-3,800   **FLD**

A 1930s Danish Louis Poulsen Emperor brass and glass chandelier, by Poul Henningsen (1894-1967), minor repair to one socket.

24in (61cm) diam

$5,000-5,700   **DRA**

An early-to-mid 20thC French glazed earthenware and patinated metal table lamp, by Jean Besnard (1889-1958), signed, rewired, with new paper shade.

27in (68.5cm) high

$7,000-7,500   **DRA**

A pair of 1930s-50s Art Deco chrome dome table lamps, rewired and PAT tested.

21in (53.5cm) high

$2,800-3,300   **TDG**

An Art Deco carved alabaster and bronze-mounted table lamp, on a cold-painted bronze base, later shade.

c1925   *base 10½in (26.5cm) high*

$1,050-1,200   **ROS**

An Art Deco gilt patinated spelter figural lamp, stamped "Foreign," on onyx base, cracks to shade, in need of rewiring.

20in (51cm) high

$1,500-2,000   **TEN**

An Art Deco bronzed metal lamp, with opaque glass ball shade.

25½in (65cm) high

$700-750   **BE**

A cold-painted bronze and ivory figural table lamp, by Roland Paris and C. Morin, signed "C. Morin."

c1930   *22½in (57cm) high*

$2,500-3,200   **ROS**

A Herbert Terry Anglepoise wheeled trolley lamp, model no.1227.

c1935-55   *73in (185.5cm) high*

$1,500-1,900   **TDG**

DECORATIVE ARTS

ESSENTIAL REFERENCE—TIFFANY LAMPS

Tiffany Studios began as Tiffany Glass Company in 1885.

- It was founded by Louis Comfort Tiffany (1848-1933), the son of one of the founders of Tiffany & Co. He had trained as a painter in New York and Paris, later specializing in stained glass.
- In 1893, Louis Comfort Tiffany created and trademarked Favrile glass (see also pages 520-521).
- In 1895, the firm made its first Tiffany lamp. This was not designed by Louis Comfort Tiffany himself but by Clara Driscoll, one of the company's designers.
- Typically in the Art Nouveau style, Tiffany lamps usually consist of a leaded slag glass shade and a patinated metal base. The shades were produced by fusing hundreds of pieces of colored glass together.
- Tiffany lamps became incredibly popular and are still prized by collectors today, often fetching very high prices.

An early 20thC Tiffany Studios leaded slag glass "Arrowroot" shade, on associated reproduction patinated metal base, metal "TIFFANY STUDIOS NEW YORK" tag to shade, some cracks to glass, loss of one piece.

26¼in (66.5cm) high

$53,000-63,000 **DRA**

A Tiffany Studios "Dogwood" table lamp, on bronze library base, the shade with "Tiffany Studios New York" tag, base signed, some hairlines.

26in (66cm) high

$60,000-65,000 **MORP**

CLOSER LOOK—TIFFANY "DRAGONFLY" TABLE LAMP

The leaded glass shade is decorated with dragonflies, each with striated red and cream wings, deep red bodies, and blue eyes.

These are set against a heavily texture, striated green and amber background, embellished with oval green glass cabochons.

The leading and etched bronze wing overlays are finished in a rich brown patina.

The shade rests on a Tiffany Studios faux turtleback bronze base, finished in a two-tone patina of dark brown and gold dore.

A Tiffany Studios "Dragonfly" table lamp, fully signed, some tight hairlines, rewired.

23in (58.5cm) high

$65,000-80,000 **JDJ**

A Tiffany Studios "Linenfold" table lamp, shade signed "Tiffany Studios New York 1927 PAT, APPL'D FOR," base signed, some small cracks, some discoloration to base.

24in (61cm) high

$18,000-23,000 **JDJ**

An early 20thC Tiffany Studios "Lotus" table lamp, metal "TIFFANY STUDIOS NEW YORK" tag to shade, base stamped, some cracks.

26½in (67.5cm) high

$70,000-80,000 **DRA**

A Tiffany Studios "Shell" table lamp, base stamped "TIFFANY STUDIOS NEW YORK 9936," metal tag "TIFFANY STUDIOS NEW YORK," some cracks to glass.

c1900 *21in (53.5cm) high*

$14,000-18,000 **DRA**

A Tiffany Studios "Woodbine" table lamp, shade with applied labels stamped "TIFFANY STUDIOS/ NEW YORK," base impressed "TIFFANY STUDIOS/ NEW YORK" and numbered "333," some heat cracks.

c1910 *19¾in (50cm) high*

$19,000-25,000 **WES**

A Tiffany Studios banded floral table lamp, on a bronze base, signed to shade "Tiffany Studios New York," base signed "Tiffany Studios New York 21667" with Tiffany logo.

23in (58.5cm) high

$44,000-50,000 **JDJ**

A 1920s Tiffany Studios table lamp, blue wave-pattern Favrile glass shade on acid-etched gilt bronze base, shade etched "L.C.T. Favrile," base stamped, rewired, replaced socket and paddle switch.

17¾in (45cm) high

$27,000-38,000 **DRA**

A Tiffany Studios ten-light lamp, with gold Favrile lily shades, in bronze fixture with lilypad foot, signed, replacement switch, rewired, flakes and chips.

21in (53.5cm) high

$19,000-25,000   **JDJ**

A pair of Tiffany Studios "Jeweled" bronze and blue Favrile ribbed glass candlesticks, engraved "L.C.T. 4846" and "4849," bases signed.

c1910   *23¼in (59cm) high*

$15,000-19,000   **DOY**

An early 20thC Tiffany Studios adjustable counterbalance desk lamp, "Wave" pattern shade, base stamped, shade etched "L.C.T. Favrile," some flecks to glass, one bubble.

14in (35.5cm) high

$7,500-10,000   **DRA**

An early 20thC Tiffany Studios floor lamp, with Favrile glass wave pattern shade, base stamped, shade etched "L.C. Tiffany-Favrile," some chips.

56in (142cm) high

$6,500-7,500   **DRA**

A 1920s Tiffany Studios glass "Linenfold" table lamp, stamped "TIFFANY STUDIOS NEW YORK 590," baseplate replaced, broken pull chain, some oxidation to base.

19in (48.5cm) high

$4,400-5,000   **DRA**

An early 20thC Tiffany Studios leaded slag glass hanging shade, with metal tag, with modern reproduction hardware and chains, some cracks.

62in (157.5cm) high

$13,000-15,000   **DRA**

A early 20thC Tiffany Studios "Acorn" hanging shade, with metal "TIFFANY STUDIOS NEW YORK" tag, minor cracks, installed associated wheel for use as a chandelier.

20in (51cm) wide

$9,500-10,500   **DRA**

An early 20thC Tiffany Studios "Turtleback' chandelier, leaded slag glass with Favrile glass tiles, metal tag to shade, some cracks to glass.

55in (139.5cm) high

$28,000-33,000   **DRA**

A Tiffany Studios "Turtleback" lantern, with iridescent turtleback tiles and bronze wire coins.

28in (71cm) high

$70,000-80,000   **MORP**

A Handel "Hawaii" opal glass table light, signed "HANDEL," with bronze foot.

Philip J. Handel and Adolph Eydam founded Eydam and Handel in 1885 in Meriden, Connecticut. By 1903 Handel had bought out his partner and the firm became the Handel Company. The firm was best known for its distinctive reverse-painted glass lampshades.

c1910 *23½in (60cm) high*

$3,200-3,800 QU

CLOSER LOOK—HANDEL "AQUARIUM" LAMP

The finial topping of the lamp is formed as a trident.

This Handel lamp is decorated with reverse-painted panels of underwater scenes, showing fish swimming among aquatic plants.

Each panel is finished on the exterior with chipped ice.

The original Handel two-armed base is decorated with fish and aquatic plants, and finished in a rich brown patina with green highlights.

A Handel "Aquarium" lamp, numbered and signed "Handel," rewired with plastic cord.

14½in (37cm) wide

$65,000-75,000 JDJ

A Handel "Wisteria" table lamp, the tree trunk base with leaded branches and openwork top, signed to shade, signed to base "Handel," some hairlines and oxidation.

31in (78.5cm) high

$14,000-18,000 MORP

A Handel table lamp, reverse-painted shade acid-etched with birds of paradise and roses, fully signed, sockets replaced, scratches to heat cap, finial possibly associated.

designed c1924 *24in (61cm) high*

$6,500-7,500 DRA

A 1910s Handel Art and Crafts-style table lamp, with obverse-painted acid-etched glass shade, shade signed, some chips to shade, resoldering to shade ring.

19½in (49.5cm) high

$2,300-2,800 DRA

A Handel "Birds of Paradise" table lamp, signed, artist signed "Broggi," base signed "Handel," minor wear.

23½in (59.5cm) high

$5,000-6,300 MORP

A Handel patinated metal and iridized glass globe pendant, reverse and obverse-painted, shade signed "HANDEL 6996," minor flecks to glass, associated ceiling cap.

designed c1922 *28in (71cm) high*

$2,500-3,200 DRA

A Handel cast metal and glass torchière, reverse-painted with stylized daisies, fully signed.

15½in (39.5cm) high

$1,400-1,800 MORP

A Handel patinated metal and glass floor lamp, reverse-painted acid-etched shade, fully signed, rewired.

designed 1921 *61in (155cm) high*

$7,500-9,000 DRA

An early 20thC hammered copper and blown glass chandelier, attributed to Benedict Studios, Syracuse, New York, some scratches.

28in (71cm) high

$3,200-3,800 DRA

An early 20thC Classique table lamp, Chicago, Illinois, reverse painted and acid etched, fabric label to base, rewired, socket guts replaced, some scratches.

22½in (57cm) high

$2,300-2,800 DRA

A Duffner and Kimberly "Waterlillies" table lamp, three sockets marked "HUBBELL."

1906-11 *22½in (57cm) high*

$7,500-9,000 NA

A Duffner and Kimberly hanging leaded glass light fixture, with metal tag.

c1910 *28in (71cm) wide*

$2,300-2,800 CLAR

CLOSER LOOK—FULPER VASEKRAFT LAMP

This lamp was made by Fulper, a pottery firm based in Flemington, New Jersey (see page 466).

Fulper Arts and Crafts "Vasekraft" lamps were made c1911-18 and are distinctively shaped. This is a very rare and fine example.

The shade is made of earthenware and leaded slag glass.

The base is made of earthenware, finished with a "Leopard Skin Crystalline" glaze.

A 1910s Fulper "Vasekraft" lamp, vertical rectangular ink stamps, some grinding chips.

17¾in (45cm) high

$20,000-32,000 DRA

A Fulper "Vasekraft" glazed earthenware and slag glass hanging shade, ink stamp, some chips, restoration to rim.

c1915 *15in (38cm) diam*

$6,500-7,500 DRA

A rare patinated copper, slag glass, and wrought iron hanging lantern, by Charles Sumner Greene (1860-1957) and Henry Mather Greene (1870-1954), Long Beach, California.

Provenance: Jennie A. Reeve House, Long Beach, CA

c1903-04 *29in (73.5cm) high*

$145,000-190,000 DRA

An early 20thC Frederick Lueders patinated copper and conch shell floriform lamp, signed "DESIGNED & EXECUTED BY F.H.W. LUEDERS PASADENA CA.," rewired, some wear.

19in (48.5cm) high

$5,500-7,000 DRA

A John Morgan & Sons table lamp, with leaded glass shade with pansies, with enameled detail on bronze base, some tight hairlines.

23in (58.5cm) high

$23,000-28,000 JDJ

A 1910s-20s Pairpoint "Puffy Tulip" patinated metal and frosted glass boudoir lamp, base stamped, three chips to shade, losses to gold paint.

14¾in (37.5cm) high

$1,900-2,500   **DRA**

A Pittsburg "Native American" table lamp, reverse painted, the base with textured glass body painted with Native American tapestries, two-socket cluster, rewired.

16½in (42cm) wide

$3,800-5,000   **MORP**

A rare Gustav Stickley hammered copper and leaded slag glass lantern, with stylized flowers.

c1905   *12¼in (31cm) high*

$70,000-80,000   **DRA**

An early 20thC Gustav Stickley hammered copper and glass newel post lantern.

19½in (49.5cm) high

$4,400-5,000   **DRA**

An early 20thC Unique "Cherry Blossom" table lamp, Brooklyn, New York, some splits and cracks, rewired.

29½in (75cm) high

$1,500-2,000   **DRA**

A Dirk Van Erp (1860-1933) hammered copper and mica table lamp, open-box windmill stamp, base resoldered, some scratches to shade, rewired.

c1915   *20½in (52cm) high*

$5,000-6,300   **DRA**

A Dirk Van Erp hammered copper and mica "Bean Pot" table lamp, open-box windmill mark, some scratches.

c1913-15   *10½in (26.5cm) high*

$5,500-7,000   **WES**

One of a pair of early 20thC Arts and Crafts hammered iron and patinated metal chandeliers, with slag glass lanterns, some cracks, both needing rewiring.

33in (84cm) high

$800-950 the pair   **DRA**

An Arts and Crafts leaded glass table lamp, with patinated floral-decorated three-socket standard.

c1920   *25in (63.5cm) high*

$1,800-2,500   **CLAR**

A Liberty & Co. Art Nouveau silver and enameled spoon, commemorating King Edward VII and Queen Alexandra, the bowl detailed "AC ERVII," detailed "CYMRIC Rd391475," small chips to enamel.

The department store Liberty & Co. opened in London in 1875 as a furniture and drapery store known as East India House. It expanded in the late 19thC, commissioning and creating carpets, ceramics, clothing, furniture, and silver. It registered its own silver hallmark in 1894; the majority of its silver was made in Birmingham.

1901 *4¾in (12cm) high ¾oz*
$1,900-2,500 **BELL**

A Liberty & Co. silver Cymric Coronation Spoon, by Archibald Knox (1864-1933), inscribed "AC ER VII," stamped "L&C Cymric," Birmingham.
1902 *6¼in (16cm) long*
$500-650 **LSK**

A set of six Liberty & Co., London "Cymric" silver and enamel coffee spoons, by Archibald Knox, stamped maker's marks "L&Co," hallmarked Birmingham.
1929 *4¼in (11cm) long*
$800-950 **L&T**

A Liberty & Co. Arts and Crafts silver and enamel napkin "Cymric" ring.
1904 *2in (5cm) diam 1¼oz*
$500-650 **APAR**

A Liberty & Co. Art Nouveau silver and enamel menu card holder, with registration number.
1906 *1½in (4cm) long ¼oz*
$500-650 **WW**

A Liberty & Co. Art Nouveau silver vase, stamped maker's marks "L&Co," hallmarked Birmingham.

This piece was designed by Oliver Baker for the "Cymric" range; the original design for 1900 indicated the collar should be enameled. Only one example dated 1901 is known. It is more commonly found in pewter.
1900 *5½in (14cm) high 32⅞oz*
$3,800-4,400 **L&T**

A Liberty & Co. Art Nouveau "Cymric" silver box and cover, stamped maker's marks "CYMRIC/L&Co," hallmarked London.
1902 *5¼in (13.5cm) high 15¼oz*
$1,200-1,400 **L&T**

A Liberty & Co. copper-framed mirror with ceramic cabochons, with "Liberty" label.
c1905 *24¾in (63cm) wide*
$2,000-2,300 **TDG**

A Liberty & Co. pewter "Tudric" rose bowl, by David Veazey, with inscription "THE MUSK OF THE ROSE IS BLOWN AND THE WOODBINE SPICES ARE WAFTED ABROAD," stamped "011."
c1900 *12¼in (31cm) wide*
$400-500 **L&T**

A Liberty & Co. pewter "Tudric" flower vase and liner, by Archibald Knox, stamped "MADE IN ENGLAND/TUDRIC/0957."
c1900 *8¾in (22cm) high*
$500-650 **L&T**

A pair of Liberty & Co. pewter "Tudric" candlesticks, by Archibald Knox, stamped "MADE IN ENGLAND/ENGLISH PEWTER/0223."
c1905 *9¼in (23.5cm) high*
$900-1,000 **L&T**

A Tiffany & Co. mokume and silver cup and saucer, marked "5044/900," French import marks.

Mokume is a Japanese metalworking technique which produces a mixed-metal laminate of layered patterns, imitating wood grain. Tiffany & Co. design director Edward C. Moore owned several examples of Japanese mokume, and in the late 1870s his firm mastered the technique.

c1878   *saucer 4in (10cm) wide*

$8,000-9,500   **DRA**

A Tiffany & Co. sterling silver water pitcher, marked "7097/4523."

1882-91   *8in (20.5cm) high 34⅝oz*

$2,500-3,200   **DRA**

A 20thC Tiffany & Co. bronze floor vase, stamped "Tiffany & Co. 19039D," light scratches.

18in (45.5cm) high

$1,300-1,800   **DRA**

A Tiffany Studios enameled copper dragonfly tray, stamped "TGDCO. TIFFANY STUDIOS NEW YORK 2/9064," small losses to enamel.

The design is closely related to the "Swirling Dragonfly" leaded shade.

c1900   *14¾in (37.5cm) diam*

$38,000-44,000   **DRA**

A Tiffany Studios bronze and glass scarab inkwell, stamped "TGDCO. TIFFANY STUDIOS NEW YORK 25056," with dark overcoat.

c1900   *4¼in (11cm) high*

$5,500-7,000   **DRA**

A Tiffany Studios picture frame, marked "Tiffany Studios New York 949," inscribed "1858 A.F-HMc A. 1908."

The glass backing of red, purple, blue, and green gives the effect of a sunset when back lit.

7in (17.5cm) high

$1,150-1,250   **JDJ**

A 1920s Tiffany Studios cedar and gilt and enameled bronze cigar box, no.134, stamped "LOUIS C. TIFFANY FURNACES INC FAVRILE 134," minor wear to gilding.

7in (18cm) wide

$2,000-2,500   **DRA**

A 1920s Tiffany Studios acid-etched gilt bronze and glass "Zodiac" picture frame, stamped "TIFFANY STUDIOS NEW YORK 920," some wear.

14in (35.5cm) high

$2,500-3,200   **DRA**

A Tiffany Studios Chinese-style bronze inkwell, with original glass insert, signed "Tiffany Studios New York 1753," some wear to patina.

6in (15cm) wide

$1,600-2,000   **JDJ**

ESSENTIAL REFERENCE—GEORG JENSEN

Georg Jensen (1866-1935) was the son of a Danish knife grinder. He was apprenticed as a goldsmith and also worked as a modeler in a porcelain factory.

● **He opened a pottery workshop in 1898, but soon gave it up to work as a silversmith and designer. In 1904, he founded his own silversmith shop, the Georg Jensen Co.**

● **He took inspiration from the Arts and Crafts and Art Nouveau movements to create his distinctive style. He is known for his hollowware and jewelry (see page 364).**

● **He encouraged his designers to work in their own styles, and worked with many talented people, including Gundorph Albertus (1887-1969), Henning Koppel (1918-81), Harald Nielsen (1892-1977), Johan Rohde (1865-1935), and Vivianna Torun Bülow-Hübe (1927-2004).**

● **George Jensen died in 1935. Georg Jensen Co. is still operational today.**

A Georg Jensen sterling silver and wood tea caddy, model no.136.

c1915-30   *5¼in (13.5cm) high*

$6,500-7,000   **DOY**

A Georg Jensen sterling silver centerpiece bowl, model no.252.

c1915-30   *10¼in (26cm) diam 42oz*

$9,500-10,500   **DOY**

A Georg Jensen sterling silver compote, "Grape" pattern, model no.265A.

designed 1918 11in (28cm) high 38¼oz

$5,500-7,000   **FRE**

A Georg Jensen sterling silver beaker, no.338, with a band of rosettes and garnet cabochons, marked, some wear

1925-32   4½in (11.5cm) high 7⅛oz

$4,400-5,000   **DRA**

A Georg Jensen sterling silver footed bowl, "Louvre" pattern, no.19A, marked.

1925-32   8in (20.5cm) diam

$2,800-3,800   **DRA**

A Georg Jensen sterling silver water pitcher, designed by Johan Rohde, no.432A, marked.

1933-44   9in (23cm) high 17¼oz

$3,200-3,800   **DRA**

A Georg Jensen sterling silver toast rack, designed by Oscar Gundlach Pedersen, no.510, marked, light scratches.

1933-44   6in (15cm) long 7⅜oz

$4,400-5,000   **DRA**

A Georg Jensen sterling silver serving platter, "Acorn" pattern, designed by Gundorph Albertus, no.642S, marked, minor scratches.

1945-77   16¾in (42.5cm) diam 44⅞oz

$4,400-5,000   **DRA**

A Georg Jensen sterling silver bowl, designed by Henning Koppel (1918-81), with artist's monogram and maker's marks "A11/HK/GEORG JENSEN/ STERLING/DENMARK/925S/980A."

This asymmetrical bowl was designed in 1948 and received the gold medal at the 1951 Milan Triennale. An example of this model is kept in the collection at Goldsmiths' Hall, London.

designed 1948   15¾in (40cm) wide 124¾oz

$12,000-14,000   **L&T**

A Georg Jensen silver "blossom" pattern oval tray, post-1945 mark, marked "DENMARK," "GEORG JENSEN," "STERLING," and "2E."

22¼in (56.5cm) long 53oz

$9,000-10,000   **NA**

DECORATIVE ARTS

A pair of Edwardian J. Aitkin & Son silver-mounted photograph frames, later cold enamel accents, Birmingham, refurbished, some surface scratches.

1909   *7¼in (18.5cm) high*
$1,000-1,250   **FELL**

A set of four early 20thC Japanese Art Nouveau silver and jade cups, impressed with the marks of the English-owned Arthur & Bond Company of Yokohama and with a "Sterling" mark.

4¼in (11cm) diam silver 9⅜oz
$950-1,050   **JN**

An Artificers Guild Arts and Crafts silver powder pot and cover, with chrysoprase finial and punch borders, London.

1919   *4½in (11.5cm) diam 12oz*
$3,800-4,400   **WW**

An early 20thC J.E. Caldwell & Co. sterling silver "Chrysanthemum" vase, Philadelphia, fully marked, numbered "3975," some dents and abrasions.

17½in (44.5cm) high 49½oz
$1,900-2,500   **WES**

A pair of James Dixon & Son Arts and Crafts silver candlesticks, probably designed by Jan Eisenloeffel (1876-1957), Sheffield, some dings, filled.

1919   *8¾in (22cm) high*
$2,300-2,800   **TEN**

An Elkington & Co. silver tea and coffee set, pattern no.16644, with engraved Japanese-style decoration, Birmingham.

1891   *60¼oz*
$2,500-3,200   **PW**

ESSENTIAL REFERENCE—CHRISTOPHER DRESSER

Christopher Dresser (1834-1904) was Britain's first professional and independent industrial designer.

● **Dresser embraced new production techniques in color, pattern, material, and ornamentation, and he worked with innumerable manufacturers.**

● **His aim was to make high-quality and beautifully designed products available to the widest possible audience. His work looks astoundingly "modern" even today.**

● **He combined new 19th-century technology with traditions from a range of cultures, influenced by his study of botany and his travels in Japan in the 1870s.**

● **This rare teapot is one of a group of remarkable designs produced by Dresser for James Dixon & Sons of Sheffield from 1879-83. He produced approximately 80 designs for the firm.**

A James Dixon & Son silver teapot, designed by Christopher Dresser, with ebony handle, with engraved presentation, Sheffield, with Victorian lozenge marks, stamped serial numbers "2278/N27/14-11."

1882   *5½in (14cm) high*
$19,000-23,000   **L&T**

A Gieves Ltd. Art Deco silver tea and coffee set, with Bakelite handles, Birmingham.

Provenance: With original Thurlow Champness & Son of Abbegate Street, Bury St Edmunds, purchase receipt dated April 6, 1968, for a total of £105 ($250).

1933   *coffee pot 7in (17.5cm) high 57oz*
$1,500-2,000   **LSK**

A pair of Goldsmiths & Silversmiths Co. Art Deco silver candelabra, London, some dings.

1937   *9¾in (24.5cm) high 34oz*
$2,300-2,800   **TEN**

A late 19thC Gorham sterling silver tazza, with silver-gilt and copper accents, for Theodore B. Starr, New York, engraved to underside "Emma Paige Eells Oct. 11th 1880," some losses.

12½in (32cm) diam 35oz
$3,200-3,800   **DRA**

A Guild of Handicraft silver and enamel box, the inset cover painted by William Mark (1868-1956), signed, maker's mark "GofH Ltd," London, scratched number "4196," bent cover, deep mark to base, some other wear.

1902   *5in (12.5cm) long*

$7,500-9,000   **TEN**

A rare Guild of Handicraft Arts and Crafts silver dish, liner and spoon, by Charles Robert Ashbee (1863-1942), London, with handle set with a green chrysoprase cabochon, minor scratches and wear.

1903   *7in (17.5cm) wide*

$13,000-15,000   **CHEF**

A pair of William Hutton & Sons Art Nouveau silver and enamel photograph frames, London.

1903   *8in (20.5cm) high*

$2,500-3,200   **ROS**

A George Lawrence Connell Ltd. hammered silver rocket bowl, London.

1909   *10½in (26.5cm) diam 52oz*

$3,200-3,800   **LSK**

A Chase Brothers of Sheffield Glasgow School teaspoon, designed by Charles Rennie Mackintosh for Cranston's tea rooms.

This was a minor part of Mackintosh's commission to furnish Miss Cranston's Willow Tea Rooms in Glasgow, which included Makintosh's iconic chairs. The original Willow Tea Rooms, dating from 1903, opened again to the public in 2018, following a £10m ($12.6m) restoration. The tearooms are now called Mackintosh at the Willow and there is a visitors' center next door.

$400-500   **HAN**

A Danish Anton Michelsen sterling silver pitcher, designed by Kay Fisker (1893-65), fully marked, some scratches.

1947   *9in (23cm) high 19oz*

$1,400-2,000   **DRA**

ESSENTIAL REFERENCE—H.G. MURPHY

H.G. Murphy (1884-1939) was an influential Arts and Crafts and Art Deco designer of jewelry and silverware.
- He was born in Birchington-on-Sea in Kent and grew up in London.
- After an apprenticeship to Arts and Crafts designer Henry Wilson, he established retail premises in Marylebone in 1928 called the Falcon Studio.
- By the early 1930s, Murphy's success was established. He received silver commissions from city institutions, churches, and schools as well as for making jewelry in silver and gold.
- In 1938, Murphy received the award of Royal Designer for Industry (RDI) from The Duke of Gloucester and Harry was appointed the Faculty's First Master.
- In the late 1930s, Murphy's health began to deteriorate. He died on July 10, 1939.

A Falcon Studio Art Deco silver teapot, in the French manner, by H.G. Murphy, carved ivory handle and finial, with Falcon Studio mark.

1930   *8½in (21.5cm) long 23¾oz*

$11,000-12,000   **WW**

A Falcon Studio matched three-piece silver café-au-lait set, by H.G. Murphy, with Falcon Studio mark.

1931/37   *max 12¼in (31cm) high 79oz*

$10,000-11,000   **WW**

A silver bishop's crozier, by Ramsden and Carr, London, engraved "OMAR RAMSDEN ET ALWYN CARR ME FECERUNT."

1908   *69½in (176.5cm) high 12oz*

$3,800-5,000   **WW**

A silver caddy spoon, by Omar Ramsden, the handle set with three chrysoprase.

1917   *3¼in (8.5cm) long 1⅜oz*

$2,500-3,200   **DUK**

A Reed & Barton sterling silver tea and coffee service.

tray 27¾in (70.5cm) wide 302oz

$5,500-7,000   **POOK**

A Walker & Tolhurst Arts and Crafts silver bowl, probably designed by Gilbert Marks, stamped maker's mark "WWBT," London.

1894   9in (23cm) diam 24oz

$3,800-4,400   **WW**

A Christofle & Cie electroplated metal teapot, modeled as a zoomorphic creature, with ivory spacers, stamped marks, designed by Emile Reiber, dated.

This design is based on an antique Japanese bronze in the Henry Cernuschi collection. This is listed by the Musee d'Orsay as being prepared for the 1878 Exposition Universelle.

1878   9in (23cm) wide

$3,200-3,800   **WW**

A silver tea service, by Robert Scott, Sheffield and Glasgow.

1921-25   169¼oz

$2,300-2,800   **WAD**

A Tuttle Silversmiths silver cocktail shaker, Boston, Massachusetts, in the form of a milk churn, initialed "W."

c1923-29   12¼in (31cm) high 41½oz

$2,500-3,200   **TEN**

A John T. Vansant & Co., sterling silver water pitcher, Philadelphia, marked "English Sterling 925," nicks to rim.

c1880   8½in (21.5cm) high 27½oz

$2,500-3,200   **DRA**

A Hukin & Heath silver-plated tureen, cover, and ladle, with ebony handles, designed by Christopher Dresser (1834-1904), stamped "Designed By Dr C Dresser" and "H & H 2123."

12¼in (31cm) wide

$6,500-7,500   **BE**

A silver-plated soup ladle, by Christopher Dresser, with ebonized wood handle, with date lozenge mark.

1880   11½in (29cm) long

$2,300-2,800   **L&T**

A Guild of Handicrafts silver-plated dish and cover, by Charles Robert Ashbee (1863-1942), the cover set with moonstone cabochon, stamped "GofHLtd."

c1901   9¼in (23.5cm) wide

$2,500-3,200   **L&T**

A W.M.F. Art Nouveau electroplated "Echo" strut mirror, stamped marks.

c1905   14¼in (36cm) high

$650-750   **L&T**

A pair of Neo-Grec parcel-gilt and patinated bronze vases, by Ferdinand Barbedienne and Ferdinand Levillain, inscribed "F. BARBEDIENNE" on base and "F. LEVILLAIN" on body.

Ferdinand Levillain (1837-1905) began his career as a master bronze artist as an apprentice in the studio of sculptor Francois Jouffroy. By 1861, while still in his early 20s, Levillain was already exhibiting at the Paris Salon. He won a silver medal at the 1889 Paris Exposition Universelle. These vases exemplify the sculptor's fruitful collaboration with bronzier Ferdinand Barbedienne 1871-c1890.

c1875   *19in (48cm) high*

$9,000-10,000   **DN**

A 1910s Roycroft nickel silver and hammered and wrought copper buttressed vase, by Karl Kipp (1881-1954), orb and cross mark, some wear.

8¼in (21cm) high

$4,400-5,000   **DRA**

ESSENTIAL REFERENCE—FREDERIC SHIELDS

Frederic Shields was an illustrator, designer, mural decorator, stained glass designer, and enamellist.
- **He was born in Hartlepool, England, and brought up in extreme poverty. As a young man he worked as a commercial engraver, studying at evening classes in London and later Manchester.**
- **His illustrations for Defoe's "History of the Plague" (1862) and "Bunyan's Pilgrim's Progress" (1864) brought him to the attention of John Ruskin and Dante Gabriel Rossetti, who invited him to visit them in London.**
- **In 1876, he settled in London. Rossetti offered him space in his own studio and helped and encouraged him with his work.**

An Arts and Crafts copper and enamel casket, by Frederic James Shields (1833-1911), stamped monogram to lid and clasp.

c1890   *6¼in (16cm) wide*

$5,500-7,000   **L&T**

A copper vase, by John Pearson, struck "J.P. 1908" and numbered "2772."

6in (15cm) high

$650-750   **SWO**

An Arts and Crafts copper and enamel decorated wall sconce, small dent to corner.

24¾in (63cm) high

$3,200-3,800   **APAR**

A Roycroft hammered copper and enamel vase, after a design by Walter Jennings, with Italian enamel decoration.

c1910-15   *7in (18cm) high*

$4,400-5,000   **WES**

A Stickley Brothers hammered copper jardinière, impressed "241."

c1910   *15in (38cm) wide*

$2,500-3,200   **CLAR**

A William Hutton & Sons Art Nouveau pewter butter dish, attributed to Kate Harris, Sheffield, with lid and glass liner.

c1910   *8¾in (22cm) wide*

$650-750   **TDG**

A pair of W.M.F. Art Nouveau pewter and brass figural candelabra, model no.269 and no.269A, faint stamped maker's marks.

c1906   *10½in (26.5cm) high*

$1,900-2,500   **ROS**

ESSENTIAL REFERENCE—FRANZ BERGMAN

Franz Bergman and his son, also named Franz Bergman, were important Austrian bronze manufacturers.

● Franz Bergman Sr. (1838-94) was born in Bohemia and worked as a metalwork finisher. In 1860, he founded a bronze factory in Vienna.

● Franz Bergman Jr. (1861-1939) took over the factory after his father's death. Bergman was not a sculptor himself, but directed his factory in the production of a range of cold-painted and patinated bronze sculptures.

● Animal figures were common, as were sculptures inspired by Asian and Arabian people.

● Bergman also made erotic figures. These are sometimes stamped "Namgreb"—Bergman in reverse.

A late 19thC Franz Bergman cold-painted bronze figure, cast as an Arab scribe reading the Koran, stamped marks, on matched hardwood stand.

5½in (14cm) wide

$2,000-2,500   **HT**

An early 20thC Franz Bergman cold-painted bronze Arab horseman, stamped "B" within urn and numbered.

9in (23cm) high

$3,200-3,800   **DN**

A Franz Bergman cold-painted bronze Arab trader shrouding a female nude, marked "Nam Greb" and "B" within urn.

9¾in (25cm) wide

$2,500-3,200   **HAN**

A 19thC Franz Bergman cold-painted bronze elephant, carrying two hunters and a fallen lion.

9¾in (25cm) high

$2,500-3,200   **HANN**

A late 19thC Franz Bergman cold-painted bronze lamp, cast as a Middle Eastern carpet seller, marked "B" within urn and "GESCH," wired for electricity.

18½in (47cm) high

$6,500-7,500   **ROS**

An Austrian cold-painted bronze lamp base of chess players, in the style of Franz Bergman, base stamped "AUSTRIA."

17¼in (44cm) high

$3,200-3,800   **BRI**

A Franz Bergman cold-painted bronze porcupine, indistinct stamp number and "GESCHUTZT," some losses, spraining to quills.

6in (15cm) long

$3,200-3,800   **TEN**

A late 19thC Franz Bergman cold-painted bronze figure of a lion, urn mark.

7in (18cm) long

$1,000-1,150   **L&T**

A Franz Bergman cold-painted bronze kingfisher, on veined marble dish, broken at ankles.

4¾in (12cm) long

$450-550   **WW**

An Austrian cold-painted bronze model of a game bird, stamped "B" within urn, for the Bergman manufactory.

c1900   *10½in (26.5cm) high*

$3,200-3,800   **DN**

A pair of late 19thC Austrian cold-painted bronze parrots, some losses to painted finish, some rubbing.

11¾in (30cm) high

$5,500-7,000   **GORL**

A cold-painted bronze table lamp, by Anton Chotka (1881-1955), in the form of an Arabian scene, signed, on a marble plinth.

13¾in (35cm) high

$4,400-5,000   **HAN**

A late 19thC Austrian cold-painted bronze cockerel, on slate base.

7½in (19cm) high

$550-650   **REEM**

A 1920s Austrian gilt bronze of a young Turkish girl, by E. Wante, signed, on onyx base.

10½in (26.5cm) high

$1,050-1,200   **JN**

A late 19thC to early 20thC Austrian cold-painted bronze model of an owl, in the manner of Bergman, on a marble plinth.

6in (15cm) high

$650-750   **WW**

A late 19thC cold-painted bronze bulldog, paint finish dirty.

7¼in (18.5cm) long

$800-950   **GORL**

A late 19thC Austrian cold-painted bronze puppy, stamped "Depose" twice, with kite registration mark, wear to paint.

7½in (19cm) long

$700-800   **REEM**

A late 19thC Austrian cold-painted bronze puppy, "Depose" mark and kite registration mark, wear to muzzle.

6¾in (17cm) long

$1,050-1,200   **REEM**

A late 19thC to early 20thC Austrian cold-painted cast bronze basset hound, stamped "Geschutzt."

5¾in (14.5cm) long

$500-650   **TOV**

A late 19thC to early 20thC Austrian cold-painted bronze lizard.

7¼in (18.5cm) long

$950-1,050   **WW**

A French bronze figure of a bear, "Ours Dans Son Auge," by Antoine-Louis Barye (1796-1875), signed "BARYE," inscribed "F BARBEDIENNE FONDEUR."

5¼in (13.5cm) long

$15,000-20,000 **TEN**

A bronze figure, "The Glint Of The Sea," by Chester Beach (1881-1956), signed "BEACH" with foundry stamp "KUNST FOUNDRY NY," on marble plinth.

9¾in (25cm) high

$750-900 **L&T**

A Spanish bronze group, "Dancing Ladies," by Joachin Bilbao Martinez (1864-1934), signed, stamped "CODINO INOS/ MADRID."

16¾in (42.5cm) high

$1,300-1,900 **L&T**

A French bronze bull, by Rosa Bonheur (1822-99), signed "ROSA B" to base.

7in (17.5cm) high

$1,500-2,000 **L&T**

A French bronze bull, by Isidore Jules Bonheur (1827-1901), signed "I BONHEUR" and stamped "PEYROL EDITEUR."

Bonheur was a regular Paris Salon exhibitor and the bull was one of his most popular subjects. This bronze was cast by his brother-in-law, Hippolyte Peyrol.

21½in (54.5cm) long

$7,500-9,000 **WW**

A patinated bronze "Verliebtes Mädchen" or "Girl in Love" model, by Arno Breker (1900-91), Germany, signed, with Venturi Arte foundry stamp and "195/300."

11½in (29cm) high

$2,800-3,800 **CHEF**

A bronze figure of a worker, by Aimé-Jules Dalou, signed, with "Susse" Freres foundry stamp and indistinct inscription "SUSSE FRES EDTS PARIS."

Dalou was a founder of the Société Nationale des Beaux-Arts, and a commander of the Legion of Honor known for his realistic and unpretentious depiction of the human form. Dalou openly sympathized with the working classes, and his alignment with the Paris Commune in 1871 resulted in his exile to London until 1879. Despite this, his works were commissioned in Paris—from the monumental sculpture at the Place de la Nation to numerous decorative sculptures lining the new boulevards of the city.

7¾in (20cm) high

$2,500-3,800 **L&T**

A study of bacchanalian nymphs and young satyr, after Clodion (1738-1814), signed to base, "Clodion 1762," rich dark brown patination.

29½in (75cm) high

$3,800-5,000 **BE**

A pair of 19thC bronze Marley horses, after Guillaume Coustou.

21¼in (54cm) high

$1,500-2,000 **PW**

A bronze figure, "Le Grand Paysan," by Aimé-Jules Dalou (1838-1902), signed and inscribed, with foundry stamp.

17in (43cm) high

$5,500-6,500 **L&T**

A French "Pro Patria" Classical bronze of a winged angel and young man, by Edouard Drouot (1859-1945), signed and inscribed.

23½in (59.5cm) high

$1,500-2,000   JN

A late 19thC French patinated bronze model of a standing geisha, by Vincent Desiré Faure de Broussé.

Vincent Desiré Faure de Broussé (c1876-1908) was born in Paris and apprenticed to the renowned portrait sculptor Jean-Jules Salmson. He is recorded to have exhibited at the Salon from 1876, and was known for creating figural sculpture influenced by examples from the Florentine Renaissance. Although this statue depicts a Japanese-inspired subject, the contrapposto pose of the figure, her serene facial features, and naturalistically heavily draped garment still recall Faure de Broussé's interest in Renaissance sculpture.

32¼in (82cm) high

$3,800-5,000   DN

A French gilt bronze figural group, "Orpheus and Eurydice," by Paul Jean Baptiste Gasq (1860-1944), with an applied plaque.

32in (81cm) high

$6,500-7,500   DN

Judith Picks

This charming bronze is based on the original statue of Peter Pan, which still stands in Kensington Gardens, London. Both were designed by Sir George Frampton, who was commissioned to make the larger statue by J.M.Barrie in 1911. Frampton (1860-1928) was a central figure of the New Sculpture movement, and produced many public monuments, including a number of statues of Queen Victoria. His original sculpture of Peter Pan is perhaps his most famous. The statue was placed in Kensington Gardens on April 1912, overnight and without permission, so that it might seem to the local children that it had appeared by magic.

A patinated bronze model of Peter Pan, by Sir George James Frampton RA, monogrammed "GF" and inscribed "PP" within a circle in the maquette, on a Connemara marble socle, dated.
1921   20in (51cm) high

$16,000-20,000   DN

A French patinated bronze model of a maiden, "Retour des Hirondelles" ("Return of the Swallows"), by Adrien Étienne Gaudez (1845-1902).

Gaudez studied under Francois Jouffroy at the Ecole des Beaux-Arts in Paris, making his debut at the Paris Salon in 1864. He worked almost exclusively in bronze and produced a wide array of sculpture, ranging from genre subjects to military and patriotic themes. His earlier work was Classical, but some of his later pieces, such as this model, can be categorized as Art Nouveau.
c1900   38¼in (97cm) high

$5,000-6,300   DN

A bronze figure of a donkey, by August Gaul (1861-1921), on marble base, signed "A. GAUL/AG," with foundry mark "H. NOACK/BERLIN/FRIEDENAU," on marble plinth.

Gaul was a noted sculptor and lithographer with a strong interest in depicting animals. He was one of the founding members of the Berlin Secession in 1898. This sculpture of a walking donkey forms part of a series of six sculptures entitled "Eselei" (folly) studying the various movements of a donkey.

5¾in (14.5cm) long

$6,500-7,500   L&T

A bronze figure, "Perseus Arming," by Sir Alfred Gilbert R.A. (1854-1934), on a verde antico marble plinth.

Alfred Gilbert was born in London and joined the Royal Academy in 1873 before going on to study at the École des Beaux-Arts, Paris and becoming one of the most influential sculptors of his generation and the New English Sculpture movement.

15¾in (40cm) high

$50,000-63,000   L&T

A bronze figure, "Comedy and Tragedy: Sic Vita," by Sir Alfred Gilbert R.A., on a ebonized wood plinth.

15¼in (39cm) high

$32,000-38,000   L&T

A patinated bronze nude, "Message of Love," cast from a model by Pierre Le Faguays, on veined marble base, signed in the cast to base rim "Le Faguays" and foundry mark.

22½in (57cm) high

$2,300-2,800   WW

A French Classical bronze faun, by Eugene Lequesne (1815-87), signed "E. LEQUESNE, SUISSE STAMP."

20in (51cm) high

$1,600-2,300   **JN**

A 19thC bronze study of two rutting stags, by Clovis Edmond Masson (1838-1913), on a marble base, signed.

21¾in (55cm) long

$1,900-2,500   **FLD**

A bronze horse, "French Cheval A La Barriere," by Pierre Jules Mene (1810-77), the horse named "Djinn," signed "P. J. MENE."

14½in (37cm) long

$2,300-2,800   **JN**

A French bronze Arab on horseback, by Ferdinand Pautrot (1832-74), signed, lacking musket.

19¾in (50cm) high

$2,500-3,200   **WHP**

A Joan of Arc bronze, after Henri Honore Ple (1853-1922), signed "Henri Ple," stamped "Elkington & Co," on a marble base.

37¾in (96cm) high

$3,800-4,400   **BE**

A bronze figure of a woman tying her sandal, "La Toilette d'Atalante," by Jean Jacques Pradier (1790-1852), signed, with Susse foundry stamp, minor wear.

12¾in (32.5cm) high

$4,400-5,000   **TEN**

A Susse Frères gilded bronze figure, "Danseuse au tambourin" from "Le Jeu de l'Echarpe," by Agathon Léonard and Léonard van Weydeveldt, Paris, marked "ALeonard Sculp, SUSSE FRES EDITEURS PARIS."

c1901   21¾in (55.5cm) high

$20,000-32,000   **QU**

A bronze figure, "Teucer," by Sir William Hamo Thornycroft RA, signed "HAMO THORNYCROFT."

Thornycroft admired the Elgin marbles, and his early works were in a Greek style. The champion Greek archer Teucer was one of the heroes of Homer's story of the Trojan War.

16¾in (42.5cm) high

$28,000-38,000   **L&T**

A standing bronze, by Sir William Hamo Thornycroft RA (1850-1925), depicting a member of 129th Duke of Connaught's Own Baluchis, signed and inscribed.

14½in (37cm) high

$9,000-10,000   **JN**

ESSENTIAL REFERENCE—DEMETRE H. CHIPARUS

Demetre H. Chiparus (1886-1947) was born in Romania and later moved to Paris.
- In Paris, he studied at the Ecole des Beaux Arts before working for Etling and the Les Neveau de J. Lehmann foundry, chiefly as a designer and sculptor.
- He mostly worked in chryselephantine (bronze and ivory), depicting stylized exotic women, often dancers, sometimes figures from the Russian Ballet, French theater, or early movies.
- His figures are generally very detailed, with impressive decorative effects.

A gilt and patinated bronze and ivory figure, "Ayouta," by Demetre H. Chiparus, on onyx base, signed "D Chiparus."

Ivory was commonly used in Art Deco figures. With new laws on the trade of ivory, figures with more than 10 percent ivory may be banned. Figures such as this one, with less than 10 percent ivory, may remain on the market, but the prices are struggling in the uncertainty of legal status. Art Deco figures without any ivory content are on the rise in comparison.

c1925 *11½in (29cm) high*
$11,000-12,000 **IEN**

A gilt-bronze and marble sculpture, "Accident de Chasse" ("The Hunting Accident"), by Demetre H. Chiparus, signed, some chips and wear.

16½in (42cm) wide
$2,500-3,200 **DRA**

A patinated ormolu figure, "The Dancer of Lebanon," by Demetre H. Chiparus, on onyx base, signed.

15in (38cm) high
$8,000-9,500 **BE**

A bronze sculpture, "Dancer of Olynthus," by Demetre H. Chiparus, on a veined onyx base with light fitting, etched "Chiparus" to base, cast number to her foot

13in (33cm) high
$8,000-9,500 **WW**

A silvered-bronze and ivory figure "Leaving the Opera," by Dimitri H. Chiparus, on onyx base, signed "D.H. Chiparus, Etling Paris."

c1930 *9in (23cm) high*
$5,000-6,300 **ROS**

Judith Picks

This impressive figure by Demetre H. Chiparus is entitled "Antinea." In Greek and Roman mythology, Queen Antinea was the granddaughter of Neptune and Clito, the last kings of Atlantis, and through Cleopatra Selene, also a descendent of the Ptolemies of Egypt. Antinea was said to keep an underground mausoleum of red marble with 120 alcoves, where she housed the numbered and labeled bodies of her former lovers, lost soldiers, and explorers. This detailed bronze and ivory figure has been in the same family for the last 40 years.

A cold-painted and patinated bronze and ivory figure, "Antinea," by Demetre H. Chiparus, the base marked "Etling Paris," signed "D H Chiparus" in the marble, some chips to marble.
c1928 *26½in (67.5cm) high*
$65,000-80,000 **ECGW**

A large cold-painted bronze and ivory figure, "Les Amis de Toujours" ("Friends Forever"), by Demetre H. Chiparus, on veined marble base, signed "Chiparus."

26in (66cm) wide
$50,000-63,000 **WW**

DECORATIVE ARTS

ESSENTIAL REFERENCE—JOSEF LORENZL

Josef Lorenzl (1892-1950) was a significant Art Deco designer and sculptor.

- He worked for several Austrian manufacturers, including Vienna Arsenal and Goldscheider (see page 467-468).
- He worked in ceramics and metal, and produced small sculptures in bronze, ivory, and sometimes chryselephantine. The figures often have a patinated silver or gilt finish and stand on an onyx or marble base.
- Lorenzl's sculptures are generally of women and reflect the fashions of the 1920s and 30s.

An ivory and cold-painted bronze figure, by Josef Lorenzl, on onyx base, signed in the cast "LORENZL."
c1925   *10¼in (26cm) high*
$2,800-3,500   **TEN**

A silvered and cold-painted bronze figure, "Allegory of Victory," by Josef Lorenzl, on onyx base, signed.

The same model was sold from the former sample stock of the Bergman factory, Vienna.
c1925   *11¾in (30cm) high*
$2,300-2,800   **TEN**

A bronze figure, by Josef Lorenzl, on onyx plinth, stamped "Lorenzl, real Bronze, Made in Austria."
c1930   *12½in (32cm) high*
$1,900-2,500   **ROS**

A cold-painted bronze figure, by Josef Lorenzl, on onyx base, signed "R.Lor Austria."
c1930   *13½in (34cm) high*
$3,200-3,800   **ROS**

A figurine, "Bridgitte," by Josef Lorenzl.
c1930   *13½in (34cm) high*
$3,800-4,400   **TDG**

A patinated gilt bronze dancer, by Josef Lorenzl, on onyx base, signed, fracture to wrist, chip to base.
11½in (29cm) high
$1,900-2,500   **CHEF**

A green patinated bronze nude maiden, by Josef Lorenzl, on onyx base, signed, some wear.
23in (58.5cm) high
$3,800-4,400   **CHEF**

A cold-painted bronze dancer, by Josef Lorenzl, on onyx base, signed, chip to base, discoloration around eye, wear to legs.
9¾in (25cm) high
$2,900-3,500   **TEN**

A patinated bronze dancer, by Marcel-André Bouraine, on a marble plinth, signed "M. Bouraine," stamped "Bronze," chips to extremities.

19¼in (49cm) high

$1,900-2,500 **GORL**

A gilt-bronze and ivory Classical maiden, cast from a model by Leonie Boehm-Henes, marble base, signed, one finger missing.

13¾in (35cm) high

$2,500-3,200 **WW**

A bronze figure, "Girl with Hoop," by Marcel-André Bouraine (1886-1948), on a marble base, signed "a Bouraine."

c1925 *12in (30.5cm) high*

$5,500-6,500 **TEN**

A bronze sculpture, "The Call" by Charles Charles, Patrouilleau foundry, signed "C. Charles."

A patinated metal sculpture, "Woman with Dogs," by A. Delatour, on marble base with onyx, signed "A Delatour."

33¼in (84.5cm) wide

$1,300-1,800 **WW**

c1930 *22½in (57cm) long*

$5,000-5,400 **TDG**

Judith Picks

Erté's career was an unusual one. Born Romain de Tirtoff in St. Petersburg in 1892, he moved to Paris in 1910, disobeying his family's wishes for him to become a naval officer. To avoid the embarrassment of his family, he took on the pseudonym "Erté" (after his initials, R.T.). In Paris, he achieved great success as a designer and fashion illustrator.

Erté's Art Deco sculptures unusually date not from the 1920s and 30s but from the later half of the 20thC. At the age of 75, during the Art Deco revival of the 1960s, Erté was encouraged to embark on a new career, re-creating the designs of his younger days. He began to create elegant bronze sculptures, such as this one, and was still working just two years before his death in 1990.

A spelter figural group, "Seduction," by Pierre Le Faguay (1892-1962), on a marble plinth, signed "FAYRAL."

Fayral was the pseudonym of Pierre Le Faguay.

c1925 *25½in (65cm) wide*

$2,500-3,200 **L&T**

An Art Deco bronze sculpture, "Elegance," by Erté (1892-1990), signed and numbered "116/250," lacking dog's leash, some wear, dated.

1980 *15½in (39.5cm) high*

$2,300-2,800 **DRA**

An Art Deco bronze sculpture, "Chinese Legend," by Erté, signed and numbered "238/500," some abrasions, dated.

1988 *22½in (57cm) high*

$2,300-2,800 **DRA**

A cold-painted bronze figure, "Dancer with Thyrsus," by Pierre Le Faguays, on a marble base, signed "Le Faguays," "Etling Paris" on base.

c1930 *10¾in (27.5cm) high*

$3,200-3,800 **ROS**

A bronze figure of a dancer, by Georges Flamand (1895-1925), on onyx socle, signed, chips to base.

11¾in (30cm) high

$1,050-1,200   **GORL**

A patinated bronze and ivory figure, "Dance of the Harlequinade," cast from a model by A. Gilbert.

22in (56cm) high

$7,000-7,500   **WW**

A cold-painted bronze figure, "Stella," by Maurice Guiraud-Riviere (1881-1947), on marble base, signed.

c1930   *11in (28cm) high*

$5,000-6,300   **ROS**

A patinated cold-painted bronze and ivory figure, "Temple Dancer," by Gerda Iro (Gerdago), on onyx base, signed, with foundry mark.

19in (48cm) high

$20,000-32,000   **WW**

A cold-painted bronze, by Godard, mounted on a slate base, signed.

c1930   *25½in (65cm) wide*

$3,200-3,800   **ROS**

A Hagenauer silver-plated and ebonized model of a dancer, stamped "Hagenauer Wien Made in Austria," figure detached from base.

c1930 12½in (31.5cm) high

$1,600-2,300   **BELL**

A gilt and patinated bronze and ivory figure, "Sleep of the Pierrot," by A. Gilbert (1884-1961), on marble base, stamped, signed "A Gilbert."

c1925   *12¼in (31cm) wide*

$5,000-6,300   **TEN**

A silvered bronze model, "Thyrse Dancer," by J.D. Guirande, on marble base, signed.

26½in (67cm) high

$3,200-3,800   **WW**

A cold-painted and gilt patinated bronze and ivory figure, by Samuel Lipchytz (1880-1943), on a marble base, signed.

c1925   *8½in (21.5cm) high*

$1,500-2,000   **TEN**

A cold-painted and gilt patinated bronze figure, "Hoop Girl," by Franz Mazura, on marble base, signed.

c1925   15¾in (40cm) high

$3,800-5,000   **TEN**

A cold-painted bronze and ivory figure "The Respectful Splits," by Paul Philippe (1870-1930), on onyx base, signed.

c1920   12½in (32cm) wide

$7,500-9,000   **ROS**

A cold-painted and gilt bronze figure, "Russian Dancer," by Paul Philippe, stamped to foot "144," on onyx base, signed.

c1925   16¾in (42.5cm) high

$5,000-5,700   **TEN**

A silvered and cold-painted bronze and ivory figure, "Pierrette," by Paul Philippe, on onyx base, signed "Philippe" and "R.u.M" (Rosenthal und Maeder).

c1925   8¼in (21cm) high

$4,400-5,000   **TEN**

A patinated bronze figure, "Dancer with Cymbals," by Charles d'Orville Pilkington-Jackson (1887-1973), on slate, signed and dated.

1922   31½in (80cm) high

$13,000-18,000   **WW**

A cold-painted bronze and ivory figure "Snake Dancer," by Professor Otto Poertzel (1876-1963), on bronze base cast with two snakes, on onyx plinth, signed.

c1930   10¾in (27.5cm) high

$6,500-7,500   **ROS**

A gilt and patinated bronze and ivory figure, "Lieselotte," by Johann Philipp Ferdinand Preiss, model no.3754, on a marble base, signed.

Ferdinand Preiss (1882-1943) was a German sculptor. He specialized in ivory and chryselephantine (bronze and ivory) figures.

c1925   7in (17.5cm) high

$3,800-4,400   **TEN**

A cold-painted bronze and ivory figure, "Girl Fencer," by Ferdinand Preiss, on marble base, signed.

c1930   7in (18cm) high

$6,500-7,500   **ROS**

A cold-painted and gilt patinated group of ballet dancers, by Bruno Zach, signed, on onyx marble base, some wear and filler, visible arm join, possibly repainted.

Bruno Zach (1891-1945) was born in the Ukraine. He studied at the Vienna Academy and produced sculpture in Art Nouveau, Art Deco, and Asian styles. His work often features sparsely clad women in stockings and garters.

c1920   17in (43cm) high

$3,800-4,400   **TEN**

MODERN MARKET

Where other areas have faltered financially, interest in, and prices for, outstanding post-World War II design has, in many cases, quadrupled. The market is fed by the quantity of items available. Design in this period was completely international and, with the added impetus of the Internet, so is the collecting market. Moreover, many pieces are found in large numbers and are consequently relatively affordable, making this area accessible to younger buyers; the styles are also in tune with a younger taste.

While the seeds of midcentury modern lay in the Scandinavian "Soft Modernism" of the 1930s, the designers who started working during and after World War II were excited by the possibilities of new materials and the demands of an enthusiastic consumer class. Designers such as Charles and Ray Eames in the United States said their mission was "getting the most of the best to the greatest number of people for the least amount of money." Of course, many of the Eames' original designs can no longer be purchased for "the least amount of money," because they are now highly prized icons of design. But these designs have been copied over the years, and although the replicas won't make the prices of anything like the originals, you can still get "the look."

As David Rago, of leading auction house Rago, says, "We're still seeing less strength in midcentury 'factory' furniture (Knoll, Eames, etc.), though it still does quite well. Instead, I'm watching prices rise for studio work by Nakashima, Powell, Evans, Castle, and so on. Wharton Esherick is perhaps the temporary victim of too little production and strong prices realized in the past. His work seems among the bargains in the market at this time."

The Modern movement is by its very nature diverse. It covers everything from the great studio craftspeople, including potters, such as the Natzlers and Peter Voulkos, to 1960s plastic and Postmodern pieces by designers such as Joe Colombo and Ettore Sottsass. There is something in this area to suit all tastes and pockets, for example, Stuart Devlin, the noted Australian/British silversmith and goldsmith, designed some highly individual furniture in the 1970s, as well as award-winning silver and gold.

Glass from the 20th century greats—the designers and factories of Scandinavia and Murano—continues to sell well, and buyers like the vibrant colors and modern forms. Big names are another plus factor, and prices for the work of luminaries, such as Murano-trained American designer Dale Chihuly, have quadrupled in recent years. However, there is a great deal of glass on the market that is in the style of "the greats" and appeals to a younger market. A particular favorite of mine are the whimsical "pulcinos" (little chicks) designed by Alessandro Pianon for Vetreria Vistosi in 1962 (see page 580).

As I mentioned in the previous edition of *Miller's Antiques Handbook and Price Guide*, there is growing interest in a newcomer to the growing 20th century glass stable in the form of postwar Czech glass, triumphed by my friend and colleague Mark Hill in his book *Hi Sklo Lo Sklo* (2008). Currently, the low end of the market ($60–650) is the most popular, and as people become more comfortable with the unusual names of the designers, this market seems only set to rise.

Top Left: A sculptural studio pottery vase, by John Ward, with artist's seal.

c1993   9¾in (25cm) high

$13,000-15,000   **CA**

Above A Nakashima Studio walnut and hickory lounge chair with arm, by George Nakashima, signed with client name.

1960   33½in (85cm) high

$10,000-11,000   **DRA**

MODERN DESIGN

A French Edition Rougier steel, bamboo, and rattanwork wicker chair and ottoman, attributed to Janine Abraham and Dirk Jan Rol.

c1955   36½in (92.5cm) high

$1,900-2,500   QU

A pair of 2000s Italian Cappellini teak stools/side tables, designed by Barber & Osgerby.

29½in (75cm) wide

$3,200-3,800   DRA

A 1970s Stendig "Nonstop" leather and felt sofa in 14 sections, designed by Ueli Berger, Eleanora Peduzzi-Riva, and Heinz Ulrich, Switzerland, with fabric label.

154in (391cm) long

$5,500-6,500   DRA

A pair of 1950s Italian Tecno P32 enameled steel, brass, and upholstery lounge chairs, by Osvaldo Borsani (1911-85), with manufacturer labels, some stains and fading.

33in (84cm) high

$4,400-5,000   DRA

A 2000s Erda Favela pine and birch plywood chair, by Fernando Campana (b.1961) and Umberto Campana (b.1953), Brazil/Italy.

30½in (77.5cm) high

$5,500-6,500   DRA

A sculpted walnut and leather "Crescent Rocker," designed by Wendell Castle (1932-2018), Scottsville, New York, signed and dated.

1980   40in (101.5cm) long

$18,000-23,000   DRA

A B&B Italia "Dadone" leather three-seater sofa, by Antonio Citterio, on chromed frame.

$1,500-2,000   WHP

A Comfort cream leather "Elda" chair, designed by Joe Columbo.

designed 1963

$4,400-5,000   SWO

An early 1960s Hille club armchair, designed by Robin Day (1915-2010), leather upholstery on a teak underframe.

designed 1962   31½in (80cm) wide

$700-800   L&T

A Bonacina Pierantonio egg-shaped rattan hanging chair, designed by Nanna Ditzel, fitted with a chain and stand.

1957

$950-1,050   **SWO**

An "S" Chair variant, designed by Tom Dixon.

40¼in (102cm) high

$1,900-2,500   **SWO**

A Herman Miller laminated rosewood and leather lounge chair and ottoman, designed by Charles and Ray Eames.

designed 1956

$9,000-10,000   **ECGW**

A Swedese bentwood and woolen upholstery "Lamino" chair, by Yngve Ekstrom, stamped mark.

c1965

$750-900   **WHP**

ESSENTIAL REFERENCE—PAUL EVANS

Paul Evans (1931-87) was an important 20thC studio furniture maker.

● He trained as a silversmith at the Cranbook Academy of Art in Bloomfield Hills, Michigan.

● In 1955, he moved to New Hope, Pennsylvania, where he met fellow craftsman Phillip Lloyd Powell. He and Powell shared a showroom for the next ten years. Together, they produced unique pieces, often fusing together materials, such as stone, wood, glass, and metal.

● Evans's background in welding, metalwork, and jewelry design strongly influenced his furniture designs.

● In 1966, he relocated to Plumsteadville, Pennsylvania, and set up his own studio.

● Evans also designed pieces for the furniture company Directional.

● He retired to Massachusetts in 1987 and died later that year.

A sculpture-front steel cabinet, by Paul Evans, with 23ct gold leaf, painted wood, cleft slate and felt decoration, welded "Paul Evans 68 D.R.," some scuffs, and oxidation.

1968   *75in (190.5cm) long*

$140,000-190,000   **DRA**

ESSENTIAL REFERENCE—CHARLES AND RAY EAMES

Charles and Ray Eames were two of the most important 20thC American designers.

● Charles Eames (1907-78) was born in St. Louis, Missouri. He studied architecture at Washington University for two years before being expelled for his advocacy of the radical architect Frank Lloyd Wright.

● Eames established his own architectural studio in 1930 with Charles Gray.

● In 1938, Eames received a fellowship to the Cranbrook Academy of Art in Bloomfield Hills, Michigan. Here, he met his future wife, design student Ray Kaiser (1912-88).

● They married in 1941 and together experimented with molded plywood. They were commissioned by the research and development division of the U.S. Navy, for whom they created various molded forms of splints, stretchers, and gliders for use by the Allies during WWII.

● After the war, Charles and Ray Eames turned to domestic furniture, developing designs for molded plywood and fiberglass chairs as well as the iconic Eames Lounge Chair, desks, storage units, sofas, tables, and more.

A Herman Miller birch plywood, laminated plywood, enameled Masonite, fiberglass, and enameled steel first edition ESU-400, by Charles Eames and Ray Eames, some dents and finish loss, reglued handles, one leg bent.

c1951-52   *59in (150cm) high*

$38,000-44,000   **DRA**

An Ercol settee or daybed, with a detachable back, some scuffing, split to left arm, recent cushions.

82in (208cm) wide

$1,050-1,200   **SWO**

A sculptured welded and patinated steel and bronze glass-topped dining table, no.PE21, by Paul Evans, oxidation to base, scratches.

1969   *95½in (242.5cm) long*

$23,000-28,000   **DRA**

A lithographic transfer-printed and lacquered four-leaf screen on casters, by Piero Fornasetti (1913-88), printed to one side with "Battaglia Navale" pattern and to the other side with "Lesene" pattern.

c1954   *57in (145cm) wide*

$7,500-9,000   **ROS**

MODERN DESIGN

A pair of 2000s German Vitra corrugated cardboard and Masonate "Wiggle" chairs, by Frank Gehry (b.1929), manufacturer labels.

34in (86.5cm) high

$3,200-3,800 DRA

An Archie Shine LTD "Hamilton" rosewood sideboard, by Robert Heritage, on tapered legs.

c1958 *90¼in (229cm) wide*

$1,900-2,500 ROS

A 1960s Danish Mogens Kold rosewood and crossbanded sideboard, by Arne Hovmand Olsen, with "sled"-type base, minor stains.

94½in (240cm) long

$2,500-3,200 WHP

A leather upholstered egg chair, by Arne Jacobsen (1902-71).

42in (106.5cm) high

$1,150-1,400 DOY

A pair of 1950s handmade teak and upholstery armchairs, by Pierre Jeanneret (1896-1967), from Punjab University, Chandigarh, India/France, new upholstery and stuffing.

Literature: "Le Corbusier Pierre Jeanneret: The Indian Adventure, Design-Art-Architecture" Touchaleaume E., Moreau G. & Vigo M.

34½in (87.5cm) high

$20,000-25,000 DRA

A pair of 1960s Danish Selig teak and upholstery lounge chairs, by Poul Jensen (1905-90), manufacturer labels, some scuffs.

33½in (85cm) high

$7,000-7,500 DRA

A pair of mid-20thC Belgian bronze and glass industrial display cabinets, with mirror bottoms and rubber feet, metal "DE JONCKHEERE-ANDRES, PLACE DU SAMEDI-BRUXELLES" label, some scratches and chips, some oxidation.

71in (180.5cm) high

$11,000-12,000 DRA

A "Judas" rosewood dining table, designed by Finn Juhl (1912-89), with two leaves, with inlaid silver buttons, marked "Illums Bohligus."

c1950 *55in (139.5cm) long*

$34,000-38,000 CLAR

A set of eight Niels Vodder Egyptian rosewood chairs, designed by Finn Juhl, branded "Niels Vodder Cabinetmaker Copenhagen Denmark Design Finn Juhl," one lacking mark.

36in (91.5cm) high

$80,000-90,000 CLAR

ESSENTIAL REFERENCE—VLADIMIR KAGAN

Vladimir Kagan (1927-2016) was an important midcentury furniture designer.

● He was born in Germany. His family were Jewish and left the country to escape Nazisim in 1937, moving first to France and later to the United States.

● Kagan took architecture courses at Columbia University but did not graduate. In 1947, he went to work for his father, who was a cabinetmaker.

● He took his first major commission in 1947 and opened an independent store in New York City in 1948. From 1950, he parterned with Hugo Dreyfuss, forming Kagan-Dreyfuss.

● Kagan's designs mixed the simplicity of Danish Modern masters, such as Finn Juhl and Hans Wegner, with the organic shapes of designers like Isamu Noguchi. He wanted to create furniture that was suitable for everyday living.

● The market for Kagan's designs remains very strong and notable collectors today include Brad Pitt, Demi Moore, Uma Thurman, and Tom Cruise.

A 1980s Vladimir Kagan Designs embroidered wool, leather, and sculpted walnut rocking chair, designed by Vladimir Kagan and after Erica Wilson, New York, refinished frame.

Erica Wilson, wife of Vladimir Kagan, operated a Manhattan needlepoint store until 2005. This fabric was created after one of her designs.

designed 1950s   *38½in (98cm) high*
$13,000-18,000   DRA

An pair of early 1960s Karpen Furniture Co. turned wood, brushed aluminum, and upholstery lounge chairs, with labels, minor sun fading and wear.

35½in (90cm) wide
$5,500-6,500   DRA

A 1950s Kagan-Dreyfuss sculpted walnut and upholstery "Floating Seat and Back" sofa, designed by Vladimir Kagan (1927-2016), one repair, some fraying

94in (239cm) wide
$18,000-25,000   DRA

CLOSER LOOK—WRITING DESK

This writing desk is made of chrome-plated steel and oak, with a rosewood veneer.

The desk is part of a furniture series designed by Bodil Kjaer (b.1932), a Danish architect and designer, for E. Pedersen & Son.

It was in high demand in the early 1960s, and starred prominently in two James Bond movies, "From Russia with Love" and "You Only Live Twice."

The actor Michael Caine and Prince Philip, Duke of Edinburgh, are said to have been some of the first customers who purchased this model.

A writing desk.
c1959   *78¾in (200cm) wide*
$18,000-23,000   QU

A pair of 1950s Danish E. Kold Christiansen chromed steel and leather "PK22" lounge chairs, designed by Poul Kjaerholm, extensive oxidation, some stains and tears.

28in (71cm) high
$2,300-2,800   DRA

A 1960s Knoll Associates walnut, enameled wood, birch, and chromed steel cabinet, designed by Florence Knoll (b.1917), no.541, some scratches.

75½in (192cm) long
$5,000-6,300   DRA

A Memphis "Kyoto" table, designed by Shiro Kuramata, manufactured by Ishimaru Co. Ltd., Tokyo, Japan, made of "Star Piece" terrazzo and chromium-plated steel, stenciled "SHIRO KURAMATA/FOR MEMPHIS MILANO."

c1983   *28¾in (73cm) high*
$11,000-12,000   PHI

A 1960s Brazilian rosewood and leather sofa, by Percival Lafer, with upholstery labels, some scratches.

90in (228.5cm) wide
$4,400-5,000   DRA

A 1950s Darrell Landrum enameled iron and upholstery sofa, refinished, reupholstered.

76in (193cm) long
$5,500-6,500   DRA

A pair of G-Plan "Housemaster" armchairs, designed by Ib Kofod Larsen, with black leather cushions.

32¼in (82cm) high

$1,900-2,500 SWO

A 1980s Belgian Georges Mathias polished and etched brass, agate, and enameled steel coffee table, light scuffs, and finish loss.

45¾in (116cm) long

$6,500-7,000 DRA

ESSENTIAL REFERENCE—GEORGE NAKASHIMA

George Nakashima (1905-90) was one of the most talented 20thC studio furniture makers.

● **He was born in Washington and studied architecture at the University of Washington, MIT, and L'Ecole Americaine des Beaux Arts in France.**

● **His work for the architect Antonin Raymond sent him to Pondicherry, India, where he began his second career as a furniture maker.**

● **Confined at the Japanese-American internment camp in Minidoka, Idaho, during World War II, Nakashima, his wife, and his daughter were released through the sponsorship of Raymond and settled in Bucks County, Pennsylvania, where Nakashima was able to work on his furniture designs.**

● **His work incorporated Japanese design and practices, Modernist ideas, and high-level craftsmanship. His interest in the natural quality and form of different woods can be seen in his furniture. His work was quite unique.**

One of a pair of 1940s Danish Fredericia rosewood bookcases, designed by Borge Mogensen (1914-72), stamped, refinished.

63in (160cm) high

$4,400-5,000 the pair DRA

A Jordan Mozer Studios LLC carved and kevlar-reinforced resin and leather prototype "Frankie" chair, designed by Jordan Mozer (b.1958), Chicago, IL, signed.

2007 *46in (117cm) high*

$13,000-19,000 DRA

A Nakashima Studio figured walnut single pedestal turned-leg desk, by George Nakashima, unmarked, some fading and some chips to top.

1955 *72in (183cm) long*

$13,000-18,000 DRA

A Nakashima Studio cherry wood and webbing long chair with armrest, by George Nakashima, unmarked, refinished, rewebbed.

1958 *66in (167.5cm) long*

$38,000-44,000 DRA

A Nakashima Studio figured walnut, hickory, and rosewood "Conoid" bench, by George Nakashima.

Provenance: Originally made for Toby Royston (1913-2009), who lived in Folly Cottage in Exton, Pennsylvania. The cottage is a Frank Lloyd Wright-designed home built in the 1960s by Wright's protégé, John Howe, and Wright's son-in-law, William Wesley Peters, of Taliesin Associated Architects. It was ultimately dubbed "Folly" due to the length and unexpected expense of the project. Royston commissioned exceptional pieces of furniture from George Nakashima to decorate the home.

100in (254cm) long

$50,000-63,000 DRA

A George Nakashima walnut and pandanus cloth hanging wall case, by George Nakashima, signed with client name, some scuffs, scratches, and stains.

1963 *84in (213.5cm) long*

$44,000-50,000 DRA

A pair of 1950s Herman Miller rosewood, plastic-coated metal, and aluminum "Thin Edge" cabinets, designed by George Nelson (1908-86).

34in (86.5cm) wide

$3,800-5,000 DRA

A 1970s Artifort "Mushroom" model 560 chair and ottoman, designed by Pierre Paulin, France/Netherlands, with manufacturer's labels, some fading.

chair 36in (91.5cm) wide

$4,400-5,000 DRA

A Charlotte Perriand "Shadow" chair, of "Shuiro" colored molded plywood, made by Tendo Mokko.

This chair comes from a private order of six copies in this shade made in 1975.

designed 1954 24¾in (63cm) high

$70,000-80,000 ARTC

A late 20thC Isa rosewood, leather and vinyl "Sheriff" chair and ottoman, designed by Sergio Rodrigues (1927-2014), replaced straps.

chair 45in (114.5cm) long

$2,500-3,200 DRA

ESSENTIAL REFERENCE—CHARLOTTE PERRIAND

Charlotte Perriand (1903-99) was an influential furniture designer and key figure in the Modernist movement.

● **She was born and raised in Paris, and she studied at the École de l'Union Centrale des Arts Décoratifs.**

● **She worked for the designer and architect Le Corbusier from 1927, and from 1937 she collaborated with the industrial designer Jean Prouvé, with whom she later designed furnishings for student accommodation at the Cité Internationale Universitaire in Paris.**

● **Throughout her life, she worked with a range of designers and architects. Her work has been displayed at numerous exhibitions.**

● **She is known for her bold designs, blunt geometric forms, and versatile approach to different materials, from wood and molded ply to anodized aluminum and melamine.**

A rare Charlotte Perriand "House of Mexique" bookcase, of lacquered aluminum and solid wood, with lacquered "pointe de diamant" aluminum sliding doors.

1952 72½in (184cm) wide

$110,000-120,000 ARTC

Judith Picks

The "Allegro" dining suite was a landmark in postwar British furniture design. It was designed in collaboration between Neil Morris of Morris of Glasgow and Sir Basil Spence. It was awarded a diploma by the Council of Industrial Design in January 1949, and exhibited at Glasgow Today and Tomorrow and the Scottish Industries Exhibition later that year. Its manufacture process was inspired by wartime innovation. During World War II, the Southampton-based helicopter manufacturers, Cierva Autogiro, had developed techniques of laminating and shaping wood to make strong and light helicopter blades— these blades were supplied by Morris of Glasgow by 1946, and the same technology was used in creating the "Allegro" suite. It was an incredibly expensive process. In 1950, a single chair was advertised at £31 18s 3d (about $90); the average British annual income then was just £101 (about $280). The furniture went into a limited production and surviving examples are rare.

An H. Morris & Co. laminated wood "Allegro" armchair, by Sir Basil Spence (1907-76), Glasgow, labeled.

designed 1947-48 33½in (85cm) high

$15,000-19,000 L&T

A Jean Royère "Flaque" low table, of straw marquetry-covered wood.

c1955 49¾in (126.5cm) long

$570,000-760,000 PHI

An "Ovalia" fiberglass and aluminum easy chair and stool, by Henrik Thor-Larsen for Torlan, with built-in loudspeakers.

1968 chair 52in (132cm) high

$5,000-6,300 QU

A Carlton laminated wood bookcase, by Ettore Sottsass (1917-2007), Memphis, Italy, nicks on edges and corners.

1981 77¾in (197.5cm) high

$20,000-32,000 DRA

A late 1950s to early 1960s "Wentworth" afromosia teak day bed, by Toothill, retailed by Heals, with copper piping and supports.

$2,500-3,200 WHP

CLOSER LOOK—"RACKET" CHAIR

This chair is by Helge Vestergaard-Jensen (1917-87), a Danish furniture designer known for his elegant and minimal design.

The frame is made of teak and brass, with an upholstered cushion.

It is designed as an abstract interpretation of a racket.

The "racket" is made of nylon string and microfibers.

A 1950s Danish "racket" chair, with decal label, some scuffs and scratches, some repairs.

46in (117cm) high

$12,000-14,000 **DRA**

A set of six Mazzei chromed steel and enameled fiberglass "Fortuna" chairs, designed by Leonardo Volpi, marked, some peeling paintwork.

1996 *31½in (80cm) high*

$1,050-1,200 **DRA**

A 1960s Danish Johannes Hansen teak, chromed steel, and aluminum desk, by Hans Wegner, some wear and marks.

Hans Wegner was a 20thC Danish Modernist designer. He learned woodworking as a boy, studied design in Copenhagen, and worked for Erik Møller and Arne Jacobsen before establishing his own furniture studio in the early 1940s. From the late 1940s until the 1960s, he collaborated with Johannes Hansen to realize his designs.

69in (175.5cm) wide

$1,300-1,800 **DRA**

A 1960s Danish Ry Mobler teak and mat-chromed steel four-bay wall unit, designed by Hans Wegner (1914-2007), from the RY 100 series.

162½in (413cm) wide

$3,800-5,000 **DRA**

A 1960s Danish A.P. Stolen teak and upholstery "Papa Bear" chair and ottoman, by Hans Wegner (1914-2007), minor stains.

chair 39in (99cm) high

$9,000-10,000 **DRA**

A N. Eilersen rosewood and leather "Model No. 4" armchair, designed by Illum Wikkelso.

$450-550 **WHP**

A 1950s Danish two-door rosewood cabinet, attributed to Kai Winding, one small filled chip.

45¾in (116cm) wide

$1,300-1,900 **DRA**

A figured maple credenza, by Craig Yamamoto, with Shoji doors.

84in (213.5cm) wide

$950-1,050 **POOK**

A L'Atelier "Jacaranda" desk, designed by Jorge Zalszupin, with rosewood patchwork design.

c1960 *74¾in (190cm) wide*

$3,800-4,400 **CHOR**

A 1960s Galerie Beyeler wool and cotton tapestry, after Alexander Calder, made for Beyeler Gallery, Basle, marked "Calder."

80in (203cm) high
$11,000-12,000
QU

A Pinton Studios "Many Triangles" wool rug, signed, by Alexander Calder (1898-1976).

81in (205.5cm) wide
$18,000-23,000
DRA

A "Trilli" wool carpet, by Aappo Härkönen for Mattokutomo Oy.

1960   93in (236cm) wide
$1,300-1,900
QU

A Larsen Design Studio cotton, vinyl, nylon, and polyester magnum fabric, designed by Jack Lenor Larsen (b.1927), United States.

Originally designed for the Phoenix Civic Plaza Symphony Hall curtain, this design's popularity kept it in production until 1992.

designed 1970   193in (490cm) wide
$1,500-2,300
DRA

A 1960s Danish "Geometri" upholstery fabric, by Verner Panton (1926-98), unmarked.

$250-380
DRA

A Hammer Prints Ltd. "Barkcloth" textile panel, by Nigel Henderson (1917-85) and Sir Eduardo Paolozzi (1924-2005), hand screen printed on cotton twill, stretched on a frame.

After his return to London from Paris in 1949, Paolozzi started teaching in the textile design department of the Central School of Art and Design. He produced screen prints that were often inspired by organic forms and paper collages that reveal his interest in abstract expressionism. In 1954, he and the artist Nigel Henderson set up Hammer Prints Ltd. to publish screen-printed textiles, ceramics, and wallpapers.

c1954   74¾in (190cm) long
$3,800-4,400
L&T

A hand-tufted floor rug, by Barbara Rae RA (b.1943), depicting an Australian scene, woven by the Edinburgh Tapestry Company, Dovecot Studios, Edinburgh, signed and labeled.

c1995-97   65in (165cm) wide
$4,400-5,000
SWO

Two pairs of David Whitehead & Sons Ltd. "foliate heads" pattern curtains, designed by John Piper (1903-92), screen printed rayon, maker's marks "DAVID WHITEHEAD FABRICS/DESIGNED BY JOHN PIPER."

Piper's original painting for this textile was exhibited in "Painting into Textiles" in 1953. Foliate Heads were a favored theme for Piper, who used them in scarf, rug, and tapestry design throughout his career.

c1954   118in (300cm) long
$3,200-3,800
L&T

A 1960s-70s Finish Rya wool rug, with wave pattern in warm tones.

64in (162.5cm) wide
$400-450
DRA

A 1950s wool tapestry panel, by Marc Saint-Saëns (1903-73), depicting a cellist, signed in the tapestry "MARC SAINT-SAËNS."

80in (203cm) high
$750-900
L&T

ESSENTIAL REFERENCE—LUCIE RIE

Lucie Rie (1902-95) was one of the most important studio potters of the 20thC.

● **She was born in Vienna and studied at the Vienna Kunstgewerbeschule before setting up her own pottery in 1925.**

● **After being forced to flee Austria in 1938, she went to Great Britain, where she established a pottery workshop in London. She made buttons at first, later shifting focus to a range of crafted hollowware.**

● **From 1946 to 1958, the German ceramist Hans Coper (1920-81) worked alongside her. He, like her, was a refugee. He left in 1958 to set up his own studio, but the pair remained friends all their lives.**

● **She received recognition during her lifetime, being awarded the CBE in 1981 and being made a dame in 1991; but it is only recently, since 2014, that her pottery has reached the heights of price it sees today.**

A porcelain footed bowl, by Dame Lucie Rie, the rim with fluxing and running bronze glaze, impressed seal mark, fleabite to rim, overall crazing.

7in (17.5cm) diam

$50,000-63,000   **WW**

A stoneware footed bowl, by Dame Lucie Rie, with yellow glaze and bronzed manganese rim, with artist's seal, faint crazing and pitting.

7in (17.5cm) diam

$32,000-38,000   **CHOR**

A porcelain bottle vase with flaring rim, by Dame Lucie Rie, incised with two bands and radiating sgraffito lines, impressed seal mark.

6in (15.5cm) high

$38,000-44,000   **WW**

A "Poppy Head" stoneware vase, by Hans Coper, impressed seal mark.

11¾in (30cm) high

$65,000-80,000   **WW**

A stoneware "Cycladic" arrow-form vase, by Hans Coper, with a black glaze, impressed with artist's seal.

1970   9¼in (23.5cm) high

$130,000-190,000   **PHI**

A 1970s porcelain conical bowl, by Dame Lucie Rie, with a golden manganese glaze, with sgraffito on the exterior, impressed with artist's seal.

9¼in (23.5cm) diam

$100,000-110,000   **PHI**

A stoneware bowl, by Dame Lucie Rie, raised monogram to base.

10in (25.5cm) diam

$38,000-44,000   **MJB**

A porcelain footed bowl, by Dame Lucie Rie, in a golden bronze glaze with radiating sgraffito lines, impressed seal mark.

7¾in (19.5cm) diam

$44,000-50,000   **WW**

CLOSER LOOK—"CYCLADIC" ARROWHEAD VASE

The "Cycladic" series was made in Frome, England, in the mid-1970s and represents the last, most critically acclaimed of Coper's work.

Coper's "Cycladic" arrowhead-form vases are very rare, with only four or five examples of each variation.

This vase is in the form of an arrowhead. It would have been fired in two pieces and joined later by a short metal pin.

A stoneware "Cycladic" vase, by Hans Coper, impressed seal to underside.

12in (30.5cm) high

$500,000-630,000   **BE**

The vase is set on a manganese base with an incised spiral.

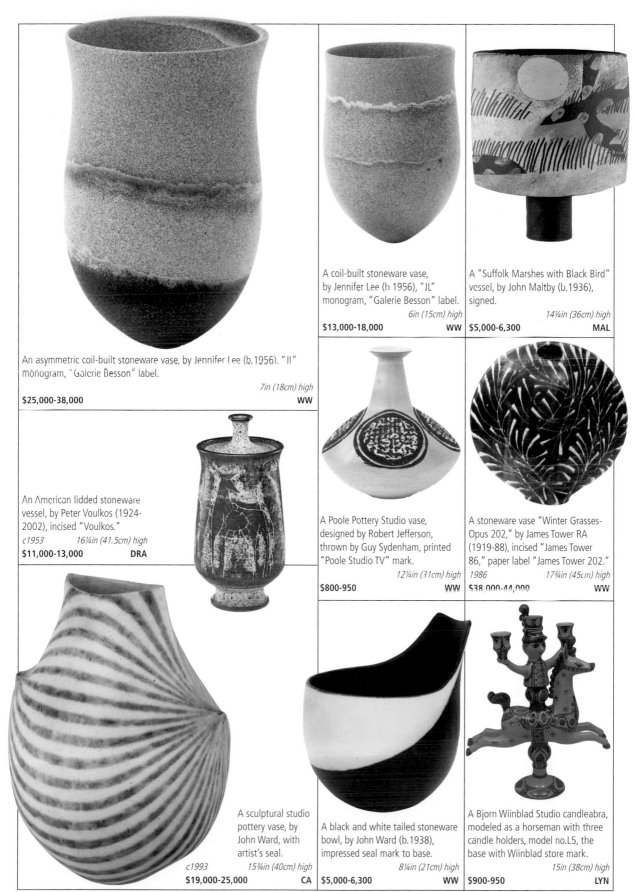

An asymmetric coil-built stoneware vase, by Jennifer Lee (b.1956), "JL" monogram, "Galerie Besson" label.

7in (18cm) high

$25,000-38,000   **WW**

An American lidded stoneware vessel, by Peter Voulkos (1924-2002), incised "Voulkos."

c1953   16¼in (41.5cm) high

$11,000-13,000   **DRA**

A coil-built stoneware vase, by Jennifer Lee (b.1956), "JL" monogram, "Galerie Besson" label.

6in (15cm) high

$13,000-18,000   **WW**

A "Suffolk Marshes with Black Bird" vessel, by John Maltby (b.1936), signed.

14¼in (36cm) high

$5,000-6,300   **MAL**

A Poole Pottery Studio vase, designed by Robert Jefferson, thrown by Guy Sydenham, printed "Poole Studio TV" mark.

12¼in (31cm) high

$800-950   **WW**

A stoneware vase "Winter Grasses-Opus 202," by James Tower RA (1919-88), incised "James Tower 86," paper label "James Tower 202."

1986   17¾in (45cm) high

$38,000-44,000   **WW**

A sculptural studio pottery vase, by John Ward, with artist's seal.

c1993   15¾in (40cm) high

$19,000-25,000   **CA**

A black and white tailed stoneware bowl, by John Ward (b.1938), impressed seal mark to base.

8¼in (21cm) high

$5,000-6,300   **WW**

A Bjorn Wiinblad Studio candleabra, modeled as a horseman with three candle holders, model no.L5, the base with Wiinblad store mark.

15in (38cm) high

$900-950   **LYN**

An Aldermaston Pottery tin-glazed charger, by Alan Caiger-Smith MBE (b.1930), painted monogram, painted date mark.

1980   *17¼in (43.5cm) diam*

$1,600-2,000   **WW**

A Jean Cocteau pottery charger, enameled with a bull, signed "Jean Cocteau 1957" and "Villefranche," marked "Edition Originale de Jean Cocteau Atelier Madeline-Jolly 3/25," with certificate of authenticity.

12¾in (32.5cm) diam

$3,800-4,400   **JDJ**

An Arabia glazed earthenware charger, by Birger Kaipiainen (1915-88), Helsinki, Finland, applied with fruit and berries, painted "KAIPIAINEN ARABIA" mark, some crazing.

25in (63.5cm) wide

$8,000-9,500   **CHEF**

A Madoura mottled fish ('Poisson Chiné') partly glazed earthenware plate, by Pablo Picasso (1881-1973), from a limited edition of 200, impressed "MADOURA PLEIN FEU EMPREINTE ORIGINALE DE PICASSO."

designed 1952   *17in (43cm) wide*

$19,000-25,000   **DRA**

A Madoura "Visages Et Hibou" ceramic pitcher, by Pablo Picasso (1881-1973), impressed marks "Edition Picasso," "Madoura Plein Feu."

11in (28cm) high

$9,500-10,500   **DUK**

A Richard Parkinson Pottery model of a golfer, designed by Susan Parkinson, impressed and printed marks.

15¼in (39cm) high

$900-1,000   **WW**

A 1950s Poole Pottery "Freeform" shape 698 vase, designed by Alfred Read, "PGS" pattern, printed and painted marks.

15¼in (39cm) high

$400-450   **FLD**

A Royal Copenhagen pillow-form earthenware vase, designed by Grette Helland Hansen, design no.441, shape no.3121, with factory marks and designer's mark.

7¾in (20cm) high

$140-160   **LYN**

A rare Troika Pottery pillar vase, painted marks, artist's monogram "AD" on base.

21½in (54.5cm) high

$2,500-3,200   **WW**

A Wedgwood "Vorticist" vase, by Norman Wilson, shape no.4669, printed and impressed marks, impressed "NW" monogram.

15¼in (39cm) high

$2,300-2,800   **WW**

A rare Aureliano Toso "Frammentato" vase, designed by Dino Martens.
c1955   *7¾in (19.5cm) high*
$2,500-3,200   **FIS**

An Aureliano Toso "Oriente" vase, by Dino Martens, with burst gold foil.
c1955   *13½in (34.5cm) high*
$5,000-6,300   **QU**

A glass bull's head, by Mario Badioli, with detachable wall bracket.
c1980   *15in (38cm) high*
$1,000-1,150   **CHEF**

A Barovier & Toso "Tessere ambra" vase, by Ercole Barovier.
1957   *15¾in (40cm) high*
$15,000-19,000   **QU**

A Barovier & Toso "A Spina" vase, by Ercole Barovier, engraved "barovier & toso murano."
1958   *12½in (31.5cm) high*
$10,000-11,000   **QU**

A Barovier & Toso. "Intarsio" vase, by Ercole Barovier.
1961-63   *14in (35.5cm) high*
$11,000-14,000   **QU**

An Effetre International blown glass egg, by Lino Tagliapietra (b.1934), signed and dated.
1987   *10in (25.5cm) high*
$1,900-2,500   **DRA**

A Fratelli Toso "Cathedral" vase, designed by Pollio Perelda, original factory label.
c1955-60   *13¾in (35cm) high*
$4,400-5,700   **FIS**

A Fucina degli Angeli dove, designed by Pablo Picasso, made by Ermanno Nason, marked "P.Picasso-E, Costantini Fucina Angeli-PA PA 1956," with original adhesive label "IVR MAZZEGA MURANO."

From 1954-57, master glassblower Ermanno Nason collaborated with the Fucina degli Angeli, Murano, run by Egidio Costantini. Nason modeled designs by several artists, including Georges Braque, Marc Chagall, Pablo Picasso, and Jean Cocteau.
1954   *15in (38cm) high*
$10,000-11,000   **FIS**

A Nastri blown glass vase, designed by Yoichi Ohira (b.1946), executed by Maestro Livio Serena and Maestro Giacomo Barbini, etched "Yoichi Ohira Mo. L. Serena Mo. G. Barbini 1/1 unico Friday 4 February 2000 murano."

Yoichi Ohira was born in Japan in 1946. He attended Tokyo's Kuwasawa Design School and graduated in 1969, then worked in Japanese glass factories before moving to Venice to study sculpture. He began working with glass in Murano in 1973 and went on to become the artistic director at Murano's de Majo Glassworks, then an independent artist and glass designer.
2000   *6½in (16.5cm) high*
$9,000-10,000   **DRA**

A Lino Tagliapietra blown glass dinosaur sculpture, signed and dated.

2000   *41in (104cm) high*

$19,000-25,000   **DRA**

A Lino Tagliapietra blown and battuto glass sculpture, "Fenice" (Phoenix), signed, one minor scratch, dated.

Lino Tagliapietra was born in 1934 in Murano, Italy. He was apprenticed to glass maestro Archimede Seguso at the age of 12 and by the age of 25 had been awarded the rank of maestro. Over his career, Tagliapietra has worked with many key Murano glass manufactures, such as La Murrina, Vetreria Galliano Ferro, and Effetre International. From the late 1980s, he increasingly focused on studio art glass.

2005   *17in (43cm) high*

$25,000-38,000   **DRA**

A Venini & C. "Pezzato" vase, by Fulvio Bianconi, acid stamped "venini murano ITALIA."

c1951   *9¾in (24.5cm) high*

$7,500-9,000   **QU**

A Vetreria Vistosi "Pulcino" sculpture, by Alessandro Pianon, with copper legs.

c1962   *8¼in (21cm) high*

$12,000-14,000   **FLD**

A Vetreria Vistosi "Pulcino" sculpture, by Alessandro Pianon, model no.S193.

c1962   *8¾in (22.5cm) high*

$5,000-6,300   **SAV**

A Vetreria Vistosi "Pulcino" sculpture, by Alessandro Pianon.

c1962   *6¾in (17cm) high*

$12,000-14000   **FLD**

A Vetreria Vistosi "Pulcino" sculpture, by Alessandro Pianon, model no.S189, labeled "VISTOSI."

c1962   *12in (30.5cm) high*

$4,400-5,000   **SAV**

The quirky "Pulcini" (chicks) made by Alessandro Pianon (1931-84) were first presented in an edition of the magazine "Domus" in April 1962. The series consisted of these five birds, with bodies of colored glass and legs of copper wire. The "Pulcini" had to be specially ordered so remain very rare today. Each piece was made by hand, meaning that quality—and value—can vary.

A Venini & C. vase, by Gianni Versace, with fused murrhines, engraved "Venini 2000 Gianni Versace."

c1995   *10¼in (26cm) high*

$3,200-3,800   **QU**

A Vetreria Vistosi "Pulcino" sculpture, by Alessandro Pianon.

c1962   *9½in (24cm) high*

$5,000-7,500   **SAV**

A Macchia with orange lip wrap, by Dale Chihuly (b.1941), Seattle, Washington, signed and dated.

1989 *21½in (54.5cm) high*

$11,000-12,000 DRA

A Loco Glass sculptural glass vase, by Samuel J. Herman, signed.

Provenance: From The Private Collection Of Samuel J. Herman.

14¼in (36.5cm) high

$2,500-3,200 DAWS

A Lots Road sculptural attenuated bottle, by Samuel J. Herman, with applied chips, trails, and silver chloride side wings, signed.

Provenance: From The Private Collection Of Samuel J. Herman. This bottle is from a series of six or seven unique bottles devised by Herman in response to his curiosity about how the glass would flow, and what the resulting form would be, if he let gravity take over, in addition to hot working the molten fluid glass in his usual manner.

c1982 *25¾in (65.5cm) high*

$1,500-2,000 DAWS

A Kosta "Autumn" cased glass vase, by Vicke Lindstrand, acid mark on base, engraved "LU 2011."

c1954 *6½in (16.5cm) high*

$1,900-2,500 FLD

A glass sculpture, "Blue Sliced Descending Form," by Harvey Littleton (1922-2013), signed, numbered "9-1987-2," some roughness and flakes, dated.

1987 *larger 17in (43cm) high*

$20,000-32,000 DRA

A blown glass "Crazy Quilt Teapot," by Richard Marquid (b.1945), Washington State, signed, copyrighted, and numbered, dated.

1979 *5½in (14cm) high*

$3,200-3,800 DRA

A late 1960s Mdina glass "Crizzle Stone" vase, by Michael Harris, signed.

10¾in (27cm) wide

$4,400-5,000 FLD

An Orrefors "Kraka" internally decorated glass vase, by Sven Palmquist (1906-84), signed, engraved "S.G.A 1956 1 Pris."

1956 *13¾in (35cm) high*

$1,150-1,400 ROS

A Whitefriars "Textured" range prototype "Banjo" vase lamp base, by Geoffrey Baxter, in kingfisher blue, original label.

This is a variation of the pattern 9681 vase. The piece was made as a prototype in the factory and never made it to the production stage.

13¾in (35cm) high

$2,000-2,500 FLD

A filet-de-verre fused and thermoformed glass thread vessel, "Veloce," by Toots Zynsky (b.1951), Providence, Rhode Island, signed "Z."

2016 *10½in (26.5cm) wide*

$10,000-11,000 DRA

A Studio BBPR patinated brass ceiling light, designed by Gian Luigi Banfi, Ludovico Belgiojoso, Enrico Peressutti, and Ernesto Nathan Rogers.

c1952   *24in (61cm) high*

$38,000-50,000   **PHI**

A 1990s welded and patinated steel chandelier, by Tom Dixon (b.1959), with three sockets.

34in (86.5cm) diam

$3,800-4,400   **DRA**

A pair of Danish Louis Poulsen enameled aluminum PH 4/3 ceiling pendants, by Poul Henningsen, with affixed labels.

designed 1966   10in (25.5cm) high

$1,000-1,150 the pair   **DOY**

A near pair of 1950s French Holophane enameled perforated metal and milk glass pendant lamps, by Mathieu Mategot (1910-2001), marked "HOLOPHANE FRANCE," losses to enamel, some chips and flecks.

max 25in (63.5cm) high

$3,800-4,400   **DRA**

A 1970s Italian polished aluminum and acrylic pendant light fixture, by Gaetano Sciolari (1927-94), light oxidation.

23in (58.5cm) diam

$3,200-3,800   **DRA**

A Fontana Arte glass, brass, and aluminum "Dahlia" ceiling light, by Max Ingrand.

c1955   *18in (45.5cm) diam*

$15,000-20,000   **PHI**

A Nakashima Studio walnut, holly, and fiberglass table lamp, by George Nakashima, signed with client name, replaced shade.

1973   *29½in (75cm) high*

$15,000-19,000   **DRA**

A Lightolier tripod table lamp, by Gerald Thurston, with walnut, brass, plastic, and enameled metal base and linen shade, some stains.

c1950   *24in (61cm) high*

$1,050-1,200   **DRA**

A 1940s Finish Taito Oy brass table lamp, by Paavo Tynell (1890-1973), base stamped "MADE IN FINLAND TAITO TT 546," with later shade, some wear.

22in (56cm) high

$3,200-3,800   **DRA**

A 1990s Italian chromed and enameled metal and fabric floor lamp, by Mariano Fortuny Y. Madrazo (1871-1949), lightbulb socket and wiring missing.

78in (198cm) high

$3,200-3,800   DRA

A 1960s Swedish Luxus teak, oak, linen, and brass floor lamp, by Uno Kristiansson (b.1925) and Osten Kristiansson (1927-2003), one replaced screw, replaced shade.

50in (127cm) high

$1,300-1,800   DRA

An Arredoluce nickeled brass, enameled steel, aluminum, and leather triennale floor lamp, by Angelo Lelii (1911-79), stamped "MADE IN ITALY," some scuffs.

c1960   59½in (151cm) high

$5,500-6,500   DRA

An Arredoluce Monza brass "Calla" floor lamp, by Angelo Lelii.

c1955   78in (198cm) high

$3,800-4,400   QU

A set of three patinated bronze floor lamps, by Andrew Lord (b.1950), with tea-dyed papier mâché shades, signed, dated, and numbered "4/10," armatures detached, wiring fraying, shades with tears.

1988   72in (183cm) high

$32,000-38,000   DRA

A French Société de Création de Modèles painted steel, painted aluminum, and walnut "Grand Totem" floor lamp, by Serge Mouille.

c1962   67¼in (170.5cm) high

$90,000-110,000   PHI

A French 1950s-60s carved and stained wood and enameled iron floor lamp, in the style of Jean Rispal, some wear.

74½in (189cm) high

$2,000-2,500   DRA

A pair of 2000s enameled metal and brass industrial-style adjustable floor lamps, with marble bases, some chips to marble.

60in (152.5cm) high

$1,150-1,400   DRA

A Nakashima Studio walnut and fiberglass floor lamp, by George Nakashima, some yellowing to shade.

1962   60in (152.5cm) high

$18,000-23,000   DRA

ESSENTIAL REFERENCE—STUART DEVLIN

Stuart Devlin (1931-2018) was a significant and influential modern goldsmith and silversmith.

● He was born in Geelong, Victoria, Australia, the son of a painter and decorator. He studied gold and silversmithing at the Royal Melbourne Technical College and later at the Royal College of Art and Columbia University, New York.

● In 1963, he won a competition to design the first decimal coinage for Australia.

● In 1965, he opened a small workshop in Clerkenwell, London.

● He was awarded a CMG in 1980, granted a Royal warrant in 1982, and served as prime warden of the Goldsmiths' Company 1996-97.

● Rejecting the prevailing taste for Scandinavian design, Devlin focused on romanticism and ornate pieces. The Duke of Edinburgh described him as "probably the most original and creative goldsmith and silversmith of his time.'

A parcel-gilt silver ice bucket, by Stuart Devlin, London, the lift-off cover with textured ball finial, with liner, some dings and discoloration.
1972   *6¾in (17cm) high 52¼oz*
$2,500-3,200   **TEN**

A silver-gilt "Flower Surprise Egg," by Stuart Devlin, opening to reveal five enameled petal flowers with leaves.
1972   *3¼in (8.5cm) high 4oz*
$550-650   **SOU**

A parcel-gilt silver rose bowl centerpiece, by Stuart Devlin, London, mounted with a silver-gilt-mounted amethyst finial.
1974   *8¾in (22.5cm) high 22oz*
$3,800-4,400   **WW**

A parcel-gilt silver cased cylinder music box, by Stuart Devlin, the rosewood interior with a Swiss Reuge Ste Croix cylinder movement playing Tchaikovsky's Piano Concerto No.1 on a single comb.
1976   *7½in (19cm) long 43oz*
$5,000-6,300   **SOU**

A pair of Swid Powell plated "Skyscraper" candlesticks, by Richard Meier (b.1934), stamped maker's marks "SWID POWELL/ SILVER PLATED."
designed 1983   *9½in (24cm) high*
$500-650   **L&T**

A pair of parcel-gilt silver three-light candelabrum, by Stuart Devlin, London.
1970   *max 15½in (39.5cm) high 108oz*
$19,000-25,000   **SOU**

A Walker & Hall matched silver "Pride" tea service, by David Mellor (1930-2009), Sheffield.
1959-60   teapot 5½in (14cm) high 74oz
$3,800-4,400   **L&T**

A silver and vase, by Fred Rich (b.1954), London, enameled with four frogs among reeds, signed "Fred Rich 94."
1994   *6¼in (16cm) high 25oz*
$18,000-23,000   **WW**

A Christofle "Como" silver-plate coffee and tea service, by Lino Sabattini (b.1925), with impressed maker's marks "GALLIA/ FRANCE/PROD. CHRISTOFLE."
designed 1956 teapot 12in (30.5cm) high
$5,000-5,700   **L&T**

'DAVOS', printed by Orell Fussli, Zurich, on paper, tape-repaired tear and creases at top edge, tears in margins, creases along folds, paper insert in upper left corner.

1901   *39in (99cm) high*

$4,500-5,000   **SWA**

'ARGENTINA (SUNNY SOUTH) AND BRAZIL', designed by Odin Rosenvinge (1880-1957), printed by Turner & Dunnett, Liverpool, minor tears in margins, unobtrusive folds.

Rosenvinge was a prolific designer of posters for various shipping companies, including the Royal Line, Anchor Donaldson Line, Allan Line, Elder Dempster Line, Orient Line and the Union Castle Line. His largest client was Cunard Line.

c1910   *33in (84cm) high*

$2,000-3,000   **SWA**

'Gleneagles Golf Course/The "Howe O' Hope" – on the "King's"', printed by Dobson Molle & Co. Ltd., Edinburgh, repaired tears, restored losses, minor restoration, unobtrusive folds.

The 'Howe O'Hope' ('Hollow of Hope') is the 15th hole on the King's course. In 1923, the Caledonian Railway was subsumed by the London, Midland and Scottish Railway.

c1920   *59½in (151cm) wide*

$10,000-14,000   **SWA**

'ARCTIC TO ANTARCTIC/ AT THE ZOO EDINBURGH', printed by Wm. Thyne Ltd., Edinburgh, minor creases.

Penguins have played a long and prominent role in the history of the Edinburgh Zoo. Founded in 1913, it was the first in the world to house and breed penguins. Six years later, in 1919, the zoo hatched its own king penguin chick. A king penguin features on the zoo's logo. Polar bears also have a long history with Edinburgh, being on display in Edinburgh as early as the 1840s when the city's first zoo opened.

c1925   *39½in (100.5cm) high*

$5,000-6,000   **SWA**

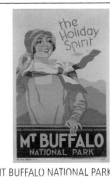

'CHEMIN DE FER DU NORD', designed by Adolphe Mouron Cassandre (1901-68), printed by L. Danel, Lille, minor creases, faded ink stamps at bottom.

1929   *39¼in (99.5cm) high*

$7,500-8,500   **SWA**

'MT BUFFALO NATIONAL PARK/the Holiday Spirit', designed by Percival Albert Trompf (1902-64), printed by Robt. Harding, Melbourne, some restoration.

c1930   *39½in (100.5cm) high*

$1,500-2,000   **SWA**

'STATE PARKS', designed by Dorothy Waugh (1896-1996), printed at US Government Printing Office, Washington, D.C., repaired tears.

Dorothy Waugh studied design at the Chicago Institute of Art, then moved to New York where she managed Alfred A. Knopf's children's book department. During the 1930s, she worked for the National Park Service as production supervisor and also provided them with actual artwork and copy. There are at least eight known images that she designed for the National Parks.

c1934   *39¾in (101cm) high*

$1,000-1,500   **SWA**

'CHATEAU D'OEX/ALPES VAUDOISES SUISSE', designed by Alex Walter Diggelmann (1902-87), lithograph.

1933   *40in (101.5cm) high*

$2,500-3,000   **L&T**

'The Golden Pass Route/ SWITZERLAND', designed by Edouard Elzingre (1880-1966), printed by Sonor, Geneva, restored losses.

1934   *40in (101.5cm) high*

$8,000-9,000   **SWA**

'NORMANDIE', designed by Adolphe Mouron Cassandre (1901-68), printed by Alliance Graphique L. Danel, Paris, minor repaired tears.

Several variations of this poster exist, all boasting the same monumental image, but differing in their text.

1935   39¼in (99.5cm) high
$23,000-30,000   SWA

'PARIS', designed by Adolphe Mouron Cassandre (1901-68), printed by Draeger, Paris, minor abrasions.

1935   39¼in (99.5cm) high
$3,000-4,000   SWA

'PARSENN/Davos', designed by Werner Weiskönig (1907-82), offset lithograph.

1936   40in (101.5cm) high
$2,000-2,500   L&T

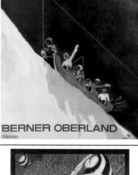

'GSTAAD/BERNER OBERLAND', designed by Alex Walter Diggelmann (1902-87), printed by J.C. Müller, Zurich, repaired tears, restoration at edges.

1937   40in (101.5cm) high
$9,000-11,000   SWA

'IMPERIAL AIRWAYS', printed by Ben Johnson & Co., London, extensive repaired tear, creases, abrasions.

This poster shows in full detail a cross-section of the Centaurus (S.812 G-ADUT), one of the Short 'C' class flying boats. In 1934, British Imperial Airways ordered 28 of the flying boats.

1937   39½in (100.5cm) wide
$3,000-3,500   SWA

'FLY BY CLIPPER TO NORWAY/THE CRADLE OF SKIING/PAN AMERICAN WORLD AIRWAYS', designed by Knut Yran (1920-98), printed by Grondahl & Son, Oslo, creases and light foxing.

This poster was used by a variety of different transportation companies, from airlines to cruise lines, each of whom overprinted it with their own particulars.

1951   39¼in (99.5cm) high
$2,000-2,500   SWA

'AUSTRALIA/THE GREAT BARRIER REEF', designed by Eileen Mayo (1906-94), printed by McLaren & Co. Pty. Ltd., Melbourne, minor overpainting.

Dame Eileen Mayo was born in Britain and studied under Henry Moore at the Chelsea Polytechnic and Fernand Léger at the Académie Montmartre. She was a painter, illustrator and printmaker, designing magazines, tapestries, stamps and posters. She moved to Australia in 1953 and designed a series of posters highlighting some of the continent's exotic wildlife, including kangaroos and koalas.

c1956   39½in (100.5cm) high
$4,500-5,500   SWA

'NEW YORK/FLY TWA', by David Klein (1918-2005), minor tears and creases.

Originally issued in 1956, the poster featured a detailed image of a TWA Constellation. The image was so popular that the airline reused it when it fully entered the Jet Age, changing the image to feature the silhouette of a jet plane.

c1960   40in (101.5cm) high
$7,000-8,000   SWA

'IRELAND/GREAT SOUTHERN RAILWAYS/THE LAND OF ETERNAL YOUTH', designed by R. Breslin for Great Southern Railways, printed by Alex. Thom & Co. Ltd.

42in (106.5cm) high
$1,500-2,000   WHYT

Judith Picks

This was one of the most iconic posters of its day, and is still recognised in the 21stC. The Chat Noir was a Parisian nightclub, which first opened its doors in 1881 on the Boulevard de Rochechouart, moving to the Rue Victor Masse in 1895. Its owner, Rodolphe Salis, is often credited with inventing the modern cabaret, which was imitated all over the world. Art nouveau painter and designer Théophile-Alexandre Steinlen actively collaborated with Chat Noir, designing the sign above the entrance to the cabaret, working on their magazine and designing this famous poster.

'TOURNÉE DU CHAT NOIR', designed by Théophile-Alexandre Steinlen (1859-1923), printed by Charles Verneau, Paris, matted and framed.
1896   *54¾in (139cm) high*
$30,000-40,000   **SWA**

'FIFTEEN YEARS OF STRUGGLE AND VICTORIES OF THE LENINGRAD KOMSOMOL', designed by the Izoram Workshop, printed by Izoram, Leningrad, replaced top margin.
1933   *56½in (143.5cm) high*
$5,000-6,000   **SWA**

'YOU CAN SHORTEN THE ROAD TO VICTORY, JOIN THE A.T.S.', designed by Gabriel Shamir (1909-92) and Maxim Shamir (1910-90), some repairs.
1943   *25½in (65cm) high*
$10,000-14,000   **SWA**

'atoms for peace/GENERAL DYNAMICS', designed by Erik Nitsche (1908-98), printed by R. Marsens, Lausanne, on paper.
This is the English language poster from the initial 'Atoms for Peace' series.
1955   *50¼in (127.5cm) high*
$5,500-6,500   **SWA**

'The Times Of The Day/Réverie Du Soir', designed by Alphonse Mucha (1860-1939), printed by F. Champenois, Paris, repaired tears, scuffing.
1899   *41¾in (106cm) high*
$10,000-14,000   **SWA**

'DRACULA', British quad film poster, printed by W.F. Clifford Printing Co. Ltd., London, restored and linen-backed.
1958   *40in (101.5cm) wide*
$13,000-16,000   **WHYT**

'COINTREAU', designed by Charles Loupot (1892-1962), printed by Les Belles Affiches, Paris.

In 1898 Francisco Tamagno designed a poster for Cointreau featuring a white Pierrot (a figure from the Commedia dell'Arte) wearing glasses licking a large bottle of Cointreau. The glasses were added by the printer to make a joke about Edouard Cointreau's bad eyesight. The detail was so successful that it was kept.
$4,500-5,000   **SWA**

'PARLATE NEL MICROFONO', designed by Ernst A. Heiniger (1909-93), printed by Ringier & Co., Zofinga, mounted on card, some losses.

Ernst A. Heiniger was an accomplished artist, designer, photographer and cinematographer. He designed a number of posters, including several promoting the use of telephones, each with a pronounced photographic element.
1951   *49½in (125.5cm) high*
$4,000-5,000   **SWA**

'FROM RUSSIA WITH LOVE/JAMES BOND IS BACK', British Quad film poster, art by Renato Fratini, framed.
1963   *40in (101.5cm) wide*
$5,000-6,000   **ECGW**

Every antique illustrated in Miller's Antiques has a letter code, which identifies the dealer or auction house that sold it. The list below is a key to these codes. In the list, auction houses are shown by the letter A and dealers by the letter D.

Inclusion in this book in no way constitutes or implies a contract or a binding offer on the part of any of our contributors to supply or sell the goods illustrated, or similar items, at the prices stated.

ADA Ⓐ
ADAM'S
www.adams.ie

APAR Ⓐ
ADAM PARTRIDGE
www.adampartridge.co.uk

ARTC Ⓐ
ARTCURIAL
www.artcurial.com

AST Ⓐ
ASTON'S
www.astonsauctioneers.co.uk

B&H Ⓐ
BURSTOW & HEWETT
www.burstowandhewett.co.uk

BAM Ⓐ
BAMFORDS
www.bamfords-auctions.co.uk

BATE Ⓐ
BATEMANS
www.batemans.com

BBR Ⓐ
BBR AUCTIONS
www.onlinebbr.com

BE Ⓐ
BEARNES, HAMPTON &
LITTLEWOOD
www.bhandl.co.uk

BELL Ⓐ
BELLMANS
www.bellmans.co.uk

BER Ⓐ
BERTOIA AUCTIONS
www.bertoiaauctions.com

BKA Ⓐ
BARBARA KIRK AUCTIONS
www.barbarakirkauctions.co.uk

BLEA Ⓐ
BLEASDALES
www.bleasdalesltd.co.uk

BLO Ⓐ
DREWEATTS & BLOOMSBURY
www.bloomsburyauctions.com

BOUR Ⓐ
BOURNE END AUCTION
ROOMS
www.bourneendauctionrooms.co.uk

BRI Ⓐ
BRIGHTWELLS
www.brightwells.com

BRO Ⓐ
BROMPTON'S
www.bromptons.co

C&T Ⓐ
C&T AUCTIONEERS &
VALUERS
www.candtauctions.co.uk

CA Ⓐ
CHISWICK AUCTIONS
www.chiswickauctions.co.uk

CAN Ⓐ
THE CANTERBURY AUCTION
GALLERIES
www.thecanterburyauctiongalleries.
com

CAPE Ⓐ
CAPES DUNN
www.capesdunn.com

CHEF Ⓐ
CHEFFINS
www.cheffins.co.uk

CHIL Ⓐ
CHILCOTTS
www.chilcottsauctioneers.co.uk

CHOR Ⓐ
CHORLEY'S
www.chorleys.com

CHT Ⓐ
CHARTERHOUSE
www.charterhouse-auction.com

CLAR Ⓐ
CLARS
www.clars.com

CM Ⓐ
CHARLES MILLER LTD.
www.charlesmillerltd.com

CUTW Ⓐ
CUTTLESTONES
www.cuttlestones.co.uk

DAWS Ⓐ
DAWSON'S
www.dawsonsauctions.co.uk

DEN Ⓐ
DENHAMS
www.denhams.com

DN Ⓐ
DREWEATTS & BLOOMSBURY
www.dreweatts.com

DOY Ⓐ
DOYLE
www.doyle.com

DRA Ⓐ
RAGO ARTS
www.ragoarts.com

DUK Ⓐ
DUKE'S
www.dukes-auctions.com

EBA Ⓐ
EAST BRISTOL AUCTIONS
www.eastbristol.co.uk

ECGW Ⓐ
EWBANK'S
www.ewbankauctions.co.uk

FELL Ⓐ
FELLOWS
www.fellows.co.uk

FIS Ⓐ
AUKTIONHAUS DR FISCHER
www.auctions-fischer.de

FLD Ⓐ
FIELDINGS
www.fieldingsauctioneers.co.uk

FLIN Ⓐ
FLINTS
www.flintsauctions.com

FRE Ⓐ
FREEMAN'S
www.freemansauction.com

GBA Ⓐ
GRAHAM BUDD
www.grahambuddauctions.co.uk

GHOU Ⓐ
GARDINER HOULGATE
www.gardinerhoulgate.co.uk

GKID Ⓐ
GEORGE KIDNER
www.georgekidner.co.uk

GORL Ⓐ
GORRINGE'S
www.gorringes.co.uk

GRV D
GEMMA REDMOND VINTAGE
www.gemmaredmondvintage.co.uk

GTH Ⓐ
GREENSLADE TAYLOR HUNT
www.gth.net

GWA Ⓐ
GREAT WESTERN AUCTIONS
www.greatwesternauctions.com

GYM Ⓐ
GOLDING YOUNG & MAWER
www.goldingyoung.com

H&C Ⓐ
HISTORICAL & COLLECTIBLE
www.historicalandcollectible.com

HALL Ⓐ
HALLS
www.hallsgb.com/fine-art

HAN Ⓐ
HANSONS
www.hansonsauctioneers.co.uk

HANN Ⓐ
HANNAM'S
www.hannamsauctioneers.com

HOLT Ⓐ
HOLTS
www.holtsauctioneers.com
Photography: Andrew Orr

HT Ⓐ
HARTLEY'S
www.hartleysauctions.co.uk

HW Ⓐ
HOLLOWAY'S
www.hollowaysauctioneers.co.uk

JDJ Ⓐ
JAMES D. JULIA INC.
(now part of Morphy Auctions)
www.morphyauctions.com

JN Ⓐ
JOHN NICHOLSON'S
www.johnnicholsons.com

JON Ⓐ
ROGERS JONES & CO.
www.rogersjones.co.uk

K&O Ⓐ
KINGHAM & ORME
www.kinghamandorme.com

KEY Ⓐ
KEYS
www.keysauctions.co.uk

KT Ⓐ
KERRY TAYLOR
AUCTIONS
www.kerrytaylorauctions.com

L&T Ⓐ
LYON & TURNBULL
www.lyonandturnbull.com

LC Ⓐ
LAWRENCES AUCTIONEERS
(CREWKERNE)
www.lawrences.co.uk

LHA Ⓐ
LESLIE HINDMAN
www.lesliehindman.com

LOC Ⓐ
LOCKE & ENGLAND
www.leauction.co.uk

LOCK Ⓐ
LOCKDALES
www.lockdales.com

LOW Ⓐ
LOWESTOFT PORCELAIN
AUCTIONS
www.lowestoftchina.co.uk

LSK Ⓐ
LACY SCOTT & KNIGHT
www.lsk.co.uk

LYN Ⓓ
LYNWAYS
www.lynways.com

M&DM Ⓓ
M&D MOIR
www.manddmoir.co.uk

MAB Ⓐ
MATTHEW BARTON LTD
www.matthewbartonltd.com

MAI Ⓐ
MOORE ALLEN & INNOCENT
www.mooreallen.co.uk

MAL Ⓐ
MALLAMS
www.mallams.co.uk

MART Ⓐ
MARTEL MAIDES AUCTIONS
www.martelmaidesauctions.com

MEA Ⓐ
MEALY'S (NO LONGER
TRADING)
www.mealys.ie

MJB Ⓐ
MICHAEL J. BOWMAN
www.michaeljbowman.co.uk

MM Ⓐ
MULLOCK'S
www.mullocksauctions.co.uk

MOR Ⓐ
MORPHETS
www.morphets.co.uk

MORP Ⓐ
MORPHY
www.morphyauctions.com

MTZ Ⓐ
AUKTIONSHAUS METZ
www.metz-auktion.de

NA Ⓐ
NORTHEAST AUCTIONS
northeastauctions.com

PBE Ⓐ
PAUL BEIGHTON
www.pbauctioneers.co.uk

PC
PRIVATE COLLECTION

PFR Ⓐ
PETER FRANCIS
www.peterfrancis.co.uk

PHI Ⓐ
PHILLIPS
www.phillips.com

POOK Ⓐ
POOK & POOK
www.pookandpook.com

PSA Ⓐ
POTTERIES AUCTIONS
www.potteriesauctions.com

PW Ⓐ
PETER WILSON
www.peterwilson.co.uk

QU Ⓐ
QUITTENBAUM
www.quittenbaum.de

RFFM Ⓐ
REEMAN DANSIE
www.reemandansie.com

RMA Ⓐ
ROB MICHIELS AUCTIONS
www.rm-auctions.com

ROCK Ⓐ
ROCK ISLAND AUCTION
COMPANY
www.rockislandauction.com

ROS Ⓐ
ROSEBERYS
www.roseberys.co.uk

SAS Ⓐ
SPECIAL AUCTION SERVICES
www.specialauctionservices.com

SAV Ⓐ
STOCKHOLMS AUKTIONSVERK
www.auktionsverket.se

SHAP Ⓐ
SHAPES
www.shapesedinburgh.co.uk

SHEF Ⓐ
SHEFFIELD AUCTION GALLERY
www.sheffieldauctiongallery.com

SHP Ⓐ
SHAPIRO AUCTIONS
www.shapiroauctions.com

SK Ⓐ
SKINNER INC.
www.skinnerinc.com

SOU Ⓐ
CATHERINE SOUTHON
www.catherinesouthon.co.uk

STA Ⓐ
STACEY'S
www.staceyauction.com

SW Ⓐ
SILVERWOODS OF
LANCASHIRE

SWA Ⓐ
SWANN GALLERIES
www.swanngalleries.com

SWO Ⓐ
SWORDERS
www.sworder.co.uk

T&F Ⓐ
TAYLER & FLETCHER
www.taylerandfletcher.co.uk

TDG D
THE DESIGN GALLERY
www.designgallery.co.uk

TDM Ⓐ
THOMAS DEL MAR LTD.
www.thomasdelmar.com

TEAR Ⓐ
MCTEAR'S
www.mctears.co.uk
Photography: Ken McArthur
Photography

TEN Ⓐ
TENNANTS
www.tennants.co.uk

TL Ⓐ
TIMELINE AUCTIONS
www.timelineauctions.com

TOV Ⓐ
TOOVEY'S
www.tooveys.com

TRI Ⓐ
TRING MARKET AUCTIONS
www.tringmarketauctions.co.uk

TW Ⓐ
THOMAS WATSON
www.thomaswatson.com

UNI Ⓐ
UNIQUE AUCTIONS
www.unique-auctions.com

VEC Ⓐ
VECTIS
www.vectis.co.uk

W&W Ⓐ
WALLIS & WALLIS
www.wallisandwallis.co.uk

WAD Ⓐ
WADDINGTON'S, TORONTO
www.waddingtons.ca

WES Ⓐ
WESCHLER'S
www.weschlers.com

WHIT Ⓐ
WHITE'S
www.whitesauctions.com

WHP Ⓐ
W&H PEACOCK
www.peacockauction.co.uk

WHYT Ⓐ
WHYTE'S
www.whytes.ie

WM Ⓐ
WRIGHT MARSHALL
www.wrightmarshall.co.uk

WRI Ⓐ
WRIGHT
www.wright20.com

WW Ⓐ
WOOLLEY & WALLIS
www.woolleyandwallis.co.uk

This is a list of auctioneers that conduct regular sales. Auction houses that would like to be included in the next edition should email us at: info@millersguides.com

UNITED STATES

ALABAMA
Buddy's Antique Auction
www.buddysantiqueauction.com

High as the Sky Auction Company
www.highastheskyauction
company.com

Tucker Auctions LLC
tuckerauctions.com

ALASKA
Alaska Auction Co.
www.alaskaauction.com

ARIZONA
Altermann Galleries & Auctioneers
www.altermann.com

J. Levine
www.jlevines.com

ARKANSAS
Ponders Auctions
www.pondersauctions.com

CALIFORNIA
Bonhams
www.bonhams.com

I.M. Chait
www.chait.com

Clark's Fine Art Gallery & Auctioneers
www.estateauctionservice.com

Clars
www.clars.com

DGW Auctioneers & Appraisers
www.dgwauctioneers.com

Ira & Larry Goldberg Auctioneers
www.goldbergcoins.com

Heritage Auctions
www.ha.com

Michaan's Auctions
www.michaans.com

John Moran Auctioneers
www.johnmoran.com

Ingrid O'Neil Sports & Olympic Memorabilia
www.ioneil.com

PBA Galleries
www.pbagalleries.com

Poster Connection
www.posterconnection.com

Profiles in History
www.profilesinhistory.com

San Rafael Auction Gallery
www.sanrafael-auction.com

Nate D. Sanders
www.natedsanders.com

Robert Slawinski
www.slawinski.com

Stack's Bowers Galleries
www.stacksbowers.com

Treasureseeker Auctions
www.treasureseekerauction.com

COLORADO
Leslie Hindman
www.lesliehindman.com

Pacific Auction Companies
www.pacificauction.com

CONNECTICUT
Automobilia Auctions
www.automobiliaauctions.com

Greenwich Auction
www.greenwichauction.net

Norman C. Heckler & Company
www.hecklerauction.com

Litchfield County Auctions
www.litchfieldcountyauctions.com

Lloyd Ralston Gallery
www.lloydralstontoys.com

Shannon's Fine Art Auctioneers
www.shannons.com

Winter Associates
www.auctionsappraisers.com

DELAWARE
Reagan-Watson Auctions
www.reagan-watsonauctions.com

FLORIDA
Auctions Neapolitan
www.auctionsneapolitan.com

Burchard Galleries Inc.
www.burchardgalleries.com

Fine Art Auctions Miami
www.faamiami.com

Kincaid Auction Company
www.kincaid.com

Kodner
www.kodner.com

Leslie Hindman
www.lesliehindman.com

A.B. Levy's
www.ablevys.com

Palm Beach Modern Auctions
www.modernauctions.com

Turkey Creek Auctions
www.antiqueauctionsfl.com

GEORGIA
Ahlers & Ogletree Auctions
www.aandoauctions.com

Great Gatsby's
www.greatgatsbys.com

Red Baron's Antiques
www.rbantiques.com

HAWAII
Malama Auctions
www.malamaauctions.com

IDAHO
The Coeur D'Alene Art Auction
www.cdaartauction.com

ILLINOIS
Bunte Auction Services
www.bunteauction.com

Hack's
www.hacksauction.com

Leslie Hindman
www.lesliehindman.com

Rock Island Auction Company
www.rockislandauction.com

L.H. Selman Ltd.
www.theglassgallery.com

The Stein Auction Company
www.garykirsnerauctions.com

Susanin's
www.susanins.com

Toomey & Co.
toomeyco.com

Wright
www.wright20.com

INDIANA
Ripley Auctions
www.ripleyauctions.com

Stout Auctions
www.stoutauctions.com

Strawser Auction Group
www.strawserauctions.com

IOWA
Tom Harris Auctions
www.tomharrisauctions.com

Jackson's
www.jacksonsauction.com

KANSAS
Woody Auction Hall
www.woodyauction.com

KENTUCKY
Hays & Associates
www.haysauction.com

LOUISIANA
Crescent City Auction Gallery
www.crescentcityauctiongallery.com

Neal Auction Company
www.nealauction.com

New Orleans Auction Galleries
www.neworleansauction.com

MAINE
Thomaston Place Auction Galleries
www.thomastonauction.com

MARYLAND
Alexander Historical Auctions
www.alexautographs.com

Guyette & Deeter
www.guyetteanddeeter.com

Richard Opfer Auctioneering
www.opferauction.com

Sloans & Kenyon
www.sloansandkenyon.com

Theriault's
www.theriaults.com

Weschler's
www.weschlers.com

MASSACHUSETTS
Douglas Auctioneers
www.douglasauctioneers.com

Eldred's
www.eldreds.com

Fontaine's
www.fontainesauction.com

Grogan & Company
www.groganco.com

Willis Henry Auctions
www.willishenryauctions.com

Kaminski
www.kaminskiauctions.com

Rafael Osona
www.rafaelosonaauction.com

Skinner, Inc.
www.skinnerinc.com

Tremont Auctions
www.tremontauctions.com

White's
www.whitesauctions.com

MICHIGAN
American Auctions
www.americanaauctions.com

Chamberlain's Auction Gallery
www.chamberlainsgallery.com

DuMouchelles
www.dumouchelles.com

MINNESOTA
Luther Auctions
www.lutherauctions.com

MISSISSIPPI
Edens
www.edensauctions.com

European Antique Auction Gallery
www.europeanauctiongallery.com

Stevens Auction Company
www.stevensauction.com

MISSOURI
Leslie Hindman
www.lesliehindman.com

Link Auction Galleries
www.linkauctiongalleries.com

Selkirk Auctioneers & Appraisers
www.selkirkauctions.com

Simmons & Company Auctioneers
www.simmonsauction.com

Soülis Auctions
dirksoulisauctions.com

MONTANA
Allard Auctions Inc.
www.allardauctions.com

NEBRASKA
The Auction Mill
www.theauctionmill.com

Omaha Auction Center
omahaauctioncenter.com

Wasner Auction Service
wanserauction.com

NEVADA
Auctions Imperial
auctionsimperial.com

Lightning Auctions, Inc.
www.lightningauctions.com

NEW HAMPSHIRE
Amoskeag Auction Company
www.amoskeagauction.com

The Cobbs Auctioneers
www.thecobbs.com

Northeast Auctions
www.northeastauctions.com

RR Auction
www.rrauction.com

William A. Smith
www.wsmithauction.com

Withington Auction
www.withingtonauction.com

NEW JERSEY
Bertoia
www.bertoiaauctions.com

Bodnars Auction
www.bodnarsauction.com

Dennis Auction Service
www.dennisauction.com

Nye & Co.
www.nyeandcompany.com

Rago
www.ragoarts.com

Time and Again Auction Gallery
www.timeandagaingalleries.com

Waterford's
www.waterfordsauction.com

NEW MEXICO
Altermann Galleries & Auctioneers
www.altermann.com

Brian Lebel's Old West Events
www.oldwestevents.com

NEW YORK
Bonhams
www.bonhams.com

Carlsen Gallery
www.carlsengallery.com

Christie's
www.christies.com

Clarke
www.clarkeny.com

Copake Auctions
www.copakeauction.com

Cottone Auctions
www.cottoneauctions.com

Doyle New York
www.doyle.com

Guernsey's Auctions
www.guernseys.com

Heritage Auctions
www.ha.com

Helios Auctions
www.heliosauctions.com

William J. Jenack Auctioneers
www.jenack.com

Kestenbaum & Company
www.kestenbaum.net

Mapes Auctioneers & Appraisers
www.mapesauction.com

Phillips
www.phillips.com

Roland
www.rolandsantiques.com

Shapiro Auctions
www.shapiroauctions.com

Sotheby's
www.sothebys.com

Stair Galleries
www.stairgalleries.com

Swann Galleries
www.swanngalleries.com

Weiss Auctions
www.weissauctions.com

NORTH CAROLINA
Brunk Auctions
www.brunkauctions.com

Chandler's Auction Gallery
www.chandlersauction.com

Richard D. Hatch & Associates
www.richardhatchauctions.com

Leland Little
www.lelandlittle.com

Raynor's Historical Collectible Auctions
www.hcauctions.com

NORTH DAKOTA
Haugland's Action Auction
hauglandsactionauction.com

OHIO
Apple Tree Auction Center
www.appletreeauction.com

Aspire Auctions
www.aspireauctions.com

Cowan's Auctions
www.cowanauctions.com

Rachel Davis Fine Arts
www.racheldavisfinearts.com

Garth's Auctions
www.garths.com

Gray's Autioneers
www.graysauctioneers.com

Fusco
www.fuscoauctions.com

Humler & Nolan
www.humlernolan.com

Dana J. Tharp Auctions
www.danajtharpauctions.com

Treadway
www.treadwaygallery.com

OKLAHOMA
Buffalo Bay Auction Co.
www.buffalobayauction.com

OREGON
Antique & Auction Company of
Southern Oregon
www.oregonauctionhouse.com

O'Gallerie
www.ogallerie.com

PENNSYLVANIA
Alderfer Auction
www.alderferauction.com

Ascendant Auction Galleries
www.ascendantauctions.com

Ashcroft & Moore
ashcroftandmoore.com

Briggs
www.briggsauction.com

Bunch Auctions
www.bunchauctions.com

Concept Art Gallery
www.conceptgallery.com

Cordier Auctions & Appraisals
www.cordierauction.com

Dargate Auction Galleries
www.dargate.com

Freeman's
www.freemansauction.com

Great Dane Auctions
www.greatdaneauctions.com

Hampton Estate Action
www.hamptonauction.com

Hartzell's
www.hartzellsauction.com

Hunt Auctions
www.huntauctions.com

Kamelot
www.kamelotauctions.com

Morphy Auctions
www.morphyauctions.com

Pook & Pook Inc.
www.pookandpook.com

Stephenson's
www.stephensonsauction.com

Teel Auctions
www.teelauctions.com

Uniques and Antiques
uniquesandantiques.com

Charles A. Whitaker
www.whitakerauction.com

Weiderseim Associates Inc.
wiederseim.com

Witman Auctioneers
www.witmanauctioneers.com

RHODE ISLAND
Bruneau & Co. Auctioneers
bruneauandco.com

SOUTH CAROLINA
Charlestone Estate Auctions
www.charlestonestateauctions.com

Charlton Hall
www.charltonhallauctions.com

Wooten & Wooten
www.wootenandwooten.com

SOUTH DAKOTA
Girard Auction & Land Brokers, Inc.
www.girardauction.com

TENNESSEE
Case Antiques
caseantiques.com

Berenice Denton
www.berenicedenton.com

Kennedy's Auction Service
www.kennedysauction.com

Kimball M. Sterling Inc.
www.sterlingsold.com

TEXAS
Austin Auction Gallery
www.austinauction.com

Bright Star Antiques Co.
www.brightstarantiques.com

Dallas Auction Gallery
www.dallasauctiongallery.com

Fortune Auction Gallery
www.fortuneauctiongallery.com

Gallery Auctions Inc
www.galleryauctions.com

Heritage Auctions
www.ha.com

Houston Auction Company
www.houstonauctionco.com

Lewis & Maese
www.lmauctionco.com

Simpson Galleries
www.simpsongalleries.com

UTAH
Silcox Auctions
www.silcoxauction.com

VERMONT
Townshend Auction Gallery
www.townshendauctions.com

VIRGINIA
Bremo Auctions
www.bremoauctions.com

Jeffrey S. Evans
www.jeffreysevans.com

Ken Farmer
www.kenfarmerllc.com

Freeman's
www.freemansauction.com

Green Valley Auctions
www.greenvalleyauctions.com

Hampton House Auctioneers
www.hamptonhouseauctions.com

Old World Auctions
www.oldworldauctions.com

Phoebus Auction Gallery
www.phoebusauction.com

Quinn's Auction Galleries
www.quinnsauction.com

WASHINGTON
Mroczek Brothers
www.mbaauction.com

Klien James Auction House
www.seattleauctiongallery.com

Pacific Galleries
www.pacgal.com

WEST VIRGINIA
Adkins Auctions
www.adkinsauction.com

GZ Auctions
www.gzauctions.com

WISCONSIN
Krueger's Auctions
www.kruegersauctions.com

WYOMING
Woodward & Associates
www.woodwardauctions.net

Wyoming Estate Services
www.wyomingestateservices.com

CANADA
ALBERTA
Heffel
www.heffel.com

Hodgins Art Auctions Ltd
www.hodginsauction.com

Lando Art Auctions
www.landoartauctions.com

BRITISH COLUMBIA
Bolylin Auction
www.bolylin.com

Gosby Antiques
gosby.ca

Heffel
www.heffel.com

Jade d'Art
www.jadeartauctions.com

Kilshaw's Auctioneers
www.kilshaws.com

Lunds
www.lunds.com

Westbridge Fine Art
www.westbridge-fineart.com

ONTARIO
888 Auctions
www.888auctions.com

A Touch of Class
www.atouchofclassauctions.com

Auction Network
auctionnetwork.ca

Dupuis
www.dupuis.ca

Empire
www.toronto.empireauctions.com

Heffel
www.heffel.com

Hua Xin Auctions
www.huaxinauction.com

Majestic Auction
www.majesticauction.ca

Medley Auctions
www.medleyauctions.com

Miller & Miller
www.millerandmillerauctions.com

Ritchies Auctioneers
www.ritchies.com

Sotheby's
www.sothebys.com

Waddington's
www.waddingtons.ca

Walkers
www.walkersauctions.com

Whitehalls
www.whitehallsauction.com

A.H. Wilkens
ahwilkens.com

QUEBEC
Empire Auctions
www.montreal.empireauctions.com

Enchères Champagne
www.champagneauctions.ca

Iegor
www.iegor.net

Kavanagh Auctions
www.kavanaghauctions.com

Pridham's
www.pridhams.ca

Dealers and specialists who would like to be listed in the next edition, or have a new address or telephone number, should email us at: info@millersguides.com. Readers should contact dealers before visiting to avoid a wasted journey.

AMERICAN DEALERS

GENERAL

Alley Cat Lane Antiques
www.rubylane.com/shops/alleycatlane

Antiques Center at The People's Store
www.peoplesstore.net

Manhatten Arts & Antiques Center
www.the-maac.com

Showcase Antiques Center
www.showcaseantiquesofcny.com

AMERICANA & FOLK ART

Elle Shushan
www.portrait-miniatures.com

Allan Katz Americana
www.allankatzamericana.com

Olde Hope Antiques
www.oldehope.com

Pantry & Hearth,
www.pantryandhearth.com

The Rookery Bookery
www.therookerybookery.com

RJG Antiques
www.rjgantiques.com

Kathy Schoemer American Antiques
www.kathyschoemerantiques.com

David A. Schorsch & Eileen M. Smiles
www.americanantiqueart.com

Patricia Stauble Antiques
patriciastaubleantiques.com

Throckmorton Fine Art
www.throckmorton-nyc.com

Jeffrey Tillou Antiques
www.tillouantiques.com

Van Tassel Baumann
www.vantasselbaumann.com

ANTIQUITIES

Artemis Gallery
www.artemisgallery.com

ARCHITECTURAL

Barbara Israel Garden Ornament
www.barbaraisrael.com

ARMS & MILITARIA

Fagan Arms
www.faganarms.com

International Military Antiques
www.ima-usa.com

Kelly Kinzle Antiques
www.kellykinzleantiques.com

Rock Island Auction Company
www.rockislandauction.com

BOOKS & MAPS

Abebooks
www.abebooks.com

Aleph-Bet Books
www.alephbet.com

Arader Galleries
www.aradergalleries.com

Bauman Rare Books
www.baumanrarebooks.com

Daniel Crouch Rare Books
www.crouchrarebooks.com

Old World Auctions
www.oldworldauctions.com

Schilb Antiquarian
www.schilbantiquarian.com

BOXES & TREEN

Steven S. Powers
www.stevenspowers.com

CARPETS & RUGS

Bettina Krainin
www.bettinakraininantiques.com

Oriental Rugs Ltd.
www.orientalrugsltd.com

Peter Pap Oriental Rugs, Inc.
www.peterpap.com

Quadrifoglio Gallery
www.quadrifogliogallery.com

CERAMICS

Elise Abrams Antiques
www.eliseabramsantiques.com

Mark & Marjorie Allen Antiques
www.antiquedelft.com

Michele Beiny
www.michelebeiny.com

H.L. Chalfant Antiques
www.hlchalfant.com

British Collectibles
www.britishcollectibles.net

Brian Cullity
www.briancullity.com

Jill Fenichell
www.jillfenichellinc.com

Samuel Herrup Antiques
www.samuelherrup.com

Katherine Houston Porcelain
www.katherinehouston.com

Leo Kaplan Ltd.
www.leokaplan.com

Polka Dot Antiques
www.polkadotantiques.com

Mellin's Antiques
www.mellinsantiques.com

Earle D. Vandekar
www.vandekar.com

CLOCKS, WATCHES & BAROMETERS

The Antique Watch Co.
www.antiquewatchco.com

Matthew Bain Inc.
www.matthewbaininc.com

Barometer Fair
www.barometerfair.com

Kirtland H. Crump
www.kirtlandcrumpclocks.com

Kelly Kinzle Antiques
www.kellykinzleantiques.com

R.O. Schmitt Fine Art
www.roschmittfinearts.com

DECORATIVE ARTS

The End of History
www.theendofhistoryshop.blogspot.com

European Bronze
www.europeanbronze.com

Evergreen Antiques
www.evergreenantiques.com

High Style Deco
www.highstyledeco.com

Holsten Galleries
www.holstengalleries.com

James Infante
www.jamesinfante.com

Macklowe Gallery
www.macklowegallery.com

Lillian Nassau
www.lilliannassau.com

Israel Sack
Tel: 212 399 6562

Pascoe & Company
www.pascoeandcompany.com

Jeffrey F. Purtell
www.steubenpurtell.com

Rago Arts
www.ragoarts.com

Retro Art Glass
www.retroartglass.com

TOJ Gallery
www.tojgallery.com

Valerio Art Deco
www.valerioartdeco.com

FURNITURE

Antique Associates
www.aaawt.com

Ark Antiques
www.arkantiques.org

Artemis Gallery
www.artemisantiques.com

Carswell Rush Berlin Inc.
www.american-antiques.net

H.L Chalfant Antiques
www.hlchalfant.com

Hyde Pak Antiques, Ltd.
www.hydeparkantiques.com

Philip Colleck, Ltd.
www.philipcolleck.com

Peter H. Eaton Antiques
www.petereaton.com

Evergreen Antiques
www.evergreenantiques.com

Samuel Herrup Antiques
www.samuelherrup.com

R. Jorgensen Antiques
www.rjorgensen.com

Eileen Lane Antiques
www.eileenlaneantiques.com

Bernard & S. Dean Levy
www.levygalleries.com

Nathan Liverant and Son
www.liverantantiques.com

Lost City Arts
www.lostcityarts.com

Olde Hope Antiques
www.oldehope.com

James L. Price Antiques
www.priceantiques.com

J.K. Russell Antiques
www.jkrantiques.com

Andrew Sindler
www.spindlerantiques.com

Sumpter Priddy Inc.
www.sumpterpriddy.com

Lynda Willauer Antiques
www.lyndawillauerantiques.com

GLASS

Elise Abrams Antiques
www.eliseabramsantiques.com

Jill Fenichell
www.jillfenichellinc.com

Leo Kaplan Ltd.
www.leokaplan.com

Lillian Nassau
www.lilliannassau.com

William Pitt Paperweights & Art Glass
www.wpitt.com

Retro Art Glass
www.retroartglass.com

L.H. Selman Ltd.
www.theglassgallery.com

JEWELRY

ALVR
www.alvr.com

Ark Antiques
www.arkantiques.org

Jewel Diva
www.jeweldiva.com

Kentshire
www.kentshire.com

Macklowe Gallery
www.macklowegallery.com

Melody Rodgers LLC
www.melodyrodgers.com

James Robinson
www.jrobinson.com

LIGHTING

Chameleon Fine Lighting
www.chameleon59.com

Lillian Nassau
www.lilliannassau.com

Paul Stamati Gallery
www.stamati.com

MODERN
Donzella
www.donzella.com

Lebreton
www.lebretongallery.com

Lobel Modern NYC
www.lobelmodern.com

Lost City Arts
www.lostcityarts.com

Mix Gallery
www.mixgallery.com

Moderne Gallery
www.modernegallery.com

Modernism Gallery
www.modernism.com

Palm Beach Modern Auctions
www.modernauctions.com

MUSIC
Norman's Rare Guitars
www.normansrareguitars.com

The Music Box Shop
www.themusicboxshop.com

ASIAN
California Asian Art Auction Gallery USA
www.caa-auction.com

Ralph M. Chait Galleries
www.rmchait.com

China Arts Auctions
www.chinaartsauction.com

Dynasty
www.dynasty.nyc

Gianguan Auctions
www.gianguanauctions.com

Floating World Gallery
www.auctions.floatingworldauctions.com

Jambhala Antiques
www.antiqueasia.org

Mellin's Antiques
www.mellinsantiques.com

Joan B. Mirviss
www.mirviss.com

Polly Latham Asian Art
www.pollylatham.com

OBJETS DE VERTU
ALVR
www.alvr.com

POSTERS
Chisholm Larsson Gallery
www.chisholm-poster.com

Poster Connection
www.posterconnection.com

Posteritati
www.posteritati.com

Swann Galleries
www.swanngalleries.com

Vintage Poster Works
www.vintageposterworks.com

SCIENTIFIC INSTRUMENTS & NAUTICAL
George Glazer Gallery
www.georgeglazer.com

Tesseract
www.etesseract.com

Boston Harbor Auctions
www.bostonharborauctions.com

SILVER & METALWARE
Argentum the Leopard's Head
www.argentum-theleopard.com

Imperial Half Bushel
www.imperialhalfbushel.com

Wayne & Phyllis Hilt
www.hiltpewter.com

James Robinson
www.jrobinson.com

Spencer Marks, Ltd.
www.spencermarks.com

SPORTING
Hall's Nostalgia
stores.ebay.com/Halls-Nostalgia

Ingrid O'Neil Sports & Olympic Memorabilia
www.ioneil.com

TEXTILES
M. Finkel & Daughter
www.samplings.com

Cora Ginsburg LLC
www.coraginsburg.com

Stephen & Carol Huber
www.antiquesamplers.com

Samplings
www.samplings.com

Vintage Swank
www.vintageswank.com

Van Tassel Baumann
www.vantasselbaumann.com

TOYS & DOLLS
Bertoia
www.bertoiaauctions.com

The Calico Teddy
www.calicoteddy.com

Gemini Antiques Ltd.
www.geminiantiquesltd.com

The Old Toy Soldier Home
oldtoysoldierauctions.com

Lloyd Ralston Gallery
www.lloydralstontoys.com

Theriault's
www.theriaults.com

Toys of Time Past
www.toysoftimespast.com

TRIBAL ART
Arte Primitivo
www.arteprimitivo.com

Marcy Burns American Indian Arts
www.marcyburns.com

Morning Star Gallery
www.morningstargallery.com

Elliott & Grace Snyder
www.elliottandgracesnyder.com

Steven S. Powers
www.stevenspowers.com

Tambaran
www.tambaran.com

Trotta-Bono
www.trottabono.com

Tribal Gatherings
www.tribalgatherings.com

CANADIAN DEALERS
CANADIANA
Peter E. Baker Antiques
www.peterbakerantiques.com

Hinton Antiques
www.hintonantiques.com

Rideau Antiques
www.rideauantiques.net

Smith's Creek Antiques
www.smithscreekantiques.com/antiques

CARPETS & RUGS
Turco Persian Rug Co.
www.turcopersian.com

CERAMICS
Baraset House
www.barasethouse.com

Eastern Townships Antiques
easterntownshipsantiques.com

Toronto Antiques on King
www.torontoantiquesonking.com

Pam Ferrazzutti Antiques
www.pamferrazzuttiantiques.com

GLASS
Eastern Townships Antiques
www.easterntownshipsantiques.com

Sean George Pressed Glass & Goblets
www.pressedglassandgoblets.com

FURNITURE
The Antique Warehouse
www.antiquewarehouse.ca

Peter E. Baker Antiques
www.peterbakerantiques.com

Baraset House
www.barasethouse.com

Elleke Claassen
www.ellekeclaassenantiques.com

Gregory Connor Antiques
www.gregoryconnorantiques.com

Faith Grant
www.faithgrantantiques.com

Land & Ross
www.landandross.com

Maus Park Antiques
www.mausparkantiques.ca

Milord Antiques
www.milordantiques.com

Rowntree Antiques
www.rowntreeantiques.com

Richard Rumi & Co. Antiques
www.rumiantiques.com

Shand Galleries
www.shandgallery.com

J. Taylor Antiques
www.taylorsantiques.com

JEWELRY
Cynthia Findlay Antiques
www.cynthiafindlay.com

Fiona Kenny Antiques
www.fionakennyantiques.com

ASIAN ART
Hua Xin Auctions
www.huaxinauction.com

Jade d'Art
www.jadeartauctions.com

Majestic Auction
www.majesticauction.ca

SILVER
Eastern Townships Antiques
www.easterntownshipsantiques.com

J.H. Tee Antiques Ltd.
www.justinteeantiques.com

Louis Wine Ltd.
www.louiswine.com

TOYS & GAMES
All Dolled Up
www.alldolledup.ca

TRIBAL ART
Waddington's
www.waddingtons.ca